THE MARPING
RATIONALISM, REI
RISE OF MODEF

DAVID BLACKBOURN was born in Lincolnshire in 1949 and studied history at Cambridge, where he was a Research Fellow of Jesus College from 1973 to 1976. He taught at London University from 1976 to 1992, before moving to Harvard as Professor of History and Senior Associate of the Center for European Studies. He has held many fellowships including the 1994 Guggenheim Memorial Foundation Fellowship and his work has been translated into six languages. Previous publications include *Class, Religion and Local Politics in Wilhelmine Germany* (1980), *The Peculiarities of German History* (with Geoff Eley, 1984), *Populists and Patricians* (1987) and *The German Bourgeoisie* (co-edited with Richard J. Evans, 1991). David Blackbourn lives with his wife and two children in Lexington, Massachusetts.

From the reviews:

'An absorbing, challenging work that gives voice to the unlettered and the disempowered . . . Fascinating, surprising and moving, this dense and authoritative book demands and deserves an attentive reading and offers rewards few historical narratives can match'   *Kirkus Reviews*

'Mr Blackbourn's engaging style and superb knowledge of the field make this book an exhilarating trip down one byway of the history of spirituality'
                    KARINA ROLLINS, *National Review* (New York)

THE
MARPINGEN
VISIONS

RATIONALISM,
RELIGION
AND THE RISE OF
MODERN GERMANY

DAVID
BLACKBOURN

Fontana Press
An imprint of HarperCollinsPublishers

Fontana Press
An Imprint of HarperCollins*Publishers*
77–85 Fulham Palace Road,
Hammersmith, London W6 8JB

Published by Fontana Press 1995
1 3 5 7 9 8 6 4 2

First published in Great Britain by
Oxford University Press 1993

Copyright © David Blackbourn 1993

David Blackbourn asserts the moral right to
be identified as the author of this work

ISBN 0 00 686341 8

Set in Plantin Light

Printed in Great Britain by
HarperCollinsManufacturing Glasgow

For Ellen and Matthew

ACKNOWLEDGEMENTS

For permission to reproduce material from copyright works or archives, the author and publisher gratefully acknowledge the following: Dietrich Orlow, *A History of Modern Germany*, 2nd edition (Prentice Hall, Englewood Cliffs, New Jersey); Wilhelm Bungert, *Heimatbuch Marpingen* (St Wendeler Druckerei und Verlag, St Wendel); Fürst Thurn und Taxis Zentralarchiv, Regensburg; Hans Back, Schmelz; and Aero-Bild Verlag, Fulda.

PREFACE

THE idea of writing this book first occurred to me nearly ten years ago, in the spring of 1982, when I came across two tantalizingly brief references to events in Marpingen. Digging around, I found a few more accounts of what had happened, including a substantial brochure (*Marpingen und seine Gnadenmonate*) in the British Library. It seemed a wonderful subject, and I decided to write about it. The book has taken longer to complete than I expected. Research and writing have been interrupted by other commitments, and the source material turned out to be far more extensive than I could have imagined. The main archival research was done in two visits to Germany, in 1984–5 and 1988. The text was substantially written between October 1988 and December 1990, partly in London and partly in Stanford, California, where I taught in 1989–90. Revisions were completed in 1991, and I have not consulted any works that appeared after the summer of 1991.

It is always a pleasure to acknowledge the debts incurred while working on a book. I should like to thank, first, the Master of Birkbeck College, London, and my colleagues in the History Department for allowing me a year of study leave in 1984–5. I shall have moved to the United States by the time this book appears, but it was conceived and much of it written in the course of thirteen happy and rewarding years at Birkbeck. I am very grateful for the generous financial support of the Alexander von Humboldt Foundation of Bonn-Bad Godesberg, which made possible the research in 1984–5 and 1988. During my time in Germany, the Institute for European History in Mainz once again served as a second home, and my thanks go to its director and staff for their friendly support.

I have benefited from the professional expertise and assistance, often well beyond the course of duty, of many German archivists in state, ecclesiastical, and private depositories. I should like to record my warm appreciation to the staff in the following archives: the Bistumsarchiv Trier, the Landeshauptarchiv Koblenz, the Bundesarchiv Koblenz, the Landesarchiv Saarbrücken, the Stadtarchiv St Wendel, the Bischöfliches Zentralarchiv Regensburg, the Staatsarchiv Landshut, the Fürst Thurn und Taxis Zentralarchiv Regensburg, and the Stadtarchiv Deggendorf. I am also grateful to the Bayerisches Hauptstaatsarchiv Munich and the Geheimes Staatsarchiv Preußischer Kulturbesitz Berlin for the efforts they made to trace material. I have drawn on the resources of many libraries, and would like to thank the staff of the following: Birkbeck College library, the University of London Senate House library, the British Library in Bloomsbury and its newspaper division in Colindale, the library of the German Historical Institute London, Heythrop College library, the library of the Institute for European History Mainz, the Mainz University library, the library of the

Priesterseminar Trier, the Stadtbibliothek Trier, the Stadtbibliothek St Wendel, and the Green Library Stanford.

I should also like to express my thanks to friends and colleagues who have provided help or advice. Claus Scharf, Ulrich Wengenroth, Martin Vogt, and Celia Applegate discussed the project with me while I was in Mainz during 1984–5, and I benefited in the same period from talking to Wolfgang Schieder in Trier. Hans Mommsen and Gerd Krumeich asked trenchant questions and helped me to think out my ideas one evening in Bochum when the work was still taking shape. Gottfried Korff, who (as I learned) had already discovered Marpingen, entertained me in Tübingen and very kindly sent me photocopies of several obscure printed source materials from the Tübingen University library. Roy Foster, Renate Hauser, and Peter Loewenberg provided me with valuable references that I would otherwise have missed. Hans Horch, learning of my work through a mutual friend, generously sent me a copy of his book on the Saarland. The fruits of my research have been delivered in one form or another to conference, seminar, and lecture audiences in Britain, Ireland, Germany, Yugoslavia, and the United States, and I am grateful for their encouragement and suggestions. I appreciate also the helpful comments made by a publisher's reader. Above all, I should like to express my warmest thanks to Frances Lannon, who generously agreed to read a draft of the entire text, giving me the benefit of her expertise and making many very valuable suggestions, both substantive and editorial. None of the above, it hardly needs to be said, bears responsibility for any errors of fact or misjudgements that the book may contain.

I have become sharply aware, in writing the book, how diverse are the subjects it deals with, or at least touches on: ecclesiastical history, theology, and the history of popular piety; the history of the Saarland; the structure of the field administration and legal bureaucracy in Bismarckian Prussia; the history of emigration, family history, the history of medicine—the list is not exhaustive. Each of these subjects has its own experts, who have produced a growing and in many cases highly impressive body of work. Without this work, often unsung, the present book could also not have been written. What I owe to it is indicated in the footnotes and the bibliography, which lists all the works consulted, as well as the archival and other primary sources used.

There are two other debts of gratitude that it is a pleasure to discharge: to the staff at Oxford University Press, and to my agent Maggie Hanbury, for their support and patience. Finally, I want to thank my family. My wife Debbie knows how much her love and companionship have meant, and I have been sustained by knowing how firmly she believed this book was worth writing. Our children, Ellen and Matthew, have helped to delay completion of the book, to its benefit. They have tolerated the absences of an academic father when he was at his desk, and put everything else in life into true perspective. I dedicate the book to them.

London,   D.B.
February 1992

CONTENTS

MAPS

TABLES

FIGURE

A NOTE ON TRANSLATION

SOME British historians of Europe seem to believe that all translation from the original is a crime against authenticity. I understand this view, but it does make things hard for the reader. I have translated German terms wherever possible, although I have also given the original of many terms (political, legal, ecclesiastical) in parentheses to help specialists. Occasionally I have done the same with a directly quoted phrase, where an important nuance might otherwise be lost, or where the language used is startling and there seemed some point in giving the original.

The Prussian state had a many-tiered system of administration. I have translated *Oberpräsident* as 'provincial governor', *Regierungspräsident* as 'district governor', *Bürgermeister* as 'mayor', and the *Gemeinderat* (in the context of a village like Marpingen) as 'parish council'. Some awkward terms remain. The most difficult is the figure between the district governor and the mayors, the *Landrat*. If the *Regierungspräsident* was something like a prefect, the *Landrat* was much more than a deputy prefect. The liberal Georg Gothein was not the only one to believe that the *Landrat* was 'the true ruler of Prussia', and his importance will be obvious in the pages that follow. I have therefore chosen to retain the original term for this distinctively Prussian figure, although I have rendered his assistant and deputy (the *Kreissekretär*) as 'district secretary'. I have also left untranslated the term *Ortsvorsteher*, (later *Gemeindevorsteher*), an officer who combined the roles of village foreman, chairman of the parish council, and communal official responsible to his superiors. The term 'village watchman' has been used for *Feldhüter*.

The following translations have been used for individuals within the Prussian legal system: 'public prosecutor' for *Staatsprokurator* (and 'senior public prosecutor' for *Oberprokurator*), 'presiding judge' for *Kammerpräsident*, 'examining magistrate' for *Untersuchungsrichter*, and 'magistrate' for *Friedensrichter*. When it comes to the two judicial institutions most often mentioned, I have translated *Friedensgericht* as 'magistrates' court' and *Landgericht* as 'superior court'. In Chapter 10 other legal institutions enter the picture, especially the various courts of appeal: here the translations I have used are always accompanied, when the institution is first mentioned, by the German original in parentheses.

The Bavarian administrative system had fewer tiers than the Prussian. Specifically, there was only one level between the provincial administration and the mayors. The administrator in question, the *Bezirksamtmann*, I have translated as 'district official', and his office as the 'district administration'.

Where I have translated the German Reichstag and the Prussian Landtag I have in each case used the term 'parliament', and have called their members 'deputies'. The term 'diet', used in some older works for the Prussian parliament, gives a falsely archaic and misleading impression. The Abgeordnetenhaus of the Prussian Landtag I have translated as 'lower house'.

Within the ecclesiastical hierarchy, I have translated *Pfarrer* as 'parish priest' and, where it is attached to the name of a particular priest, as 'Father'; for example, *Pfarrer* Neureuter is rendered as 'Father Neureuter'. His Protestant opposite number is always 'Pastor', to make the denominational distinction clear. For *Kaplan*, the young (and sometimes not so young) Catholic priest without a permanent parish of his own, I have used 'curate'; but again, where the term is used with the name of a particular curate, I have preferred to render *Kaplan* Schneider as 'Father Schneider' rather than the stilted 'Curate Schneider'. I have translated *Domkapitular* as 'canon', and used the word 'dean' for both *Dekan* (head of an administrative deanery) and *Domdekan* or *Domprobst* (who were cathedral deans), trusting that the context will make it clear in a given case which sort of dean is involved. I have followed English usage in rendering *Kirchenrat*, in the context of a village like Marpingen, as 'parochial parish council', to distinguish it from the secular parish council. *Generalvikariat* has been translated as 'vicariate-general', and *Bischöfliches Ordinariat* as 'diocesan authorities'.

This note refers to translations in the text. In the footnotes I have used standard German abbreviations in order to save space, so that there the reader will, for example, find 'District Governor Wolff' as 'RP Wolff', where the abbreviation stands for *Regierungspräsident*. These and all other abbreviations used are given in the following list.

ABBREVIATIONS USED IN THE FOOTNOTES

Abt.	Abteilung
BA	Bezirksamt(mann)
BAK	Bundesarchiv Koblenz
BAT	Bistumsarchiv Trier
Best.	Bestand
BM	Bürgermeister
BO	Bischöfliches Ordinariat
BZAR	Bischöfliches Zentralarchiv Regensburg
DAZ	*Deutsche Allgemeine Zeitung*
EM	*Die Erscheinungen in Marpingen im Jahre 1876*
Fasc.	Fascikel [= Faszikel]
FZ	*Frankfurter Zeitung*
GV	Generalvikariat
HMA	Hofmarschallsamt
KPD	Kommunistische Partei Deutschlands
KR	Königliche Regierung
KRA	Königliche Regierungsamt
KVZ	*Kölnische Volkszeitung*
KZ	*Kölnische Zeitung*
LASB	Landesarchiv Saarbrücken
LHAK	Landeshauptarchiv Koblenz
LR	Landrat
LRA	Landratsamt
MdI	Ministerium des Innern
MG	*Marpingen und seine Gnadenmonate*
MMGE	*Die Marpinger Mutter-Gottes-Erscheinungen und Wunderheilungen*
MRS	Mouvement pour le Rattachement de la Sarre à la France
MWOL	*Marpingen—Wahrheit oder Lüge?*
NBZ	*Nahe-Blies-Zeitung*
NZ	*National-Zeitung*
OP	Oberprokurator
RP	Regierungspräsident
SAStW	Stadtarchiv St Wendel
SAL	Staatsarchiv Landshut
SB	*Stenographische Berichte über die Verhandlungen ... des Landtages*
SBZ	*Saarbrücker Zeitung*
SMZ	*Saar- und Mosel-Zeitung*
SP	Staatsprokurator
SPB	*St-Paulinus-Blatt*
SPD	Sozialdemokratische Partei Deutschlands
SZ	*Saar-Zeitung*

TLZ	*Trierische Landeszeitung*
TTZ	Fürst Thurn und Taxis Zentralarchiv Regensburg
VZ	*Vossische Zeitung*

Introduction

At the beginning of July 1876, the United States of America stood on the eve of its centenary, the festive preparations only slightly clouded by news of General Custer's fate on the Little Bighorn the previous month. European eyes were fixed on the Balkan battlefields, where the revolt of Bosnia, Herzegovina, and Bulgaria against the Ottoman empire had just been joined by Serbia and Montenegro. In Germany the Eastern Crisis dominated foreign news; but after a war-scare in 1875 there was also concern with neighbouring France, whose defeat by Prussian arms just five years earlier had paved the way for German unification. Foreign alarms went together with domestic uncertainty. In the summer of 1876 the work of constructing the new state continued. While Bismarck and the liberals tested each other out and conservatism regrouped, two issues in particular underlined the fact that external unification had not brought internal unity. The struggle in Prussia between state and church, known as the *Kulturkampf*, had already heightened denominational tensions and created fear and bitterness among a substantial proportion of the Catholic minority; and by 1876 the economic recession that began three years earlier was causing serious distress and prompting calls for remedial measures.

Before July 1876 few people in Germany or elsewhere had reason to give much thought to a village called Marpingen. It was a community of 1,600 inhabitants, situated in the northern Saarland, solidly Catholic and thoroughly unremarkable. The village had done nothing to attract special attention from the Prussian district governor in Trier who was ultimately responsible for its administration, nor was the parish an object of anything more than routine interest to diocesan authority, also in Trier. Marpingen was not quite the isolated community some later depicted. Many inhabitants earned a living outside the village, peasants conducted business in nearby market towns, figures as various as the rural postman, notaries, moneylenders, and travelling musicians passed through with news. At the beginning of July, however, the attention of Marpingen was centred on hay. In a village with many head of cattle and numerous meadows, haymaking had an important place in the annual agricultural cycle. Work began at dawn, and all available hands were pressed into service. Children were no exception, and the village school had a 'haymaking holiday' (*Heuferien*). Those too young to take part or to help with the care of farm animals were entrusted with the task of gathering berries.

It was in order to gather bilberries—*Wälen* in local dialect—that, on the hot Monday of 3 July, a number of young girls found themselves in the Härtelwald, a hilly wooded area that contained many rocky gullies and lay a few minutes away from Marpingen to the south-east. There were five girls in all. Three were 8-year-olds, and fast friends: Katharina Hubertus, Susanna Leist, and Margaretha Kunz. With them in the woods were Katharina's 6-year-old sister Lischen, and another 6-year-old, Anna Meisberger. The girls had become separated as they picked berries, and were not together when the Angelus sounded and they began to make their way home. Between the wood and the village was an area of wild meadow with thick bushes around it. It was here that Susanna Leist suddenly called out, bringing Katharina and Margaretha hurrying to her, and drew her friends' attention to a 'white figure'. When the girls reached home, agitated and frightened, all three described seeing a woman in white carrying a child in her arms. There is some dispute over the initial reactions of parents, siblings, and neighbours, but it is clear that the girls remained in a state of excitement. Margaretha slept badly and prayed a lot, Katharina dreamed of the woman in white, Susanna was reluctant to go to bed at all. The following day they returned to the spot and knelt down about twenty yards away to pray. According to their account, after they had said the Lord's Prayer three times the apparition appeared again to Margaretha and Katharina—although not to Susanna Leist, the original seer. 'Who are you?' they asked the figure in local dialect, and received the reply: 'I am the Immaculately Conceived.' 'What should we do?' 'You should pray.' The children resumed their prayers, and the figure disappeared.

The apparitions continued in the days that followed. The figure, now confidently identified by adults as the Blessed Virgin, instructed that a chapel be built, encouraged the sick to come to her, and asked that water be taken from a spring some distance away in the Härtelwald. Soon other children and adults claimed to have seen the Virgin, and there were reports of miraculous healings from those who had touched the ground where the apparition stood or drunk water from the spring. Within less than a week thousands of pilgrims were streaming to Marpingen. Reports spoke of 20,000 in the village, with up to 4,000 at the apparition site singing, praying, and taking away foliage or handfuls of earth from the spot. Many further cures were made public. When the civil authorities closed off the area, the three visionaries began to claim apparitions in other parts of the village—in their homes, in barns and stables, in the school, in the graveyard and the church. The visions they described became more luxuriant. The Virgin appeared with and without the Christ-child, sometimes accompanied by angels. She was dressed now in white, now in gold or azure. The apparitions also took on darker tones. On one occasion the girls reported seeing the Virgin clad in black, on another they described a celestial procession passing over the graveyard. The devil also appeared.

Marpingen became a *cause célèbre*. Journalists, priests, and the sellers of pious memorabilia descended on the village, as well as pilgrims from Germany and abroad. Supporters and opponents of events there dubbed Marpingen 'the German Lourdes', even 'the Bethlehem of Germany'.[1] 'It is an undeniable fact

[1] Landesarchiv Saarbrücken, Best. Einzelstücke Nr. 107, Zusammenstellung des wesentlichen In-

that the whole world is talking about Marpingen', wrote one sympathetic commentator.[2] 'Marpingen has become the centre of events that have shaken the
world', suggested another.[3] The hyperbole was forgivable. A pub brawl in a
different part of Germany began when one man insulted another by calling him
a 'Marpinger'. (A local court found him guilty of slander and sentenced him to
a fine of 15 Marks or three days in gaol.[4]) One newspaper ran an editorial
under the headline 'Stambul and Marpingen'.[5] Bismarck himself reportedly
made slighting remarks about Marpingen and Lourdes.[6] The interest of the Iron
Chancellor reflected another element of the village's new celebrity, for among the
outsiders who came to Marpingen in the wake of the apparitions were local and
district administrative officials, examining magistrates, gendarmes, soldiers, and
a criminal policeman from Berlin. They suspected sedition, riotous assembly,
and deception: public order and the dignity of the state were supposedly at stake.
The apparition movement collided with the machinery of state, and the result
was a protracted struggle that was to extend from Marpingen and surrounding
areas of the Saarland to the courtrooms of the Rhineland and the Prussian
parliament in Berlin. Even Kaiser Wilhelm I was prompted to send a telegram to
the provincial authorities asking to be told what was happening.

Pondering on what had happened from a different perspective was a man on
whom the drama placed a heavy burden. 'The events are so tremendous,' wrote
the Marpingen parish priest, 'that a true account of them would already fill a
book.'[7] The book that follows may not be the one that Jakob Neureuter had in
mind, but it does try to present a true account of what happened in Marpingen,
why, and with what consequences.

Most people associate modern apparitions with the celebrated examples—
Lourdes, Knock, Fatima. These have become canonical in a double sense. In
formal ecclesiastical terms, they belong to the very small number of cases that
were authenticated by the church after a canonical enquiry. In theory this meant
only that there could be no objection to Catholic support for them; in practice
the church made great efforts to develop the cult of the Virgin at Lourdes and
other favoured sites. These apparitions were also canonical in the sense that
literary critics use the term to describe 'great texts' that have come to be regarded

halts der Untersuchungsacten betreffend die Mutter-Gottes-Erscheinungen in Marpingen. Saarbrücken den 9. August 1878. Kleber Untersuchungsrichter [LASB, E 107], 484; 'An der Gnadenstätte
von Marpingen', *Die Gartenlaube* (1877), 669; *Marpingen und seine Gnadenmonate . . . von einem Priester
der Diöcese Münster, der wiederholt Marpingen besucht hat* [MG] (Münster, 1877), 16.

[2] *Marpingen—Wahrheit oder Lüge? Dem christl. Volke vorgel. v. einem Unbetheiligten* [MWOL] (Münster,
1877), 4.
[3] *Die Marpinger Mutter-Gottes-Erscheinungen und wunderbaren Heilungen. Dem katholischen Volke
dargestellt von einem geistl. Priester aus der Diöcese Paderborn* [MMGE] (Paderborn, 1877), 13.
[4] Report from Deutz in the *Elberfelder Zeitung*, cit. *Saar- und Mosel-Zeitung* [SMZ], 17 Oct. 1876.
[5] *Breslauer Zeitung*, cit. *Germania*, 13 Jan 1877. 'Stambul' was, of course, Istanbul, an allusion to the
war in the Balkans.
[6] J. Rebbert, *Marpingen und seine Gegner. Apologet. Zugabe zu d. Schriften u. Berichten über Marpingen,
Mettenbuch u. Dittrichswalde* (Paderborn, 1877), 9.
[7] LASB, E 107, 430: draft of an undated letter seized by authorities.

as making up an accepted literary canon. Indeed, the celebrated apparitions can
be regarded as texts of a sort. What the Virgin wore, where she stood, and what
she said, all were recorded in detail, reproduced in print, and endlessly pored
over. These accounts of authenticated cases established the archetypal qualities
of the modern Marian apparition. They had a demonstrable effect on other
visionaries, and served as a reference point for those priests and publicists who
argued for other apparitions to be included within the canon.[8] Lourdes, Knock,
Fatima, and the small number of other cases approved by the church represented
only a tiny fraction of all the apparitions that were claimed. Alongside the great
tradition was a little tradition of alleged revelations that never became canonical.
Even if we exclude the apparitions recorded in Africa, the Americas, and Asia,
there have been thousands of such cases in Europe alone during the last century
and a half. German-speaking Europe, contrary to what one might expect, has
been one of the most important settings of modern apparitions. Marpingen itself
was only one of three major, widely reported cases of its kind in the 1870s (the
others were in the Prussian Ermland and Bavaria), and it prompted a host of
obvious imitators. These Lourdes writ small, whether in Germany or Italy,
France, or Spain, attracted their own chroniclers.

   Modern Marian apparitions have generated an enormous literature among
Catholic writers. This varies in tone from austere entries in theological encyclo-
pedias to effusive popular accounts (including, in the case of Lourdes, novels
and films). Some of the most scholarly writing has predictably been concerned
with approved apparitions. The work of René Laurentin on Lourdes, and the
Pontmain visions of 1871, is exemplary.[9] There is also valuable work dealing
with apparitions more generally, especially where both authenticated and non-
authenticated cases receive consideration. Examples include Bernard Billet's
Vraies et fausses apparitions dans l'Église and the writings of the English Jesuit
Herbert Thurston.[10] The large volume of hagiographical literature is discouraging
at first sight, but it does provide a sense of the recurring motifs in reported
apparitions.[11] Pious contemporary accounts of individual cases are generally

---

   [8] For an approach to the apparitions that sees them as 'fictions' and compares them to contemporary
'Lives of Jesus', see J. Kent, 'A Renovation of Images: Nineteenth-Century Protestant "Lives of Jesus"
and Roman Catholic Alleged Apparitions of the Blessed Virgin Mary', in D. Jasper and T. R. Wright
(eds.), *The Critical Spirit and the Will to Believe* (Basingstoke, 1989), 37–52.
   [9] R. Laurentin (with Bernard Billet and Paul Galland), *Lourdes. Dossier des documents authentiques*,
7 vols. (Paris, 1958–66). Vols. iii, iv, and vii were co-edited with Bernard Billet, vols. v–vi with Billet
and Paul Galland; R. Laurentin and A. Durand, *Pontmain. Histoire authentique*, 3 vols. (Paris, 1970),
i. *Un signe dans le ciel*.
   [10] B. Billet *et al.* (eds.), *Vraies et fausses apparitions dans l'Église* (Paris, 1973); H. Thurston, *Beauraing
and Other Apparitions: An Account of some Borderline Cases in the Psychology of Mysticism* (London,
1934).
   [11] See e.g., P. Sausseret, *Erscheinungen und Offenbarungen der allerseligsten Jungfrau Maria*, 2 vols.
(Regensburg, 1878); B. St. John, *The Blessed Virgin in the Nineteenth Century: Apparitions, Revelations,
Graces* (London, 1903); R. Ernst, *Maria redet zu uns. Marienerscheinungen seit 1830* (Eupen, 1949);
J. D. Delaney (ed.), *A Woman Clothed with the Sun: Eight Great Apparitions of Our Lady in Modern
Times* (New York, 1960).

more useful than compilatory works in the same vein, for the sharpness of detail
has not yet been rubbed smooth by repetition and it is often possible to see locally
specific features alongside the 'timeless' elements.

The non-Catholic literature on Marian apparitions is smaller but more diverse:
it includes fiercely hostile diatribes and works that explore the possible meaning
of the events from positions that are agnostic or sceptical but not always unsympathetic. Émile Zola's fictional account of Lourdes distributes its sympathies
more broadly than most anticlerical works, providing room for a generous portrait
of the central visionary figure, a range of clerical attitudes, and compassion for
those whose afflictions took them to the Pyrenean town.[12] Most anticlerical
philippics were less nuanced, paying little attention to the visions or seers and
emphasizing instead the political and commercial interests served by the apparitions. In other words, they provide a photographic negative of hagiographical
accounts. Another common non-Catholic approach to the apparitions has been
psychological. Contemporaries such as Krafft-Ebing interpreted visionary claims
in terms of religious mania and 'hysteria' with their origins in sexual disturbance
or emotional shock.[13] The explanatory potential of this approach should not be
dismissed, and a Catholic writer like Thurston (a direct contemporary of Freud)
also employs psychological terms in discussing dubious modern apparitions.
There is nevertheless a danger of reductionism, as there is in modern, post-
Freudian interpretations. The work of Michael P. Carroll on the psychological
origins of Marian apparitions shows the strengths and weaknesses of the
approach.[14] His close examination of particular case histories draws out and
combines pieces of evidence about the visionaries' lives with readings that are
often ingenious and sometimes illuminating. But the explanations still threaten
to explain away: it is scarcely more desirable to diagnose the visionaries as a
bundle of symptoms than it is to view the visions exclusively as a sign of divine
grace or as clerically and commercially inspired bunkum. Moreover, the close
reading of individual case histories is not matched by a similar sensitivity to time
and place, to the everyday events, social structures, and belief systems that joined
the individuals and families concerned to their neighbours.

The two levels are brought together in an outstanding work by William Christian on apparitions in fifteenth-century Spain. Alongside a careful, textual reading
of the visionaries' accounts, he places their experiences within the social structure
of Spanish rural society and explores the meanings they would have had for

[12] É. Zola, *Lourdes*, transl. E. Vizetelly (London, 1894).
[13] R. Krafft-Ebing, *Lehrbuch der gerichtlichen Psychopathologie* (Stuttgart, 1875), 200–2: 'Beob. 86. Hysterischer Irresein. (Religiöser Wahnsinn.)'; *Lehrbuch der Psychiatrie auf klinischer Grundlage für practische Ärzte und Studirende*, 3 vols. (Stuttgart, 1879–80): ii. 90–3 ('Die religiöse Verrücktheit'); ii. 116–17 ('Transitorische Irreseinzustände'); iii. 87–90 ('Zur religiösen Verrücktheit').
[14] M. P. Carroll, *The Cult of the Virgin Mary: Psychological Origins* (Princeton, NJ, 1986). See also Carroll's *Catholic Cults and Devotions: A Psychological Inquiry* (Kingston, Montreal, and London, 1989); and D. Blackbourn, 'The Catholic Church in Europe since the French Revolution: A Review Article', *Comparative Studies in Society and History*, 33 (1991), 778–90.

contemporaries. The book succeeds as an investigation into 'the world of images in the minds of the people of rural Castile and Catalonia'.[15] Christian's work belongs to the rich historiography of medieval and early modern popular religion, which has yielded insights into the significance of apparitions along with much else.[16] Comparable work on modern apparitions is much more difficult to find. It is probably a reflection on French historiography as well as the primacy of French apparitions in nineteenth-century Europe that the latter should have received most attention. Thomas Kselman examines the famous French apparitions with a sharp appreciation of their place in popular religious sentiment; Judith Devlin does the same for less celebrated cases, in a book concerned with a variety of rural popular beliefs.[17] Beyond France, interest in apparitions or in other manifestations of popular piety has been minimal, not least in German-speaking Europe. Despite recent signs of change, the predominant emphasis in works on Catholicism has been on ecclesiastical, organizational, and political history, rather than on the mentalities of the faithful.[18]

Marian apparitions have generally attracted the attention of historians where they have played a political role. It is the political uses that were made of Lourdes, the overt clerical mobilization of the large-scale pilgrimages there, that have been emphasized.[19] The same has generally been true of the way in which mainstream historians have approached the Fatima events of 1917, and the great wave of apparitions that accompanied the onset of the Cold War in the late 1940s. A recent work by Nicholas Perry and Loreto Echeverría includes discussion of many European apparitions, from France in the 1830s to Yugoslavia in the 1980s, in terms of the political aspirations that they helped to crystallize.[20] In the last

[15] W. A. Christian, *Apparitions in Late Medieval and Renaissance Spain* (Princeton, NJ, 1981), 9. On the modern period, see also W. A. Christian, 'Tapping and Defining New Power: The First Months of Visions at Ezquioga, July 1931', *American Ethnologist*, 14 (1987), 140–66; and W. A. Christian, *Person and God in a Spanish Valley* (Princeton, NJ, 1989), esp. 52–75.

[16] See C. W. Bynum, *Holy Feast and Holy Fast: The Religious Significance of Food to Medieval Women* (Berkeley, Calif., 1987); B. Nolan, *The Gothic Visionary Perspective* (Princeton, NJ, 1976); R. C. Finucane, *Miracles and Pilgrims: Popular Beliefs in Medieval England* (London, 1977).

[17] Thomas Kselman, *Miracles and Prophecies in Nineteenth-Century France* (New Brunswick, NJ, 1983); Judith Devlin, *The Superstitious Mind: French Peasants and the Supernatural in the Nineteenth Century* (London and New Haven, Conn., 1987).

[18] Recent exceptions include J. Sperber, *Popular Catholicism in Nineteenth Century Germany* (Princeton, NJ, 1984); G. Korff, 'Formierung der Frömmigkeit. Zur sozialpolitischen Intention der Trierer Rockwallfahrten 1891', *Geschichte und Gesellschaft*, 3 (1977), 352–83; G. Korff, 'Zwischen Sinnlichkeit und Kindlichkeit. Notizen zum Wandel populärer Frömmigkeit im 18. und 19. Jahrhundert', in J. Held (ed.), *Kultur zwischen Bürgertum und Volk* (Berlin, 1983), 136–48; W. Schieder (ed.), *Volksreligiosität in der modernen Sozialgeschichte* (Göttingen, 1986). See also R. van Dülmen, 'Religionsgeschichte in der historischen Sozialforschung', *Geschichte und Gesellschaft*, 6 (1980), 36–59.

[19] See Kselman, *Miracles and Prophecies*; M. Marrus, 'Pilger auf dem Weg. Wallfahrten im Frankreich des 19. Jahrhunderts', *Geschichte und Gesellschaft*, 3 (1977), 329–51. For a brief but rounded discussion, see R. Gibson, *A Social History of French Catholicism 1789–1914* (London, 1989), 145–51.

[20] N. Perry and L. Echeverría, *Under the Heel of Mary* (London, 1988). The authors' trenchant anti-clericalism gives their book force, although their insistent tone is sometimes self-defeating. See also W. A. Christian, 'Religious Apparitions and the Cold War in Southern Europe', in E. R. Wolf (ed.), *Religion, Power and Protest in Local Communities: The Northern Shore of the Mediterranean* (Berlin, 1984), 239–66.

decade, Marpingen too has made its first appearances in German historical scholarship, especially in the illuminating work of Klaus-Michael Mallmann on working-class politics, religion, and social protest in the Saarland.[21]

There is no doubt that modern apparitions were commonly triggered by larger events: periods of wartime or post-war stress, political conflict, socio-economic crisis. It is also plain that many apparitions had an impact in turn on contemporary political conflicts, above all in helping to foster Catholic identity against the claims of the state or the challenge of anticlericals. I was first led to Marpingen by passing references in two older books that mentioned events there in the context of the *Kulturkampf*.[22] There is overwhelming evidence, as this book tries to demonstrate, of the link between the apparitions and a combination of political persecution, material distress, and social change. That is true not only of the original events in Marpingen, but of the revitalized apparition movement in the twentieth century.

Some may feel that this is all we need to know about the events themselves— that they are of minimal intrinsic concern, interesting chiefly because of their trigger-function, essentially a symptom or reflection of larger, more important things (politics, society, economy). This conviction is curiously in harmony with the attitude struck by the church authorities towards apparitions that had been approved, when they were keen to hustle the visionaries out of the way lest the humble original actors become too much the focus of a secondary cult that obscured the 'real' meaning of events. I am reluctant to hurry the visionaries and their fellow villagers out of the way prematurely (or to introduce them in too peremptory a fashion). To do so would foreshorten our perspective on the apparitions, elide the different meanings they are able to yield. These were undeniably episodes that occurred within an immediate political and economic framework of *Kulturkampf* and Great Depression. The official and popular response they evoked then breathed into the apparitions almost a separate existence as matters of state. But the experience of the three girls, their families, and neighbours was also rooted in the particularities of life in Marpingen, as a parish, as a productive entity, as a web of family and village relationships. The advent of the apparitions can be fully understood only if we penetrate the lives and beliefs of Marpingen's inhabitants at a time when much was changing, materially and mentally (and the two can hardly be disconnected): the size of the village, its

---

[21] Mallmann mentions Marpingen briefly in *Die Anfänge der Bergarbeiterbewegung an der Saar (1848–1904)* (Saarbrücken, 1981), 86; but see esp. 'Volksfrömmigkeit, Proletarisierung und preußischer Obrigkeitsstaat. Sozialgeschichtliche Aspekte des Kulturkampfes an der Saar', in *Soziale Frage und Kirche im Saar-Revier* (Saarbrücken, 1984), 213–21; and '"Aus des Tages Last machen sie ein Kreuz des Herrn"? Bergarbeiter, Religion und sozialer Protest im Saarrevier des 19. Jahrhunderts', in Schieder (ed.), *Volksreligiosität*, 164–7. See also Gottfried Korff's contribution to the Schieder collection, 'Kulturkampf und Volksfrömmigkeit'.

[22] Julius Bachem, *Erinnerungen eines alten Publizisten und Politikers* (Cologne, 1913), first published as *Lose Blätter aus meinem Leben* (Freiburg, 1910); Eduard Hüsgen, *Ludwig Windthorst* (Cologne, 1911).

relationship to the outside world, patterns of employment, the structure of family life, forms of popular devotion.

If I entered Marpingen through the *Kulturkampf*, I found myself staying there for other reasons, and in the work that follows try to present what happened from an 'internal' and an 'external' perspective. The book examines what the apparitions meant for those who shared the immediate world of the visionaries, as well as what Marpingen came to signify for others. The intention is to bring these two worlds together, as they were in fact brought together by events. It is an attempt to develop the approach of an earlier book on Catholics and politics in Württemberg during the Wilhelmine period.[23] There I tried to examine the interplay between the meaning of politics—its aims and organization, the language in which it was couched—for leaders in the state capital of Stuttgart and those in local communities. The present work has obvious differences. Its immediate focus is narrower, its scope and time-scale are larger. But the interplay and connections between different worlds of meaning are central to the undertaking. It has become common in the last decade or so for historians to take a 'small case', a local incident, and draw out the larger historical pattern woven into it. This has yielded outstanding results in the works of Emmanuel Le Roy Ladurie, Natalie Zemon Davis, and Carlo Ginzburg.[24] Among German historians, David Sabean's *Power in the Blood* has also shown how fruitful the approach can be.[25] Like William Christian's study of Spanish apparitions, these are all works that deal with the late medieval and early modern periods. There is no intrinsic reason for this particular monopoly.

One reason why such cases attract historians of an earlier period is obviously the documentation they leave behind. Studies of this kind are made possible in the first place because the incident became a source of interest to ecclesiastical or civil authorities, thus generating evidence for the historian. But the same applies to the modern period; it is certainly true of Marpingen. The apparitions caused a stir that activated the pens of clerical and civilian administrators, policemen, and magistrates. Without the unwitting source material they created the present study could not have been written.

I have used archival material from seven major depositories in writing this book. The two most important lie at opposite ends of the Mosel valley, in Trier and Koblenz. The Bistumsarchiv in Trier contains extensive files on the Marpingen apparitions. The material includes letters, memoranda, and depo-

[23] D. Blackbourn, *Class, Religion and Local Politics in Wilhelmine Germany: The Centre Party in Württemberg before 1914* (London and New Haven, Conn., 1980).

[24] E. Le Roy Ladurie, *Montaillou: Cathars and Catholics in a French Village 1294–1324* (London, 1978); E. Le Roy Ladurie, *Carnival: A People's Uprising at Romans 1579–1580* (London, 1980); N. Z. Davis, *The Return of Martin Guerre* (Cambridge, Mass., 1983); C. Ginzburg, *The Cheese and the Worms: The Cosmos of a Sixteenth-Century Miller* (London, 1980).

[25] D. W. Sabean, *Power in the Blood: Popular Culture and Village Discourse in Early Modern Germany* (Cambridge, 1984).

sitions on the original events variously authored (or recorded) by the parish priest, the visionaries and their families, other villagers, those who claimed they or their children had been miraculously cured, and visitors to Marpingen. The files allow us to reconstruct the course of the ecclesiastical enquiry set up with great difficulty by the diocesan authorities (there was no bishop in 1876–7 because of the *Kulturkampf*), and there is evidence on the impact of state intervention in the affair. Later folders contain extensive material on the twentieth-century revival of the apparition movement. This rich holding has proved an essential source, and I have supplemented it with use of the Marpingen parish archives.

The Landeshauptarchiv in Koblenz contains the administrative records of the Prussian Rhine Province for the nineteenth century.[26] It has a file on Marpingen that shows the response of the Prussian authorities, local, provincial, and national, and constitutes a prime source for the efforts of both civilian and military arms of the state to grapple with events. The archive also houses much valuable material that helps us to understand the circumstances of Marpingen and surrounding areas of the Saarland in the 1870s and earlier decades. I have used files on matters such as emigration, political movements, religious practices and organizations, and the prosecution of the *Kulturkampf*.

There is some additional material on the administrative response to Marpingen in the local Stadtarchiv at St Wendel. More extensive and illuminating is a further depository of Prussian material in the Landesarchiv Saarbrücken, which contains evidence on the regional response to the Marpingen events. More important, the archive possesses the comprehensive summary-cum-transcription of statements, intercepted letters, impounded documents, records of interrogations, gendarme reports, and the like, drawn up by a Prussian examining magistrate prior to the legal action eventually initiated against inhabitants of Marpingen and others in 1879. The full documentary record from which the examining magistrate worked contained ten volumes. It was destroyed by Second World War bombing, but the summary runs to almost five hundred handwritten pages and provides an invaluable source on virtually every aspect of the apparitions.

Light is cast on Marpingen from a different angle by material in the archive of the Bavarian Thurn und Taxis family, best known perhaps for the private postal service they operated for several centuries (and for the family brewery that still exists). Princess Helene of Thurn und Taxis travelled to Marpingen in the summer of 1877, together with a large retinue of servants, one of many Catholic aristocrats from Germany and beyond drawn to the miraculous events. The detailed account of her expenses that survives offers a valuable insight into aristocratic patronage of the apparitions. Princess Helene played a more central part in supporting another series of German apparitions closer to the family home. These took place in Mettenbuch, Lower Bavaria, and began nearly six

---

[26] I also used the papers of the Catholic academic Georg von Hertling in the Bundesarchiv Koblenz to get a measure of educated Catholic opinion in the 1870s, but these proved to be of disappointingly limited value.

months after their counterparts in Marpingen. They are extensively documented, and I have used this material to augment the sources on Marpingen and to provide a basis for comparisons. The Bavarian evidence helpfully supplements the Saarland evidence in several ways. The files of the diocesan Bischöfliches Zentralarchiv in Regensburg have much to say about the setting of the Mettenbuch apparitions and the church response. The Regensburg material also permits comparisons to be made between the dominant figure among the Marpingen seers, Margaretha Kunz, and her counterpart in Mettenbuch, Mathilde Sack. A combination of the evidence in Regensburg and the Staatsarchiv Landshut also provides better information about alleged miraculous cures ascribed to Mettenbuch than it is possible to piece together for Marpingen.

The Bavarian material is particularly instructive in the contrasts it reveals. The size and nature of the holdings on Mettenbuch in ecclesiastical and state archives already indicate differences between the course of events there and in Marpingen. The diocesan archive is in many respects a fuller source for the immediate events than its counterpart in Trier, because in Regensburg an untrammelled clerical authority was in place at the time when the apparitions were reported. The Bishop of Regensburg could mount a regular canonical enquiry, whereas the official response in Trier was desperately improvised. The contrast holds true of the state archives. The ripples of official anxiety in Prussia, reaching to Berlin, had no counterpart in Bavaria. The holdings in Landshut show that the issue was dealt with largely by local officials in Deggendorf, watched over by the provincial authorities in Landshut: Munich was not involved.[27]

The availability of the Mettenbuch evidence is very valuable in examining the Marpingen case. So is the sheer range of material on Marpingen itself, coming as it does from clerical and lay authorities, and from different levels within each. This provides plenty of opportunities for control and corroboration of the sources. The fact that so much of our material was compiled for internal consumption within the civil or ecclesiastical bureaucracy concerned is a further advantage. Some strikingly unbuttoned candour is to be found in both. None of this means, of course, that the evidence speaks for itself. Priests and bishops, policemen and magistrates, viewed events through a particular optic and had special interests to plead or preserve. More important, the bulk of the direct evidence we have comes filtered through the clergy and officials who recorded it. Their reports, letters, or interrogations are the medium through which we hear the visionary children, their families, and supporters. This is an obvious and familiar problem. In practice the richness of the sources helps. In the case of Margaretha Kunz, for example, it is true that we generally hear her voice only when she is being questioned; but at least we can hear what she reportedly said at different times to her mother, the parish priest, a variety of visiting priests,

[27] A letter of 21 July 1988 from the Bayerisches Hauptstaatsarchiv Munich notes the absence of holdings on Mettenbuch. It is possible that further digging would unearth material, but the fact that a well-organized archive has nothing catalogued under Mettenbuch is in itself indicative.

pilgrims and sympathetic publicists, half a dozen different magistrates and civilian officials, the warden of a state orphanage and his wife, a senior detective, and nuns in several different convents. Her cruel misfortune as a girl and a young woman subjected from the age of 8 to close scrutiny of one kind or another allows us many opportunities to observe her (as well as to observe the observers). In her case, as more generally, much of the evidence has to be read against the grain. Used in this way it can tell us much more about Marpingen than those who recorded it were interested in, although there remain many lacunae, many points where I wish the evidence enabled me to say more. The wartime loss of the complete witness statements is especially regrettable. It means that one is left trying to reconstruct some important aspects of village geography and social relations from fragmentary evidence.

Archival material provides the foundation of this book, but it is not the only evidence. There are printed sources of various kinds on which I have drawn. Particularly useful is the transcript of the two-week trial in 1879, together with the record of the Prussian parliamentary debate on Marpingen that took place in the previous year.[28] I have also made extensive use of press reports and the large pamphlet literature, both friendly and hostile. For all the recycling of information and mutual plagiarism that went into these reports and brochures, they sometimes provide sharp detail as the authors struggled to pick up local knowledge. Unlike harassed officials with austere masters, journalists and publicists were inclined actually to describe Marpingen for their readers. They were, of course, notably one-eyed observers: Catholics depict guileless visionaries and pilgrims innocent of unruliness or alcohol consumption, liberal anticlericals portray an undifferentiated mass of ignorance. Like all sources they have to be read for their silences, their more or less conscious suppressions, the avenues of thought they close off. But that point can be turned round: we can see how evidence was put together into plausible, coherent narratives of what was 'really' happening. I have tried to show how Catholic priests and lay publicists incorporated the apparitions into a larger narrative frame in which faith and simple-hearted goodness were pitted against the arrogance of rationality and power. There was a parallel liberal-progressive discourse (shared by many officials) that posed the issue as a battle between the forces of light and darkness, science and superstition. These mental and emotional constructs play an important part in this book.

It may be helpful to indicate the organizational scheme of the book. It is divided into three parts. The first offers a progressively sharper focus on the scene of the apparitions. It begins in Chapter 1 with an examination of Marian apparitions

---

[28] *Der Marpinger Prozeß vor dem Zuchtpolizeigericht in Saarbrücken. Nach stenographischer Aufnahme*, ed. Georg Dasbach (Trier, 1879) [Henceforth: *Prozeß*]; *Stenographische Berichte über die Verhandlungen der durch die Allerhöchste Verordnung vom 3. Oktober 1877 einberufenen beiden Häuser des Landtages. Haus der Abgeordneten* (Berlin 1878), ii, 46th Sitting, 16 Jan 1878, 1151–81. [Henceforth: *SB*, with date and page numbers.]

in Europe from the French Revolution to the 1870s, in an attempt to identify
a pattern or typology. Chapter 2 moves to Marpingen itself and explores
what might have predisposed the village population to support the claims
of the three girls. Chapter 3 considers the question of timing, placing the
apparitions in the context of material, religious, and political tensions during the
1870s.

Part II is the centrepiece of the book. It looks at the apparitions through
different eyes, and examines their significance at different levels. Where Part I
progressively narrows the focus towards the immediate events, Part II moves in
the opposite direction. The thematic chapters track the widening importance of
Marpingen, moving outwards from the visionary children to the chain of events
they set off, from the village world where the story began to the larger political,
legal, and ecclesiastical worlds with which the apparitions became intertwined.
Chapter 4 considers the visions and the visionaries, together with the reactions
of their families and fellow villagers. Chapter 5 looks at those who went to
Marpingen as pilgrims, the many 'miraculous cures' that were claimed, and the
diverse forms of commercialization that emerged in the wake of the apparitions.
Chapter 6 examines the role played by the parish priest and other clergy, the
problems they faced, and the issues that divided them. One difficulty all faced
was the way in which Marpingen quickly became interlocked with politics.
Chapter 7 examines the full panoply of administrative, legal, and military measures taken by the state. It tries to explain why the initial response was repressive,
and how the state became locked into persevering with a tough stance. Chapter
8 then addresses the question of how Catholics responded to the harsh measures
taken against them. The final chapter of Part II examines the liberal-progressive
view of the apparitions and state repression. The analysis of liberal reactions
provides a counterpoint to the way in which Catholics viewed the apparitions,
and suggests how liberals saw Marpingen as a touchstone of the struggle between
progress and backwardness.

Part III is concerned with the complex aftermath of events. Chapters 10 and
11 are companion studies in embarrassment. The first examines how the the fall-
out from the apparitions worked its way through the Prussian administrative,
legal, and political systems, culminating in the parliamentary debate of 1878 and
the trial the following year. Chapter 11 turns to the parallel problems faced by
the church, as it struggled against the background of the *Kulturkampf* to mount
an enquiry. The fudging of the issue by the church helped ultimately to keep the
issue of the apparitions alive. The long and in many ways extraordinary epilogue
to Marpingen, right down to the 1960s, is the subject of the final chapter.
Marpingen did not become the German Lourdes, but it was not for want of
effort. An examination of the periodic revivals of interest in the apparitions, and
the advent of new visionary claims, offers a reprise of many of the themes sounded
in the book. Village struggles, demographic and social upheaval, economic crisis,
political turbulence in an age of war, fascism, and cold war: all help to explain

why the apparitions of 1876–7 continued to exercise their hold on the Catholic imagination in Marpingen and beyond.

It should be clear already what sort of approach I take to the events described in this book. To take them seriously is in itself a declaration of sorts. Even twenty years ago a mainstream historian—of modern Europe, at least—would hardly have done so. Marian apparitions occupied a kind of historical limbo along with other manifestations of superstition and delusion. If the role of religion in modern Europe was generally neglected, popular religious phenomena were truly the lost souls of historiography. They were usually passed over, and what attention they did receive was slighting. They were, at best, a sign of how slowly modernization spread its benefits, at worst the symptom of a worrying irrationalism. Writers might be urbane, sorrowful, or chiding, according to individual taste; they seldom paid such matters the compliment of viewing them levelly. But historians, while they may laugh at or chide each other, should not seek easy amusement at the expense of historical actors, or instruct them in their errors. Our role is not to emulate Auden's 'governess in the dead of night | giving the universe nought for behaviour'. This old commonplace has become a new commonplace in the last decade or so, and this has been reflected especially in the attention—the respectful attention—paid to many forms of popular culture. Certainly in the field of modern European history, this change has so far found expression largely in the study of non-religious movements or beliefs, for reasons that are obvious only if one accepts that this was a predominantly secular age. I do not.

There are obvious gains to be had from a sympathetic study of popular religious mentalities and movements. I hope that this study demonstrates some of them. There are potential pitfalls too. One is them is to abdicate the properly critical stance of the historian by confusing it with improper presumption, throwing out the 'cold abstraction' of theory along with the arrogance of modern certainties. We are well rid of the second, but need to hang on to the first. German historians of 'everyday life' have faced particular criticism on this score, and I find myself siding with the critics.[29] A related pitfall is the sentimentality that sometimes attends studies based on a small community. I trust that the venality and fractiousness so evident among the inhabitants of Marpingen has helped to save me from this, although it remains very difficult to use the word 'community' without lending it a certain cosiness. I have tried to remain alive to the danger.[30]

In trying to cast off the arrogance of the present we not only give the victims

---

[29] See J. Kocka, 'Theorien in der Geschichtswissenschaft', in P. Leidinger (ed.), *Theoriedebatte und Geschichtsunterricht* (Paderborn, 1982), 7–27; and—more vigorously—H.-U. Wehler, 'Neoromantik und Pseudorealismus in der neuen "Alltagsgeschichte"', in Wehler, *Preußen ist wieder chic* (Frankfurt am Main and Berlin, 1983), 99–106. On the history of everyday life, see G. Iggers (ed.), *The Social History of Politics: Critical Perspectives in West German Historical Writing since 1945* (Leamington Spa, 1985), 'Introduction', esp. 40–3; L. Niethammer, 'Anmerkungen zur Alltagsgeschichte', *Geschichtsdidaktik*, 5 (1980), 231–42.

[30] Some of the dangers of conceptual looseness associated with the term are discussed with great penetration by David Sabean, *Power in the Blood*, 27–30.

of the past a voice, but cast the apparent victors of the past in a different light. I was constantly impressed as I prepared this study by the dark undertones of progressive attacks on the apparitions, by the violent language of a scientific and pseudo-scientific certainty that helped to legitimize harsh repression. There is everything to be said for examining what the prophets of modernity stood for in a case such as Marpingen, and I have tried to do that. But this too exacts a price if we are not careful. It has probably become more difficult now to extend historical sympathy to those whose standpoints would, not so long ago, have been broadly shared by historians. Who now wants to make the effort to understand why a Rudolf Virchow—doctor, pathologist, scientific popularizer, and self-conscious progressive—thought that civilization itself was at stake over affairs like Marpingen? It has become for historians an unfashionable frame of mind, and those who were once disdainful are now in their turn disdained. Easier by far to summon up empathy for an oppressed Saarland villager seeking solace in the Blessed Virgin than to understand the martinets of modernity. Easier too, perhaps, to see why Marpingen felt itself a village under siege than to appreciate why local officials feared for public order. But if we are to take mentalities seriously we must also try to enter—and enter generously—into the world of a Virchow or a district official. In aiming to steer between censure and sentimentality, I have tried to do that in this book.

PART I

The Background

1

Apparitions of the Virgin Mary in Nineteenth-Century Europe

Marian apparitions were among the great collective dramas of nineteenth-century Europe. They drew scores of thousands of men and women to obscure valleys and remote mountains where the Virgin Mary had allegedly appeared, a figure that rose to hundreds of thousands at a place such as Lourdes. The apparitions were perhaps the most spectacular sign of a religious revival that is one of the outstanding characteristics of the nineteenth century, although one of the least well studied. They also represented an ambiguous counterpoint to the more familiar social and political upheavals of the period.

Such events were not, of course, original to the nineteenth century. Private revelations have been recorded throughout the Christian era, although their form has changed significantly over the centuries. The still-living Mary is supposed to have appeared to St James in Saragossa during his mission to convert Iberia. Further Marian apparitions were claimed by saints in Italy, France, and Spain during the fourth and fifth centuries, and by the Archbishop of Toledo around 667. By the eighth century chroniclers were already describing a case closer to the form taken by so many later apparitions, in which the Virgin allegedly appeared to an English swineherd in 708 or 709.[1] By the eleventh century the motif of the humble female visionary was well established, but through to the end of the late medieval period the typical visionary remained adult and male, often a priest. It was the period after 1400 that fully established the modern type of Marian apparition, where the visionary was increasingly likely to be female rather than male, a child rather than an adult, lay rather than clerical. A classic, even stereotypical case was the 'shepherd's cycle' type of vision so common in Spain.[2] Apparitions also seem to have grown in significance in the early modern period, at least if we judge them by their capacity to create cults and devotional sites of lasting importance. Nearly one in five of the still extant pilgrimage centres established in the years 1400–1530 was based on the story of an apparition; many others associated with miracles or the finding of sacred objects had an apparitional

[1] M. L. Nolan and S. Nolan, *Christian Pilgrimage in Modern Western Europe* (Chapel Hill, NC, 1989), 275.
[2] Christian, *Apparitions*.

element. This pattern persisted, with some variations, through the period of the
Counter-Reformation.[3]

Nothing entirely novel was therefore involved when, after an eighteenth-
century lull, apparitions were again reported in growing numbers after the French
Revolution. To talk of medieval and modern types of apparition is to make a
misleadingly absolute distinction and write off the importance of the early modern
period. Nevertheless, something new clearly was happening in the nineteenth
century. For all the changes that took place in the idiom of Marian apparitions
from about 1400, it remains true that there was no period before the nineteenth
century in which children were more favoured than adults, or female visionaries
outnumbered males. Both were distinctively modern developments.[4] The same
can be said of the centrality the vision itself assumed in modern apparitions. The
apparitions seen by early medieval saints were incidental features in the lives
whose legends they embellished: it was the saint who was the object of the cult.
In later apparition stories connected with the discovery of sacred objects, it was
the object—the relic or statue—that had primary importance. That changed in
the nineteenth century. The classic medieval cults of the Virgin of Guadalupe in
Spain or the Black Madonna of Czestochowa in Poland, both fourteenth-century
in origin, were centred on miraculous objects; the classic modern cult was centred
on an apparition such as Lourdes. Novel also were the almost exclusive association
of apparitions with the Virgin Mary, the messages that accompanied the visions,
and the place that the apparitions acquired within the devotional life of the
church.[5] Taken together, these developments marked a qualitative change, the
creation of a new idiom.

It was a French creation, and the elements that made up the new idiom came
largely from three apparitions that took place in France in a period of less than
thirty years. In 1830–1 a novice nun, Cathérine Labouré, saw a series of visions
at her convent in the Rue du Bac, Paris, in which the Virgin asked her to have a
miraculous medal struck depicting the event.[6] Sixteen years later, two young
cowherds—the 14-year-old Mélanie Calvat and the 11-year-old Maximin
Giraud—reported seeing a vision outside the remote Alpine village of La Salette
(Department of the Isère), when Mary appeared and proclaimed God's anger at

[3] Nolan and Nolan, *Christian Pilgrimage*, 277–85.
[4] Nolan and Nolan, ibid. 272–4, argue convincingly against the medieval–modern distinction drawn
by Victor and Edith Turner in *Image and Pilgrimage in Christian Culture: Anthropological Perspectives*
(Oxford, 1978). But they are too reluctant to recognize what was new in the 19th cent., and their
preoccupation with the origins of apparition sites makes them less alert to the different ways in which
these pilgrimage sites developed.
[5] Turner and Turner, *Image and Pilgrimage*, 27. Guadalupe had its origins in 1326, Czestochowa in
1382.
[6] R. Laurentin, *The Life of Cathérine Labouré 1806–1876* (London, 1983); Carroll, *Cult of the Virgin
Mary*, 165–8; Kselman, *Miracles and Prophecies*, 91–2; Joseph I. Dirvin, 'The Lady of the Miraculous
Medal: Paris 1830', in Delaney (ed.), *A Woman Clothed*, 63–86.

the impiety of the region.[7] Then, in 1858, came the most celebrated case of all, when another young shepherd girl, Bernadette Soubirous, saw a figure in the grotto of the Massabielle near the Pyrenean town of Lourdes. In the course of eighteen separate visions the figure announced itself as the Immaculate Conception, directed Bernadette to a healing spring, and ordered that a chapel be built on the site. At Lourdes all the elements of the classic modern apparition fused: the simplicity of the humble visionary, the delivery of a message, the initial scepticism of the parish priest, the hostile reaction of the civil authorities, claims of miraculous cures, and finally the purposive creation of an official cult by the church.[8]

The last point is important. One reason why these apparitions are widely familiar, Lourdes above all, is because they obtained official church approval. The same is true of a small number of other nineteenth-century cases, including Pontmain in France (1871), Pompeii in Italy (1876), and Knock in Ireland (1879). But the total number of alleged apparitions ran to many hundreds. More seem to have been reported in Italy and France than elsewhere, but there were cases right across Europe, from Spain and Normandy to Bohemia and Polish Prussia. They can be found throughout the century, from the 'winking Madonnas' of Italy in the 1790s to the apparitions seen by a group of children at Tilly-sur-Seulles in the Calvados in 1896–9.[9] Most writers have concentrated on the officially endorsed cases, and there are obvious reasons for this. Those who believe in the authenticity of the approved apparitions have an interest in emphasizing the true at the expense of the false. For all historians of the subject, clerical approval has created superior documentation. I nevertheless want to consider the fullest possible range of apparitions, canonical and non-canonical. This has clear advantages if we are looking for patterns, whether in the lives of the visionaries or the circumstances in which their visions occurred. Nor does this procedure do violence to any obvious distinction between more 'plausible' (approved) and 'implausible' (non-approved) cases. No such clear distinction can be convincingly made. True, anyone who reads accounts of nineteenth-century apparitions is likely to register the differences between the humble, gracious, and guileless Bernadette Soubirous and many of her patently improbable imitators (including

[7] Kselman, *Miracles and Prophecies*, 62–8; John S. Kennedy, 'The Lady in Tears: La Salette 1846', in Delaney (ed.), *A Woman Clothed*, 89–112; Carroll, *Cult of the Virgin Mary*, 149–56; J. Spencer Northcote, *Celebrated Sanctuaries of the Madonna* (London, 1868), 178–229.

[8] The basic source for Lourdes is the 7-vol. compilation of documents and commentary by René Laurentin (with Bernard Billet and Paul Galland), *Lourdes. Dossier des documents authentiques*. See also A. Neame, *The Happening at Lourdes, or the Sociology of the Grotto* (London, 1968); Carroll, *Cult of the Virgin Mary*, 156–65.

[9] Sources for individual apparitions are given below. It is not easy to find evidence on the less celebrated cases. Despite taking its title from an apparition of the early 1930s, Thurston, *Beauraing*, provides probably the best account of non-approved 19th-cent. apparitions. This work by a sceptical Jesuit can be used alongside the devotional work of Sausseret, *Erscheinungen*, and the anticlerical book by Perry and Echeverria, *Under the Heel*, both of which refer to a wide range of cases. There is no listing of 19th-cent. apparitions to rival Bernard Billet's *Vraies et fausses* on the twentieth.

those at Lourdes). But the criteria of personal character and subjective good faith
provide a poor litmus test. Certain approved apparitions had features that worried
many clergy—one of the seers at La Salette told the saintly *curé* of Ars that the
whole affair was a fraud, and later gave his name to a liqueur called Salettine.[10]
Conversely, there can be no doubt about the good faith of the visionaries in many
non-approved cases. By attaching too much importance to the good or bad faith
of the visionaries—to their conscious intentions—we may also pay too little
attention to the unconscious impulses that moved them. Unless we are prepared
to see divine intercession at work in separating a small number of cases from all
the rest, there is no good reason to narrow our enquiry to the hallowed few.

In practice, apparitions unfolded in diverse ways as they passed through
different phases. The first phase was the initial local event: the story related by
the visionaries, and the immediate reaction of family, neighbours, fellow villagers
and parish priest (or fellow nuns and superior). At this stage the pattern shows
the greatest degree of uniformity over time and across Europe. Many cases,
lacking any support, went no further. Those that did went through a second
phase when the local event achieved a wider resonance. Pilgrims and the curious
arrived in larger numbers, and attempts at commercial exploitation grew; the
clergy was often overwhelmed and sometimes divided; and the political significance of the apparitions' message, together with real or assumed threats to
public order, drew the interest of civil authority. The course of events now showed
greater variations, and this became more marked in the final stage. The vast
majority of apparitions became the small change of history. They collapsed under
the weight of their inherent improbability, withered in the face of clerical reproach
or firm police action, or simply petered out as the circumstances that had given
them a larger meaning changed. In these cases, the events usually continued to
be celebrated as a purely local, unofficial cult, although they could sometimes
blaze back into life. In a very small number of cases, however, the events became
something more. Approved and cultivated by the church, they developed—
or were developed—into a formidable official cult, often with a clear political
purpose.

The cycle provides a useful framework for trying to make sense of a phenomenon that held different levels of meaning. I want to start by looking at the
visionaries themselves, attempting to isolate common features of their lives which
might explain why they experienced—or claimed to have experienced—what
they did. I turn then to the patterns of response: the geographical circumstances,
social tensions, and political pressures that led the immediate community to
accept the truth of the apparitions, and others to follow them. Finally, I try to
track the apparitions against developments in the nineteenth-century church,
considering the degree to which the church encouraged forms of popular piety
that made apparitions more likely, and examining how the church tried to control

---

[10] Karl Rahner, *Visions and Prophecies* (London, 1963), 61; Perry and Echeverria, *Under the Heel*,
104–5.

the mass movements and popular enthusiasm unleashed by events. For we are faced, in the end, with the fact that Lourdes enjoyed a brilliant career while the majority of apparitions were attributed to hallucination, superstition, or the designs of the devil.

Women and Children

In the majority of cases recorded in the nineteenth century, celebrated or obscure, the seers were children or women. The general image we have of them, strongly emphasized in devotional accounts, is that they belonged to the poor and vulnerable. Is this accurate? The evidence suggests that it is.[11] There are some exceptions—a Rimini seer of 1850 was the adopted daughter of a countess—but the youthful visionaries came predominantly from poor rural backgrounds.[12] It is certainly true of the best-documented cases. Mélanie Calvat at La Salette was the daughter of an impoverished pit-sawyer and mason. She had often been forced to beg for food before leaving home at the age of 8 to work as a cowherd on a series of farms around the town of Corps. Her fellow cowherd, Maximin Giraud, was a carter's son.[13] Bernadette Soubirous provides the archetypal case. A sickly and asthmatic child, she was the eldest of six children born to a poor miller and his wife. Her father lost the use of his left eye when Bernadette was 8, and his mill (part of the marriage settlement) two years later. As a bankrupt, he took casual and 'dishonourable' jobs that included the collecting and disposal of scrap metal, old bones, dirty hospital dressings, and rags. Bernadette sometimes joined her father rag-picking. In 1856, two years before the apparitions, the family was unable to pay its rent and was lodged in the old lock-up in Lourdes. The following year Bernadette's father was arrested for theft, although the charge was dropped through lack of evidence.[14]

In most of the cases that lacked this prominence our information is more sketchy. But where it is more precise, the indications are clear. The pilgrimage to Our Lady of Redon-Espic in the Périgord was based on an apparition claimed by the shepherdess Marie-Jeanne Grave in 1814. Seven young shepherds, shepherdesses, and farm servants saw visions of the Virgin in the diocese of Valence in 1848–9.[15] Similar reports came from three shepherd children in Dolina (Austria) in the same period.[16] It was a shepherdess, Veronica Nucci, who claimed

[11] Nolan and Nolan, *Christian Pilgrimage*, 289, suggest that a good quarter of modern visionaries 'were from the middle class' (see also 288, table 7–15). But their sample is very small (only 45 modern, i.e. post-1780 cases are considered), and the fact that it is derived from shrines still extant in the 1980s may skew the figures.

[12] On Rimini, and the Countess Baldini's adopted daughter, see Sausseret, *Erscheinungen*, 259–62.

[13] Kennedy, 'The Lady in Tears', 90–1.

[14] Laurentin, *Lourdes*, i. 75 ff., 131–5; J. Hellé, *Miracles* (London, 1953), 48–57; Carroll, *Cult of the Virgin Mary*, 158–9.

[15] Gibson, *Social History*, 146, 149.

[16] Nolan and Nolan, *Christian Pilgrimage*, 286.

to have seen the Virgin at Ceretto in Italy in 1853, and the farm servant Mathilde
Sack together with four peasant children made similar claims in the Bavarian
village of Mettenbuch in 1877.[17] It may be that among the cases where we have
little to go on beyond a vague rural, village background, the visionaries came
from middling or reasonably well-off families—as was the case in Pontmain,
where we have better evidence.[18] But the signs point towards significant numbers
of farm servants and—especially—shepherds and cowherds. In the nineteenth
century, as in the 'shepherd's cycle' of an earlier period, many child visionaries
practised a lowly and poorly respected profession, widely distrusted because
the shepherd (like the knacker) handled animal skins and worked outside the
community.[19]

  The pattern is comparable, but more complicated, when it comes to adult
visionaries. This is partly because of the significant numbers of female religious
among them, who commonly—not invariably—came from a point above the
lower rungs of rural society. Take the celebrated case of Cathérine Labouré, a
fixed point in all the devotional works on the subject. She is often presented as a
simple Burgundian peasant child from a large family.[20] This gives a misleading
picture of her material circumstances. She was indeed the eighth of ten surviving
children, but her father was the largest peasant in the area, an employer of farm
servants and a former mayor of his village. Several of Cathérine's brothers were
settled in comfortable petit-bourgeois circumstances in Paris. Three of them (a
wine merchant, a restaurateur, and a bottle merchant) started businesses typical
of the sons of the more substantial Burgundian peasantry in the capital; one was
a pharmacist, another a clerk. At the age of 12, Cathérine herself was mistress of
a large farm.[21] This was a long way from minding sheep or picking rags.

  But Cathérine Labouré was the exception that proves the rule. Most of the
adult visionaries about whom we have information resembled more closely the
widow Beirne and the other poor tenant farmers of Knock, or Marie Bergadieu,
known as Berguille and dubbed 'the Ecstatic Woman of Le Fontet'. She was in
her mid-forties when supposedly vouchsafed a series of Marian visions in 1873–
4. Born to a poor sharecropping family in the Gironde, she lived a life of peasant
hardship and watched all but two of her children die in infancy.[22] Another
visionary of the same period illustrates a third type, alongside female religious
and poor peasant women. Estelle Faguette of Pellevoisin was a 31-year-old
chambermaid to the Countess de la Rochefoucauld, unmarried and suffering

[17] On Veronica Nucci, Sausseret, *Erscheinungen*, 253–6; on Mathilde Sack and Mettenbuch, see
below, Ch. 4.
[18] See Laurentin and Durand, *Pontmain*, i. *Un signe dans le ciel*, esp. 14–20.
[19] On 'dishonourable professions', see W. Danckert, *Unehrliche Leute. Die verfemten Berufe* (Berne,
1963); K. S. Kramer, 'Ehrliche/unehrliche Gewerbe', in *Handwörterbuch zur deutschen Rechtsgeschichte*
(Berlin, 1971), 855–8. It is a sign of the esteem enjoyed by shepherds that syphilis was named after
one.
[20] Cf. Ernst, *Maria redet*, 20; St John, *The Blessed Virgin*, 1–18.
[21] Laurentin, *Life*, 16–36; Dirvin, 'The Lady of the Miraculous Medal', 63–4.
[22] Devlin, *Superstitious Mind*, 154–5.

from an ulcer of the bowels, peritonitis, and consumption, when she experienced a series of visions in 1876. The Virgin related that her mother's heart had been touched by Estelle's simple piety and extended to her the hope of a cure.[23] Estelle Faguette's sufferings may have been especially severe, but she was not alone as a servant seer. Others included Mary McLoughlin, the priest's housekeeper in Knock, talked about in the area for her 'little fault' with the bottle, and Marie Courrech, perhaps the best-documented of all the subsequent visionaries at Lourdes, who was a servant to Mayor Lacadé.[24] Further research may well uncover further evidence on the role played by seers who were unmarried servants, a background they shared with the English visionary and prophet Joanna Southcott.[25]

Dependent or outsider status, as much as sheer poverty, are the recurrent themes in the lives of the visionaries. To these we should add the experience of emotional vulnerability resulting from bereavement or fractured family circumstances. Some caution is needed here. Infant mortality remained high in Europe until the latter part of the nineteenth century, while epidemics, malnutrition, and war acted as 'the giant orphan-makers'.[26] We should not exaggerate the peculiarity of the visionaries. It is nevertheless striking how far emotional loss and unhappy families provide a common thread linking their lives prior to the apparitions. That, not poverty, is the key to Cathérine Labouré. She was 9 when her mother died, and the young girl climbed tearfully on to a chair to embrace an image of the Virgin in the dead woman's room and 'take Mary as her mother'. After two years farmed out to an aunt and uncle, vinegar merchants who proved as sour as their merchandise and showed her little affection, Cathérine returned to assume the burden of running the family farm. She found her father violently at odds with her growing religious vocation, was sent against her will to help in her widowed brother's Paris restaurant (she felt this as an 'expulsion'), and entered the convent only when a sympathetic brother and sister-in-law paid the dowry her father refused to provide.[27] In the case of La Salette, emotional loss and conflict were interwoven with material privation. Maximin Giraud was brought up by a grandmother after his mother died when he was 2. His father remarried quickly, and the young boy was apparently much abused by his stepmother.[28] Bernadette Soubirous suffered similar experiences. Quarrelling and bitterness gripped the family home. Bernadette's mother had ceased to nurse her soon after her birth, when a fallen candle burned her breast, and appears to have

[23] Ernst, *Maria redet*, 39–41; T. de Cauzons, *La Magie et la sorcellerie en France*, iv (Paris, 1911), 611–13; Perry and Echeverría, *Under the Heel*, 135–6; William J. Walsh, *The Apparitions and Shrines of Heaven's Bright Queen*, 4 vols. (New York, 1904), iv. 119–48.
[24] On McLoughlin, see Mary Purcell, 'Our Lady of Silence: Knock 1879', in Delaney (ed.), *A Woman Clothed*, 158; on Marie Courrech, Laurentin, *Lourdes*, ii. 62–71, 85–9.
[25] See J. F. C. Harrison, *The Second Coming* (London, 1979); J. K. Hopkins, *A Woman to Deliver her People* (Austin, Texas, 1982).
[26] E. Simpson, *Orphans* (New York, 1987), 135.
[27] Laurentin, *Life*, 16–47; Ernst, *Maria redet*, 20.
[28] Carroll, *Cult of the Virgin Mary*, 153–4.

neglected her eldest daughter. In 1857 Bernadette was sent back to live with her former foster-mother in the town of Bartrès, where she was ill-treated and overworked as a shepherd and farm servant. Her return from this Cinderella existence took place in January 1858, three weeks before the first vision of the Virgin Mary.[29]

Illness or ill-use, bereavement, fostering or departure from the family home: these marked the lives of the seers. A parallel pattern of experiences can be found in the backgrounds of others whose prophecies, visions, and status as mystics were not associated, or associated only in part, with Marian apparitions. A well-known example is the early nineteenth-century Westphalian seer, Anna Katherina Emmerich, who received remarkably prolonged revelations from the Virgin Mary, one of which—dictated to the Romantic writer Clemens Brentano—was later published as *The Life of the Virgin Mary*.[30] Brentano, who took down thousands of pages describing these and other visions of the Old and New Testaments and church history, observed that in the illness that preceded her major revelations she was 'nursed by rough and awkward hands ... abandoned by all and ill-treated like Cinderella'.[31] Or take the Belgian girl Louise Lateau, whose trances and stigmata became so celebrated in the 1860s that she was studied by over a hundred doctors and two hundred theologians in the space of three years.[32] She was born in 1850 in Bois d'Haine (between Mons and Charleroi); her father died of smallpox when she was a baby, and she was sent into domestic service at the age of 11 by the widow Lateau, an unbending and rather cold woman 'of almost unpleasant frankness'. Recalled home to work as a dressmaker, she gave herself up to what one observer who came to know the family well described as 'slavery' in order to help her mother.[33] A concentrated set of events probably helped to trigger her stigmata. In 1866, two years before they appeared, there was a cholera outbreak in Bois d'Haine which eventually claimed fourteen lives. Louise nursed six victims with great fortitude, but the following year herself suffered a series of debilitating illnesses that may have been in part a cry for attention. In 1867 she suffered in turn from chlorosis and quinsy; this was followed by an outbreak of eczema and attacks of neuralgia that began in the last months of the year and continued into 1868, when she began to vomit blood. Weakened by a strict diet, she was given the last rites on 15 April 1868. Four days later her first menstrual cycle began; five days after that came the first stigmata.[34]

Louise Lateau's case obviously lends itself to psychological interpretation and suggests how long-term anxiety and a sense of neglect might have been brought

[29] Hellé, *Miracles*, 49–50; Ernst, *Maria redet*, 29–32; Carroll, *Cult of the Virgin Mary*, 158–9.
[30] H. Graef, *Mary: A History of Doctrine and Devotion*, 2 vols. (London, 1963), ii. 386; Perry and Echeverría, *Under the Heel*, 79–80.
[31] Hellé, *Miracles*, 191.
[32] F. F. M. Lefebvre, *Louise Lateau of Bois d'Haine: Her Life, her Ecstasies, and her Stigmata. A Medical Study* (London, 1873), 38.
[33] Ibid. 39
[34] Ibid. 4–14

to a head by a series of more immediate events, in this case the onset of puberty coupled with the effects of the cholera outbreak and her own desire to be the nursed rather than the nurse.[35] It is possible to discern a comparable trigger among many who experienced visions of the Virgin, usually a break in the continuity of everyday life which served to focus anxieties. Maximin Giraud had left home to work as a cowherd only weeks before he saw his first vision; Bernadette Soubirous had just returned from the neglect and exploitation of Bartrès to a home where she desperately sought security. A break of this kind, the crossing of a threshold, was common. Usually we find some sort of domestic emotional upheaval, in conjunction with a change in other aspects of their life. Sometimes this was a matter of beginning school or being on the eve of confirmation; sometimes it was associated with being fostered out or sent to work away from home. In the case of adult visionaries the role played by illness and bereavement seems to have been foremost. Estelle Faguette had been diagnosed as seriously ill; the former novice who saw apparitions in the Umbrian parish of Spoleto in 1862 had been forced to forgo a convent life because of rheumatism.[36] The earliest (non-Marian) apparitions claimed by Marie Bergadieu began after the death of a daughter; the Marian apparitions followed a dramatic visit to Lourdes in 1873 where she believed herself miraculously cured of a dubiously diagnosed cancer.[37]

It is not difficult to understand the emotional consolations the presence of the Virgin Mary brought to children and adults alike. For some she clearly represented a true mother. As we have seen, Cathérine Labouré had 'taken Mary for her mother'. There was a striking parallel to this in the case of the German-American girl Therese Schaffer. Adopted at the age of 10, she had promised the Virgin that she would become a nun when her mother died. Her vision, which occurred in a St Louis hospital in 1871 during a serious illness, might be seen as the embracing of Mary as a mother whose love was constant.[38] But there is no shortage of European examples. Interpretations which emphasize an emotional surrogate of this kind obviously make most sense when the visionary in question was literally motherless: Cathérine Labouré, Maximin Giraud, the adopted girl who had a vision at Rimini in 1850, Mathilde Sack in Mettenbuch. Such an approach also illuminates a case like that of Thérèse Martin, the later St Teresa of Lisieux. Severely distressed by the death of her mother Zélie when she was 4, Thérèse then had to face the departure into the convent of her elder sister and substitute mother, Pauline. Thérèse suffered a nervous illness for a period of six months, which apparently ended after an apparition of the Virgin in May 1883.[39] This

---

[35] For a psychological interpretation, see Carroll, *Cults and Devotions*, 86–7, 92, 95–7, 101–2.

[36] Sausseret, *Erscheinungen*, 287–92.

[37] Devlin, *Superstitious Mind*, 154–5.

[38] Sausseret, *Erscheinungen*, 292–5; Walsh, *Apparitions and Shrines*, iv. 45–55.

[39] M. Furlong, *Thérèse of Lisieux* (London, 1987), 34–51. Furlong describes Thérèse (49) as 'disturbed and angry at her desertion by a series of mothers'. Thérèse herself recounts the experiences in her *Autobiography of a Saint*, transl. R. Knox (London, 1960), 42–4, 64–74.

angle of approach also helps to explain those visionaries, including Bernadette Soubirous, whose biological mothers neglected or even rejected them.

The emotional balm provided by the experience of the apparitions may be easier to pin down with precision among younger seers, but it was not restricted to them. Adult visionaries also belonged to the vulnerable and weak. To the sick the Virgin offered relief, while the bereaved or isolated obtained an affirmation of their worth and the means to act out their grief. The Virgin Mary offered the certainty that she would not spurn her children—irrespective of biological age— and emotional comfort in the face of worldly troubles seems to have been a mainspring in many apparitions. Even when the Virgin told the visionaries that they would have to suffer in her cause, the suffering was invested with meaning and the certainty of release. The consolation gained from the visions emerges even from the visual descriptions given by the seers. Along with the rich unsullied colours—the pure whites, blues, azures, and golds—of the Virgin's apparel, and the dazzling but benign light that surrounded her, accounts spoke of Mary's incomparable beauty and gentleness. Some of these descriptions, especially later in the century, may be rightly regarded as the reproduction of a well-worn visual idiom—the pictorial counterpart to the narrative conventions within which the visionaries' stories were obviously framed. (Unsympathetic critics referred to their 'dreadful uniformity'.[40]) Even the more hackneyed accounts often suggest a genuine emotional intensity, however, and some convey a sense that the face and voice of the Virgin, the visions of angels and paradise, were the materials out of which the seers constructed an imagined better world.

The contrast between the everyday world and the world of the visions also offered subversive possibilities. Eugène Barbedette, one of the Pontmain seers, was asked by a group of lay women and religious in Fougères whether any of them bore a resemblance to the Virgin. 'None,' he replied: 'beside the Blessed Virgin you are all ugly.'[41] The bold levity of the remark reminds us of the greatly enhanced status enjoyed by visionary children especially. Generally poor, overworked, and powerless, they now became the centre of attention. The children were the conduit through which divine dissatisfaction was expressed, and there are instances where it appears that they were revenging themselves, more or less consciously, on the hard adult world. Marie-Jeanne Grave, in the Périgord, reported the words of the Virgin that her parents would die if they continued to blaspheme, together with the village mayor (their landlord), who had scoffed.[42] The Virgin of La Salette announced her son's anger that Sunday was not being observed as a day of rest, a point with obvious relevance to children who were forced to work seven days a week; at Lourdes the first rash of Bernadette's

[40] *VZ*, 15 Oct. 1876.
[41] Laurentin and Durand, *Un signe*, 65.
[42] Gibson, *Social History*, 146.

imitators included several servant girls.[43] In many cases the young seers were able, through the words of the Virgin, to convey strictures on the morals of the adult world and issue apocalyptic warnings.[44] An obvious anticlerical animus was present in some incidents. A priest from Rimlingen who spoke out against the long series of apparitions that occurred in Alsace during the early 1870s received a written warning from the Virgin that he would be punished in hell if he did not believe. The orthographical errors in the warning eventually drew suspicion on a 13-year-old girl, who confessed to authorship.[45]

This was an unusually transparent case, but the effect of all the apparitions was to invert the normal relationship between the children and their priests, employers, and neighbours. Through the words of the Virgin the young seers determined who should approach the site of the apparition, how they should behave, the procedures that would lead to a miraculous cure. They instructed that chapels be built, told of secrets they could not divulge, prophesied woe for sinners and sceptics. Where the children foretold the death of individuals, they seemed to dispose—if only as messengers—of life itself. Their experiences, in short, brought enhanced status, even (or perhaps particularly) when their demeanour remained simple and unspoiled. Everyday travails were replaced by the attention and respect of adults, including sometimes the cream of society and potentates of the church. If so many of the children had indeed lived Cinderella lives before their visions, they now experienced that sudden and happy reversal of fortunes so characteristic of Cinderella and other folk-tales.

Among older girls and women we find a similar combination of meanings in the words attributed to the Virgin. Sometimes they were angry, lashing the mighty for their sins and warning of a terrible reckoning. An 18-year-old girl from Normandy, imprisoned in Rouen for arson, returned to her village and predicted, on the Virgin's authority, that many priests would die if a chapel were not constructed in honour of Our Lady of La Salette.[46] The harsh strictures and dire warnings reported by Estelle Faguette in the 1870s were matched by those of a host of other young French women seers of the period, like the stigmatist and visionary in Fraudrais (Loire-Inférieure) who spoke in the voices of the Virgin and the Archangel Michael, warning of a time of troubles and the razing of Paris.[47] The notion of reversal was usually less apocalyptic and extravagant. Yet it was there by implication in every case. At the very least, the respect conferred by the apparition gave women an opportunity normally denied them to slough

[43] The fullest account of the imitative visionaries is in Laurentin, *Lourdes*, ii. 57–90. See also Kennedy, 'The Lady in Tears', 93–4; Devlin, *Superstitious Mind*, 161.

[44] V. Turner and E. Turner, 'Postindustrial Marian Pilgrimage', in J. Preston (ed.), *Mother Worship* (Chapel Hill, NC, 1982), 156–64.

[45] A. F. vom Berg [Adam Fauth], *Marpingen und das Evangelium* (Saarbrücken, 1877), 26–7. On the Alsatian apparitions, see also Thurston, *Beauraing*, 121–2.

[46] Devlin, *Superstitious Mind*, 152–3.

[47] Ernst, *Maria redet*, 39–41, on Estelle Faguette; de Cauzons, *La Magie*, iv. 610–11, on the visionary of the Fraudrais, and 597–617, on others of the same kind.

off harsh responsibilities: like illness, the status of visionary was a resource of the
weak, a means of escape. But the drama of the apparition also offered a veiled
means of protest against real or imagined ill-treatment.[48]

Many of these elements seem to be present in the apparitions that took place
in the Bohemian village of Philippsdorf in 1866.[49] Magdalena Kade was a 30-
year-old unmarried weaver's daughter. After some sort of severe shock at the age
of 19 she had a long history of illness, including abscesses and convulsions that
ended in unconsciousness. Her father died when she was 13 and her brother
Joseph inherited the family home; her mother, who had inherited the family's
smallholding, died in 1861. After her father's death Magdalena continued to live
in the house now owned by her brother, sharing it with his large family, until she
moved out and lived with the Kindermann family in Philippsdorf in October
1864. Towards the end of 1865 she was the victim of a series of scurrilous
lampoons (*Pasquille*) by a neighbour who later admitted his campaign of persecution to the parish priest. This was the background, then, when illness among
the Kindermann family led to Magdalena, herself ill, being fetched home by her
brother ten days before Christmas 1865. There she lay in bed beneath a picture
of the 'suffering mother', surrounded by a 'swarm of small children' and her
brother's lodgers. Her apparitions began four weeks after she had returned home,
three weeks after she had been given the last rites. The complete cure promised
by the Virgin materialized, and Magdalena became the centre of attention of
local doctors. The events surrounding this former victim of scurrilous gossip also
prompted a local cult of 'Mary the Salvation of the Sick', publicized by the
parish priest's pamphlet on the 'extraordinary events and miraculous cures' in
Philippsdorf.[50] Thousands of pilgrims streamed to the village and Magdalena
found herself taken seriously by visiting priests and lay Catholics of position and
influence. Here, no less than in Lourdes or La Salette, was an upside-down
world.

Visions for Troubled Times

What was true for the visionaries themselves was true also for their families and
fellow villagers, whose lives were profoundly affected by events. Initially, at least,
this prospect was often unwelcome and the seers were greeted with scepticism.
Bernadette Soubirous was beaten by her mother for lying, berated for her 'little
carnivals', abused in the streets by neighbours, and slapped by a woman who

[48] This argument is pressed, thoughtfully if perhaps a little repetitively, by Devlin, *Superstitious Mind*,
who applies it to possession and hysteria as well as visions and prophecies.
[49] For the following, see Sausseret, *Erscheinungen*, 244–9, and Walsh, *Apparitions and Shrines*, iv.
59–70.
[50] Father Franz Storch, *Maria, das Heil der Kranken. Darstellung der außerordentlichen Vorfälle und
wunderbaren Heilungen, welche im Jahre 1866 zu Philippsdorf in Böhmen sich ereignet haben* (Georgswalde,
n.d.) I have been unable to locate a copy of this brochure.

accused her of 'putting on comedies'.[51] 'You are little liars' was the first response of Mme Barbedette to the Pontmain visionaries: 'Be quiet, everyone is already looking at us.'[52] Outright suspicion and fears of scandal were the initial reactions of many—not all—parish priests. The same response occurred everywhere in the early stages. Where children were concerned, they were seldom regarded as particularly saintly and it was asked why they should have been singled out for special favour. An element of family rivalry can often be detected here. The events also threatened to disrupt normal economic activity as the pious or curious were drawn into the drama. As the news spread it became increasingly likely that the village would suffer the unwelcome attentions of local police and civil administrators. In a place like La Salette, already marked down by the authorities as a den of banditry, this was hardly good news.[53]

And yet so many apparitions overcame these initial obstacles to their acceptance. Why? In some cases the role taken by the local priests undoubtedly played a part. Suspicion was their instinctive reaction; but many seem to have approached the apparitions with a fairly Manichaean question—were they a true sign of grace, or the work of the devil? If they felt able to eliminate the latter, they were readier to believe the former. The persistence of the children and their reluctance to confess then reinforced this conclusion. Many priests, it is true, conscientiously believed that they were cultivating a cool detachment, but this often amounted to tacit support for the children's account. The Abbé Guérin in Pontmain strove to remain neutral, but his suggestion that the children 'saw' because they were less worldly than the adults gave an unmistakable cue to his parishioners. So did the reaction of Sister Vitaline, who taught at the village school. Unable to suppress her excitement, she told boarders at the school what had happened, causing them to join the growing crowd; she then drew up a chair in the middle of the visionaries and helped them to construe the 'letters in the sky' that formed the centre-piece of the apparition.[54] The pattern was similar in La Salette. The elderly Abbé Perrin tried not to commit himself, but after hearing the children's story he told them tearfully that they had seen the Blessed Virgin, and alluded indirectly to the subject in his sermon at high mass the following day. He was rapidly transferred to another parish, but the Abbé Mélin of Corps soon proved to be equally trusting.[55] A similar sequence of events can be seen elsewhere.

This does not provide a full explanation, however. There were plenty of examples—the Abbé Peyremale in Lourdes is the best known—where the local priest remained sceptical long after the authenticity of the apparitions had been generally accepted in the locality. Here the priest was, at best, a follower rather

[51] Laurentin, *Lourdes*, i. 152–3; P. Marnham, *Lourdes: A Modern Pilgrimage* (London, 1980), 4–5.

[52] Laurentin and Durand, *Un signe*, 23–5.

[53] On the reputation of La Salette, Sausseret, *Erscheinungen*, 193–4.

[54] Laurentin and Durand, *Un signe*, 28, 37, 46.

[55] Kselman, *Miracles and Prophecies*, 142; St John, *The Blessed Virgin*, 121; Sausseret, *Erscheinungen*, 176; Northcote, *Sanctuaries*, 183, 187.

than a leader.[56] Some suffered unpopularity because of their sceptical stance; and many apparitions achieved a high level of local acceptance whatever the position taken up by the priest. One explanation much favoured by the anticlerical press was material self-interest. The apparitions attracted pilgrims, and pilgrims spent money. They brought custom to the taverns and local carters, required accommodation at inns or in private houses, bought bottles and cans in which to carry home the miraculous water. It is true that as the celebrity of apparition sites grew, commercialization increasingly meant the invasion of outside stallholders, postcard sellers, and rosary vendors. It is also worth pointing out that action by the civil authorities might damage local trade. In Lourdes the Imperial bureaucracy threatened to run a proposed new railway around Lourdes if the town did not come to its senses. 'You'll see, that little nuisance has lost us the railway,' remarked Mayor Lacadé of the future St Bernadette.[57] There was the further problem that the arrival of pilgrims in very large numbers could have undesirable side-effects as fields and crops were trampled. Apparitions had much the same impact on arable land and meadows as a gold rush. But there were compensations. Father Grand of Saint-Saturnin, a supporter of the fake mystic Rosette Tamisier, observed to one sceptical villager: 'You fool! Within a year this whole district will be another California.'[58]

The prospect of profit played an undoubted role in winning local support for the apparitions. The families of both Magdalena Kade and Bernadette Soubirous were, for example, beneficiaries. Bernadette herself wrote to her sister requesting her not to sell pious objects, without success. When her brother began to do the same thing she was resigned to asking only that he not sell them on Sundays.[59] But the extent of local enrichment spread well beyond immediate families. Lourdes is the classic example. The policeman Philippe Viron, who took a celebrated photograph of Bernadette, entered the photographic business commercially.[60] The family which owned the land on which the grotto stood became immensely wealthy. Mayor Lacadé, who had worried that the apparitions would lead to the town losing its railway link, later drew up plans for the sale of *Eau Lacadé* and the development of Lourdes as a spa.[61] In the case of Lourdes itself, nobody could imagine the full extent of the commercialization that would follow. The railway did arrive in the town, but not until 1866, and the full development of the hotels and the spread throughout the town of the medals, rosaries, plaster statues, crosses, and chains so deplored by later visitors like Zola and Huysmans did not happen overnight.[62] But those who lived in places where later apparitions

[56] Kselman, *Miracles and Prophecies*, 142–7.
[57] Hellé, *Miracles*, 40, 248; Neame, *Happening*, 158–9.
[58] Hellé, *Miracles*, 270.
[59] Marnham, *Lourdes*, 77–8. Cf. Laurentin, *Lourdes*, vi. 78–9.
[60] Laurentin, *Lourdes*, vii. 15.
[61] Hellé, *Miracles*, 45, 83.
[62] On the railway and the growth of the town, see Laurentin, *Lourdes*, vii. 13–27. The sharp-tongued aesthete and convert Huysmans gives the best description of the gross commercialization that had

occurred could hardly fail to be aware of the possibilities. This was implicit in all subsequent expressions of local enthusiasm for 'the Rhenish Lourdes' or 'the Mayo Lourdes'.

We should nevertheless hesitate to ascribe too much importance to material self-interest in determining local responses. The fact that these were often poor and isolated communities suggests another powerful sentiment at work: the sense of local pride. To be the place where an apparition occurred brought kudos as well as material rewards. Such an event quite literally put a place on the map and offered the chance to pursue old rivalries by new means. We see this element most obviously in play when an apparition was followed shortly afterwards by a host of patent 'imitations' in the immediate locality. The Rimini apparition of 1850 led to a chain of similar cases in Fossombrone, Lugo, Sant'Arcangelo, Sant'Agate, and Montbarrocio.[63] The Alsatian apparitions at the beginning of the 1870s had a similar character.[64] Local rivalries almost certainly played a part in the positive reception given to more celebrated apparitions. This might be village-to-village rivalry, or resentment towards a local market town during a period when there was rural–urban tension over the trade in wood, cattle, or quarry-stone.[65] Events at La Salette provided the chance to score over the dominant regional town of Corps.[66] Lourdes had a different problem. It was surrounded by spa towns: Argelès, Bagnères-de-Bigorre, Barrèges, and the smart new resort of Cauterets (where Bernadette Soubirous herself took the waters in hope of a cure).[67] After 1858 it leap-frogged them all, in fame as well as fortune.

It is also striking how many nineteenth-century apparition sites were surrounded by places of Marian devotion and pilgrimages, without themselves having previously attracted much attention. This is true of several northern French and German locations, although the most striking examples are to be found in Italy. Vicovoro, where apparitions occurred in 1863, was a large village midway between Rome and Subiaco, where St Benedict began the monastic order to which he gave his name. Campocavallo, where similar events took place thirty years later, was just a few miles from the celebrated pilgrimage centre of Loreto.[68] Lourdes is once again the classic case. In common with the surrounding area of the Bigorre it had long been dominated by the Benedictine abbey at Saint-

occurred by the beginning of the twentieth century, offering a closely observed account of the progression from the cheap trinkets in old Lourdes to the 'gewgaws de luxe' as the visitor approached the Avenue of the Grotto. See J. K. Huysmans, *The Crowds of Lourdes* (London, 1925), 27–8.

[63] Thurston, *Beauraing*, 76–85.

[64] Berg, *Marpingen*, 26–7.

[65] See the discussion of tensions like this in H. Rubner, 'Waldgewerbe und Agrarlandwirtschaft im Spätmittelalter und im 19. und 20. Jahrhundert', in H. Kellenbenz (ed.), *Agrarisches Nebengewerbe und Formen der Reagrarisierung* (Stuttgart, 1975), 97–108.

[66] E. Weber, 'Religion and Superstition in Nineteenth-Century France', *Historical Journal*, 31 (1988), 407.

[67] Marnham, *Lourdes*, 52–3.

[68] K. S. Latourette, *Christianity in a Revolutionary Age*, i. (New York, 1958), 327; Thurston, *Beauraing*, 87 ff. On Loreto, see Northcote, *Sanctuaries*, 65–106.

Savin.[69] Lourdes was also ringed by eight or nine established centres of Marian pilgrimage, several of them based on miraculous legends that prefigured the story of Lourdes itself. Our Lady of Garaison was noted for the apparition of an early sixteenth-century shepherdess: it boasted a grotto, a spring, and stories of miraculous cures. Médoux traced its origins as a pilgrimage centre to a seventeenth-century apparition seen by another shepherdess, Liloye, a 'rough draft of Bernadette'. At Bétharram there was the legend of a shining statue of the Virgin found in a bush. It also had a grotto, a spring, and tales of cures. Bétharram was revived as a pilgrimage centre in the 1840s and was very active in the following decade until eclipsed by Lourdes.[70]

The affirmation of local identity, no less than the prospect of material reward, thus fuelled local acceptance of the apparitions. Both worked against potential fears that the impact of events would harmfully disrupt normal life. But that prompts a further question: just how 'normal' was life in La Salette, Lourdes, Pontmain, and the rest when the apparitions took place? The answer is that running through the history of nineteenth-century apparitions was a background of severe economic crisis at the times when they took place. Popular receptiveness to the visionaries' accounts was heightened because the Blessed Virgin's words seemed to provide an explanation of hard times.

We are, of course, dealing with communities that were notably poor at the best of times: the shepherds, peasants, and quarrymen of Lourdes, the weavers of Philippsdorf, the tenant farmers of Knock. A recent writer has pointed out that even the place-names around Pontmain—Fougères, Landivy, Désertines—suggest bracken, brush, and untilled land.[71] There is nevertheless a striking correlation between the timing of the apparitions and the economic cycle. The events at La Salette occurred during the last great general crisis of famine across western Europe, the hungry forties. In La Salette the potato and other crops had failed in 1845, and by September 1846—when the apparitions began—had visibly failed again. The message of the Virgin in fact spoke directly to this material distress, which was explained as a sign of divine anger: 'I showed it to you last year in the potato harvest but you paid no heed to it.' She went on to warn of a great famine to come, when the wheat would turn to dust and the grapes and nuts would rot. But if men repented, there would be plenty: 'rocks will turn into wheat, potatoes will be found sown in the ground'.[72] Small wonder that such a message struck a responsive chord. The background to Bernadette Soubirous's visions was similar. Cholera had claimed many lives in Lourdes in 1854-5, and in 1856-7 there was famine in the Pyrenean departments when the

[69] The Bavarian apparition site of Mettenbuch was also overshadowed by the major Benedictine abbey of Metten.

[70] Neame, *Happening*, 27-8, 98; Huysmans, *Crowds*, 1-11. It was Huysmans (p. 8) who drew the parallel between Liloye and Bernadette.

[71] Weber, 'Religion and Superstition', 408.

[72] Kselman, *Miracles and Prophecies*, 62-3; Devlin, *Superstitious Mind*, 160; Sausseret, *Erscheinungen*, 167-72; St John, *The Blessed Virgin*, 111-17.

crops failed and the vines were ravaged by phylloxera.[73] Bernadette's own family was not the only one in Lourdes to have suffered extreme poverty in the period leading up to the first apparition in February 1858.

The two best-known apparitions of the 1870s unfolded against a similar background. The events in Pontmain began in January 1871, during an exceptionally harsh winter when the wolves were encroaching close to the farms in search of food, and epidemics of typhoid and smallpox had broken out.[74] The apparition reported in 1879 in the County Mayo village of Knock took place at a time of chronic agricultural crisis. The value of the principal Irish crops fell by over £14 million between 1876 and 1879, and the production of potatoes dropped from over 4 million tons to just over 1 million in the same period. The failure of this staple in three consecutive years brought distress on a scale not seen since the potato famine of 1847, and there was a tense mood among a population faced with starvation and evictions.[75] Mayo was at the storm-centre of discontent. Eighteen families in the immediate area of Knock had suffered recent eviction, and a public demonstration had been held in the village in June 1879.[76] One historian has even suggested that the apparitions were a product of hallucinations caused by malnutrition, specifically by pellagra contracted from poor-quality relief rations of 'Indian meal' or maize.[77] There is an obvious danger of reductionism with an approach of this kind, but we should not exclude the possibility that poverty and poor diet had a direct bearing on events. Piero Camporesi, for example, has brilliantly illuminated the links between starvation, adulterated food, and the dreams of the poor in early modern Europe.[78] Famine, whether in Knock, Lourdes, or La Salette, had physiological as well as psychological effects: visionaries and their supporters were often hungry or poorly fed, just as they were often unwell.

At a time of catastrophe the intercession of the Virgin brought consolations of many kinds to the poor—and Lourdes is typical in that it was the poor, beggars,

---

[73] Laurentin, Lourdes, i. 128–9; Devlin, Superstitious Mind, 161. Cathérine Labouré's apparition also occurred at a time of economic crisis in 1830, and achieved its resonance during an outbreak of cholera which arrived in France as the first 'miraculous medals' were struck in the summer of 1832. The medals often served as talismans against cholera. See Weber, 'Religion and Superstition', 406.

[74] Laurentin and Durand, Un signe, 13–14; Devlin, Superstitious Mind, 75, 97.

[75] In 1879 over a thousand families, with a total of nearly 6,000 people were evicted: F. S. L. Lyons, Ireland since the Famine (London, 1973), 165.

[76] Purcell, 'Our Lady of Silence', 148–9; J. Lee, The Modernisation of Irish Society 1848–1918 (Dublin, 1973), 66–78; S. Clark, Social Origins of the Irish Land War (Princeton, NJ, 1979), 247; Carroll, Cult of the Virgin Mary, 209–11; T. Neary, I Comforted Them in Sorrow: Knock 1879–1979 (Knock, Co. Mayo, 1979), 16–17. The Land League, formed in the autumn of 1879, first took shape nearby in Irishtown, Co. Mayo.

[77] See E. M. Crawford, 'Indian Meal and Pellagra in Nineteenth-Century Ireland', in J. M. Goldstrom and L. A. Clarkson (eds.), Irish Population, Economy, and Society: Essays in Honour of the late K. H. Connell (Oxford, 1981), 131 n. 38. Crawford notes that 77% of the population in the parish of Knock were on relief rations of maize at the time, and the symptoms of pellagra were widespread. I am grateful to Roy Foster for drawing this article to my attention.

[78] P. Camporesi, Bread of Dreams: Food and Fantasy in Early Modern Europe (Oxford, 1989).

servants, and slate quarrymen, who were the first to accept Bernadette's account.[79]
Mary's appearance brought comfort, for had she not singled out the most humble
for a sign of grace?[80] Her message that plenty could be restored by faith and
repentance was a source of hope. Indeed the apocalyptic message itself yielded a
form of emotional consolation: it confirmed that things were as bad as people
believed, yet gave them a warrant to express their fears as well as providing a
vocabulary with which to do so. Judith Devlin has referred to this kind of social
release as a 'black carnival', and argued that the apocalyptic aspect of apparitions
often amounted to 'an inverted form of protest' that rejected reality and consigned
both catastrophe and redemption to an other-worldly realm of the imagination.[81]
The message of the apparitions offered explanation of a sort by placing the harsh
blows of the here-and-now within the framework of a moral universe. There are
perhaps some parallels with popular reactions to the Black Death in the fourteenth
century, when anxiety and the impulse to expiation attached themselves to the
cult of the stern but merciful *Mater Dolorosa*.[82]

Nineteenth-century epidemics like cholera and smallpox went hand in hand
with famine. They were also closely linked, as they had been in previous centuries,
with war and political upheaval.[83] These too provide a key—perhaps the single
most important—to the widespread support for Marian apparitions. The first
great wave of visions in modern Europe occurred in the aftermath of the French
Revolution. Within France a series of alleged miracles preceded the great counter-
revolutionary uprising in the Vendée.[84] Marian apparitions and moving or
weeping statues were reported in Italy, especially from the Papal States, during
the Napoleonic campaigns of the 1790s.[85] They had their counterparts in the
many visions, miracles, prophecies, celestial signs, and cases of stigmata that
were claimed in occupied Germany.[86] A further set of apparitions was closely
associated with the political upheavals of restoration Europe in the 1830s and
1840s. Cathérine Labouré's first apparition occurred on 18 July 1830, as political

---

[79] Devlin, *Superstitious Mind*, 161–2.

[80] On the miraculous events as a source of comfort, see Hellé, *Miracles*, 12. On the motifs of humility
and simplicity that underlined the apparitions as a cult of the poor, Kselman, *Miracles and Prophecies*,
esp. 107–9.

[81] Devlin, *Superstitious Mind*, 160–3.

[82] See Marina Warner, *Alone of All her Sex: The Myth and Cult of the Virgin Mary* (London, 1976),
215–6. See also Norman Cohn's classic study, *The Pursuit of the Millennium* (London, 1957).

[83] Richard J. Evans, 'Epidemics and Revolutions: Cholera in Nineteenth-Century Europe', *Past and
Present*, 120 (1988), 123–46. Epidemics were, of course, spread by the movements of armies, and
attacked civilian populations that were especially vulnerable. On the connection in earlier periods
(particularly the 17th cent.) between war and apparitions, miracles and the finding of sacred objects,
see Nolan and Nolan, *Christian Pilgrimage*, 222–3.

[84] C. Tilly, *The Vendée* (London, 1964), 255. See also T. Tackett, 'The West in France in 1789: The
Religious Factor in the Origins of Counterrevolution', *Journal of Modern History*, 54 (1982), 715–45.

[85] Thurston, *Beauraing*, 68–76; Carroll, *Cult of the Virgin Mary*, 195–6; G. Turi, '*Viva Maria!' La
reazione alle riforme leopoldine (1790–1799)* (Florence, 1969), 243–87, and appendix III, pp. 310–12;
A. J. Heriot, *The French in Italy, 1796–1799* (London, 1957), 112–13, 263–4, 268.

[86] T. C. W. Blanning, *The French Revolution in Germany: Occupation and Resistance in the Rhineland
1792–1802* (Oxford, 1983), 236–9.

crisis came to a head in France. It preceded the outbreak of revolution by just nine days, and the sequence of her later visions paralleled the chronology of post-revolutionary events.[87] The revolutions of 1848–9 also provided the background to a series of similar events, including visions in the Vosges and Valence, and a cluster of miraculous occurrences in Italy that echoed those of the 1790s.[88]

The clearest case of apparitions that shadowed political upheaval can be seen in the 1860s and early 1870s, when the creation of new states in Italy and Germany redrew the map of Europe. The events in Philippsdorf took place in 1866, as tension led to war between Austria and Prussia over the German question. The village itself lay just on the border, in an enclave of Habsburg Bohemia surrounded by German Saxony.[89] The struggle for Italian unification was accompanied by a renewed wave of apparitions, especially around the crucial year of 1870. A series of visions in 1869–70 in the sanctuary of Santa Maria della Croce, near Cremona, was followed by reports of a moving statue in Soriano (Calabria) in 1870, during the invasion of the Papal States by Victor Emmanuel. Rome itself was the scene of a similar case in 1871.[90] The Franco-Prussian war of 1870–1 provided the backdrop to another cluster of apparitions. The appearance of the Virgin and her 'sign in the sky' at Pontmain in January 1871 is the most familiar, but a more extensive series of apparitions took place at the same time in Krüth, Wittelsheim, and other Alsatian villages.[91]

The seers themselves were undoubtedly affected by the anxieties these upheavals generated. A striking number had seen their own immediate security threatened. Maria Catalani, who claimed one of a series of apparitions in Rome in 1816, had been injured during the sacking of the papal palace at Terracina by Polish troops in 1798 (an injury she claimed had now been miraculously cured).[92] There are some parallels here with the visions of Anna Katherina Emmerich, which began in 1798 with French troops in occupation of the western parts of Germany. In some of the earliest visions she reported being taken by her guardian angel to battlefields where she had helped the dying. Four years later she entered the Augustinian convent in Dulmen as a novice, but was forced to return home shortly afterwards when Jérôme Bonaparte became king of Westphalia and the convent was dissolved.[93] A similar fate must have seemed imminent to Cathérine Labouré, who could hardly have remained untouched by the violent anti-clericalism and sacking of churches that formed a counterpoint to her revelations. The immediate position of Magdalena Kade was equally insecure. At the time

---

[87] Kselman, *Miracles and Prophecies*, 77–8; Weber, 'Religion and Superstition', 406.
[88] On the visions of Rosine Horiot in the Vosges, see Devlin, *Superstitious Mind*, 151; on the apparitions in Valence, Gibson, *Social History*, 149; on Italy, Thurston, *Beauraing*, 76–85
[89] Sausseret, *Erscheinungen*, 243–4.
[90] Thurston, *Beauraing*, 85–7, 102–6; Sausseret, *Erscheinungen*, 267–9.
[91] 'Wunder in Elsaß', *St Bonifatius-Kalender für das Jahr 1893*, 89–104; Berg, *Marpingen*, 26–7; Thurston, *Beauraing*, 121–2.
[92] Sausseret, *Erscheinungen*, 305–10.
[93] Hellé, *Miracles*, 188–200.

when the Virgin appeared to her, she was living in one of the row of houses in Philippsdorf closest to the border with German Saxony. Her brother's lodgers included factory workers employed in the Saxon towns of Gersdorf and Spree-dorf, and it is hard to imagine that some of the tension of 1866 did not communicate itself to her through this channel.[94] Five years later Joseph and Eugène Barbedette saw the Lady in the Sky at Pontmain at a time when they were anxious about their half-brother serving in the Franco-Prussian war, while in Rome that same year a statue of the Virgin moved in answer to the plea of a woman whose son had just been conscripted: 'O Mother to whom everything is possible, when will you finally free us from the Piedmontese who snatch our children from us?'[95]

Belief in the intercessionary power of the Virgin offered hope to the individual; it also fed a collective faith in the apparitions. For moving statues and apparitions followed the line of hostilities. Pontmain, from which thirty-eight soldiers had been mustered, was threatened by an advancing Prussian army that had just won the battle of Le Mans and seemed set to overrun the diocesan town of Laval. Large-scale movements of troops and wounded and the sound of gunfire audible in the village meant that, as one account puts it, 'fear ruled' and local peasants had hidden what money, corn, wine, and linen they possessed.[96] The appearance of the Mother of Hope and the Queen of Peace struck a chord, and the halting of the Prussian advance and subsequent armistice were attributed to her intercession.[97] The Alsatian apparitions of the early 1870s were no less clearly prompted by the experience of war, although their theme was more bellicose.[98] If the Virgin of Pontmain was the harbinger of peace, the Virgin in Alsace characteristically brandished a sword against Prussia. A wave of subsequent apparitions lasting until 1874 developed variations on the same theme.[99]

Apparitions and Politics

We are not dealing solely with a general fear of war and political change, but with fear of what those particular wars and changes would bring. In the twentieth century the political spectre was communism: that was what fuelled the response

[94] On the physical location of the Kade home, and the proximity of the border, see Sausseret, *Erscheinungen*, 243–4.

[95] Laurentin and Durand, *Un signe*, 16, 20; Sausseret, *Erscheinungen*, 267–9.

[96] Laurentin and Durand, *Un signe*, 14.

[97] In the Rimini apparition of 1850 rumours abounded that two Austrian officers had been converted by the appearance of the Virgin and had laid down their swords as a sign of respect: Sausseret, *Erscheinungen*, 259–62.

[98] See de Cauzons, *La Magie*, iv. 607, on the 'intense patriotic anguish' of these years in France.

[99] 'Wunder in Elsaß', 89–104; Berg, *Marpingen*, 26–7; Thurston, *Beauraing*, 121–2. One group of 9-year-old children claimed to have seen the child Jesus wielding a sword against German soldiers and creating disunity in their ranks. In the case of Anna Katharina Emmerich there had been very similar rumours, with the French and German roles reversed. In one such rumour, two French soldiers supposedly jumped into the visionary's room through a window but fled when they saw a light like a halo around her head. See Hellé, *Miracles*, 188–200.

to the celebrated Fatima apparitions of 1917, and their many successors after 1945.[100] In the nineteenth century the perceived political enemies were anticlerical liberalism and the ambitions of the modern state. That message was proclaimed, with appropriate national variations, in apparitions of the Virgin from Napoleonic Italy to Bismarckian Germany. Italy's miraculous Madonnas in the 1790s, like their counterparts elsewhere in French-occupied Europe, were one sign of a broad backlash of popular Catholic sentiment. The credence given to such episodes betrays a desperate search for security (or revenge) in the face of revolutionary change. The impact of the French armies and the new regimes they established can hardly be exaggerated. The church had touched everyday life in old-regime Europe at almost every level. It was landlord, employer, consumer, educator, and purveyor of charity, as well as guardian of the faith.[101] In the Papal States and the numerous principalities of the Holy Roman Empire it wielded temporal power. The political and institutional aspects of this dominance were now overturned in a matter of years. Two Popes were deposed and forced into exile in France, where one of them died.[102] Not only was the temporal power of the church broken in Rome, but the ecclesiastical principalities in the former Holy Roman Empire were abolished as the map of Europe was radically reshaped. Church lands were secularized and foundations wound up, civil marriage was introduced, religious pilgrimages and processions were curtailed or abolished. True, the initial zeal of the revolutionary armies was later tempered by the Concordat of 1801 and Napoleonic pragmatism. But there was no reversal of the most important institutional changes, and the attitude of the French satellite regimes, with their shallow local roots, remained incorrigibly lofty about Catholic 'backwardness'.[103]

It was against these radical changes and scornful temporary masters that the Catholic reaction directed itself. Sometimes it took organized form, especially if outraged religious sentiment fused with nationalist (or localist) resentment. Spain is the best-known example, where the French and their local allies were violently at odds with popular feeling and opposition took the form of guerrilla war. The Tyrolean revolt of Andreas Hofer and the Sanfedist movement in Italy shared many of the same characteristics.[104] In comparison with these movements, the

[100] See below, Ch. 12.
[101] See the essays in W. J. Callahan and D. Higgs (eds.), *Church and Society in Catholic Europe of the Eighteenth Century* (Cambridge, 1979).
[102] Latourette, *Christianity*, i. 147. It was Pius VI who died. On the humiliating fate of his successor, Pius VII, see ibid. 349–50.
[103] The anticlerical militancy of the people's armies at home is wonderfully brought out by R. Cobb, *The People's Armies* (New Haven, Conn., and London, 1987), 442–79, and the actions of the revolutionary armies in one part of occupied Europe can be followed in Blanning, *French Revolution in Germany*, 207–54. On the Napoleonic occupations, see O. Connelly, *Napoleon's Satellite Kingdoms* (New York, 1969).
[104] E. J. Hobsbawm, *The Age of Revolution 1789–1848* (London, 1962), 107, 194; H. Reinalter, *Aufklärung—Absolutismus—Reaktion. Die Geschichte Tirols in der zweiten Hälfte des 18. Jahrhunderts* (Vienna, 1974), 235–6; E. E. Y. Hales, *Revolution and Papacy, 1769–1846* (London, 1960), 116–28;

waves of popular enthusiasm that greeted apparitions of the Virgin were clearly spontaneous and reactive rather than organized and active. Given the apparent dominance of women among both visionaries and their enthusiasts, one is tempted to see a sexual division of labour in operation. Outraged Catholic men attacked the brave new world of the French with main force; fearful Catholic women took comfort and hope from the Virgin Mother. However, any such gender division was far from absolute, and the distinction between revolts as active and apparitions as passive forms of resistance is very blurred at the edges. The civil authorities certainly saw mass gatherings at the sites of apparitions, and the heightened emotions that were aroused, as a source of potential danger. The evidence from Italy suggests that apparitions and miracles served to legitimize resistance as much as deflect it into quietist channels.

The apparitions that took place during the French occupation were intensely political. They were read as a sign of divine anger against irreligious despoilers, and a source of reassurance that the reign of Godlessness would come to an end. Both interpretations were to recur when subsequent apparitions seemed to speak to a sense of Catholic isolation or persecution. This was most obviously the case in France during the great nineteenth-century cycles of revolution and counter-revolution, clericalism and anticlericalism. Cathérine Labouré's vision coincided with the overthrow of the ultra-clerical Bourbon monarchy, which was to issue in an attack on Jesuit headquarters in Paris in July 1830, the desecration of Notre Dame, and the sacking of the archbishopric in the capital city twice in eight months. The Virgin appeared in blue and white, the colours of royalist France fused with the emblems of innocence and purity. Her reported concern with 'evil times' fitted the prevailing mood of the faithful, and the miraculous medal requested by the vision and struck in 1832 clearly had the status of a talisman. Within four years, 15 million medals had been made; by 1842 the figure was 100 million.[105] Later apparitions echoed the political message of 1830. Lourdes was widely interpreted as a sign of support for the legitimist cause against the Second Empire. Pontmain was located in the classically 'white' part of France, close to the Breton border and the old *Chouan* capital of Fougères, where the 1818 revelation of the nun Sister Nativité had identified the revolution with Antichrist. Soon after the apparition royalists presented an image of 'Our Lady of Hope of Pontmain' to the Count of Chambord, pretender to the French throne.[106] (The Belgian stigmatist Louise Lateau reportedly smiled at the mention of Chambord's

Turi, 'Viva Maria!', 248 ff. Heriot, *The French in Italy*, 186–7, draws an explicit parallel between guerrilla campaigns in Italy and Spain.

[105] St John, *The Blessed Virgin*, 1–18; Kselman, *Miracles and Prophecies*, 91–2; Weber, 'Religion and Superstition', 406.

[106] Weber, 'Religion and Superstition', 408; M. Oraison, 'Le Point de vue du médecin psychiatre clinicien sur les apparitions', in Billet *et al.* (eds.), *Vraies et fausses*, 130–1. Sister Nativité's vision took place at almost the same time as the Marian apparitions of two girls in Bourg in May 1819. See also Devlin, *Superstitious Mind*, 152, and Kselman, *Miracles and Prophecies*, 124.

name.[107]) Marie Bergadieu related that the great king Henri V would come to save France and sinful Paris be destroyed: her visions were taken up by the legitimist, clerical press. The apocalyptic prophecies of the Pellevoisin apparitions bore a similar political message, the Virgin excoriating the faithlessness of France and warning of a 'time of trials'.[108]

The link between the real or perceived political persecution of Catholics and the incidence of apparitions was not confined to France. Successive waves of apparitions in Italy followed the contours of political conflict, increasing in number at times when church autonomy, religious orders, clerical education, and the integrity of the Papal States were most at risk, especially around the middle of the century and in the years 1869–71. In Ireland the events at Knock are inseparable from resentment over the Protestant ascendancy, heightened by the particularly severe crisis of the 1870s. In Germany, as we shall see, the apparitions of the 1870s took place during a fierce church–state struggle, the *Kulturkampf*, when many Catholics were gripped by panic. Both supporters and opponents agreed on the importance of this background.[109]

It is no surprise that governments reacted with alarm to the apparitions. They occurred at times of unusual tension and they attracted large crowds whose behaviour was unpredictable. The numbers involved were impressive, given the difficult terrain and poor communications at so many apparition sites. Two months after the apparitions began at La Salette there were perhaps 500 people on the hillside, mainly from around Corps. But even before the snows had cleared in the following spring larger crowds started to arrive from a much wider area, and an estimated 50,000 were present on the anniversary of the first vision.[110] At Lourdes the crowd grew from several hundred a week after the first apparition to around 8,000 two weeks later.[111] Near to large towns the numbers could be greater still. The miraculous events at Vicovoro in 1863 were first reported on 22 July; by the Feast of the Assumption on 15 August there were 10,000 pilgrims present, many from nearby Rome.[112] News spread through rumour carried by hawkers, colporteurs, shepherds, and others, and pilgrims travelled on foot or by cart. It is clear that these means of communications still served to alert local interest even in the 1870s. On 26 January 1871, just nine days after the vision in the sky, 500 pilgrims from the neighbouring parish of Landivy arrived in Pontmain; the thousands who followed, from Maine, Normandy, and Brittany, still came predominantly on foot.[113] By the 1870s, however, the telegraph and the

[107] De Cauzons, *La Magie*, iv. 609.

[108] Devlin, *Superstitious Mind*, 154; Walsh, *Apparitions and Shrines*, iv. 119–48; de Cauzons, *La Magie*, iv. 611–13; Ernst, *Maria redet*, 39–41.

[109] The theme of 'political apparitions' is central to Perry and Echeverria, *Under the Heel*, who sometimes develop it with more vigour than subtlety.

[110] Sausseret, *Erscheinungen*, 185–6; St John, *The Blessed Virgin*, 126.

[111] Ernst, *Maria redet*, 30.

[112] Sausseret, *Erscheinungen*, 263–7.

[113] Laurentin and Durand, *Un signe*, 55.

press were already spreading news of these events more quickly, and the railway extended the area from which pilgrims were drawn.

The civil authorities were not concerned about numbers alone. Pilgrims crowded the highways and strained the minimal provisions for public order in rural areas. They also threatened to spread epidemics. More than that, the apparitions attracted large numbers of those whose mobility was least expected or desired: women, children, the poor. For all those who took part, the pilgrimages offered a degree of emancipation from everyday social structures and conventions. They represented, in Victor Turner's phrase, a 'bout of nomadism'.[114] How the pilgrims behaved was important. Like the crusades, to which some writers compared them, the mass pilgrimages to new Marian apparition sites combined religious and secular strands.[115] They were marked by a heightened spiritual intensity, and the very novelty of the miraculous events meant that the solemnity of collective singing and prayer was often accompanied by more unrestrained, even crazed behaviour. Pilgrims at the apparition sites stripped the foliage from trees and bushes to carry home as talismans; latecomers carried off earth, attributing to it magical healing properties similar to those of the miraculous spring water. At some of the sites scores, even hundreds, of pilgrims themselves claimed to have seen visions or celestial signs; rumours circulated about unbelievers who had been struck down or found their horses lamed. The apparitions brought the animistic and superstitious aspects of popular religious belief to the surface.[116]

At the same time the behaviour of the pilgrims had a festive, ludic quality. This doubtless derived in part from the sheer improbability of the dramatic hillside settings, where hundreds of candles burned and large crowds prayed and sang in unison. Eyewitnesses of the scene at La Salette spoke years later with wonder of the 'spectacle'.[117] But the pilgrimage sites were also festive in a more worldly sense. They attracted hawkers and stallholders, musicians and confidence tricksters; alcohol was speedily made available, and the confining bonds of everyday life were loosened. These elements could disturb even governments which might be sympathetic to the Virgin's message, as the experience of Restoration France demonstrated.[118] In fact, of course, apparitions tended to achieve their greatest resonance precisely at those times when the civil power was unsympathetic. There was therefore a natural inclination to view the events not only as examples of fraud and deception, but as politically motivated too. This, as well as general considerations of public order, resulted in efforts by the civil authorities concerned to nip events in the bud and prevent the gathering of crowds, efforts that were generally unsuccessful.

[114] V. Turner, 'Pilgrimages as Social Processes', in Turner, Dramas, Fields and Metaphors: Symbolic Action in Human Society (Ithaca, NY, 1974), 171.
[115] St John, The Blessed Virgin, 275, for the comparison with the crusades.
[116] See below, Ch. 5, for a detailed examination of German pilgrims in the 1870s.
[117] Sausseret, Erscheinungen, 187.
[118] On the Bourg incident of 1819 and government alarm, see Devlin, Superstitious Mind, 152.

Lourdes illustrates the general pattern very well. Bernadette Soubirous herself was questioned in turn by the local police commissioner, an imperial prosecutor, and an examining magistrate. All sought to extract a confession from her, and Police Commissioner Jacomet made her father promise that she would be prevented from visiting the grotto. Following correspondence between the Minister of Public Worship and the local Prefect of the Tarbes, attempts were also made to have Bernadette declared insane. At the same time, soldiers were sent to Lourdes and a brigade of mounted police stiffened the local force. The grotto itself was placed under an interdict and surrounded with palings.[119] These measures proved remarkably ineffective. The restriction on Bernadette's movements did not withstand the growing force of local opinion and was lifted by the mayor of Lourdes. The presence of soldiers and gendarmes at the site also proved no deterrent to pilgrims, and when the grotto was barricaded in June 1858 the barricades were demolished and reconstructed again three times before the parish priest urged his flock to avoid openly resisting the civil authorities. Eventually orders to open the grotto to the public were given by Napoleon III himself, whose 2-year-old son and heir had been sent to Lourdes by the Empress Eugénie and 'cured' of sunstroke contracted in Biarritz.[120] But this bizarre dénouement should not obscure the fact that the might of the state had already been humbled.

Did the authorities at Lourdes and elsewhere over-react to events? In some respects they obviously did. Behind the actions of officials at all levels, and not only in the case of Lourdes, we can discern a kind of educated rage that such events were possible in the most modern of centuries. Traces of eighteenth-century Enlightenment thought mingled here with a more specifically nineteenth-century belief in progress. To purposive official state-builders and their self-consciously 'modern' supporters, particularly among the professional middle classes, such instances of ignorance and superstition were monstrous aberrations in the age of steam and mass education. In the event officials painted themselves into a corner with their bluster, and shows of force proved counter-productive— although it is by no means certain that a policy of benign neglect would have proved more successful. The authorities were also wide of the mark when they saw political inspiration behind the apparitions. Catholic and clerical political movements certainly tried to exploit them, most notably in France, but they invariably jumped on to bandwagons that were already rolling. Some Catholic politicians who defended the church against the incursions of the state were, in fact, equivocal about the apparitions and the popular enthusiasm they unleashed. This was particularly the case in Germany, as we shall see.[121]

---

[119] Kselman, *Miracles and Prophecies*, 180–3; St John, *The Blessed Virgin*, 224–6, 243, 254–9. Detailed accounts of the civil authorities' actions are to be found throughout the 7 vols. of Laurentin, *Lourdes*, interwoven with evidence about the visions themselves and the clerical response.

[120] On the Emperor and Lourdes, Laurentin, *Lourdes*, iv. 51–64.

[121] See Kselman, *Miracles and Prophecies*, 113–40, on the clerical-political exploitation of the apparitions in Third Republic France, and below, Ch. 8 on the ambivalence among Centre Party politicians in Germany.

The popular movements were spontaneous, not organized; but the civil authorities were nevertheless right to detect a broad political meaning in the behaviour of the crowds, if for the wrong reasons. Where they saw subversive inspiration, the reality was an instinctive popular reaction, but one that contained its own political logic. Like nineteenth-century bread rioters, the crowds at apparition sites were neither manipulated, nor simply mobs. The reaction to attempted restrictions on access to the sites showed a determination to defend their territory that we associate with urban social movements. The latter built barricades and the former pulled them down; both acted with an eye both to logistic practicality and the symbolic importance of public space.[122] In other ways, too, the behaviour of apparition crowds gives us a window on forms of collective Catholic action that have received far less attention from historians than, say, popular working-class movements. To take two examples: the many accounts of singing and praying in the face of gendarmes or soldiers often suggest a form of passive resistance, while the ubiquitous flowers, rosaries, lighted candles, vigils, and processions all indicate the confident parading of a common set of symbols. In fact, Catholic pilgrims appear to have acted with a considerable degree of self-consciousness when they brandished their own potent religious icons against those of civil authority. The great state-building process in nineteenth-century Europe, whether it took place within a monarchical, imperial, or republican form, challenged the authority and jurisdiction of the church. It also developed its own symbols of allegiance, in the form of flags, anthems, and monuments.[123] The pilgrimage badges, Marian hymns, and miraculous spring-waters of the apparition crowds were a rival set of emblems. They were an illustration of the hold the church militant had on the popular Catholic imagination in nineteenth-century Europe.

The Role of the Church

The resonance of the apparitions testifies to the remarkable Catholic revival in nineteenth-century Europe, at a time when *bien-pensant* opinion believed allegiance to the church was bound to wither in the face of modern science and education. A popular movement that saw hundreds of thousands of pilgrims descend on Lourdes with papal blessing would have seemed improbable in the 1780s. In the first place, the church of the 1780s took a far more austere line on

---

[122] The classic works are those of George Rudé, including *The Crowd in the French Revolution* (Oxford, 1967) and *The Crowd in History* (London, 1981). For a rare attempt to discuss the role of religion in this context, see O. Hufton, 'Women in Revolution, 1789–96', *Past and Present*, 53 (1971), 90–108.
[123] See E. J. Hobsbawm, *The Age of Empire 1875–1914* (London, 1987), ch. 6 ('Waving flags'), and E. J. Hobsbawm, 'Mass-Producing Traditions: Europe, 1870–1914', in Hobsbawm and T. Ranger (eds.), *The Invention of Tradition* (Cambridge, 1983), 263–307. Maurice Agulhon's *Marianne into Battle: Republican Imagery and Symbolism in France 1789–1880* (Cambridge, 1981) is an exemplary study of one way in which French republican identity was fostered.

the pious claims of unlettered shepherd girls. In the latter part of the eighteenth century, powerful advocates of the Catholic Enlightenment sought to temper, even to eliminate, many forms of popular belief and practice. Their targets included the large numbers of popular feast days and pilgrimages, materialist cults like the benediction of cows, and the emotional 'excesses' of private revelations or visions. They extended to what one of them called 'indiscreet modes of devotion' towards Mary.[124] The reformers stood for a bracing and rationalized faith, stripped of baroque piety and maudlin excess.[125] The movement for reform was associated particularly with the doctrinal supporters of Jansenism and Febronianism, but it was not confined to them and had many supporters in the Curia and among influential bishops in the national churches. Here was another sign of the change that occurred in the nineteenth-century church. On the eve of the French Revolution the papacy possessed neither the centralized organization nor the prestige within the church that were later to make Pius IX's personal attachment to the cult of the Virgin so important. Buffeted by political pressure from the Bourbon monarchs of France, Spain, and Portugal, Rome was forced to allow a large measure of autonomy to the Gallican church in France and to 'enlightened', Josephinist-minded bishops in German-speaking Europe.[126]

Both the inner and outer lives of the church were therefore very different towards the end of the eighteenth century from what they became in the great age of Marian apparitions. The contrast is summed up by the suppression in 1773 of the Jesuits, who were to be so closely associated with the Marian revival. The dissolution of the order showed the vulnerability of Pope Gregory XIV to external pressure, and symbolized the turn away from the highly emotional, even sensual forms of piety the Jesuits had always encouraged. It was a reminder of the more general decline in the numbers and the vitality of orders and congregations in the period, a result partly of suppression (a French royal commission in 1786 closed down a thousand religious communities), partly of internal decay and a decline in new foundations.[127] The diminution of the Pope's authority was paralleled by a shrinking of the church's material and human resources.[128] The French Revolutionary and Napoleonic wars seemed to bring these troubles to a head. It led to the persecution of priests, the dislocation of the church's pastoral

[124] The Italian priest Ludovico Muratori, author of *The Science of Rational Devotion*, cited in Perry and Echeverría, *Under the Heel*, 53. For Muratori's influence in German-speaking Europe, see C. Dipper, 'Volksreligiosität und Obrigkeit im 18. Jahrhundert', in Schieder (ed.), *Volksreligiosität*, 88.

[125] Korff, 'Zwischen Sinnlichkeit und Kindlichkeit'; E. Hegel, *Die Katholische Kirche Deutschlands unter dem Einfluß der Aufklärung des 18. Jahrhunderts* (Opladen, 1975); Callahan and Higgs (eds.), *Church and Society*, 8–9, 62–3, 71–5, 136; and Dipper, 'Volksreligiosität', on Reform Catholicism, Josephinist and cameralist reformers, and popular piety.

[126] K. O. von Aretin, *The Papacy in the Modern World* (London, 1970), 15–44; Perry and Echeverría, *Under the Heel*, 49–62; Latourette, *Christianity*, i. 45–55; G. R. Cragg, *The Church and the Age of Reason 1648–1789* (London, 1960), 209–33.

[127] Latourette, *Christianity*, i. 138; Callahan and Higgs (eds.), *Church and Society*, 9, 20–1, 42–4.

[128] The fate of the Jesuits presented the spectre of another threat to the authority of the universal church, for the Jesuits had always played a major missionary role in the Spanish and Portuguese empires, now clearly in terminal decline.

activity, and the auctioning off of vast amounts of church land in the process
known as secularization. It also brought the widespread loss of temporal sov-
ereignty, nowhere more obviously than in the territory of the former Holy Roman
Empire, which finally disappeared in 1803.[129] And yet, paradoxically, these
developments also helped to lay the foundations for the Catholic revival of the
nineteenth century. The losses of church land made the national churches more
dependent on Rome, thus strengthening the 'ultramontane' backlash of popular
sentiment among Catholics, of which the Marian apparitions and similar manifestations in the 1790s represented a first wave. Indeed, the events of the revolutionary era did much to discredit reforming, 'enlightened' tendencies within
the church and strengthened the hand of those who had always warned against
the Jansenists and their like.[130] The post-Napoleonic settlement was unable to
restore the Pope's diplomatic and political influence in Europe, but the authority
of the Pope within the church had been greatly increased and some of the
conditions created for a revival of its inner life. There was an intimate connection
between this revival and the rash of nineteenth-century apparitions. In the course
of the century there was a marked renewal of emotionally laden forms of piety
reminiscent of the Counter-Reformation, in which external, physical forms of
devotion played a central role. An obvious example was the cult of the Sacred
Heart, itself a devotion that began with a series of apparitions in late seventeenth-
century France.[131] The trend was underpinned by a more zealous clergy, the
revival of old teaching orders, the emergence of new congregations and sodalities,
and the holding of popular missions. These features were initially more apparent
in France and Italy than elsewhere, but from around the 1840s they increasingly
became characteristic of Catholicism in Europe as a whole.[132] The cult of the
Virgin was central to the new piety. Consider the new orders and congregations
created in the nineteenth century. In France alone the years up to the end of the
1850s saw the founding of the Daughters of Mary Immaculate, the Society of
Mary (the Marists), the Congregation of the Immaculate Heart of Mary, the
Little Brothers of Mary, the Sisters of Our Lady of Charity of the Good Shepherd,
the Sisters of the Holy Humility of Mary, and many more.[133] These bodies
were often concerned with missionary work overseas, but there were numerous

[129] On the revolution, see Gibson, *Social History*, 30–55, and J. McManners, *The French Revolution
and the Church* (London, 1969); on the dechristianization campaigns, Cobb, *People's Armies*, 442–79;
and on the Napoleonic regimes, Connelly, *Satellite Kingdoms*.

[130] Aretin, *Papacy*, 19–20.

[131] Carroll, *Cults and Devotions*, 132–53; Latourette, *Christianity*, i. 359–60; R. Aubert, *Le Pontificat
de Pie IX (1846–1878)* (Paris, 1950), 464–66, and 466–69 on 'external' devotions generally. The visions
of Christ were seen by Marguérite-Marie Alacoque, a young nun in Paray-le-Monial, between 1673
and 1690. Sacred Heart revelations were associated much more with nuns or clergy than were Marian
apparitions.

[132] On Germany, see Sperber, *Popular Catholicism*; on France, Gibson, *Social History*; on Ireland, E.
Larkin, 'The Devotional Revolution in Ireland, 1850–75', *American Historical Review*, 77 (1972), 625–
52.

[133] Latourette, *Christianity*, i. 337–43; Perry and Echeverria, *Under the Heel*, 84–90.

confraternities and sodalities devoted to the Virgin at parish level. The confraternity in honour of the Immaculate Heart of Mary, established in 1836 by the priest of Notre Dame des Victoires in Paris, had nearly 18,000 associations by 1880 with 25 million affiliated members.[134] Once again, France set the pace in these developments, but as the century progressed a similar pattern emerged in Belgium, Germany, Switzerland, Austria, and elsewhere. Alongside Marian confraternities, we should also note the revival of pilgrimages to places associated with the Virgin, and the growth of Marian medals, statuary, and hymns. Perhaps the most important strand within the burgeoning cult of the Virgin was the emphasis on Mary Immaculate who was free of the taint of sin, a powerful symbol of purity in dangerous and troubled times.

Under the impact of European Romanticism and the growth of neo-scholasticism in Catholic theology, many aspects of the cult of the Virgin enjoyed a respectability at the highest levels of the church that had been absent in the second half of the eighteenth century.[135] The papacy threw its own growing prestige behind the cult. Pope Gregory XVI was a strong supporter of Marian devotions. He carried a picture of the Madonna when personally leading a procession in Rome during a cholera outbreak, and helped to place the question of Mary's Immaculate Conception, disputed in the church for centuries, back on the agenda.[136] The role of Pope Pius IX was still more important. It was widely known that he attributed the remission of severe childhood epilepsy, which had jeopardized his career as a priest, to the Virgin's intercession. He also saw it as a sign of the Virgin's favour that he escaped imprisonment when forced to flee Rome in 1848.[137] In this way, as well as through increasingly Romanized liturgies and hymn-books, the papacy encouraged the cult of Mary. Pius IX's enunciation of the doctrine of the Immaculate Conception of the Virgin in 1854 crowned these developments and set the tone for the 'Marian century' that followed.[138]

The changed tenor of Catholic devotions in the nineteenth century created an atmosphere in which visions were more likely to occur, and to be treated sympathetically when they did. We need only look at the central motif of the Immaculate Conception in the visions of Cathérine Labouré, Bernadette Soubirous, and others to see how changing doctrine and popular piety reinforced each other. This newly charged atmosphere was especially important for the two groups which featured prominently in virtually all Marian and non-Marian

[134] St John, *The Blessed Virgin*, 94.

[135] G. A. McCool, *Catholic Theology in the Nineteenth Century* (New York, 1977), 129 ff.; Aretin, *Papacy*, 93–104. On the cult of the Virgin, G. Miegge, *The Virgin Mary: The Roman Catholic Marian Doctrine* (London, 1955); Warner, *Alone of All her Sex*.

[136] Warner, *Alone of All her Sex*, 236–54. Gregory XVI promised plenary indulgences to wearers of medals in honour of the Immaculate Conception; he also gave permission to the Dominican order and a number of churches to include the word *immaculata* in the preface of the mass of the Blessed Virgin: Latourette, *Christianity*, i. 265.

[137] W. Delius, *Geschichte der Marienverehrung* (Munich, 1963), 254.

[138] On Pius IX and Marian devotions, Aubert, *Le Pontificat*, 466–9, and on the triumph of Roman liturgy, ibid. 473–4.

visions of the nineteenth century: women and children. The Catholic Church
was notably feminized in the course of the nineteenth century. Not only was
there an enormous growth in the numbers of women who entered orders and
congregations; women also started to form a larger proportion of church atten-
ders, as the line between practising and non-practising Catholics was more
sharply drawn and a European pattern became widely established that men left
religious matters to their wives and daughters.[139] Religion was coming to be seen
as a woman's sphere. That women predominated among adult visionaries was
therefore, in part, a simple reflection of this larger change. But there is a further
point. The feminization of Christianity raised particular difficulties in the Catholic
Church. If Protestant women could measure the feminization of the church by
increases in their own power, Catholic women were in a more ambiguous position.
They were central to the Catholic revival, yet exercised their faith within a church
run on strictly hierarchical lines and dominated by a male clergy.[140] Women
parishioners were formally powerless, while it is possible to see the burgeoning
female orders and congregations as a sort of ecclesiastical siding—albeit a large
one—away from the main line of church authority. The figure of the Virgin
Mary, moreover, the perfect example of a 'softening' of theology and religious
symbolism in the nineteenth century, was of course a figure that had been defined
for centuries by male clergy and presented a model at once chaste, domesticated,
and submissive.[141]

All of these things are true, but they are partial truths. The church also seemed
to (and sometimes did) offer women a respite from powerlessness. They looked
to the priest as a means of evading the domination of husband, father, or brother,
as a 'countervailing locus of power'.[142] Female religious escaped the trials of
nineteenth-century reproduction, and enjoyed a degree of autonomy and authority seldom available to women outside the order or congregation.[143] The disproportionate number of women among the passionate supporters of Marian
apparitions—the 'pious women' who invariably arrived on the scene—can be
seen in similar terms. If female visionaries themselves gained comfort or escape
from harsh demands, their supporters also gained. For village women it was their
world that now eclipsed the normal world of affairs, however briefly. Women

[139] H. McLeod, *Religion and the People of Western Europe 1789–1970* (Oxford, 1981), 28–35; Gibson, *Social History*, 104 ff., 180–90; F. Lannon, *Privilege, Persecution, and Prophecy: The Catholic Church in Spain 1875–1975* (Oxford, 1987), 60–2.

[140] For two very different views on this, see J. Galot, *L'Église et la femme* (Paris, 1965) and Mary Daly, *The Church and the Second Sex* (New York, 1968).

[141] A. Douglas, *The Feminization of American Culture* (New York, 1978) is a classic statement of this case concerning Protestantism. On similar trends in 19th-cent. Catholicism, see Miegge, *Virgin Mary*, ch. 7, and B. Pope, 'Immaculate and Powerful: The Marian Revival in the Nineteenth Century', in C. Atkinson, C. Buchanan, and M. Miles (eds.), *Immaculate and Powerful: The Female in Sacred Image and Social Reality* (Cambridge, Mass., 1985), 193–4.

[142] Gibson, *Social History*, 187.

[143] S. O'Brien, '*Terra Incognita*: The Nun in Nineteenth-Century England', *Past and Present*, 121 (1988), 110–40; Gibson, *Social History*, 117–19; C. Clear, *Nuns in Nineteenth-Century Ireland* (Washington, DC, 1988).

travelled together as pilgrims to apparition sites, cultivating a female sociability that was the lay equivalent of the networks created among female religious. All could petition the Blessed Virgin for help with reproductive or marital problems, the drunken husband or the violent father.[144] And the figure they petitioned was not by any means associated only with female submissiveness. In the Marian century the Virgin remained a richly ambiguous symbol, fusing the potent myths of virginity and motherhood, combining the 'womanly' virtues with power.[145]

The emphasis in the nineteenth century on simple, uncomplicated piety also increased the attention paid to children—and brought the church closer to popular sentiment, where the wise child was a familiar figure of legend and folklore.[146] There was a growing tendency to admit children to communion at an earlier age, and a more intensive preparation for confirmation. (It is striking how many youthful visionaries were undergoing instruction for confirmation at the time of their apparitions.) Children, brought earlier and more fully into the life of the church, were subject to heightened religious emotions. There is a general point here, and a particular one. The general point is that Catholic children lived in a world increasingly suffused with the songs, perfumes, and flowers of a rather cloying new piety, exposed to highly physical representations of all kinds depicting the Sacred Heart of Jesus or the sorrows of the Virgin. We get a glimpse into the intense emotional world of nineteenth-century visionaries from accounts of their games. The children at La Salette were constructing an altar or *paradis* of flowers and stones when their apparitions began.[147] The childhood pastimes of another visionary, Thérèse Martin of Lisieux, suggest a similar degree of emotional susceptibility to spiritual experiences.[148] The religious world of visionary children was increasingly one which made their visions more likely.

More specifically, any experience of this kind was increasingly likely to be cast in a Marian idiom. The influences in this direction were relentless. Children saw statues or pictures of the Virgin, sang songs in her honour, and wore devotional objects dedicated to her.[149] Even in remote areas they might well be enrolled in a Marian sodality, or be close to those who were or had been members of one. Sometimes it is possible to make direct links between influences of this kind and a particular visionary. It is surely significant, for example, that two aunts of Bernadette Soubirous who accompanied her to the grotto had been Children of

[144] F. Mernissi, 'Women, Saints and Sanctuaries', *Signs*, 3 (1977), 101–12.

[145] The theme of the Virgin Mary as 'a polyvalent figure who appears in many guises' is subtly explored in Warner, *Alone of all her Sex* (quotation, p. xxiv). See also Pope, 'Immaculate and Powerful', 190.

[146] See Devlin, *Superstitious Mind*, 148–9.

[147] St John, *The Blessed Virgin*, 113.

[148] Furlong, *Thérèse of Lisieux*, 33, 40, 46, 50, 52.

[149] Several details of the Pontmain apparition closely recalled those to be found in a statue of the Virgin in the village church, itself modelled on the statue of Our Lady of Hope in the recently founded sanctuary in Saint-Brieuc: Laurentin and Durand, *Un signe*, 36. The Knock apparition also bore close similarities to a statue in the church at Lecanvey, from which the widow Beirne and her daughters had just returned: Ernst, *Maria redet*, 42–6; Thurston, *Beauraing*, 125–7.

Mary, a product of the cult around the miraculous medal of Cathérine Labouré.[150]
As Lourdes itself became the object of a cult, there are many indications that
Marian apparitions became a powerful idea in children's minds. Lourdes became
a kind of template. After the 1850s visions seem much more often to have followed
the pattern set by events in the Pyrenees; even the colours changed, as the
multicoloured apparel of earlier (local) apparitions yielded to a more standardized
white and blue.[151] Some local comparisons make the point. Many remarkable
occurrences were reported in Germany during the 1790s—miraculous crucifixes,
stigmata, a plague of caterpillars falling on snow—but apparitions of the Virgin
were not among them.[152] The Virgin was central to almost all the miraculous
claims of the 1870s, however, and the three most important incidents resembled
Lourdes very closely. The French village of Tilly-sur-Seulles in the Calvados
offers the possibility of an even more specific comparison. In the 1840s, the
factory foreman Eugène Vintras acquired a following with prophecies allegedly
vouchsafed him in visions of a ragged old man. Fifty years later the village became
news again as the site of miraculous apparitions, but now it was children who
were the visionaries and the Virgin Mary who featured in their visions. One of
the seers, the 14-year-old Louise Polinière, was a shepherdess.[153]

We are dealing here with a growing Marianization—and standardization—of
nineteenth-century visions and prophecies. This occurred from around the
middle of the century, and was certainly a welcome development to the church.
For the period up to the 1840s had seen a proliferation of apocalyptic, revelatory
cults that seemed to rival the official Catholic faith. In Germany renegade priests
led their (largely female) supporters in millenarian movements that prophesied
the coming of Antichrist, before taking their followers to new communal lives in
America during the 1850s, in a move that paralleled the emigration of the radical
'48ers.[154] In France a farrago of sects thrived between the Restoration and 1848.
The vermin-ridden mendicant Digonnet was believed by his supporters in the
Forez to be the reincarnation of Elijah, his followers styling themselves 'béguines'
after the free religious communities of women that sprang up in Europe from the
late twelfth century. Unfrocked priests ministered within the Universal Gnostic
Church, or the Johannite Church. The visionary and prophet Eugène Vintras
railed against misrule in France and founded the Carmel, or Society of Mercy, a

---

[150] Neame, *Happening*, 90; Carroll, *Cult of the Virgin Mary*, 160–1. The priest who taught Bernadette
her catechism at Bartrès also likened her to the children of La Salette: Hellé, *Miracles*, 73.

[151] Pope, 'Immaculate and Powerful', 176. The great exception to standardization on the Lourdes
model is Italy, where the long-established local variant on intercessions of the Virgin, namely pictures
and statues that moved and wept, persisted through the 19th cent.

[152] Blanning, *French Revolution in Germany*, 237–8.

[153] On Vintras, de Cauzons, *La Magie*, iv. 595–7; Devlin, *Superstitious Mind*, 151–2. On the apparitions
of the 1890s, Thurston, *Beauraing*, 128–31; de Cauzons, *La Magie*, iv. 615–16.

[154] See H. Treiber, '"Wie man wird, was man ist". Lebensweg und Lebenswerk des badischen
Landpfarrers Ambros Oschwald (1801–1873) im Erwartungshorizont chiliastischer Prophezeiungen',
Zeitschrift für die Geschichte des Oberrheins, 136 (1988), 293–348.

polygamous sect whose aim was to hasten the rule of the Holy Spirit.[155] Within this religious undergrowth were sects with a radical political message.[156] But even when the sects were reactionary in their politics—and Vintras prophesied the imminent accession of the legitimate King Louis XVII in France, as well as supporting the doctrine of the Immaculate Conception before it was officially enunciated—the church was predictably unhappy with these popular movements and their questionable leaders. Vintras was condemned by Popes Gregory XVI and Pius IX. When his popularity remained unbroken he was accused of sorcery and performing satanic sexual rites, and the church applauded the suppression of the cult by the state.[157]

Famine, epidemic, and political turmoil in nineteenth-century Europe produced despair, but they also had the capacity to unleash apocalyptic fears and millenarian hopes. The warm, even rapturous response to Marian apparitions was not a phenomenon apart. It had affinities, sometimes even overlapped, with other well-observed ways in which men and women of the nineteenth century made sense of their threatening world, whether through support for religious and utopian prophets, attempts to harness magic, or the interpretation of celestial omens.[158] From a clerical perspective, Marian visions and revelations promised to be safer, while drawing strength from other sources of popular legitimacy. Marian apparitions often combined other elements, whether in the form of vision and celestial omen (Pontmain and others) or vision and prophecy (Cathérine Labouré, La Salette, Pellevoisin) in a form of homespun syncretism. The nineteenth-century church went with the grain of popular religious sentiment, but not indiscriminately, nor without a push in the approved direction. Even then it risked creating dangers for itself. Like the sorcerer's apprentice, the church risked unleashing or sanctioning forces it could not control. Visions that were palpably fraudulent, or in which children reported the presence of the devil, caused embarrassment and alarm. Some apparitions contained an anticlerical component; all heightened popular expectations in ways that threatened to cut across

[155] De Cauzons, La Magie, iv. 594–600. On prophets and politics in France more generally, Kselman, Miracles and Prophecies, 68–83.

[156] Treiber, 'Wie man wird, was man ist'; R. Wirtz, 'Die Begriffsverwirrung der Bauern im Odenwald 1848. Odenwälder "Excesse" und die Sinsheimer "republikanische Schilderhebung"', in D. Puls (ed.), Wahrnehmungsformen und Protestverhalten. Studien zur Lage der Unterschichten im 18. und 19. Jahrhundert (Frankfurt am Main, 1979), 81–104. A specifically Protestant movement of this sort is imaginatively analysed by J. Mooser, 'Religion und Sozialer Protest. Erweckungsbewegung und ländliche Unterschichten im Vormärz am Beispiel Minden-Ravensburg', in H. Volkmann and J. Bergmann (eds.), Sozialer Protest (Opladen, 1984), 304–24. See E. Berenson, Popular Religion and Left-Wing Politics in France, 1830–1852 (Princeton, NJ, 1984), on the religious idiom of radical politics in France.

[157] De Cauzons, La Magie, iv. 595–7; Devlin, Superstitious Mind, 151–2.

[158] See E. J. Hobsbawm, Primitive Rebels: Studies in Archaic Forms of Social Movement in the 19th and 20th Centuries (Manchester, 1959); V. Lanternari, The Religions of the Oppressed: A Study of Modern Messianic Cults (London, 1963). Recent writers on 19th-cent. France have illuminated the different links between prophecy, religion, and protest: Devlin on popular religious and non-religious beliefs in rural society, Kselman on prophecy and politics, Berenson on the strong religious dimension in French utopian and socialist movements of the 1830s and 1840s.

the lines of clerical authority. As Émile Zola observed, the events at Lourdes could be seen as the beginning of a new religion, setting the experiences of a marginal, ill-educated girl against an established, male hierarchical church.[159] It is hardly surprising that so many parish priests were instinctively sceptical; and where they were not, their bishops issued suitably firm instructions.

Some cases, of course, never reached the level of sustained diocesan attention. Where the visionary was a convicted arsonist, or reported the Virgin violently hostile to the local clergy, the parish priest was unlikely to be indulgent. The same was true where a rash of clearly imitative apparitions spread through a particular locality. The reaction was usually to apply the sort of pressure also brought to bear on dubious stigmatists. Most of these did not pass the test of a stern interrogation; some did not pass the test of soap and water. But where this approach did not stifle the phenomenon, or an apparition did not automatically disqualify itself, a church enquiry was necessary. Under the canon law of the post-Tridentine church there were strict rules governing new claims for private revelations and miracles. None could be accepted without a formal enquiry set in train by the appropriate bishop; any opinion expressed prior to that lacked validity and was conditional on the church's final judgement.[160] The eighteenth-century Pope Benedict XIV re-emphasized that the church granted its appro-bation only after a rigorous examination of the evidence. Even then, the church did not approve the revelation in question, or require assent to it by the faithful; it merely deemed that the revelation was not inimical to the faith. The church's judgement came in the form of a *nihil obstat*; it permitted rather than entailed belief.[161]

That, at least, was the theory. In practice there was considerable variation in the rigour of the enquiries held at diocesan level, and the extent to which their outcome was influenced by opinion among clergy and laity. The most rigorous canonical commissions deliberated for years. Generally organized by the bishop's vicar-general, they typically consisted of members of the cathedral chapter and theologians from a local seminary. They took detailed statements from the vision-aries themselves, usually the result of repeated questioning; they considered evidence from hundreds of witnesses; and they took into account medical evi-dence, both on the state of mind of the visionaries, and on the precise status of any miraculous cures that had been claimed. Cases were officially recognized by the church only after the commission of enquiry had satisfied itself that deception, vanity, collusion between the persons involved, auto-suggestion, hallucination, and diabolical influence could be excluded from consideration.[162] The desire of

[159] Zola, *Lourdes*, esp. 184–98, 470–91.

[160] The rules on this were laid down at the 25th session of the Council of Trent, in Dec. 1563.

[161] On Benedict XIV and canon law on the subject, see Ernst, *Maria redet*, 11–16; H. Holstein, 'Les Apparitions Mariales', in D'H. du Manoir (ed.), *Maria. Études sur la Sainte Vierge*, v (Paris, 1958), 773–6; Billet *et al.* (eds.), *Vraies et fausses*, 169–72.

[162] On the procedure, L. Lochet, *Muttergottes-Erscheinungen* (Freiburg, 1958), 39–44. For examples, see Laurentin, *Lourdes*, v and vi, on Lourdes; Laurentin and Durand, *Un signe*, 68–74, on Pontmain.

the church to protect its own position is understandable, and the measures it took to avoid debasing the currency of true revelations were often grimly impressive.[163]

Yet all this rigour can be rather misleading. It was certainly not much in evidence in many Italian cases. The apparitions and miraculous cures associated with Maria Catalani in Rome, in 1816, were authenticated by an ecclesiastical commission less than four months after the first apparition had been reported. Veronica Nucci, the Tuscan visionary of Ceretto in 1853, had already become a novice before the ecclesiastical commission began its work.[164] Prudence and the desire for discretion may have prompted this, especially as the girl's noviciate was being served in the distant Papal States; but it must have made it more difficult for the enquiry to conclude that her claims were groundless. In an 1862 incident of a moving statue of the Virgin in the Umbrian district of Montefalco, the Bishop of Spoleto and his vicar-general swelled the numbers of pilgrims by visiting the site and blessing the statue.[165] The ecclesiastical authorities in Italy seem to have approached their obligations under canon law less critically than their counterparts north of the Alps. This may be explained, in part, by the fact that moving statues and apparitions that took place in or around churches appeared less potentially threatening than visions that occurred in grottos, away from the symbolic control of the priest. But it probably owed as much to the indulgence of the Italian hierarchy. It is worth noting that the rather unsatisfactory later life of the La Salette visionary Mélanie Calvat ended, after spells as a Carmelite nun in Darlington and Marseilles, in a form of exile in southern Italy under the spiritual protection of two sympathetic bishops.[166]

The later behaviour of the children of La Salette might reasonably have given the French church cause to reflect on the rigour of its procedures. Certainly many sceptical voices were overruled in the enquiry set up by the Bishop of Grenoble, but the pressure on him was greater from the opposite direction. Even while his commission was considering evidence in the summer of 1847, weighty figures in the French church such as the Bishops of La Rochelle and Langres, and the later Bishop of Orléans, Dupanloup, visited La Salette and supported the authenticity of the apparitions. The Bishop of La Rochelle wrote a pamphlet on the subject, and when the octogenarian Bishop of Grenoble still hesitated, troubled by the childen's talk of secrets, the Archbishop of Lyons and the Bishop of Belley were among those who pressed the claims of the visions. The pastoral letter announcing that the apparitions were 'characterized by all the conditions

---

[163] In the course of the enquiry into Louise Lateau she was asked on one occasion to resist her ecstasy and to continue working. The result, according to one North American bishop, was that she worked while blood flowed copiously over her body and hands on to her sewing machine. This is reported in Lefebvre, *Louise Lateau*, 26; Lefebvre, a Catholic doctor, made a detailed examination of Louise Lateau at the request of the church.

[164] Sausseret, *Erscheinungen*, 256–9, 305–10.

[165] Ibid. 287–92.

[166] St John, *The Blessed Virgin*, 185–201.

of truth' was read from all the pulpits of the Grenoble diocese on 10 November 1851.[167]

The procedures at La Salette were flawed, but there was at least a gap of five years between the apparitions and the official judgement. In the case of Lourdes it was four years, in that of Pontmain three years. This is not evidence, in itself, of an increasing rush to judgement. The church authorities were much more prepared for dealing with such cases by the beginning of the 1870s, and the speed of communications had improved enormously in the quarter-century that separated La Salette from Pontmain. There are nevertheless indications of a growing willingness to suspend disbelief. Take the issue of suspected diabolical origins of the apparitions. In earlier years, the appearance of the devil in an apparition was regarded within the church as damning evidence. The absence of such an element in the apparitions of La Salette and Lourdes was thought to weigh in their favour. This was to change. In 1866 a nun in the Congregation of the Daughters of Mary in Anglet claimed a vision of the Virgin in which she had been shown demons let loose on earth, wreaking devastation. The Virgin taught her a prayer that would scatter the devil's spirits. The Bishop of Bayonne supported her claims by ordering that half a million copies of the prayer be printed.[168] Five years later, the Bishop of Laval canvassed the opinion of internationally recognized theologians and canon lawyers when considering his judgement on Pontmain, but expressly rejected their doubts about the diabolical components of the apparitions.[169] Approval was also given to the Pellevoisin apparitions of 1876 in which the devil had featured prominently.[170]

Pope Pius IX did much to ease acceptance of the new cult by his known support for individual apparitions, starting with La Salette, where he confirmed his favour with a flurry of papal briefs and rescripts—eight in the months of August and September 1852—conferring privileges on priests who visited La Salette and confraternities that took its name.[171] In the case of Lourdes, the Pope let it be known that he viewed Bernadette Soubirous's vision as a sign that vindicated his promulgation of the doctrine of the Immaculate Conception just four years earlier.[172] The endorsement of Rome would not have counted for much in the 1780s; but the Pope now had the authority to set the tone within the church, as the years from the 1840s to the 1870s saw the triumph of ultra-montanism, or papal supremacy. This was partly a matter of organization. The promotion of Roman rites and liturgy, the more regular summoning of bishops

[167] See St John, *The Blessed Virgin*, 126–36, 148–58; Kselman, *Miracles and Prophecies*, 150–3; Gibson, *Social History*, 147, 149; Northcote, *Sanctuaries*, 189–96. Details on the composition and findings of the ecclesiastical commission can be found in J. Sabbatier, *Affaire de La Salette* (Paris, 1857), 6–8, a contemporary work giving a lively insight into the ecclesiastical, legal, and journalistic controversies that continued to surround the case.
[168] Sausseret, *Erscheinungen*, 303–5.
[169] Laurentin and Durand, *Un signe*, 68–74.
[170] Ernst, *Maria redet*, 39; Thurston, *Beauraing*, 127–8; de Cauzons, *La Magie*, iv. 611–12.
[171] St John, *The Blessed Virgin*, 160–1; Perry and Echeverria, *Under the Heel*, 104.
[172] Perry and Echeverria, *Under the Heel*, 121–2.

to Rome, the growing intervention in diocesan disputes—all served to remind the bishops of the Vatican's authority.[173] It was also, in part, a matter of personnel. By the third quarter of the nineteenth century a growing number of European bishops and senior religious were themselves ultramontanes, and supported the embracing of popular piety favoured by the Pope. This too made the official endorsement of individual apparitions more likely.

Those who were fundamentally sceptical about the apparitions were not likely to have their doubts stilled by the course of events between the 1840s and 1870s; rather the contrary. But these decades did much to remove doubts on another score: that the cult of the apparitions might undermine the authority of the church. The pontificate of Pius IX showed that the church could successfully channel powerful currents of popular piety; that it could take up the fears and aspirations unleashed by the apparitions of the Virgin and give them institutional shape. In a period bounded by the anticlerical challenge of 1848 and the European-wide church–state struggles of the 1870s, Marian apparitions were a symptom of popular Catholic sentiment; they were also a potentially powerful weapon in the hands of the church. In these years the church domesticated a potentially anarchic wave of popular sentiment. The original visionary children were removed from the limelight and placed in orders where they were forbidden to talk about their revelations. The fillip they had given to the Marian cult was not to be compromised by popular enthusiasm for the secondary cult that had grown up around the children themselves. The new Bishop of Grenoble, Monsignor Ginouilhac, expressed this with admirable clarity when he spoke to a vast assembly of pilgrims at La Salette on the ninth anniversary of the original apparition: 'The mission of the shepherd children is at an end, and that of the church begins. They may go their way and be lost sight of; they may even prove unfaithful to a great grace received; but the fact of the apparitions will not be shaken on that account.'[174]

That was the negative side: ensuring that popular devotion to the Virgin should flow in orthodox channels. But the church went well beyond that, assimilating elements of the new cult into the liturgy and pressing the apparitions into the service of the 'Marian century'.[175] In this way the apparitions were incorporated into the papacy's fight against the nineteenth century, symbolized by the promulgation of infallibility in 1870 and the *Syllabus of Errors* six years earlier. The extraordinary organizational flair with which the church exploited the major apparitions showed how selectively it rejected the nineteenth century. In the 1864 *Syllabus of Errors*, Pius IX hurled eighty paragraphs of condemnation at the

[173] Latourette, *Christianity*, i. 279.
[174] Sausseret, *Erscheinungen*, 190; St John, *The Blessed Virgin*, 167.
[175] On the liturgical changes, see Lochet, *Muttergottes-Erscheinungen*, 34–5. It was appropriate that at the end of the Vatican Council of 1869–70 the ceremonial proclamation of papal infallibility, originally scheduled for 29 June, the feast of St Peter and St Paul, should have been made on 18 July, the anniversary of the day on which the Pope had first received the prophecy communicated at La Salette. See J. B. Bury, *History of the Papacy in the Nineteenth Century* (London, 1964), 126.

modern world, concluding notoriously that it was an error to believe that 'the Roman Pontiff can and should reconcile himself to and agree with progress, liberalism, and modern civilization'.[176] But the church enthusiastically adopted many technical means of 'modern civilization' in order to achieve its objectives. The organization of mass pilgrimages to the apparition sites and the development of the sites themselves provide classic examples. The Papal States may have been slow to introduce the steamship and the railway (Pope Gregory XVI is credited with the remark 'chemin de fer, chemin d'enfer'), but in the second half of the nineteenth century the church became remarkably adept at using modern means of communication to further the cult of the Virgin.[177]

Nowhere did this unfold more impressively than in France. A French Pilgrimage Committee was set up in 1872 under the auspices of the Augustinian Assumptionists. The same year saw the first French National Pilgrimage to La Salette. In 1873 over 3 million pilgrims visited French shrines, including a quarter of a million at Lourdes, to which the first national pilgrimage was organized in that year. In the same decade organized national pilgrimages also visited Lourdes from Belgium (1873), Poland, Italy, and Germany (1875), Spain and Ireland (1876), and Portugal and Switzerland (1877).[178] The role of the Assumptionists was important and telling, for they had specialist skills in journalism and the techniques of modern organization.[179] The logistics of pilgrimage transportation were becoming increasingly complex by the end of the century. In 1873 pilgrims travelled to Lourdes by two special trains; thirty years later eighteen were required.[180]

Successful organization on this scale built on the experience of mounting popular missions and the planning of special occasions, such as the exhibition of the Holy Coat at Trier in 1844, which attracted half a million visitors.[181] The church also learned something from the great exhibitions of the nineteenth century.[182] This applied not just to transportation, but to the development of the apparition sites. La Salette provided the first modest indications of a pattern that was later to assume much grander dimensions. A path was constructed to allow pilgrims easier access to the site; when they reached it they found two convents,

---

[176] Full text in A. Fremantle, *The Papal Encyclicals in their Historical Context* (New York, 1956), 143–52.

[177] Latourette, *Christianity*, i. 265. Quotation from Gregory XVI in Aretin, *Papacy*, 69.

[178] St John, *The Blessed Virgin*, 182–3, 275–6; Aubert, *Le Pontificat*, 467; Neame, *Happening*, 121–3; Marrus, 'Pilger auf dem Weg'; Perry and Echeverria, *Under the Heel*, 132–5. On the links between apparitions and politics in the Third Republic, see Kselman, *Miracles and Prophecies*, 113–40.

[179] On their organizational and journalistic flair (they ran two pilgrimage papers, *La Croix* and *Le Pèlerin*), see Pope, 'Immaculate and Powerful', 185–6.

[180] St John, *The Blessed Virgin*, 276. The logistics were complicated by the special needs of the sick, transported to Lourdes in the celebrated 'white trains' described by witnesses as various as Émile Zola (*Lourdes*) and Ruth Cranston, *The Miracle of Lourdes* (New York, 1955). It is worth noting that in the 1890s the journey from Paris to Lourdes still took 22 hours: Neame, *Happening*, 29.

[181] W. Schieder, 'Kirche und Revolution. Sozialgeschichtliche Aspekte der Trierer Wallfahrt 1844', *Archiv für Sozialgeschichte*, 14 (1974), 419–54. Clerical sources suggested as many as a million visitors.

[182] Korff, 'Formierung', 356–7.

and between them a sanctuary that could hold 2,500 people.[183] At Lourdes construction was on a much larger scale. Major work began in 1866, the year that the railway reached the town. By 1872, one year after the Paris Commune in which the Archbishop of Paris had been murdered, the site was ready to host a major show of strength: 20,000 pilgrims were present for a national rally presided over by nine bishops.[184] Then, on 3 July 1876, thirty-five bishops and 5,000 priests were among the 100,000 Catholics present at the consecration of a statue in honour of the Virgin.[185] The 1870s were the pivotal decade as land purchases allowed the construction of a new road, the Boulevard of the Grotto, from the railway station direct to the apparition site. The self-contained Lourdes 'domain' assumed its modern form. It soon sprouted new buildings: hospitals, offices, the medical bureau. Above all, new religious buildings and statuary arose, illuminated for maximum effect like their profane counterparts. Coloured lights lit up the Basilica of the Immaculate Conception on the eve of special festivals, and outlined the bulging roof of the Church of the Rosary so that it resembled 'a giant gingerbread cake sprinkled with red seeds'. The huge cast-iron statue of the Virgin on the Esplanade was similarly 'aureoled with a circle of electric almonds'.[186]

Organization was also the keynote when it came to the control of pilgrims at a site like Lourdes. This was very much in line with the marked tendency in the nineteenth-century church to impose maximum discipline on spontaneous and potentially threatening aspects of the religious revival. One sign of this was the attempt to clamp down on pilgrimages (especially those involving overnight stays) undertaken without the leadership of the parish priest.[187] After the initial flood of unorganized pilgrims to Lourdes, observers were soon commenting on the way in which priests led their flocks to the site with almost military discipline, harrying them in the case of one 'lazy flock of Bretons ... as if they were sheep-dogs'.[188] A Lourdes hymn was adopted in 1873, banners and the wearing of regional dress were encouraged. Priests became preoccupied with the 'management of crowds'; Lourdes became an 'enormous machine'.[189]

The question soon arose whether the day-to-day running of major apparition sites could be left to the local diocese. The answer was that it could not, and religious orders moved in to assume specialist responsibility. In Lourdes it was the Garaison Fathers of the Immaculate Conception who took over the domain,

---

[183] Sausseret, *Erscheinungen*, 164.

[184] Neame, *Happening*, 121.

[185] Aubert, *Le Pontificat*, 468.

[186] Huysmans, *Crowds*, 81, 89. Huysmans (80) described the Church of the Rosary as a cross between a hippodrome, a casino, and a railway round-house. The Church of the Sacred Heart was completed in 1875, the Basilica of the Immaculate Conception in 1876, the Church of the Rosary in 1889. On the development of the site see Laurentin, *Lourdes*, i. 29–78; Hellé, *Miracles*, 83–4.

[187] On Germany, see Sperber, *Popular Catholicism*, 63–73; on France, Marrus, 'Pilger auf dem Weg' and Gibson, *Social History*, 150–1.

[188] 'Zwei Tage in Lourdes', *Die Gartenlaube* (1876), 603; Huysmans, *Crowds*, 38.

[189] Huysmans, *Crowds*, 105, 112.

which was formally separated from the parish of Lourdes—not without a great deal of friction.[190] In Pontmain religious were installed at the site within eight months of the favourable canonical judgement. They were centrally concerned with the subsequent development of Pontmain, including the construction of their own accommodation, the buying up of the barn outside which the original visionary children had stood, and the building of a sanctuary (raised to the status of a basilica in 1905). In the 1890s they also began publication of the *Annales de Pontmain*, which included the first systematic recording of all allegedly miraculous cures.[191]

The spectacular development of both French and non-French apparition sites in the last decades of the century reflected a broader organizational *élan* in the church during those years. It was a golden age of organized mass pilgrimages. Two million made the journey to Trier in 1891 for the second showing of the Holy Coat; five years later 200,000 visited the small Saarland town of St Wendel during the two weeks in which the bones of the patron saint were on display.[192] Large, organized pilgrimages also became common in Spain and Italy during the same period.[193] The phenomenon was not confined to Europe. The Quebec shrine of St Anne of Beaupré had been a pilgrimage centre since the late seventeenth century, but until the 1870s the number of annual visitors never exceeded 12,000. Then the construction of a new church in 1876 (raised to the status of a minor basilica in 1887), the organization of parish confraternity visits, the publication of the *Annales de la Bonne Sainte Anne*, and the zeal of the Redemptorist order brought an extraordinary increase in numbers. By 1880 there were 36,000, by 1890 105,000, by 1900 135,000, and by 1905 168,000.[194] Comparable developments can be found in Mexico, the Philippines, and elsewhere.[195]

One historian has described how the crowds who flocked to see the exiled Popes Pius VI and Pius VII at the beginning of the century showed a 'vast if unorganized loyalty'.[196] By the end of the century the church had done much to organize that loyalty. In Europe, as elsewhere, the great leap forward came in the last decades of the century, but the 1870s saw the decisive developments. This was certainly true of the Marian cult built around the apparitions. It was the decade in which several of the most prominent original seers died: Cathérine

---

[190] The whole period from the first arrival of the Garaison Fathers in 1866 until the death of the parish priest Father Peyremale in 1877 was one of friction, feuding, and faction. See Neame, *Happening*, 112–20. The vindictiveness—and the lawsuits—continued after Peyremale's death, greeted by the leader of the Garaison Fathers with unbecoming pleasure.

[191] Laurentin and Durand, *Un signe*, 59–76.

[192] Korff, 'Formierung'; M. Müller, *Die Geschichte der Stadt St Wendel* (St Wendel, 1927), 559–61.

[193] Perry and Echeverría, *Under the Heel*, 142–5. On the development of the apparition site at Knock, see Neary, *I Comforted Them*, 70–87.

[194] Turner, *Image and Pilgrimage*, 27; C. G. Herbermann *et al.* (eds.), *The Catholic Encyclopedia*, i (New York, 1907), 539–40.

[195] Perry and Echeverría, *Under the Heel*, 144–8.

[196] Latourette, *Christianity*, i. 157–8. The potential support was clear even in the dark days of the 1780s: 60,000–100,000 came to each of the Pope's several daily blessings in Vienna during Easter 1782. See Dipper, 'Volksreligiosität', 85.

Labouré and Maximin Giraud in 1876, Bernadette Soubirous in 1879. But the movement had already been assimilated by the church, which aimed to dispose briskly of dubious apparitions and to construct a powerful official cult out of those it considered exemplary. The basilicas, organized pilgrimages, processions, and confraternities served this purpose.

The church had a number of reasons in the 1870s for rallying Catholics behind the new cult as a political show of force. They included the vulnerable position of the Pope after the final stage of Italian unification, and the violent church–state struggles of the 1870s. But the effect of promoting the official cult with such vigour, at a time of political uncertainty and economic depression, was unpredictable. The 1870s witnessed the greatest wave of new Marian apparitions that Europe had ever seen. Some of these, such as Pontmain, Pompeii, and Knock, were officially endorsed and taken up by the church. The majority were not.

2

The Place: A Changing Village in the Saarland

Immediately after his inauguration in November 1867, Bishop Eberhard of Trier issued a pastoral letter, in which he reflected on the great variations within his diocese. Alongside the 'noise and bustle' of new industrial regions to which people were thronging, stimulated by 'the railway lines along which the iron horse rushes', were rural areas that were 'completely remote, cut off from communications, isolated, sometimes almost inaccessible'.[1] Ostensibly at least, Marpingen belonged to the second category as surely as did those parts of the diocese in the Eifel and the Hunsrück. The village was situated in the Saar–Nahe hill country, with its raw climate and difficult terrain. The Als valley in which Marpingen lay was over 800 feet above sea-level, and surrounding peaks—notably the local landmark of the Schaumberg—reached nearly 2,000 feet.[2] To the east of the village were old Roman roads that had once linked Straßburg to Trier and Mainz to Metz, but in the nineteenth century the main lines of communication passed Marpingen by. During the 1850s and 1860s, as the railway expanded and communities pushed their claims for inclusion in the network, Marpingen remained miles distant from the nearest railhead. As one writer noted in the 1870s, it was 'not marked on normal maps'.[3]

Yet Marpingen was not a completely remote community. Bishop Eberhard's stark distinction between urban and rural areas was less true of the Saarland than it was of most industrializing regions in Germany, and the rural isolation he described in the 1860s was in many ways already a thing of the past. The church itself was one of the agents of change. Eberhard's pastoral letter was followed by an extensive series of visitations throughout the Trier diocese, symbolizing one aspect of a steady centralization in nineteenth-century church life.[4] Marpingen did not escape this trend. The village was already familiar with priests (and

[1] J. J. Kraft, *Matthias Eberhard, Bischof von Trier. Ein Lebensbild* (Trier, 1878), 116–17.
[2] W. Bungert, *Heimatbuch Marpingen* (Marpingen, 1980), 21.
[3] W. Cramer, *Die Erscheinungen und Heilungen in Marpingen, Gläubigen und Ungläubigen erzählt* (Würzburg, 1876), 6.
[4] On the mounting tempo of episcopal visitations between the 1840s and 1870s, and a corresponding increase in decanal activity, see J. Marx, *Geschichte der Pfarreien der Diözese Trier*, i. *Allgemeines* (Trier, 1923), 518–19.

MAP 1. Imperial Germany

schoolteachers) who had not been born there and imported new ideas. The zealous young priest who arrived in 1864 from busy Koblenz was only one in a fairly long line, although his firm ideas on discipline and piety represented the sharper interventionist thrust of the church into the lives of its parishioners after the middle of the century.

This was just one of many ways in which Marpingen, like similar communities, became less self-contained during the nineteenth century. Population growth prompted emigration, and emigrants sent back remittances and news. The rural postman, notaries, moneylenders, bailiffs, knife-grinders, and travelling musicians pursued their occupations in Marpingen. Villagers went regularly to traders and moneylenders in nearby Tholey for provisions and credit, or to sell their cattle; others had business in the commercial and administrative town of St

Wendel, two hours away by foot. This traffic testified to the way in which even an upland village was penetrated in the nineteenth century by powerful market forces. As rural producers in Marpingen were gradually freed from the old cycles of dearth, they became locked into the equally inexorable cycles of the market. By the middle of the 1870s, around half of the adult males also found employment outside the village. In an earlier generation they would have emigrated; now they found work in the coalfields of the Saar basin, setting off at dawn on Monday and returning only on Saturday evening. This brought novel tensions into every aspect of village life.

Politically, too, Marpingen could hardly remain unaffected by events outside the confines of the village. Like a number of other apparition sites, it was situated on a borderland and had a history of political uncertainty to match. In the fifty years from the 1760s Marpingen was incorporated in six different states; then the Catholic region to which it belonged was sold in 1834 to Protestant Prussia. If the period of political turbulence left its mark, so did the experience of learning to live with Prussian stability. Borderlands are potential battlegrounds. Marpingen had learned this during the Thirty Years war, and the lesson was re-learned in the era of Napoleon and Bismarck.

This chapter is about a community fundamentally transformed in the nineteenth century. Whether we look at agricultural crises and the advent of the 'miner-peasant', at the administrative and political structures within which Marpingen was located, or at changing patterns of religious practice, we see a period of transition and uncertainty. Change, not isolation, provides the context of the apparitions that began in the 1870s.

Peasants and Miners

Marpingen lay in a basin-shaped site where several streams drained into the north–south flowing Als. It was a village of scattered fields and houses linked by paths, tracks, and foot-bridges. As the village grew, its shape was determined by a hilly topography studded with streams and marshes, woods and rocky outcrops.[5] Roads followed the pattern of housing. The result was a tangle of crooked streets and alleys apparent from nineteenth-century maps and ground-plans, and indicated still by street names like Altgasse, Neugasse, and Ringelgasse. The village was also internally differentiated in spatial terms. Beyond the basic division between the *Unterdorf* and *Oberdorf*, the upper and lower parts of the village, nineteenth-century Marpingers were aware of living in the Gottrod, the Härtel, the Helmesborn, or one of the other seventeen districts whose names derived

---

[5] K. Hoppstädter and H.-W. Hermann, *Geschichtliche Landeskunde des Saarlandes*, i. *Vom Faustkeil zum Förderturm* (Saarbrücken, 1960), 15–16, refer to a 'varied hill country with an agreeable alternation of wooded hilltops and precipices, open fields, damp meadows, shadowed gullies, and sunny hillsides'.

from the old field-names (*Flurnamen*).[6] Sub-village identities were no doubt fostered by size as well as topography. By the 1870s, after nearly two centuries of population growth, Marpingen was one of the largest villages in the area. Its inhabitants numbered 145 in 1617. This was more than halved by the devastation and epidemics of the Thirty Years war, and the population did not recover its former level until the late seventeenth century. During the eighteenth century it then rose sharply, from 170 in 1707 to 462 in 1790. By 1803 it had reached 620, and, as Table 2.1 shows, during the first half of the nineteenth century the population continued to grow quickly, as it did throughout Germany.

TABLE 2.1. *Population growth in Marpingen, 1803–1885*

Year	Population
1803	620
1830	950
1843	1,113
1855	1,268
1865	1,450
1875	1,622
1855	1,743

Source: Bungert, *Heimatbuch Marpingen*, 193.

Until the middle of the century Marpingen was almost entirely dependent on agriculture. Of the 1,250 hectares within the village limits, slightly over a fifth were taken up by woodlands, water, roads, houses, and farms. Of the remaining 980 hectares, 64 per cent were arable, 3 per cent garden-plots, and 33 per cent meadow or grazing land. The soil was of only moderate quality, typical of the hilly northern Saarland, but it supported a variety of crops grown for sale, subsistence, or use as animal feed, including rye, oats, and root vegetables, with the potato making headway from the eighteenth century. Some flax was grown for local weaving. The village also had substantial stocks of horses, cattle, and pigs (numbers of sheep were declining sharply in the nineteenth century), together with goats and poultry.[7] The range of agricultural activities corresponded to a village social hierarchy that ran downwards from the richest *Pferdebauern*, or 'horse peasants', through the 'cattle peasants' (*Kuhbauern*) and much more

---

[6] The best source of information on the shaping of the village is Bungert, *Heimatbuch*, 317 ff., 341 ff. Brief outsiders' descriptions can be found in *MMGE*, 10–11 and *MG*, 13. In the early 1830s, the peasant and linen-weaver Anton Recktenwald and his wife Barbara moved from the crowded Alte Klosterstraße and built a small house on the Rheinstraße, the old Roman road to the east of Marpingen, which became a significant new settlement: Bungert, *Heimatbuch*, 335–6.

[7] Bungert, *Heimatbuch*, 114, 121, 126, 143–4, 370 ff.; W. Laufer, 'Bevölkerungs- und siedlungsgeschichtliche Aspekte der Industrialisierung an der Saar', *Zeitschrift für die Geschichte der Saargegend*, 29 (1981), 132–3.

numerous small peasantry (the 'goat peasants', or *Ziegenbauern*), to day labourers and those who traded in feathers or engaged in other 'dishonourable occupations'.[8] Scattered mineral deposits in the village provided a modest resource for the lower classes. In the 1820s and early 1830s some twenty 'poor people' of Marpingen extracted small amounts of iron ore which they transported for sale in Neunkirchen; others dug lumps of coal which they burnt themselves or sold.[9] Otherwise, economic activity fitted around an agricultural framework. Linen-weaving and stone-quarrying were the subsidiary occupations of peasants or agricultural labourers (the local stone was good, but was barely exploited for anything other than local use until the twentieth century[10]). Millers and local craftsmen—blacksmiths, nail-makers, wheelwrights, cartwrights, coopers, cobblers, masons, and carpenters—served peasant needs.

At the top of the social hierarchy were the village notables, drawn first of all from the wealthier peasants, who would usually have farm servants and would certainly employ members of small-peasant families.[11] They were joined by a small number of millers, innkeepers, and those who combined these activities, like Johannes Hubertus, a landowner who was proprietor of the Dewese inn and sold everything from bootnails, dyes, and building materials to sugar, flour, and seed.[12] These were the closest Marpingen came to possessing a resident middle class. There were no merchants, moneylenders, or notaries: the peasants generally went to Tholey or St Wendel for these services. There was no doctor in Marpingen throughout the nineteenth century.[13] The village also contained no resident officials, not even minor officials such as a local mayor or magistrate. At different times, under different regimes, the local mayor was to be found in the neighbouring communities of Tholey, Bliesen, Ottweiler, and Alsweiler: he was never resident in Marpingen itself.

There was one exception to this absence of resident officials. The Catholic priest and the village schoolteachers were the only local notables in Marpingen not concerned with the land in one way or another, and even this exception was qualified. Both had to tread warily where the villagers' agricultural interests were concerned. The clergy, as we shall see, became painfully involved with the question of peasant debt. Successive teachers in Marpingen, like village teachers elsewhere in Germany, found themselves under heavy pressure from parents who

---

[8] On Johannes Kreuz and other dealers in feathers, see LASB, E 107, 23, 255–6; on 'dishonourable occupations', Danckert, *Unehrliche Leute*.

[9] Bungert, *Heimatbuch*, 209–11.

[10] One exception was the stonecutter Peter Recktenwald, from the Rheinstraße settlement, who delivered sandstone for the St Wendel railway bridge in 1860: ibid. 336.

[11] This social hierarchy received architectural expression in the different size and form of the farmhouses constructed by horse-, cattle- and goat-peasants: ibid. 324–30. On peasant notables generally, see H. Wunder, *Die bäuerliche Gemeinde in Deutschland* (Göttingen, 1986), 121, 126.

[12] Bungert, *Heimatbuch*, 419.

[13] BAT, 70/3676, 134: Father Schmitt to GV Trier, 3 June 1901. A check of the *Adreß-Kalender, Regierungs-Bezirk Trier*, for the years 1871 (122–5) and 1876 (138–42) also showed no doctor in the village, the nearest doctors in the 1870s being in St Wendel, Tholey, and Heusweiler.

resented the costs of the school and the removal of children from the fields, especially at harvest time. In the early nineteenth century Marpingen had a teacher called Becker who married into the village and turned a prudently blind eye to non-attendance. Widespread truancy, 'rough treatment' of the teacher, and indifference among peasants on the school advisory board were still so common in the 1840s that the parish priest, Father Bicking, asked to be relieved of his post as local school inspector.[14] Even when larger numbers of better-trained teachers came to the village later in the century, their position remained uneasy. The official enquiries carried out in the wake of the 1876 apparitions give us a vivid account of young, college-trained teachers who had little contact with villagers and clung rather desperately to each other and to teachers in neighbouring villages for companionship.[15]

Until the middle of the nineteenth century agriculture was the focus of work, recreation, and family life for the majority of Marpingers. It governed the cycle of work and the timing of feasts; it was even the basis of village nicknames.[16] Larger peasants producing for the market were concerned with draught animals and cash crops. Most had more modest horizons. Thirty poor peasants petitioned the Saxe-Coburg-Gotha government in 1833 for a place where the goatherd could legally graze their animals. If this proved impossible, their petition argued, they would 'in a short time become nothing more than day labourers', or 'beggars'.[17] This was an indication of the mounting pressures on small property-owners in the village. The French occupation after 1793 had removed the burden of serfdom and tithe payments from the peasantry, but it also confirmed two other late eighteenth-century developments with potentially adverse effects on marginal peasant producers. One was the abolition of collective husbandry under a village *Gehöferschaft*, whereby land was periodically reallocated. The other was the consolidation of holdings and the passing of common land into private hands.[18] The effect of these changes was to strengthen private property ownership and stimulate a livelier market in

---

[14] H. Derr, 'Geschichte der Pfarrei Marpingen', dissertation (Trier, 1935), 68–72. There is a copy of Derr's typescript in the seminary library, Trier.

[15] This material was largely collected during the interrogations of the Marpingen teacher, Fräulein André: LASB, E 107, 278–95. The Catholic parts of the Rhineland remained under-supplied with teachers even in the 1870s, as officials themselves admitted: K. Ohlert, 'Das Volksschulwesen', in J. Hansen (ed.), *Die Rheinprovinz 1815–1915*, ii. (Bonn, 1917), 19–20.

[16] Bungert, *Heimatbuch*, 117.

[17] Ibid. 202–3.

[18] H. Horch, *Der Wandel der Gesellschafts- und Herrschaftsstrukturen in der Saarregion während der Industrialisierung (1740–1914)* (St Ingbert, 1985), 36–41, 57–64, 89–98, 146–7; Bungert, *Heimatbuch*, 146–50; J. Müller, *Die Landwirtschaft im Saarland. Entwicklungstendenzen der Landwirtschaft eines Industrielandes* (Saarbrücken, 1976), 18–20. The process of consolidation is well described in H. Weyand, 'Die Stückelteilung und Bannrenovation im Oberamt Schaumburg: Ein Beitrag zur Untersuchung Grundherrlicher Bauerndörfer des 17./18. Jahrhunderts', *Zeitschrift für Agrargeschichte und Agrarsoziologie*, 20 (1972), 161–85. The *Gehöferschaft* was a relatively unusual arrangement in Germany, associated particularly with the Hunsrück: M. Müller, *Säkularisation und Grundbesitz. Zur Sozialgeschichte des Saar-Mosel-Raumes* (Boppard, 1980), 53.

land, the negative consequences of which were felt with particular force by small peasants during the agricultural crises that punctuated the nineteenth century.

The underlying problem in these crises was the pressure on land created by a sharply rising population, particularly under the partible inheritance system bequeathed by the French civil code.[19] The result was the subdivision and parcellization of holdings. This was less acute in Marpingen than in some other parts of the Saarland, such as the area around Merzig, but the continuing pressure of population, coupled with low output, meant that a growing number of small and middle peasant holdings were unable to support a family without some form of supplementary income.[20] The evidence of this could be seen in the rising numbers of agricultural labourers and the declining number of farm servants.[21] Those who clung to their marginal holdings lived on the edge of subsistence. A sudden economic disruption, such as occurred when Marpingen lost French markets for its cattle and grain after 1815, and again when Saxe-Coburg-Gotha joined the Prussian *Zollverein* in 1830, threatened the most vulnerable with indigence.[22] The same was true during harvest failures and periods of agricultural depression, like the mid-1830s and much of the 1840s, when there was severe poverty in Marpingen.[23] The Prussian *Landrat* of St Wendel spelt out the implications of this in 1843:

By far the largest number of agriculturalists only possess holdings sufficient to feed their families and cover their dues (*Abgaben*) from the yield. If there is a bad harvest, then the necessities of life are lacking and in order to maintain his family the peasant is forced to contract debts, reduce his herd of cattle, or later to sell a part of his holding.[24]

The crucial point here was the nature of the debt that was contracted. Cheap credit was almost impossible to obtain. This problem was certainly not unique to the Saarland; but organizations offering low rates of interest to the peasantry were particularly lacking there until a very late stage. Even after mid-century, Raiffeisen organizations and state-sponsored peasant loan banks were slow to

[19] Horch, *Wandel*, 95–6.
[20] J. J. Kartels, 'Die wirthschaftliche Lage des Bauernstandes in den Gebirgsdistricten des Kreises Merzig', *Schriften des Vereins für Sozialpolitik*, 22 (1883), 187–239; K. J. Rivinius, 'Die sozialpolitische und volkswirtschaftliche Tätigkeit von Georg Friedrich Dasbach', in *Soziale Frage und Kirche im Saarrevier* (Saarbrücken, 1984), 165–73; Horch, *Wandel*, 150; Müller, *Landwirtschaft*, 19.
[21] Horch, *Wandel*, 247–55. On the broadly similar pattern throughout Prussia, see K. Tenfelde, 'Ländliches Gesinde in Preußen. Gesinderecht und Gesindestatistik 1810 bis 1861', *Archiv für Sozialgeschichte*, 19 (1979), 189–229.
[22] See Müller, *St Wendel*, 212, on the way that 'poverty knocked at the door of the small peasant' in the area after 1815.
[23] Derr, 'Pfarrei Marpingen', 13, 22, 26. The classic account of over-population, agrarian crisis, and pauperism is Wilhelm Abel, *Massenarmut und Hungerkrisen im vorindustriellen Europa* (Hamburg, 1974).
[24] Quoted in J. Mergen, *Die Auswanderungen aus den ehemals preußischen Teilen des Saarlandes im 19. Jahrhundert*, i. *Voraussetzungen und Grundmerkmale* (Saarbrücken, 1973), 288.

arrive.[25] A Christian Peasant Association that offered benefits such as cheap insurance to the Saarland peasantry was founded more than twenty years later than its counterparts elsewhere in the Prussian Rhine Province.[26] In Marpingen, long-term mortgage loans from the church maintenance fund and church foundations were advanced in the period around 1820, although by the time they came to maturity in the middle of the century the parish priest was disillusioned about continuing the practice.[27]

If money could not be raised through family connections, the most usual resort was to the moneylender—or, in the language of contemporary writers, the *Wucher*, or usurer. The smaller peasants often had no alternative but to take out secured loans at high rates of interest. The moneylenders—in the case of Marpingen they were based mainly in Tholey—had networks of informers in the villages who let them know who was in difficulty, and were prepared to 'work' their villages with great energy.[28] One contemporary writer suggested, no doubt with some exaggeration, that the Saarland moneylenders were active 'from 3 o'clock in the morning until 10 o'clock at night'. The cattle dealers seem to have been equally diligent.[29] The moneylenders also exploited the new vigour of the land market and peasant efforts to extend their holdings, as well as the opportunities for litigation that frequent subdivision and boundary disputes provided.[30] A dyspeptic Coburg official commented in 1816 that the salient characteristics of the peasantry in the area around St Wendel were pride, envy, boastfulness, greed, and grubby self-interest.[31] Thirty years later one of his Prussian successors referred only a little more politely to 'egoism, acquisitiveness, and mistrust'.[32] The inhabitants of Marpingen certainly attracted their share of judgements like this. Father Bicking attacked their 'litigiousness . . . deceit, and malice in business matters' and their 'hard-hearted self-interest'; his successor Father Sartorius remarked that the greatest error of the village peasantry was to 'want to play the diplomat' in business matters, and to practise 'double-dealing and duplicity,

[25] O. Beck, *Die ländliche Kreditnoth und die Darlehenskassen im Regierungsbezirk Trier* (Trier, 1875), paints a gloomy picture and notes (pp. 9, 12–13) that in the Saarland the real advances by the 1870s had come in workers' consumer co-operatives rather than in peasant co-operative banks. Of the 32 Raiffeisen organizations in the Rhine Province at the time he wrote, not one was in the Trier administrative area. In his earlier *Land- und volkswirtschaftliche Tagesfragen für den Regierungsbezirk Trier* (Trier, 1866), 91, Beck argued that within the left-bank areas of the Rhine Province the southern region was 'very removed' from the activities of the state's agricultural association.
[26] The Rhineland Bauernverein was founded in 1862, the Trierischer Bauernverein in 1884. See Rivinius, 'Dasbach', 173–80.
[27] BAT, 70/3676, 34–8: Father Bicking to GV Trier, 4, 7, and 16 Dec. 1849, and 22 Feb. 1850.
[28] E. R. Knebel, 'Der Wucher im preußischen Saargebiete', *Schriften des Vereins für Sozialpolitik*, 35 (1887), 127.
[29] Kartels, 'Die wirthschaftliche Lage', 208; Knebel, 'Der Wucher', 129. On moneylenders and cattle dealers around St Wendel, see Müller, *St Wendel*, 212.
[30] Müller, *Landwirtschaft*, 24–7; Knebel, 'Der Wucher', 138; G. F. Dasbach, 'Der Wucher in den Dörfern des trierischen Landes', *Schriften des Vereins für Sozialpolitik*, 35 (1887), 153.
[31] Horch, *Wandel*, 601 n. 134.
[32] G. Bärsch, *Beschreibung des Regierungs-Bezirks Trier*, 2 vols. (Trier, 1849), i. 27.

artifice and crooked ways'.[33] We need to exercise some caution on this point. Our sources are generally officials, priests, and notaries, who took a patronizing attitude towards the peasantry and were not always alive to the difference between need and greed. They may also have attributed to vanity and acquisitiveness what was in fact the product of a strategy designed to maintain family holdings.[34] Whatever the causes, the effects were indisputable. The cycle of debt and foreclosure was described by Father Bicking in a series of anxious letters to his superiors in 1849. He noted that the church maintenance fund and the Hoff'sche foundation (established by Matthias Hoff, parish priest in 1812–38) had debtors who owed as much as 200 thaler, with unpaid back-interest of 40 thaler. More problematic still, land which formed the security for mortgage loans had since been sold, sometimes more than once. In at least one case mortgaged land had changed hands and then been included in a forced sale of property.[35] Untangling these skeins of debt was complicated by the relatively small number of names shared by villagers (around one Marpinger in ten was called Recktenwald), but the major problem was the sheer volume of debt. Bicking referred to the 'increasing indebtedness of the larger part of the inhabitants'. It was a measure of the general crisis that in early 1850 both parish and church council were advocating that the church take advantage of the 'opportunities offered by the frequent compulsory auctions taking place here' to buy up cheap land for renting out.[36] The forced sale or auctioning of property became part of the rhythm of weekly life. Saturday afternoon, kept free of work because of an oath originally sworn by the villagers in 1699, became the favoured day for the striking of notarial agreements and the auctioning of land and furniture.[37] The problem of debt was particularly acute in the crisis years of the 1840s, although a notary from Tholey reported a lively level of forced public auctions of land and houses during the 1860s.[38] Some of the foreclosed property was bought by 'outsiders', among them Protestants and Jews, which created friction with the villagers.[39]

The Tholey notary, Heß, suggested another reason why Marpingen had 'gone downhill' and become 'impoverished'. He was referring to the division and 'squandering' of large parts of the communal woodland.[40] Heß's account was

[33] Derr, 'Pfarrei Marpingen', 27, 37.

[34] See M. Segalen, Love and Power in the Peasant Family (Oxford, 1983); P. Bourdieu, 'Marriage Strategies as Strategies of Social Reproduction', in R. Forster and O. Ranum (eds.), Family and Society. Selections from the Annales: Économies, Sociétés, Civilisations (Baltimore, 1976), 117–44. These draw on French material; for Germany, see H. Medick and D. W. Sabean (eds.), Interest and Emotion: Essays on the Study of Family and Kinship (Cambridge, 1984); and for a close analysis of one village, U. Jeggle, Kiebingen: Eine Heimatgeschichte (Tübingen, 1977).

[35] BAT, 70/3676, 34–6: Bicking to GV Trier, 4, 7, and 16 Dec. 1849.

[36] BAT, 70/3676, 38: Bicking to GV Trier, 22 Feb. 1850.

[37] Derr, 'Pfarrei Marpingen', 29.

[38] MMGE, 22: Heß to Prince Radziwill, 28 Nov. 1876.

[39] Derr, 'Pfarrei Marpingen', 29. See also the report in the SMZ, 4 Nov. 1876, referring to outside landholders in the village.

[40] MMGE, 22: Heß to Prince Radziwill, 28 Nov. 1876; and Derr, 'Pfarrei Marpingen', 26, on the sale of one particular parcel of land in the 1840s.

strongly tinged with moral disapproval, but he put his finger on an important point. The situation was actually more serious, as well as more complex, than he suggested. The woodlands were a potentially valuable source of fuel, bracken, moss, and leaf-mould or 'forest straw' (*Laubstreu*); they also provided grazing for goats, pigs, and sheep. The woods had always served as a safety-valve during times of particular peasant hardship. In the nineteenth century this safety-valve was threatened in a number of different ways. The creeping advance of arable, the excessive felling of trees during the French occupation, and further incursions during the 'hunger years' after 1817 all reduced the area of woodland.[41] This was exacerbated by the sale of communal woodland into private hands, with resales sometimes taking it out of the village altogether.[42]

Perhaps most serious of all, however, was the campaign by the nineteenth-century state to restrict peasant use of the remaining communal woodlands in the name of rational forestry management. In the Saarland there had been fierce social struggles at the end of the eighteenth century as the peasantry asserted customary rights to graze animals and collect wood. These struggles sharpened when the area became part of Prussia.[43] Prussian officials claimed to represent the general interest against the sectional concerns of wood dealers and bark tanners, and against peasants allegedly ignorant of their own best interests. They clamped down severely on grazing and the gathering of wood, leaf-mould, and bracken.[44] The result was a series of confrontations between the peasantry and forestry officials.[45] Matters came to a head during the 1840s, when the effects of acute material distress led to constant skirmishing between peasantry and state, and convictions for wood thefts reached unprecedented levels. In this respect the situation in the Saarland was similar to that in Prussia as a whole.[46] The potential for conflict did not disappear after 1848, for Prussian forestry officials continued to assert their right to protect woodland from the 'selfishness' and short-sightedness of peasant communes.[47] The conflict that occurred in Marpingen after the apparitions, when villagers and state officials fought over access to the woods, gains an extra dimension of meaning from the history of social struggles that preceded it. Indeed, the very presence of three young girls gathering

[41] O. Beck, *Die Waldschutzfrage in Preußen* (Berlin, 1860), 513; A. Bernhardt, *Geschichte des Wald-eigentums, der Waldwirtschaft und Forstwirtschaft in Deutschland*, 3 vols. (Berlin, 1872–5), iii. 124–5. Arable already accounted for more than 50% of all land in Marpingen by the end of the 18th cent.

[42] See Kartels, 'Die wirthschaftliche Lage', 210.

[43] Horch, *Wandel*, 57–64, 93–8, 145–6, 232–4.

[44] Beck, *Waldschutzfrage*; Beck, *Tagesfragen*, esp. 48–61 and 72–6.

[45] O. Beck, *Beschreibung des Regierungs-Bezirks Trier*, 3 vols. (Trier, 1868–71), ii. 218.

[46] The pioneering modern work on wood-thefts and other forms of 'everyday criminality' was done by Dirk Blasius. See *Bürgerliche Gesellschaft und Kriminalität: Zur Sozialgeschichte Preußens im Vormärz* (Göttingen, 1976); *Kriminalität und Alltag. Zur Konfliktgeschichte des Alltagslebens im 19. Jahrhundert* (Göttingen, 1978).

[47] See Beck, *Tagesfragen*, 61, and the same author's *Waldschutzfrage*. On the St Wendel area, see the material in LASB, Best. Landkreis St Wendel, Nr. 476. The papers of Georg Dasbach, founder of the Trier Bauernverein, indicate that this 'fierce struggle between peasantry and forestry administration continued up to the end of the century': BAT, 85/282b, 138.

berries in the Härtelwald acquires a further layer of significance when we recall officials who complained that 'children are frequently misused in the theft of the fruits of the forest'.[48]

The central point is that the safety-valve represented by communal woodland was progressively closed in the course of the nineteenth century. One result, especially in the 1830s and 1840s, was widespread emigration.[49] In Marpingen long-distance migration was already well established in the eighteenth century. The entire St Wendel district proved a major source of colonists when the Habsburg monarchy tried to create bulwarks of German settlers against the Turks on the middle Danube. The area just north-west of Marpingen, around Tholey and Lebach, was known as 'Turkey' because so many had emigrated in this way. Marpingers were well represented in the eighteenth-century waves of colonization. In the 1760s as many as fifty inhabitants left the village for the Hungarian Banat.[50] This movement of population was permanently commemorated in 1777 when a returning emigrant, Johannes Thomé, had a cross erected in the village in gratitude for his safe homecoming.[51]

Long-distance emigration from the area resumed in the decades after the Napoleonic wars, reaching a high-point in the 1840s. It took place on a greater scale from the rural districts of St Wendel and Merzig than from any other part of the Saarland.[52] This area now became noted for the numbers it sent to the United States, rather than to other European countries or to destinations like Brazil and North Africa (although three Marpingen inhabitants with nine dependants did receive permission to emigrate to Algeria in 1844).[53] America was the principal goal of Marpingen emigrants, and the process gained momentum as the letters and remissions of relations encouraged others to follow.[54] It is impossible to identify all the individuals concerned. The personal details we possess suggest emigrants of some substance. Of the three Marpingen heads of families who applied to emigrate to Algeria in 1844, one—the carpenter Hufnagel—had assets of over 1,200 thaler, the other two almost 900 thaler between them.[55] We also know that one of the America-bound emigrants in 1847 was the senior churchwarden Michel Puhl.[56] The depression of land prices as properties flooded the market at periods of peak emigration deterred many from selling up and leaving; but the numbers who did leave suggest that emigration from the Marp-

---

[48] Bernhardt, Geschichte des Waldeigentums, iii. 143, criticized the freedom from prosecution of under-12s.

[49] Müller, Landwirtschaft, 19.

[50] Hoppstädter and Hermann, Geschichtliche Landeskunde, i. 101; Bungert, Heimatbuch, 165–77. The records also show large-scale emigration to the same destination from the neighbouring villages of Alsweiler, Berschweiler, and Urexweiler.

[51] Bungert, Heimatbuch, 174–6.

[52] Horch, Wandel, 162.

[53] Mergen, Auswanderungen, 138, 199, 216–17.

[54] Bungert, Heimatbuch, 178–81.

[55] Mergen, Auswanderungen, 216–17.

[56] BAT, 70/3676, 18.

ingen area, as from other German areas of partible inheritance such as Württemberg, was a common resort of smaller peasants, although not of the landless.[57] During the peak emigration year of 1846, not only were the figures of the St Wendel district running ahead of those elsewhere in the Saarland or the administrative area of Trier, but the mayoral district that included Marpingen (Alsweiler) was strikingly over-represented within the St Wendel district as a whole.[58]

Emigration gives a measure of economic crisis in Marpingen during the hungry forties. Neither poverty nor emigration disappeared after the middle of the century: even in the relatively prosperous 1850s continuing shortage of credit and indebtedness encouraged peasants to see 'emigration as their salvation', a view encouraged by the many agents active in the area.[59] The historian of St Wendel has described the families travelling in their covered wagons over the Baltesweiler heights to Trier, and on through Luxemburg to Antwerp.[60] The arrival of the railway in the 1860s brought a new kind of problem to rural areas in the form of foreign competition, especially French and Hungarian. Emigration figures rose again in the mid-1860s, and even more in the following decade.[61] By the 1870s, however, the storm-centre of rural crisis and mass emigration had shifted to the northern parts of the St Wendel district, away from Marpingen and neighbouring villages. The reason for this is plain: in the decades after 1850 Marpingen and the surrounding areas were pulled firmly into the orbit of the industrial Saarland. At the time of the apparitions agricultural depression was still a factor of undoubted importance; but the tensions and crises in the village were increasingly those generated by dependence on the coalfields to the south.

That was a result of the peculiar pattern of industrialization in the Saarland. In the middle of the century the Saar already boasted a number of industries, including glass, ceramics, and tanning as well as some mineral extraction and engineering, but in the following two decades the area was transformed by coal and iron. Extensive canal and railway building programmes opened up new markets in eastern France, the Rhineland, Belgium, and southern Germany, and helped to create the heavy-industrial triangle of the Saarland–Lorraine–Luxemburg.[62] It was, above all, the explosive development of the coal industry

---

[57] Mergen, Auswanderungen, 155–8; Horch, Wandel, 154. Heavy emigration caused the population of Württemberg to fall by 75,000 between 1849 and 1855: Das Königreich Württemberg. Eine Beschreibung von Land, Volk und Staat (Stuttgart, 1863), 314–15.
[58] Of the 468 authorized emigrants from the 7 mayoralties in the St Wendel district, 38% were accounted for by the Alsweiler mayoralty: Bungert, Heimatbuch, 180.
[59] Beck, Ländliche Kreditnoth, 200.
[60] Müller, St Wendel, 246.
[61] Beck, Tagesfragen, 9, and Ländliche Kreditnoth, 200.
[62] H. Klein, 'Geschichte des Landkreises Saarbrücken', in Grenze als Schicksal—150 Jahre Landkreis Saarbrücken (Saarbrücken, 1966), 63–7; P. Keuth, 'Die wirtschaftliche Entwicklung im Landkreis Saarbrücken', in Grenze als Schicksal, 113–21; Hoppstädter and Hermann, Geschichtliche Landeskunde, i. 111.

which led contemporaries to talk of a 'black California'.[63] In 1850 the town of
Dudweiler produced 73,000 tons of coal with a labour force of under 700; twenty
years later the output was 600,000 tons and the labour force nearly 3,000 strong.[64]
Rapid industrialization based on coal, iron, and railways did not in itself make
the Saarland exceptional in the Germany of the 1850s and 1860s. It was the
composition of the work-force that was unusual. The first miners and industrial
workers from the Saar valleys were soon followed by small peasants and dwarf
holders from nearby districts, pushed by the shortage of land and pulled by the
prospect of a new source of income. The surplus rural population of the Palatinate
and Lorraine was drawn for similar reasons.[65] But the rush to the Saarland was
not quite of Californian proportions. As labour shortages made themselves felt,
efforts to recruit in other coalfields and in areas like the Harz met with limited
success: wage levels were comparatively low and incomers often experienced
hostility and returned home. Above all, housing was in desperately short supply.
The difficulties of local topography were compounded by the reluctance of
Prussian forestry officials to release woodland to the state mining administration
for the construction of workers' colonies. The policy of attracting workers from
outside the area was finally given up in the late 1860s.[66]

The solution to the labour shortage in the industrial belt was the characteristic
Saarland institution of the worker-peasant, or miner-peasant.[67] The type is exemplified in the figure of Nikolaus Warken, charismatic leader of the miners' movement in 1889–93, who always retained the rural holding inherited from his father
and returned to farm it in 1893 when dismissed as a strike leader.[68] The worker-
peasants of the Saar did not sell up their holdings or move their homes and
families, but commuted to the pits and iron works from a rural base. That is the
explanation for the fact that Saarland miners were drawn from an extraordinarily
large number of different places: by the end of the 1850s coalfield workers already
lived in 400 different towns and villages.[69] There was an intermediate zone from

[63] Laufer, 'Aspekte', 154.
[64] R. Saam, 'Die industrielle und siedlungsgeographische Entwicklung Dudweilers im 18. und 19.
Jahrhundert', Zeitschrift für die Geschichte der Saargegend, 22 (1974), 112.
[65] K. A. Gabel, Kämpfe und Werden der Hüttenarbeiter-Organisationen an der Saar (Saarbrücken,
1921), 29–30.
[66] K. Fehn, Preußische Siedlungspolitik im saarländischen Bergbaurevier (1816–1919) (Saarbrücken,
1981), 41–7, 248; Hoppstädter and Hermann, Geschichtliche Landeskunde, i. 107–8.
[67] K. Fehn, 'Das saarländische Arbeiterbauerntum im 19. und 20. Jahrhundert', in H. Kellenbenz
(ed.), Agrarisches Nebengewerbe und Formen der Reagrarisierung (Stuttgart, 1975), 195–214; M. Zenner,
'Probleme des Übergangs von der Agrar- zur Industrie- und Arbeiterkultur im Saarland', in Soziale
Frage und Kirche im Saarrevier (Saarbrücken, 1984), 70–1. The worker-peasant was also a Württemberg
institution, and there were common characteristics. See H. Hoffmann, Landwirtschaft und Industrie in
Württemberg (Berlin, 1935). The Saarland resembled the central German Erzgebirge, which combined
industrial concentration and the characteristic mixture of proletarian and rural populations, more than
it did other mining areas like the Ruhr.
[68] K.-M. Mallmann, 'Nikolaus Warken', in P. Neumann (ed.), Saarländische Lebensbilder, i.
(Saarbrücken, 1982), 130, 149.
[69] H. Steffens, 'Einer für alle, alle für einen? Bergarbeiterfamilien in der 2. Hälfte des 19. Jahrhunderts',
in T. Pierenkemper (ed.), Haushalt und Verbrauch in historischer Perspektive (St Katharinen, 1987), 196.

which daily commuting was made possible by the railway, but large numbers travelled from more outlying areas, living for six days of the week in crude dormitory accommodation (*Schlafhäuser*) near their place of work. In 1875, 35 per cent of all Saar miners were weekly commuters of this sort.[70]

The rapid expansion of mining affected Marpingen in a number of ways. The village itself contained very small deposits of both iron ore and bituminous coal. After these had been scavenged by the village poor in the 1820s, formal prospecting and mining concessions were issued by both the Saxe-Coburg and Prussian governments. Coal was in fact mined for thirty-five years in the Härtelwald, scene of the later apparitions, and in two neighbouring districts. But the frequent changes of concession-holder bear witness to the geological difficulties and the small amounts of coal produced by open-cast mining methods. The different sites produced an annual average of under 200 tons between them, much of it sold under the terms of the concession to villagers themselves at a favourable price. Mining never employed more than nine men in Marpingen, and ceased completely in 1861 when the extension of the Saarland railway network made the modest output unprofitable.[71]

It was not mining in the village itself, but the impact of the southern coalfields, which transformed Marpingen in the space of a generation. This was partly a matter of straightforward migration to the industrial belt, indicated by the declining rate of increase of the village population (see Table 2.1). The poor now had an opportunity to leave Marpingen that did not require the capital needed for overseas emigration. Many were initially drawn away from agricultural employment by railway construction, especially on the Nahe–Rhine line.[72] (The Neunkirchen–Bad Kreuznach stretch of the line employed 10,000 men.[73]) Others reached the coalfield via the half-way house of wood-cutting for the mines.[74] Day labourers and poorer peasants were most heavily involved in this movement of population. Much more important, however, were the *Fernpendler* who commuted to the mines and turned Marpingen into a classic village of worker-peasants. The only miners resident in Marpingen in 1850 were the handful working in the village's own pits. By 1867 there were eighty miner-peasants, who together with their dependants made up a third of the village inhabitants. By 1875 the number had risen to 195, and with their dependants they accounted for just over a half (51.4 per cent) of the population. A decade later the proportion had reached nearly 60 per cent.[75] Employment in the mines clearly attracted small peasants. This is strongly suggested by the fact that most of those Marpingen miners who

[70] Fehn, *Siedlungspolitik*, 231; H.-W. Hermann and H. Klein, 'Zur sozialen Entwicklung im Landkreis Saarbrücken', in *Grenze als Schicksal—150 Jahre Landkreis Saarbrücken* (Saarbrücken, 1966), 135; Laufer, 'Aspekte', 148–51. In 1900 the figure was still 25%, in 1909 20%.
[71] Bungert, *Heimatbuch*, 208–23.
[72] Müller, *St Wendel*, 247 ff.
[73] Horch, *Wandel*, 610 n. 110.
[74] Laufer, 'Aspekte', 144.
[75] Bungert, *Heimatbuch*, 301.

owned land in 1875 (around a quarter) kept goats rather than cattle.[76] But the low figure for property-owning demonstrates the extent to which the coalfield also provided employment for the sons of peasant families that owned more substantial property. The surplus population of young men with no immediate inheritance prospects matched the labour demands of the expanding mines. The figures on average family size suggest that the proportion of younger, unmarried miners rose over the years.[77] There was nevertheless a gradual rise in the proportion of Marpingen miners who owned land and fixed property, as sons inherited from their parents.[78] The miners in the village therefore enjoyed different circumstances from their counterparts in the coalfield itself. The latter might own a vegetable garden, a potato plot, and a goat in the cellar; the former either were, or had the prospect of becoming, true peasant proprietors.[79]

There is no doubt that the opening up of work in the mines had positive effects for Marpingen. It provided employment opportunities that were not restricted to miners alone. One of the best-respected figures in the village, the master carpenter Jakob Schario, worked in the coalfield.[80] Mine work brought money into the village and took the edge off rural poverty. For the miners themselves the new means of employment could offer material rewards without the sense of proletarianization.[81] 'We country people' was the way the miner Jakob Kirsch referred to men like himself, when he talked about his daughter Magdalena's 'miraculous' cure in 1876, and the pleasure with which he described her once again carrying heavy cattle fodder lent practical illustration to his point.[82]

Many contemporaries and later writers painted an idealized picture of the Saarland worker-peasant. They contrasted his healthy attachment to the land and enjoyment of the benefits conferred by 'traditional' peasant life with the urban cesspool of the coalfield itself, and the breakdown of domesticity that supposedly occurred there.[83] Some of these commentators were Catholic priests. The Marp-

---

[76] Horch, *Wandel*, 391. Compare the pattern in the Westphalian village of Quernheim in the post-1848 period, where it was small peasants and their sons who went into the cigar-making industry: J. Mooser, 'Soziale Mobilität', esp. 186–7.

[77] In 1875 the average number of dependants per miner (principally children, although it also included dependent parents, grandparents, brothers, and sisters) was 1:2.93 in Marpingen, higher than the ratio among Saar miners as a whole (1:2.78). Subsequently the Marpingen ratio fell, while it rose in the Saarland as a whole. With the Marpingen figures given first, the ratios were 1:2.95/1:3.15 (1885), 1:2.61/1:3.13 (1890), 1:2.29/1:2.89 (1895). Differences in family size do not provide an alternative explanation for these figures: if this were taken into account, the difference would be even greater. Ratios calculated from the tables in Bungert, *Heimatbuch*, 301, and Steffens, 'Einer für alle', 195.

[78] Horch, *Wandel*, 378, 638 n. 131.

[79] On the differences, see Steffens, 'Einer für alle', 198–9; and on the determination of the Marpingers not to be mere 'goat-peasants', Bungert, *Heimatbuch*, 305–6.

[80] LASB, E 107, 132.

[81] See Mallmann, *Anfänge*, 43–6; Fehn, 'Arbeiterbauerntum', 197.

[82] *MWOL*, 18.

[83] See the comments of the *Landrat* of Saarbrücken on fathers who had no time and mothers who were 'themselves badly brought up, irresponsible, lazy, and [had] little sense of order, cleanliness, or domesticity': LHAK, 442/6383, 237–52: LR Saarbrücken to KR Trier, 1 Feb. 1885; also the officials

ingen clergy took a less sanguine view of the worker-peasant: while acknowledging that mining income had helped the village, they criticized the moral effects. As Father Sartorius put it in 1863, Marpingen had changed since the middle of the century and some had been tainted by 'violence, extravagance, and recklessness'.[84] The Arcadian myth was naturally at work here, but there is no reason to doubt a kernel of truth in the clerical charge. The Saar coalfield was indeed a harsh and violent place. At a time when shifts were growing longer (from 8 hours in the 1850s to 10 hours in the 1870s), housing conditions were appalling, and three-quarters of the work-force were treated annually for illnesses that included pneumonia, pleurisy, and epidemic diseases, the social life of the miner was always likely to disappoint fastidious mine officials and clergy. Alcohol abuse and crimes of violence ran at high levels.[85] In the raw violence of its social relations, the early industrial Saarland lived up to the Californian comparison. The mainly young men of Marpingen who worked there could hardly remain unaffected by the pressures.

In fact, they bore additional strains because of their divided lives. Marpingen's miners belonged without exception to the 35 per cent of Saarland miners in 1875 who were away from home all week. They worked in the pits of Altenwald, Maybach, Itzenplitz, and Dechen, in the mining inspectorates of Sulzbach, Friedrichstal, Reden, and Heinitz. The closest of these pits was 20 km. distant, a four-hour walk over rugged country. The construction of the St Wendel–Neunkirchen railway in 1860 was a major help only to those who worked in Heinitz, and further railway connections that eased the journey to work were not built until the end of the century. Most Marpingen miners walked, making their way along a 'miners' path' that ran from the cross on the nearby Exelberg, past Hirzweiler and Hüttigweiler to Wemmetsweiler, where the routes to the various pits diverged.[86] They belonged to the 'hardfeet', or *Hartfüsser*, so called because of the sound made by their cobbled boots on the streets of the pit villages as they marched to work.[87] They made this journey twice a week, early on Monday morning when they left home and late on Saturday evening when they returned. During the week they lived in dormitories thrown up at speed to meet the accommodation crisis. One clergyman realistically likened them to barracks, for a warden imposed a military-style discipline that included lights out, codes of dress, and a ban on the knocking out of pipes. Rooms were damp, sanitary arrangements primitive, and outbreaks of disease common. As the mining

cited in Steffens, 'Einer für alle', 187–92. On the idealization of the worker-peasant, see K. Pauli, *Der Arbeiterbauer im Saarland* (dissertation; Heidelberg, 1939).

[84] Derr, 'Pfarrei Marpingen', 36.

[85] Horch, *Wandel*, 306–7, 310–15, 393–4 on work-intensification, illness, and violence respectively; H. Steffens, *Autorität und Revolte. Alltagsleben und Streikverhalten der Bergarbeiter an der Saar im 19. Jahrhundert* (Weingarten, 1987), chs. 3–4.

[86] Bungert, *Heimatbuch*, 302–4.

[87] Hoppstädter and Hermann, *Geschichtliche Landeskunde*, i. 111; Hermann and Klein, 'Zur sozialen Entwicklung', 135; Bungert, *Heimatbuch*, 303.

administration admitted in the late 1860s, most of the dormitories were 'over-crowded and leave much to be desired hygienically'.[88]

Marpingen miners lived, in short, like *Gastarbeiter*. There were corresponding compensations, above all in the emotional warmth and *esprit de corps* of a collective life that revolved around communal cooking and eating. But that only highlighted their alienation from the larger work-force. The sacks of potatoes and other provisions brought from home earned them the nickname the 'satchel-men'; it also created suspicion that they were better fed than other miners. This was not the only source of hostility. The fact that they lived in the closed world of the dormitory barracks, the fear that they would undercut wage levels, even their accents which were mocked as rustic: all isolated the miners of Marpingen and similar villages from the solidarities that developed among those who were permanently resident.[89]

But if the weekly commuters took the village world with them into the coalfield, they also brought the coalfield world back with them into the village.[90] In neither place were they truly at home. Miners shared an intensely male life at the pit, and lived in an extended all-male 'family' outside work: they were generally better informed about their neighbour in the next bunk than they were about their own families.[91] A thirty-hour weekend at home was hardly long enough to resume familiarity with a world shaped for most of the week by women, children, and old people. Younger unmarried men reacted against the sexual morality of the village, and began to resist the marriage and inheritance strategies of the peasant family.[92] Married men, no longer at home during the week to organize work and represent the family to the outside world, felt their role as head of the household usurped by their wives and their patriarchal authority dented. This was a potent source of tension within marriages.[93] The pressures faced by the wives who remained in the village were perhaps even greater. They had the extra physical burden of looking after the agricultural holding, charged now with 'male' tasks like ploughing, sowing, and reaping, feeding large animals as well as goats and geese, carrying materials for the construction of new outbuildings.[94] They also had to assume a new role as figures of authority within mother-centred families.

---

[88] K. Hoppstädter, '"Eine halbe Stunde nach der Schicht muß jeder gewaschen sein". Die alten Schlafhäuser und die Ranzenmänner', *Saarbrücker Bergmannskalender* (1963), 77–9, referring to dormitories in Heinitz and Sulzbach that housed Marpingen miners; Steffens, *Autorität und Revolte*, 198–211.

[89] Hoppstädter, 'Eine halbe Stunde nach der Schicht'.

[90] Zenner, 'Probleme', 67.

[91] Steffens, 'Einer für alle', 215; Gabel, *Kämpfe*, 29–30.

[92] Horch, *Wandel*, 381. On the regulation of the moral life of young people in the peasant village, see H. Rosenbaum, *Formen der Familie* (Frankfurt am Main, 1982), 77–8.

[93] Parallels in Württemberg during the same period are discussed in J. Kuczynski, *Geschichte des Alltags des deutschen Volkes 1600–1945*, iv. *1871–1918* (Berlin, 1982), 414–15.

[94] Bungert, *Heimatbuch*, 305. We should not, of course, underestimate the heavy work-load that normally fell on the wife in a peasant family: during the busy summer when working days were long they might be working 16 hours a day. See Rosenbaum, *Formen der Familie*, 81. It was the *type* of work that changed when the men were absent.

While absent fathers, paradoxically, were able to develop an emotionally closer relationship with their children—no longer the ubiquitous delegator of work, but the cherished weekend visitor bearing gifts—it was mothers who, conversely, took on the task of organizing the household work of the farm.[95] There was, of course, another side to these role-changes. The new pressures faced by miners' wives in villages like Marpingen also gave them a new authority. They not only took a large share of responsibility for the farm; it was also they who, more than ever, maintained family and neighbourhood social ties, and represented the family in dealings with school authorities and other officials. All of this represented a potential increment of power and autonomy. It was a development that ran parallel to the enhanced status of miners' wives in the coalfield itself. They increasingly assumed representative functions within the family, and at the same time contributed significantly to family income and carved out a sphere of responsibility for themselves by taking in lodgers.[96] Yet the wives in weekly-commuter villages probably paid a higher price for their new autonomy than women in the coalfield. They were far less informed about, indeed were excluded from the male world of work, while their customary sphere of influence in matters such as family marriage strategies was undermined by the departure of older sons to the pit. The assumption of additional responsibilities on the farm did nothing to alter the patriarchal property arrangements sanctified by the civil code, but it readily brought them up against village prejudice about 'refractory' (aufsässige) women and 'weak' men.[97]

Between the end of the eighteenth century and the 1870s Marpingen underwent a double transformation. The first dismantled the system of Gehöferschaften and common land and replaced it with peasant individualism and a free market in land. The second turned the village increasingly into an annexe of the Saarland coalfield. There are comparisons to be made with the process that transformed the English village of Highley in Shropshire, first through enclosures and then through the advent of mining. If Marpingen seems to have weathered the double transition with less resilience than Highley, this may be because the latter did not

---

[95] On the new affective relationship between fathers and children, see Horch, Wandel, 365–8; Hoppstädter, 'Eine halbe Stunde nach der Schicht', 79. Compare the changing gender roles in the Austrian mining village of Grünbach, described in Eva Viethen, 'Tradition und Realitätseignung— Bergarbeiterfrauen im industriellen Wandel', in H. Fielhauer and O. Bockhorn (eds.), Die andere Kultur. Volkskunde, Sozialwissenschaften und Arbeiterkultur (Vienna, Munich, and Zurich, 1982), 241–59. For some perceptive observations on the new burdens that fell on women, see Steffens, 'Einer für alle', 199–200, 215–16.

[96] On miners' wives in the coalfield, see K.-M. Mallmann, '"Haltet fest wie der Baum die Äst". Zur Rolle der Frauen in der Bergarbeiterbewegung 1892/93', Saarheimat, 24 (1980), 89–92. This area of research was opened up by L. Niethammer and F. J. Brüggemeier, 'Wie wohnten Arbeiter im Kaiserreich?', Archiv für Sozialgeschichte, 16 (1976), 61–134.

[97] Mallmann, 'Haltet fest', 91; Horch, Wandel, 346–7. On the displeasure excited by 'inverted roles' in the family, and the Saarland form of charivari—the Schaware or Schalwari—with which this could be punished, see N. Fox, Saarländische Volkskunde (Bonn, 1927), 369 ff.

physically lose its men in the same way.[98] Marpingen became a form of
Weiberdorf—a village without men.[99] True, it did not face the problems of the
Eifel village depicted in Clara Viebig's celebrated novel, from which the men
were permanently absent in the Westphalian industrial belt, returning just twice
a year.[100] Nor was the situation comparable to the Friulian village of Verzegnis,
whose adult male population was away for months at a time in pursuit of seasonal
agricultural work—a village we know about because of an outbreak of 'collective
hysteria' among the women of Verzegnis in 1878.[101] Social transformation nevertheless created anxieties and uncertainty, not least in the realm of family life.
These provide an essential part of the background to the events that began in
July 1876.

Borderlands

The economic and social upheaval that Marpingen experienced from the second
half of the eighteenth century was more than matched in the political sphere. In
the fifty years after the mid-1760s the small area to which the village belonged
was caught up in a dizzy reel of territorial exchanges and treaties. The dance
was hardly interrupted by the post-Napoleonic settlement in Europe, for the
dispositions of the Allies were the prelude to revolution and a further change of
masters.

Marpingen had been part of the Duchy of Lorraine for 500 years when, in
1766, the duchy was incorporated into France and the village thus became briefly
part of the French eastern border. An exchange of territory in 1787 then made
the Schaumburg district to which Marpingen belonged even more briefly part of
the Duchy of Pfalz-Zweibrücken. When the Duke of Zweibrücken fled before
the French Revolutionary armies in 1793, Marpingen once again became part of
France and remained within the Department of the Moselle for twenty years.
After the defeat of Napoleon in 1814, the area was initially subject to a joint
Austrian–Bavarian provisional administration; it was then temporarily administered by Prussia for a few months in 1816, before being ceded to the Duchy of
Saxe-Coburg-Gotha as a reward for one of Prussia's allies in the war against
Napoleon. The Duke of Saxe-Coburg-Gotha named his new parcel of land
the Principality of Lichtenberg. Marpingen remained part of it until the duke,

---

[98] G. Nair, *Highley: The Development of a Community 1550–1880* (Oxford, 1988). As Nair shows,
miners migrated to Highley to work in the mines and left again as the pits ran down.
[99] On *Weiberdörfer* in the Saarland, see Fox, *Saarländische Volkskunde*, 389; Kartels, 'Die wirthschaftliche Lage', 197, 202–4, 212–14; Steffens, 'Einer für alle', 214–16.
[100] Clara Viebig, *Das Weiberdorf. Roman aus der Eifel* (Berlin, 7th edn., 1901).
[101] L. Petit, 'Une epidémie d'hystéro-demonopathie, en 1878, à Verzegnis, province de Frioul, Italie',
Revue Scientifique, 41 (10 Apr. 1880), 974A–975A; Devlin, *Superstitious Mind*, 251 n. 47. I am grateful
to Luciana Borsatti, who first drew Verzegnis to my attention. D. R. Holmes, *Cultural Disenchantments:
Worker Peasantries in Northern Italy* (Princeton, NJ, 1989), deals with similar cultural dislocations in
the Friuli, especially in the village of Rubignacco, part of the commune of Cividale del Friuli.

disillusioned by political unrest in 1832, decided to sell the territory to Prussia in 1834 in exchange for 80,000 thaler a year.[102]

The most obvious legacy of this territorial carousel was a fractured relationship towards political authority. Impermanence became the norm as rulers, taxes, and systems of conscription came and went. This was hardly favourable soil for the would-be state builders of the late eighteenth and early nineteenth century. It was common enough for contemporary resentment against a ruler to be couched in terms of the 'good old law'; in the area around Tholey and St Wendel experience had provided a rich variety of rulers in a short space of time, whose real or imagined virtues could be deployed against a given incumbent. This may explain something of the political turbulence of the area, certainly up to the 1830s. The revolutionary armies which unseated the severe Pfalz-Zweibrücken regime were welcomed until French taxes, conscription—and, no doubt, the epidemics that accompanied troop movements—led to disillusionment.[103] The new Saxe-Coburg regime was equally uncertain about its new subjects. One official, reporting on the area in 1816, believed that 'frequent changes and perpetual war' were among the reasons why the inhabitants embraced 'revolutionary principles', demonstrated 'insubordination, even where there is no stronger resistance', and made 'insulting remarks about their superiors'.[104] The report offers an insight into the anxieties of the official mind in the immediate aftermath of the Vienna settlement—and in this case the anxieties proved well-founded. While liberal critics in the tiny capital of St Wendel objected to the arbitrary rule and petty repression of the Saxe-Coburg regime, craftsmen in the town and peasants in surrounding areas protested about the severe economic crisis, the burden of taxes, and financial maladministration. The decision of the principality in 1830 to join the Prussian Customs Union, which suppressed a lucrative smuggling trade, and the revolutionary examples of France, Belgium, and the Palatinate, were enough to send the area up in revolt in 1832. It was the only part of the Saarland that experienced insurrection in the 1830s, and Prussian troops had to be sent from Saarlouis to restore order.[105] This was the prelude to the arrival of Prussian rule two years later.

In 1834 the refractory population of the Principality of Lichtenberg became Prussian subjects, incorporated into the administrative district of Trier in the

[102] M. Bär, *Die Behördenverfassung der Rheinprovinz seit 1815* (Bonn, 1919), 93 ff.; Bungert, *Heimatbuch*, 94–113, 195–205; Müller, *St Wendel*, 189–91, 229. See also the maps in the end map-folder of Hoppstädter and Hermann, *Geschichtliche Landeskunde*, ii.

[103] Bungert, *Heimatbuch*, 195–7. On the French occupation and local reactions in the Rhine–Mosel area, see H. Molitor, *Vom Untertan zum Administré. Studien zur französischen Herrschaft und zum Verhalten der Bevölkerung im Rhein–Mosel Raum von den Revolutionskriegen bis zum Ende der napoleonischen Zeit* (Wiesbaden, 1980); and on the Saar region specifically, F. and A. Ecker, *Der Widerstand der Saarländer gegen die Fremdherrschaft der Franzosen 1792–1815* (Saarbrücken, 1934). The final French withdrawal was accompanied by a severe epidemic of typhus.

[104] Horch, *Wandel*, 601 n. 134.

[105] J. Bellot, *Hundert Jahre politisches Leben an der Saar unter preußischer Herrschaft (1815–1918)* (Bonn, 1954), 16–18; Müller, *St Wendel*, 199–231; Bungert, *Heimatbuch*, 204–5.

Rhine Province. The new rulers were to prove more lasting, and they brought stability—but at a price. The Saar area was the southernmost appendix of a region, the Rhine Province, that proved generally problematic for the Prussian state, for its acquisition shifted the centre of gravity of Prussia westwards and raised problems it was slow to recognize or deal with.[106] These were partly organizational problems of state-building, as large chunks of new territory with varied traditions had to be digested. The administrative district of Trier, for example, was created in 1816 out of twenty-eight different territorial units, even before the acquisition of Lichtenberg in 1834 caused a further reorganization.[107] But there was also the problem of suspicion in the core Prussian state towards the 'alien' west, with the result that while lower officials might be natives of the area, senior administrators tended to be brought in from outside and antagonized the local population with their stiffness and constant talk of how things were done 'at home'.[108] Almost all of the senior officials in the state-owned mines, so crucial to the local economy, were non-native. But the problem was much broader, given the ambition of the Prussian state to keep its bureaucratic hand on everything from forests and pharmacies to the licensing of theatrical troupes.[109] This was a general problem of the Rhine Province, where the local population resented heavy-handed and 'outside' administration, especially of such sensitive matters as taxation and conscription.[110] The sense of alienation was exacerbated in the case of the Saarland by the absence of any local university or technical high school (such as the Rhineland possessed in Bonn and Aachen) which might have trained a local administrative élite.[111] This reinforced the common perception in the Saarland that it was viewed by its new rulers simply as a source of taxes, conscripts, and coal. It is hardly surprising that the historian of St Wendel described relations between the local inhabitants and the Prussian state as 'more than frosty for decades'.[112]

There was an important denominational element to the chilliness. Like the rest of the Rhine Province, the Saarland was a largely Catholic region faced by self-consciously Protestant rulers. Prussia had a Protestant dynasty, a Protestant state church, and an officer corps with high social status and almost no Catholic members.[113] Some in Berlin clearly believed that Prussia also had a Protestant mission, although few went as far as foreign minister Ancillon, who called in

---

[106] See R. Vierhaus, 'Preußen und die Rheinlande 1815–1915', *Rheinische Vierteljahrsblätter*, 30 (1965), 152–75.

[107] Beck, *Beschreibung*, i. 17.

[108] H. Klein, 'Die Saarlande im Zeitalter der Industrialisierung', *Zeitschrift für die Geschichte der Saargegend*, 29 (1981) 99; Müller, *St Wendel*, 239–44.

[109] T. Ilgen, 'Organisation der staatlichen Verwaltung und der Selbstverwaltung', in J. Hansen (ed.), *Die Rheinprovinz 1815–1915* (Bonn, 1917), i. 87–148, esp. 97.

[110] On emigration to avoid conscription, see Mergen, *Auswanderungen*.

[111] 'Ehrung für Karl August Schleiden', *Saarheimat*, 24 (1980), 129–30.

[112] Müller, *St Wendel*, 544.

[113] Vierhaus, 'Preußen und die Rheinlande', 167–8, who also notes that those members of the Catholic aristocracy who chose a military career tended to prefer the Austrian army.

1832 for a 'Protestantization of the Catholic Rhineland'.[114] Protestant officials
had a near-monopoly in most branches of administration, at least in the upper
and middle levels.[115] Potential social conflicts therefore had an added religious
dimension where Catholic peasants or miners faced Protestant forestry or mine
officials. There were, at the same time, contentious issues that affected Catholics
directly and produced a sullen if not hostile attitude towards the state. One was
the way that Catholic (but not Protestant) parishes on the left bank of the Rhine
were starved of funds for church building, especially before 1848.[116] Another was
the vigorous reaction of the Prussian state to the mixed marriages policy of the
Catholic Church, where the open confrontation that took place in Cologne in
1837 (the so-called 'Cologne events') spilled over into areas like the Saarland.[117]
But it was the underlying attitudes that Catholics perceived, as much as particular
incidents, that rankled: the abiding suspicion shown towards Catholic festivals
and pilgrimages, the tendency even among the most well-intentioned of officials
to patronize the Catholic population. The reaction of the Catholic Father
Piblinger of Kleinbittersdorf was no doubt exceptional—he omitted the normal
prayer *Domine salvum fac regem* from his services and declared that he would rather
live under the Turks than the Prussians—but underlying Catholic discontent was
revealed in the actions of clergy and laity in 1848.[118] The Saarland remained
relatively calm in 1848: Catholics were less politically active than they were in the
northern parts of the Trier diocese, and there was nothing to compare with the
radical, insurrectionary movement that emerged in the neighbouring Bavarian
Palatinate.[119] There were, however, riots (and wood thefts) in villages around St
Wendel, as well as in Mettlach, Merzig, and the Warndt, and Prussian troops
intervened as they had in 1832.[120]

The following decade was an era of reaction in the Saarland, as elsewhere in
Prussia. It may be a legend that officials from the eastern provinces were sent in
to wave the big stick during the years of reaction—of all the *Landräte* active in
the Saar region after the revolution, one was from Pomerania, the remainder

[114] K. Bachem, *Vorgeschichte, Geschichte und Politik der deutschen Zentrumspartei*, 9 vols. (Cologne,
1927–32), i. 148; F. E. Heitjan, *Die Saar-Zeitung und die Entwicklung des politischen Katholizismus an
der Saar 1872–1888* (Saarlouis, 1931), 17.
[115] Heitjan, *Saar-Zeitung*, 15–17.
[116] Kraft, *Matthias Eberhard*, 38–40.
[117] On the Cologne events, F. Keinemann, *Das Kölner Ereignis: Sein Widerhall in der Rheinprovinz
und Westfalen*, 2 vols. (Münster, 1974); C. Weber, *Aufklärung und Orthodoxie am Mittelrhein 1820–
1850* (Munich, Paderborn, and Vienna, 1973), 79–87. LHAK, 403/13676, 17–39, on mixed marriages
in the diocese of Trier; and Klein, 'Die Saarlande', 103, on the Saarland.
[118] Klein, 'Die Saarlande', 99.
[119] LHAK, 403/16730 contains abundant evidence on oppositional priests and the popular support
they enjoyed, in towns like Trier and Koblenz, and villages like Gommelshausen (rural district of
Trier) and Grausdorf (Wittlich district). On the Saarland in 1848–9, see Bellot, *Hundert Jahre*, 22–34;
Horch, *Wandel*, 196–204; Mallmann, *Anfänge*, 47–9.
[120] Bellot, *Hundert Jahre*, who is mainly concerned with organized political movements, tends to
underestimate popular protest. See Klein, 'Die Saarlande', 106; Müller, *St Wendel*, 233.

came from western provinces[121]—but the reactionary turn of the 1850s did not need East Elbians for its implementation. The St Wendel district showed that. The local *Landrat*, Engelmann, and his district secretary had been remarkably liberal in 1848. Both were transferred as a result. The new *Landrat*, Rumschöttel, who arrived in September 1848 and was still in post during the Marpingen apparitions nearly thirty years later, was a Rhinelander by birth but a notable hardliner.[122] Similar changes of personnel took place in the neighbouring Saar districts of Merzig and Saarbrücken. A tough new regime followed, in which the *Landräte*, under instructions from above, tried to stifle any signs of disloyalty among their subjects. This did not change fundamentally with the revival of political and associational life at the end of the 1850s. In fact the emergence of a strong liberal-progressive opposition in the Saarland, as elsewhere in Prussia during the so-called constitutional conflict, caused renewed efforts to control the press and lean on officials believed to favour the opposition, especially at election time. During the run-up to the 1863 elections the *Nahe-Blies-Zeitung* in St Wendel was one of the newspapers that succumbed to pressure to carry officially inspired news.[123] Officials of all kinds faced disciplinary action, in line with a tough directive from Berlin reminding provincial authorities that the problem of disloyal officials should be combated 'thoroughly and vigorously':

If a lax view of the duties they owe their Royal Master has crept in among some officials, it is high time to remind them as forcefully as possible about the meaning of their oath of service, and if some officials have gone so far in disregarding their obligations as openly to defy the regime that represents the Royal Will, then the use of all lawful means is called for to break their resistance and, according to circumstances, to punish them or at least render them harmless.[124]

Disciplinary action was taken against fire brigade members in Saarbrücken because they had taken part in a festive reception for the Progressive politician Rudolf Virchow.[125] Postal officials throughout the administrative district of Trier were warned that 'loyalty and obedience' were required, and senior officials were expected not only to demonstrate this by voting in the right way themselves, 'but also to influence the subordinate officials, junior officials, and contractual servants of the Crown towards the policies laid down, by verbal encouragement and instruction, so that there can be no ignorance, uncertainty, or false conception among direct and indirect state officials about the requirements of His Majesty's Government.'[126] There was pressure of a similar kind during the 1866 elections

[121] Bellot, *Hundert Jahre*, 95.
[122] Klein, 'Die Saarlande', 106; Müller, *St Wendel*, 239–46.
[123] Bellot, *Hundert Jahre*, 61.
[124] LHAK, 403/8806, 37–42: MdI Berlin to Governor Rhine Province, 20 Apr. 1863.
[125] Bellot, *Hundert Jahre*, 62.
[126] LHAK, 442/6660, 185: *Circulaire an die Herren Vorsteher der Königlichen Post-Anstalten im Ober-Post-Directions-Bezirke Trier, exclusive der im Auslande gelegenen,* from Director of Posts Meyer, Saar-louis, 17 Oct. 1863. If necessary, post office counters were to close so that officials could do their electoral duty.

on mine, post, railway, and forestry officials, who faced disciplinary action and even dismissal for stepping out of line.[127]

Among the officials whose loyalty the *Landrat* was expected to monitor were Catholic clergymen. One might expect fewer complaints about the clergy after 1848 than before, given the improved position of the Catholic Church and the greater warmth of church–state relations.[128] Viewed by the state as a potential ally against revolutionary unrest, the church enjoyed greater autonomy and received more generous financial treatment.[129] For their part, the bishops of Trier asked Catholics to vote for conservative candidates favoured by the government. But there was still considerable friction at a lower level. The fledgling Catholic press, and the organizational activities of certain priests, caused a steady stream of minor conflicts with state authority in the 1850s and 1860s.[130] In the Saarland there was official unease about the organization of Catholic miners by Dean Johann Hansen of Ottweiler, a former member of the Left in the Prussian constituent assembly of 1848–9.[131] Local priests also proved very unreliable supporters of governmental candidates at elections. In the 1866 elections to the Prussian lower house, the *Landräte* of the region reported gloomily on the role played by priests. In Ottweiler, with few exceptions, they betrayed a 'regrettable lukewarmness'.[132] In Saarlouis there had been only 'feeble and lukewarm participation' in the election, despite the conservative advice of the Bishop of Trier, and some of the clergy 'even voted openly for the opponents of the government'.[133] From St Wendel it was reported that the Catholic clergy had generally demonstrated 'the greatest indifference', and produced 'all manner of excuses' for failing to fulfil their electoral duties.[134]

Looked at in more detail, these reports suggest a differentiated political picture within the Saarland. While the Saarbrücken district remained solidly anti-governmental, Ottweiler—under the powerful influence of the industrial magnate Stumm—was already turning to pro-governmental candidates. St Wendel was closer to Saarbrücken in its continuing allegiance to oppositional politicians.

[127] Examples in LHAK, 442/6660, 102 and 441, on railway and postal officials respectively.
[128] See the friendly toasts ('to King and Pope') exchanged at the festive inauguration of Bishop Eberhard of Trier in 1867 by the new bishop and the resident divisional commander in Trier, at a gathering attended by all the leading civil and military officials of the area: Kraft, *Matthias Eberhard*, 109–10.
[129] Ibid. 37–41, 53–4.
[130] LHAK, 430/16730 has details of the continuing conflict between District Governor Sebaldt of Trier and the *Trier'scher Volksbote*. For the case of Father Dorbach of Bernkastel, whose trouble with the authorities over the non-registration of associations led to surveillance of meetings by gendarmes and to legal proceedings, see LHAK, 442/7853, 371–2, 411–18: Dorbach to KR Trier, 11 Jan. 1854 and 18 Nov. 1854. On the early Catholic press in the area, see Heitjan, *Saar-Zeitung*, 19–20.
[131] See R. Schock, 'Johann Anton Joseph Hansen', in P. Neumann (ed.), *Saarländische Lebensbilder*, ii (Saarbrücken, 1984), 170–9; Gabel, *Kämpfe*, 32–4; Rivinius, 'Dasbach', 121.
[132] LHAK, 442/6660, 37–9: LR Ottweiler to MdI Berlin, 7 July 1866.
[133] LHAK, 442/6660, 141–2, 148–9: LR Saarlouis to MdI Berlin, 4 and 20 July 1866.
[134] LHAK, 442/6660, 231–2: LRA St Wendel to KR Trier, 8 Aug. 1866.

TABLE 2.2. *Saarland votes in the Landtag elections of 1866*

	Conservatives	Progressives	Undecided
Ottweiler	100	59	0
Saarbrücken	44	189	8
St Wendel	45	95	8
TOTAL	189	343	16

Source: LHAK, 442/6660, 37–9.

Too much should not be read into the voting figures. Turn-out was low under the three-class Prussian franchise (although much higher in 1866 than in 1863), and the electoral process was also indirect: the figures in the table refer to the votes of the college of electors (*Wahlmänner*), not to the original voters.[135] It is nevertheless clear that the constituency to which Marpingen belonged remained strongly committed to progressive candidates at a time when the general trend was towards conservative-governmental candidates. It is possible to break the figures down further. Within St Wendel, there were four strongly progressive areas: the town of St Wendel, the districts of Baumholder and Leitesweiler, and the group of villages that constituted the mayoral district of Alsweiler—Alsweiler, Bliesen, Urexweiler, Winterbach, and Marpingen.[136] Tholey was a 'loyal' island within this oppositional area.[137] The Alsweiler district therefore contradicted the local official's general rule that the rural areas were 'indifferent to political matters, but fundamentally conservative'—and this despite the strong pro-governmental lead that came from the government-appointed but locally respected mayor of Alsweiler, Arimond.[138] This probably owed something to the rebellious traditions of the area: the parish priest was still claiming in the 1860s that some Marpingen peasants were 'infected with wicked revolutionary ideas'.[139] But the oppositional temper was no doubt kept alive by simmering forest disputes and the burden of taxation, especially communal taxation. It was the progressives' exploitation of the tax issue that the *Landrat*'s office in St Wendel singled out as one of the two main reasons why the area did not defer politically to its local mayor in 1866.[140]

The other reason he advanced was the local sense of 'the disadvantages— personal and material—of war'. This was classic border country, with experience

---

[135] Turn-out in the St Wendel constituency rose from 22% in 1863 to 34% in 1866: Bellot, *Hundert Jahre*, 62, 79.
[136] LHAK, 442/6660, 231–40: a lengthy report by the new trainee official (*Regierungs-Assessor*) Strauss, from LRA St Wendel to KR Trier, 8 Aug. 1866.
[137] LHAK, 442/6660, 31: LR Ottweiler to KR Trier, 7 July 1866.
[138] LHAK, 442/6660, 231–40: LRA St Wendel to KR Trier, 8 Aug. 1866.
[139] Nikolaus Sartorius, cited in Derr, 'Pfarrei Marpingen', 37.
[140] LHAK, 442/6660, 231–40: LRA St Wendel to KR Trier, 8 Aug. 1866. On the high burden of communal taxation, and the resentment it caused, see Kartels, 'Die wirthschaftliche Lage', 209–10.

dating back to the Thirty Years war of what hostilities could mean. Vauban's fortifications were nearby, and the area around St Wendel had been devastated by the French construction of a security corridor in the late seventeenth century; a century later it was the site of marches and counter-marches by French and Allied armies, occupied and billeted in turn by French, Austrian, and Prussian troops.[141] The vulnerability of the borderland continued to be felt under Prussian rule. For the Prussian state, the Rhine Province as a whole was a border area; the Saarland was a border within a border.[142] That was why Saarlouis—ironically, given its reputation as a 'French nest'—was one of Prussia's leading garrison towns.[143] The entire area was treated as a security zone at times of political tension: even under Coburg rule the Prussians sent an observation corps to the Belgian–Luxemburg border in the autumn of 1830.[144] In 1848 Prussian troops were stationed there to repel any threat from the revolutionary west or the Bavarian Palatinate; in 1866 the Bavarian border was guarded by gendarmerie, customs, and forestry officials.[145] It was an area into which troops were poured at the first hint of trouble, giving its inhabitants a further sense that they lived on the margin.

There was a further, painfully ironic element in the tension on the Saarland border in 1866. It was customary for the Prussian regime to doubt the loyalty of the local population; on this occasion the population had reason to doubt the loyalty of the Prussian regime. Through the spring and summer of 1866, pre-war anxiety was heightened on the Saar by rumours that Bismarck was preparing to sell off the state-owned mines to a French syndicate, as a possible prelude to ceding the area to France in exchange for acquiescence in the Prussian annexation of Schleswig-Holstein. The press speculation had a factual basis: at the end of April Bismarck did propose the sale of the Saarland mines, to prevent losses to the state if the area should be lost in the course of war. There was obviously a strong element of political calculation in all this: voters were to be frightened off voting for progressive candidates in the election with the threat of what might happen if the government had to raise revenue from the sale of the mines rather than through parliamentary appropriations. But however much bluff was involved, it could work only by sowing fear and uncertainty in the minds of the Saarland population.[146]

[141] Hoppstädter and Hermann, *Geschichtliche Landeskunde*, i. 99–101; Müller, *St Wendel*, 103–41, 169–89.

[142] The local history published in 1966 to celebrate the 150th anniversary of the administrative district of Saarbrücken bore the title *Grenze als Schicksal*—the border as destiny.

[143] The ratio of soldiers to civilians in Saarlouis was 1:2.5 in 1840, the highest proportion of troops in any Prussian town: A. Lüdtke, 'The Role of State Violence in the Period of Transition to Industrial Capitalism: The Example of Prussia from 1815 to 1848', *Social History*, 4 (1979), 202. On the reputation of Saarlouis as a 'French nest', see Heitjan, *Saar-Zeitung*, 18; Bellot, *Hundert Jahre*, 83; Ecker and Ecker, *Widerstand*, 54.

[144] Klein, 'Die Saarlande', 100–2.

[145] Müller, *St Wendel*, 250.

[146] B. A. Boyd, 'Rudolf Virchow: The Scientist as Citizen', dissertation, N. Carolina: Chapel Hill,

There was a final crucial point about the 1866 war: its effect on the denomi-national balance of the future Germany. Catholic reactions to the outcome of the war between Prussia and Austria came close to a collective panic. The impact was no doubt more severe among the population of the southern states than it was among those already accustomed to Prussian rule (although there was serious Catholic rioting in Berlin), but the effects in the Saarland should not be underestimated, particularly at a time when sectarian conflict was growing in an area of mixed denominations.[147] By chance, Prussian voting took place on the day that the battle of Königgrätz laid the basis for a Protestant-dominated Lesser Germany, although the outcome was not yet known. There is evidence that the softening up of the local population had swung some fearful voters behind the regime, but the opposition still won a clear victory.[148] The votes in the Alsweiler mayoral district went overwhelmingly to the Progressive candidates Duncker, Sello, and Virchow, to a party that opposed authoritarian 'Borussian' politics and expressed misgivings about war against Austria fought on Bismarck's terms.[149]

In the years that followed, liberal and progressive standard-bearers of this sort became less attractive to Catholic voters. This was not so much because liberals accepted the *fait accompli* of 1866; it was more because of the manner in which, in temporary alliance with Bismarck, they sought to shape the new German state that came into existence between 1866 and 1871. For one of the most prominent features of the 'liberal era' of the 1870s was an offensive against the Catholic Church in which Progressive politicians and the new Reich Chancellor co-operated. In fact, the name given to that conflict—the *Kulturkampf*—was coined by Rudolf Virchow, the Progressive politician who in 1863 had so delighted a popular crowd from surrounding rural districts when he spoke during the annual market in St Wendel.[150] By the 1870s Progressives of this stamp no longer offered a political home to Catholic voters. In areas of the Rhine Province where the Catholic press and associations had already emerged in the 1850s and 1860s, the Catholic Centre Party was able to build on this structure and consolidate a political movement opposed to Bismarckian repression and liberal anticlericalism alike. In the Saarland, and especially in rural areas like the district of St Wendel, there was very little political organization among Catholics. Their form of resist-ance to the *Kulturkampf* was to take a rather different form.

1981, 104–5; Bellot, *Hundert Jahre*, 70–80; F. Stern, *Gold and Iron: Bismarck, Bleichröder and the Building of the German Empire* (London, 1977), 38–9, 74, 76–7.

[147] G. C. Windell, *The Catholics and German Unity, 1866–71* (Minneapolis, 1954); H. Lacher, 'Das Jahr 1866', *Neue Politische Literatur*, 14 (1969), 83–99, 214–31.

[148] Bellot, *Hundert Jahre*, 75–84, who probably over-emphasizes the fall in the oppositional vote from 80% to 65%, and certainly exaggerates the 'loyalty' of the Catholic clergy, who were not 'unequivocally on the side of the government' (p. 78).

[149] LHAK, 442/6660, 231–40: LRA St Wendel to KR Trier, 6 Aug. 1866. All five *Wahlmänner* in Alsweiler voted Progressive.

[150] Bellot, *Hundert Jahre*, 63.

A Religious Revival

The political upheavals that Marpingen experienced from the end of the eighteenth century could hardly leave the religious life of the village unaffected. The most dramatic changes came as a result of French occupation. Until the arrival of the revolutionary armies the parish was part of the diocese of Trier, and for centuries the nominal parish priest had been the abbot of the nearby Benedictine abbey in Tholey. These links were broken when Marpingen became a part of the French Republic in 1793 and the parish was attached to the diocese of Metz, where it remained until 1824.[151] The congregation was still unfamiliar with German hymns fifteen years later. (It was not until 1848 that episcopal questionnaires in Trier dropped the question asking whether children were taught German language and geography in school.[152]) Under the adverse conditions of French rule church documents disappeared, no accounts were prepared for ten years, and the parish lost its fields, meadows, and woodlands in the process known as secularization—a modest local version of events in Trier, where monasteries became barracks and convents were transformed into coal-depots.[153] Pastoral care was seriously disrupted. When the long-serving Father Mauritius Klock died in 1795 there was a gap of two years before Father Heinrich Licht took his place; but Licht refused to swear the oath of allegiance to the French Republic and was evidently hampered in carrying out his clerical offices. Thirty-two children were prepared for first communion in 1793, none in the four following years. Not until 1803–4 did pastoral care return to something approaching normality.[154]

Incursions of this sort into the life of the church encountered varied reactions in Germany. In some places they emboldened local anticlericals; in others they met with popular resistance.[155] Given later events in the village, one might expect the latter to have been true in Marpingen. In fact the tone was set by villagers

[151] Marpingen, along with the parishes of Alsweiler, Bliesen, Oberthal, and Namborn, found itself just on the wrong side of the line drawn by the French when they carved out a new (and smaller) diocese of Trier: Marx, *Geschichte der Pfarreien*, i. 7, 10.
[152] P. de Lorenzi, *Beiträge zur Geschichte sämtlicher Pfarreien der Diöcese Trier*, i. *Regierungsbezirk Trier* (Trier, 1887), 646–7; Derr, 'Pfarrei Marpingen', 12, 19, 27; Marx, *Geschichte der Pfarreien*, i. 531. The parish priest from 1812 to 1838, Matthias Hoff, had studied in Sedan and was ordained in Verdun. Even in the 1850s there were still parishes on the western border of the diocese that used churches on French soil, because of government reluctance to provide the money for new church construction. See Kraft, *Matthias Eberhard*, 38–40.
[153] Derr, 'Pfarrei Marpingen', 11–13. On secularization in Trier, see Müller, *Säkularisation und Grundbesitz*, 85–105; and more generally the contributors to A. Langner (ed.), *Säkularisation und Säkularisierung im 19. Jahrhundert* (Munich, Paderborn, and Vienna, 1978).
[154] Derr, 'Pfarrei Marpingen', 11–12; Bungert, *Heimatbuch*, 517. These local problems mirrored the problems at diocesan level, where Trier faced enormous difficulties in pursuing its normal visitation of parishes. See Marx, *Geschichte der Pfarreien*, i. 515–18. On the adverse effects of secularization and diocesan reorganization see Marx, 5–8, 251–62, 277–9, 283–4; Ecker and Ecker, *Widerstand*, 220–4.
[155] An older, nationalist historiography exaggerated the degree of resistance (see Ecker and Ecker, *Widerstand*); Blanning, *French Revolution in Germany*, emphasizes it as a corrective to works preoccupied with the 'German Jacobins'. For a judicious overview, see Molitor, *Vom Untertan*, 203–10.

who took the opportunity to settle old scores. Father Licht had his windows broken and attempts were made to drive him out of Marpingen.[156] Events in Tholey, where the records of the abbey were burnt in the market-place when French troops arrived, may hold the key to this hostility. Marpingen had paid tithes to the abbey until the levy was abolished by the French. It had also been administered for centuries by a succession of Benedictine monks from the abbey: there was no parish priest resident in the village until the 1780s.[157] The sense of stepmotherly treatment could only have been reinforced by the odious reputation Tholey enjoyed by the later eighteenth century. One visitation numbered it among the 'most corrupt' of the religious foundations in Trier, dominated by 'insubordination, disputes, drunkenness, and other forms of dissipation'.[158] The 'rebellious spirits' of Marpingen noted by the historian of the parish had their counterparts in neighbouring areas of the Schaumburg that had lived in the shadow of the abbey.[159]

Contemporaries often associated impiety of this kind with the experience of war, but the poor reputation of Marpingen persisted through the first half of the nineteenth century. Father Hoff complained in the 1830s about 'frequent excesses', particularly the amount of dancing on feast days and holidays. His successor Father Bicking had a lengthier and more detailed catalogue of complaints: 'With the exception of a few pious and honest households the moral state of this parish shares all the shortcomings and defects of the whole district.' Lack of interest in church services, card-playing, spirits-drinking and enthusiasm for the tavern, dancing through the night on feast days, the negligent upbringing of children, irresponsibility, crude sensuality: these were 'quite general' in the parish.[160]

The singularity of these complaints should not be exaggerated. German priests of the time routinely denounced the excessively worldly celebration of church festivals, and condemned behaviour such as talking and smoking during church services. There were parishes where members of the congregation had to be physically restrained from leaving the church during the sermon.[161] One common clerical charge seems, in fact, not to have surfaced in Marpingen. That was the frequently voiced concern over the moral dangers posed by unsupervised pilgrimages, especially when young people were concerned, and above all in the case of pilgrimages that entailed overnight stays.[162] In Marpingen it was the behaviour of young people all too close to home that attracted condemnation.

---

[156] Derr, 'Pfarrei Marpingen', 11–12, 20.
[157] Handbuch des Bistums Trier (Trier, 1952), 892–3; Lorenzi, Beiträge, 646–7; Bungert, Heimatbuch, 196, 513–15.
[158] Horch, Wandel, 126.
[159] Derr, 'Pfarrei Marpingen', 11–12. Before the arrival of the French, inhabitants of the Schaumburg district of Pfalz-Zweibrücken also felt themselves to be treated in a 'stepmotherly' fashion by their secular ruler: Ecker and Ecker, Widerstand, 52.
[160] Derr, 'Pfarrei Marpingen', 22, 27–9.
[161] Sperber, Popular Catholicism, 14–16. Parishioners also avoided sermons in the Saarland, the women returning to their kitchens, the men repairing to the tavern: Fox, Saarländische Volkskunde, 264.
[162] Sperber, Popular Catholicism, 18–30.

Young men 'roamed around the alleyways at night' and indulged in 'senseless shouting and bellowing' during dances.[163] It was the young men of Marpingen, again, who engaged in fights with gangs from neighbouring villages over disputed 'territory'. As the saying went, 'whoever goes through Urexweiler without being duped and through Marpingen without being thumped can go through the whole world'.[164] This form of village patriotism, in which initiation rites played their part, was common in the Saarland and often manifested itself during a parish feast, or *Kirmes*.[165] It may have been especially prominent in Marpingen because of the 'outsiders' who had acquired land within the village, and became the butt of such aggression.

Father Bicking suggested a further reason for the poor moral standards of Marpingen. During a period of plague in 1699, the heads of households in the village had called on the Virgin to intercede and swore to keep Saturday afternoons holy. The oath was renewed in 1814 at a time when the French withdrawal brought another epidemic to the village.[166] In the following decades, however, the oath increasingly served the purpose of freeing Saturday afternoons for worldly pleasures. Bicking reported sternly to his superiors in Trier that the 'notorious indolence' of the Marpingers was widely attributed by neighbours to the effects of the oath, which had so accustomed villagers to 'the sweetness of doing nothing' that the effects carried over into the rest of the week.[167] The oath also encouraged card-playing and the 'sales tippling' that accompanied business transactions on Saturday afternoons and went on into the night. And it provided the occasion for physical attacks on 'outsiders' who owned land in the village and tried to work it in defiance of the oath. For all these reasons the parish priest set his face against the oath.[168]

Drinking, card-playing, dancing, unruly young people: these are familiar enough sources of conflict between priest and parishioners. Even the issue of the oath fits into a recognizable pattern: elsewhere it was a parish feast or the meetings of a religious brotherhood that the clergy claimed had degenerated into pretexts for worldly self-indulgence.[169] Events in the first half of the nineteenth century nevertheless suggest an unusual degree of spite and hostility in relations between the inhabitants of Marpingen and successive parish priests. Father Licht had his windows broken; Father Hoff had differences with his flock over dancing and the question of standards in the village school; Father Bicking had problems over almost everything, encountering verbal and physical abuse that may have led him eventually to leave Marpingen and become the parish priest of Hupperath.[170]

---

[163] Father Bicking in 1843, cited in Derr, 'Pfarrei Marpingen', 27–8.
[164] *Gemeinde Marpingen, Heimatkundliche Lesestoffe*, 23 (1984), 19–23, quotation 23.
[165] Fox, *Saarländische Volkskunde*, 421–5; Horch, *Wandel*, 379–80. Relations between Marpingen and Urexweiler were particularly bad: *Gemeinde Marpingen*, 23 (1984), 19.
[166] *MG*, 15–16; *MMGE*, 13; Derr, 'Pfarrei Marpingen', 20–1.
[167] Derr, 'Pfarrei Marpingen', 30.
[168] Ibid. 29.
[169] Sperber, *Popular Catholicism*, 33–5.
[170] Derr, 'Pfarrei Marpingen', 35.

Several of Bicking's conflicts suggest that the background of material distress soured relations between the village and its priest. When he asked that part of the proceeds from the sale of the Kaiserborn woods be used to help repair the leaking roof and rotting pews in the church, his request was rejected even by the members of the parochial church council.[171] There were further disputes over the mismanagement of church accounts. Towards the end of 1847 Bicking reported that the elderly parish bookkeeper Michel Recktenwald had produced no accounts for the previous year, and there were items of income and expenditure dating back two and even three years that had not been entered. Recktenwald had been 'indifferent and negligent' and the auditor was incapable of doing anything about it. Worse still, no action had been taken by the parochial church council because 'its members are themselves defaulting debtors of the church maintenance fund'. Bicking complained that unless he had assistance he would be obliged to intervene himself—'a hateful business for a priest'.[172] In the event, Dean Creins from St Wendel tried unsuccessfully to unravel the accounts, and it was left to Bicking to uncover the full extent of the maladministration. It transpired that the church maintenance fund and a church foundation had incurred losses resulting from irregular loans to parochial church council members and others. Michel Recktenwald died in the spring of 1848, and it was eventually decided to take legal action against his heirs.[173]

Relations between priest and parishioners seem to have been exceptionally bad during the 1840s. The illegitimacy rate in Marpingen also reached a high-point at this time.[174] But the same decade also saw the first signs of a renewal of piety and clerical authority in the village. An important first stage in this process was the replacement of the 1699 oath with a Brotherhood of the Sacred and Immaculate Heart of Mary which parishioners were encouraged to join. The initiative for this came from Father Bicking. The statutes of the brotherhood were approved by Trier in July 1847 and it was inaugurated three weeks later on the Feast of the Assumption.[175] It became the norm for villagers to join the brotherhood after their first communion. A second, symbolically important step was taken at the same time: the restoration of the Marienbrunnen. This was a well close to the parish church, whose history went back to a medieval legend. During the draining of a swamp a miraculous image had supposedly been found; it was placed in a shrine by the newly dug well and became an object of veneration, attracting

[171] Derr, 'Pfarrei Marpingen', 26.

[172] BAT, 70/3676, 20: Bicking to GV Trier, 25 Oct. 1847.

[173] BAT, 70/3676, 25, 30, 34–7: Bicking to GV Trier, 8 Apr. 1848, 26 June, 4, 7, and 16 Dec. 1849, 2 Feb. 1850. Dean Creins was in Marpingen in Nov. 1847: for his report, ibid. 22–4.

[174] See the table appended to Derr, 'Pfarrei Marpingen'. Even at its peak the rate reached only 10%, considerably lower than in some other parts of Catholic Germany, notably Bavaria.

[175] MMGE, 13; Die Erscheinungen in Marpingen im Jahre 1876. In geordneter Reihenfolge nebst den damit zusammenhängenden Ereignissen zusammengestellt [EM] (Saarlouis, 1877), 6–7; Derr, 'Pfarrei Marpingen', 30–3. The renewal of brotherhoods was fairly common in Trier in mid-century, although in many parishes (especially in urban areas) the vehicle of Catholic renewal was the more 'lay' form of the Verein, or association. See Marx, Geschichte der Pfarreien, i. 442–3.

pilgrims in considerable numbers. Both image and shrine fell into disrepair, however, and in 1846 the latter was knocked over by a passing cart. On the same day that the Marian brotherhood was inaugurated a new votive column was erected on the old site.[176] Later writers saw this double renewal in 1847 as a turning-point. The Marienbrunnen now attracted increased numbers of visitors again, especially on Marian festivals, and became a popular meeting place for the women of Marpingen. The new brotherhood also proved successful, and there were further indications of change: illegitimacy rates fell, attendance at mass rose.[177] Bicking's successor, Nikolaus Sartorius, noted in 1863 that 'the moral condition of the parish has improved markedly'.[178] As the naming of the brotherhood indicated, the purposive renewal of popular piety in Marpingen was built on the Marian traditions of the village, whose patron saint was the Virgin and whose parish festival was held on the Feast of the Assumption.[179]

The new departure was strengthened by the arrival of Jakob Neureuter as parish priest in 1864.[180] Ordained only four years earlier, Neureuter was a zealous young priest who shared with his sister, who accompanied him to Marpingen, a fierce devotion to the Virgin Mary.[181] Inheriting an uncatalogued library of 'worthless works', he spent over 200 marks on a glass bookcase and improved the collection. Among the new works was a book on Lourdes.[182] There is evidence that he was generous with references to Our Lady of Lourdes during his sermons.[183] The son of an artist and a gifted amateur himself, Neureuter also painted a life-size Virgin and Child for the village church, with materials donated by veterans of the Franco-Prussian war as a votive offering.[184] Further improvements to the Marienbrunnen followed in the 1870s. These were among the outward signs of a renewal of piety that would have seemed unlikely just a few

[176] Derr, 'Pfarrei Marpingen', 32–3, 54–61; N. Thoemes, *Die Erscheinungen in Marpingen. Historische Darstellung nach an Ort und Stelle gesammelten schriftlichen und mündlichen Mittheilungen und nach eigenen Erfahrungen* (Stuttgart, 1877), 9–10. It cannot be assumed that the finding of the image was mere legend. 'Found objects' of this kind often were uncovered in Christian Europe, having been hidden during a period of conflict, or placed in an obscure location as a votive offering and forgotten during a period of war or plague: Nolan and Nolan, *Christian Pilgrimage*, 257–66.

[177] *MMGE*, 12; Derr, 'Pfarrei Marpingen', 33–4, 63.

[178] Derr, 'Pfarrei Marpingen', 37.

[179] Bungert, *Heimatbuch*, 549.

[180] BAT, 70/3676, 85. Bungert, *Heimatbuch*, 556–7, follows Derr, 'Pfarrei Marpingen', 37, in mis-dating Neureuter's arrival to 1865.

[181] J. Frohschammer, 'Die Glaubwürdigkeit der Wunderheilungen in Lourdes und Marpingen', *Die Gartenlaube* (1878), 166.

[182] Cf. the inventory on Neureuter's arrival in 1864 and on his departure 31 years later: BAT, 70/3676, 81–4; BAT, 70/3676a, 188–91. During a house-search in 1876 a German translation of Henri Lassère's *Notre Dame de Lourdes* belonging to Neureuter was found in the possession of the parish priest of Heusweiler: *MWOL*, 57.

[183] He had apparently taken a vow with a number of fellow priests to refer to Lourdes during his sermons: Father Rupp of Primstal to Hermann Derr, historian of the parish, cited in Derr, 'Pfarrei Marpingen', 43.

[184] LASB, E 107, 376; E. Radziwill, *Ein Besuch in Marpingen. Nebst einem Anhang, enth. alle Correspondenzen u. Actenstücke, welche über die Marpinger Angelegenheit in letzter Zeit in der 'Germania' erschienen sind* (Berlin, 1877), 7.

decades earlier. A Berlin detective, pursuing his enquiries in Marpingen after the apparitions, observed with distaste that it was 'teeming with images of the Virgin'.[185]

The changes in Marpingen belonged to a large-scale religious revival in Germany during the third quarter of the nineteenth century, marked by the reassertion of clerical authority and the renewal of popular piety.[186] The 1844 pilgrimage to the Holy Coat in Trier, which found an enormous response in the Saarland, symbolized both aspects of the new departure.[187] It was the starting-point of changes that occurred in the diocese over the following decades. These were partly administrative, and they were facilitated by the larger funds and the greater degree of autonomy granted by the state to the church in the years after 1848. Diocesan organization became tighter, seminary education was overhauled, the preparation of priests for their pastoral role became more rigorous.[188] There were parallel changes in matters of religious substance as well as clerical organization. Here too there was a form of centralization. In practice this meant Romanization, which in turn meant a growing emphasis on the figure of the Virgin Mary. This was reflected in liturgical changes, and in a new edition of the diocesan hymnal in which motifs like the Immaculate Conception were very apparent.[189] It could be seen in the special encouragement given to pilgrimages with Marian connections, and in the increasingly common celebration of May as 'Mary's month', a practice that began in Italy and France and spread to Germany in the course of the nineteenth century.[190] The new emphasis also found expression in that characteristic preoccupation of the period, statuary.[191] These developments had their opponents in Trier, but those like Cathedral

---

[185] Police Commissar Meerscheidt-Hüllessem, *SMZ*, 20 Dec. 1876.

[186] Sperber, *Popular Catholicism*, 39–98; G. Korff, 'Heiligenverehrung und soziale Frage. Zur Ideologisierung der populären Frömmigkeit im späten 19. Jahrhundert', in G. Wiegelmann (ed.), *Kultureller Wandel im 19. Jahrhundert* (Göttingen, 1978), 102–11; W. K. Blessing, *Staat und Kirche in der Gesellschaft. Institutionelle Autorität und mentaler Wandel in Bayern während des 19. Jahrhunderts* (Göttingen, 1982), 84–98. We can trace the revival in the fortunes of a pilgrimage like the Aachen Procession of Relics, or the renewed interest in a saint like Boniface: H. Schiffers, *Kulturgeschichte der Aachener Heiligtumsfahrt* (Cologne, 1930); L. Lenhart, 'Die Bonifatius-Renaissance des 19. Jahrhunderts', in *Sankt Bonifatius. Gedenkgabe zum zwölfhundertsten Todestag* (Fulda, 1954), 533–85.

[187] Schieder, 'Kirche und Revolution'. On the impact in the Saarland, see Fox, *Saarländische Volkskunde*, 254.

[188] Kraft, *Matthias Eberhard*, 146; Marx, *Geschichte der Pfarreien*, i. 49–55, 316–55; Horch, *Wandel*, 388–9.

[189] A. Heinz, 'Im Banne der römischen Einheitsliturgie. Die Romanisierung der Trierer Bistumsliturgie in der zweiten Hälfte des 19. Jahrhunderts', *Römische Quartalschrift für Christliche Altertumskunde und Kirchengeschichte*, 79 (1984), 37–92; A. Heinz, 'Marienlieder des 19. Jahrhunderts und ihre Liturgiefähigkeit', *Trierer Theologische Zeitschrift*, 97 (1988), 106–34. B. Schneider, 'Die Trauben- und Johannesweinsegnung in der Trierer Bistumsliturgie vom Spätmittelalter bis zum ausgehenden 19. Jahrhundert', *Archiv für mittelrheinische Kirchengeschichte*, 37 (1985), 57–74, shows how older, local liturgical forms were eclipsed by Marian ones.

[190] K. Küppers, 'Die Maiandacht als Beispiel volksnaher Frömmigkeit', *Römische Quartalschrift für Christliche Altertumskunde und Kirchengeschichte*, 81 (1986), 102–12; Delius, *Marienverehrung*, 263.

[191] In 1859 a 22 ft. statue of the Virgin on a 125 ft. plinth was erected in Trier, an initiative of Bishop Arnoldi: Thoemes, *Die Erscheinungen*, 8.

Dean Holzer who tried to stem the ultramontane trend were increasingly in the minority.[192]

The changes that occurred in Marpingen from the 1840s to the 1870s represented in microcosm what was happening in the Trier diocese at large, as longstanding Marian traditions were renewed and new 'traditions' nurtured, under the close control of an increasingly active clergy.[193] But the new intensity of religious life in the village also owed something to events in the Saarland. The most important development was the growth of sectarian antagonism in the third quarter of the nineteenth century. Marpingen itself was almost entirely Catholic—there was only one non-Catholic inhabitant in 1871—but the surrounding area was a denominational patchwork quilt as a result of frequent territorial changes since the sixteenth century.[194] The St Wendel district was troubled by a succession of disputes in the 1850s and 1860s, often arising when the two denominations were forced to share the same church. The village of Offenbach was a striking example. In 1859 the Catholic Father Wald wrote to the civil authorities in Trier that there was 'no year in which complaints and charges are not put forward'.[195] At the root of the problem was the fact that the Catholic population had formerly belonged to the parish of St Julian, which became part of the Bavarian Palatinate in 1803. Thereafter they shared a church with local Protestants. Discord arose in 1821 and in 1844–6, before erupting again more seriously at the end of the 1850s. The denominations squabbled over almost everything: the ownership of the church bells and the times when they should be rung, the displaying of flags in church, the days of the week when church services were to be held and the times that they should start and finish. There were mutual charges that services were deliberately prolonged to spite members of the other denomination. Father Wald and his Protestant opposite number, Pastor Schneegans, were unable to resolve the dispute, and the local mayor was obliged to place restrictions on the use of the church to restore 'peace and order'. The quarrel exercised the minds of Prussian civil servants from mayoral level, via the officials in St Wendel and Trier, right up to the Rhineland provincial administration in Koblenz. A further dispute then arose in Offenbach in the 1860s, when Protestants complained about the construction of a Catholic parsonage at local expense. On this occasion the problem spread when the administration in Trier decided that the village of Kappeln should share the building costs. Kappeln Protestants complained that there 'were not even Catholic servants' in their community, and fought the

[192] The struggles between ultramontanes and liberals in Trier are analysed with great acumen in C. Weber, *Kirchliche Politik zwischen Rom, Berlin und Trier 1876–1888* (Mainz, 1970). The acerbic Franz-Xaver Kraus recorded the rise of Marian-centred ultramontanism in Trier with liberal distaste: Kraus, *Tagebücher*, ed. H. Schiel (Cologne, 1957).

[193] On the strength of Marian traditions in Trier, see Fox, *Saarländische Volkskunde*, 252–61; Thoemes, *Die Erscheinungen*, 2–7; Kraft, *Matthias Eberhard*, 121.

[194] Bungert, *Heimatbuch*, 519; *MMGE*, 11. The St Wendel district had an almost exactly equal number of Catholics and Protestants.

[195] LHAK, 403/10611, 283–317: Wald to KR Trier, 23 Sept. 1859. For the following account, see ibid. 251–358.

decision—unsuccessfully—up to the appeal court in Berlin. This dispute lasted a full ten years, from 1863 to 1873.[196]

Offenbach and Kappeln were just two among many episodes of sectarian squabbling in the St Wendel district during these years. In Weierbach a dispute over a shared church simmered through the 1850s and broke out in open hostility in 1860.[197] In Oberreidenbach, Protestants protested about contributing to the salary of the sacristan in Catholic Sien, and Protestant members of the town council objected to the building of a Catholic parsonage in Sien with council funds.[198] But the incident which probably had most impact on Marpingen was in Berschweiler, where a lively argument in 1863–4 turned on the extent to which communal funding in a mixed district gave Catholics rights in a Protestant church.[199] The Berschweiler dispute was one that the inhabitants of Marpingen would have followed very closely, for this was a neighbouring village with which it enjoyed close links—the mother of one of the Marpingen 'visionaries' was born there.

The effects of a different form of sectarian antagonism were brought into Marpingen from the industrial belt. The root cause here was the way in which the denominational geography of the region was turned inside out by migration. Some overwhelmingly Catholic towns, such as St Ingbert, had growing numbers of Protestant inhabitants.[200] More commonly, as in the Köllertal and on the Middle Saar, it was Protestant areas that faced an influx of Catholics.[201] The increasingly hard line taken by the Catholic Church on mixed marriages was one reason for friction; it was reinforced by atavistic Protestant fears of being swamped by 'backward' Catholics.[202] For workers who commuted from villages like Marpingen, being treated as inferiors by the indigenous Protestant population was a normal part of the experience of working in the coalfield.[203]

The sense of denominational identity among Catholic miners was also positively fostered by the activities of the church among the working class in the 1850s and 1860s. Throughout these decades numerous popular missions were mounted, mainly by the fiery Redemptorists, in the towns of Bliesransbach, Dudweiler, Lebach, Merzig, Saarbrücken, Saarlouis, and Saarwellingen.[204] These were another fruit of more relaxed relations between church and state after 1848.

[196] LHAK, 403/10611, 573–98, 629–715.
[197] LHAK, 403/10611, 429–58.
[198] LHAK, 403/10611, 599–628; 403/10612, 11–26.
[199] LHAK, 403/10611, 517–52.
[200] W. Krämer, Geschichte der Stadt St Ingbert, 2 vols. (St Ingbert, 1955), ii. 146–8, 227.
[201] See the map in Laufer, 'Aspekte', 156.
[202] On Protestant attitudes towards 'inferior' Catholics, see ibid. 154–5; Rivinius, 'Dasbach', 121–2.
[203] Mallmann, 'Aus des Tages Last', 155–6; Horch, Wandel, 398–400. On similar denominational tensions in the Ruhr coalfield, see S. H. F. Hickey, Workers in Imperial Germany: The Miners of the Ruhr (Oxford, 1985), 78–81.
[204] LHAK, 442/6438, 171, 179–83, 241–3, 247–8, 277–80, 307–11, 331–4, 349–50, 393, 399–407, 427–30, 449–64. The Redemptorists had a reputation for hell-fire preaching at their missions; the Jesuits were more cerebral in approach: E. Gatz, Rheinische Volksmission im 19. Jahrhundert (Düsseldorf, 1963), 96, 111.

Some mission preachers did cause anxiety among local officials (and even parish priests); but before the middle of the century the Prussian state had banned such popular missions altogether.[205] There must be some doubt, it is true, whether these missions had much impact on workers from commuting villages like Marpingen. The missions were not very accessible to shift-working miners, and the comments of some local officials on the missions' ineffectiveness underline the general rule that they had greater success in older, long-established working-class areas than in raw new settlements of 'workers' colonies'.[206] Clerical efforts to organize miners on an occupational basis were a different matter. The principal organizations were the St Barbara Brotherhoods and the miners' associations, or *Knappenvereine*, the former modelled on Marian brotherhoods and sodalities, the latter on the journeymen's associations pioneered by Father Adolf Kolping.[207] The prime mover in setting them up in the region was Dean Hansen of Ottweiler. The first St Barbara Brotherhood was established in 1855, the first *Knappenverein* four years later: by the 1880s there was a formidable network throughout the Saarland, one of many manifestations of the growing attention the church was paying to the 'social question'.[208] These organizations were much less likely than the popular missions to prompt misgivings on the part of the parish clergy, for it was they who were expected to provide the leadership—the local priest would normally be the *Präses*, or chairman. Unlike the missions, the *Knappenvereine* and St Barbara Brotherhoods also offered something more than sporadic exhortations to renewed faith. Through their meetings, processions, banners, and rituals they provided a sense of structure and community, institutionalizing the comforts of the faith. Marpingen had a brotherhood, as did the neighbouring commuter villages of Alsweiler and Urexweiler.[209] It had no *Knappenverein* by name, but there was a Miners' Burial Fund which later changed its name to the Catholic Miners' Association Marpingen. This was established in 1867. By 1872, when its first banner was dedicated, the organization had 180 registered members.[210]

The message of both missions and miners' organizations was strongly paternalist. Mission priests emphasized 'the duty of parents to bring their children up to

[205] The Luxemburg Redemptorist Father Zobel got into trouble with the Prussian administration because of his vivid language, especially the immediacy with which he recounted the sins of the flesh: LR Merzig to KR Trier, 24 June 1852, LHAK, 442/6438, 29–34, and ibid. 39–44, 47–57, 191–2, and 207, recounting his banning from Prussia and recriminations against the Luxemburg government.
[206] LHAK, 442/6438, 29–34: LR Merzig to KR Trier, 24 June 1852. On the varying effectiveness of the missions in different areas, see Gatz, *Volksmission*, 170–2.
[207] Mallmann, *Anfänge*, 52. On Kolping, see Sperber, *Popular Catholicism*, 85–91; M. Schmolke, *Adolf Kolping als Publizist. Ein Beitrag zur Publizistik und zur Verbandsgeschichte des deutschen Katholizismus im 19. Jahrhundert* (Münster, 1966).
[208] Schock, 'Hansen', 170–9; Gabel, *Kämpfe*, 32–4; Rivinius, 'Dasbach', 121. On the not very successful efforts of the church to improve the number of places of worship for Catholic workers in the Saarland, see E. Klein, 'Bergfiskus und Kirche an der Saar im 19. Jahrhundert', *Zeitschrift für die Geschichte der Saargegend*, 23/24 (1975–6), 157–93; Zenner, 'Probleme', 74–6.
[209] Mallmann, *Anfänge*, 52.
[210] Bungert, *Heimatbuch*, 614–15. The Burial Fund changed its name in 1905.

obey clerical and civil authority'.[211] And for all that Dean Hansen had been a
member of the Left in the Berlin constituent assembly of 1848–9, the ethos of
the miners' brotherhoods and associations was quietist. Their statutes made it
plain that they sought to 'reconcile the worker to his lot', to foster his 'resignation'
and 'patience'.[212] Poems, songs, and verse-plays published by miners' organizations pressed the same message. In one characteristic play a pit-deputy con-
vinces a group of miners that they themselves are to blame for their economic
problems, and one of the miners agrees that they should 'stay peacefully quiet
when things are tight'.[213] Control in the associations was firmly in the hands of
the clergy, who laid down precise regulations (backed by fines) governing matters
such as smoking, behaviour during parades, the touching of hats to officials, and
the doffing of hats to priests.[214] The church aimed to discipline popular sentiment
within the community of the faithful. 'The priest can do more than the police',
as one celebrated clergyman put it.[215] The ideal of loyalty and discipline was
encapsulated in the visit of the Suffragan Bishop Eberhard of Trier to Püttlingen
in the early 1860s, when hundreds of miners accompanied the bishop to church
in a 'truly magnificent torchlit procession'.[216]

There must be some question whether the message of the church was fully
accepted. Scepticism is in order on the one hand because of the evidence on
violence and drunkenness in the coalfield. But there is an even more important
point: the same workplace and religious solidarities that developed among miners,
and were fostered in institutions favoured by the clergy, could outrun clerical
precepts of quietism. An example of this is the Catholic miners' strike in October
1871 at the Dechen pit, one in which many men from Marpingen worked,
over the abolition of morning prayers before the shift.[217] That piety did not
automatically exclude militancy was demonstrated elsewhere in western Germany
during the 1860s in the attraction that Lassallean socialism exerted on Catholic
workers.[218] It was to be demonstrated still more spectacularly in the Saarland
itself in the early 1890s in the figure of the miners' leader Nikolaus Warken. A St
Barbara Brotherhood member and a pilgrim to the Holy Coat in Trier in 1891,
he was quite prepared to talk of 'a drop of petrol' as the solution to coal stocks

---

[211] This from the Redemptorist mission at Merzig in 1867: LHAK, 442/6438, 404.

[212] Schock, 'Hansen', 170–9.

[213] The play, *Steiger und Knappen*, was used in the Saar coalfield. See *Spiele für Knappenvereine*
(Paderborn, 1874), copy in LHAK, 442/7854, 265–336.

[214] See e.g., the *Statuten des Katholischen Bergmann Vereins zu Altenwald* (1874), copy in LHAK,
442/7854, 109–24. Many Marpingers worked in the Altenwald pit. Similarly paternalistic statutes of
journeymen's associations are in LHAK, 442/7853, 457–60, 737–44.

[215] Christoph Moufang, head of the seminary in Mainz, a close ally of Bishop Ketteler, and one of
the most politically active clergy of the 1850s and 1860s, cited in J. Götten, *Christoph Moufang. Theologe
und Politiker 1817–1890* (Mainz, 1969), 98.

[216] Kraft, *Matthias Eberhard*, 92.

[217] Mallmann, *Anfänge*, 58–9. Horch, *Wandel*, 385–6, gives the date as 1872. More Marpingen miners
worked in Dechen than in any pit except Altenwald: Bungert, *Heimatbuch*, 302.

[218] H. Grote, *Sozialdemokratie und Religion* (Tübingen, 1968).

that jeopardized the miners' cause in the militant actions of 1889–93.[219] The same combination of piety and radical behaviour was to characterize the conduct of many miners in Marpingen in 1876–7, natives and pilgrims alike.

There can be no denying the strength of the Catholic religious revival in the third quarter of the nineteenth century, but it was not completely under clerical control. This was true in a twofold sense. There is, first, the question of clerical authority and discipline. It is hardly surprising that assiduous pastoral activity failed to root out entirely what the clergy thought of as 'excesses'; the more striking point is that, as the miners at Dechen showed, powerful currents of popular piety could themselves provide the moral justification for 'excesses' that took the form of resistance to worldly authority.[220] The events in Marpingen in the mid-1870s were to demonstrate how hard the clergy would find it to contain renewed religious sentiment within approved channels. Clerical control of the religious revival was incomplete in a second sense. A price had been paid for the renewed piety in the 1850s and 1860s. The efforts of the clergy in villages such as Marpingen had been more effective than those of earlier 'enlightened' reformers partly because they went with the grain of popular belief. Rather than offer a head-on challenge to the more crypto-materialist, superstitious aspects of common belief, they tried to stamp these with a more acceptable form, often centred on the Virgin.[221] The encouragement of the devotion to May as 'Mary's month' is a good example, for it was superimposed on popular attachment to the ringing of bells in May to drive out evil spirits.[222] The stories of Our Lady of Lourdes that children heard from their priest and in the Catholic school were similarly overlaid on popular beliefs about the appearances of mysterious 'women in white'.[223] But there were dangers in what Küppers calls this appropriation of popular (volksnahe) belief.[224] The 'superstitions' of which the church disapproved had not been driven out, merely driven underground. They were to emerge again in the circumstances of the 1870s.

[219] Mallmann, 'Nikolaus Warken', 127–52.

[220] Clifford Geertz has drawn a distinction between religious 'ethos' (how things *should* be) and religious 'world-view' (how things are *perceived* to be). Religion commonly reinforces the 'fit' between the two, but at times of rapid upheaval that seem to threaten a way of life the gap between the two can lend a powerful spiritual-religious dimension to a broader social crisis. See C. Geertz, *The Interpretation of Cultures: Selected Essays* (London, 1975), esp. 126–7.

[221] On popular religious beliefs in the Saarland, Fox, *Saarländische Volkskunde*, 248 ff.

[222] Küppers, 'Maiandacht', esp. 102–9.

[223] On the Alsweiler 'woman in white' of the late 1830s or early 1840s, see LASB, E 107, 323.

[224] Küppers, 'Maiandacht'.

3

The Time: Economic Crisis and
Political Repression in the 1870s

Prussian victory over France in 1870 laid the basis of the German Empire
that came into being the following year. The formation of the new state seemed
to many contemporaries to mark the beginning of a new age. One of them
later wrote that the events of the 1870s were like a spring wind, signalling 'the
end of the Middle Ages, the beginning of the modern era'.[1] The sentiment
was widespread. Pride in the might of German arms, symbolized in the
celebration of Sedan Day as a national festival, was joined to pride in German
material and cultural achievements. Unification was widely perceived as
providing a framework within which the railway and the telegraph, the
educational system and the rule of law, would make an Age of Progress still
more complete.[2] This sense of buoyancy was fuelled by the heady upward
movement of all the economic indicators during the so-called *Gründerzeit*, the
post-unification boom of 1871–3.

There was, however, a darker side to all this. Even during the industrial and
financial boom there was a major strike-wave that indicated the lack of social
unity in the new nation.[3] Then, in 1873, the overheated economy crashed and
Germany entered a period of depression. This unleashed anxieties and caused a
hunt for scapegoats. Parts of the Catholic community were among those who
blamed the liberal economic system in general, and 'Jewish capital' in particular,
for the sudden reversal. Anti-Semitism was an extreme manifestation of Catholic
resentment and panic in these years, another sign of the fractured social basis on

[1] The theatre director Heinrich Hart, cited in G. A. Craig, *Germany 1866–1945* (Oxford,
1978), 56.
[2] See D. Blackbourn and G. Eley, *The Peculiarities of German History: Bourgeois Society and Politics
in Nineteenth-Century Germany* (Oxford, 1984), 185–8.
[3] U. Engelhardt, 'Zur Entwicklung der Streikbewegungen in der ersten Industrialisierungsphase
und zur Funktion von Streiks bei der Konstituierung der Gewerkschaftsbewegung in Deutschland',
Internationale Wissenschaftliche Korrespondenz zur Geschichte der deutschen Arbeiterbewegung, 15 (1979),
547–69; L. Machtan, 'Zur Streikbewegung der deutschen Arbeiter in den Gründerjahren (1871–
1873)', ibid. 14 (1978), 419–42; L. Machtan, *Streiks im frühen deutschen Kaiserreich* (Frankfurt am
Main, 1983).

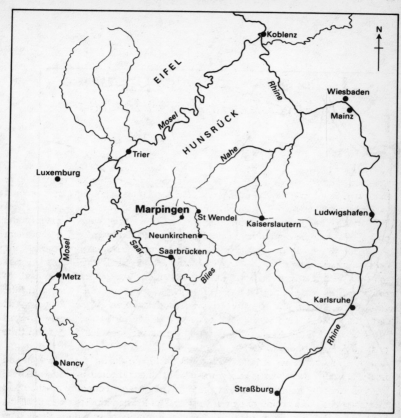

MAP 2. Marpingen: Location

which the German Empire rested.[4] Shoe-horned by the events of 1866–71 into a
Lesser Germany in which they were a minority of about a third, Catholics were
generally ill at ease in the celebratory atmosphere that followed the Franco-
Prussian war. Sedan Day, for example, was all too obviously seen by many who

[4] On the search for scapegoats, see H. Rosenberg, *Große Depression und Bismarckzeit. Wirtschaftsablauf, Gesellschaft und Politik in Mitteleuropa* (Berlin, 1967), 58–117. On Catholic anti-Semitism
in the 1870s, when the themes of economic depression and *Kulturkampf* were often yoked together,
see D. Blackbourn, 'Catholics, the Centre Party and Anti-Semitism', in Blackbourn, *Populists and
Patricians: Essays in Modern German History* (London, 1987), 168–87; E. Heinen, 'Antisemitische
Strömungen im politischen Katholizismus während des Kulturkampfs', in E. Heinen and H.-J. Schoeps
(eds.), *Geschichte in der Gegenwart. Festschrift für Kurt Kluxen zu seinem 60. Geburtstag* (Paderborn,
1972), 259–99.

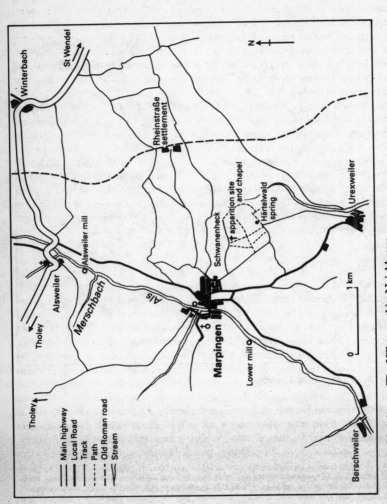

MAP 3. Marpingen: The Village and its Neighbours

Source: Wandkarte des Kreises Sankt Wendel entworfen und gezeichnet von Philipp Frierich Schmitt Verlag (Kreuznach, 1893).

celebrated it as an anti-Catholic occasion, and Catholics boycotted it accordingly.[5] The onset of economic depression also coincided with the opening of the *Kulturkampf*, the struggle between church and state initiated by Bismarck as a campaign against the alleged Catholic 'enemy within'. This had a much more violent impact on the daily life of Catholics than is often recognized. Bismarck was supported by liberals of various persuasions, who saw the opportunity for a final settling of accounts with clerical 'obscurantism' and 'medievalism'. In so far as the bombast about progress survived the economic and social upheavals of the 1870s, it became increasingly directed at the hapless Catholic community and its spiritual leaders.[6]

At a time of economic downturn and general uncertainty, Catholics therefore had additional reasons for anxiety. Their response took various forms. The one with which we are most familiar is organizational: the development of the Catholic Centre Party, of Catholic associations and newspapers. But Catholics also reacted in less formal, political ways to what they perceived as an attack on their whole way of life. There was, on the one hand, a discernible pattern of dumb insolence towards civil authority, which occasionally tipped over into physical resistance to the implementation of the *Kulturkampf*. There was, on the other, a heightening of religious fervour and apocalyptic sentiment. It is against this background that events in Marpingen should be seen.

The Great Depression

Whether Germany and other countries experienced a 'Great Depression' throughout the period 1873–96 remains a subject of controversy.[7] There is general agreement, however, that 1873 saw the onset of a serious recession that lasted to the end of the decade, even if the position improved for industry (but not agriculture) in the 1880s. There is also little doubt what triggered the depression. In the years 1871–3 an enormous investment boom took place in Germany, on the back of the indemnity paid by the French after their defeat. More was invested in newly founded limited companies in three years than in the whole period 1851–70.[8] The mood of confidence injected into the money markets by unification turned to over-confidence, and led to an investment bubble. Small investors as well as large companies were caught up in speculative railway, property, and industrial ventures. Markets in Germany (and Austria) collapsed in May 1873,

---

[5] On the celebration of the nationalists' 'Saint Sedan', see Blessing, *Staat und Kirche*, 181, 190–1, 198, 236; on Catholic boycotts, J. B. Kissling, *Geschichte des Kulturkampfes im Deutschen Reiche*, 3 vols. (Freiburg, 1911–16), ii. 279; W. Jestaedt, *Der Kulturkampf im Fuldaer Land* (Fulda, 1960), 134–5.

[6] See below, Ch. 9.

[7] Rosenberg, *Große Depression*; V. Hentschel, *Wirtschaft und Wirtschaftspolitik im wilhelminischen Deutschland* (Stuttgart, 1980); G. Eley, 'Hans Rosenberg and the Great Depression of 1873–96', in Eley, *From Unification to Nazism* (London, 1986), 23–41.

[8] Rosenberg, *Große Depression*, 41. The figures are 2,400 million marks for the period 1850–70, 2,900 million in 1871–3.

with a domino effect that spread throughout western Europe and into Russia and the USA.[9] The immediate effect on German industry was a sharp fall in the share index and dividends, followed by a longer period of falling prices and slower growth-rates. The impact of the recession and the attempt to preserve profits led to a wave of lay-offs.

The Saarland was severely hit. The recession was felt most in the regions where heavy industry predominated, and the mushroom growth of the area in the 1850s and 1860s had been based almost exclusively on coal and iron. This lack of diversification was partly the result of an unwillingness among businessmen to invest in a vulnerable border region, a handicap that was only gradually overcome after the acquisition of Lorraine in 1870.[10] The effect was 'a struggle for existence' for Saar industry as weak demand led to reduced output, shrunken profits, and redundancies.[11] At the Burbach iron works a profit-rate of 40 per cent at the beginning of the 1870s was cut to 6.7 per cent in 1875–6; dividends were halved and the numbers employed fell from 2,089 in 1873 to 1,264 in 1877.[12] Mining faced similar problems. At the Dudweiler pit, coal output had doubled between 1855 and the early 1870s, but fell in the second half of the decade. The number of miners fell sharply: not until the late 1890s did the work-force again reach the levels of the early 1870s.[13] Redundancies occurred throughout the coalfield, made easier by new conditions of service introduced in September 1866, which removed the privileged status formerly enjoyed by established miners in the quasi-corporate *Knappschaft*. With the depression a further erosion of their position took place and the period of notice was once again reduced. Between 1876 and 1879, nearly 1,800 colliers and hauliers were dismissed, almost 10 per cent of miners working underground.[14] Those who remained in employment faced insecurity, declining real wages, and worsening conditions. The state mining authorities had always pursued a low-wage policy that kept rates below those paid in other mining areas.[15] Now those rates were cut in a desperate attempt to reduce costs. In 1874 underground workers earned on average 3.58 marks a shift; by 1879 this had fallen by 16 per cent to 2.99 marks a shift.[16] The reduction was greater than the decline in living costs. One of the general characteristics of the 'Great Depression' period was the favourable effect of declining prices on real wages. In Britain this was apparent in the 1870s; in Germany real wage levels did not improve until the following decade.[17] Figure 3.1 shows that, following the substantial gains made in nominal and real wages during the boom of the early 1870s, the wage–cost

[9] C. Kindleberger, *Manias, Panics and Crashes: A History of Financial Crises* (London 1978), 132–3.
[10] Keuth, 'Die wirtschaftliche Entwicklung', 117.
[11] Gabel, *Kämpfe*, 32.
[12] Horch, *Wandel*, 221, 225.
[13] See the table in Saam, 'Entwicklung', 112.
[14] Herrmann and Klein, 'Zur sozialen Entwicklung', 136; Mallmann, 'Volksfrömmigkeit', 202.
[15] Klein, 'Die Saarlande', 110–11.
[16] Mallmann, 'Volksfrömmigkeit', 203.
[17] Rosenberg, *Große Depression*, 47.

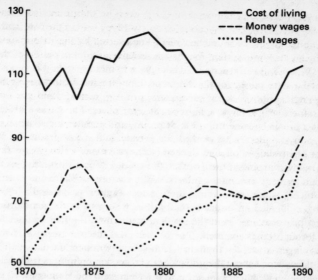

FIGURE 3.1. *Money wages, living costs, and real wages of Prussian state miners in the Saarland, 1870–1890.*

Note: In each case, 1900 = 100.

Source: Horch, *Der Wandel der Gesellschaft*, 304.

scissors opened dramatically in the second half of the decade, before a steady improvement in wages made itself felt through the 1880s. Pressure on wages was accompanied by demands for higher productivity, as the maximum length of shift was increased to twelve hours. Like savings on materials, this increased the chance of accidents, which occurred with greater frequency as tiredness rose and concentration fell towards the end of the shift.[18]

Material distress and the loss of status enjoyed by 'established' men did not lead to any notable industrial or political militancy. The Social Democratic Party (SPD) achieved very little success on the Saar, by comparison with other areas, and the month-long Ruhr miners' strike in June–July 1872 found no echo in the Saarland—although Prussian mining officials were concerned that if they exported coal to Westphalia to relieve the situation there, they might import industrial action into the Saarland.[19] The preconditions for industrial action were

[18] Steffens, *Autorität und Revolte*, 128–9, and 119–30 on work-rhythm and work-discipline generally; Horch, *Wandel*, 214.

[19] H. Pelger, 'Zur sozialdemokratischen Bewegung in der Rheinprovinz vor dem Sozialistengesetz', *Archiv für Sozialgeschichte*, 5 (1965), 377–406; H. Lademacher, 'Wirtschaft, Arbeiterschaft und Arbeiterorganisationen in der Rheinprovinz am Vorabend des Sozialistengesetzes', *Archiv für Sozialgeschichte*, 15 (1975), 111–43; Mallmann, *Anfänge*, 58–70; Horch, *Wandel*, 317–18.

worse everywhere after the onset of the depression than they had been during the strike-wave in the boom years of the early 1870s, and in the Saarland activity was inhibited by the semi-military discipline exerted by the state mine-owners, aided by an elaborate system for the surveillance and intimidation of the work-force.[20] Where industrial action did take place in these years it was almost always outside the state mines (or the works of the repressive iron magnate Stumm): among engineering workers, hat makers, printers, masons, and glass cutters.[21] When miners struck, it was against private employers. There was a strike in May 1873 at a privately owned pit near Saarlouis, and another the same summer by young pony-minders who worked for private subcontractors at the state-run mine of Altenwald—a pit, like Dechen (scene of a major strike two years earlier), where many Marpingen men worked.[22] Prussian officials nevertheless detected 'a certain ferment' among the miners.[23] While wrong in blaming this on socialist and Jesuit 'agitators', they were right to detect a suppressed mood of desperation and anger. Denied an outlet by authorities who sent in the gendarmes at the slightest provocation—as in the incident at Altenwald—their feelings found an outlet through other channels. One of them was the movement that converged on Marpingen after July 1876, in which so many miners participated. There is very little evidence about the impact of the recession on miners from Marpingen itself, although we know something about feelings in the Heinitz pit where many of them worked. One miner later recalled: 'Until the year 1875 times were bearable. From then on the work-time got longer and longer and the earnings smaller.'[24] Few Marpingen miners would have belonged to the 'established' labour force whose relatively privileged position was being eroded: employment in the pit had come too suddenly and recently for that. By the middle of the 1870s the village had nevertheless come to depend on industrial earnings, and in 1876 the parish council noted the adverse effect of 'poor wages'.[25]

The same document also referred to the problems facing agriculture, a reminder that primary producers were among the main victims of the depression. The first half of the 1870s was a period of suddenly fluctuating fortunes for agriculturalists. There were widespread harvest failures in 1870–1, aggravated in the Marpingen area by the effects of the nearby war.[26] The following years saw a short boom, as the rapidly growing economy boosted purchasing power and ensured a buoyant land market, before the onset of a sustained fall in agricultural

[20] Steffens, *Autorität und Revolte*, 28–9; Mallmann, *Anfänge*, 66–70; Lademacher, 'Wirtschaft, Arbei-terschaft', 137–40.

[21] Klein, 'Die Saarlande', 114–15; Steffens, *Autorität und Revolte*, 26–7.

[22] Mallmann, *Anfänge*, 58–60.

[23] Mallmann, 'Volksfrömmigkeit', 201.

[24] A Heinitz miner in 1889, cited in Mallmann, 'Volksfrömmigkeit', 203.

[25] LASB, E 107, 434: petition of parish council of 28 Sept. 1876 to provincial governor Koblenz. The context should be noted: the petitioners were arguing that the villagers were too poor to pay a 4,000 mark surcharge.

[26] On the combination of harvest failures and billeting, see Beck, *Ländliche Kreditnoth*, 48–9, 121–2, 128, 163.

TABLE 3.1. *Registered emigration from the administrative district of Trier, 1870–1875*

District	1870	1871	1872	1873	1874	1875
Bernkastel	35	43	74	21	9	12
Bitburg	26	47	73	37	18	18
Daun	30	53	26	17	3	NR
Merzig	15	50	42	24	24	5
Ottweiler	4	44	41	6	4	2
Prüm	36	44	35	24	14	10
Saarburg	23	40	54	37	46	22
Saarbrücken	14	20	17	14	8	5
Saarlouis	65	45	54	45	10	12
Trier (town)	20	33	23	16	14	5
Trier (country)	92	141	110	76	26	20
St Wendel	57	73	59	39	4	13
Wittlich	23	97	72	21	13	3
TOTAL	440	730	680	377	191	127

Note: Damage to the pages giving overall figures for 1875 (883–90) means that these figures have been reconstructed from the returns for individual districts. NR = not recorded.

Source: LHAK, 442/1505, 154–60, 276–82, 406–10, 540–7, 714–890.

prices that was one of hallmarks of the 'Great Depression'. The major cause of this secular decline in prices was the influx of cheap grain, meat, and other produce from Europe and overseas, as new land was opened up and transportation costs fell steeply. As it contemplated the harvest prospects in the summer of 1876, the *Kölnische Zeitung* looked back grimly on the previous three years and observed that agriculturalists in the Rhine Province had experienced 'little pleasure, only vexation'.[27]

There were variations in the overall pattern, especially within a part of the province as diverse as the administrative district of Trier. The emigration figures for the region offer a useful picture both of the problems faced by agriculture in more and less industrialized districts, and of the fluctuations in agricultural fortunes over time. Both are important if we wish to place the Marpingen area in context. Tables 3.1 and 3.2 make it clear that the major sources of emigration in this period were the more purely agricultural districts in the north, centred on the Mosel valley, the Eifel, and the Hunsrück. Taking the figures for registered and unregistered emigrants together, Bitburg had the largest number in every year from 1872 to 1875; it was followed by the rural districts of Trier, Bernkastel, and Prüm. The Saar districts which in previous years had been high on the list (Merzig, St Wendel) now showed much smaller numbers of emigrants. Indeed, if we take into account the figures for immigration as well, the fairly modest losses

[27] *KZ*, 22 July 1876.

TABLE 3.2. *Registered and unregistered emigration from the administrative district of Trier, 1872–1875*

District	1872	1873	1874	1875
Bernkastel	186	58	13	52
Bitburg	286	131	58	59
Daun	97	48	18	NR
Merzig	72	37	33	14
Ottweiler	46	18	14	4
Prüm	117	55	47	29
Saarburg	86	52	47	37
Saarbrücken	43	80	16	25
Saarlouis	156	69	44	28
Trier (Town)	35	26	26	5
Trier (Country)	250	102	53	40
St Wendel	73	57	10	28
Wittlich	195	57	32	4
TOTAL	1,642	790	411	325

Source: As Table 3.1.

in some Saarland districts (Merzig, Saarburg, Saarlouis, St Wendel) was balanced by net gains in the industrialized districts of Ottweiler and Saarbrücken. We can see this pattern at work even within the St Wendel district. Not only did the district as a whole have relatively fewer emigrants as it came within the orbit of the industrial Saarland; where we have figures for individual mayoral districts, they show that emigration was highest in the areas most dependent on agriculture, Baumholder and Grumbach, rather than in the Alsweiler mayoralty that contained mining villages like Marpingen and Urexweiler.[28]

These figures do not mean there was no agricultural depression in the Saarland; they do show that the arrival of industry had soaked up much of the surplus rural population that elsewhere in the Trier administrative district still had no resort but emigration. For the worker-peasant villages of Merzig or St Wendel, agricultural and industrial recession were interlocked to a far greater degree. We can gain a better idea of this double crisis if we consider the emigration statistics in a different way—as an indicator of the rapid year-by-year fluctuations in the first half of the 1870s. If we take the St Wendel and Merzig districts, the trend is clear. The numbers leaving were artificially depressed in 1870 as bad harvests and the dislocations of war made emigration difficult. The rise in 1871–2 represented the backlog of those wishing to leave, and now—crucially—able to do so on the back of buoyant prices for agricultural produce and land. The fall-off, which was very sharp indeed in 1874–5, followed the downward movement of prices that limited

[28] LHAK, 442/1505, 122–30, gives figures for St Wendel mayoral districts in 1870.

opportunities for emigration once again, although for different (and more long-term) reasons than those which had applied in 1870–1.

Throughout the Trier administrative district, and beyond, emigration fell off steeply with the onset of the 'Great Depression' and did not rise again until 1880.[29] What is notable about districts like St Wendel and Merzig is the way that the pattern of boom and recession was shaped by the interlacing of agricultural and industrial production. The brief golden interlude of high agricultural prices was fuelled by rising wages in the coalfield. Rising family incomes in worker-peasant households encouraged the acquisition of new land and the construction of new farm buildings. There was a speculative element to this—the rural equivalent of urban property speculation during the *Gründerzeit*—and land became overpriced as its value was bid up by worker-peasants.[30] This was good—while it lasted—for would-be emigrants, releasing land on to a buoyant market. The problems were all the more serious when industrial wages, agricultural prices, and land values fell at the beginning of the depression, leaving peasant and worker-peasant households with high levels of debt contracted in the good years, and stagnant or declining incomes. The result was the cycle of debt, credit shortage, and usurious loans described by writers in the 1870s and 1880s such as Otto Beck, Georg Dasbach, and E. R. Knebel.[31] The final stage for many was foreclosure.[32] At the time of the apparitions in Marpingen, one generally unsympathetic outside observer (a gendarme) noted that 'the bailiff often has to distrain property'.[33] The sudden onset of industrial depression intensified the economic problems of rural producers in the area. It also decanted large numbers of the itinerant poor from the industrial regions of Westphalia and the Lower Rhine into districts like St Wendel, where—in the words of the local historian—they became a 'scourge'.[34]

[29] K. J. Bade, *Vom Auswanderungsland zum Einwanderungsland* (Berlin, 1983), chs. 1–2, esp. table 3, p. 31. See also the editor's own contributions to K. J. Bade (ed.), *Population, Labour and Migration in 19th- and 20th-Century Germany* (Leamington Spa, 1987).

[30] Kartels, 'Die wirthschaftliche Lage', 208. On the active role played by miner-peasants in the land market, see Beck, *Ländliche Kreditnoth*, 112, and Müller, *Landwirtschaft*, 24–7.

[31] Beck's *Ländliche Kreditnoth*, which includes accounts from figures like local magistrates and teachers who were involved in credit co-ops, was published in 1875; Dasbach's and Knebel's descriptions of usury and its roots were both published in the *Schriften des Vereins für Sozialpolitik* for 1887. For a modern account of the problem, see T. Bark, *Vertragsfreiheit und Staat im Kapitalismus* (Berlin, 1978), on the laws concerning usury and interest-rates in the period 1850–1900.

[32] This was particularly true following the revised Prussian land law of 1872, which laid down the equal treatment of land and other forms of property when it came to matters like land transfer, indebtedness, and distraint, thus meeting the demands of liberal reformers bent on 'removing those attributes of land debts which render them less valuable to the capitalist than other similar investments, and [of] making such debts negotiable on the capital markets, where larger amounts of capital are available for investment': E. I. Becker, *Die Reform des Hypothekenwesens als Aufgabe des norddeutschen Bundes* (Berlin, 1867), cited in M. John, *Politics and the Law in Late Nineteenth-Century Germany* (Oxford, 1989), 92 (and 90–3 more generally).

[33] Gendarme Hentschel: *Prozeß*, 163.

[34] Müller, *St Wendel*, 276.

The *Kulturkampf*

One of the few figures in German public life to write about Marpingen in his memoirs was Julius Bachem, the Catholic lawyer, politician, and publicist, who later defended villagers from charges arising out of events there. Writing nearly forty years later, he tried to convey the impact of repressive measures against Catholics which formed the political background to the apparitions. The phrase he came up with was 'Diocletian persecution'.[35] The episode that prompted Bachem to this harsh description was the *Kulturkampf*, the conflict between church and state in Prussia that lasted through most of the 1870s. Like comparable episodes in other European countries at the time, the struggle had complex origins.[36] It was, in part, a 'domestic preventive war' against the Catholic minority in Prussia and the new Reich, depicted by Bismarck as an enemy within.[37] In addition to genuine anxieties, particularly about the Polish Catholics in the Prussian east, there was also an element of Bismarckian calculation at work. By exploiting liberal anticlerical sentiment that came to a head in the wake of the Pope's pronouncement of infallibility in 1870, he probably wished to deflect the political aspirations of liberal majorities in the German and Prussian parliaments by drawing them behind a struggle against the Catholic Church. It was a lead that liberals were more than happy to follow.[38]

The *Kulturkampf* consisted of a series of legislative measures spanning the period 1871–6. Some were enacted in the German national parliament, such as the 'pulpit paragraph' of 1871 prohibiting the abuse of the pulpit for political purposes, and the expulsion of the Jesuits from Germany the following year. But the major thrust of the *Kulturkampf* came in Prussia, and centred on the 'May Laws' of 1873 which sought to establish firm state control over the education and appointment of clergy.[39] It was the almost complete failure of these measures that led to a second wave of punitive legislation, designed to break the will of the recusant clergy and the Catholic laity who supported them. The principal weapons were laws passed in the Prussian parliament in 1874–5, allowing the authorities to seize church property where priests had been illegally appointed,

---

[35] Bachem, *Erinnerungen*, 133.

[36] W. Becker, 'Der Kulturkampf als europäisches und als deutsches Phänomen', *Historisches Jahrbuch*, 101 (1981), 422–46.

[37] H. Bornkamm, 'Die Staatsidee im Kulturkampf', *Historische Zeitschrift*, 179 (1950), 41–72, 273–306.

[38] Two useful surveys of the older literature on the *Kulturkampf* are R. Morsey, 'Bismarck und der Kulturkampf. Ein Forschungs- und Literaturbericht 1945–1957', *Archiv für Kulturgeschichte*, 39 (1957), 232–70, and R. Morsey, 'Probleme der Kulturkampf-Forschung', *Historisches Jahrbuch*, 83 (1964), 217–45. More recently, see M. L. Anderson, *Windthorst: A Political Biography* (Oxford, 1981), 130–200; Sperber, *Popular Catholicism*, 207–52; D. Blackbourn, 'Progress and Piety: Liberals, Catholics and the State in Bismarck's Germany', in Blackbourn, *Populists and Patricians*, 143–67.

[39] The centrality of the Prussian *Kulturkampf* should not cause one to forget the parallel struggle in Baden. See L. Gall, 'Die partei- und sozialgeschichtliche Problematik des badischen Kulturkampfes', *Zeitschrift für die Geschichte des Oberrheins*, 74 (1965), 151–96; J. Becker, *Liberaler Staat und Kirche in der Ära von Reichsgründung und Kulturkampf* (Mainz, 1973); G. Zang (ed.), *Provinzialisierung einer Region. Zur Entstehung der bürgerlichen Gesellschaft in der Provinz* (Frankfurt am Main, 1978).

to expel the incumbents, and—through the 'bread-basket law'—to remove state subsidies from any priest who refused to declare support for the government measures. This period contained the most nakedly repressive episodes in the *Kulturkampf*, as priests went on the run, clergy were imprisoned and expelled, church property was confiscated on a large scale, and state commissioners were sent in to administer it. By the end of the conflict, 1,800 priests had been gaoled or exiled and 16 million marks of church property seized.[40]

The *Kulturkampf* had a severe impact in the diocese of Trier. In December 1873 the diocesan seminary in Trier was closed down, and on 6 March 1874 Bishop Matthias Eberhard became the second Prussian bishop to be arrested, receiving a fine of 130,000 marks and a prison sentence of nine months. He died six months after his release from gaol, exactly one month before the Marpingen events began.[41] By the time of his death, 250 priests had come before the courts, 230 of the 731 parishes in the diocese were 'orphaned', and 150,000 Catholics were without a priest. Nearly 200 parishes still had no official incumbent at the end of the 1870s.[42] The parish clergy bore the brunt of state repression, as Prussia in the 1870s became a less bloody version of France in the 1790s. Priests whose descriptions were posted in wanted notices went on the run disguised as peasants or riverboat captains and in one case as a Jewish hawker; others slipped into villages in the early hours of the morning to celebrate mass illegally.[43] Persecution reached its height in 1874–5, but Catholic life had been severely disrupted in a variety of ways long before then. Popular missions, never more intensive than in the years 1866–71, came to an abrupt end as the Jesuits and Redemptorists were expelled from the diocese, along with the Franciscans, Minorites, Capuchins, and other orders.[44] There was a government crack-down on pilgrimages, supposedly in the name of morality.[45]

Surveillance and repression also affected Catholic associational life in the diocese. Action was particularly rigorous where it was suspected that Catholic organizations and social movements of workers were intertwined—in the case of journeymen's associations, for example, or the 'red curates' who encouraged 'pernicious agitation and inflammatory remarks against employers, against the

---

[40] The repressive aspects are explored in detail by M. Scholle, *Die Preußische Strafjustiz im Kulturkampf 1873–1880* (Marburg, 1974)

[41] *Bericht über die Gefangennehmung des Herrn Bischofs Dr. Matthias Eberhard sowie über die Austreibung der Professoren aus dem bischöflichen Priesterseminar zu Trier* (Trier, 1874); F. R. Reichert, 'Das Trierer Priesterseminar im Kulturkampf (1873–1886)', *Archiv für mittelrheinische Kirchengeschichte*, 25 (1973), 65–105; Kraft, *Matthias Eberhard*, 205 ff. The first bishop to be imprisoned, on 3 Feb. 1874, was the Archbishop of Posen and Gnesen.

[42] K. Kammer, *Trierer Kulturkampfpriester* (Trier, 1926), 162; Weber, *Kirchliche Politik*, 20, 61.

[43] No fewer than twelve priests were named in one wanted notice of Nov. 1874: Kammer, *Kulturkampfpriester*, 148.

[44] Ibid. 191.

[45] SAStW, C/56, 70–1: circular from RB Trier to *Landräte*, 16 June 1873, warning about the use of spirits and immorality, esp. in overnight pilgrimages.

propertied classes, the bourgeoisie, the capitalists, etc'.[46] But government measures extended right across the range of associational life: local officials were ordered to furnish comprehensive lists of all associations in their areas, indicating their membership, leaders, aims, and links with other organizations.[47] Thus the authorities in Trier informed *Landräte* in December 1873 that in view of the dissemination of written material favouring the ultramontane cause they should subject the charitable Borromeo Association to 'the strictest possible surveillance'.[48] Even the St Raphael Association that aided Catholic emigrants was suspected of engaging in nefarious activities 'under the leadership of ultramontane agitators'.[49] Government activity in this sphere reached its height in the pressures brought to bear on the German Association of Catholics, founded in 1872 and generally known as the Mainz Association after the non-Prussian town where its headquarters was registered. Through the prohibition, surveillance, and closure of meetings under the 1850 law of association, through presssure on local leaders and on officials who joined it, and eventually through the shutting down of branches, the authorities succeeded in suppressing the organization.[50]

The pattern of persecution in the Saarland resembled that to be found in other parts of the Trier diocese and administrative district. 'May Law' priests suffered the same treatment. Father Peter Boever, for example, was appointed illegally as curate to the parish of Wiesbach: he spent five months on the run, then served a prison term in Saarbrücken before being exiled in Luxemburg for ten years.[51] Catholic associations were subject to the same surveillance. The authorities solemnly examined the statutes of the Dudweiler Brotherhood of the Most Sacred Heart of Mary for possible transgressions of the law of association; the *Landrat* of Saarlouis suspected the Catholic Reading Association in that town of political intentions.[52] A 'keen eye' was to be kept on journeymen's associations, and the Mainz Association was the object of particular attention.[53] The impression is nevertheless unmistakable that the Prussian authorities spent less time on the Saarland than they did on districts further north, particularly around Trier,

[46] LHAK, 442/7853, 621–3: MdI Berlin to KR Trier, 15 July 1874, on the 'danger to public order' of journeymen's associations. On 'red curates', SAStW, C/56, 96–8: MdI Berlin to KR Trier, 10 Mar. 1874.
[47] There is extensive material on this in LHAK, 442/7853 and 442/7854.
[48] LHAK, 442/6383, 111: KR Trier to *Landräte*, 20 Dec. 1873.
[49] Mergen, *Auswanderungen*, 99.
[50] On measures used against the Mainz Association, LHAK, 403/6695, 253–68 and 442/7853, 621–3. On the closure of branches in the Trier district, LHAK, 442/7853, 715–17, 747–52, and 442/7854, 1–2. On the Mainz Association more generally, see Kissling, *Geschichte*, ii. 309–25, and Sperber, *Popular Catholicism*, 211–15.
[51] Kammer, *Kulturkampfspriester*, 37–9.
[52] On the Dudweiler Brotherhood, LHAK, 442/7854, 599–605. On the Saarlouis Reading Association, LHAK, 442/7853, 747–55: LR Saarlouis to KR Trier, 10 Aug. 1874.
[53] On journeymen's associations, see RB Trier to LR St Wendel, 19 Dec. 1874, copy in SAStW, C/56, 128.

TABLE 3.3. *Priests convicted before July 1876 of illegally performing clerical duties in the Diocese of Trier*

Trier administrative district		Koblenz administrative district	
Trier (town)	21	Koblenz	11
Wittlich	11	Neuwied	7
Bernkastel	7	Mayen	7
Trier (country)	7	Cochem	5
Daun	7	St Goar	4
Bitburg	7	Ahrweiler	3
Saarlouis	6	Adenau	2
Ottweiler	5	Kreuznach	2
Prüm	4	Zell	2
Saarburg	3		
Merzig	2		
Saarbrücken	2		
St Wendel	1		
TOTAL	83		43

Source: LHAK, 403/15716: Verzeichnis derjenigen Geistlichen, welche auf Grund # 23 Abs. 2 des Gesetzes vom 11.5.1873 zur gerichtlichen Untersuchung gezogen und verurteilt sind. Diözese Trier.

Koblenz, and the Mosel valley that joined them. Associations in the Saarland apparently attracted less attention than those elsewhere.[54] In the case of prosecutions against the clergy, impressions are reinforced by hard evidence. Table 3.3 shows clearly that by far the largest number of clerical convictions under this heading, at least before the events in Marpingen occurred, were obtained against priests active along the Trier–Koblenz axis.[55] The numbers in the Saarland were very modest by comparison: there were more prosecutions in the town of Trier than in all six Saar districts combined. Prosecutions of priests for membership of the Mainz Association show a similar pattern.[56] The figures on priests expelled from the administrative district tell the same story (see Table 3.4).

This evidence points to a lower level of *Kulturkampf* persecution in the Saarland than in other parts of the Trier diocese. One reason for this might be the reluctance of officials in some (although not all) parts of the Saarland to implement the *Kulturkampf* legislation. Distaste for government policy was certainly shown by Count Helldorf, *Landrat* of Ottweiler, and Rudolph de Lasalle Louisenthal zu Dagstuhl, *Landrat* of Merzig.[57] The latter retired early in 1875, and was later to

[54] I base this esp. on the 785-page contents of LHAK, 442/7854, dealing with enquiries about and prosecution of associations that discussed 'public affairs' and 'political matters'.
[55] For the effect on these figures of prosecutions after the Marpingen events had begun, see Table 7.1 below.
[56] See LHAK, 403/6695, 253–68.
[57] Klein, 'Die Saarlande', 116–17.

TABLE 3.4. *Place of residence of priests expelled from the administrative district of Trier, 1874–1875*

Bernkastel	4	Saarburg	2
Prüm	4	Saarlouis	2
Trier	4	Adenau	1
Daun	3	Kreuznach	1
Wittlich	3	Merzig	1
Bitburg	2	St Wendel	1
Ottweiler	2	TOTAL	32
Saarbrücken	2		

Note: Adenau and Kreuznach were in the administrative district of Koblenz, all the others in the district of Trier.

Source: LHAK, 442/10419: 'Ausweisungen kath. Geistlicher 1874–1884'.

be compromised by the behaviour of his family during the events in Marpingen.[58] This might explain some of the tetchiness shown by the authorities in Trier, when warning local *Landräte* that if they allowed meetings of the Mainz Association they would be responsible for any subsequent 'breaches of public security and order'.[59]

But simply counting cases can also give a misleading impression of the *Kulturkampf* in the Saarland. One reason why comparatively less time was taken up by Catholic associations in the area was simply the lower density of Catholic organizations in the Saar districts compared with, say, Trier.[60] The modest number of priests convicted and expelled was also, in one respect, a matter of chance. Only where new appointments were made after May 1873 was the cycle of fines, imprisonment, illegal services, and expulsions set in motion, and there appear to have been fewer such appointments in the Saarland. Where 'May Law' priests were appointed, and the *Landrat* and his local officials took a hard line, the outcome could be as violent in the Saarland as anywhere else.[61] The Namborn case, in the St Wendel district, was to spark the most serious *Kulturkampf* conflict in the Trier diocese before Marpingen itself. In the summer of 1873 the parish priest of Namborn retired, and the Bishop of Trier defied the May Laws by appointing Father Jakob Isbert to the vacant parish without informing the Prussian authorities in Trier. In November 1873, *Landrat* Rumschöttel of St Wendel publicly proclaimed Isbert in breach of the law, but the priest continued to perform his pastoral duties, making his base just over the nearby Oldenburg

[58] See below, pp. 160, 262–3 on Louisenthal and his family.

[59] See instructions and advice to *Landräte* from RP Trier, 6 Jan. 1873, SAStW, C/56, 56 ff. This may help to explain why no charges were brought against Dean Hansen of Ottweiler for his activities in the Mainz Association. See LHAK, 403/6695, 253–68.

[60] See below, pp. 113–15.

[61] On the incidents that accompanied the state action against 'May Law' priests in Bliesransbach, Dillingen, Dudweiler, Haustadt, Neunkirchen, and Wiesbach, see Kammer, *Kulturkampfpriester* 136–49.

border and visiting Namborn clandestinely at night. The number of summonses against him reached double figures, and in the summer of 1874 Isbert was sentenced *in absentia* to a total of 32 months in prison.[62] On 6 July 1874 he was finally caught in Namborn by Mayor Woytt and a gendarme, but when they attempted to take him to St Wendel, in order to deliver him to prison in Saarbrücken, the church bells were rung and a large and threatening crowd surrounded them. Only the intervention of Father Alt of nearby Hofeld enabled the officials to remove Isbert. Similar scenes were then repeated at St Wendel station. The local mayor had ordered the platforms to be sealed off, but up to a thousand Catholics stormed the station and military assistance was required. Twenty-three arrests were made and two days later *Landrat* Rumschöttel ordered the riot act to be read. The direct challenge to the authority of the state in Namborn occurred in the same month as the attempt on Bismarck's life by the Catholic journeyman cooper Kullmann, and against that background those found guilty of organizing the affray were given harsh sentences: four received prison terms of three years, one eighteen months, and another six months.[63]

Namborn was an exceptional case. The severity of the sentence passed on Father Isbert had no precedent—the Prussian authorities intended custodial sentences for clergy to be a measure of last resort, and where such sentences were imposed the priests in question were normally released and expelled after a much shorter period.[64] Isbert was the only priest in the diocese of Trier who was not released by late November 1875.[65] Namborn was also exceptional because of the levels of violence it unleashed. Two days after Isbert's capture, *Landrat* Rumschöttel was already making anxious arrangements about the prevention of disturbances on his release.[66] The case raised more serious questions of public order than any previous episode in the Trier administrative district, and was in many ways a direct forerunner of the Marpingen affair.

What happened in Namborn undoubtedly had an impact on the inhabitants of Marpingen. The parish itself escaped the most severe effects of the *Kulturkampf*. The harshest direct impact was probably that of the 'bread-basket law': the state share of the parish priest's income had been rising in Marpingen, and its removal almost certainly had a greater effect there than it did in wealthier

---

[62] The court judgements against Isbert can be found in LHAK, 403/15716, 12–13. Kammer, *Kulturkampfpriester*, 156, claims that there were 11 judgements against Isbert; I have been able to find only 10.

[63] BAT, B III, 11, 14/6 [1], 96–9; Müller, *St Wendel*, 270–3; Bellot, *Hundert Jahre*, 137; Mallmann, 'Volksfrömmigkeit', 211–12.

[64] LHAK, 442/10419, 23–7: Circular of MdI Berlin, 22 June 1874, concerning implementation of law on illegal performance of clerical offices.

[65] Kammer, *Kulturkampfpriester*, 156. LHAK, 442/10420 contains the weekly running totals of Catholic priests imprisoned under the May Laws in Saarbrücken and Trier. The lists show that the clerical prison population was at its height in June 1874 and declined steadily through to the summer of 1875. After July 1875 imprisoned priests were a rarity.

[66] SAStW, C/56, 104–5: LR Rumschöttel to Mayor Müller of St Wendel, 8 July 1874.

Rhenish parishes.[67] The villagers were forced to dig into their pockets at a time of economic crisis, and the extra sacrifices obviously produced tension and resentment.[68] Otherwise the central concern of the May Laws with the education and appointment of new clergy did not touch the parish. Father Neureuter had been in Marpingen since 1864, and until the apparitions began he had still not (like many priests in the diocese) been relieved of his post as a school inspector.[69] But events in Namborn inevitably affected a neighbouring parish within the same deanery. The crowds that mobbed the station in St Wendel included many from surrounding rural areas, and the villain of the piece was a man with whom the inhabitants of Marpingen had a quarrel of their own. Rural Mayor Woytt of Alsweiler acquired the local nickname 'The Devil of St Wendel' for his part in the Namborn affair; for Marpingers he was also the man who insisted on a contribution of 900 thaler a year from the village towards his salary, against the 600 thaler voted by the parish council.[70] The bad blood between mayor and village was to play its part in events after July 1876.

The *Kulturkampf* not only brought relations between Catholics and the Prussian state to a new low point; one of the least studied effects of the conflict was to heighten communal tension. The delicate balance between the denominations made this particularly important in the Saarland. In the 1870s the Protestant sense of historic superiority was heightened and Catholics became increasingly conscious of inhabiting a social-cultural 'ghetto'.[71] The estrangement of the two communities was signalled by the exchange of ritual insults such as 'Blo'kopp' (Catholic) and 'Luttrischer Dickkopp' (Protestant).[72] In St Wendel the limited tolerance of earlier years disappeared.[73] The *Kulturkampf* also raised the temperature of communal tension in the surrounding areas, where relations had already become strained in the 1850s and 1860s. In Berschweiler renewed conflict broke out over burials in the shared village churchyard.[74] The events in Marpingen broke out against the local background of what one newspaper described as 'tense relations' between the two communities.[75]

[67] On the sources of clerical income in Marpingen, see BAT, 70/3676, 43–6, 81–4. See Sperber, *Popular Catholicism*, 247–9, on the greater impact of the bread-basket law in poorer, left-bank Rhenish parishes.

[68] BAT, 70/3676a, 158–9: Neureuter to GV Trier, 30 Oct. 1893.

[69] Thoemes, *Die Erscheinungen*, 14–15.

[70] Radziwill, *Besuch*, 6. On the financial burden on villages of rural mayors, Kartels, 'Die wirthschaftliche Lage', 229.

[71] J. Bachem, 'Wir müssen aus dem Turm heraus', *Historisch-Politische Blätter*, 137 (1906), 376–86, is a celebrated Catholic criticism of this siege-mentality. On this ghettoized 'milieu-Catholicism', see C. Amery, *Die Kapitulation oder deutscher Katholizismus heute* (Reinbek, 1963).

[72] Fox, *Saarländische Volkskunde*, 268–9.

[73] Müller, *St Wendel*, 602–3.

[74] SZ, 10 Sept. 1876; NBZ, 30 Sept. and 12 Oct. 1876. Cf. the 'duel of bells' in the Palatine village of Kaulbach, where a Catholic chapel was constructed by a local priest in 1875 as a symbol of the Catholic presence in a predominantly Protestant area: Nolan and Nolan, *Christian Pilgrimage*, 237, 371 n. 21.

[75] SMZ, 16 July 1876.

The Hope of Deliverance

State persecution, Protestant hostility, and a heightened sense of anxiety—these produced varied Catholic responses. The most familiar of these was organizational. The *Kulturkampf* turned the Centre Party into a major political vehicle for Catholic interests. The Catholic press burgeoned in the same period, and the founding of new associations and the growth of existing ones confirmed Germany's reputation as the 'classic land' of Catholic associational life.[76] These organizational developments were generally less evident in the Saarland, however, than in other parts of the Rhine Province; and they were least in evidence in the area around St Wendel. There the Catholic backlash took a more 'primitive' form. The circumstances of the *Kulturkampf* unleashed elemental religious emotions that drew on the revived popular piety of previous decades.

The *Kulturkampf* gave a great fillip to the growth of the Centre Party. Founded in 1870, the party won an estimated 83 per cent of the Catholic vote in the Reichstag election of 1874.[77] The Rhine Province was a region where the Centre achieved impressive levels of political mobilization, but this was not uniformly the case and sub-regional variations were especially apparent on the left bank of the Rhine. In the administrative district of Trier, both the town itself and its rural hinterland were heavily politicized. The zealous younger clergy of Trier, led by Georg Dasbach the later peasant organizer, threw themselves into robust political campaigning. It was a measure of their success that they alarmed not only the government but Bishop Eberhard, who warned against 'drawing the uneducated people into political decisions'.[78] The efforts of Dasbach and others helped to turn the northern part of the Trier administrative district into a political bastion of the Centre Party. Things were very different in the Saarland, where the party polled well below the levels that might have been expected from the denominational make-up of the region. Of the three Reichstag and Prussian parliamentary seats in the region, the Centre captured only one. In the constituency Ottweiler-St Wendel-Meisenheim it was a narrow but consistent loser.[79]

Borderland fears of France, played on by the 'national parties', and the intimidation of his work-force by the industrial baron Stumm certainly did not help the Centre. On the other hand, a denominationally mixed population was something that, elsewhere, usually helped to bring out the Catholic vote. It is hard to escape the conclusion that in this case organization—or the lack of it—was a key

[76] *Handbuch der Kirchengeschichte*, ed. H. Jedin, vi. 2. *Die Kirche zwischen Anpassung und Widerstand (1876 bis 1914)* (Freiburg, 1973), 220.
[77] J. Schauff, *Die deutschen Katholiken und die Zentrumspartei* (Cologne, 1928), 75.
[78] U. Fohrmann, 'Georg Friedrich Dasbach—Gedanken über einen Ultramontanen', in *Soziale Frage und Kirche im Saarrevier* (Saarbrücken, 1984), 88–9; H. Thoma. *Georg Friedrich Dasbach. Priester, Publizist, Politiker* (Trier, 1975).
[79] Bellot, *Hundert Jahre*, 128–50; Heitjan, *Saar-Zeitung*, 21–86. Heitjan presents an upbeat account of the Centre's fortunes that is undermined by the electoral evidence of his text. Apart from the two seats in the Saarland, there was only one other seat within the whole diocese of Trier which the Centre did not control.

ingredient. The party was underdeveloped in the Saarland compared with the
north of the Trier administrative district. The dependence of the Saarland Centre
on outside speakers and parliamentary candidates—from Trier, Cologne,
Boppard—was one sign of this. So, more fundamentally, was the relative paucity
of Catholic newspapers and associations, the substructure on which Centre Party
successes elsewhere rested. In the decade 1871–81 the number of Catholic
newspapers in the Rhine Province as a whole rose from thirty to sixty-five, the
number of subscribers from 70,000 to 170,000.[80] The growth of the press was
more sluggish in the Trier district than it was on the right bank of the Rhine; but
it was incomparably livelier in Trier itself than in the Saarland, not least because
of the efforts once again of Georg Dasbach, founder of the popular Sunday
paper, the *St-Paulinus-Blatt*, and its daily stable-mate, the *Trierische Landeszeitung*.[81] Apart from the Saarlouis *Saar-Zeitung*, founded in 1872, there was
not a single Catholic newspaper in the Saarland until the *St Johanner Volkszeitung*
appeared in 1884—and it, characteristically, was merely the local edition of a
Trier newspaper with a different masthead and a Saarland supplement.[82]

Associational life followed the same pattern. Historians of the Saarland during
the *Kulturkampf* have noted the founding of Catholic associations in the 1870s,
and taken by itself the activity in the region looks impressive.[83] The Saarlouis
district had a Catholic Reading Association, a Boniface Association, a Mission
Association, a Young Women's Association, an Association of the Childhood
of Jesus, and a Rosary Association, as well as several branches of the Mainz
Association.[84] Journeymen's associations and branches of the Mainz and Borromeo Associations could be found throughout the region.[85] But set against the
mushrooming organizations in other areas, it is the modesty of associational life
in the Saarland that stands out. The mayoral district of Bonn contained twenty-
six associations; the rural district of Trier had no fewer than sixty-nine.[86] The

[80] H. Thoma, 'Wie es zur Gründung des "Paulinus" kam', *Paulinus*, 20 Apr. 1975, copy in BAT,
85/282a.
[81] Fohrmann, 'Dasbach', 91–5, 101; Thoma, 'Wie es zur Gründung des "Paulinus" kam', *Paulinus*,
20 Apr. 1975. The *St-Paulinus-Blatt* sold 14,500 copies by the end of 1875, a year after it was founded.
[82] Heitjan, *Saar-Zeitung*, 24 ff.; Fohrmann, 'Dasbach', 101.
[83] Klein, 'Die Saarlande', 116; U. Fohrmann, *Trierer Kulturkampfpublizistik im Bismarckreich* (Trier,
1977), 27–33; Mallmann, 'Volksfrömmigkeit', 208–10.
[84] LHAK, 44/7853, 747–55: LR Saarlouis to KR Trier, 10 Aug. 1874. See also the list in LHAK,
442/7854, 157–61.
[85] The Borromeo Association predated the *Kulturkampf*. The organization's accounts for 1871 show
that there were Saarland branches by that date in Bliesransbach, Dillingen, Dudweiler, Ensdorf,
Fraulautern, Friedrichsthal, Merzig, Neunkirchen, Ottweiler, Püttlingen, Saarbrücken, Saarlouis,
Saarwellingen, St Wendel, Sulzbach, and Wallerfangen: LHAK, 442/6383, 99–106. Branches of the
Mainz Association existed by August 1874 in Burbach, Dillingen, Emmersweiler, Eppelborn, Geis-
lautern, Großrosseln, Lebach, Lisdorf, Merzig, Neunkirchen, Ottweiler, Picard, Püttlingen, Saarlouis,
Schiffweiler, Schwalbach, Schwarzenholz, Steinbach, St Wendel, Völklingen, Wadern, Wehrden, and
Wiesbach: LHAK, 442/7853, 747–52; LHAK, 442/7854, 39–93.
[86] LHAK, 403/6695, 397 ff., a file containing lists of associations from every administrative district
in the Rhine Province. On the rural district of Trier, LHAK, 442/7854, 231–45. LHAK, 442/7853 is
also a major source of information on the subject.

acid test of comparison suggests that the Catholic response to the *Kulturkampf* remained organizationally more flaccid in the Saarland than elsewhere.

This applies particularly to the area around Marpingen. The St Wendel district was sparse in Catholic associations even by the standards of the Saarland. True, the town itself (which contained a large number of craftsmen) had a Catholic journeymen's association with 110–15 members, a Borromeo Association with 50–60 members, and a branch of the Mainz Association which before its closure had reached a membership of eighty-five.[87] But the number of associations noted by local officials was small compared with the numbers reported in a northern part of the Trier administrative district such as Bitburg, or even in a Saarland area like Merzig.[88] A whole swathe of associations that elsewhere mobilized Catholic sentiment during the *Kulturkampf* was simply absent in St Wendel; and no organizations were set up in St Wendel (as they were in other Saarland and non-Saarland areas) to express institutional support and collect money for the Pope.[89] Newspaper circulation told the same story. The *St-Paulinus-Blatt* had fewer subscribers in St Wendel than in any of the thirteen areas making up the administrative district of Trier. There were more than three times as many in Merzig, well over four times as many in Ottweiler.[90] Outside the town of St Wendel itself, organization was even more patchy. There was, it is true, a well-supported branch of the Mainz Association based on the villages of Alfsassen and Breiten, with just over a hundred members drawn from the peasantry, craftsmen, and day labourers, and the Borromeo Association had auxiliary branches in Urexweiler and Tholey, although not in Marpingen which lay between them.[91] Mayor Müller of St Wendel also reported that a large Catholic meeting at the end of August 1873, which attracted over 500 people to hear speakers who included Dasbach, was attended 'almost exclusively' by small peasants and miners from outside the town. The mayoralty of Alsweiler was one of the areas from which they apparently came.[92] But Mayor Woytt of Alsweiler, hardly a man to overlook Papist machinations when there was the slightest sniff of them, painted a rather different picture in July of the following year. Apart from a few members of the Mainz Association known to him, his enquiries had failed to uncover any Catholic associational life, and he was sure none existed. Nor could they exist, 'because the villages out in the countryside lack suitable personalities to provide leadership'.[93]

[87] On the journeymen's and Borromeo associations, see LHAK, 442/7854, 35–55 and 249–51. A full membership list of the Mainz Association can be found in SAStW, C/56, 56–8.

[88] For the Bitburg list, LHAK, 442/7854, 3–34; for Merzig, ibid. 65–74. A complete list of associations in the Trier administrative district is in LHAK, 403/6695, 525–605. The list for St Wendel, one of thirteen districts, occupies under 2 pages out of 81 (ibid. 602–3).

[89] LHAK, 442/6438, 59: LR St Wendel to KR Trier, 6 May 1875.

[90] See the table in Fohrmann, *Kulturkampfpublizistik*, 347.

[91] SAStW, C/56, 59–62, on the Mainz Association. LHAK, 442/6383, 99–106, for a list of Saarland branches of the Borromeo Association.

[92] SAStW, C/56, 75: Mayor Müller's report of 27 Aug. 1873 on the meeting held 3 days earlier.

[93] LHAK, 442/7854, 45: Mayor Woytt of Alsweiler to LR St Wendel, 30 July 1874.

The accounts given by the mayors of St Wendel and Alsweiler seem contradictory at first glance. One argued that small peasants and miners from the area around Alsweiler, Urexweiler, and Marpingen had flocked to hear Catholic speakers in the local market town. The man on the spot claimed that there were no Catholic organizations in the area, because it lacked local leaders. There is actually no contradiction. Mayors Müller and Woytt inadvertently pointed to the different forms that the Catholic response to the *Kulturkampf* might take. In some areas, particularly in the earlier stages of the conflict, these reactions assumed a highly organized form; in others they were largely spontaneous. Even at the high-point of the organized Catholic response to the *Kulturkampf*, in the summer of 1873, attendance at the August meeting in St Wendel did not lead to the harnessing of such sentiment by an 'official' movement. To explore the nature of this more inchoate, unorganized sentiment is to come closer to an understanding of why, just two years after Mayor Woytt's complacent report, there were 20,000 Catholics encamped in Marpingen.

Even in areas where the Catholic response to persecution took the classic organized form of associations, petitions, and processions, there was a highly charged emotional undertow to popular sentiment. We can see this in the town of Trier. Catholics there were organized in clubs and made formal representations about the May Laws, but the arrest of Bishop Eberhard in March 1874 released more elemental passions. *Landrat* Spangenberg could hardly proceed with his prisoner to the gates of the prison because 'the people threw themselves to the ground, tore their hair, and one heard lamentations that pierced the soul'. As the bishop turned to give a last blessing to the Catholic crowd, 'the agitation of the masses at this final moment was so great, their wailing and moaning so heart-rending, and the emotion that seized even sturdy men so powerful, so overwhelming, that the whole scene is indescribable'.[94] As outright repression increased in 1874-5, and the government suppressed organizations like the Mainz Association which had channelled popular feeling, incidents of this kind became more frequent. They were rarely as violent as the Namborn episode. More often, the accounts of the rumours and panics that swept through Catholic communities in these years suggest an overriding sense of desolation and desperation.[95]

Where there was no Catholic bourgeoisie to organize associations and petitions, and the parish clergy were unwilling or unable to do so, a more diffuse emotional response that sometimes turned into collective panic was uppermost from the start.[96] These Catholic reactions were not shapeless, but they did not take their shape from organizations. They manifested themselves in other ways, one of

[94] Kraft, *Matthias Eberhard*, 209-10.

[95] See e.g. the rumours about the pardoning of Father Christian Müller of Schoeneberg that spread around the Bad Kreuznach area: Kammer, *Kulturkampfpriester*, 121-2.

[96] There is no work on Catholic petition movements, or on the role of bourgeois clubs and associations during the *Kulturkampf*, but there is material in several local studies. See Jestaedt, *Kulturkampf im Fuldaer Land*; L. Ficker, *Der Kulturkampf in Münster*, ed. O. Hellinghaus (Münster, 1928); H. Schiffers, *Der Kulturkampf in Stadt und Regierungsbezirk Aachen* (Aachen, 1929).

which was a passionate longing that the Pope might somehow deliver German Catholics from their vale of tears. Bishop Ketteler of Mainz, one of the leading figures in German political and social Catholicism, warned of this: 'I disapprove of . . . a certain bragging and boasting about the power of the Pope, as if he were in a position to cast down his enemies and muster the whole world against them with a single word'.[97] This longing was part-mystical, part-militant. In individual cases, the craving for deliverance could take pathological form. When a new mental hospital opened in Merzig in the summer of 1876, the first two male patients were a man who believed he was the Pope and another who claimed to be a papal legate.[98] Catholic uncertainty and the desire for reassurance also expressed themselves in the importance attached to omens and prophecies. The widely known 'Lehnin'sche prophecy' was thought to have predicted the coming of the *Kulturkampf*; in some Catholic circles there was a yearning for 'supposed signs of a supernatural divine intervention or the expectation of such'.[99] Cases of stigmata and similar manifestations were also reported in the same period, like that of Elisabeth Flesch of Eppelborn who 'sweated blood'.[100]

Above all, the Catholic longing for divine intercession against worldly troubles attached itself to the Blessed Virgin. This was hardly surprising, given the revival of Marian devotions in previous decades and the fact that many other forms of popular piety had been eclipsed or even supplanted by the central figure of the Virgin. While Marian hymns, prayers, and medals offered a source of reassurance, the church hierarchy called *in extremis* for Catholics to rededicate themselves to the Virgin. After the arrest of the Archbishop of Posen and Gnesen in early February 1874, the German bishops urged the faithful: 'Take refuge in the Mother of Mercy and pray for the mighty intercession of all our transfigured brothers and protectors who sit at the throne of God, that the days of tribulation may be shortened'.[101] Bishop Eberhard of Trier made even more direct reference to the protection of the Virgin. After his release from gaol in 1875 he visited the Marian pilgrimage church of Eberhards-Clausen, where he talked with feeling about the 'simple countryman' to whom a miraculous image of the Virgin had been revealed 'at a time of sorrow when widespread confusion reigned'. The parallels with the present were obvious, as the bishop went on to note how thousands of pilgrims had been drawn to the site seeking aid and comfort through the intercession of the Mother of Mercy. Since that time, he concluded, the diocese had stood 'under the protection' of the Virgin.[102] The phrase had particular resonance in the district of Trier, for it was also the title of a popular prayer, 'Unter deinem Schutz und Schirm', requesting intercession.[103] That the

---

[97] Kissling, *Geschichte*, ii. 306.
[98] *SMZ*, 15 Aug. 1876.
[99] Kissling, *Geschichte*, ii. 306.
[100] LASB, E 107, 131; *Prozeß*, 189
[101] Kraft, *Matthias Eberhard*, 205.
[102] Ibid. 224–6.
[103] Text of the prayer in *EM*, p. 4 of appendix.

prayer should be recited regularly was to be one of the messages conveyed by the Virgin in Marpingen.

Intercession could, of course, mean different things. There is no doubt that many Catholics longed for a physical sign of the Virgin's presence, and the period was punctuated by many claims of Marian apparitions. Even before the *Kulturkampf*, the war and post-war uncertainty after 1866 led to many such reports, especially in German borderlands. In 1868 a young boy in Eckwertsheide, a half-forgotten pilgrimage centre near the Silesian town of Neisse, claimed to have seen an apparition in the pilgrimage chapel and been cured of lameness. The local bishop rejected the authenticity of the apparition, but it was eagerly supported by the *Schlesisches Kirchenblatt* and enjoyed great popular support even after episcopal interdiction.[104] Apparitions were then reported on Germany's eastern and western borders in the early 1870s. One of the most remarkable was in Leng, a Polish-speaking Prussian village in Silesia, near Ratibor. Several peasants from the village had purchased an old wooden church, formerly the place of worship in nearby Ostrog until a new stone building replaced it. When the wooden church was in its new location a fungus grew through a crack in the floorboards of the sacristy and spread into a pancake-shaped form. The development of cracks in the fungus then created the image of a face which purportedly resembled that of the Virgin Mary. A secondary school pupil wrote about the miraculous event, and the image was painted by an artist from Gleiwitz. A glass case was reverently placed over the fungus, now referred to as the *Obraz Najświętszej Panny Maryji na grzybie*—The Image of the Most Blessed Virgin Mary in the Mushroom—and when beads of condensation appeared on the case they were construed as diamonds, pearls, and stars. Thousands of pilgrims travelled to Leng to pay their respects. Eventually the parish priest of Ostrog and a fellow priest threw away the by now putrid fungus, but support for the Leng 'apparition' proved more difficult to uproot.[105]

A much more extensive series of apparitions was reported on Germany's western border during the same period. It began with the Alsatian apparitions in Krüth and Wittelsheim during the Franco-Prussian war and continued into the 1870s.[106] In April 1873 further apparitions of the Virgin were reported in the Lorraine village of Guisingen; a month later several children between the ages of 8 and 12 claimed to have seen the Virgin, who warned of a 'great bloodbath', in the Palatine village of Medelsheim.[107] Then came reports of an apparition in the village of Rohrbach.[108] These apparitions were as palpably dubious as the image

[104] Details of these events circulated again after events in Marpingen. See report in the *DAZ*, 29 Aug. 1876.

[105] *KZ*, 6 Sept. 1876.

[106] 'Wunder in Elsaß'; Berg, *Marpingen*, 26–7; Thurston, *Beauraing*, 121–2.

[107] A. Hoffmann, 'Aberglaube und religiöse Schwärmerei in der Pfalz im 19. Jahrhundert', *Archiv für mittelrheinische Kirchengeschichte*, 27 (1975), 212–13; K. Lillig, 'Die Wallfahrtskapelle vom "Heiligen Kreuz und den Sieben Schmerzen Mariä" bei Medelsheim', *Saarheimat*, 23 (1979), 273–6.

[108] *SMZ*, 19 July 1876.

of the Virgin in Leng. The cluster of Alsatian apparitions that followed Krüth were clearly imitative, and the same was true in Medelsheim (one of the Medelsheim seers had been taken by her father to Guisingen shortly before proclaiming her own visions). In none of these cases did the report of events suggest much grace or dignity: one of the boys in Medelsheim apparently tried to shake the Virgin down from the tree on which she was perched, while another girl claimed that the Virgin had hopped on to her hand and stayed there a while before disappearing.[109] The Virgin of Rohrbach supposedly appeared in a plum tree. The fact that the apparitions nevertheless found such a widespread and ready response indicates the state of popular sentiment in the area.

On the western margins of the new German state, economic crisis and the *Kulturkampf* exacerbated what was already a widespread mood of anxiety generated by the Franco-Prussian war. Apprehension and a mood of heightened religious fervour were apparent in the area around Marpingen, where the events of 1876 had already been prefigured by several incidents in the preceding year. Marpingen was close to Eppelborn, the home of Elisabeth Flesch. Even closer was Dirmingen, where a striking prelude to the Marpingen apparitions occurred in May 1876. The incident arose out of a seemingly unspectacular event: Father Schwaab of Urexweiler was walking his dog in the Dirmingen woods with a schoolteacher friend when the dog was suddenly alarmed by a falling spruce tree. The spot in the woods was already associated in folk memory with magical events: a forester had supposedly been beaten by an unknown hand, and someone else claimed to have seen thousands of cats there.[110] Popular sentiment proceeded to turn the incident into a form of apparition. Rumour had it that Father Schwaab had seen a woman whose sudden disappearance was followed by a whirlwind that toppled the spruce. The priest denied any supernatural occurrence, but according to the forester Louis Bruch the affair caused 'great excitement' throughout the district. The tree became known as 'the spruce of the spirits': some avoided it, others carved crosses in the wood and stripped the tree and its neighbours of their bark, which they cooked and ate or fed to their cattle. The mysterious woman was believed to be the Virgin Mary ascending to heaven.[111]

It would be surprising if word had not spread to Marpingen of such 'miraculous' events in a neighbouring parish. Father Schwaab's human companion in the Dirmingen woods was the brother of the schoolteacher Grady, whose friendship with the Marpingen teacher André was often to take her to the 'German Lourdes' in the months that followed.[112] Perhaps more important, one of the

[109] Hoffmann, 'Aberglaube', 212.
[110] On the role played by cats in popular beliefs, see R. Darnton, *The Great Cat Massacre, and Other Episodes in French Cultural History* (New York, 1984), 75–104.
[111] During investigation into Marpingen, statements on the Dirmingen incident were taken from Father Schwaab, senior forester Joseph Mallmann, local forester Louis Bruch, and district school inspector Christian Schroeder, all of whom testified at the subsequent trial in Saarbrücken. See LASB, E 107, 340–4; *Prozeß*, 30, 141, 148, 184–5.
[112] *Prozeß*, 185.

young women in Urexweiler who spread a version of events heard from Father
Schwaab's housekeeper was Katharina Kunz, a distant relation of the Marpingen
Kunz family whose daughter Margaretha was one of the three visionaries of 3
July 1876.[113] The rumours of what had occurred in Dirmingen would also have
had a familiar ring to inhabitants of Marpingen. Some decades before there had
been stories of a mysterious 'woman in white' seen in the Alsweiler mill, the mill
where Margaretha Kunz's father Jakob had worked.[114] Marpingen had its own
woman in white less than five years before the Marian apparitions began, when
a village woman claimed to have seen a white-clad figure resembling Father
Neureuter's dead sister provide 'miraculous accompaniment' for the priest on
one of his journeys.[115]

The apparitions began in Marpingen while the village was suffering the effects
of severe agricultural and industrial recession, and at a time of religious persecution. The Bishop of Trier had recently died after his spell in gaol; Father
Isbert of Namborn still sat in gaol, while the man who arrested him—Mayor
Woytt, the 'Devil of St Wendel'—continued to conduct what Marpingers saw
as a vendetta against their village. Events in Dirmingen had prompted 'great
excitement' just five weeks earlier. The mood of expectation, the sense that
something would happen in the village, is conveyed by the parish priest. In an
entry in his notebook, Father Neureuter later recalled his feelings on the eve of
the apparitions. 'I always had the thought that Marpingen would be tested.'[116]
The events that began on 3 July 1876 were to test Neureuter and the villagers of
Marpingen more than the priest could have imagined.

[113] LASB, E 107, 344. Katharina Kunz's father and Margaretha Kunz's paternal grandfather were
brothers.
[114] LASB, E 107, 323.
[115] LASB, E 107, 110, 447–8, 466. This incident occurred in the autumn of 1871.
[116] LASB, E 107, 424: undated entry in Neureuter's notebook.

PART II

The Apparitions

4

The Visionaries and their World

The Visionaries

Margaretha Kunz, Katharina Hubertus, and Susanna Leist took no part in the haymaking that was occupying Marpingen at the beginning of July 1876. All three were 8-year-olds with older brothers and sisters to carry out this and other physically demanding jobs: Kunz was the youngest of ten, Leist the second-youngest of nine, Hubertus the middle child of five.[1] But they had been entrusted on 3 July with another task often given to younger peasant children. As Susanna's father later remarked: 'I let the child go into the woods because she couldn't help me with my work; she could pick berries there.'[2] The social status of their families is difficult to establish precisely. 'Poor, but with enough to live on' was how the parish priest later described their circumstances.[3] What scraps of evidence we have suggest that the girls came from middling *Kuhbauer* families, although (as we shall see) the Kunz family was more ambiguously placed. They certainly owned meadows and barns, while Johann Leist was known to be in funds at the beginning of 1877 after selling a pair of draught oxen and a cow.[4] Margaretha Kunz had an uncle in Marpingen, the peasant Stephan Kunz IV, who can be classed as a village notable; another uncle in Alsweiler was a cartwright.[5] The glimpses we occasionally get into the interiors of their homes are consistent with this: they indicate substantial farmhouses (stone or half-timbered) of the kind associated with *Kuhbauern*, containing separate rooms for different domestic functions, not the cramped cottages of the small peasantry. Father Neureuter warmly praised the respectability of the three families; the notary Heß of Tholey knew the Kunz and Hubertus families and described them as 'people of exemplary honesty'.[6]

The three girls, all born in 1868, were friends. They came from the part of the

[1] Details of the families in N. Thoemes, *Unsere Liebe Frau von Marpingen. Geschichtliche Darstellung nach persönlichen Forschungen und Erlebnissen* (Trier, 1878), 15; *EM*, 9.
[2] LASB, E 107, 301.
[3] BAT, B III, 11, 14/4, 2: Neureuter to Bishop Korum Trier, 25 Oct. 1902; *MG*, 36.
[4] The ownership of land, barns, and animals has been pieced together from LASB, E 107, 109, 317–18; BAT, B III, 11, 14/3, 21, 32, 42; *Prozeß*, 85.
[5] On Stephan Kunz, see LASB, E 107, 79, 431–2; BAT, B III, 11, 14/4, 117. It was common in Marpingen for identically named members of the same family clan to add the number after their names. On the uncle in Alsweiler, see LASB, E 107, 370.
[6] LASB, E 107, 307.

village nearest to the Härtelwald woods, began attending school at the same time, and played together regularly. The argument is so often made that peasant children grew up in a world without play that it is worth remarking how often they were described by diverse witnesses as playing (although not, of course, with toys: the toy farm was the prerogative of the urban middle-class child).[7] Perhaps the main point here is the fact that their play struck many later supporters of the apparitions as a sign of the girls' sheer ordinariness. In other ways, too, they were unexceptional. If it is striking how often they were ill—one of the three was commonly missing from their later vigils at the site—then that only underlines the vulnerability of children in these years. All three girls contracted rubella in late summer 1876, and all were to catch scarlet fever during an epidemic in the first half of 1877— but so did 250 other children from the village.[8] Nor was there anything out of the ordinary in their behaviour at school, where they were considered 'well-behaved and diligent'. The supernumerary teacher Lambert Lichtherz later claimed hc had been told by the girls' teacher, Fräulein André, of her dissatisfaction with their conduct before the apparitions. But André denied this, and it seems unlikely in view of her subsequent behaviour towards them.[9]

Is there anything in the lives of these children and their seemingly ordinary family backgrounds that might help to explain what happened? The starting-point here must be the figure of Margaretha (or Gretchen) Kunz. Although the youngest of the visionaries, she was powerfully built like her mother and was easily the largest of the three girls.[10] A contemporary photograph of the three seers shows her dominating the group physically.[11] She was also by common consent the cleverest. Dr Nikolaus Thoemes, who did so much to disseminate the 'miracle of Marpingen' with his pamphlets, believed that Kunz was 'generally more developed than the other two'.[12] The word that seemed to occur to everyone who met her was geweckt—bright or sharp. For the priest Felix Dicke, who spent a long time in the village, she was 'somewhat brighter than the other two'. The teacher André thought her 'very bright', compared with the average Susanna Leist and the rather backward Katharina Hubertus.[13] She impressed the merchant Jacob in Tholey as 'bright and fearless', while the superintendent of the institution in Saarbrücken in which all three girls were later confined believed she was

[7] On peasant children and the absence of play, see Rosenbaum, Formen der Familie, 93–7; on children and toys, H. Retter, Spielzeug. Handbuch zur Geschichte und Pädagogik der Spielmittel (Weinheim and Basle, 1979); I. Weber-Kellermann, Die Kindheit. Kleidung und Wohnen, Arbeit und Spiel (Frankfurt am Main, 1979).

[8] BAT, B III, 11, 14/3, 24; F. Lama, Die Muttergottes-Erscheinungen in Marpingen (Saar) (Altötting, n.d.), 61.

[9] LASB, E 107, 98–9.

[10] On her mother, see LASB, E 107, 325.

[11] The same group photograph is reproduced in Bungert, Heimatbuch, 229 and Lama, Muttergottes-Erscheinungen, 36.

[12] Thoemes, Die Erscheinungen, 21.

[13] MMGE, 14 ; LASB, E 107, 99.

'brighter than the others and appears to influence them'.[14] Margaretha also differed from her two companions in having no father. He had been killed in a mill accident in December 1867, five months before Gretchen was born. It would be surprising if she did not experience some resentment from her brothers and sisters, as the last-born of an unusually large family, another mouth to feed in suddenly straitened circumstances (and another claimant on the modest family property). We do know that the life of the family changed after the death of Jakob Kunz. Gretchen's sister Magdalena became a servant girl in the village and her elder brothers went down the pit.[15] The family also had to come to terms with other problems. Jakob Kunz had debts when he died, having lost the Alsweiler mill when it was subject to forced sale. His widow took legal action on the grounds of wrongful distraint in an unsuccessful attempt to use an oversight in the contract of sale as a means of recovering part of the property.[16]

The fatherless Margaretha Kunz had thus seen her family forced to adjust to changed and difficult circumstances. There are several points here that recall the lives of other visionary children. There are certainly some parallels with Mathilde Sack, a tailor's daughter who was the central figure of the Mettenbuch apparitions in Bavaria which began in 1877. Mathilde, it is true, was older—14 at the time of the first Mettenbuch apparitions. She had also led a more varied, even picaresque life compared with Gretchen Kunz, having left an unhappy family home near Straubing to live in Nuremberg and Amberg, where she lodged for a time with a factory worker's wife of ill repute, and worked variously for a confectioner, a gold-beater, and in domestic service. In the unsympathetic words of the Bishop of Regensburg, she had 'knocked about in the world' at an age when most girls were 'frightened to mix with people'.[17] She and Margaretha Kunz nevertheless had things in common. Both were bright, rightly regarded as the dominant characters in their respective apparitions. The other children were 'under her influence', said the schoolteacher Mayr of Mathilde.[18] Both had suffered recent bereavement, both had to come to terms with a fractured family life and a threat to family respectability. Margaretha had lost her father under painful circumstances and seen her older brothers leave home to work as miners.

[14] On the merchant Jacob, LASB, E 107, 87; on Riemer, Radziwill, *Besuch*, 3–4. Riemer's testimony might be thought biased, but Radziwill (who was working to release the children) called him 'friendly and kind', and Riemer's views only echo those of almost everyone who met Margaretha.

[15] LASB, E 107, 75; the notary Hetz to Prince Radziwill, 28 Nov. 1876, cited in *MWOL*, 13–15. It was not unusual for the children of middling peasants to go into service, although there is no mention of it happening in the Leist or Hubertus families.

[16] LASB, E 107, 307.

[17] The details on Mathilde Sack are drawn from the reports, interrogation transcripts, and correspondence in BZAR, F 115, Fasc. IV, 'Untersuchung der Angaben der Mettenbucher Mädchen in Waldsassen—1878 u. 1879', and the unnumbered folder entitled 'Mettenbuch. Mathilde Sack in Waldsassen'. There is also relevant material in Fasc. I, e.g. Fasc. I, 11, 12: 'Bericht des Pfarramtes Metten über die behaupteten Erscheinungen der Mutter Gottes, 23 Juli 1877', and Fasc. I, Beilage 1: 'Protokoll der Vernehmung der Mathilde Sack, Schneiderstochter, 14 J. alt, bezüglich der Mutter-Gottes-Erscheinungen zwischen 1. und 21. Dez. l. J.', Metten, 25 Dec. 1876.

[18] SAL, 164/2, 1162: 'Besprechung mit Lehrer Mayr von Berg vom 7. Mai 1877'.

Mathilde's mother had died three years before the apparitions, her father had been gaoled, and she finally left her stepmother's home to live with an aunt in Mettenbuch when her brother went into the army. There is, finally, the question of domestic or farm service that seems to run through the lives of so many seers. In the summer before she went to Mettenbuch, Mathilde had lived in Amberg with the Scherer family, whose son had known her father. The daughter of the house later claimed that Mathilde had been taken in 'more out of charity than as a servant', but it seems clear that Mathilde was in fact dismissed by a mistress dissatisfied with her services, as well as unhappy with her quarrelsome behaviour and supposedly poor moral character.[19] The 8-year-old Margaretha Kunz hardly faced a future of this kind; but she may have faced the prospect of following her elder sister into service, in circumstances closer to those in which Mathilde Sack found herself after November 1876, when she went to work as a farm servant in her aunt's house.[20]

There are uncanny echoes in both life-histories of another, more celebrated visionary, Bernadette Soubirous, the daughter of a bankrupted and imprisoned miller, sent out to work as a farm servant. To what extent were the German seers in the 1870s prompted by the example of Lourdes? The timing alone suggests some influence. The first apparition was reported in Marpingen on the very day that 100,000 Catholics, including thirty-five bishops, were celebrating the crowning of a statue to the Blessed Virgin at Lourdes.[21] It was a time when details about Lourdes and Bernadette's apparitions were widely reported in the Catholic press, when Catholics in Germany would have been giving voice to their sense of regret that the Virgin had not yet graced German soil. The pervasive influence of Lourdes went back further, however, although it undoubtedly grew after the first organized national pilgrimage from Germany took place in 1875. The Marpingen children had certainly heard about Bernadette Soubirous and other visionaries. Their homes contained no popular pamphlets on the subject, unlike the Kraus home of two of the Mettenbuch seers, whose mother had literature on both La Salette and Marpingen itself.[22] But their schoolteacher André had talked

[19] BZAR, F 115, Fasc. IV: 'Protokoll über die vom 20. bis zum 23. September 1878 zu Waldsassen gepflogenen Untersuchung im Betriff der Mettenbucher Erscheinungen'; 'Protokoll aufgenommen im Kloster der Cisterzienserinen zu Waldsassen am 7. November 1878'.

[20] On Mathilde Sack's move to Mettenbuch, BZAR, F 115, Fasc. I, 11, 12: 'Bericht der Pfarramtes Metten über die behaupteten Erscheinungen der Mutter Gottes', 23 July 1877; F 115, Fasc. IV: 'Protokoll aufgenommen ... am 7. November 1878'. On the social-psychological dimensions of farm service, see R. Schulte, 'Dienstmädchen im herrschaftlichen Haushalt. Zur Genese ihrer Sozial-psychologie', *Zeitschrift für bayerische Landesgeschichte*, 41 (1978), 879–920.

[21] St John, *The Blessed Virgin*, 378.

[22] Frau Kunz told a visitor from Cologne that Marpingen 'was a remote village and she did not read the public prints' (*öffentliche Blätter*). The vigilant authorities could find no such material in the homes of the Kunz, Leist, or Hubertus families. On the widow Kraus, who 'liked to read', and her favourite reading-matter, BZAR, F 115, Fasc. V: 'Protokoll aufgenommen im Kloster Metten am 28. Dez. 1878', with 'Katharina Kraus (Mutter)' written in the top right-hand corner. The copy of the statement is dated 30 Dec. 1878. (Fasc. V is entirely concerned with the questioning of Frau Kraus's son, Franz-Xaver.)

about these and other apparitions, and may even have done so just before the Marpingen events began.[23] The children also received instruction concerning the Immaculate Conception from the parish priest, and Frau Kunz later recalled to a visitor that Father Neureuter had talked about the apparitions at Lourdes in a sermon.[24]

Some officials were convinced that the girls' parents, Frau Kunz in particular, had inspired the children's accounts. Despite their investigative zeal, no evidence at all could be found to substantiate this. One witness claimed he had heard from 'a peasant in Marpingen' that Frau Kunz was the originator of recent stories about a similar 'miracle' at Alsweiler, but the same vague charge was later made against Frau Leist, and in neither case could the authorities make much of it.[25] The likeliest explanation remains the simplest. The children lived in an atmosphere suffused with piety—one of Katharina Hubertus's sisters hoped to become a nun—and would have heard stories about apparitions from their parents and older children, including their own sisters.[26] Starting school then marked a sudden change in their lives, and brought them into more regular contact with such accounts. School instruction probably heightened the susceptibilities of the Marpingen children in the same way that the experience of being prepared for confirmation certainly influenced a number of the Mettenbuch and Dittrichswalde children. (The 13-year-old Augusta Frafryusdi had just successfully completed her final confirmation class on the evening of her first vision at Dittrichswalde, and the apparition announced itself as the Immaculate Conception on the day of her first communion.[27]) The Marpingen apparitions included scenes, from the Annunciation to the temptation of Christ, that exactly echoed passages in the Schuster school bible that the girls had studied in catechism classes.[28] Fusing these susceptibilities together was the chance of time and place. The time when the Marpingen apparitions began would have been marked by particular devotions to the Virgin Mary, even without the drama of the Lourdes coronation ceremony. The Marian festival of the Visitation that fell on 2 July was especially important in German-speaking Europe; and the following day was one on which, every year since the late seventeenth century, pilgrims from throughout the Trier diocese had travelled to the Marian shrine at Beurig.[29] This was the day on which the

[23] Margaretha Kunz later told at least one person that André had talked about Lourdes shortly before the Marpingen apparitions began, although the girl was inconsistent in what she said on the subject; but so too was André, and the district school inspector Schroeder was one who found André's confused denials unconvincing. See LASB, E 107, 75–6, 84, 102–4; Prozeß, 76.

[24] LASB, E 107, 49. There is confirmation in a source sympathetic to the parish priest: Sausseret, Erscheinungen, 233. See also above, p. 89.

[25] LASB, E 107, 323; Prozeß, 146.

[26] Barbara Hubertus later realized her ambition when she entered the Order of the Poor Child Jesus: BAT, B III, 11, 14/3, 10; Bungert, Heimatbuch, 559.

[27] 'Die Erscheinungen der unbefleckt Empfangenen in Dittrichswalde', Der Sendbote des göttlichen Herzens Jesu, 14 (1878), 56–8.

[28] LASB, E 107, 106–9, 113–17.

[29] On the importance of the Visitation in Germany, Nolan and Nolan, Christian Pilgrimage, 62; on

three girls found themselves still in the Härtelwald woods as dusk fell and the Angelus sounded.[30]

When they returned home that first evening with their stories of a 'woman in white', the initial reaction of their parents was, on the face of it, sceptical. Susanna Leist's father told her she was talking nonsense (*dummes Zeug*), and suggested she had simply seen a village woman. Katharina Hubertus was given no food that evening by her father; her mother promised her a new dress if she stopped her romancing. Frau Kunz also resorted to carrot and stick, promising her daughter a new dress if she told the truth and punishment if she continued to lie: 'Your brother Peter will beat you half to death, and you will go to hell and not to heaven.'[31] The parents were, of course, on the defensive when they recounted these reactions to the parish priest, and still more so when questioned by the Prussian authorities. This comes through clearly in their statements ('I can't watch out for each of my children, I have nine', protested Leist's father).[32] This special pleading has to be set against other evidence suggesting a rather more active part in the shaping of the apparitions, even if one that fell short of the conspiratorial 'instigation' suspected by the authorities. None of the parents in Marpingen encouraged the girls with quite the deliberation of Frau Kraus in Mettenbuch, who cajoled her own children to emulate the claims of her niece, Mathilde Sack.[33] They nevertheless prompted the girls in a variety of ways. Frau Leist seems to have played the principal role. When the three girls returned from the woods on the first evening, frightened and excited about the 'woman in white', they had to pass the Leist house. Frau Leist was among the group of villagers who first heard the story, and according to the later account of Margaretha Kunz she said to the childen: 'Go back into the woods tomorrow, pray, and if you see her again ask who she is; if she says she is the Immaculately Conceived, then she is the Blessed Virgin.'[34] There is further evidence of this if we read between the lines of Susanna Leist's own response to the question: who

Beurig, Thoemes, *Die Erscheinungen*, 4. The Dittrichswalde apparitions also began just two days before an important date in the local church calendar, the feast of St Peter and St Paul: 'Die Erscheinungen der unbefleckt Empfangenen', 56–8.

[30] Frohschammer, 'Die Glaubwürdigkeit', argues that the atmosphere created by dusk and the ringing of the Angelus made the children especially susceptible to 'seeing'. For an explanation of Mettenbuch that also attaches importance to the time of day, see the account of the psychiatrist Dr Grasky given to the district official of Deggendorf: SAL 164/2, 1162: 'Rücksprache mit Irrenhaus-Direktor Dr Grasky vom 4. Mai'.

[31] LASB, E 107, 301–4, 322; BAT, B III, 11, 14/3, 2–5; and BAT, B III, 11, 14/4, 2–3.

[32] LASB, E 107, 301.

[33] BZAR, F 115, Fasc. V: 'Protokoll aufgenommen im bischöfl. Palais zu Regensburg am 20. November 1878 über die Vernehmung des Xaver Kraus von Mettenbuch bezüglich angeblicher Erscheinungen, geschlossen und unterzeichnet, den 22. November 1878'. The plausibility of Franz-Xaver Kraus's testimony about his mother's part in events is increased by the fact that his artless admissions were interspersed with no less artless and highly unconvincing denials of her role. See also BZAR, F 115, Fasc. I, 22: 'Familienschema der Kinder von Mettenbuch'.

[34] BAT, B III, 11, 14/3, 63–4.

had suggested they return to the woods? She said nothing for a quarter of an hour, then replied: 'It was *not* my mother.'[35]

Frau Leist also played a significant part in trying to 'improve' on the description of the Virgin given by the children. When questioned, she reported the girls talking of a figure wearing a blue sash, before this detail had been mentioned by any of the children.[36] Examining magistrate Emil Kleber and a detective brought in from Berlin both saw this as a highly incriminating piece of evidence pointing to parental instigation. The more likely explanation is that, to the rather vague account given by the girls, Frau Leist added a detail, the blue sash, which had figured in the description of the Lourdes apparition and corresponded more closely to her own idea of what the Virgin 'ought' to look like. There is a further example of the way in which the events of the first day were retrospectively shaped into a pattern more closely resembling the apparition at Lourdes. The three girls had been accompanied in the woods by two others: the 6-year-old Lischen Hubertus, Katharina's younger sister, and another 6-year-old, Anna Meisberger. At a very early stage the two children surplus to the requirements of a classic apparition à la Lourdes were tacitly dropped from the account: as the narrative crystallized with constant retelling it featured only Margaretha, Susanna, and Katharina. If the girls' parents were not solely responsible for this, they certainly did nothing to impede the construction of a more 'satisfactory' account.[37]

As the apparitions continued, the parents' behaviour continued to encourage belief in the authenticity of the girls' accounts. This is particularly true of the originally sceptical parents. Once they had suspended their initial disbelief, they argued strongly for the authenticity of the visions. Take the case of Johannes Hubertus, Katharina's father. On 17 July 1876 he told an examining magistrate that he 'paid no attention to the matter and went about my work'.[38] This was simply untrue. He was the first of the parents to accompany the girls to the apparition site when he went there on 5 July, together with the teacher Bungert and the retired miner Nikolaus Recktenwald (his brother-in-law). This was probably the occasion when he conducted a series of rather flawed tests to determine whether the girls were telling the truth (their eyes were covered to see if they claimed to see the apparition in the same place), an examination that apparently convinced him. He and his wife were both at the site on the evening of the same day when another of his daughters, Barbara, claimed that her bad foot had been cured. He was also seen at the site on later occasions, giving progress reports to pilgrims on whether or not the Virgin had appeared. Hubertus

---

[35] At an interrogation on 31 Oct. 1876: LASB, E 107, 60–1.

[36] LASB, E 107, 302. Frau Kunz also tried to improve on the apparition (or perhaps on Frau Leist's theological grasp). Hearing from her daughter that the figure had called itself the 'Immaculately Conceived', Frau Kunz remarked that 'She must have said the Immaculate Conception': BAT, B III, 11, 14/3, 5.

[37] LASB, E 107, 58; *Prozeß*, 96.

[38] LASB, E 107, 299.

suggested to Father Neureuter at an early stage that some sign should be erected at the site, and was the first to mention the building of a chapel to the priest. Once Hubertus had overcome the initial fear that his daughter and her companions were deliberately lying, his conviction was apparently absolute. He did not demur at the increasingly elaborate forms assumed by the apparitions, and the first alleged apparition of the Virgin in the village itself, on 24 July, took place in the Hubertus house. Neureuter's notes record that Hubertus himself 'heard' the singing and praying of the angels who accompanied the apparition on 3 August.[39]

The parents encouraged the apparitions in other ways. They not only went to the site, but put questions to the apparition through the children. They also permitted the three girls to remain there for such lengthy spells that they became exhausted, and—for all their reported insistence that the children should not become swollen-headed or self-important—were evidently prepared to display them for the admiration of others. Johannes Leist claimed not to share his wife's enthusiasm for what had happened, indeed on occasion said he had never believed in the apparitions (he 'had been a soldier and didn't want to set himself up against authority'); but we find him showing Susanna off with paternal pride to the merchant Schwan of Tholey.[40] Frau Margaretha Hubertus told the authorities that when pilgrims came, they 'fetched my child out of the house and I let her go, though reluctantly'. This does not square with the experience of one pious visitor from the Netherlands shortly after Christmas 1876, who later wrote an account in the Amsterdam *Tyd*. Frau Hubertus was happy that he should talk to the seers (all three were in her house at the time) and encouraged them to write down what they had seen, although she drew the line at photographs.[41] Other accounts suggest that the children were encouraged to read out the descriptions of the apparitions they had written in exercise books, and to sign pictures— presumably commercial reproductions of the Madonna of Marpingen—for visitors.[42] Sympathetic and hostile accounts show that hundreds of pilgrims were welcomed by the girls' parents into their homes, particularly if they were priests or visitors (generally women) of high social station. One 'lady' from Koblenz stayed for ten days with Frau Kunz to help with the preparation and serving of meals. During the particularly crowded period of late August 1877, a Belgian priest recalled having to spend the night in a chair at either the Leist or Hubertus house.[43]

[39] See LASB, E 107, 308–11, 321–2; BAT, B III, 11, 14/3, 10–11, and BAT, B III, 11, 14/4, 3.

[40] *Prozeß*, 229; LASB, E 107, 123–5.

[41] LASB, E 107, 300; *MWOL*, 82. The Dutch visitor was there on 29 Dec. 1876.

[42] *MWOL*, 92–3; LASB, E 107, 161. On one occasion Herr Hubertus, according to the mayor's secretary Schuh from Eppelborn, told his daughter after some time: 'Don't write any more'. The hostile Schuh believed that Hubertus was irritated because no money had been forthcoming. On commercial reproductions of the image of the Virgin, see below, Ch. 5.

[43] Sausseret, *Erscheinungen*, 227, 231. See also LASB, E 107, 237.

'One Big Lie'

Looking back on events as a 20-year-old convent servant, shortly to become a novice nun, Margaretha Kunz observed coolly that the 'great mistake' had been 'to believe us immediately instead of calming us down'.[44] This formed part of a statement admitting that the visionaries' claims were 'one big lie'.[45] Confessions of this kind were not without precedent. Maximin Giraud of La Salette later made damaging admissions, as we have seen, and one of the Pontmain seers subsequently withdrew her claims.[46] Margaretha Kunz also made similar confessions to various state officials at the time, although in every case these earlier retractions were in turn retracted.[47] It is possible to argue, and many did, that all of these confessions were made under some sort of duress. Officials could frighten the young girl with the fate that awaited her mother if she persisted with her fabrications; the ecclesiastical authorities could threaten her with the still more terrible punishment she might expect—and they also held the key to Margaretha becoming a novice. Yet taking all this into account, the circumstances of her confessions does not undermine their content, and what she admitted is compellingly plausible.

Her admissions underline the way that the visionaries' stories were shaped by others. Margaretha Kunz makes it clear that it was not only the idea of the Immaculate Conception that was suggested to the children after they reported the 'woman in white'; so were other aspects of the apparition and the words she used. When the children were asked if the Virgin wore a golden crown and carried the child Jesus, they readily agreed. The suggestions that a chapel be built ('of stone, not of wood') and the sick be brought to the site were also reported by the girls as answers to questions put by others.[48] As new suggestions were made, the seers incorporated them into their accounts. Thus the idea of the devil 'was put into our minds by imprudent observations and questions'.[49] This may be how the girls came to describe the 'poor souls from purgatory' shown to them by the Blessed Virgin and released by their prayers.[50] Belief in the physical manifestation of tormented souls, crying for release, was a strong element in local popular piety; it was just the sort of matter on which the visionaries were likely

---

[44] BAT, B III, 11, 14/3, 63-4.

[45] BAT, B III, 11, 14/3, 59-65. These pages of folder 3 contain the handwritten confession, a typed copy, and the envelope (marked *Secretum*) in which the confession was placed. It was dated Thorn, Convent of St Joseph, 26 Jan. 1889. See also below, Ch. 11.

[46] On Maximin Giraud, see above, p. 20; on Jeanne-Marie Lebossé of Pontmain, see Laurentin and Durand, *Un signe*, 79-100.

[47] LASB, E 107, 48-86.

[48] BAT, B III, 11, 14/3, 63-4.

[49] Ibid.

[50] Ibid. See, later in the same folder, the unfavourable ecclesiastical view of this episode: BAT, B III, 11, 14/3, 43-9: judgement of Bishop Laurent of Chersones on the apparitions, dated Simpelveld [Netherlands], 9 May 1880, section VI, points 1-4.

to be pressed.[51] What Margaretha Kunz described retrospectively is an apparition narrative being constructed through a process of suggestion and accretion. This is consistent with other evidence. To take an overt example, in September 1876 the children referred vaguely to a shining head hovering over the Blessed Virgin in one apparition. The visiting theologian Matthias Scheeben showed them a picture of St Nicolas of Flue that he carried with him, and the visionaries promptly agreed that this was the very head they had seen.[52]

The later account given by Margaretha Kunz differs from contemporary narratives because the evidence is direct; it differs from the various retractions made to officials at the time because, with the need to shield individuals from possible prosecution lifted, responsibility for encouraging the girls is now brought home more directly to adults in Marpingen. The inspiration for the idea of the Immaculate Conception is now attributed to Frau Leist, not to 'words that I read two or three years earlier during a parish feast in the prayerbook of a girl from outside the village'.[53] Another feature of the apparitions, the appearance of the devil, is now linked to unfortunate remarks by adults (including visiting priests), not just to pictures seen in the Schuster school bible. Taken as a whole, however, the later confession is very bland, failing to mention many points and lacking detail on others. This may be attributed partly to forgetfulness about events that had happened twelve years earlier, partly to involuntary suppression, partly to motives of self-exculpation and the understandable desire to top and tail the story into the right shape for a convent audience. The author of the confession presents the cool and chastened recollections of a young woman who has distanced herself from the 8-year-old Margaretha Kunz.[54] There is no good reason to doubt the underlying truth of the later admission, but it is best read in conjunction with other evidence on the three visionaries. The contemporary retractions, not surprisingly, have more immediacy. They also give a richer sense, in their evasions as well as their admissions, of what the apparitions meant to the children at the time. Read alongside contemporary accounts of the children's behaviour from third parties, they suggest that the experience of the apparitions was far from simple and cannot be interpreted solely as an adult construct. The visionaries were both playful and desperate. They were in part constructing for themselves the image of a better life and enjoying the intoxication of their novel status; they were also burdened with guilt and driven on by fear.

The classic Marian visions of the nineteenth century contained an intense vision of a better world, of peace, hope, or plenty. Even the less spiritually compelling seers reported visions whose beauty contrasted starkly with the realit-

---

[51] For a Marpingen example, BAT, B III, 11, 14/4, 16. The 'poor souls in purgatory' also played a part in the Mettenbuch apparition: B. Braunmüller, *Kurzer Bericht über die Erscheinungen U. L. Frau bei Mettenbuch* (Deggendorf, 1878), 5–8.
[52] *MMGE*, 55. The author of the pious brochure in which this story appeared clearly saw it as evidence supporting the authenticity of the apparitions.
[53] Cf. BAT, B III, 11, 14/3, 63–4; LASB, E 107, 58.
[54] But see below, Ch. 11, pp. 351–7 on Margaretha Kunz's chequered later career as a nun.

ies of everyday life. The Virgin's face was gentle and surrounded by radiant light, her clothes rich and sumptuous. When apparitions took place at times of agricultural crisis, as they so often did, the children told of the plenty that would replace want. A number of these motifs occurred (although not as prophecies) in the Mettenbuch visions. The children described angels carrying the Virgin's train, so that it was possible to see she had 'golden shoes and white stockings'. They had 'seen angels eating grilled fish from a golden table', and they described the Virgin's instructions that they make up and drink daily from a concoction that sounds like a rustic ambrosia.[55] The Marpingen apparitions were, by contrast, remarkably lacking in intensity or a sense of rapture. Drawing on half-remembered fragments from books or catechism classes, prompted by parents and other adults, the girls talked conventionally about the beauty of the Blessed Virgin, adding details of familiar Bible stories like the Annunciation.[56] The overriding impression is one of fragmented descriptions lacking any real centre. In other apparitions the Virgin assumed a fixed appearance, graced a particular spot, and delivered a single powerful message. In Marpingen the children described a Virgin in motley who flitted from place to place and had no special message. The exchanges they reported seldom rose above the level of banality, their prophecies concerning missed appointments rather than sublime matters of war, peace, and famine.[57]

The apparitions described by the Marpingen children did not so much represent the eruption of the divine into everyday life, as subject the divine to an everyday regimen. We can see this in the lengthy, commonplace exchanges the seers reported having with the Virgin, who sometimes sat, sometimes joined them in their games as they rolled down the hillside. It is even more apparent in the list of places where they claimed to have seen her: in their homes, in the barn and stables, in various houses in Marpingen, and in a shop in Tholey, in the school, the church, the graveyard.[58] This aspect of the apparitions created doubts among some clerical observers, and it is worth exploring what it might have meant to the visionary children. Most obviously, of course, if the apparitions were to continue after the authorities blocked off the Härtelwald, they would have to do so within the village. This inevitably meant a certain domestication of the Virgin. But we can go further than that. In recounting the appearance of Mary in these places, by 'naming' houses and meadows, the children were able to employ

[55] BZAR, F 115, Fasc. I, Beilage I: 'Protokolle der Visionäre. Neujahr 1877 mitgetheilt' (the statements themselves were taken down on 24 Dec. 1876); Fasc. V: 'Vernehmung des Fr. Xav. Kraus in Regensburg. Nov. 1878. Weitere Vernehmungen in Metten. Dezbr. 1878': 'Protokoll ... über die Vernehmung des Xaver Kraus', 22; SAL, 164/2, 1162: 'Besprechung mit Lehrer Mayr von Berg vom 7. Mai 1877'.
[56] The details the children gave of the Annunciation followed exactly the passages in Schuster's illustrated bible they had worked through in school since Easter 1876: LASB, E 107, 106–8.
[57] On the children's predictions, LASB, E 107, 129–30. Cf. the Mettenbuch seer, Theres Liebl: 'A great war will afflict the land. Much blood will flow. But if there is much praying, this will not happen for eleven or twelve years': BZAR, F 115, Fasc. I: Beilage marked 'Ad 20', 'Protokoll, Metten d. 6. November 1877'.
[58] BAT, B III, 11, 14/3, 43–9: Bishop Laurent's report of 9 May 1880, section I, 1–3.

familiar village landmarks. There was doubtless a reassuring element to this: a Blessed Virgin who could be associated with Schäfer's meadow, or with the large round stone that stood at the edge of the upper village, was rendered benign, placed firmly within a bounded world. At the same time, the visionaries' message that the Virgin Mary had graced these everyday spots cast the places themselves in a new light. It also enhanced the status of the messengers, for the children—through their privileged position—placed their own stamp vicariously on property and places that were normally the concern of adults.

This element of reversal continued what had begun at the original apparition site. Access to the site had been jealously guarded by the seers. Neither the parish priest nor the priest from Heusweiler was to approach it; at one point the children brought Father Neureuter the instruction (*Weisung*) of the Virgin that he should cease his close contact with and observation of them.[59] On several occasions they indicated with a shake of the head that particular individuals were not to approach.[60] The children announced which prayers had to be recited and the spring from which water should be drunk (not the Marienbrunnen near the church, but one in the Härtelwald). In other ways, too, the visionaries underlined their special status. They spoke of secrets, and told pilgrims that celestial omens would be explained.[61] Katharina Hubertus said she had been told to become a nun.[62]

There was sometimes a palpably playful air to the behaviour of the children. When the sympathetic Dr Thoemes pressed them on one occasion about the appearance of the Virgin, they answered pertly: 'she has gone now'.[63] The merchant Huber from Urexweiler found the three girls sitting in a tree and asked them about the apparitions. They gave no answer, and laughed when he offered them a gold coin.[64] While the well-disposed teacher André remained in Marpingen, the apparitions in the schoolroom had something of the same puckish character.[65] There are parallels in the Mettenbuch case. On one occasion the children were followed and watched by the peasant Strobel, who believed himself well hidden until the children turned towards him and one of them said: 'look, there's another angel'.[66] In Marpingen the playfulness contained a malicious

[59] LASB, E 107, 446.

[60] BAT, B III, 11, 14/3, 12; *EM*, 54. This was recorded in the notes of several priests and added to the evidence compiled by examining magistrates: LASB, E 107, 6, 184.

[61] LASB, E 107, 129–30; *EM*, 81.

[62] BAT, B III, 11, 14/3, 40.

[63] Thoemes, *Die Erscheinungen*, 89.

[64] LASB, E 107, 91–2. The issue of whether the children, and Kunz in particular, accepted money from pilgrims took up much police time. The balance of evidence suggests that she did, although she was extremely careful when her mother was present. See e.g. *Prozeß*, 197–8.

[65] See LASB, E 107, 104–5. Only after School Inspector Schroeder ordered André to send the children out of the school whenever they reported a new apparition did they cease to talk about them during lessons.

[66] SAL, 164/2, 1162: 'Besprechung mit Lehrer Mayr von Berg vom 7. Mai 1877'. Compare Franz-Xaver Kraus's 'obstinate' reply to the gendarme Dörfler in Mettenbuch: 'Now that you want to know

streak, as it surely did when the children claimed to see the devil in the house of the pious church bookkeeper Fuchs.[67] In the response to figures such as Dr Thoemes, the Urexweiler merchant, and the bookkeeper it is also possible to detect an element of contempt. During the period that she and her two companions spent incarcerated in a Saarbrücken orphanage, Margaretha Kunz confided to a sceptical older girl: 'you are not as stupid as the stupid gentlemen; they are more stupid than we children'.[68]

An awareness of their own power, playfulness, malice, even (in the case of Kunz at least) a certain contempt: all were elements in the conduct of the children. Without doubt the children were encouraged to play their roles by the uncritical, even complaisant reaction they encountered from parents, villagers, and a growing number of visiting admirers. As the gendarme Hentschel argued, 'through the daily arriving visitors, among them many ladies and gentlemen and people of high rank, who, usually accompanied by priests, did not disdain to visit the blessed children, to pamper them, and eventually make them gifts, the children ... were totally spoiled'.[69] But the attention paid by villagers and pilgrims cut two ways: it was also a burden on the children that sometimes became intolerable. Pilgrims crowded in and around their parents' homes, asking the children to repeat what they had seen and pestering them to sign pictures. In the words of one visiting priest, they found themselves in a 'state of siege'.[70] Other pilgrims went to the school to see the little visionaries, and waylaid them outside, or fetched them away from their games. They were exposed to constant public demand: one day they were kept at the apparition site from 8 a.m. to 11 p.m., until almost collapsing from exhaustion.[71] This may account for some of the tetchiness, the sudden silences, and the occasional discomfiting of questioners. These were children of 8, after all, who yawned, stretched, and readily became bored when subjected even to friendly questioning.[72] The pressures on them also help to explain a number of the more elaborate later apparitions, as the children were driven to reckless invention. This was certainly true of one such case, the dubious 'prediction' that a young child, Jakob Schnur, would die, and the related description of a funeral procession in the sky over Marpingen. Margaretha Kunz later said that these had been 'invented to satisfy the people who wanted ever more miracles'.[73]

The children faced other difficulties. One was the problem of what to say to

about it, I'm definitely not telling you anything': SAL, 164/2, 1162: 'Meldung des Gendarmen Dörfler am 6. Mai 1877'.

[67] LASB, E 107, 117. The children claimed to have driven the devil out—not with consecrated water, but with water from the newly 'miraculous' spring.
[68] LASB, E 107, 73–4.
[69] Report of gendarme Hentschel on the period of late Aug. and early Sept. 1877: LASB, E 107, 166.
[70] Sausseret, Erscheinungen, 226. See also Cramer, Die Erscheinungen, 17.
[71] MMGE, 39; MG, 23.
[72] BAT, B III, 11, 14/3, 16–17: comments of the Poor Child Jesus nuns in Echternach on the reactions of the children to questioning.
[73] LASB, E 107, 64–5.

members of the clergy. In the early stages they could expect harsh questioning: the children were very fearful when first interviewed by Father Neureuter, and this may have been another reason for the instruction that the clergy keep away from the apparition site. In October 1876, when Margaretha Kunz was in her uncle's house in Alsweiler, the local parish priest tried to question her 'but she ran away without telling him anything'.[74] Visiting priests came to Marpingen regularly throughout the fourteen months of apparitions, and among them were sceptical spirits. Some had 'tests' they wanted to apply.[75] Perhaps most difficult of all, however, was the situation they found themselves in with Neureuter, after he had accepted the truth of their claims and paid the price by spending time in gaol. By that stage, at the latest, the prospect of admitting that everything rested on falsehood must have seemed insurmountably daunting.

Alongside the expectations of public and priests, the children faced pressure from the state authorities. In addition to two comprehensive medical examinations, they were interrogated fourteen times—and Margaretha Kunz more often than that—by a variety of officials, including two examining magistrates (Emil Kleber and Ernst Remelé), the magistrate Gatzen of Tholey, *Landrat* Rumschöttel of St Wendel, senior administrative and legal officials from Trier and Saarbrücken, and a detective from Berlin.[76] These interrogations were conducted in Marpingen, Tholey, St Wendel, and at a Protestant-run orphanage in Saarbrücken to which all three girls were removed (without the prior knowledge of their parents) following a guardianship court judgement of 6 November 1876.[77] The girls remained in the Prinz Wilhelm- und Mariannen-Institut for nearly five weeks, from 9 November to 12 December. They were not ill-treated there. Prince Edmund Radziwill, who took up the case on the parents' behalf, found Herr Riemer the warden 'friendly and kind', while his wife adopted a more-in-sorrow-than-anger position; but the girls were confined to the institution, separated from their parents, severely restricted in their visitors, and kept under close observation.[78] They were homesick, and concerned about what would happen to themselves and their parents. There was particularly severe pressure on Margaretha Kunz, who was kept apart from her two companions at night, and was often in tears.[79]

It is hardly surprising that their experience provoked anxiety. The apparitions claimed by the girls during a number of their interrogations, and by Margaretha

[74] LASB, E 107, 370.
[75] On the responses of the clergy, both credulous and sceptical, see below, Ch. 6.
[76] The figure of 14 is given by Neureuter in a much later report to Bishop Korum of Trier, written from Kesten am Mosel, 25 Oct. 1902: BAT, B III, 11, 14/4, 17. The evidence in LASB, E 107, 48–86, suggests the number of formal interrogations was slightly lower than this, but if informal questioning is included, the figure is almost certainly an underestimate, especially for Kunz. She claimed to have been questioned 28 times: BAT, B III, 11, 14/3, 63–4.
[77] LASB, E 107, 62; LHAK, 442/6442, 39–49; *MWOL*, 69–73; Radziwill, *Besuch*, 3, 10–16.
[78] Radziwill, *Besuch*, 3. A good idea of the regime in the institute can be gleaned from the summary of the children's statements while there, in LASB, E 107, 64–81.
[79] See the evidence of Frau Riemer and Helene Schmidt in *Prozeß*, 59–66, 73–7.

in Saarbrücken, suggest that the Virgin had become a form of talisman, whose presence was invoked against harm.[80] The central problem for the girls was that events had mushroomed and brought serious political and legal repercussions. Margaretha later expressed her incomprehension 'that the whole thing went so far', until 'it reached a stage where I could no longer go back'.[81] The chronology suggests that after local enthusiasm for the events reached a first high-point on 6 July the girls drew back out of anxiety, for they reported no further apparitions for some days. But they were no longer in control of the situation. The gravity of their position clearly affected all three, and their mutual loyalty suffered under the pressure, particularly the relationship between Kunz and Leist. Susanna Leist claimed after the first day not to have 'seen' for a period of weeks, although she continued to accompany her companions. In Saarbrücken she alternated between 'scornful' reactions to Margaretha's claims of further apparitions and warnings to her friend that 'you talk too much, you'll betray everything'. Kunz retorted: 'I know what I can say—I'm cleverer than you.'[82] Like their counterparts in Mettenbuch, the Marpingen children were driven by the pressure of events to squabble among themselves.[83] What followed was a cycle of confessions and retracted confessions, as the girls were torn between their parents and those who questioned them (or from whom they sought friendship) in Saarbrücken. Margaretha suffered particularly. Singled out by all who questioned her as the ringleader, she had plainly reached an emotional condition in which she was highly receptive to those whose real or affected kindness seemed to offer a way out of her troubles. Her confidants included Frau Riemer and an older girl in the Saarbrücken institution, Lina Schmidt; they also included the detective from Berlin who was present at most of the interrogations, and on whom Margaretha appears to have developed a desperate kind of dependence. He spoke more often to her than to the other two, her reactions alternating between petulance and the desire to unburden herself. Frau Riemer recalled asking Margaretha if she liked him, and receiving the answer: 'Like *him*? This whole mess (*Sauerei*) is his fault. It wouldn't have happened if he'd stayed in Berlin.' Yet she became sad when he went away, and seemed almost to pine for him.[84] The detective offered his own self-satisfied newspaper account of his success with the 8-year-old girl: 'Gretchen, you can tell tales to the stupid peasants, but to me, dear Grete, you will tell the truth. Come here and sit on my lap and then tell me the whole truth.' And this, it seems, she eventually did—'tearfully'.[85]

---

[80] On these apparitions, see BAT, B III, 11, 14/3, 24–6.

[81] BAT, B III, 11, 14/3, 63–4.

[82] Conversation in the presence of Herr and Frau Riemer and an older girl, Helene Schmidt: LASB, E 107, 76–7.

[83] On Mettenbuch, see Franz-Xaver Kraus's account of conflicts between himself, his brothers and sisters, and Mathilde Sack, in BZAR, F 115, Fasc. V.

[84] *Prozeß*, 59–60.

[85] *SMZ*, 20 Dec. 1876, citing the *Berliner Tageblatt*, in which it was later established that it was Meerscheidt-Hüllessem himself who recounted his experiences in Marpingen under the by-line 'from a reliable correspondent'.

There was also emotional pressure from the other direction, especially—once again—on Margaretha Kunz. On 26 November, her mother and Frau Hubertus went to Saarbrücken, but were refused permission to visit their daughters. Frau Kunz was given the opportunity to speak to Margaretha when the girl appeared at a window, however, and two witnesses report her saying: 'When you are in court, say what you've said before.' It was a message that she found other ways of impressing on her daughter. When Emma Walter, another inmate of the orphanage, followed Frau Kunz into Saarbrücken to return an umbrella the visitor had left behind, Margaretha's mother whispered that she should tell Gretchen to stick to her story. Two days later a 'small man from Marpingen', probably Margaretha's legal guardian, Stephan Kunz, also visited the institution and delivered the same message from the courtyard. After Margaretha's departure, Emma Walter found a letter under her mattress, addressed 'Dear Gretchen' and repeating the earlier admonition.[86] In these circumstances, the homesickness felt by the girls for Marpingen and their families must have been offset by fear of what awaited them there if they went through with their retractions.

The pressures that faced them at home are illustrated by an incident that occurred at the end of November, shortly after the visit of Frau Kunz and the conversation at the window. The children had then been in Saarbrücken for over two weeks, and Margaretha Kunz had already embarked on a cascade of statements in which she pointed the finger at a succession of young women from Marpingen and neighbouring villages (as well as the schoolteacher André) as prime movers in the initial stages of the apparitions. One of these statements concerned an 11- or 12-year-old girl who lived in a 'small house' in the Eulenwald district of Marpingen (later identified, when it hardly mattered, as the house of the cobbler Michel Puhl).[87] The Riemers were sufficiently impressed by this story, which seemed to contain the suggestion that the girl in question had actually acted the part of the 'woman in white', that they had Margaretha repeat it to one of the examining magistrates and to a young trainee legal official (*Referendar*), Dr Jakob Strauß. The latter was a Catholic who had grown up near Marpingen, and later became well respected among the local clergy as a generous, charitable man. In the autumn of 1876 Strauß was asked by his superiors, as a Catholic, to evaluate Margaretha Kunz and her claims. He tried to win her trust, taking her to his parents' home in Schiffweiler (his mother was a firm believer in the apparitions). It was in the garden of his parents' house that Strauß first formed a highly negative judgement on the 8-year-old, who appeared willing either to agree or disagree that there was a 'Virgin in the clouds' when offered money.[88]

[86] See the evidence of Frau Riemer and Emma Walter, *Prozeß*, 65–8, 72–3; and LASB, E 107, 79 .

[87] LASB, E 107, 64–70. Margaretha also referred at different times to another girl of the same age living near to them, who had 'schooled' the three girls, and to a 15- or 16-year-old from Bliesen, who wore pigtails and lived near the house where Margaretha's sister had been a servant. This may have been the daughter of the tradeswoman Margaretha Wagner. See LASB, E 107, 75–6.

[88] BAT, B III, 11, 14/5, 26: Rector Peter Nikolay of Trier to Karl Kammer, 12 Jan. 1957. Nikolay (who spoke of Strauß's generous character) was recalling a story he had heard from the legal official

On 29 November he and the girl travelled from Saarbrücken to Marpingen, where Margaretha was to tell her mother the truth and they would look for the 'small house'. When they arrived at the Kunz home, Strauß first spoke alone to Frau Kunz and to one of Margaretha's elder sisters and explained the situation. Both indignantly denied that Gretchen could have lied to them. When Margaretha herself was called into the room she 'became extremely agitated and was silent'; but she nodded when Strauß asked if her earlier accounts had been untruthful. Frau Kunz then reacted 'with violent grief and anger', sobbed convulsively, and told Gretchen: 'You are no child of mine if you lied.' At which her daughter, herself tearful, declared that the retraction was a lie, and the original story true. When Dr Strauß asked about the little house, Gretchen told him 'with a kind of impertinent aplomb' that there was no point in looking for it, as she had invented the whole thing.[89] Strauß later declared that the children 'lied with an impudence and impertinence . . . such as I have never found in a criminal'.[90] His violent reaction no doubt expressed the sense of hurt and embarrassment felt by a young Catholic official who had pinned his hopes on a policy of kindness. The magistrate Gatzen of Tholey was less harsh in his judgement. The incident between Margaretha and Dr Strauß resulted, he believed, either from the 'pressure of the parents on the children or the children's fear of being punished.'[91]

The events of 29 November provided a foretaste of what was to happen when all three girls were permanently returned to Marpingen two weeks later. None of their confessions survived the return. All three were interrogated further by the examining magistrates Ernst Remelé and Emil Kleber, and on one occasion Susanna Leist broke down and claimed that Kunz had invented the whole thing. Interviewed together with her parents in June 1877, however, Leist once again retracted; so did Kunz and Hubertus, interviewed later in the presence of their mothers.[92] Illness then took some of the pressure off the visionaries: the girls succumbed to the epidemic of scarlet fever that swept through Marpingen, and Margaretha Kunz also suffered from a contusion of the foot, stomach pains, and a high temperature that may have been a residue of her bout of scarlet fever. On 7 August she was considered sufficiently ill by the parish priest to receive the last sacraments at home. But there was considerable doubt about the genuineness of her illness, and the symptoms of early August may have been consciously or unconsciously triggered by anxiety over renewed interrogation. For on 9 August the authorities renewed their offensive, with the visitation of Marpingen by state

---

in the early years of the century. Of course, the form taken by Strauß's well-meaning but irregular 'test' of Margaretha Kunz was likely to create uncertainty in the mind of the child over how to respond.

[89] LASB, E 107, 68–71; *Prozeß*, 77–80.
[90] *Prozeß*, 82.
[91] LASB, E 107, 297.
[92] Kleber's notes give the date of the interview with Leist and her parents as 2 June 1877, the interview with Kunz, Hubertus, and their parents as 15 June: LASB, E 107, 82–3. The trial transcript (*Prozeß*, 36) has Kleber referring to July, probably a stenographic error.

prosecutor Masson of Saarbrücken.[93] This proved as unproductive as previous efforts to break the will of the girls when they were surrounded by their families. The prime target of the visit, Margaretha Kunz, was in bed when the state prosecutor arrived at her house; when he pulled aside the curtains to her bed she turned her back on him and laughed. This was to be the last effort to extract confessions from the girls during the period, up to September 1877, when they were still claiming apparitions. There were two later attempts, however. In November 1877, Margaretha Kunz was confronted with Lina Schmidt, her former companion in the orphanage, but denied all knowledge of the confessions she had made.[94] On 14 February 1878, all three girls were interrogated for a last time by Emil Kleber, and maintained the truth of their original statements.[95]

Villagers and the Apparitions

When Margaretha Kunz said much later that things reached a stage where she 'could no longer go back', it is clear she was not referring only to the pressures the children faced from their parents. They were also trapped by larger village expectations. The events of 3 July struck a powerful chord in Marpingen, and within two days the crowd at the site had grown to over a hundred. As initial scepticism melted away, the villagers committed themselves to the apparitions in numerous ways. They maintained vigils at the site, placed flowers and a cross there, erected crude wire fencing around the site, and stewarded 'the place' when the crush of pilgrims threatened to get out of control. A cult of the 'German Lourdes' developed, bringing income to the village but also the unwanted attentions of a suspicious state. It is not hard to see why the three girls should have hesitated to admit that it was all based on a lie.

How did support for the apparitions spread? In a village the size of Marpingen, and one which had grown on both sides of a fairly steep valley, not all the inhabitants learned simultaneously of what had happened. Nor, when they had heard the news, did all automatically accept the truth of it and rush *en masse* to the site. Both the timing and the pattern of the way in which support for the apparitions grew deserve attention. All the evidence suggests that in the first two days it remained a minor affair.[96] On the first evening, knowledge of what had happened that afternoon seems to have remained fairly localized, although it was already the object of intense interest among the women and children who lived near the Leist and Hubertus houses, which were very close to each other. On the following day this interest transferred itself to the apparition site, but the numbers of those involved remained small and the events were still a matter of concern

[93] On this visitation, see LASB, E 107, 29, 92–4.
[94] LASB, E 107, 84.
[95] Ibid. 85–6.
[96] See e.g. the account given by the linen-weaver Schu, who was haymaking in a meadow close to the apparition site throughout the days of 3–6 July: LASB, E 107, 154.

only to the families and their immediate neighbours in the upper village, closest to the Härtelwald. Of the little group that gathered on 4 July, the twenty children included siblings of the three girls, and four of the six adults—five of them women—were related to the visionaries. Three of them (Anna and Jakob Blies, and the widowed Maria Blies) were related to Susanna Leist; Eva Langendörfer was related to Hubertus.[97] The other two women present, Katharina Schnur and Elisabeth Schnur, were neighbours in the upper village. While curiosity and a pious disposition doubtless encouraged those present to visit the apparition site, it is likely that they also had a watching brief on behalf of the Hubertus, Kunz, and Leist family interest.

The crucial change came on the following two days. On the afternoon of 5 July the group at the site remained small, but its composition was now significantly different. The girls' families were now directly represented for the first time through the presence of Frau Kunz and Katharina Hubertus's parents.[98] This lent encouragement to the children: it was also a declaration of serious family intent, and likely to be interpreted as such by the wider audience. In addition to Hubertus, there were other adult males at the site on 5 July. They included the publican Peter Schnur and the schoolteacher and village sexton Nikolaus Bungert, who had a meadow—one of the largest in the village—near the Härtelwald. In the evening, when the number present had risen to about a hundred, the men also included Nikolaus Recktenwald, who was to play a crucial role in events. Recktenwald was a 38-year-old miner who had not worked since September of the previous year because of rheumatism aggravated by the campaigns of 1866 and 1870–1 in which he had fought. A close neighbour of the young seers, he was one of the first to hear about the apparitions when his wife told him on the evening of 3 July. Recktenwald had been at the site on the afternoon of the 5th, and was fetched back there in the evening after the children reported that the Virgin answered 'Yes' to the question 'Should the sick be brought here?' At Recktenwald's request the children guided his hand to the Virgin's foot; he touched it, and was told by the children the two prayers he should say every day for eight days. Recktenwald claimed that he then felt a powerful force run through his body, a feeling like 'ice-cold water'; and with this he felt himself cured.[99]

Accounts of the apparitions agree that Recktenwald's alleged cure had a decisive impact on village opinion. As the news made its way round Marpingen it intensified interest in events at the Härtelwald and dispelled the initial scepticism of many who had been inclined to discount the claims of three 8-year-old girls. One commentator likened the population of Marpingen on the morning of 6 July to a 'hive of bees about to swarm'.[100] The crowd that gathered at the site that day

[97] Details on those present on 4 July in LASB, E 107, 139–40; *EM*, 13–17; Thoemes, *Die Erscheinungen*, 18.
[98] LASB, E 107, 142.
[99] LASB, E 107, 264–71; *EM*, 15–22; *MWOL*, 9–11; Thoemes, *Die Erscheinungen*, 22–6.
[100] *MMGE*, 31.

was not disappointed, for they witnessed an even more dramatic sequence of events. The evening saw two further cures reported. One was of the 7-year-old Magdalena Kirsch, bedridden for six months with consumption, who had refused solids for several weeks.[101] The second concerned the 4-year-old Theodor Klos, who had complained for sixteen months of severe pains in the back and chest. He was partly deformed and had been diagnosed by a doctor as suffering from a chipped vertebra.[102] Both children claimed an instant release from pain after touching the Virgin's foot. The young Klos also believed he had seen her, but this claim was overshadowed by events that were interpreted as an even clearer sign that the story told by the three girls deserved credence. On the same evening, following the experience of the two sick children, the 17-year-old Anna Hahn and four men in their forties—Jakob Klos, Jakob Leist, Nikolaus Ames, and Nikolaus Leist—became the first adults to claim they had seen the apparition.[103] Anna Hahn lost consciousness during her apparition; the four men seemed overcome with awe, but described the Virgin bathed in a light that 'shone like the midday sun' and crowned by a diadem set with stones that 'twinkled like stars', holding the Christ-child on one arm. The cures of the two children, following Recktenwald's experience the previous day, had already lowered the threshold at which disbelief was suspended. The descriptions of the men now worked powerfully on those present, who prayed fervently until midnight. The following morning a cross was erected at the apparition site, with a sign that read 'Here is the place'.[104]

There is no doubt about the rising emotional temperature on 5 and 6 July, but it would be a mistake to see village reactions as an undifferentiated mass enthusiasm. The point about the events of those two days was that the claims of the three girls had now received the sanction of adults, and particularly of men who were taken seriously. Hubertus, Schnur, and Bungert lent the girls' stories a degree of legitimacy simply through their presence—although Bungert was never a keen enthusiast.[105] More important was the testimony of Recktenwald and the adult visionaries, for these were men of good local repute. Recktenwald was the respected veteran of two military campaigns. Nikolaus Leist's claim to have seen the Virgin was reinforced by the fact that he was generally known from an earlier experience, in which he had fallen under a cart but survived unhurt because 'someone lifted the cart in a miraculous way' as the wheels ran over him.[106] In other words, while the claims of the three original seers ran potentially counter to normal relations of authority in the village, they became acceptable when they seemed to be confirmed by adult males with good village reputations. At that

[101] Cramer, *Die Erscheinungen*, 36–41; *MWOL*, 16–18; *Prozeß*, 114–18.
[102] *MWOL*, 19–21; *MMGE*, 32; Thoemes, *Die Erscheinungen*, 34–5.
[103] *EM*, 31–6; *MMGE*, 32–4; Thoemes, *Die Erscheinungen*, 36–40; *MWOL*, 21–3; *MG*, 20–2.
[104] *MMGE*, 33–4.
[105] On Bungert, see LASB, E 107, 141.
[106] *MG*, 21–2.

point the miraculous experience described by three 'simple country girls' could safely be celebrated.

The importance of these structures of response in the village is underlined from a different perspective if we look at how support for the apparitions spread into the village along the lines of family, neighbourhood, and kinship networks. The leading actors on those two days were still members of family and neighbourhood clans from the upper village. Nikolaus Leist, one of the four adult male visionaries, was Susanna Leist's uncle on her father's side and the uncle of Katharina Hubertus on her mother's side.[107] Recktenwald and Schnur were next-door neighbours who lived near to the homes of the Leist and Hubertus girls, and to the Blies family from which Frau Leist came.[108] But these were also men with wider connections. As a member of the Leist family was to put it many years later, 'the village notables (Dorfobrigkeit) now began to concern themselves with the affair'.[109] Nikolaus Recktenwald, in so many ways a key figure, was related through his wife Margaretha to the master carpenter Jakob Schario.[110] Schario was a figure of some standing in the village, despite his youth (he was just 23 in 1876). When Prince Edmund Radziwill came to Marpingen in November 1876 and took up the case for returning the three girls from Saarbrücken, Schario was one of the two 'well-respected' inhabitants Radziwill summoned to tell him the background to the affair, and in the spring of 1877 he succeeded Peter Fuchs as parish bookkeeper.[111] He also became one of the 'most zealous advocates' of the apparitions. Schario was suspected by the authorities—wrongly, but plausibly—to be the person who had constructed the cross erected at the apparition site; he was certainly involved in plans for the construction of a chapel in the Härtelwald, and accommodated many prominent pilgrims at his home.[112] Schario also had two other sisters who played a part in advancing the cause of the apparitions. One of them, Barbara Backes, was a noted 'enthusiast'; the other, Elisabeth Dörr, was a neighbour of the Kunz family who accompanied Margaretha to the apparition site and put questions to the Virgin through the child.[113]

Recktenwald's neighbour Peter Schnur—who encouraged both Recktenwald himself and the mother of the sick child, Magdalena Kirsch, to seek a cure at the site—was also a prominent figure in Marpingen. A publican and a future Ortsvorsteher (the only government-appointed official in the village) he had influence that stretched beyond the upper village. It was a testimony to his standing that both the parish priest Neureuter and Mayor Woytt of St Wendel should have

[107] LASB, E 107, 238.
[108] Ibid. 274.
[109] BAT, B III, 11, 14/5: Report of Sister Elisa Haben of Bad Münster am Stein, 17 Nov. 1946. She was the daughter of Susanna Leist's older sister Margaretha, recounting what she had heard from her mother.
[110] LASB, E 107, 274. Margaretha Recktenwald was Schario's older sister.
[111] Radziwill, Besuch, 5–6, 14.
[112] LASB, E 107, 195–7. On the accommodation of pilgrims, see BAT, B III, 11, 14/4, 88.
[113] BAT, B III, 11, 14/3, 13–14; LASB, E 107, 7, 138–9; Prozeß, 168–70.

singled him out for mention. Years later, Neureuter observed that during the *Kulturkampf* Schnur 'opposed me in the most ungrateful and callous manner'.[114] His harsh judgement receives a kind of back-handed confirmation in the fact that Woytt considered Schnur the 'most suitable personality' in the village for the post of *Ortsvorsteher*.[115] The fact that this awkward customer threw his weight so strongly behind the apparitions (he played 'a dubious role in the whole business' according to one examining magistrate) was undoubtedly important in spreading support throughout the village.[116]

Schario and Schnur were not the only village notables who lent support to the affair. The man whom Schario succeeded as parish bookkeeper, the former *Ortsvorsteher* Fuchs, also played an important part, especially in taking down statements about apparitions and cures.[117] Another active notable was the miller Johann Thomé. He was the other man, along with Jakob Schario, called to give a progress report to the newly arrived Prince Radziwill.[118] Woytt, whose view of the village population was generally uncomplimentary, called him 'the most sly and treacherous person in Marpingen and a tireless fighter for the swindle there'.[119] Thomé was certainly involved in the selling of 'miraculous water' and in plans to construct a chapel in the Härtelwald.[120] Mention should be made, finally, of Stephan Kunz, a village notable who was also Margaretha's legal guardian (*Vormund*). It was he who delivered the message in Saarbrücken that she should stick to her story, and he is also known to have visited the Härtelwald, although his role in the affair seems otherwise to have been slight.[121] His actions may well have been governed by the dictates of family honour.

The cast of those who advanced the cause of the apparitions in Marpingen therefore included some of the most prominent men in the village. Of those mentioned above, four (Peter Fuchs, Stephan Kunz, Peter Schnur, and Johann Thomé) were members of the parish council in 1870.[122] Two of them (Kunz and Thomé) were also among the five *Wahlmänner*, or electors, who represented Marpingen under the indirect system of voting at the Prussian parliamentary elections held in 1876.[123] The group included a former and a future *Ortsvorsteher*,

---

[114] BAT, 70/3676a, 158–9: Neureuter to GV Trier, 30 Oct. 1893.

[115] LASB, E 107, 143.

[116] The examining magistrate was Emil Kleber, cited LASB, E 107, 143. On Schnur's activities, see ibid. 129, 142–4, 265; *Prozeß*, 103–4.

[117] See LASB, E 107, 22–3, 88, 111, 145, 431.

[118] Radziwill, *Besuch*, 5–6, 14.

[119] LASB, E 107, 197.

[120] For a summary of the evidence collected by the authorities against Thomé, see LASB, E 107, 21–3, 196–7, 227.

[121] LASB, E 107, 79, 431–2.

[122] BAT, 70/3676, 90, gives a list of parish council members voting on a routine matter referred to them by the parochial parish council. These men made up 4 of the 9 members at the time, not including Mayor Arimond, Woytt's predecessor. A fifth member—the *Ortsvorsteher* at the time when the apparitions began, Jakob Geßner—was undoubtedly a sympathizer, but found himself in a very exposed position and tried for prudential reasons to avoid outright identification with the affair.

[123] The full list of the five *Wahlmänner* is given in *NBZ*, 24 Oct. 1876.

THE VISIONARIES AND THEIR WORLD

and consecutive church bookkeepers. This support must be kept in perspective. In the first place, the part played by these men was likely to exercise the minds of the investigating authorities simply because they were prominent village figures, personally known (and mostly disliked) by the local mayor. Some of them were bound to attract attention because of their occupations, most obviously in the case of the publican Peter Schnur. There is thus an inbuilt tendency for the available sources to exaggerate their role in events. It is also true that heavy-handed state intervention drew into the affair some prominent village men who apparently played no part in the initial events, but were reacting to the secondary issue of repression. This was the position of Johann Thomé, and in a slightly different sense of Stephan Kunz.[124] It should be remembered, finally, that there were village notables whose names simply never appear in the thousands of pages of statements taken by the investigating authorities, men who clearly lent the apparitions no active support. All of this said, it is nevertheless striking how the visionaries received legitimation at an early stage through the presence at the apparition site or the active encouragement of prominent village figures. The seers' parents belonged to the moderately substantial class of *Kuhbauer* (albeit somewhat declassed in the case of Kunz), and their supporters included men of substance: landed peasants, craftsmen, a miller, and a publican. The 'German Lourdes' was never a cult of the village underclass.

There is, however, another obvious strand that runs through the early stages of the apparitions. That is the part played by the members of miners' families. There were, of course, no working miners in Marpingen during the crucial period from Monday 3 July to Friday 7 July, but there were temporarily unemployed or invalid miners, as well as miners' wives and children. Together they account for an impressive number of the incidents that helped to turn the apparitions from a neighbourhood event into a village drama. Gretchen Kunz herself had brothers in the pit. The first 'miraculous cure' was claimed by Nikolaus Recktenwald, a miner kept away from work by rheumatism; the second and third were professed by the miners' children Magdalena Kirsch and Theodor Klos. Two of the four men who claimed to have seen an apparition of the Virgin on the evening of 6 July, the 41-year-old Jakob Leist and the 48-year-old Jakob Klos, were ex-miners who had retired through ill health. A 'fifth man' was involved in that episode, but did not talk about his own alleged apparition until months later. He was the 23-year-old Anton Hahn, another miner, who had been away from work with an injured foot.[125]

By the time Marpingen's working miners returned on the evening of Saturday 8 July, the critical events had already occurred and the apparitions were regarded

---

[124] The bulk of the evidence on Thomé's involvement concerned his hostility to the actions of Mayor Woytt and the Prussian army, and his involvement in the campaigns to return the children to their parents and lift the financial burden imposed on the village. The same is true of Stephan Kunz, although he was less active than Thomé.

[125] LASB, E 107, 241, 251.

as an established fact. I have found no indication at all of miners who expressed scepticism or discontent with what had happened in their absence, and the strong likelihood is that such a reaction would have been uncovered by the extensive investigations if it had been there to uncover. The fathers of Magdalena Kirsch and Theodor Klos joyfully accepted the apparently miraculous cures of their children and allowed accounts of what had happened to be published. Miners also supported the apparitions in other ways. The wire that villagers placed around the apparition site was brought from the Cetto pit.[126] A significant number of miners were present when the Prussian army intervened in Marpingen on 13 July, and miners later provided many of the witnesses at the trials arising out of the incident. The presence of these working miners in Marpingen on a Thursday suggests that some at least were absenting themselves from work, as the authorities anxiously surmised.[127] There were also many miners among those fined for visiting what became the no-go area of the woods, or providing illegal bed-and-breakfast for pilgrims. Even the fragmentary collection of summonses that survives includes the names of the miners Matthias Barbian, Stephan Fuchs, Michael Kunz, Stephan Lambert, Johann Leist, Nikolaus Leist, Nikolaus Lerman, Michael Meisberger, Jakob Scheib, and Peter Joseph Thomé.[128]

The fact that many of these summonses were served on miners' wives is a reminder that it was they who were permanently in Marpingen throughout the apparitions. In many ways they remained—as they had been at the outset—the more active partners in events, and several miners' wives were themselves summonsed, including Elisabeth Fuchs, Katharina Fuchs, Elisabeth Leist, Katharina Müller, and Margaretha Teigel.[129] Elisabeth Schnur, the mother of the 'good child' Jakob whose dubiously prophesied death became a central episode of the apparitions, was the wife of the miner Peter Schnur.[130] Miners' wives were not the only women belonging to mining families who were involved in the movement surrounding the apparitions. So, too, were the mothers (and mothers-in-law) of active miners—women such as Frau Kunz, Margaretha's mother. The same applies to miners' sisters, as the case of another widowed Frau Kunz demonstrates. Frau Anna Kunz ran the household of her brother, the miner Johann Leist, and was summonsed in December 1877 for the illegal accommodation of pilgrims.[131]

[126] LASB, E 107, 132.
[127] On the events of 13 July and the trial of Matthias Scheeben that followed from them, see BAT, B III, 11, 14/3, 27; *KVZ*, 27 and 28 May 1877. See also below, Ch. 7, pp. 232–5.
[128] BAT, B III, 11, 14/4, 97, 113, 115–16, 122–5, 130, 151, 158, 170, 172, 178, 180–1. There must have been other miners among those summonsed for whom we have no details on occupation. These were summonses given to Neureuter, which he kept and in a few cases annotated. They clearly represent only a proportion of the total number issued. Johannes Leist on one occasion told the priest of '30 people' who had been summonsed, but could remember only 13 names; Neureuter referred to other summonses that were torn up.
[129] BAT, B III, 11, 14/4, 98, 107, 162, 167–8, 183.
[130] LASB, E 107, 112.
[131] BAT, B III, 11, 14/4, 122–3.

These examples indicate the central part played by women in the village response to the three visionaries. If the public presence of male notables in the Härtelwald was important in securing approval for the apparitions, women were crucially involved in numerous ways. Women were the first to visit the site, and continued to show their support by visiting the Härtelwald and placing flowers at the spot.[132] While the woods were open, the gatherings of women which had formerly taken place around the Marienbrunnen near the church transferred themselves to the newly miraculous spot on the other side of the village.[133] It was generally women who took sick children to the site in the hope of a cure, women who had a central role in the 'domestic' task of accommodating visitors to the village. Indeed, it may be in less publicly visible areas that women contributed most of all to the continuing village enthusiasm for the apparitions. It was, above all, informal networks of women, gathered together in their homes, in the streets, and in the fields, through which the latest news of the apparitions was spread. We can identify some of these networks of sociability, such as the one that linked Jakob Schario's sisters Barbara Backes, Elisabeth Dörr, and Margaretha Recktenwald both to the upper village neighbours of the Kunz, Leist, and Hubertus families, and to other zealous supporters of the apparitions like Angela Kles.[134] Mostly, however, their existence can be read only between the lines in the hundreds of statements that police and examining magistrates took in Marpingen during 1876–7, as a ubiquitous web of contacts.[135]

Given the form taken by the sexual division of labour in Marpingen, these women's networks transcended the male occupational divisions of mining and agriculture. Male networks of sociability, by contrast, were more divided between the coalfield and the village. There is no evidence at all, however, that the male response to the apparitions was divided on occupational or socio-economic lines. Neither the parish priest nor any of the visiting clergy so much as hinted at this. It is perhaps even more telling that months of intensive questioning by hostile outsiders who were looking for divisions among the villagers produced no indication that the events were disproportionately taken up (or cold-shouldered) by one particular group—whether miners, the peasantry, or one particular group of them, or the village underclass. What positive evidence there is suggests the contrary. If miners fetched wire to place around the apparition site, peasants helped to steward it and one of the village joiners built the cross that was erected there.[136] The lower class of Marpingen were also among the supporters of the apparitions. Those summonsed for transgressions of one sort or another, mainly for entering the woods or accommodating pilgrims illegally, included peasants, miners, craftsmen, day labourers, a linen-weaver, and the son of a dealer in

[132] On women and flowers, LASB, E 107, 134.
[133] BAT, B III, 11, 14/3, 55.
[134] On Angela Kles, see LASB, E 107, 275–8.
[135] A fragment of an overheard conversation can be found in BAT, B III, 11, 14/4, 115.
[136] The cross was built by the joiner Becker: *Prozeß*, 105.

butter.[137] Support for the apparitions apparently cut across class lines, just as it transcended the endemic factionalism of the village.

There are many explanations for this impressive solidarity. Most obviously, villagers believed in the apparitions. The Marianization of popular piety had been at work in Marpingen for a generation, apparitions had recently occurred nearby, and so many aspects of what was reported in July 1876 matched local expectations of such an event. It happened at the right time: Lourdes was fresh in the mind because of the ceremony there on 3 July, and the coincidence of dates was readily seen as an omen. It also happened in the right place, at the edge of the village, on that border with which the miraculous and supernatural was strongly associated where the man-made abutted on to the natural, in this case the border between meadows and woods.[138] (The various 'women in white' who had been seen in the area also roamed this borderland.) Finally, the narrative presented by the children, suitably 'improved' by adults close to them, was instantly recognizable and reassuring. This seemed to be the longed-for sign at a time of tribulation. That there were almost immediately adult visionaries, to confirm what the three girls had said, suggests the emotionally heightened mood of the village in early July 1876; so does the evident rapture displayed by villagers (especially women) at the apparition site. Like a revolutionary situation, the sudden, dramatic, and extraordinary break with the everyday seemed to intensify feelings. In Marpingen it prompted renewed devotions, as belief in the apparitions was fed by continuing reports of miraculous cures and prophecies. The popular convictions that surfaced with the apparitions—animistic faith in the curative powers of the special water, the belief that the Virgin caused ill fate to befall her detractors (or their livestock)—were not always welcome to the parish priest.[139] One sign of the heightened emotional temper in Marpingen can be seen in the claims made by dozens of other village children—the *Konkurrenzkinder*, or 'rival children'—that they too had seen the Virgin and hosts of angels, climbed ladders to heaven, and met St Peter at the gates, or released suffering souls from purgatory. The first of these children was Theodor Klos, cured on 5 July; the largest number was reported in July and August of 1877, as the impending end of the original apparitions in early September issued in a final spasm of popular piety in the village.[140]

Reasons for the positive local response to the apparitions should be sought in the profane as well as the sacred (they are often difficult to separate cleanly). Many of the summonses that rained down on the village were, after all, the result

[137] See BAT, B III, 11, 14/4, 71–4, 80–6, 88–177.
[138] See Weber, 'Religion and Superstition', 421.
[139] See below, Ch. 5, on the rumours that circulated among pilgrims to Marpingen, and Ch. 6 on the dilemmas faced by the clergy.
[140] A list of the 'rival children' can be found in BAT, B III, 11, 14/4, 14, 67. On their claims, see LASB, E 107, 126–8; *Prozeß*, 193–6.

of commercial activities associated with the apparitions: providing accommodation for pilgrims, selling earth from the apparition site or water from
the 'miraculous' spring. One close observer, the trainee schoolteacher Metzen,
suggested that the men in the village began to believe in the apparitions only
when the flood of visitors persuaded them of the advantages.[141] This was a line
of argument consistently followed by the state authorities, and the commercial
opportunities opened up locally by events were obviously important. How
important they were will be considered in detail in the following chapter.

The apparitions also promised benefits of a less tangible kind to Marpingen,
for they put an unremarkable village on the map and made it, for a short time, a
centre of attention. 'How things can change overnight', wrote Andreas Schneider
from Trier to his brother, the parish priest in Alsweiler: 'who would ever have
imagined that one day Marpingen would get itself talked about?'[142] In the aftermath of the apparitions, writers of newspaper articles and pamphlets were certainly not stinting in the accolades they heaped on the village. It became the
'Rhenish Lourdes', the 'German Lourdes', even 'the Bethlehem of Germany'.[143]
'It is an undeniable fact that the whole world is talking about Marpingen,' observed
one writer; 'Marpingen has become the centre of events which have shaken the
world,' wrote another.[144] Even those used to being big fish in their own small pool
could hardly have remained unaffected by such flattering attention. In normal
times, however, Marpingen was overshadowed even by its neighbours, and had
particular reason to cherish the events that turned this situation upside down. In
administrative terms, the village had long been treated in a stepmotherly fashion.
Under successive regimes in the eighteenth and nineteenth centuries it had been
subject to district or cantonal regimes in Tholey or St Wendel, and to mayoral
rule from Guidesweiler, Urexweiler, Bliesen, and Alsweiler.[145] This, despite the
fact that Alsweiler, for example, was considerably smaller. In the past this had
fuelled long-standing and vigorous village rivalry, measured in the currency of
boundary disputes and periodic fisticuffs.[146] In celebrating the apparition of the
Virgin and its emergence as the German Lourdes, Marpingen could continue
the rivalry with Alsweiler and Urexweiler by other means.[147] The same applied
to relations between the village and Tholey. Just as Mettenbuch was overshadowed
by the eighth-century Benedictine foundation of Metten, so Marpingen had long

[141] LASB, E 107, 155.
[142] LASB, E 107, 355: Andreas Schneider to Father Konrad Schneider, 10 Sept. 1876.
[143] See *Germania*, 2 Dec. 1876, citing the *Deutsche Vereinscorrespondenz*; MG, 16; LASB, E 107, 349–
51, 484; K. Schorn, *Lebenserinnerungen. Ein Beitrag zur Geschichte des Rheinlands im neunzehnten
Jahrhundert*, 2 vols. (Bonn, 1898), ii. 260.
[144] *MWOL*, 4; *MMGE*, 13.
[145] Beck, *Beschreibung*, i. 66–73.
[146] See Bungert, *Heimatbuch*, 117, 139–40.
[147] There was corresponding scepticism from many in Alsweiler, including Margaretha Kunz's uncle,
the cartwright Jakob Fuchs, who questioned his niece closely 'without getting a sensible answer', and
concluded that there 'was nothing in it': LASB, E 107, 92. See also ibid. 200, on Fuchs and other
Alsweiler sceptics.

been dominated by its powerful tithe-lord.[148] In the final quarter of the nineteenth century, villagers remained heavily dependent on the merchants, tradesmen, moneylenders, cattle-dealers and notaries who were concentrated in Tholey. The apparitions helped to settle old scores here, as well; certainly the Marpingers flaunted them to the tradesmen of Tholey with a marked braggadocio, as if to indicate that they were no longer so poor and vulnerable. One incident contained darker undertones. Tholey had a significant number of Jewish traders, and a rumour went round Marpingen that the Blessed Virgin had instructed people 'not to shop any longer with the Jews'.[149]

Whatever combination of piety, avarice, and pride led villagers to accept and support the apparitions, Marpingen was to pay a high price for its presumption. It will already be clear that the Prussian state took a keen interest in the events of 1876–7. The full extent of its investigative and repressive zeal will be considered in Chapter 7. This too led to a closing of village ranks against outsiders. It is striking that the apparitions did not divide the village in any discernible way. As we have seen, the apparitions were not appropriated or used by any particular occupational group or class. As far as one can tell, they did not lead to rivalry between the upper village and other parts of Marpingen. Nor did opinion polarize along the lines of the old factional disputes that had plagued the village in the years before 1850, and were to do so again at the end of the century.[150] Village pride cemented support for the apparitions. The claims of the 'rival children' met, it is true, with a good deal of scepticism. One miner found two of these children in the graveyard during the summer of 1877, claiming that they had seen his recently buried four-week-old child, dressed in white and surrounded by angels. He told them curtly that the child had been buried in black, and chased them off.[151] But there were virtually no open sceptics when it came to the three original visionaries. The policeman Kinzer of Namborn observed that 'in the whole of Marpingen the only opponents of the Virgin Mary swindle known to me are the miller Scherer, Stephan Kunz, and Michel Thomé, the father of the publican'.[152] (The Stephan Kunz in question was a 72-year-old, and is not to be confused with Margaretha's guardian, Stephan Kunz IV.) The examining magistrate Emil Kleber was able to add just three more names. The peasant

[148] Even today Marpingen is 'somewhat marginalized' by Tholey and St Wendel: *Gemeinde Marpingen*, 23 (1984), 18. On Metten, closed down by the Bavarian state in 1803 but reopened in 1830, see *Handbuch der Historischen Stätten Deutschlands*, vii. *Bayern*, ed. K. Bosl (Stuttgart, 1961), 418–20. The 1868 apparition site of Eckwertsheide in Silesia was overshadowed by the Franciscan house of Annaberg: description in *DAZ*, 29 Aug. 1876.
[149] LHAK, 442/6442, 31–3: LR Rumschöttel St Wendel to RP Wolff Trier, 9 Oct. 1876; LASB, E 107, 125–6. Villagers were supposedly asked instead to shop at the Schwan store (with 'Schwanen-Fritz'). The question obviously arose whether the shopkeeper in question had set the rumour in motion, but the magistrate Gatzen of Tholey was convinced this was not the case. It is most likely that the story originated with resentful inhabitants of Marpingen.
[150] Derr, 'Pfarrei Marpingen', 48–9, 68–71.
[151] LASB, E 107, 127.
[152] LASB, E 107, 195.

Matthias Kunz (also unrelated to the visionary) had spoken out against the apparitions and forbidden members of his family to visit the apparition site; the day labourer Recktenwald 'scoffed at the whole affair' and later told the detective from Berlin that there was bound to be 'a clique of swindlers behind the whole thing'; and the trainee schoolteacher Metzen dismissed the apparitions as 'nonsense'.[153] The parish priest, finally, noted a conversation he had overheard between the peasant Huber and another male villager, in which one of them remarked: 'If I had the children in school, I would beat them half to death.' 'Otherwise,' recorded the priest in his notebook, 'everyone believes, except for the young trainee teacher [Metzen]. The schoolmasters of the district have mocked like Pharisees.'[154]

This makes a total of precisely eight identifiable sceptics in a village of 1,600. One of these (Recktenwald) may have been trying to ingratiate himself with the police; certainly by 1878 the former day labourer had become a *Polizeidiener*.[155] Another (Huber) was apparently 'converted' to the truth of the apparitions by 9 July.[156] Why were there apparently so few sceptics in Marpingen, whereas a schoolteacher who knew Mettenbuch well suggested that although there were 'many' in the village who believed in the apparitions, 'perhaps half joke about them'?[157] An important part of the answer is suggested by Huber's experience, for strong moral pressure was undoubtedly exerted on those who expressed misgivings. The trainee teacher could afford to be cold-shouldered by the village; he would soon be moving on. The same was not true of teachers who were established in the village, like Bungert and Fräulein André. The latter, who had been in Marpingen for ten years and taught the three seers, found herself in a particularly difficult position. Colleagues from neighbouring villages, Metzen, and her own successor all remarked how she fell silent when the subject was raised, and she told the investigating authorities plaintively that she had not tried to stop the three girls' activities 'because I did not believe it was my job, and I would have had little success alone against the entire population'.[158] On another occasion, taxed by the district school inspector with the question why she had not tried to convince the three girls of their 'vanity and delusion', André retorted that 'she could not oppose the whole village'.[159] Similar pressures must have operated on other potential sceptics. The miller Peter Scherer no doubt felt secure enough to stand out against village wisdom; certainly he was the most outspoken

[153] LASB, E 107, 154–5, 195.

[154] Undated entry in Neureuter's notebook: LASB, E 107, 426. Elsewhere in the Rhine Province, teachers took it upon themselves to report to the state authorities on what they regarded as clerical mischief. See e.g. the letter of the teacher Breidbach of Zell to the Governor of the Rhine Province, 31 July 1873: LHAK, 403/6695, 247–50.

[155] LASB, E 107, 155.

[156] LASB, E 107, 132, 143.

[157] SAL, 164/2, 1162: 'Besprechung mit Lehrer Mayr von Berg vom 6. Mai 1877'. See also ibid., 'Meldung des Gendarmen Dörfler am 6. Mai 1877'.

[158] LASB, E 107, 279–83.

[159] LASB, E 107, 104.

opponent of the apparitions, and delivered damning verdicts on the role of visiting priests.[160] Stephan Kunz and Michel Thomé seem to have become more circumspect as time went on.

In late November 1876 a Marpingen correspondent of the liberal *Saar- und-Mosel-Zeitung* observed: 'It is at least possible that even in the "Rhenish Lourdes" there were doubting Thomases, but why have they not dared to express their doubts openly to their bigoted fellow citizens?'[161] One reason why the moral pressure on sceptics grew stronger rather than weaker must be sought in the negative side of Marpingen's celebrity, in the notoriety that carried the visionaries off to Saarbrücken and brought gendarmes, soldiers, and a high-ranking Berlin detective into the village. In this respect, too, the day labourer Recktenwald and the miller Scherer were exceptions. Recktenwald joined the police and Scherer blamed the apparition supporters for exposing the village to the attention of police and army.[162] The great majority in the village reacted differently. A wall of silence went up against outsiders, and any private doubts were suppressed. Open scepticism now became a form of betrayal.

---

[160] LASB, E 107, 182, 200; *Prozeß*, 146.
[161] *SMZ*, 2 Dec. 1876. Early in November the detective from Berlin supposedly handed the village watchman a piece of paper headed 'to the loyal citizens of Marpingen', inviting those who rejected the apparitions to give their names. According to the story, not a single signature had been forthcoming after three days: *Germania*, 14 Nov. 1876; Radziwill, *Besuch*, 33.
[162] LASB, E 107, 200.

5

Pilgrims, Cures, and Commercialization

Pilgrims

The events in Marpingen remained a matter of local interest for only a few days. By the end of the first week pilgrims were starting to arrive from outside the village, and on Sunday 9 July the Härtelwald was completely full for the first time.[1] The second week saw the arrival of pilgrims in numbers exceeding those visiting Lourdes in 1876.[2] The parish priest recorded the following description in his notebook on 11 July:

Evening. Enormous enthusiasm. Even after 10 o'clock at night I heard four processions coming from Sotzweiler. They came the whole night from every direction, bringing their sick in carts. The Blessed Virgin is immeasurably generous. I have been reading this evening about Lourdes; it strikes me as feeble compared with the mighty current that here is breaking through all barriers. Processions despite May Laws and Culturkampf. At half-past eleven I could still hear the rolling of the wagons on which they were bringing the sick.[3]

The next day Marpingen was host to around 20,000 visitors, with up to 4,000 in the Härtelwald at any one time. The crush of pilgrims already threatened to exhaust supplies of food and drink in the village, and Neureuter observed that he would have to hear confessions 'day and night' to satisfy the demand.[4] There was general agreement that 12 July marked the beginning of what Father Schwaab of Urexweiler called the 'great rush'.[5] Carts and pilgrims on foot crowded the roads and tracks in all directions; Neureuter recorded that 'the carts even come down the Tholey mountain at night, a road that can hardly be travelled in the day'. A schoolteacher in Dörsdorf was unable to conduct his classes because of the noise made by passing pilgrims.[6] The stream of people was not to abate for fourteen months, although the numbers fluctuated over that period.

---

[1] *MMGE*, 34; LASB, E 107, 6 ff., 154. According to the linen-weaver Schu, who was haymaking in his nearby meadow in the first days after the apparitions began, only 'a few people' went to the site before 6 July.

[2] Lourdes, with its direct rail link and special trains, was drawing around 7,000 pilgrims a day in the spring of 1876. See 'Zwei Tage in Lourdes', 602–6.

[3] LASB, E 107, 424.

[4] Cramer, *Die Erscheinungen*, 16–19; *EM*, 53; LASB, E 107, 339.

[5] LASB, E 107, 339.

[6] Ibid. 418; *Prozeß*, 126.

At official pilgrimage sites, large crowds congregated on particular, firmly established days or times of the year. The pilgrimage to Marpingen followed a more complicated rhythm. Numbers were generally much greater (as one would expect) on Sundays and on dates with a particular importance in the church calendar. These included Easter and Christmas, when a candle-light vigil was held in the Härtelwald.[7] There were also predictably large gatherings for Marian festivals such as the Assumption, Mary's Nativity, the Immaculate Conception, the Visitation, Candlemas, and the Annunciation.[8] This paralleled the pilgrimage cycle at the other German apparition sites of Dittrichswalde and Mettenbuch.[9] The church calendar partly explains the vast increase in the number of visitors to Marpingen in the summer of 1877. There were two major Marian festivals in this period (the Visitation on 2 July, the Assumption on 15 August). Seasonal factors (weather, harvest) probably played a role as well.[10] But there were also important local reasons for the build-up. The annual parish festival in Marpingen (the *Kirmes*) took place at the end of August: the number of pilgrims increased then, just as it did in Mettenbuch during the period of local festivities known as the *Deggendorfer Gnadenzeit*.[11] Most important of all, 3 July 1877 was the first anniversary of the apparitions, and 3 September the date on which—according to the children—the Virgin would appear for the last time. The two months in between saw a 'colossal increase' in the volume of pilgrims.[12] In July the numbers taking holy communion in the parish church rose sharply. In early August weekday visitors were running at 600 a day, rising to at least twice that by the end of the month. The numbers increased dramatically on major occasions. On the morning of 13 August the gendarmes reported around 150 pilgrims in the village; by the afternoon of the following day, the eve of the Feast of the Assumption, there were 9,000.[13] It is a measure of the crowds that a quarter of all the money donated by pilgrims in the second half of the month was given on the one day of 15 August. The sum involved, 300 marks, was ten times the amount left annually in church offertory boxes in a normal year.[14] The parish festival on 19 August saw an estimated 7,000–8,000 people in the village during the day, with perhaps 4,000 remaining there through the evening.[15] These figures were exceeded in the predicted last days of the apparitions. As many as 30,000 visitors

[7] *Germania*, 3 Feb. 1877; *SPB*, 11 Feb. 1877; *SMZ*, 22 Feb. 1877; *MWOL*, 91.

[8] *MWOL*, 91.

[9] An estimated 13,000 were present in Dittrichswalde on the Feast of the Assumption, compared with a daily average of around 2,000. Mary's Nativity on 8 Sept. brought 50,000: 'Die Erscheinungen der unbefleckt Empfangenen', 59–61. On Mettenbuch, see Braunmüller, *Kurzer Bericht*, 19–21.

[10] Nolan and Nolan, *Christian Pilgrimage*, 54–61, on seasonal pilgrimage cycles.

[11] Braunmüller, *Kurzer Bericht*, 19–21.

[12] LASB, E 107, 483.

[13] Rebbert, *Marpingen und seine Gegner*, 116; LASB, E 107, 162.

[14] LASB, E 107, 224–5, has a detailed break-down of the money left, admittedly based on gendarmes' estimates. But see also the confirmation of the sums involved by church bookkeeper Jakob Schario: *Prozeß*, 161–2.

[15] LASB, E 107, 163.

went to Marpingen in the first three days of September: reports indicated that
the road from St Wendel was completely filled by pilgrims.[16] Thereafter the
numbers fell off markedly. From 100 to 150 a day immediately after 3 September,
the figure was down to a handful in December.[17] By March 1879, a gendarme
reported that the pilgrims were 'mainly just girls and women from the locality'.[18]

The way in which the crowds built up at Marpingen showed the same widening-
ripple effect that we find in other nineteenth-century apparitions. Dittrichswalde
provides a good example. The first apparitions were reported there on 27 June
1877. In the first week pilgrims came largely from the immediate vicinity; in the
second week they began to come from other parts of the Ermland; by the third
week large numbers of visitors were reported from West Prussia, Posen, and even
across the Russian border. There were now 2,000 pilgrims a day, and up to
10,000 on Sundays.[19] In Marpingen, too, news of the events 'spread like wildfire'
in the immediate locality before any word of it reached the press.[20] There were
obvious channels of communication, such as hawkers, tinkers, travelling
musicians, and other itinerants. From Monday 11 July news must have been
carried through the Saar coalfield by Marpingen miners returning from their
weekend at home. Word also spread via market towns like Tholey, which were
clearing-houses for news, and through figures like the Urexweiler blacksmith who
heard the story at an early stage from passers-by and relayed it.[21] Above all, news
was transmitted by those who had visited Marpingen themselves. As a result of
these various forms of dissemination, individuals and small knots of pilgrims
were joined by larger groups from Saarland localities which made their way in
processional form to the apparition site—the 'unified detachments' (geschlossenen
Trupps) that so alarmed the officials who observed them.[22] The speed with which
information and rumour spread can be seen in the case of Nikolaus Schorn, a
tailor from Haustadt who visited Marpingen on the Saturday evening of 5 August
and claimed to have been cured of his lameness. As he and his wife returned
home that evening in their borrowed cart, they were delayed in Sotzweiler by a
'great throng of curious people', and when they reached Haustadt a large crowd
was gathered in front of their house from the 'whole surrounding area'.[23]

By the beginning of August Marpingen had long been attracting pilgrims from
outside the Saarland, the spread of its celebrity no doubt accelerated by the
publicity that followed military intervention on 13 July. Six days after that the
Saar- und Mosel-Zeitung was already referring to visitors from Cologne, Koblenz,

---

[16] LASB, E 107, 169, 483; MG, 42.
[17] LASB, E 107, 154, 167.
[18] Prozeß, 162.
[19] 'Die Erscheinungen der unbefleckt Empfangenen', 59–61.
[20] SMZ, 19 July 1876. See also Berg, Marpingen, 8.
[21] LASB, E 107, 339.
[22] LASB, Best. LRA Saarbrücken, 1, 739: Bekanntmachung LR Rumschöttel, St Wendel, 13 Aug.
1876.
[23] EM, 69.

and Lorraine, and by 30 July Neureuter had received a letter from a priest in Moravia who had read about Marpingen in the *Schlesische Volkszeitung*.[24] The letters received by Neureuter showed just how widely Marpingen had become known. His correspondents came not only from Bonn, Koblenz, Mönchen-Gladbach, and numerous smaller towns in the Rhine Province, but from almost every part of the Reich: Baden, Bavaria, Hanover, Hessen, Saxony, Silesia, Thuringia, West Prussia. There was also keen interest beyond the German borders. In the autumn of 1876 alone, the parish priest had letters from Belgium, Luxemburg, The Netherlands, Switzerland, Austria, Italy, and the USA.[25] Prince Radziwill, who was in England before he set off for Marpingen from Ostend in November 1876, noted that the apparitions were also 'beginning to excite attention' across the Channel.[26]

If word of mouth spread news of Marpingen through the immediate locality, it was the press that spread it throughout Germany and beyond. Ironically, the hostile liberal press first took up the affair. The *Saar- und Mosel-Zeitung* was already congratulating the government on 15 July for its firmness in dispatching the army to Marpingen; it followed up the next day with a scathing attack on the 'crassest stupidity' of events there.[27] Other local liberal papers like the *Nahe-Blies-Zeitung* devoted attention to Marpingen, joined by part of the national liberal press.[28] There was no shortage of later Catholic commentators who saw divine purpose in the fact that news of the apparitions was spread by the enemies of the church. The Catholic press was much slower off the mark, fearing initially that the apparitions might prove an embarrassment. The *Trierische Landeszeitung* did not provide its readers with an account of the apparitions until 22 July, the Sunday *St-Paulinus-Blatt* not until 23 July. But they soon made up for their early restraint, challenging the mocking stories carried in the liberal press with accounts of miraculous events. It was through the Catholic press that claims of alleged cures achieved wide currency. The *Saar-Zeitung* was the prime mover in this. On 3 August it published the first of many statements by those who claimed cures at Marpingen. The press also provided a forum for the priests Neureuter and Schneider to express their conviction that the apparitions were authentic. Influential Catholic newspapers took up these local press reports. Among them was the *Kölnische Volkszeitung*, the best-selling Catholic daily in Germany.[29] While guarded about the authenticity of the apparitions and cures, it provided very full coverage and carried articles by the Cologne academic Matthias Scheeben, a

[24] *SMZ*, 19 July 1876; LASB, E 107, 193: Father Pettera of Malspitz to Neureuter, 30 July 1876.
[25] Details of Neureuter's correspondence in LASB, E 107, 170–80, with further references ibid. 376–449 and 78–80 (the latter concerning the parallel correspondence of Father Schneider of Alsweiler, who helped Neureuter with the flood of letters).
[26] Radziwill, *Besuch*, 3.
[27] *SMZ*, 15 and 16 July 1876.
[28] See below, Ch. 9, for a detailed analysis of liberal press coverage.
[29] J. Lange, *Die Stellung der überregionalen katholischen deutschen Tagespresse zum Kulturkampf in Preußen (1871–1878)* (Frankfurt am Main and Berne, 1974), 29.

frequent visitor to Marpingen and one of the leading theological supporters of the apparitions.[30] The Berlin-based *Germania* tried more actively to put Marpingen on the map. Its editor was the combative priest and Reichstag deputy Paul Majunke, who had published a book on Lourdes.[31] He took a personal interest in Marpingen and was another frequent visitor to the village. His paper provided a platform for Catholic priests and publicists to write at length about Marpingen, and it supported the idea that a chapel be built at the site. The hostile view that Marpingen was being promoted as a 'German Lourdes' had a good deal of justice when it came to *Germania*.[32] On 16 August the paper published the opinion of Father Schneider: 'it can rightly be said that Marpingen is becoming a second Lourdes'. The comparison was sustained in many further articles.[33] By the autumn of 1876, the press war over the apparitions had made Marpingen familiar to newspaper readers throughout Germany. For many it was, of course, an object of mockery: in October a man in Deutz who had called someone a 'Marpinger' during a public house quarrel was fined 15 marks and given three days' custody for slander.[34] There was also a lightly mocking tone in the comment of the *Breslauer Zeitung* in early 1877 that 'an edition of a newspaper which carries no news from Marpingen is laid aside as indignantly as one which contains nothing Turkish'.[35] But liberal irony and hostility stoked up Catholic press coverage of events (German newspapers of the period referred constantly to the stories run by their opponents), thus widening the circle of Catholics who knew about Marpingen.

There were limits to the number of readers reached by the Catholic press, which was far less developed than its liberal counterpart and did not yet boast the extensive network of small-town newspapers that was to emerge in the 1890s. The *Kölnische Volkszeitung* may have been the most-read Catholic newspaper in Germany, but its circulation was only 8,600 in the mid-1870s.[36] While Catholic academics received their opinions about Marpingen (and helped to form those of others) in the pages of the *Kölnische Volkszeitung*, *Germania*, or the *Schlesische Volkszeitung*, more humble Catholics depended on the patchy local press—augmented by popular pamphlets. These popularly written accounts of the apparitions and cures played a major part in capturing the interest of potential pilgrims. They generally consisted of newspaper articles put together between soft covers and sold for a few pfennigs. *Die Erscheinungen in Marpingen* by Nikolaus Thoemes had originally appeared as a series of seventeen articles in *Germania* between 5 and 31 October 1876; W. Cramer's *Die Erscheinungen und*

[30] On Scheeben and his role, see Chs. 7 and 10.
[31] See P. Majunke, *Die Wunder von Lourdes* (Berlin, 1873).
[32] Berg, *Marpingen*, 15; Schorn, *Lebenserinnerungen*, ii. 260.
[33] See e.g. *Germania*, 2 Dec. 1876, 20 Feb. 1877 ('Marpingen und Lourdes').
[34] *SMZ*, 17 Oct. 1876, citing the *Elberfelder-Zeitung*.
[35] Cited in *Germania*, 13 Jan. 1877. 'Turkish' was, of course, a reference to the war going on in the Balkans.
[36] Lange, *Die Stellung*, 29.

Heilungen in Marpingen began life as the November 1876 edition of Cramer's own Marian monthly, *Herz-Maria-Blüthen*. As popular pamphlets they appeared with far larger print-runs than in their original form and were frequently reprinted. Thoemes also published his account with the Diemer Verlag in Stuttgart, which was in turn reprinted by Schoenhaar of Saarlouis, and in a revised version by Groppe of Trier.[37] Yet another pamphlet, by the priest Felix Dicke, went rapidly through eight editions.[38] Peddled by hawkers, like the candles and medals that were also produced to celebrate Marpingen, these accounts reached a mass audience. Thoemes's booklet was advertised to colporteurs as 'a draw (*Zugartikel*) of a kind seldom on offer'. It was reported in February 1877 that Saarbrücken and the surrounding countryside were 'inundated with massive quantities' of a pamphlet about Marpingen. Similar pamphlets achieved 'widespread circulation' around St Wendel through colporteurs.[39]

Modern means of communication, the press and the popular pamphlet, helped to familiarize the Catholic public with events in Marpingen; the railway gave them the opportunity to go there in person. The growing railway network was an important enabling element in the revival of Catholic piety in the nineteenth century, making possible mass pilgrimages to places like Lourdes. The same was true of German apparition sites of the 1870s, as would-be pilgrims thumbed their timetables and checked their connections. Extra carriages had to be added to accommodate the demand and railway traffic grew enormously at the nearest railheads of the three apparition sites: Bisellen for Dittrichswalde, Deggendorf for Mettenbuch, St Wendel for Marpingen.[40] In none of these cases were the connections particularly good: one cleric travelling from Paderborn to St Wendel found himself changing at Düsseldorf, Düren, Trier, and Saarbrücken, while the alternative route via Bingerbrück was very slow.[41] By the middle of the 1870s, however, Germans were perfectly familiar with railway travel and hardly deterred by a lengthy or complicated journey. Huge crowds were therefore decanted out of the stations nearest to the apparition sites, the wealthier travelling on by landau, the rest in carts with seats of straw, or on foot—a comfortable two hours in the case of the walk from St Wendel to Marpingen.[42] The very wealthiest could, of course, hire a special train, as the Princess Helene of Thurn und Taxis did on the Munich–Tutzing stretch of the return journey from one of her three visits to

[37] LASB, E 107, 450–3. See also Rebbert, *Marpingen und seine Gegner*, 7. On the concern felt by the administrative and judicial authorities over Thoemes's pamphlets, see LHAK, 442/6442, 95–103, and on the subsidizing of a rival, anti-apparition brochure with money from the Ministry of the Interior in Berlin, ibid. 81–93.

[38] Dicke's pamphlet (*MMGE*) was published anonymously. On reprints, see LASB, E 107, 479.

[39] LASB, E 107, 453; *SMZ*, 6 Feb. 1877.

[40] 'Die Erscheinungen der unbefleckt Empfangenen', 59–61; 'Bei der Madonna von Dietrichswalde', *Die Gartenlaube* (1878), 29; 'An der Gnadenstätte', 666; Müller, *St Wendel*, 274 ff.

[41] *MMGE*, 8; 'An der Gnadenstätte', 666.

[42] Bungert, *Heimatbuch*, 233; Cramer, *Die Erscheinungen*, 6.

Mettenbuch.[43] For the most part, though, the princess and her entourage used the public railway system, as she did on her visit to Marpingen in August 1877. The party in this case numbered seventeen (thirteen travelling first-class, four second-class), and the transportation to the apparition site of the princess and assorted ladies- and gentlemen-in-waiting, personal maids, valets, footmen, dressers, and other servants enriched the railways by over 650 marks, not including the cost of meals and tips in station restaurants.[44]

It was probably the visit of the Princess Helene to Marpingen which prompted a gendarme to remark that 'all classes were represented among the pilgrims, from the princess down to the day labourer'.[45] A more friendly observer was equally impressed by the presence of 'high and low, rich and poor, educated and uneducated'.[46] The wide social range of the pilgrims is alluded to in many different sources, whether sympathetic accounts, hostile accounts, or the evidence turned up by the legal investigations, but it is difficult to come by anything very systematic. The visitors' books signed by pilgrims that I have been able to consult cover only the period after the Second World War.[47] Some inferences are nevertheless possible if we proceed with care. A starting-point is the area of striking agreement in Catholic and liberal accounts about who the pilgrims were, despite sharp disagreements on the significance they attach to their conclusions. Both dwell on the presence of aristocratic and other high-born visitors, one side obviously impressed, the other moved to scorn and sarcasm. At the same time, both emphasize the overwhelmingly 'popular' character of the pilgrims. For sympathetic Catholic observers the simple faith of the masses had brought them to Marpingen, even if 'over-educated' Catholics were more inclined to stay away. Liberal accounts frequently make the same point, but draw a very different conclusion. The mass of pilgrims spotted at St Wendel station were people 'whose stupid appearance betrays immediately that they belong to the lowest classes, and indeed not to the most intelligent among them'.[48] The implication of these descriptions seems to be that it was the middle classes that were missing. A working hypothesis might therefore be that the pilgrims were drawn particularly from the highest and lowest in Catholic society, and much less from those in between.

[43] TTZ, Hofmarschallsamt [HMA] 2700/3031: 'Abrechnung. Über eine Reise I[hrer] K[öniglichen] Hoheit von Tutzing nach Metten und zurück, August 13–19 1878'. The cost of the special train was 160 marks, a small proportion of the total cost of the journey, which was over 2,000 marks.
[44] TTZ, HMA 2699/2803, 2809–10: 'Reise Rechnung. Über eine Reise I[hrer] K[öniglichen] H[oheit] von Tutzing nach Marpingen'. The exact figure was 655 marks, out of a total cost of 3,332 marks for the trip.
[45] Gendarme Hentschel's testimony in Prozeß, 162. Hentschel certainly noted Princess Helene's presence. See his report for 15 Aug. 1877, in LASB, E 107, 162.
[46] MG, 41.
[47] BAT, B III, 11, 14/7–8: Pilgerliste 1944–7. I have been unable to consult a further list in family possession, an excerpt from which is reproduced in Bungert, Heimatbuch, 230–3. The excerpt contains a disproportionate number of the high-born.
[48] 'An der Gnadenstätte', 666.

There is certainly no doubt about the attraction that Marpingen exerted on upper-class Catholics. Observers of all persuasions referred in 1876–7 to 'well-dressed visitors' and *Herrschaften*; they also talked more specifically about the numerous 'persons of high birth' and 'ladies of the highest estate'.[49] The historian of St Wendel observed that after Prince Radziwill's visit in November 1876, a visit to Marpingen 'became the done thing' (*zum guten Ton wurde*) among the Catholic aristocracy of Germany and Austria, and the evidence bears him out.[50] One of the earliest was the Baroness Louisenthal of Dagstuhl, a local estate of over 500 acres that had once belonged to a Hohenzollern. A passionate supporter of the apparitions, the baroness first visited Marpingen on 15 July 1876, and returned twice more later in the year.[51] Her visits ceased only after strong pressure had been exerted by the authorities on her husband (a former *Landrat*), and because she feared to jeopardize the position of an ageing family priest, a non-national who faced expulsion from Germany.[52] Further 1876 visitors included members of two other prominent Catholic families: the Count and Countess Stolberg, together with the countess's mother (a Ballestrem by birth), and the Countess Spee, a Galen by birth.[53] But it was during the summer of 1877, in the period from shortly before the Feast of the Assumption on 15 August until 3 September, that the main aristocratic influx took place. Marie, Queen Mother of Bavaria, and Princess Friedrich Karl, sister of the Austrian Kaiser, were present in this period; so were the Princess Thurn und Taxis, the Princess Löwenstein, and the Countess of Lippe.[54] These were indeed 'the cream of the German aristocracy'—certainly of the Catholic aristocracy—as one visiting priest admiringly put it. On 22 August it was rumoured that Archduke Johann was in Marpingen, and on 3 September that the former Queen Isabella of Spain and a Dutch prince were there incognito.[55]

This impressive aristocratic presence was offset by a marked bourgeois absence—a *male* bourgeois absence, at least. The examining magistrate Emil Kleber compiled a report running to 500 pages dealing with the main incidents in Marpingen, and summarizing the numerous statements taken from participants, witnesses, and gendarmes. Just half a dozen businessmen have found their way

[49] LASB, E 107, 163–6, 168: gendarme reports; LHAK, 442/6442, 679: LRA St Wendel to RP Wolff Trier, 11 Apr. 1877; *MG*, 37, 41; Schorn, *Lebenserinnerungen*, ii. 260.

[50] Müller, *St Wendel*, 275.

[51] LASB, E 107, 86, 389–91. A thumbnail sketch of the Louisenthal family is provided by Kraus, *Tagebücher*, 257, 270–1. The family acquired the estate of Dagstuhl in 1807; it had belonged to the Count of Hohenzollern-Hechingen until the French occupation. See H. Nießen, *Geschichte des Kreises Merzig* (Merzig, 1898), 234–5.

[52] For the pressure on her husband and household, see BAT, B III, 11, 14/4, 39–40; LASB, E 107, 390; and below, Ch. 7.

[53] LASB, E 107, 361–2; *Prozeß*, 84 (which gives the Countess Spee as 'Spree'); *MWOL*, 44–5; *TLZ*, 5 Sept. 1876. H. Reif, *Westfälischer Adel 1770–1860* (Göttingen, 1979), 435–49 is excellent on the religious piety to be found among these heavily intermarried Catholic aristocratic families.

[54] LASB, E 107, 162 (in a slip of the pen, examining magistrate Kleber has written 1876 for 1877); *MG*, 46; Rebbert, *Marpingen und seine Gegner*, 55; Sausseret, *Erscheinungen*, 229.

[55] LASB, E 107, 166; *MG*, 46.

into this record. One was a hotel owner from the spa town of Neuenahr, who went to Marpingen seeking a cure for his mentally ill daughter.[56] Another, the merchant Caspar, helped to draft the statement by the Dörr family of Humes about the cure of their son Jakob.[57] A few other merchants from nearby Tholey and Urexweiler apparently visited Marpingen out of curiosity.[58] There is no single reference in the examing magistrate's summary, or in any other source, to pilgrims who were industrialists, managers, or technicians, no mention at all of any pilgrim from the middle and upper ranks of the bureaucracy, whether a grammar school teacher or a judge, no pilgrim engaged in the exercise of a profession such as law, medicine, engineering, or architecture.

The social composition of those who went to Marpingen reflected, in part, the skewed distribution of Catholics in the overall population, for Catholics were markedly under-represented in the propertied and educated middle classes. The relative paucity of Catholics with the educational qualifications to enter the bureaucracy and professions—the so-called *Bildungsdefizit*—was already a matter of public debate in the 1870s; the absence of Catholics among German entrepreneurs and managers was later to form part of the background to Max Weber's celebrated thesis on the Protestant ethic and the spirit of capitalism.[59] But the strikingly apparent under-representation at Marpingen of the Catholic business and professional middle class not only mirrored the general social structure of Catholic Germany; it also said something about the Catholics who were members of those classes, and especially of the educated middle class. For there were, of course, Catholic doctors, lawyers, and officials, but they were precisely the Catholics about whom the clergy complained that they were 'too close to the Protestants and lukewarm', that they led worldly lives and read novels.[60] These were the Catholics who distrusted 'excessive' Mariolatry and found episodes like Marpingen more of an embarrassment than an inspiration.[61]

The exception that proved the rule of the missing Catholic middle classes was the clergy. It can be seen as the functional equivalent in Catholic Germany of the

[56] LASB, E 107, 236.

[57] Ibid. 90.

[58] Ibid. 86–92, on the merchants Ehses (Zeltingen), Jacob (Tholey), and Huber (Urexweiler).

[59] The Görres Society, founded in 1876, had as one of its aims to improve this state of affairs by emphasizing to Catholics the importance of education and scholarship. BAK, Nachlaß Hertling, 28: Schriften u. Reden Hertlings, contains material on the objectives of the society. For the debate on Catholic educational and economic 'backwardness', see J. Rost, *Die wirtschaftliche und kulturelle Lage der deutschen Katholiken* (Cologne, 1911); A. Neher, *Die wirtschaftliche und soziale Lage der Katholiken im westlichen Deutschland* (Rottweil, 1927).

[60] See Gatz, *Volksmission*, 97–8.

[61] See the attack in *Germania*, 9 Feb. 1877, on a Catholic factory owner who had expressed himself scandalized about Marpingen. Other Catholic editors took a different view, esp. in private. The personal distaste for aspects of the popular piety of Marpingen in the liberal-Catholic circles around the *Kölnische Volkszeitung* was expressed by Julius Bachem in his memoirs; the editor of the *Essener Volkszeitung* wrote to Father Schneider on 19 Aug. 1876 in very critical vein (LASB, E 107, 357–9). The scepticism, even indignation, among 'thinking Catholics' was exploited by Protestant writers: see Berg, *Marpingen*, 40.

non-Catholic professional middle class and intelligentsia—although its social origins were lower. The overall reaction of the clergy to the apparitions was not uniform or simple, and it warrants detailed consideration elsewhere.[62] Here it is worth noting that those priests who did support the apparitions made up an important part of the general body of pilgrims. Leaving aside the priests from neighbouring parishes who spent lengthy periods in Marpingen assisting Father Neureuter, and the 'priest-publicists' like Edmund Prince Radziwill and Paul Majunke, many hundreds of clergy went to the village as ordinary pilgrims. Of the 500 or so visitors in the village on 28 August 1877, around forty were members of the clergy.[63] The exceptionally large crowd present on 3 September included 'hundreds' of priests from all parts of Germany as well as Belgium and the Netherlands.[64] Some idea of the geographical spread of clerical visitors can be gleaned from those—a small minority of the total—who were caught and prosecuted for the illegal celebration of mass in Marpingen. They included priests not only from the Rhine Province and the nearby Palatinate, but from Baden, Westphalia, and East Prussia.[65]

The aristocracy and the clergy were the most visible pilgrims, but the great majority of those who travelled to Marpingen had more humble backgrounds. In this they resembled participants in the great 1844 pilgrimage to the Holy Coat in Trier and those who flocked to other contemporary apparition sites.[66] Some belonged to the small trading classes: butchers, grocers, publicans, shopkeepers.[67] They were joined by members of the lower middle class such as primary school teachers, clerks, and minor officials. These were generally people whose names entered the official record without their being suspected of any crime, usually because they were interviewed as witnesses. That is how we know about the presence in Marpingen of the hairdresser Grischy of Saarbrücken and the grocer Gertrude Hermes of Neumagen.[68] The apparitions evidently attracted considerable numbers of those engaged in domestic service, among whom the servants or housekeepers of priests seem to have been well represented (one of the pilgrims was a chambermaid of the celebrated Bishop Ketteler of Mainz).[69] Reports also make frequent mention of craftsmen, including dyers, masons, cabinet-makers, carpenters, and cobblers, as well as peasants and day labourers. These are pilgrims whose precise identity is most difficult to pin down, although

[62] See below, Ch. 6.

[63] LASB, E 107, 165.

[64] MG, 41.

[65] Details in LHAK, 403/15716, 130–1, 134–9, 144–7, 154–5, 158–61. On the difficulty of catching the priests in the act of breaching the Kulturkampf legislation, as seen through the eyes of a frustrated gendarme, see LASB, E 107, 168–9.

[66] Schieder, 'Kirche und Revolution'.

[67] The occupations in what follows are drawn from LASB, E 107, unless otherwise stated. There are isolated references in other sources to petty-bourgeois pilgrims. Thus Prince Radziwill, on his journey to Marpingen, shared his carriage with a publican from the Cologne area: Radziwill, Besuch, 3–4.

[68] Prozeß, 147; LASB, E 107, 313.

[69] On Ketteler's chambermaid, see NBZ, 26 and 29 Aug. 1876.

they are the ones who alarmed local officials when they flocked to the apparition site—often in groups of hundreds—from villages in the districts of Merzig and Saarlouis.[70] They were least likely to stay the night in Marpingen or to attract any special attention from chroniclers of the apparitions. Except when apprehended by gendarmes, they are present in most accounts simply as 'masses'. It is from the evidence of these infractions, as well as from the striking numbers of carts that clogged the roads and tracks around Marpingen, that their participation must be inferred. It was, for example, a peasant from Lauschied who was convicted at Saarbrücken in early March 1877 of leading an illegal procession to Marpingen.[71] Other peasants and day labourers from outside the village were among those charged with offences in Marpingen itself.[72]

Marpingen was, finally, a miners' pilgrimage. As we have seen, Marpingen miners and their families were closely associated with the apparitions from the start. All the evidence indicates that the same was true across the whole region. Whether we look at those who claimed cures, those present at the site on the evening that the army intervened, or those who subsequently tangled with gendarmes stationed in the Härtelwald, miners were prominent.[73] Pilgrims came from all areas of the coalfield, including towns in the Palatinate such as St Ingbert.[74] But the largest numbers came from the Köllertal and from the string of part-agricultural, part-mining villages on the northern fringe of the coalfield. These villages, closely resembling Marpingen itself in population and social structure, recur again and again in references to pilgrims. They included Dirmingen, Eppelborn, Heusweiler, Illingen, Köllerbach, Lebach, Münchwies, Theley, Uchtelfangen, and Urexweiler.[75] It was in mining villages of this kind that a further wave of reported Marian apparitions occurred in 1877.[76]

If Marpingen drew pilgrims disproportionately from the Catholic lower classes, it also attracted more women than men. This is true across class lines. It is plain enough among the social élite that princesses, countesses, and baronesses vastly outnumbered princes, counts, and barons. The point is underlined, among these letter-writing classes, by the much larger correspondence that Neureuter had with aristocratic women than with their male counterparts.[77] Indeed, it is clear from one such correspondence that the Countess Spee had initially been refused

---

[70] LASB, Best. LRA Saarbrücken, I, 735–9; *KZ*, 26 Aug. 1876; Mallmann, 'Volksfrömmigkeit', 216–17.

[71] *SMZ*, 4 Mar. 1877.

[72] See below, Ch. 7. The *Nahe-Blies-Zeitung* suggested (5 Sept. 1876) that of the 280 people who appeared before the court in St Wendel the previous day charged with pilgrimage-related offences, 'most belonged to the working class (*Arbeiterstand*)'.

[73] On cures, see below, pp. 173–4; on miners and resistance to the power of the state, see pp. 267–8 below, Ch. 8.

[74] *MWOL*, 93, on a party of 400 pilgrims from St Ingbert in early 1877.

[75] LASB, E 107, has numerous mentions; see also Klein, 'Geschichte', 73. On the size and character of these villages, Hoppstädter and Hermann, *Geschichtliche Landeskunde*, i. 113–14, and Laufer, 'Aspekte', 162.

[76] See below, Ch. 6; Klein, 'Die Saarlande', 117; Mallmann, 'Volksfrömmigkeit', 220–1.

[77] LASB, E 107, 408–12; *Prozeß*, 212.

permission by her husband to visit Marpingen.[78] 'Ladies', titled or otherwise, were frequently to be found in the houses of the visionary children, or making up the little groups that kissed and wept over those who claimed to be cured.[79] The crowds that surrounded later 'visionaries' had a similar composition.[80] It seems likely from the descriptions we have that these women included many who were the wives and daughters of the absent bourgeois men. That also seems indicated by the account of a group of fifty or sixty people 'in town dress' who disembarked at St Wendel, and were 'almost exclusively members of the fair sex of a certain age'.[81] There is one particular case where we have better documentation. Frau Privy Councillor Dorothea Dreyerkmann of Soest was such a keen supporter of the apparitions that she settled permanently in Marpingen after her husband died.[82]

The same gender pattern recurs further down the social scale. Again and again pilgrims are recorded as 'the wife of the dyer Bingemer', 'the wife of the former postman Philipp Schu', 'the wife of the cobbler Gerber of Tholey', 'the wife of the publican Franzen from Neumagen and a female neighbour'.[83] The evidence points in the same direction when it comes to pilgrims who were numbered rather than named. There are many descriptions like those of the gendarme Metzen, who saw 'about twenty female persons (Frauenzimmer) going to the pilgrimage place in small groups'; a party was spotted from Furschweiler that contained twelve women and one man.[84] Women also made up the majority of those present at the apparition site itself, as they did at all such places, including palpably fraudulent ones like the Gappenach mill near Mülheim where a 'Virgin in the bottle' appeared.[85] These findings come as no great surprise. Like the well-documented attraction of women to earlier religious movements (the Trier pilgrimage of 1844, the millenarian movement of the maverick Catholic priest Ambros Oschwald in the 1840s and 1850s) they are one more sign of the 'feminization' of nineteenth-century Catholicism.[86]

Why did pilgrims make the journey to Marpingen? The apparitions obviously

[78] LASB, E 107, 408–12.
[79] LASB, E 107, 165–6, 237; Prozeß, 93.
[80] e.g. those flocking around Elisabeth Thies, who claimed to have seen the Virgin, St Michael, and a vision of a chapel at the apparition site: MG, 34.
[81] 'An der Gnadenstätte', 666. Compare the report of another writer from Dittrichswalde who witnessed a group of 17–20-year-old girls 'from the middle social class' bound for the apparition site: 'Bei der Madonna', 29. Among Neureuter's Belgian correspondents, the inevitable aristocrats and priests were joined by a quarry-owner's wife: LASB, E 107, 415.
[82] BAT, 70/3676a, 149–59.
[83] LASB, E 107, 184, 215, 313. Frau Franzen was also accompanied by her daughter: Prozeß, 85.
[84] LASB, E 107, 155; Kammer, Kulturkampfpriester, 160.
[85] According to one observer, the crowds gathered around the 'miraculous acorn tree' in Dittrichswalde were three-quarters female: 'Bei der Madonna', 30. On the preponderance of women at Gappenach, see SMZ, 27 Mar. and 7 Apr. 1877. The incident is discussed more fully below in Ch. 6.
[86] On Trier, see Schieder, 'Kirche und Revolution', 427; on Oschwald, see Treiber, 'Wie man wird, was man ist'. In the millenarian movement of Joanna Southcott in 19th-cent. England, 63% of those on a surviving list of 7,000 members who had been 'sealed' were women: Hopkins, A Woman to Deliver her People, 77.

tapped a source of intense spiritual hunger among German Catholics. Pilgrims went to give thanks for the revelation of the Virgin, as an act of penance, to obtain grace by being there and touching the sacred soil. Many sought the intercession of the Blessed Virgin: in addition to cures for themselves or members of their family, they might be seeking help with a problem of reproduction or fertility, the recovery of a stricken farm animal, a good harvest, the freedom of a son from conscription, guidance over a major decision, even help with a pending examination. These were the same concerns that prompted thousands of readers of popular journals devoted to the Virgin Mary or the Sacred Heart to send their pleas for intercession.[87] It was not strictly necessary to visit an apparition site in person. Large numbers of believers clearly prayed to Our Lady of Marpingen (or Mettenbuch, or Dittrichswalde) from home, or asked others who travelled there to do so on their behalf. Sometimes these arrangements were formalized. Theres Köstelbacher had a young daughter, and a husband (an ex-gendarme) confined to the lunatic asylum in Deggendorf: she was supported by her relations on condition that she prayed for them in Mettenbuch.[88] Others sent professional pilgrimage-goers with their requests. One elderly woman told a reporter from the *Gartenlaube* that she had been to Marpingen on twenty-two occasions with commissions of this kind, as well as twelve times to Altötting and seven times to Maria-Einsiedeln. She had been doing the rounds of apparition sites for thirty years, since taking over the role when the previous village woman who looked after pilgrimages (*Wallfahrtsbesorgerin*) had suffered a bad fall.[89] Like her French equivalents, the *voyageuses*, she was the third party who provided the means of requesting intercession at the site to those who were unable to travel.[90]

But for pilgrims the journey itself was important. As writers such as Victor Turner and Iso Baumer have suggested, journeys of this kind create meanings for those who make them.[91] It was widely believed that any sacrifice or discomfort entailed by the pilgrimage was itself a source of blessings and grace for others— for the living, or for the 'poor souls' in purgatory whose sufferings played such a prominent part in popular Catholic sentiment of the period.[92] The journey also tended to create a temporarily heightened sense of community among pilgrims as they streamed towards their common goal; and as they approached that goal,

[87] Every issue of a journal such as *Die Sendbote des göttlichen Herzens Jesu* contained numerous requests of this kind. The somewhat jaundiced author of 'Bei der Madonna', 30, recounts the Dittrichswalde seers being asked by pilgrims to put requests to the Virgin Mary about pigs, goats, and chickens.
[88] SAL, 164/2, 1164, has extensive correspondence on this case, mainly because the young daughter claimed an apparition during a visit in 1881.
[89] 'An der Gnadenstätte', 667.
[90] Devlin, *Superstitious Mind*, 45.
[91] V. Turner, *Process, Performance and Pilgrimage. A Study in Comparative Symbology* (New Delhi, 1979); Turner, 'Pilgrimages as Social Processes'; Turner and Turner, *Image and Pilgrimage*; I. Baumer, *Wallfahrt als Handlungsspiel. Ein Beitrag zum Verständnis religiösen Handelns* (Frankfurt am Main and Berne, 1977), esp. 42–5.
[92] Turner, *Process, Performance and Pilgrimage*, 137.

the 'place' itself worked powerfully on the emotions of the travellers. Many descriptions of Marpingen pilgrims indicate how arrival at the blessed place released desperate spiritual longings and an almost painful sense of rapture. Father Neureuter recorded in his notebook: 'Deep emotion, some in tears as they ask for holy masses to be said. They could hardly state what they wanted through their sobbing, then turned away and held a handkerchief to their faces.'[93] The depth of religious passions was even more evident at the apparition site, which provided a tangible, physical focus for powerful emotions. In the words of the Baroness Louisenthal: 'The prayers you address to heaven in this privileged place have more power than the others.'[94]

Some clerical writers describe the scene in highly sanitized terms. In one account the pilgrims conducted themselves 'calmly and with dignity'; another writer relished the contrast between pilgrims who prayed, sang, and said their rosaries quietly, while the gendarmes 'walked among the crowd with cigars burning'.[95] This decorum is inherently implausible in crowds of thousands, and is contradicted by the majority of accounts. Sympathetic and unsympathetic observers are agreed that pilgrims stripped the foliage and the bark off all the bushes and trees around the site, scrambled for earth (which they sometimes ate), carried heavy jugs and milk cans to fill with 'miraculous water' at the spring, and broke off pieces of melted wax from votive candles, in their desire for physical talismans to take home with them.[96] The wire put up around the apparition site, and the action of local men and visitors like the hefty cobbler Umhofer from Winterbach, who tried to keep access free for the sick, were obviously necessary to prevent the crush of pilgrims and maintain some kind of order.[97] But the wire was soon trampled down, and none of these efforts at the site could prevent members of the crowd—'mostly quite young girls'—from fainting.[98] Those who lost consciousness were likely then to find themselves surrounded by hopeful pilgrims eager to learn of another possible visionary.

In addition to the fervour with which they greeted each new claim of a vision or cure, pilgrims were highly receptive to reports of other supernatural phenomena connected with Marpingen. A group of around 150 congregated by a quarry outside St Wendel to gaze at the sky where a procession of pilgrims had been reported 'floating through the air'.[99] Another group of pilgrims from Losheim lost their way in the dark, and believed they had been guided to their

[93] LASB, E 107, 387–8: undated entry in Neureuter's notebook.

[94] 'Les prières que vous addressez au ciel dans cet endroit privilégié ont plus de forces que les autres': LASB, E 107, 391, Baroness Louisenthal to Neureuter, 2 Sept. 1876.

[95] MWOL, 90–1; MG, 45.

[96] LASB, E 107, 153–63; Cramer, Die Erscheinungen, 13, 15, 55; MWOL, 92; 'An der Gnadenstätte', 667. One female schoolteacher took away a leaf from the site which she kept under the glass of a mounted picture of Marpingen: LASB, E 107, 405: Felix Dicke to Neureuter, 24 Aug. 1876.

[97] LASB, E 107, 135; Cramer, Die Erscheinungen, 16. On the similar measures needed to protect the apparition site at Dittrichswalde, 'Bei der Madonna', 30.

[98] LASB, E 107, 163.

[99] KZ, 23 Aug. 1876. The incident took place on 16 August.

goal by a 'miraculous star of Marpingen'.[100] Early in 1877 rumours spread that a virulent plague was imminent, and only those who possessed the miraculous water of Marpingen would be spared. In some versions the plague would afflict cattle as well as humans.[101] A report that the Belgian stigmatist Louise Lateau had smiled at the mention of Marpingen spread among the pilgrims and took its place in the local mythology.[102] There were numerous reports from Marpingen itself and from nearby railway stations of religious passions that bordered on mania, and the historian of St Wendel wrote coldly of 'ugly goings-on' as 'somnambulists and hysterical women saw heaven and hell open and hordes of demons roaming around the area'.[103] Incidents of this kind were reported in sympathetic as well as hostile accounts. It was also a friendly source that recorded similar events in Dittrichswalde on the evening of 8 September 1877 (the feast of Mary's Nativity), when panic and collective hysteria swept through the crowd of 50,000 as pilgrims reported hearing lions roar and seeing a ball of fire.[104]

There was clearly an element of cathartic release involved for pilgrims caught up in the great emotional drama surrounding the apparitions. The occasion touched every sense—sight, sound, touch, smell: it resembled a Wagnerian total work of art, a *Gesamtkunstwerk*.[105] The pilgrimage journey also offered a sense of release in another way. The pilgrimage was a break with the everyday; it provided temporary relief from the daily round—from the immutability of one's place in the local community, from quarrels with neighbours, from the constraints of work and those who wielded authority (even the priest who heard confession was new, unfamiliar). We should not underestimate the importance of this element— of the brief respite from the demands of work, the temporary sloughing off of responsibility—for those such as women and miners who were disproportionately represented among the pilgrims. To this was added what Victor Turner has called the sense of *communitas*.[106] If miners took their solidarities with them on pilgrimage, it is likely that the journey itself and the atmosphere that prevailed at the apparition site also helped to foster a sense of commonality among the wives and widows who set out alone or in small groups for Marpingen.

The solemnity of the purpose did not preclude enjoyment: sacred and profane cannot be neatly separated in the pilgrimage drama. Among the pilgrims (generally middle-class or clerical) who recorded their experiences, a striking feature is their pleasure in the enjoyment of the landscape—the hills, valleys, woods, and 'restfully murmuring brooks'—and the delight in describing and

[100] *EM*, 78–81.

[101] Berg, *Marpingen*, 44; *SMZ*, 6 Feb. 1877.

[102] LASB, E 107, 191–2 (examining magistrate Kleber gives the name as 'Lateaux').

[103] Müller, *St Wendel*, 274, an account that is taken over in his history of the parish by Derr, 'Pfarrei Marpingen', 40. See also the report in the *SMZ* of 19 Oct. 1876 about a 20-year-old domestic servant at Saarbrücken station who believed herself to be the Virgin Mary, wept and prayed, and thought she was surrounded by angels.

[104] 'Die Erscheinungen der unbefleckt Empfangenen', 61.

[105] Baumer, *Wallfahrt*, 49, makes the analogy.

[106] See e.g. Turner, 'Pilgrimages as Social Processes'.

naming the local topography.[107] The pilgrimage had a restorative function and provided material for the amateur geologist or homespun Baedeker. It had an even more obvious festive aspect. Eating, drinking, overnight stays, and heightened sociability had always been a part of pilgrimages. The 'dense, shouting, and yelling crowds' that left St Wendel station included those whose first pilgrimage was to the local hostelry; and some tin flasks were filled with miraculous water only after they had been emptied of wine or schnapps on the way.[108] Pilgrims to Dittrichswalde passed the railway journey with noisy choruses of the popular song 'Wir fahren auf der Eisenbahn, so lang' es uns gefällt', and loud cheers went up when beer barrels bound for Dittrichswalde were spotted at Osterode station.[109] This aspect of the pilgrimage had its darker side. Violence accompanied the heightened emotions, petty crime fed on the opportunities presented. In Mettenbuch the mentally retarded wife of a shoemaker was badly beaten by her husband and another woman after making some kind of scene at the apparition site, while bystanders looked on. Purses, clothes, and washing were stolen; spoons, glasses, and bedlinen disappeared from local inns.[110] Marpingen attracted a variety of petty thieves and confidence men, and the offertory box in the parish church was broken into three times during the winter of 1876–7.[111]

In their combination of the solemn and the festive, with an admixture of the lawless, the pilgrimage to apparition sites resembled those secular 'pilgrimages' undertaken by nationalist organizations, ex-servicemen's associations, and students on occasions such as Sedan Day or the Kaiser's birthday, when the devotions were habitually lubricated by alcohol.[112] Marpingen also had in common with nationalist gatherings that both drew strength from the political conflicts of the 1870s. In early September 1876 the Catholic journalist Hermann Kühn wrote to Neureuter that 'the apparitions obviously have a direct connection with the *Kulturkampf*'.[113] One popular pamphlet writer expressed a general view when he suggested that German Catholics had been obliged 'to look with envy on France' since the apparitions of La Salette and Lourdes; but now events in Marpingen were taken as a sign that they were not to be left without succour in their time of need.[114] Marpingen attracted pilgrims because it was the 'German Lourdes',

[107] Cf. Sausseret, *Erscheinungen*, 22–35.

[108] 'An der Gnadenstätte', 666–7.

[109] 'Bei der Madonna', 29.

[110] SAL, 164/2, 1163: BA Deggendorf to MdI Lower Bavaria, 12 Dec. 1877.

[111] Examples of petty theft and confidence tricksters in LASB, E 107, 139, 166; *Prozeß*, 132–5; NBZ, 10 Oct. 1876. On the robberies of the offertory box, LASB, E 107, 232: statement by Neureuter on 17 Nov. 1877.

[112] See the description of the Sept. 1877 'Kaiser-Festlichkeiten' in Düsseldorf, when drunken ex-servicemen littered the hedges and many appeared the worse for wear on the parade-ground, in Rebbert, *Marpingen und seine Gegner*, 114. R. Chickering, *We Men Who Feel Most German. A Cultural Study of the Pan-German League, 1886–1914* (London, 1984) provides more disinterested evidence on the same subject.

[113] LASB, E 107, 194: Kühn to Neureuter, 2 Sept. 1876. Kühn worked for *Germania* and for the Bavarian *Historisch-Politische-Blätter*.

[114] *MMGE*, 7.

because—in the words of another of Neureuter's correspondents—'the Blessed Virgin has bestowed the honour of a visitation on our oppressed Rhineland'.[115] Against a background of persecution, the apparition was not merely a sign of grace; to many it signified the intercession of the Virgin against the persecutors. Pilgrims at the site sang Marian hymns that invoked the protection of the Virgin, such as 'Unter deinem Schutz und Schirm', with their thoughts plainly on the military and police forces of the Prussian state. Marpingen was a refuge, for the same reasons that the pilgrimage to Our Lady of Vorburg in the Bernese Jura gained a new intensity during the Swiss *Kulturkampf* in the same period.[116] In both cases the siege-mentality was not entirely defensive. Many of the rumours that made the rounds among Marpingen pilgrims were militant in temper, suggesting that the enemies of the faith were to be routed. One characteristic story that was widely circulated concerned a Protestant merchant who had supposedly mocked events in Marpingen and been punished by the sudden and inexplicable death of his horses.[117] Rumours spread that when soldiers cleared the 'place' a large cross appeared, surrounded by four large, very bright candles, and the soldiers received something like an electric shock when they tried to remove it. Another rumour had it that an angel appeared there at night with a flaming sword.[118] Female pilgrims on a train bound for Marpingen were overheard claiming that police efforts to suppress the movement would fail: the Virgin Mary had resolved to appear to the king, so all the world would see that they had been right. In the words reportedly used by one of the pilgrims: 'We are the power!'[119]

Cures

The prospect of a cure for themselves or their children was one of the major reasons why people went to Marpingen. All manner of afflicted made the journey: reports refer to the blind, the deaf and dumb, the rheumatic and arthritic, epileptics, the mentally disturbed, and those who had survived epidemics like typhoid or smallpox but still bore the scars. Many travelled by railway, some in special trains.[120] Others managed the journey on foot, or were carried by cart. They ranged in age from the four-month-old daughter of the peasant Katharina Becker from Winterbach, a child with cramps and severe abdominal pains, to the 63-year-old widow from Mainzweiler, Maria Zimmer, who had suffered for ten years with rheumatism.[121] Those seeking cures made their way or were helped to

---

[115] LASB, E 107, 177: letter to Neureuter from a curate in Bonn. Cf. Cramer, *Die Erscheinungen*, 5.
[116] I. Baumer, 'Kulturkampf und Katholizismus im Berner Jura, aufgezeigt am Beispiel des Wallfahrtwesens', in G. Wiegelmann (ed.), *Kultureller Wandel im 19. Jahrhundert* (Göttingen, 1978), 88–101; Baumer, *Wallfahrt*, esp. 27, 53–5.
[117] *Prozeß*, 25–6; LASB, E 107, 428–9.
[118] *KZ*, 27 July 1876.
[119] *NBZ*, 10 Oct. 1876.
[120] See reports of trains from Lorraine, and from Spichern and Alstingen, in *SMZ*, 6 Feb. 1877.
[121] On the Becker case, *Prozeß*, 173–4; Radziwill, *Besuch*, 22; *MWOL*, 24; *EM*, 40–2. On the Zimmer case, Cramer, *Die Erscheinungen*, 45–6; *MWOL*, 26–9.

the apparition site; their hands were guided to the spot on which the Virgin had stood, and they said the prescribed prayers. Most drank the 'miraculous water' from the Härtelwald. Witnesses reported that some also ate earth.[122]

For those unable to visit Marpingen in person, hope of a cure rested on use of the miraculous water. It was normal for pilgrims to take water home with them, for their own use and for sick relations. One joiner travelled from Trier to Marpingen on foot during the bad weather of February 1877 in order to take water home to his bedridden wife. He carried a twelve-litre jug, his companion a six-litre jug.[123] The jugs, flasks, and bottles carried by the pilgrims are an invariable part of the descriptions we have. Those who could not acquire water in this way addressed themselves to the parish priest, who found himself buried in correspondence as a result. Thus the Countess Spee requested some for a daughter who had suffered for fourteen years with an inflamed hip, for her daughter-in-law Countess Droste-Nesselrode who had rheumatism and epilepsy, and for her husband who was also ill at the time.[124] Marpingen temporarily eclipsed other pilgrimage places and shrines associated with miraculous cures. In that sense too it was the German Lourdes. A businessman from the town of Lüdinghausen near Münster informed Neureuter in August 1876 that he had travelled to Lourdes the previous year, but had been unable to take his sick wife with him: 'And now the Blessed Virgin has come two-thirds of the way to meet us.'[125]

Many believed that their hopes had been realized. There was a flood of reported cures in the first month, and the claims continued steadily thereafter.[126] By the end of August there was 'hardly any place in the whole surrounding district which does not boast one or more people who have been cured'.[127] At the end of December Neureuter told a Dutch visitor that the number of cures had reached 300–400.[128] The period from July to early September 1877, which saw the largest-ever crowds of pilgrims in the village, also witnessed a new burst of alleged cures. There were fifteen on the two final days of the apparitions, 2 and 3 September.[129] Writing in the autumn of that year, Joseph Rebbert referred to 'many hundreds' of cures.[130] The claims did not stop with the apparitions. There was often a

---

[122] The procedure that had to be followed is described in MG, 47. Margaretha Kunz and two men from Niederhofen witnessed earth being eaten. A 2½-year-old boy from Wiesbach who had weak limbs following a serious (probably epidemic) illness was given earth to eat by his parents: LASB, E 107, 91, 153.

[123] SMZ, 1 Mar. 1877.

[124] LASB, E 107, 408–12. Neureuter was generally reluctant to send water, and the countess had been forbidden by her husband to visit Marpingen, so Neureuter suggested she make her devotions at home and dispatched Father Dicke to her with water.

[125] LASB, E 107, 355–7, quotation, 356: letter from an (unnamed) merchant, 17 Aug. 1876.

[126] BAT, B III, 11, 14/4, 4–10, 13–16.

[127] TLZ, 2 Sept. 1876.

[128] 'L. v. H. Ein Niederländer in Marpingen', Germania, 26, 27 Dec. 1876, 1, 3 Feb. 1877; MWOI, 83.

[129] MG, 43.

[130] Rebbert, Marpingen und seine Gegner, 35.

considerable time-lag between a cure supposedly being effected by miraculous water and the details being publicized. The case of a priest's niece from the Tutzing area of Bavaria, allegedly cured of a lame leg after drinking water brought back from Marpingen by her uncle in 1877, was recounted in a Stuttgart newspaper only in the spring of 1878, and Neureuter first received direct information about it in September of that year.[131] Katharina Eberz of Roes claimed a cure from chorea (St Vitus's dance) after drinking water obtained by her brother in February 1877, although word did not reach the parish priest of Marpingen until July 1880. A point of interest in this case is that Katharina Eberz described drinking Lourdes water without effect on three occasions.[132] It is clear that the water was still being used years after the apparitions had ceased. In one harrowing case in 1880, drops of it were put without her knowledge into the food and drink of a deranged nun believed by her fellow religious in Aachen to be possessed by the devil.[133] In the same year Anna Thomé of Hölzweiler, near Saarlouis, claimed that the water had restored her voice.[134] Heinrich Hennes of Cologne was still claiming relief from an unspecified ailment through use of Marpingen water in 1894.[135]

Detailed information about most of the alleged cures is hard to come by. Rumours abounded, but most of the stories that circulated were vague. That applies even to the cases of those who claimed to have been cured in Marpingen itself; it is still more true of later, geographically dispersed claims about the effects of drinking the water. This problem is not unique to Marpingen. The district official in Deggendorf, following up two cures reported in Mettenbuch, observed: 'it is absolutely characteristic that one learns least about the allegedly miraculous cures in Mettenbuch itself, and that news of them mainly spreads far away'.[136] In a subsequent letter to his opposite number in Regen, enquiring about a peasant whose burned hand had supposedly been healed, the same official complained about the difficulty of getting hard information:

I should like to take the opportunity to add that according to the rumours that are circulating many inhabitants of the Regen district have already been described as miraculously cured, but that when detailed enquiries are made into cases such as this the bad conscience of those who spread the news usually makes it impossible to establish the name or place of residence of the person concerned.[137]

Evasiveness prompted by fear of the repercussions or public mockery also

---

[131] This was the case of the 17-year-old Therese Graf, described as a 'young girl in the Starnbergersee area' in the *Katholisches Sonntagsblatt*, 7 Apr. 1878: cutting in BAT, B III, 11, 14/4, 33. A letter from the priest concerned was sent on 18 Sept. 1878: ibid. 56.

[132] BAT, B III, 11, 14/4, 46–8 includes statement of Katharina Eberz and a local doctor. Cf. the 1879 material on the alleged cure of Maria Klaß of Bitburg, ibid. 57, 65–6.

[133] See the correspondence in BAT, B III, 11, 14/4, 62–4.

[134] BAT, B III, 11, 14/4, 58: letter of Anna Thomé to Neureuter, 11 Dec. 1880, plus notes from her current and previous parish priests on her ailment. Thomé came originally from the Bitburg area.

[135] BAT, B III, 11, 14/4, 60: letter of 21 Nov. 1894.

[136] SAL, 164/18, 697: BA Deggendorf to BA Viechtach, 19 June 1877.

[137] SAL, 164/15, 814: BA Deggendorf to BA Regen, 22 Nov. 1877.

hampered official efforts to obtain information about cases connected with Marpingen. It is hardly surprising that many were reluctant to talk about cures, when even a correspondent of Neureuter's asking for water to cure her deafness asked that the packet be posted from outside the village 'in order that those who, even in Losheim, mock religion notice nothing'.[138] In some cases, the only evidence consisted of the crutches left in the parish church.[139]

There are nevertheless reported cures about which more detailed evidence is available. There are some two dozen cases where the individuals and families concerned spoke to priests or Catholic publicists, and details of their cures were subsequently printed in the press, principally in the *Saar-Zeitung*, the *Trierische Landeszeitung*, or *Germania*. These accounts were reprinted in popular pamphlets, and tended to be the cases on which the investigating authorities concentrated. Their enquiries also turned up some additional cases, and other alleged cures are recounted in correspondence with Neureuter that has survived in the ecclesiastical archives. From this material I have been able to compile a sample of forty-five cases.[140] Excluded from this are all individuals identified only in terms such as 'a woman of 27', where there is a danger of double-counting, and those where no gender is specified, usually when the designation is simply 'child'.[141] In each of the forty-five cases we have the name and sex of the person allegedly cured; the age is known in twenty-eight cases, and the place of residence in all but four. The sample probably constitutes something under 10 per cent of all alleged cures, but it provides the basis on which at least some general observations can be hazarded.

The clearest finding concerns the breakdown by gender of those claiming cures. Medieval miracle-cures were more often claimed by men than women;[142] the opposite was true by the nineteenth century, as the Marpingen evidence shows. Women and girls were markedly over-represented in the sample, as they were among visionaries and supporters of the apparitions. Thirty-five of the forty-five (78 per cent) were female, only ten (22 per cent) male. Among adults, the female : male ratio was 22 : 5, among children 13 : 5. If children of 12 and over are added to the 'adult' category, the female : male ratio becomes a still more striking 26 : 5. In other words, 84 per cent of all those aged 12 or over who claimed to have been cured were female. That is very close indeed to the distribution of cures at Lourdes: of the sixty-four cases deemed to have been miraculous by the

[138] LASB, E 107, 175.
[139] Ibid. 185.
[140] The sample was compiled from the following sources: LASB, E 107, 90, 163–6, 181–90, 264–74, 347; BAT, B III, 11, 14/4, 4–10, 13–16, 19–20, 24, 33, 46–8, 55–70; *Prozeß*, 30, 90–1, 114–18, 128–9, 173–4; Cramer, *Die Erscheinungen*, 12–13, 19, 32–41, 44–54; *EM*, 40–53, 66–73; *MG*, 39–43; *MWOL*, 16–39; Thoemes, *Die Erscheinungen*, 22–36, 43–59, 72–8; Lama, *Die Muttergottes-Erscheinungen*, 24–5, 43.
[141] LASB, E 107, 187. Some cases are also noted in BAT, B III, 11, 14/4, where cured individuals are identified by gender and age, but not by name.
[142] R. C. Finucane, *Miracles and Pilgrims*, 142–6. Finucane has a breakdown of 61% male, 39% female from a French and British sample of 2,300.

Medical Bureau, fifty-two (82.5 per cent) involved women.[143] It is also worth noting that in the great majority of instances where we have reports of sick children being taken to Marpingen by one parent, it was the mother. In fact, in the case of the baby daughter of the Beckers from Winterbach, the father made it clear that they went to Marpingen on his wife's initiative, and refused the Catholic publicist Dr Thoemes permission to use details of what had happened in his *Germania* articles.[144]

We have the ages, at the time they were cured, of twenty-eight individuals. Of these, only six were male, and there is no indication of any clustering around particular ages in this very small group. The female twenty-two, on the other hand, contain two prominent groups: five girls of 11 or 12 years old, and five women between the ages of 38 and 49. These were precisely the ages in which there were large numbers of female visionaries. The age-distribution of those cured highlights the general prominence of infants and children among their number. Of the sub-sample of twenty-eight, just under a third (nine) were 10 or younger; exactly half (fourteen) were 12 or younger. Many cases excluded because of incomplete information indicate that the proportion of infants and children may be under-represented in the sample. Again, parallels with the visionaries themselves—in Marpingen and elsewhere—are suggested; for if few children went to Marpingen unaccompanied, there are certainly cases where those who claimed cures had badgered their parents into going. Like the emergence of young 'rival' visionaries (*Konkurrenzkinder*), the age-distribution of the cured underlines the importance of children.

The geographical distribution of the alleged cures also conforms closely to what we know about those who were generally attracted to Marpingen. There is evidence here on forty-one cases in the sample. One was Belgian. Of the remaining forty individuals, just five came from towns (two from Paderborn, one each from Elberfeld, Koblenz, and Trier). Analysis of the other cases underlines just how much Marpingen was a miners' pilgrimage. Twenty-one of the thirty-five cures were reported either from the coalfield proper or from miner-peasant villages such as Marpingen itself, Wiesbach, and Urexweiler. The remaining fourteen cures were distributed among surrounding rural areas, with the Eifel, the Hunsrück, and the Mosel valley most prominent. The geographical pattern suggests a certain imitative effect. One cluster of cures occurred in the miner-peasant village of Wiesbach, another in the Bitburg district of the Eifel, confirming other indications that news of cures spread rapidly through rural areas of that kind and prompted imitations.

We have less detailed information about the social class of the families which claimed cures, although the evidence we do possess seems fairly unambiguous. There were seventeen cases in which the precise occupation of the person cured

---

[143] Marnham, *Lourdes*, 185.
[144] In the event, Thoemes did include material about the Becker cure in his pamphlet. On this case, see *Prozeß*, 173–4; *MWOL*, 24; *EM*, 40–2; Radziwill, *Besuch*, 22.

is known—or the principal source of income of the family concerned if that person is a child or lists herself as 'wife'. Eight were miners. Four were peasants, one was a peasant and cooper, another a day labourer. Two were craftsmen, a cobbler and a tailor (the two poorest, most proletarianized crafts). The final case stands out, for it was the only non-German cure in our sample and the individual concerned was the Princess Emilie Drion of Gosselies in Belgium.[145] This conforms to a pattern observable since the early modern period, whereby the initial cures of 'humble' persons triggered the interest of the socially more elevated (another contrast with medieval Europe, when the upper classes were much more prominent among the miraculously cured).[146] This sociological breakdown once again produces what we might expect from the overall composition of the pilgrims and users of Marpingen water. The beneficiaries of alleged cures came almost entirely from mining, peasant, and poor craft backgrounds, leavened by a numerically small but conspicuous aristocratic presence. The only respect in which the statistics may misrepresent the true situation is the use of the husband's occupation where, as is almost always the case, the occupation of the wife (or widow) is not stated. It seems very likely, given the districts involved, that many of these families were actually miner-peasant households. The overall picture is nevertheless clear, and additional indirect evidence points in the same direction. Neureuter received one letter of thanks for a cure on headed notepaper,[147] but the majority of cases where inferences about occupation are possible suggest that the families of miners, peasants, or small traders were involved. That emerges especially from publicized cures, where the events were witnessed by neighbours whose occupations are given. Typical was the case of Katharina Schorr, 5-year-old daughter of the widow Katharina Schorr of Wiesbach: the cure of her lame right leg was witnessed by two miners and a day labourer.[148]

The material we have on Mettenbuch largely reinforces the Marpingen evidence. From the enquiries of the ecclesiastical and state authorities, together with the accounts of those who advertised their good fortune, I have been able to identify fifty-six adults and children who claimed to have been cured. The full name, the sex, and place of residence is known in every case; the occupation (or the occupation of the parents in the case of children) is recorded in most.[149] Among adults, there were twenty-six women (68 per cent) to twelve men (32 per cent). When it comes to children, the figures are at first sight surprising. In an almost exact mirror-image of the Marpingen findings, boys outnumber girls two to one (12 : 6). But we should bear in mind that, in Mettenbuch as in Marpingen, it was commonly the mother or a female relation (typically an aunt) who seized

[145] LASB, E 107, 188–9; Lama, Die Muttergottes-Erscheinungen, 43.

[146] For the much greater upper-class numbers of the cured in medieval England (esp.) and France, see Finucane, Miracles and Pilgrims, 142–6; on the pattern that became established from the early modern period, Nolan and Nolan, Christian Pilgrimage, 247–8.

[147] BAT, B III, 11, 14/4, 50–1.

[148] Cramer, Die Erscheinungen, 53; MWOL, 38.

[149] The sources are those given in Table 5.1.

the initiative in taking the child to the apparition site. In at least one known case, an innkeeper's son from Metten who had rickets, the father was initially very sceptical.[150]

The geography of the Mettenbuch cures was similar to Marpingen's, but even more regionally concentrated. There is no fully recorded cure from outside Bavaria, although one report (not included in the sample) refers to an unnamed day labourer from Glashütte in Bohemia whose lameness had been cured.[151] Only two of the sample of fifty-six came from larger towns (a restaurateur from Furth, a middle-aged single woman of unspecified occupation from Passau). The overwhelming majority came from the market towns and villages of Lower Bavaria, with notable concentrations in the nearby districts of Deggendorf, Regen, and Viechtach, which provided ten cases between them.[152] Small clusters of two or three cures elsewhere (in Prackenbach, Sattelpeilnstein, Dünzling) suggest a familiar pattern of imitation.

The sociology of those cured indicates broad similarities to Marpingen, but also some differences, as shown in Table 5.1.

TABLE 5.1. *Family occupation of those claiming cures at Mettenbuch*

	Men	Women	Children	All
Merchant	—	—	1	1
Tradespeople	2	2	3	7
Craftsmen	3	7	2	12
Peasants	2	5	4	11
Smallholders, Cottagers	5	2	3	10
Servants	1	2	1	4
Quarrymen, railway workers	—	—	3	3
TOTAL	13	18	17	48

Sources: BZAR, Fasc. I, VIIb: 'Äußere Wirkungen (Heilungen)', Fasc. II: 'Bericht über angebliche Wunder-Heilungen 1877'; SAL, 164/15, 814; 164/18, 697; Braunmüller, *Kurzer Bericht*, 29–63.

The absence of the bourgeoisie is striking: it would have been complete, but for the grandchild of a merchant. On the other hand tradesmen, craftsmen, and their families show up very strongly. Half of all the women in the sample where the family occupation is known came from this milieu. The trades and crafts concerned were varied. The cured children included a miller's son, the son of an innkeeper couple, a butcher's daughter, a weaver's daughter, and a photographer's

---

[150] Braunmüller, *Kurzer Bericht*, 54.
[151] Ibid. 29.
[152] This certainly understates the real numbers involved. There were at least 4 other cases in Regen, not included in the sample because of incomplete information. See SAL, 164/15, 814: BA Deggendorf to BA Regen, 22 and 25 Nov. 1877, 6 Apr. 1878, 29 Sept. 1878, and replies; Braunmüller, *Kurzer Bericht*, 29.

son. The adult women had husbands or fathers who were millers, coopers, potters, sieve-makers, and weavers; one was a small tradeswoman, the ubiquitous *Krämerin* commonly found at apparition sites. The men included a restaurateur, a cartwright, and two joiners. Taken together, crafts, trades and small businesses account for 40 per cent of those cured.[153] They represent a cross-section of the provincial artisanate and petty bourgeoisie, from the more marginal weavers to substantial crafts and trades (millers and butchers were generally among the wealthiest in any village or market town). By contrast with Marpingen, no one from the Cinderella crafts of shoemaking and tailoring appears in the sample.[154] The peasantry account for a further 23 per cent. It is impossible to be sure how substantial their holdings were, although in one case at least a grateful peasant widow was wealthy enough to endow the parish church in Metten with 300 marks for masses to be read. The peasantry was outnumbered, although not dramatically so, by the combined categories of cottager and smallholder (21 per cent) and farm or domestic servant (8 per cent).[155] It is worth noting that the alleged recovery of a bedridden domestic servant—Theres Kroiß of Deggendorf—was the first major, 'exemplary' cure that attracted others through the publicity it achieved.[156] The proletarian element, finally, was small: a mere 6 per cent. Additional, more fragmentary evidence excluded from the sample suggests a similar pattern. In the district of Regen, cures were also claimed by people from the households of a gingerbread baker, a farm servant, a weaver, and a joiner.[157] As in Marpingen, those who claimed cures came from the peasantry, the rural poor, and the small trading classes. But in Mettenbuch they seem to have been somewhat more substantial; above all there was no equivalent to the miners who formed the largest single group in Marpingen.

What drove such people to seek cures for themselves or their children? We should not neglect the most obvious reason: the tyranny of disease in this period, to the extent that to contemporaries health meant simply being alive, such was the threat of death.[158] This was most spectacularly manifested by the continuing importance of epidemics and infectious diseases—what two recent writers have

[153] The figure would be slightly higher with the inclusion of one man who described himself as a 'cottager and mason', but I have taken the first part of this description as the more important.

[154] On the internal divisions within crafts and trades in Germany, see D. Blackbourn, 'Between Resignation and Volatility: The German Petty Bourgeoisie in the Nineteenth Century', in *Populists and Patricians*, 84–113.

[155] One of the cases involving a domestic servant was unusual, for it concerned a man employed as a knacker and huntsman by an aristocratic house.

[156] Theres Kroiß wrote to her sister in Munich about her supposed cure, and the case found its way into *Germania* and other Catholic newspapers. See BZAR, Fasc. I, 'Bericht des Pfarramtes Metten über die behaupteten Erscheinungen der Mutter Gottes', IV: Ereigniße nach dem Schluße der Erscheinungen und ihr allmähliches Bekanntwerden in weiteren Kreisen', 23 July 1877.

[157] SAL, 164/15, 814: BA Deggendorf to BA Regen, 22 and 25 Nov. 1877, 6 Apr. 1878, 29 Sept. 1878, and replies.

[158] R. Spree, *Health and Social Class in Imperial Germany. A Social History of Mortality, Morbidity and Inequality* (Oxford and New York, 1988), 31.

called 'the *ancien régime* of disease'.[159] Cholera had hit the Saarland severely in
1859–63 and again in 1866.[160] The Franco-Prussian war brought a major outbreak
of smallpox, which was followed by diphtheria, influenza, and scarlet fever. In
Marpingen 250 children were affected by a scarlet fever epidemic in 1877,
including all three visionaries. Forty-eight children under the age of 14 were
among the seventy-seven who died in the first half of the year.[161] In Prussia during
the 1870s, one child in four still died before reaching the age of 1, and a
major decline in infant mortality did not occur until the end of the century.[162]
Contemporary expectations about illness and death are suddenly revealed by a
chance remark during the trial that followed events in Marpingen. When the
visionaries' 'predictions' of imminent deaths in the village came up for discussion,
the presiding judge observed matter-of-factly: 'If a 1-year-old child is ill, it can
be assumed that it will probably die' (*so liege die Vermuthung nahe, daß es wohl
sterben werde*).[163]

If infants and children were most vulnerable, serious illness and the prospect
of early death were also an ever-present reality for adults. Prussian mortality rates
reached their peak in the early 1870s, when life expectancy was 38.5 years for
women, only 35.5 years for men.[164] It is striking how the lives of adults who had
a role in the Marpingen affair were punctuated by serious illness. The parish
priests of Marpingen and Alsweiler both contracted smallpox during the outbreak
in 1870–1. Neureuter was nursed by his sister, who died after catching the disease
herself.[165] The original presiding judge at the Saarbrücken trial had to stand
down after contracting diphtheria; a prominent witness, the senior official Karl

---

[159] C. Herzlich and J. Pierret, *Illness and Self in Society* (Baltimore and London, 1987), 3–23, who
draw principally on French evidence.

[160] Fox, *Saarländische Volkskunde*, 263. There had also been major outbreaks of cholera in the Saarland
in 1835–7 and 1849. On the latter outbreak, affecting the entire Trier administrative district, see LHAK,
403/16730, 95–9.

[161] On the smallpox epidemic generally, see A. Mitchell, 'Bürgerlicher Liberalismus und Volksgesundheit im deutsch–französischen Vergleich 1870–1914', in J. Kocka (ed.), *Bürgertum im 19. Jahrhundert. Deutschland im europäischen Vergleich*, 3 vols. (Munich, 1988), iii. 408; and for its effects in
Marpingen and the surrounding area, Müller, *St Wendel*, 266; Lama, *Muttergottes-Erscheinungen*, 61;
Berg, *Marpingen*, 42–3. Spree points out that measles, diphtheria, rubella, croup, scarlet fever, typhus,
and child-bed fever accounted for under 10% of deaths in Prussia in 1877, but these figures apply to
adults as well as infants, and are based on towns of over 15,000: Spree, *Health and Social Class*, 41.

[162] I. Hardach-Pinke and G. Hardach (eds.), *Deutsche Kindheiten 1700–1900* (Kronberg, 1978), 30;
Spree, *Health and Social Class*, 35–6 (and ch. 2, pp. 55–102, on infant mortality generally). An older
source suggests rising levels of infant mortality up to the 1870s: A. Peiper, *Chronik der Kinderheilkunde*
(Leipzig, 1951), 142. The exception to the later downturn in infant deaths from infectious diseases
was smallpox, against which compulsory immunization was successfully introduced in 1874: C.
Huerkamp, 'The History of Smallpox Vaccination in Germany: A First Step in the Medicalization of
the General Public', *Journal of Contemporary History*, 20 (1985), 617–35; Mitchell, 'Liberalismus und
Volksgesundheit', 408 ff.

[163] *Prozeß*, 101.

[164] Spree, *Health and Social Class*, 35; G. Hohorst, J. Kocka, and G. A. Ritter (eds.), *Sozialgeschichtliches Arbeitsbuch II: Materialien zur Statistik des Kaiserreichs 1870–1914* (Munich, 1978),
33–4.

[165] LASB, E 107, 110; BAT, 70/3676, 92: Neureuter to GV Trier, 6 Aug. 1871.

Schorn, was also forced to miss the trial through serious illness.[166] The ubiqui-
tousness of illness, and the pressure it placed on families, can be glimpsed from
a letter written by Rudolf Virchow. Himself a doctor and pathologist, as well as
one of the fiercest contemporary liberal critics of 'miraculous cures', Virchow
writes here as a father cataloguing illness in his own household:

Unfortunately illness has not ceased in my house this winter. My family has seen the
addition of a boy, but my mother has died. The other children have had, one after the
other, influenza, chickenpox, pneumonia, and bronchitis, and now they are all suffering
from measles, some of them seriously. My wife is naturally recovering only slowly from all
this.[167]

Priests, senior officials, and doctors belonged to the more comfortably situated
in society. High levels of morbidity and low life expectancy affected the poor
most harshly. Cumulative ill-health made peasants, labourers, and miners more
vulnerable to the 'great killers'—tuberculosis, pleurisy, pneumonia, and strokes
as well as infectious diseases.[168] This is not surprising given the long hours of
work, the high rate of accidents, the cramped, insanitary conditions in which they
lived, the absence of fresh air and exercise, and the poor diet, especially in the
coalfield. Miners had the highest rate of illness of any industry except construction. They were subject daily to violent changes of temperature between the
coal-face and outside, and were prone to arthritis because of the positions in
which they had to work, and to respiratory diseases such as pneumoconiosis and
emphysema that came from breathing coal-dust. The sheer physical demands of
the work left many miners in a state of semi-permanent exhaustion and weakened
their resistance to infections such as influenza. The result was that invalidity
shortened the working lives of miners more than it did any other group of workers.
Early retirement through invalidity also took its toll in lost income, exacerbating
the adverse domestic conditions which also underlay much of the endemic
sickness in mining households.[169]

Doctors were, of course, among the contemporaries who made this very point,
although they tended to do so in highly moralistic terms. For the mine doctor
Teich of Dudweiler the problem lay in 'barbarism, brutality, and dissipation',
'superstition and limited intelligence', as well as 'poverty and distress'.[170] Teich's
suggestion that the poor upbringing of children perpetuated this moral-biological

---

[166] Prozeß, 2, 94.
[167] Virchow to Wilhelm Wittich, 6 Mar. 1858, in M. Stürzbecher, Deutsche Ärztebriefe des 19.
Jahrhunderts (Göttingen, 1975), 105.
[168] A classic literature developed around 1914 on the sociology of illness. See M. Mosse and G.
Tugendreich, Krankheit und soziale Lage (Munich, 1913, reprinted Göttingen, 1977); F. Müller-Lyer,
Soziologie der Leiden (Munich, 1914); A. Grotjahn, Soziale Pathologie (Berlin, 1915). Spree's Health
and Social Class is a sophisticated modern analysis of morbidity, mortality, and social inequality, R. J.
Evans, Death in Hamburg: Society and Politics in the Cholera Years 1830–1910 (Oxford, 1987) a case-
study of social inequality in the face of epidemic disease.
[169] Hickey, Workers in Imperial Germany, 122–6; U. Frevert, Krankheit als politisches Problem 1770–
1880 (Göttingen, 1984), 227–8; Horch, Wandel, 309–15.
[170] Cited Laufer, 'Aspekte', 154. See also Horch, Wandel, 309–10.

morass was a common one. It formed part of the growing emphasis which doctors were starting to place, from around the 1860s, on the importance of 'hygiene', with the accompanying assumption that it was the deviant behaviour of the poor, and especially the working class, in matters such as cleanliness, sobriety, diet, and exercise that was the largely self-induced cause of their higher levels of disease.[171] These attitudes surface in more muted form in the medical certificates and related testimony of doctors who examined alleged cures, where it is commonly suggested that the journey to Marpingen, the fresh air, and the exercise had contributed most to the 'cure'. This was the judgement of Dr Brauneck from St Wendel on the alleged cure of the miner's daughter Magdalena Kirsch, and of Dr Bähr from Tholey on the cure of Katharina Schug.[172] It is not surprising that the doctors involved in the Marpingen case should have expressed another complaint: that those who claimed cures had gone to the site, drunk the water, and eaten the earth—but not consulted a doctor. Injured *amour propre* no doubt reinforced their view that those who sought cures in Marpingen had wilfully and perversely embraced superstition and turned their backs on science.[173]

There are several questions that we need to ask at this point. To what extent was medical treatment actually available to such people, to what extent did it address their needs, and was it welcome in the form in which it was available? This was undoubtedly a watershed period in medical research and treatment: from the 1870s there were numerous advances in diagnostic skills, surgery, and the relief of pain. Science-based medicine began to command greater respect than it enjoyed during the 'crisis of confidence' in the middle of the century. But there were still important limits to what medicine could achieve.[174] The great epidemic diseases remained impervious to medical advance, leaving among those who survived them a legacy of suffering which is evident from the Marpingen evidence. There was still little relief that doctors could offer to those suffering from stomach ulcers, or from the crippling arthritis and rheumatism so prominent among those who claimed miraculous cures. The widow Maria Zimmer of Mainzweiler, for example, had been told by a doctor in Ottweiler that she had 'incurable' rheumatism.[175] Moreover, it was only with the development of the pharmaceutical industry from the 1880s that a new range of pain-killing and fever-

---

[171] See U. Frevert, 'The Civilizing Tendency of Hygiene: Working-Class Women under Medical Control in Imperial Germany', in J. C. Fout (ed.), *German Women in the Nineteenth Century* (New York, 1984), esp. 323–4; Frevert, *Krankheit*, 185–241, esp. 207–41; A. Labisch, '"Hygiene ist Moral—Moral ist Hygiene"—Soziale Disziplinierung durch Ärzte und Medizin', in C. Sachße and F. Tennstedt (eds.), *Soziale Sicherheit und soziale Disziplinierung* (Frankfurt am Main, 1986), 265–85; P. Weindling, 'Hygienepolitik als sozialintegrative Strategie im späten Deutschen Kaiserreich', in A. Labisch and R. Spree (eds.), *Medizinische Deutungsmacht im Sozialen Wandel des 19. und frühen 20. Jahrhunderts* (Bonn, 1989), 37–55.

[172] *Prozeß*, 116–18, 129.

[173] See e.g. *KZ*, 10 July 1877, and Berg, *Marpingen*, 42–3.

[174] Spree, *Health and Social Class*, 163–5. The phrase 'crisis of confidence' comes from C. Ferber, cited ibid. p. 163.

[175] Cramer, *Die Erscheinungen*, 45–6; *MWOL*, 26–9.

reducing preparations became available.[176] There was also medical resistance to some potentially valuable new fields. One of these was paediatrics, still generally frowned on as 'unnecessary' by the medical establishment of the period. Requests that it be examined as a subject in its own right were rejected by the medical faculties of the Prussian universities in 1874, journals in the subject established themselves only with difficulty, and the German Paediatric Society (Deutsche Gesellschaft für Kinderheilkunde) was not formed until 1883, later than its equivalents in many other European countries.[177]

More important still, the decisive factor for the majority of the population was the extent to which advances in research and treatment, pioneered in clinics or laboratories and discussed in the journals, filtered through to ordinary practices. That depended, in the first place, on the actual availability of a doctor. As the population grew rapidly in Prussia from the middle of the nineteenth century, the number of doctors lagged behind. Indeed, the number graduating in Prussia in 1867–71 fell in absolute numbers. In the 1860s and 1870s the number of doctors per inhabitant was lower than in the period before 1848; not until 1876 did the trend reverse itself as the numbers started to outstrip the rise in population.[178] In Prussia in 1876 there were fewer doctors per 10,000 inhabitants (3.3) than in the Reich as a whole (3.7), and far fewer than in a city like Hamburg (6.7).[179] Even these figures tell only part of the story. If we are considering those from the villages of the Saarland, the Eifel, or the Hunsrück who sought cures in Marpingen, we need to bear in mind the crass discrepancy between the rural and urban provision of doctors. In 1876, three-quarters of the population lived in communities with a population under 5,000; but well over half of the doctors lived in towns of 5,000 or more, and the proportion was rising.[180] Thus, while the provision of doctors in the Rhine Province, at 3.6 per 10,000, was above the Prussian average, the doctors were concentrated in major urban centres such as Cologne, Düsseldorf, and Trier, and in smaller administrative centres (Kreisstädte), leaving rural areas relatively neglected. Doctors simply did not want to live in the countryside if they could avoid it. One who was forced to for financial reasons complained bitterly that he lived 'in the village instead of the Kreisstadt in order to provide my four poor children with some kind of upbringing', and hoped for a more 'respectable' future.[181] The chronic disparities in the supply of doctors can be seen within the administrative district of Trier, where official handbooks show a heavy concentration of doctors in Trier itself, and in St Johann-Saarbrücken. Similarly, the number of doctors in the administrative

[176] C. Huerkamp, Der Aufstieg der Ärzte im 19. Jahrhundert (Göttingen, 1985), 132–6.
[177] Peiper, Chronik, 97–105.
[178] Huerkamp, Aufstieg der Ärzte, 65, 148.
[179] Hohorst, Kocka, and Ritter (eds.), Sozialgeschichtliches Arbeitsbuch II, 152.
[180] Huerkamp, Aufstieg der Ärzte, 139–51, and table, p. 151. See also Spree, Health and Social Class, 111–14, 165, on the rural under-provision of doctors.
[181] The Kreisphysikus of Erkelenz (Aachen district) to Virchow, 31 Jan. 1868, cited in Stürzbecher, Ärztebriefe, 177–8.

centre of St Wendel comfortably exceeded the numbers in rural areas like the Alsweiler mayoralty.[182] A large village like Marpingen still had no doctor at the beginning of the twentieth century.[183] It is hardly surprising that rural areas lagged far behind at a time when the statistics show a steadily increasing proportion of the population consulting doctors.

Saarland miners were in a special position. They had access to a salaried mine doctor (Knappschaftsarzt) under the state-paternalist arrangements that existed in the mines of the Saar.[184] These doctors did not provide free treatment for the dependants of miners, however.[185] The principal function of the mine doctors was to keep the miners in a fit state to work: they tended strongly to a censorious insistence that the 'unhealthy' way of life of miners' families (especially the domestic shortcomings of their wives) bore a large share of responsibility for frequent illnesses.[186] The perceived arrogance of doctors was undoubtedly one reason, together with non-availability and cost, why the sort of people who put their trust in Marpingen were often reluctant to consult a medical man. It was obvious that many (especially younger) doctors who set themselves up in working-class or poor rural areas were doing so only until such time as they could move on to a more lucrative practice. Medical men were also more likely to be curt and brisk in their manner towards lower-class patients, with whom they would seldom enjoy a family–doctor relationship.[187] As a result, the growing insistence within the nineteenth-century medical profession on the authority of the doctor—he issued the 'orders', the patient was expected to 'obey'—would generally take a more didactic, even hectoring form in dealings with lower-class families. Bourgeois families might receive advice about the virtues of a holiday in the mountains or the time when their children should begin music lessons; peasants and miners were more likely to hear a lecture about their insanitary living conditions or diet.[188] This form of condescension caused resentment. A good example can be seen in the circumstances surrounding the alleged cure of 7-year-old Magdalena Kirsch, whose parents claimed she was able to walk again and hold down food after a six-month illness during which they 'had expected her death daily'. When the authorities requested the St Wendel medical officer of health (Kreisphysikus), Dr Brauneck, to examine her, he did so fleetingly

[182] Adreß-Kalender . . . Trier (1871), 122–5; Adreß-Kalender . . . Trier (1876), 138–42, 166–7.
[183] BAT, 70/3676, 134: Father Schmitt to GV Trier, 3 June 1901.
[184] See e.g. Horch, Wandel, 280–2.
[185] The presiding judge at the later trial in Saarbrücken erroneously believed that the Knappschaftsärzte did provide treatment for dependants. See Prozeß, 115.
[186] See Frevert, 'The Civilizing Tendency'; and G. Heller, 'Körperliche Überbelastung von Frauen im 19. Jahrhundert', in A. Imhof (ed.), Der Mensch und sein Körper von der Antike bis heute (Munich, 1983), 137–56, who argues that the physical burdens on mothers esp. was compounded by the burdens they faced as the main objects of moralizing 'hygiene' campaigns.
[187] Huerkamp, Aufstieg der Ärzte, 120, 162–4; Frevert, Krankheit, 215.
[188] Huerkamp, Aufstieg der Ärzte, 162–3; Frevert, Krankheit, 230–41. The process of 'medicalization' is also discussed in Spree, Health and Social Class, 178–83, Labisch, 'Hygiene', Weindling, 'Hygiene-politik', and (from a somewhat conspiratorial standpoint) in G. Göckenjan, Kurieren und Staat machen. Gesundheit und Medizin in der bürgerlichen Welt (Frankfurt am Main, 1985).

and pronounced her a 'potato belly' (*Kartoffelleib*), a phrase he later described somewhat unconvincingly as a 'technical expression'.[189] It is easy to understand the frustration felt by Brauneck, who believed that 'a form of mania' was abroad in the area, had lost many Catholic patients because of his sceptical stance, and found himself faced with a family that had not sought medical assistance during the six-month illness of a child.[190] The complaint of the girl's father about the phrase 'potato belly', which was published as a newspaper statement, also contained more than a touch of pathos: 'Even though I am a poor miner and have not studied, like the doctor, I hope that all those who read this my letter will accept what I say as the truth, for I state here on my conscience and as God is my witness that I wish to testify to nothing but the truth!' Disputing that his daughter had 'eaten portions of potato three or four times a day', Kirsch tried to set the doctor straight: 'No, no, Herr Doktor, you are quite wrong. I am very surprised that you made such a statement about my daughter to the Herr District Governor. I would be ashamed to talk such rubbish (*so dummes Zeug zu schwätzen*) to the Herr District Governor.' After a further jibe about 'what anybody could see, who hasn't studied doctoring', Kirsch concluded: 'We may be poor country people, but we have enough common sense and feeling for what is true, and cannot be so easily fooled (*lassen uns nicht so leicht was vormachen*).'[191]

The Kirsch case is illuminating in several ways. The failure to have their daughter treated indicates the strain of fatalism among the poor about illness, especially the illness of children. In a common phrase among those who shunned doctors: 'You really own your child only after the first year; before that it is just on loan.'[192] A similar sense of resignation can be found among adults. Maria Scheid of Gronig, who suffered from chest pains and was probably consumptive, had 'no hope' of recovering.[193] Barbara Leidinger, a lame and bedridden miner's wife from Eiweiler, had visited no doctor for eleven months before her supposed cure, but 'resigned myself to my fate and submitted myself to God's will'.[194] Fatalism went together with a widespread popular scepticism about what doctors could actually achieve, evident enough among those who claimed cures from Marpingen. Margaretha Wittling of Stennweiler had consulted several doctors over her 'nervous convulsions' and been given drops to take, but ceased to take medicines 'partly because I no longer had any confidence in the doctor, partly because I was too poor'. Anna Sebastian of Remmesweiler had been diagnosed as suffering from gout over a period of eight years, but 'the medical treatment

[189] *Prozeß*, 114–18; Cramer, *Die Erscheinungen*, 36–41; *MWOL*, 16–18.
[190] Brauneck's belief that the local Marian cult had become 'a form of mania' was expressed in his report of 3 Sept. 1876 on the three visionaries: LASB, E 107, 99. One writer claimed that Brauneck had 'lost his entire practice in Catholic areas' because he was sceptical of 'miraculous cures': Berg, *Marpingen*, 38.
[191] A full copy of the statement is in *MWOL*, 16–18.
[192] Quoted in Frevert, 'The Civilizing Tendency', 334.
[193] *MWOL*, 31–2.
[194] Cramer, *Die Erscheinungen*, 53–4.

was unsuccessful'. Some, indeed, made the popular association of doctors with illness, not cures: 'all the medicines prescribed seemed only to reduce my strength,' said the bedridden Barbara Leidinger.[195]

Jakob Kirsch and his wife also contrasted the 'common sense' of simple folk with the 'rubbish' talked by those who had 'studied doctoring'. The attitude here was very much that of the peasant who criticized a certain type of veterinary surgeon, 'the gentleman with the top hat and kid gloves' who was supposedly deficient in practical knowledge, or complained of agricultural officials who used 'Latin names and complicated chemical formulae'.[196] When it came to doctors, attacks on the 'overeducated' and arrogant in the name of robust common sense often had another side to them: the stubborn defence of customary healing methods. This might include resort to the herbalist, the bone-setter, the wise woman, the piss-prophet, or the faith-healer—in short, to one of the many 'quacks' who still outnumbered doctors in many rural areas.[197] It might equally be expressed in the belief that the earth from a particular spot, the bark from a particular tree, or the water from a particular spring had healing properties. Such beliefs often provided the pre-Christian underpinning for the faith placed in the miraculous character of 'the place' graced by the Virgin, and the waters associated with it.[198] We have already seen how pilgrims struggled to acquire physical talismans from the site, whether earth, foliage, or—particularly—water. Pilgrims journeyed to Marpingen as others did to spa towns like Bad Dürkheim or the recently opened Bad Neuenahr, seeking cures or relief from their afflictions. They went, however, under the banner of faith, not science. That the German Chemical Society had analysed the waters and pronounced them strikingly deficient in curative properties was irrelevant;[199] pilgrims believed in the power of the Virgin Mary as intercessor, and in the power of the water. The faith that

---

[195] Details in Cramer, *Die Erscheinungen*, 47–50, 53–4. See, more generally, Huerkamp, *Aufstieg der Ärzte*, 139–40; W. Alber and J. Dornheim, '"Die Fackel der Natur vorgetragen mit Hintansetzung alles Aberglaubens". Zum Entstehungsprozeß neuzeitlicher Normsysteme im Bereich medikaler Kultur', in J. Held (ed.), *Kultur zwischen Bürgertum und Volk* (Berlin, 1983), 163–81; and (on France), Devlin, *Superstitious Mind*, 212–13.

[196] See Blackbourn, *Class, Religion and Local Politics*, 160; I. Farr, 'Populism in the Countryside: The Peasant Leagues in Bavaria in the 1890s', in R. J. Evans (ed.), *Society and Politics in Wilhelmine Germany* (London, 1978), 137.

[197] Alber and Dornheim, 'Die Fackel der Natur', esp. 174–8; Spree, *Health and Social Class*, 110–14, 161 ff. Recent writers have rightly warned us not to accept a simple dichotomy between 'fringe' and 'orthodox' medicine (or to accept the homogeneity of either); but the line of division was more clearly drawn in the last decades of the nineteenth century than it was earlier. See W. F. Bynum and R. Porter (eds.), *Medical Fringe and Medical Orthodoxy 1750–1850* (London, 1987); R. Cooter, *Studies in the History of Alternative Medicine* (London, 1988).

[198] Fox, *Saarländische Volkskunde*, 269–71, on such beliefs in the Saarland. Many Catholic pilgrimage sites were associated with 'uncontaminated' places marked by a particular stone, tree, or source of water, pointing to pre-Christian origins: Nolan and Nolan, *Christian Pilgrimage*, 292–3. For a longer historical perspective on the belief in the curative powers of water, see R. P. Masani, *Folklore of Wells, Being a Study of Water-Worship in East and West* (Bombay, 1918), esp. 41–2, 54–65.

[199] BAT, B III, 11, 14/4, 32: newspaper clipping with details of a *Bericht der deutschen chemischen Gesellschaft* (1878), 878, with a full chemical breakdown of the contents of the water.

manifested itself among those who sought cures, and believed they had found them, was overlaid like a palimpsest on popular animistic beliefs.

The clergy were often uncomfortable with the form taken by these beliefs, and some were extremely sceptical about claims of miraculous cures.[200] But there were also priests attracted to the idea that the ultimate seat of illness was the soul, reluctant to accept that everything could be reduced to cells and organs.[201] A suspicion of 'exaggerated' rationalism also inclined many clergy to side with the 'common sense' of popular Catholic sentiment against the pretensions of the medical men. Father Schwaab of Urexweiler enthused about the alleged cure from tuberculosis of his parishioner Frau Denzer; he also publicly expressed his doubts about the competence of doctors, and interested himself in homeopathy.[202] Another priest, Father Bollig of Mertesdorf, complained about attempts to stop the dissemination of Marpingen water on the part of 'doctors plagued by professional jealousy' (Brotneid).[203] The Kirsch case, once again, illustrates a larger point, for the family received considerable help in drafting their statement against Dr Brauneck from a sympathetic priest, Father Schneider of Alsweiler.[204] Indeed the case shows how the sides lined up over the politics of cures: the Catholic poor, supported by priests and Catholic newspapers, against the state authorities, supported by doctors and the liberal press. The acrimony over the alleged cures formed only one part of a more extensive battle that came to a head in the period of the Kulturkampf, between the claims of faith and the dictates of science, between piety and progress.[205] Those on the Catholic side rightly perceived a hostility on the part of doctors that owed much to a broad progressive vision and was often tinged with liberal political sympathies.[206] Doctors, for their part, saw a threat to the 'church of medicine' and a confirmation of their view that (in Dr

[200] See below, Ch. 6, on differences within the the clergy. On the long-standing concern of some priests that popular medical beliefs were 'heathen', see Frevert, Krankheit, 55.

[201] Some Protestant clergymen also believed in miraculous cures. In the Schwelmer Gemeindeblatt, under the heading 'The Saviour Heals', Pastor Patze of Schwelm (Arnsberg district) spoke of cures effected by faith, including that of a journeyman with cancer who was cured when he 'threw himself into the arms of the Redeemer'. Cited in FZ, 7 Aug. 1876. Mostly, however, Protestants were reluctant to countenance modern (as opposed to biblical) miracles.

[202] LASB, E 107, 347; Prozeß, 30, 197.

[203] LASB, E 107, 362: Father Bollig of Mertesdorf to Father Schneider, 3 Oct. 1876. Huerkamp discusses the growing demand for a professional monopoly by doctors, and it has an important place, alongside the parallel efforts of lawyers and others, in the growing literature on 'professionalization'. See W. Conze and J. Kocka (eds.), Bildungsbürgertum im 19. Jahrhundert, Part 1: Bildungsbürgertum und Professionalisierung in internationalen Vergleichen (Stuttgart, 1985); H. Siegrist (ed.), Bürgerliche Berufe. Zur Sozialgeschichte der freien und akademischen Berufe im internationalen Vergleich (Göttingen, 1988); D. Blackbourn and R. J. Evans (eds.), The German Bourgeoisie: Essays on the Social History of the German Middle Class from the Late Eighteenth to the Early Twentieth Century (London, 1991). On 'professional jealousy' among French doctors, see M. Ramsey, 'The Politics of Professional Monopoly in Nineteenth-Century Medicine', in G. L. Geison (ed.), Professions and the French State 1700–1900 (Philadelphia, 1984), 225–305.

[204] Prozeß, 115.

[205] See below, Ch. 9.

[206] On the liberal-progressive sympathies of doctors in the St Wendel district, see LHAK, 442/6660, 232, 236: LRA St Wendel to KR Trier, 8 Aug. 1866.

Brauneck's words) behind 'a well-planned machination and mystification' the clerical forces of darkness were at work.[207]

While there is no evidence of conspiracy, it is certainly true that many dubious cures were taken up by individual priests and by parts of the Catholic press. It is worth pointing out here the contrast with the very different situation that developed at Lourdes, where the official recognition given to the apparitions led the church to demand a greater degree of rigour in the adjudication of supposedly miraculous cures. Compare the hundreds of cures that were claimed in Marpingen with the much stricter standards of evidence applied in Lourdes, where in the century after the archives of the Medical Bureau opened in 1878 just 63 out of 5,000 cures—slightly over one tenth of 1 per cent—were eventually proclaimed inexplicable on scientific or medical grounds.[208] Many purported Marpingen cures were obviously unsatisfactory. Some were patently fraudulent and accepted by no one, such as the case of the three deaf-and-dumb children of the miller Geißecker of Heinserath.[209] Other claims were given credence, yet appeared scarcely less dubious. The cure of the lame tailor Nikolaus Schorn from Haustadt was one case that raised doubts, not least because the individual involved was heavily in debt to a moneylender and benefited handsomely in financial terms from his new status as a miraculously cured man. The scepticism of the local *Landrat* was sufficiently widely shared that the account of Schorn's 'cure' was removed from the later editions of one popular Catholic pamphlet.[210] There were equally serious doubts about the real state of health of 2½-year-old Jakob Schulz of Eiweiler, prior to his supposed cure from lameness at the end of July 1876.[211] In several other cases, individuals had apparently post-dated an improvement in their condition to make it coincide more neatly with a visit to Marpingen. There was a further set of cases where any improvement that had taken place was extremely short-lived. The 12-year-old Princess Emilie Drion made an initial recovery, but then relapsed; claims were made for the cure of the young Fritz Hirtenstein of Steele, after he had drunk a medicine-glassful of Marpingen water, but his death followed a few days later.[212]

Perhaps the largest category of cases where a body like the Lourdes Medical Bureau would have rejected claims for miraculous cures outright consisted of those resting on the vague healing of a 'bad foot', a 'sore arm', or 'convulsions'.

---

[207] On the 'church of medicine', see Cooter, Introduction to Cooter (ed.), *Alternative Medicine*. Dr Brauneck's view can be found in LASB, E 107, 99.

[208] Marnham, *Lourdes*, 162. Not all supporters of Lourdes were so modest: the Assumptionist Fathers claimed nearly 3,000 cures in the years 1888–1910, or 135 per annum; another clerical partisan of Lourdes came to a total of nearly 4,000 in the period 1888–1917, or 66 per annum: Neame, *Happening*, 134–5.

[209] *Prozeß*, 93.

[210] LASB, E 107, 186. The writer in question was Thoemes, who included the Schorn cure in his *Germania* articles and the pamphlet based on them, but not in later versions.

[211] See esp. the statement of the Heusweiler chimney-sweep Hamann: LASB, E 107, 185; Cramer, *Die Erscheinungen*, 50; *MWOL*, 35–6.

[212] LASB, E 107, 187–9.

The St Wendel medical officer of health, who saw more cases than anyone else, declared flatly that he had seen no cure that was at all miraculous.[213] His verdict was echoed by every one of the other five doctors whose evidence on the subject was heard at the later trial in Saarbrücken.[214] It seems likely that any rigorous enquiry by the ecclesiastical authorities would have come to the same conclusion. That is certainly what happened at Mettenbuch, where the commission set up by Bishop Senestrey took up character references on those alleging cures, gathered detailed evidence about their claims from both doctors and priests, and co-operated closely with the local medical officer of health, Dr Appel of Deggendorf.[215] The contrast between the two cases is striking. The doctors in Mettenbuch had a church enquiry with which to co-operate; their counterparts in Marpingen aligned themselves with the state authorities and gave their opinions in court. The different circumstances, decisive in so many ways, had a major effect on the responses to alleged cures. Supporters of Marpingen, feeling themselves under siege in a diocese without a bishop, were more likely to seize on dubious cures and more free to promote them. Doctors, supporting the civil authorities and in turn backed by the liberal press, were conversely more inclined to see dissimulation and conspiracy behind every claim.

Yet, unimpressive though many cures certainly were in their claims for miraculous status, there is no reason to doubt that most were advanced in good faith. They are best understood as the product of neither supernatural intercession nor deliberate deception, but of the power of suggestion, or the cathartic effect produced by faith and heightened expectation of a cure at a time of unusual emotional excitement. This was an explanation resisted by many doctors and religious zealots alike, the former because (like the argument that the visionary children were 'hallucinating') it seemed to rule out the fraud they were sure was involved, the latter because it smacked too much of allowing scientific rationalism in through the back door. But contemporaries who stood at some distance from the claims and counter-claims often looked at cures in this way. One Munich academic and ex-priest observed that 'the supposed miraculous cures can be well enough explained as a result of excited imagination, keen expectation, and devoted trust'.[216] A doctor in Münstereifel wrote in similar terms about the case of Katharina Eberz:

In my view the physical change in the body of the sick woman must be regarded as the product of a mental stimulus. The many reports about supposed cures through the use of Marpingen water which have been spread through the countryside, but were often enough false, as I can confirm from two cases in this district, had a great effect in raising people's

[213] LASB, E 107, 181–2.
[214] See the trial evidence of Drs Cornelius, Bähr, Doinet, Katconi, and Frank: *Prozeß*, 31–2, 57–8, 90–1, 93, 128.
[215] BZAR, F 115, Fasc. I: 'Bericht des Pfarramtes Metten über die behaupteten Erscheinungen der Mutter Gottes'; 'Akten der bischöfl. Commission, vom 21. Sept. bis 14. Nov. 1877'; 'deren Gutachten'; Fasc. II: 'Berichte über angebliche Wunder-Heilungen 1877'.
[216] Frohschammer, 'Die Glaubwürdigkeit', 166.

spirits, and it is therefore very likely that a sorely tried sick person, who had no more to hope for from human help, placed her confidence in supernatural assistance, which was then, so she believed, granted her through the Marpingen water.

With conditions such as convulsions, epilepsy, and chorea which could have psychological causes, continued the doctor, it was entirely possible that psychological influences could bring about an improvement.[217]

Dr Schmitt's conclusions receive some support from the kinds of cure associated with Marpingen. Whereas long-standing shrines of local madonnas or saints were typically credited with specific properties (they cured infertility, or warded off plague), Marpingen shared with other modern apparition sites an all-purpose reputation. But a high proportion of alleged cures involved psychologically conditioned afflictions such as epilepsy, neurasthenia and nervous convulsions, aphonia (loss of voice), chorea, and neuroparalysis. This was also true at Mettenbuch and Lourdes, where nervous disorders (especially general or partial paralysis) were disproportionately represented among the cures. There are, indeed, numerous individual cases at Lourdes that are almost identical to cases at Marpingen—of coxalgia (where children gradually become unable to walk and refuse food), of paralysis following typhus, of aphonia.[218] Contemporary pioneers of psychiatry such as Charcot and Krafft-Ebing also cited many strikingly similar cases of 'hysterical paralysis', or 'religious mania' with hysterical symptoms.[219] Hysteria was invoked on occasion by doctors examining German cures. Dr Doinet referred to the condition of Maria Pfeiffer, from Sohren in the Hunsrück, as 'hysterical paralysis'.[220] Theres Kroiß, bedridden before her alleged cure at Mettenbuch, was described by the Deggendorf medical officer of health, Dr Appel, as 'a hysterical person'.[221] The same doctor, preaching the need for caution, observed contemptuously that it was 'mainly hysterical females to whom such miraculous cures happen'.[222]

There is good reason not to accept these diagnoses uncritically: hysteria is a notoriously value-laden term.[223] But the psychological approach should not be

[217] BAT, B III, 11, 14/4, 48: medical certificate (*Attest*) from Dr Schmitt of Münstereifel, 22 June 1880.
[218] Devlin, *Superstitious Mind*, 68–9; Neame, *Happening*, 140–1. I have found a similar pattern at Mettenbuch, based on the sources used for Table 5.1.
[219] J. M. Charcot, *Leçons sur les Maladies du Système Nerveux*, i (Paris, 1875), 287–8, 341–5, 355–9, cited in Devlin, *Superstitious Mind*, 67–8; Krafft-Ebing, *Lehrbuch der gerichtlichen Psychopathologie*, 200–3; *Lehrbuch der Psychiatrie*, ii. 90–3, 116–17, iii. 87–90.
[220] *Prozeß*, 90–1. See also LASB, E 107, 165–6.
[221] SAL, 164/2, 1162: 'Rücksprache mit Bezirksgerichtsarzt Dr Appel dahier am 9. Mai 1877'. See also the medical judgements on Kroiß as a 'hysterical person through and through' in BZAR, F 115, Fasc. I: 'Bericht des Pfarramtes Metten über die behaupteten Erscheinungen der Mutter Gottes, VII: Bisherige Wirkungen, welche für die Echtheit zu sprechen scheinen, b. äußere Wirkungen (Heilungen)', and elsewhere in Fasc. I and Fasc. II.
[222] Dr Appel used the dismissive term *Weibspersonen*, which is best translated as 'females', rather than 'women'.
[223] I. Veith, *Hysteria: The History of a Disease* (Chicago, 1965); and more recently, E. Showalter, *The Female Malady: Women, Madness and the English Culture 1830–1980* (London, 1987).

discarded out of hand, for it can have explanatory value if rooted in the social and mental world of the individuals concerned. Take the question of the sudden 'shocks' that often triggered nervous disorders such as neuroparalysis or aphonia. At Lourdes, and in other French cases, the traumatic shock experienced by the women and children miraculously 'cured' of these disorders had sometimes taken the form of rape or violence on the part of a husband or father.[224] Here the gender-specific connotations of the term 'hysteria', used dismissively by Dr Appel, have considerable value if looked at from another angle. We should also recall Charcot's insistence that the term hysteria be applied to men as well as women—interestingly enough, in place of the notion of hypochondria more usually applied to the male at this time. There is a familiar roll-call of nineteenth-century men for whom illness was a refuge, almost a form of occupation. One thinks of Ruskin, Carlyle, Proust, Max Weber.[225] Many of the nervous symptoms displayed by the 'cured' women and girls of Marpingen and Mettenbuch can also be plausibly seen as a response to the reality or prospect of relentless toil and hardship, as a form of flight into illness. Before she took to her bed and refused hot food, Theres Kroiß had been a servant girl whose paralysis supposedly started after she swallowed a needle.[226] Katharina Becker escaped heavy work in the fields because of her partial paralysis.[227] There were many other cases suggesting that illness could be, in part, a resort of the weak, a means of coping with anxiety or sloughing off intolerable responsibilities.[228] We are irresistibly reminded by many of those who claimed cures of the peasant wives, daughters, and farm servants who constituted so many of the visionaries themselves. The cured and the visionaries form two groups strikingly congruent in terms of gender, social class, even age structure. In fact, the two groups cannot be neatly separated, for many visionaries claimed some form of cure, while some of those who claimed cures also believed they had been vouchsafed apparitions. Whatever the individual trauma, the domestic despair, or the social pressures which prompted the nervous disorders afflicting so many of the cured, the drama of the cure must have provided emotional consolations and prestige similar to that experienced by the original visionaries.[229]

[224] Devlin, *Superstitious Mind*, 67–8. I could find no evidence about the causes of these conditions among those claiming cures at Marpingen or Mettenbuch.

[225] It should be noted that when modern sociologists of medicine refer to illness as an 'occupation' they mean something different, namely the acceptance of their condition by the person who is ill, and their willingness to fight against it and try to regain a condition of 'health' by following a prescribed regimen. See C. Herzlich, *Health and Illness: A Social Psychological Analysis* (New York and London, 1973), 119–25.

[226] SAL., 164/2, 1162. There are tantalizing parallels with a votive shrine in Eberweis, Austria, established when a tailor was 'saved' after swallowing a needle: Nolan and Nolan, *Christian Pilgrimage*, 235.

[227] *MWOL*, 24; *EM*, 40–2.

[228] This has been suggested for similar French cases by Devlin, *Superstitious Mind*, 67. More generally on 'flight into illness' and 'illness as liberator', see Herzlich, *Health and Illness*, 8, 114–19. The particular burdens that fell on women are discussed in Heller, 'Körperliche Überbelastung'.

[229] Kselman, *Miracles and Prophecies*, 62–79, explores this theme in the case of Lourdes.

Commercialization

Commercialization was inseparable from major pilgrimages. These were festive as well as solemn undertakings, and nineteenth-century pilgrims needed food, drink, and shelter as much as their medieval counterparts. Modern pilgrims, like purely secular travellers, also wanted souvenirs of their visits, a demand that was increasingly met by modern mass production in the form of pilgrimage medallions, candles, and rosaries turned out by the thousand. These artefacts provided an easy target for sceptics. One anticlerical German visitor to Lourdes in 1876 noted that on the road to the grotto one encountered 'the profane hustle and bustle of the annual market; for a quarter of an hour there was row upon row of stalls, where the commonplace spirit of speculation fed generously on pious delusions'.[230] Among the objects for sale were prayer books, pictures, rosaries, photographs, scapulars, flasks, sticks, brooches, and medallions. But it was not only non-Catholics who had serious doubts about all this. The Catholic convert Huysmans called commercialization of this sort 'the devil's revenge', and complained that the Lourdes quarrymen ('these local louts') had given up work to sell rosaries and sausages and 'bleed the pilgrims dry'.[231] The Catholic politician and lawyer Julius Bachem, who later defended inhabitants of Marpingen on charges that included the attempt to gain money through false pretences, shared with many middle-class German Catholics a strong antipathy to devotional kitsch.[232] Others expressed a more sinister hostility. There was a firm belief among some German Catholics that the profits went disproportionately into the pockets of Protestants and Jews. The publicist Hans Rost argued plaintively that it was 'a perhaps little known but undeniably regrettable truth that in Lourdes almost all the shops selling devotional materials, rosaries, prayer books, and souvenirs are in the hands of the Jews'. The same applied, he suggested, to Bavarian pilgrimages.[233] Beneath Rost's disagreeable claims there is, however, an important truth: that among the beneficiaries of modern, commercialized pilgrimages were the wholesalers and suppliers of mass-produced devotionalia, as well as transport concerns and large breweries.

Yet a major pilgrimage also enriched the local population of the town or village which was its goal. Take the case of Trier. It is true that organized commercial interests benefited from its many pilgrimages: as early as the 1770s there were reports of three large ships full of rosaries arriving for distribution during the Feast of the Annunciation.[234] But inhabitants of the town had a major part in

[230] 'Zwei Tage in Lourdes', 603.
[231] Huysmans, Crowds, 80–92; Huysmans to Henry Céard, 19 Mar. 1903, in B. Beaumont (ed.), The Road from Decadence: From Brothel to Cloister. Selected Letters of J. K. Huysmans (London, 1989), 219. See also Lochet, Muttergottes-Erscheinungen, 47.
[232] Bachem, Erinnerungen, 142.
[233] Rost, Die wirtschaftliche und kulturelle Lage, 202–3. Huysmans also propagated the view that there was widespread 'Jewish influence' behind the devotional kitsch sold at Lourdes. See Crowds, 88, 127–8.
[234] Müller, St Wendel, 593.

selling rosaries and other mass-produced objects, and they also provided bed and board for pilgrims. The abolition of various Trier pilgrimages during the Catholic Enlightenment is estimated to have cost the inhabitants 30,000 thaler a year, leading to protests and the rescinding of the ban.[235] In the nineteenth century, the two great pilgrimages to the Holy Coat in Trier have provided us with detailed descriptions of how the local population profited from the hundreds of thousands of visitors. In 1844, stalls were set up all around the cathedral, and sales of devotional objects and souvenirs were enormous: this was one target of the criticism that accompanied the event.[236] In 1891, over a thousand new businesses sprang up to serve the pilgrims. Images of the Holy Coat found their way on to medallions, brooches, purses, tie-pins, and foodstuffs, and the grossly commercialized nature of the occasion once again drew fierce attacks.[237]

Both locals and non-locals therefore benefited from the pilgrimage trade. Marpingen was no exception. It nevertheless differed from an established centre such as Trier or Lourdes in its lack of official status. This had its effect on the pattern of commercialization, as on every aspect of the Marpingen affair. It meant that there were no set days when pilgrims descended on the village, no officially sanctioned mass pilgrimages—in short, there was no pilgrimage 'season'. There was, equally, nothing like the infrastructure of shops, stalls, and hotels of the kind that developed at Lourdes. The casual commercialization at Marpingen always sailed close to the wind in legal terms. Extensive though it was, the pilgrimage trade in the village was an essentially improvised, hole-and-corner affair.

The Prussian authorities decided almost immediately that greed and intent to defraud lay behind the apparitions, and held to this view tenaciously throughout the long enquiry.[238] At the 1879 trial in Saarbrücken, desperate attempts were still being made to show that dealers in devotional kitsch had been ready before 3 July 1876, in other words that the whole episode had been cynically planned. Not a single piece of evidence was ever found to support this view of a fraudulent conspiracy, and it seems certain that the initial apparitions were spontaneous. The inhabitants of Marpingen, unsurprisingly, emphasized the damage that the whole affair had done to the local economy. Village landowners explained how the pilgrims threatened their meadows; the parish council complained on 28 September 1876, not for the first time, that police measures had caused 'interference in their trade with the outside world'.[239] A sympathetic writer agreed that 'all trade and commerce . . . came to a standstill' during this period.[240] But villagers

[235] G. Birtsch, 'Soziale Unruhen, ständische Gesellschaft und politische Repräsentation. Trier in der Zeit der Französischen Revolution', in E. Hinrichs *et al.* (eds.), *Mentalitäten und Lebensverhältnisse. Beispiele aus der Sozialgeschichte der Neuzeit. Rudolf Vierhaus zum 60. Geburtstag* (Göttingen, 1982), 151.

[236] Fox, *Saarländische Volkskunde*, 254. See also Schieder, 'Kirche und Revolution'.

[237] Cf. F. Jaskowski, *Verlauf und Fiasko des Trierer Schauspiels im Jahre 1891* (Saarbrücken, 1891); Fox, *Saarländische Volkskunde*, 257.

[238] LASB, E 107, 48 ff.: 'Einzelne Beschuldigungen . . . III: Betrug'.

[239] Ibid. 259–60, 434.

[240] Cramer, *Die Erscheinungen*, 29.

probably exaggerated these 'vexations', and there is no doubt that they quickly sought ways to make good any losses.[241] As we have already seen, the school-teacher Metzen believed that the village men overcame their doubts about the apparitions only when visitors began to arrive in force.[242] While that may not be strictly true, the evidence shows that the flood of pilgrims offered numerous profitable opportunities which villagers were not slow to accept. Public Prosecutor Petershof was wrong when he claimed in 1877 that 'the entire population of the place has as good as given up work', but there was more truth to his charge that they 'live[d] off the pilgrims'.[243]

The most obvious beneficiaries were those able to offer accommodation. In some respects, of course, a town like St Wendel was better placed to benefit from this new business than Marpingen. As a local administrative and commercial centre connected to the railway network it was geared to accommodating visitors. The town undoubtedly did well in these years. Princess Helene of Thurn und Taxis paid a hotel bill there of 368 marks in 1877.[244] The historian of the town has described these 'golden days': the guest-houses and inns were filled, and the tables were permanently laid at the Trierischer Hof, whose 'antediluvian yellow mail coach rattled continuously over the streets with new visitors'.[245] But if St Wendel was a staging post, most pilgrims wanted to stay in Marpingen itself if possible. The immediate beneficiaries of this were the village inns: Dewese and Kiewese, with their medieval origins, Beckersch, Hansnickels, Scherersch, Schneidersch, Blaumeier, and the two most recent additions, built by outside entrepreneurs in the 1870s, Trapps and Zur Post.[246] The inns found their rooms permanently taken, and no longer had to make do with the passing trade of wandering journeymen, itinerant musicians, commercial representatives, and those such as knife-grinders, tinsmiths, ropemakers, brushmakers, and tinkers who serviced the village periodically. These were halcyon days for a substantial publican like Johann Hubertus, landlord of the Dewese, where there was accommodation for as many as fifteen guests. In September 1877 alone, 206 people were recorded as staying at the Dewese, where the bill for an overnight stay would come to between 1.10 and 1.40 marks.[247]

The volumes of beer and other drink consumed at such establishments also rose greatly with the arrival of the pilgrims. On 12 July, a telegram was sent from

[241] The picture of economic life in the village that emerges from the evidence collected by examining magistrate Kleber is one of business as usual. Cattle and crops were bought and sold, merchants continued to do their business in the village. Gustav Fischer from Ottweiler provides an example: he continued to visit Marpingen fortnightly to settle up with his customers, the village's bakers: LASB, E 107, 234; Prozeß, 124–5.
[242] See above, Ch. 4.
[243] LHAK, 442/6442, 115–17: OP Petershof to MdI Berlin, 20 Sept. 1877, quotation on 116–17.
[244] TTZ, HMA 2699, 2810.
[245] Müller, St Wendel, 275.
[246] Bungert, Heimatbuch, 416. Magistrates and police conducted interrogations at Blaumeier's: BAT, B III, 11, 14/4, 74.
[247] Bungert, Heimatbuch, 417–18.

Johann Thomé's inn to a Kaiserslautern brewery requesting 150 gallons of beer: 'Marian miracle in Marpingen. Enormous pilgrimage. Send 7 Hecto[litres] to Thomé immediately on credit.' On the same day Thomé told a visitor from Ottweiler that business had been 'very good' in recent days, and added 'if only the police don't interfere'.[248] Another visitor was told by a grinning mine host that 'at present more beer was devoured (*vertilgt*) in a day than he would usually pull in a whole year'.[249] At 10 pfennigs a glass, and 15 pfennigs for a brandy, the extra profits must have been considerable. On top of that came the extra demand for bread and cheese, hot food, and tobacco. The extensive aristocratic presence in the village inns, which was very marked at the Hubertus establishment, must have given a particular fillip to the local economy, especially when they travelled with a retinue of footmen, coachmen, and the like. Even in the case of Princess Helene of Thurn und Taxis, who stayed with Neureuter, a sum of 30 marks was entered in her accounts under 'provisions for coachmen', along with 80 marks under 'tips'.[250]

Like many other clerical and aristocratic visitors, Princess Helene chose to stay with the parish priest. One result was that Neureuter's housekeeper was summonsed at least twice for the illegal lodging of guests (*gesetzwidrige Beherbergung*).[251] Other pilgrims spilled over from the village inns into private houses, through either choice or necessity. The homes of the visionary girls were particularly sought after. Many witnesses testified to the large number of guests in the Kunz, Leist, and Hubertus households. One visitor in mid-August 1877 reported that around twenty other people were drinking coffee in the room at the same time.[252] In the three weeks from 28 August to 17 September 1877, Frau Kunz put up over 100 guests; around 150 people lodged in the Hubertus and Leist homes over a somewhat longer period that late summer and early autumn.[253] The homes of later visionaries were also popular with pilgrims.[254] The use of private dwellings as guest-houses became commonplace as the number of visitors grew. Most of the information we have on the provision of board and lodging concerns August and September 1877, when the influx of pilgrims reached new levels and the gendarmes cracked down as they had not done before. Many visitors were forced to seek accommodation in neighbouring villages such as Alsweiler, and the gendarmes' reports suggest that both inns and private houses

[248] LASB, E 107, 207. The telegram was sent in the name of a brewery representative called Schoettle. See also *Prozeß*, 109.
[249] 'An der Gnadenstätte', 668.
[250] TTZ, HMA 2699, 2803: 'Hofmarschallamts-Rechnung. Belege 1877/78: Reise Rechnung. Über eine Reise I[hrer] K[öniglichen] H[oheit] von Tutzing nach Marpingen'.
[251] BAT, B III, 11, 14/4, 71, 100.
[252] LASB, E 107, 325–6: statement of mayor's secretary Schuh of Eppelborn. See also LASB, E 107, 314; *Prozeß*, 18–19, 85, 145.
[253] LASB, E 107, 303–4.
[254] Ibid. 252, on guests at the home of Peter Hahn, father of Anna and Anton Hahn who had allegedly seen apparitions on 6 July 1876.

in Marpingen were 'overcrowded'.[255] Two widows faced with fines for taking in visitors claimed that 'the whole village' shared their fear of being punished for an '"offence" of which they were *all* without exception guilty' as they tried 'to find beds and straw for the jostling crowds of people'.[256] They may have been guilty of some exaggeration, but in the period August–November 1877 nearly fifty inhabitants of the village were fined under the 1861 trade tax law for operating a guest-house illegally, most of them with previous convictions for the same offence.[257] Some of these were marginal cases. The mason's wife Elisabeth Schnur was summonsed for putting up her own relations, the peasant Jakob Saar for lodging an itinerant knife-grinder who stayed with him for a few days every year.[258] There was, on the other hand, the case of the linen-weaver Nikolaus Schu, which suggests brazenness and desperation in equal parts. Schu had suffered ill health for some years and lived with his peasant brother near the parish church. He was convicted along with many others for the illegal lodging of guests. The difference was that Schu had tried to obtain a licence to run a guest-house, which was turned down on the grounds that his accommodation was too cramped. He then applied for a licence to sell alcohol from his premises (*Erlaubnis zur Schenkwirtschaft*), and calculated unwisely that a gift of a 10-mark gold coin to the official involved would help his cause. The result was a conviction for attempted bribery.[259]

For the most part, the villagers seem to have viewed the accommodation of pilgrims as an act of Christian charity that also provided a legitimate means of augmenting modest family incomes. Those summonsed included miners, peasants, craftsmen, and one of the village teachers—although it was, in fact, often their wives who were named on the summonses.[260] The evidence we have on the prices charged is patchy and inconclusive. The master carpenter Jakob Schario allegedly put up more than ninety people in the period from August to November 1877, including many of the 'well-off', at higher than usual prices.[261] On the other hand, the miner's widow Frau Kunz and her sister charged only 20 pfennigs a night for a bed, and 10 pfennigs for a straw pallet.[262] Reports and opinions differed even on the same individual. This is particularly true of another widow Kunz, Margaretha's mother. The gendarmes were not alone in believing that she, along with the other girls' parents, charged high prices and 'profited enormously'.[263] The claim that she charged 'city prices' for coffee also seems to be borne out by the experience of one visitor who paid 50 pfennigs each for

[255] *MG*, 42; LASB, E 107, 162.
[256] BAT, B III, 11, 14/4, 122.
[257] LASB, E 107, 167. See also Kammer, *Kulturkampfpriester*, 160.
[258] BAT, B III, 11, 14/4, 71, 99.
[259] BAT, B III, 11, 14/4, 89, 177.
[260] Based on the summonses for failure to register guests, in BAT, B III, 11, 14/4, 71, 77, 85, 88–9, 91–100, 115, 122–5, 128–9, 134–8, 142, 156, 177.
[261] LASB, E 107, 197.
[262] BAT, B III, 11, 14/4, 122.
[263] LASB, E 107, 166, 303–4, quotation from the village sceptic Scherer.

coffee and cakes for himself and a companion.[264] On the other hand, two modest tradeswomen from Neumagen were guests at the house during Whitsuntide 1877 and found it 'cheap'.[265]

While St Wendel was better endowed with hotels and guest-houses, Marpingen could therefore offer improvised alternatives to take advantage of the pilgrimage trade. The same held true in other spheres of activity. There was, for example, no carriage business in this agricultural and mining village; it had never been on a major coaching route. As a result, it was professional carriage drivers from elsewhere who picked up the custom of better-off pilgrims bound for Marpingen. They included Michel Bart (St Wendel), Peter Schättler (Tholey), Peter Blatt (Ottweiler), Johann Grün and Nickel Munkes (St Johann), Peter Brösch and H. G. Jacob (Saarbrücken).[266] The St Wendel carriage drivers had particular reason to be grateful to Marpingen, having lost much of their business with the advent of the Rhine–Nahe railway.[267] But the suggestion of one writer that inhabitants of the village 'became carriage drivers' suggests that Marpingers were among those whose straw-filled carts and 'ancient conveyances' lined up outside the St Wendel station, as they improvised a means of transporting pilgrims to the village.[268] Even more important, once the pilgrims had arrived the villagers could offer them the benefits of their local knowledge. Some presented themselves as guides, a function which probably included assistance with evading gendarmes during periods when the authorities were trying to prevent access to the site. Being on the spot offered many other forms of opportunist profit. Some visitors were persuaded to part with 50 pfennigs or 1 mark for a piece of cloth on which the Blessed Virgin had supposedly stood, deemed 'good against illness'.[269] The day labourer Johannes Kreuz (known as 'Kreuzhannes') and his brother-in-law, the cobbler Michel Puhl—both men with village reputations for drunkenness— dug earth at the apparition site and sold it to pilgrims.[270] Providing earth for visitors became a common source of income among the young men of the village.

The trade in water was more widespread, as it was at Mettenbuch.[271] Some sold water drawn at the 'miraculous spring' from under the noses of the gen- darmes. This could be risky, as the many convictions for entering the Härtelwald illegally show.[272] It could also be a slow process. The hotel owner Bonn, from

[264] Prozeß, 18; LASB, E 107, 325–6: evidence of mayor's secretary Schuh of Eppelborn.
[265] Prozeß, 85; LASB, E 107, 314.
[266] Bungert, Heimatbuch, 417.
[267] Müller, St Wendel, 751.
[268] Ibid. 275; 'An der Gnadenstätte', 666–8.
[269] LASB, E 107, 236–7. Many witnesses testified to this. One man, from Püttlingen, believed it had happened in the house of Elisabeth Recktenwald (one of the later 'rival children').
[270] LASB, E 107, 253–6; BAT, B III, 11, 14/4, 80–4.
[271] Evidence on Mettenbuch in SAL, 164/2, 1161: BA Deggendorf to BM Metten, 9 July 1878 and reply of 12 July 1878; BA Deggendorf to BM Metten, 14 Aug. 1878 and reply of 16 Aug. 1878; BA Deggendorf to BM Metten, 16 Aug. 1878; BA Deggendorf to KR Lower Bavaria, 26 Sept. 1878 and 13 Nov. 1878; 164/2, 1163: BA Deggendorf to KR Lower Bavaria, 12 Dec. 1877.
[272] Source as in n. 260.

Bad Neuenahr, was in Marpingen in the summer of 1877, seeking water for his mentally ill daughter. He complained to another visitor that after eight days he had still not obtained any *genuine* Marpingen water; a man called Stephan—probably Stephan Brill—had promised him some, but apparently the gendarmes had been too watchful. Bonn eventually returned home with water he had managed to obtain himself.[273] Bonn's emphasis on 'genuine' water had a point to it, for there were those who fobbed pilgrims off with water from other sources.[274] Water was also sent to pilgrims, something that showed up in the large increase in outgoing post from Marpingen, much of it consisting of small packages that the postman Lohmeyer suspected of containing water. The extra load on the postman was so great that he acquired a dog-cart in the spring of 1877.[275] The other aspect of this trade was the sale of tin containers to hold the water. Marpingen had no tinsmith, but at least two moved into the village from Tholey to meet the new demand. Johann Thomé and other prominent Marpingen figures seem to have had a major part in the distribution network.[276] Tin containers were prominently displayed in the windows of private houses as well as on some of the stalls that sprang up in the village.[277]

The stalls and booths dealt largely in mass-produced commercial goods with a higher mark-up than the containers produced by local tinsmiths. They were much the same at all the apparition sites, with suitable alterations to fit local circumstances. Representations of the Virgin were predominant. They came in a variety of forms: postcards, mounted pictures, and images made from wood, metal, leather, cloth, plaster, soap, gutta-percha, and gingerbread. Many of the postcards showed the visionary children in the presence of the Virgin at the apparition site. They sat alongside other reproductions of religious artworks such as pictures of the saints, medallions, crucifixes, amulets, rosaries, candles, and prayer books. For sale, finally, were the popular pamphlets celebrating the apparitions.[278] These wares were sold from stalls set up in the streets of Marpingen, near the church, and around the nearby Marian spring. It is possible to reconstruct how they reached the village by looking at cases where similar goods were intercepted on the way. On 26 September 1876 Prussian officials in Saarbrücken seized a shipment of pilgrimage medallions addressed to a goldsmith called Ney.

[273] LASB, E 107, 236.
[274] See the report in the *NBZ*, 19 Oct. 1876, on a feather-dealer selling water that was not from the 'miraculous spring'. This may have been the namesake of one of the visionary children, Margaretha Kunz.
[275] LASB, E 107, 235.
[276] *Prozeß*, 171; LASB, E 107, 196.
[277] LASB, E 107, 237, reporting the full-scale inspection undertaken by the Prussian authorities on 9 Aug. 1877; *Prozeß*, 165–6; 'An der Gnadenstätte', 668. According to two witnesses, these containers were sold for 5 to 8 groschen: LASB, E 107, 313–15.
[278] On Marpingen, see LASB, E 107, 237; 'An der Gnadenstätte', 668. On Dittrichswalde, 'Bei der Madonna', 30. On Mettenbuch, SAL, 164/2, 1161–3. There are also examples of commercial pictures, medallions, and pamphlets preserved in BZAR, F 115, in two of the unnumbered folders that follow the seven numbered ones (Fasc. I–VII), namely those marked 'Angebl. Erscheinungen in Mettenbuch 1878', and 'Metten. Untersuchungen der Muttergotteserscheinungen in Mettenbuch'.

The medallions depicted the Virgin and Child, and were inscribed 'This is my dearly beloved son' on one side and 'Miraculous spring at Marpingen' on the other. The Marian prayers mentioned by the children were named around the outside. Ney had ordered fifty gross from Beysen & Becker of Paris on the advice of a hawker who had told him of a chance 'to do good business'; they had been bought wholesale at 2 pfennigs each to be sold on to the hawker at 6 pfennigs.[279] Eleven months later a further consignment of medallions was seized at Saarbrücken station, this time from Robineau Fils in Paris to the Saarlouis merchant Meeß who frequently handled such articles. From Meeß's statement it emerged that a previous order of fifteen gross from the same Paris wholesaler had been sold on to a book dealer and another merchant in Saarlouis, to the *Saar-Zeitung*, and to a number of hawkers.[280]

The trade in medallions therefore ran from distant manufacturers and wholesalers, through merchant middlemen, to retail outlets such as bookshops, hawkers, and stallholders. The same was true of popular pamphlets, postcards, and other mass-produced religious artworks. The popular accounts of Marpingen written by Dr Nikolaus Thoemes were variously published in Berlin, Stuttgart, Saarlouis, and Trier, and the publishers explicitly advertised them to attract hawkers and stallholders.[281] We get a glimpse of the business world of ephemeral religious publishing from the vain attempts made by Thoemes to raise money for the Marpingen cause by selling the reproduction rights to a drawing of the apparitions he had commissioned from a needy sculptor in Stuttgart. This involved him in negotiations with the photographer Krapp, Peter Philippi of the publishing firm J. B. Grach in Trier, and the publisher Hermann Butzon in the pilgrimage town of Kevelaer.[282] The sticking-point was partly the 4,000 marks Thoemes wanted for the copyright, partly the publishers' preference for the 'Deger Madonna', a representation of the Virgin of Marpingen commissioned from a prominent religious artist in Düsseldorf by the Belgian aristocrat whose daughter had experienced a 'miraculous' cure.[283] It was the Deger picture that eventually predominated in the hawkers' knapsacks and on the streets of Marpingen, where the postcards sold for between 50 pfennigs and 1 mark according to size.[284]

[279] LASB, E 107, 150–1; *Prozeß*, 187–8; *MWOL*, 45–6.
[280] LASB, E 107, 151–5.
[281] Ibid. 450–3. The pamphlets were also advertised direct to the public through the press. In autumn 1877 the Pfeiffer'sche Buchhandlung advertised the brochure *Marpingen: Wahrheit oder Lüge?* at 30 pfennigs in the local paper that served the area around Mettenbuch. See the *Deggendorfer Donaubote*, 5 Sept. 1877, copy in SAL, 164/2, 1162.
[282] LASB, E 107, 461–2; *Prozeß*, 179–80. Philippi was a major figure in the Catholic public life of Trier during the *Kulturkampf*, and one of the founders of the Katholischer Volksverein. See LHAK, 442/7854, 675–89.
[283] On the commissioning of the Deger Madonna, see LASB, E 107, 147–50; and on the intense interest of the authorities in this particular work, and its reproduction, see LHAK, 442/6442, 105–10.
[284] LASB, E 107, 318–19. The examples collected in the folders of the BZAR cited in n. 278 show that religious devotionalia were also imported to Mettenbuch from France.

This was an organized, essentially specialist trade, and the professionals moved into Marpingen to practise it. Within two weeks of the first apparition, the press reported that a Jewish tradesman from Tholey had established a stall in the village.[285] Other traders followed. The stallholders included the Bonnems and several others from Tholey, Johann Baus from Lockweiler, and 'many' from St Wendel. Others came from further afield, such as Katharina Mungen from Wittlich and the picture seller van Treek of Rheijdt, who made 1,100 marks from his wares between the end of August and the beginning of December 1877.[286] For many of these, the content of what they were selling would have been a matter of indifference. The hawker who ordered medallions from the goldsmith Ney in Saarlouis, a native of the Speicher district noted for its itinerant traders, had sold similar objects to the Trier pilgrims in 1844; he had also sold revolutionary cockades in 1848 and military mementoes in 1871.[287] The inhabitants of Marpingen were not entirely excluded from this business. A tradesman called Schorr sold medallions and crucifixes from a stall in the summer of 1877, and professional tradespeople like the Bonnems complained that they faced 'strong competition' from villagers as well as 'outsiders'.[288]

There was also money to be made indirectly from providing accommodation for those stallholders who did not live in nearby Tholey or St Wendel. Indeed, the picture seller van Treek set up shop in a living-room of the Leist family home, paying 9 marks a week for full board.[289] During his stay in Marpingen, van Treek would have paid his hosts around 125 marks, enough to rent a 2-*Morgen* meadow for a year and buy 10 *Zentner* of hay, and accounting for something over 10 per cent of his own considerable profits.[290] There is something symptomatic about this arrangement. The Leists fared handsomely, but their role remained ancillary. Their windfall typified the financial rewards that Marpingen's inhabitants gleaned from the whole affair. The money brought by pilgrims certainly lubricated the local economy. One merchant who had regular business in the village claimed that the offertory money left by pilgrims showed up in the increasing amounts of small change with which his bills were settled.[291] Whether or not that is true, the profits made by most villagers from offering themselves as guides, selling earth and water, or renting out rooms were improvised, opportunist, and relatively paltry.

The makings of something on a larger scale were clearly there. While medallions and rosaries poured into Marpingen from east and west of the Rhine, plans were

[285] *SMZ*, 18 July 1876.
[286] LASB, E 107, 160, 234, 318–19; *Prozeß*, 159–60; Müller, *St Wendel*, 275. On the comparable developments in Mettenbuch, see SAL, 164/2, 1162; and on Dittrichswalde, 'Bei der Madonna', 30.
[287] *Prozeß*, 187–8. The hawker, frightened off by the official interest, had not in fact collected his medallions.
[288] LASB, E 107, 159, 234.
[289] Ibid. 318. He had been turned down by the Hubertus family.
[290] On the costs of rented land and hay, see Beck, *Beschreibung*, i. 233. Two *Morgen* is about one and a third acres, 10 *Zentner* about 10 cwt., or half a ton.
[291] The merchant Gustav Fischer of Ottweiler, testifying in court: *Prozeß*, 124–5.

afoot for a more fundamental development of the village. One entrepreneur offered to build a 'sanctuarium' there, of the kind to be found at Lourdes and Pontmain; another proposed a hotel near the Härtelwald with a view over the apparition site.[292] One hostile commentator drew parallels with other apparition sites and with spa towns: 'People are hoping soon to be able to enter into competition with Lourdes . . . As in a spa that is coming into fashion, first-class hotels, elegant stores, and attractive parks will spring out of the ground like mushrooms.' By analogy with the spas, there would be 'pilgrimage seasons'.[293] The writer's barbs were not entirely unfounded. Behind urgent local demands for the building of a chapel at the site, and the talk of a 'German Lourdes', lay an evident desire to emulate the Pyrenean prototype, although it would be wrong to exaggerate the part played by commercial motives. The analogy with spas was also apposite, for the parallels between spa resorts and pilgrimage sites were not lost on contemporaries.[294] The inhabitants of Marpingen were certainly aware of them. One petition from the parish council to the Prussian provincial authorities argued plaintively that 'the removal of controls over the blessed spring would pose no greater harm to the local or general good than the daily, unrestricted filling of hundreds of bottles in Ems and Carlsbad'.[295] In fact Bad Neuenahr might have been an even better example. Situated fairly close to Marpingen, it was a resort that arose out of nothing when the wealthy wine grower Georg Kreuzberg discovered mineral springs on his newly acquired land in the 1850s. Opened by the Empress Augusta in 1858, with a Latin motto that pledged it to 'the health and comfort of the sick', Bad Neuenahr was already being referred to as a 'celebrated spa' by the Suffragan Bishop Eberhard of Trier in a diocesan visit a few years later.[296]

Marpingen turned into neither Lourdes nor Bad Neuenahr. The hotels, parks, and shops, like the basilica and sanctuarium, remained unbuilt. By a nice irony, the only person who appears to have exchanged his former job for that of mineral water manufacturer between 1876 and 1879 was one of the gendarmes on duty in Marpingen.[297] For the villagers, the windfall profits of 1876–7 disappeared as the pilgrimage movement ebbed and the stallholders moved out. The natives of Marpingen continued to earn their living as peasants and (increasingly) miners,

[292] *Prozeß*, 213; 'An der Gnadenstätte', 668.

[293] 'An der Gnadenstätte', 668.

[294] The district official in Deggendorf drew an explicit parallel between Mettenbuch and 'our more famous healing springs': SAL, 164/2, 1163: BA Deggendorf to KR Lower Bavaria, 12 Dec. 1877. See also S. L. Bensusan, *Some German Spas: A Holiday Record* (London, 1925), 14: 'There is something akin to the medieval pilgrimage in this modern movement to the spas.'

[295] LASB, E 107, 435. Bottled water was a major source of Bad Ems's prosperity; it probably enabled the less celebrated Bad Wildungen to break even. The annual output of bottles at the latter had reached 2 million by the First World War. See Bensusan, *Some German Spas*, 19–20, 41, 47.

[296] Bensusan, *Some German Spas*, 62–3; Kraft, *Matthias Eberhard*, 88–9.

[297] *Prozeß*, 58. There is a curious parallel with the case in Lourdes of the gendarme Viron, a keen amateur photographer who was the first person to photograph Bernadette Soubirous and went on to establish a highly successful photography business in the town. See Marnham, *Lourdes*, 87.

rather than as hotel attendants and the purveyors of religious kitsch. Only with the revival of demands for the recognition of the apparitions in the twentieth century did thoughts of developing the village commercially as a German Lourdes surface once again.

6

The Reaction of the Clergy

In 1877 the Catholic writer Joseph Rebbert published a booklet on Marpingen, in which he discussed the position of Catholic priests faced with such events. His emphasis was on their ability to master the situation. The clergy was 'superior to all other classes in its scholarship' and fully alive to the dangers of delusion, deception, and diabolical influence; it operated within the clear ground-lines set out by the Catholic Church and could expect the laity to follow its leaders without question.[1] Things were a little different in practice. Many priests embraced the apparitions with a passionate conviction that left little room for doubt. Others were more sceptical, expressing alarm at the direction events were taking. But the enthusiasm of the pilgrims, the rash of imitative apparitions, and the political background of the 1870s all made it more difficult to exert control over popular sentiment. The clergy found itself caught between the rules of the church, the pressure of the civil authorities, and the demands of the faithful. Particular problems inevitably arose for any priest whose own parish was the centre of attention. The situation was especially difficult in Marpingen. Jakob Neureuter not only had to cope with the sustained pressure that arose from highly publicized apparitions, but was forced to do so at a time when the *Kulturkampf* had robbed the diocese of its bishop and generally disrupted the hierarchical chain of command.

For and Against

Large numbers of priests visited Marpingen during the apparitions. At the beginning of September 1877 hundreds were present in the village, from Germany and abroad.[2] Some of them no doubt went, as Father Wolf of Neuforweiler claimed he did, because parishioners had already made the pilgrimage and they wanted to investigate events for themselves.[3] As befitted their role as members of the Catholic intelligentsia, many clergy saw themselves as fact-finders. Priests with notebooks, questioning the young seers or clustered around those who claimed cures, became a common sight in the village. It is difficult to

[1] Rebbert, *Marpingen und seine Gegner*, 39–40.
[2] *MG*, 41.
[3] *Prozeß*, 150.

reconstruct their views, but it is probable that those who made the journey to Marpingen were more predisposed to accept the authenticity of the apparitions. That is certainly indicated by their behaviour. Priests were reported weeping loudly when Margaretha Kunz recounted the story of the apparitions; many accompanied the triumphant processions of the miraculously cured to the visionaries' homes.[4] Hundreds risked arrest, and twenty were indeed prosecuted, for illegally celebrating mass in the village.[5] Many priests took Marpingen water away with them, others wrote to Neureuter requesting that he send some.[6] There is no great surprise in this. A generation of German priests, trained in the spiritually revived seminaries of the 1850s and 1860s, had imbibed and passed on to their parishioners the message of the 'Marian century'. Marpingen, like Lourdes, seemed to confirm the timeliness of the doctrine of the Immaculate Conception.[7] At a time when the *Kulturkampf* was imprisoning their fellow priests, the apparitions must have represented for many a solace: a sign of hope in a cold, hard world. As one priest wrote from Bavaria, the apparition of the Immaculate Conception was a means of restoring Christian belief 'to a present sunk in materialism'.[8] The apparitions were welcomed as a sign of such potency that it would jolt the sceptics and progress-mongers out of their complacency. In a tremulous letter to a fellow priest, enclosing water, Father Schneider of Alsweiler wrote in October 1876: 'I firmly hope and believe that things are still to happen here at which the *Kulturkämpfer* will marvel, as once did Columbus and his fellows when they discovered America.'[9] The words and deeds of the Blessed Virgin would serve to counter and confound the 'excessive rationalism' and mere head-learning denounced in the *Syllabus of Errors*. Schneider wrote scornfully to another priest about the efforts of the local mayor and school inspector, who had encouraged a new teacher in Marpingen to drive mystical thoughts out of the young visionaries' heads with the help of exercises in mental arithmetic.[10] His correspondent on this occasion was Felix Dicke, a priest from the Westphalian parish of Minden. In some respects, Dicke was less militant about the powers of the Virgin, striking a tone that was gentler and even allowed for affectionate humour about the seriousness of a fellow priest. The summer of 1876 was very dry, and Dicke had been in Marpingen when Father Eich of Heusweiler asked the Virgin, through the children, whether it would rain. Writing to Neureuter after returning home, Dicke commented: 'My mother is well, despite the storms

[4] Sausseret, *Erscheinungen*, 230; LASB, E 107, 372–3.
[5] LHAK, 403/15716, 130–1, 134–9, 144–7, 154–5, 158–61.
[6] *SMZ*, 30 Mar. 1877; LASB, E 107, 170–80: letters to Neureuter.
[7] Many priests who visited Marpingen wanted, like some of Neureuter's clerical correspondents, to establish the place of Marpingen within a sequence of apparitions. The correspondents mentioned, particularly, La Salette, Lourdes, Philippsdorf, and the experiences of the Belgian stigmatist Louise Lateau, which (perhaps because of the exiled *Kulturkampf* priests who went to Belgium) seemed to hold a particular interest for the German clergy. See LASB, E 107, 170–80; *Prozeß*, 211–15.
[8] LASB, E 107, 359–61: Father Klotz to Schneider, 19 Aug. 1876.
[9] LASB, E 107, 364: Schneider to Father Bollig of Mertesdorf, 10 Oct. 1876.
[10] LASB, E 107, 106: Schneider to Dicke, 6 Sept. 1876.

and heavy showers, which do not cease. That is the work of Father Eich with his questions. He will certainly not enquire again: "will it rain?" But the Blessed Virgin has shown him a sign of her love by giving such a sustained answer to his question.'[11] The innocent jocularity suggests the warm sense of fellowship among clergy who had met each other for the first time through the apparitions; it does not signify scepticism on the fundamental issue—the Virgin Mary's powers as an intercessor. Dicke cited the improvement in the health of his mother (she suffered from gout) as one among many examples of the 'help brought by the Blessed Virgin in Minden'.[12]

Dicke, Schneider, and the putative rain-maker, Eich, together formed a group of priests who tried to take some of the burden from Neureuter's shoulders. Eich, from a nearby parish, was involved from the first days of the apparitions. He was on close terms with Neureuter, for the latter was accustomed to spending a few days each summer in Heusweiler, helping with the pastoral duties.[13] Schneider and Dicke did not arrive until several weeks later. Schneider had severe bronchial catarrh through June and July, although he was in touch with Neureuter—his closest clerical neighbour—and wrote to the editor of *Germania* with an outline of events as early as 17 July. Dicke had been 'left cold' by the first reports of the apparitions, but was profoundly affected by Neureuter's own letter, published in *Germania* on 28 July, and set off for Marpingen within days—just as he had, on a previous occasion, gone to Bois d'Haine in Belgium, where he spent a considerable length of time with the stigmatist Louise Lateau.[14]

These priests supported Neureuter in several ways. They offered advice and helped to deal with the large number of requests for water and other correspondence. Schneider was especially active answering letters, while Dicke was dispatched on one occasion to the Countess Spee-Galen with a bottle of Marpingen water. Neureuter was reluctant to post it, but equally wary of encouraging the countess to visit Marpingen while her husband disapproved.[15] Both priests took statements from the visionaries and the cured, as well as recording the experiences of other villagers at the hands of the authorities. Dicke was instrumental in putting the various accounts of incidents in some kind of order. Neureuter's notes were chaotic, and Dicke suggested—with some self-deprecating remarks about the 'young sparrow giving advice to the experienced eagle'—that it would save time in the long run if newly arrived visiting priests could simply be referred to a fully written-up account, rather than having to be told individually about the events.[16] A narrow line separated the gathering and

---

[11] LASB, E 107, 337: Dicke to Neureuter, 11 Sept. 1876.

[12] LASB, E 107, 408: Dicke to Neureuter, 11 Sept. 1876, and ibid. 401-4. Dicke also talked of others whose health had improved, and of a bankrupt merchant who had come to an amicable arrangement with his creditors.

[13] LASB, E 107, 333-5: *Prozeß*, 12-13, 19, 29.

[14] *Prozeß*, 23-6; *MMGE*, 8, 19.

[15] LASB, E 107, 78-80, 349-75, 408-12; *Prozeß*, 20.

[16] LASB, E 107, 144-6, 407, 416.

ordering of this material from making it public. The Catholic press was hungry for information about Marpingen. They acquired it in part from the prominent priest-publicists who stayed in Marpingen, including Paul Majunke, editor of *Germania*, Edmund Prince Radziwill, who contributed to the same paper, and the Mariologist Matthias Scheeben, who wrote in the *Kölnische Volkszeitung*. But material from priests who had spent longer periods in Marpingen was always in demand. Schneider wrote a number of accounts for the local and national press; Dicke contributed two pieces to the Marian periodical, the *Herz-Maria-Blüthen*, and eventually published a full-length account with the Bonifacius press in Paderborn.[17]

It is instructive to compare the course of events in Marpingen with those in Mettenbuch. In the latter case it was members of the regular clergy from the nearby Benedictine abbey and seminary of Metten who lent their support to the parish priest, Johannes Anglhuber, himself a member of the order.[18] Word of the apparitions had spread through a village landlady to some of the seminarists; they had told their fellow pupils, and questions were raised during classes.[19] At the same time Anglhuber approached the abbot for advice. It was Father Benedikt Braunmüller who calmed his anxieties (he 'approached the matter in a more sanguine fashion'), made some notes at second and third hand, and prevailed on the parish priest to take statements from the visionary children and their parents.[20] Braunmüller acted as scribe when he and Anglhuber first took statements from the children over Christmas 1876, and he accompanied the parish priest to Regensburg to bring news of the events to Bishop Senestrey a few days later.[21] Braunmüller later brought a Capuchin colleague to talk to one of the visionaries, Anna Liebl, and published a pamphlet on the apparitions that had run through five editions by 1878.[22] In other words, at Mettenbuch it was members of the regular clergy who performed the tasks—advising the parish priest, helping him take statements, publicizing the affair—that were performed in Marpingen by members of the secular clergy. There is nothing surprising about that. Mettenbuch was next door to a major Benedictine foundation, and it is a reasonable

---

[17] *MMGE.*

[18] See the brief account of Anglhuber's career in *Heimatblätter für den Stadt- und Landkreis Deggendorf*, hrsg. von dem *Heimatverein Deggendorf und Umgebung*, 10 (1963), 365.

[19] BZAR, F 115, Fasc. I: Pater Benedikt Braunmüller to Bishop Senestrey, 10 Jan. 1877.

[20] Ibid.: 'Bericht des Pfarramtes Metten über die behaupteten Erscheinungen der Mutter Gottes, V: Verhalten des Pfarrers diesen Erscheinungen gegenüber'. This part of the report sent by Anglhuber to Bishop Senestrey on 23 July 1877 mentions Braunmüller

[21] BZAR, F 115, Fasc. I. The visit of Braunmüller and Anglhuber to Senestrey is noted at the beginning of the folder, in the material headed 'Erste Mitteilungen mit Protokollen über Vernehmung der Kinder'. Braunmüller's signature as scribe can be found at the foot of the statements themselves, contained in Beilage I.

[22] On the visit of Braunmüller and the Capuchin Father Walter to Anna Liebl, BZAR, F 115, Fasc. I: 'Auszug aus einem Briefe des Pfarrers v. Metten an Se. bischöfliche Gnaden vom 31. Dez. 1877'. The pamphlet was Braunmüller's *Kurzer Bericht*, published by J. Pfeiffer. For correspondence between Regensburg and Braunmüller over this disputed pamphlet, see BZAR, F 115, Fasc. III, Bishop Senestrey to Braunmüller, 16 Nov. 1878, Braunmüller to Senestrey, 19 Nov. 1878.

assumption that, other things being equal, the regular clergy would play an important supportive role. They had more time at their disposal, and were in a sense specialists (as we have seen, they were invariably sent in by the church to run the local sites in places where the apparitions had been approved, as the Garaison Fathers were at Lourdes).[23] But in Prussian Marpingen, unlike Bavarian Mettenbuch, there were no regular clergy to be found in 1876: they had been expelled as part of the *Kulturkampf*. There were, however, numerous beleaguered secular clergy who saw Marpingen as a beacon, and were prepared to risk the brusque treatment of the gendarmerie and even incarceration in order to witness events for themselves.

One particularly frustrated group for whom Marpingen may have offered a practical and emotional outlet was made up of young (and not-so-young) curates (*Kapläne*). Even before the 1870s the life of the curate could be awkward, as he chafed and tried to carve out a role for himself.[24] The *Kulturkampf* added new frustrations, as promotions were stalled and curates remained for years in the same post under difficult conditions. When Michael Korum was appointed to the long-vacant bishopric of Trier in 1881, he found that some of the seventy-eight curates in the diocese had been ordained as priests twelve or more years before and were still occupying their first curacy; Konrad Schneider had in fact been serving in Alsweiler since 1860.[25] Not all curates wore the title as a badge of honour like the busy and celebrated Georg Dasbach of Trier. On the other hand, there was no other Prussian curate, in Trier or elsewhere, who enjoyed the attention and respect earned by Dasbach as he relentlessly organized peasants, fought court cases, edited newspapers, and arranged political meetings.[26] To curates such as Schneider and Dicke, and to figures on the fringe of Neureuter's informal support group such as curates Schwaab of Urexweiler and Schütz of Ottweiler, Marpingen must have seemed a rewarding and important cause.[27]

Some of the differences between the situations in Bavaria and Prussia therefore emerge from the respective roles played by regular and secular clergy in Mettenbuch and Marpingen. But it is also important to recognize that the clergy as a whole was divided in its reactions to reported apparitions. These divisions ran through regular and secular clergy alike. In Mettenbuch the enthusiasm of Father

[23] Gottfried Korff has pointed out that the regular clergy were often the administrators and bene-ficiaries of established devotional sites; as such they had invariably supported them against criticism and threats to their existence during the late 18th-cent. Catholic Enlightenment: Korff, 'Zwischen Sinnlichkeit und Kindlichkeit', 141.

[24] This can be clearly read between the lines of a circular from Bishop Eberhard of Trier immediately after his inauguration in Nov. 1867, concerned with pastoral training, spiritual retreats, and the like: Kraft, *Matthias Eberhard*, 130.

[25] J. Treitz, *Michael Felix Korum, Bischof von Trier 1840–1921* (Munich, 1925), 84; Lorenzi, *Beiträge*, 643.

[26] On Dasbach's career, see the material in BAT, 85/281–2b, although it is disappointingly thin on the 1870s; also Thoma, *Dasbach*, Fohrmann, 'Dasbach'.

[27] Konrad Schneider was one of the speakers at a meeting organized by Dasbach at St Wendel in August 1873, under the aegis of the Mainzer Verein. See the report of Mayor Müller of St Wendel in SAStW, C/56, 75–84.

Braunmüller and some fellow monks was offset by the doubts of other Metten Benedictines who were 'resolutely opposed to the whole business'.[28] In the case of Marpingen, the female religious who used miraculous water in the attempt to exorcize a fellow nun have to be set against the anxiously sceptical.[29] One of the letters written to Neureuter came from Mother Josepha Gottschalk, the Prioress of the Magdalen convent at Oosterhout in the Brabant and the former head of an order that had been expelled from Upper Silesia during the *Kulturkampf*. She expressed her doubts about the apparitions on the basis of what she had read, and wondered if the Catholic press had given a false impression of events.[30] Felix Dicke, stopping off in Koblenz on one of his journeys between Marpingen and Minden, became embroiled in a fierce debate at the Franciscan convent in the Castor Straße, a debate which went on for several hours and resumed the following day. The prioress of the convent, Sister Gabrielle, who reserved her judgement and argued for a rigorous enquiry before the apparitions could be accepted, disputed with Dicke himself, and also with a Fräulein Zweiffel, a laywoman and the daughter of a rich Koblenz merchant. Fräulein Zweiffel had been to Marpingen with a female companion and expressed herself a believer. Dicke reported that this zealot was 'given a thorough ticking off' by the prioress.[31]

Marpingen was also a contentious issue among the secular clergy. After a heated discussion with other priests in early September 1876, Father Eich wrote to Neureuter: 'Immediately there arose *disputatio*, which assumed a painful character ... I resolved not to touch on M[arpingen] again in clerical company at any price.'[32] Neureuter's correspondence contains direct evidence of clerical scepticism about the apparitions in the form of letters from priests who expressed their doubts; there is also indirect evidence, such as the letter from a priest's cook in Bensberg who asked for some Marpingen water, but wanted to keep the matter secret as the priest was a sceptic.[33] Among the local clergy in the Saarland, enthusiasts like Schneider, Eich and Schwaab have to be set against those who kept their distance, like the parish priest in Tholey and others who went on the offensive against the apparitions.[34] Father Geisbauer of Bliesen preached against Marpingen from the pulpit as early as 11 and 12 July and warned his flock not to go there; parish priests in St Wendel and Illingen reportedly did the same on the following Sunday.[35] Geisbauer also disciplined a number of children in his parish by excluding them from confession for eight days.[36] We are told that

[28] SAL, 164/2, 1162: note by BA Deggendorf on a conversation with Dr Hagler of Metten.
[29] See above, Ch. 5.
[30] LASB, E 107, 171.
[31] Ibid. 405–6: Dicke to Neureuter, 11 Sept. 1876.
[32] Ibid. 334: Eich to Neureuter, 5 Sept. 1876.
[33] Ibid. 173.
[34] Ibid. 201.
[35] On Geisbauer, see LASB, E 107, 201. The disputed reports about Dietz (St Wendel) and Lenarz (Illingen), as well as Geisbauer, in *KZ*, 26 July 1876 and 3 Aug. 1876.
[36] LASB, E 107, 75. This emerged in the course of enquiries about Margaretha Wagner of Bliesen, who was suspected of encouraging Margaretha Kunz to invent apparitions in the school.

around Hasborn, in the southern coalfield, none of the local priests supported the apparitions.[37]

A prudential concern not to antagonize the civil authorities obviously accounted for some of this reserve. Even Felix Dicke was worried at the impression that would be created if nuns began to arrive in Marpingen. 'Thank God' was his reaction, on learning that the superior of the Koblenz Franciscans had put off her trip.[38] The mildly sceptical who kept their distance were probably fearful of exposing themselves to reprisals. Those who came out openly against Marpingen went a step further, using the same language as employed by government officials when they described it as a 'swindle'. In other words, some of the sceptical clergy reacted as the authorities would have liked the clergy as a whole to react, condemning the apparitions unequivocally. It may be relevant that one of the reported opponents, Father Lenarz of Illingen, was a strongly pro-government priest who had been praised by the *Landrat* of Ottweiler for his political stance during the Prussian elections of 1866.[39] Such attitudes could be found, as a minority position, in high places within the diocesan hierarchy. A beleaguered old guard in the cathedral chapter around Dean Holzer also believed that events like those in Marpingen should be condemned, and viewed the failure to do so as symptomatic of the way in which the church had turned its back on sensible co-operation with the Prussian government.[40]

That was not the only issue, of course: questions about the nature of the faith were also at stake. Figures such as Holzer and his protégé, Franz-Xaver Kraus, were predictably repelled by such Mariolatrous 'excess'. Like their counterparts among the lower clergy, the small number of theologically liberal (and often politically conservative) parish priests, they had become increasingly isolated within the church because of their root-and-branch hostility to developments within Catholicism over the previous decades. For Kraus, 'the Marpingen miracle-stories' were just another of the 'hateful and risible' outcrops of ultramontanism.[41] But other priests, whose attachment to the kind of faith promoted by Pope Pius IX was not in doubt, were equally concerned. The notebooks kept in Neureuter's house, in which visiting priests could read accounts of what had occurred, contained many critical marginalia about the nature and duration of the apparitions, especially about the incidents when the devil had reportedly appeared.[42] This concern is understandable. The children depicted the devil in a variety of guises: wearing black and white horns, as a goat, as a black-clad man

[37] This is based, however, on the much later recollection of conversations among priests which themselves took place 25 years afterwards. See BAT, B III, 11, 14/5, 126: Rector Peter Nikolay of Trier to Karl Kammer, 12 Jan. 1957.
[38] LASB, E 107, 404–5: Dicke to Neureuter, 24 Aug. 1876.
[39] LHAK 442/6660, 447–8: LR Ottweiler to KR Trier, 22 Dec. 1866.
[40] Weber, *Kirchliche Politik*, 4–19 gives an excellent introduction to the clerical politics in the cathedral chapter.
[41] Kraus, *Tagebücher*, 381, 23 Sept. 1877. Kraus had been effectively exiled from Trier because of his liberal-governmental views, and was a professor in Strasbourg.
[42] LASB, E 107, 144–6.

with a beard. On one occasion, when the children claimed to have driven him from the house of church bookkeeper Fuchs, the devil allegedly complained that it was raining, and the children shouted 'Go to hell, you'll be warm there'; one of the girls then threw him a piece of apple out of the window, and he grumbled that it contained a worm, whereupon they threw him another apple.[43] Felix Dicke was sufficiently worried by what in his booklet he called the 'dark points' of the children's accounts that he discussed the matter with several clerical and lay friends, and even wrote to a priest in Lourdes, Father Costelat, asking whether there had been parallel incidents there.[44] Despite some nagging doubts, Dicke remained 'personally convinced' that the apparitions 'rested on truth'.[45] Other priests were less easily persuaded. The regent of a seminary in Paderborn was 'taken aback' when consulted by a Catholic writer on Marpingen about the incident with the apples: he was inclined to believe in the authenticity of the apparitions, but felt that these were 'certainly curious matters which make an extremely unfavourable impression'.[46] Father Feiten of Fraulautern went further: after keeping away from Marpingen at the outset and instructing his parishioners to do the same, he felt compelled to visit the village when reports of the devil's appearance were publicized, to inform Neureuter that he suspected some of the apparitions were demonic in origin.[47]

Feiten apparently acted without discussing the matter with fellow priests. By early October 1876, however, he was part of a group of clergy airing similar doubts. The prime mover here seems to have been an academically trained priest from Wolfstein called Hammer. At the beginning of October he visited Feiten in Fraulautern, a priest called Limbourg in Schwarzenholz, and other clergy in Saarlouis and Saarwellingen, in each case to discuss Marpingen. He reported that the prevailing view among these clergy—all, as he put it, 'pious priests'— was that the apparitions were diabolical in inspiration.[48] Hammer himself initially jibbed at the suggestion that the reported appearance of the devil condemned the apparitions as a whole; but he was informed about the view taken by the Bishop of Luxemburg when investigating similar cases in Alsace, and decided to follow this up with a personal visit to the bishop. The latter's extremely damning report on the Alsatian incidents, and the parallels with Marpingen, prompted Hammer

[43] Ibid. 115–23. The incident at the Fuchs house was recorded by W. Cramer (see *Die Erscheinungen*, 118), whose pamphlet on Marpingen contained a number of references to worrying aspects of the apparitions. See also 5–8, 27–8.

[44] *MMGE*, 24; LASB, E 107, 120–2, 404; *Prozeß*, 209.

[45] *MMGE*, 24.

[46] The writer in question was Cramer, who reported this comment of Regent Batsche in a letter to Neureuter on 15 Oct. 1876. See LASB, E 107, 118–19. He also reported the comments of Dean Heinrichs in Mainz, who was unwilling to commit himself, and remarked that 'the devil often did foolish things'.

[47] Ibid. 441.

[48] The account here, and in what follows, is based on the letter written by Hammer to Dean Riedinger in Speyer, 14 Oct. 1876 (ibid. 201 ff.), and on the statements and further material, ibid. 414–15. See also *Prozeß*, 211–12.

to write a letter of warning to Canon Riedinger in Speyer, the editor of the *Sonntags-Blatt Christlicher Pilger*, in which an account of Marpingen had recently been published. Riedinger, in turn, passed on his doubts about the 'offensive' features of the apparitions to Father Dell, from the Palatine parish of Zell, who had promised him a traveller's report on his visit there; and Dell passed the correspondence on to Neureuter via Konrad Schneider, adding his own queries. Through this intense epistolary activity, the circles of doubt grew wider.

The Dangers of Popular Religion

The parallels with the Alsatian apparitions of the early 1870s were a source of particular and widespread concern. Hammer anxiously reported the Bishop of Luxemburg's words that what had happened in Krüth and elsewhere had been designed 'to expose our religion to ridicule'.[49] A Belgian priest from Liège, who hoped to write a French-language account of Marpingen, alluded to the events in Alsace when he wrote to Schneider asking if the latter was 'absolutely convinced' about the authenticity of the apparitions.[50] For these priests only two alternatives seem to have presented themselves: the inspirations were either divine in inspiration, or diabolical. Hence the importance so many of them attached to the 'holy water test', which they believed would establish whether or not the devil was at work.[51] Some priests, however, voiced further alternatives. The apparitions might, thought Edmund Prince Radziwill, be the product of 'an overwrought state of piety'; Father Eich was initially inclined to dismiss them as 'childish nonsense'.[52] These possibilities were also potentially alarming. Even if they did not raise the spectre of diabolical inspiration, they created the prospect of an unruly popular piety—which had also, after all, been one of the characteristics of the Alsatian apparitions. Eich's first instinct was to reprove his more enthusiastic parishioners and warn them that there was a difference between the possibility and the reality of a miracle. His concern was to 'curb any disorder'.[53] Other priests were similarly concerned. Father Geisbauer of Bliesen later summed up the dangers implicit in the Marpingen events. He had 'never believed in the alleged miraculous apparitions, worried that the true Marian cult might suffer and the affair could get out of hand (*ausarten könnte*), as has indeed happened in the recent period'.[54]

This may have been wisdom after the event, but Geisbauer's concerns were certainly not unfounded. The Marpingen apparitions triggered numerous imi-

---

[49] LASB, E 107, 201–5: Hammer to Riedinger, 14 Oct. 1876.
[50] Ibid. 205: Abbé Jox [? Jux] to Schneider, 15 Oct. 1876.
[51] Neureuter and Father Limbourg of Schwarzenholz did in fact conduct such a test, but decided that the results were inconclusive: *Prozeß*, 157–9.
[52] Radziwill, *Besuch*, 23; LASB, E 107, 335.
[53] *Prozeß*, 29.
[54] Geisbauer's interrogation, 26 Oct. 1877: LASB, E 107, 201.

tations, some of them geographically remote from the Saarland. In late July 1876 a group of children on an estate in Posen claimed to have seen an apparition on the road between Czekanow and Lewkow; they were soon supported by adults. This followed references to Marpingen in a local Catholic weekly, *Warta*, and speculation that similar events might happen in the east.[55] The Mettenbuch apparitions also owed something to the example of Marpingen. A further series of apparitions, of a rather different kind, was reported in the spring of 1877 from the area around Koblenz. The first occurred at the Gappenach mill near Pölch, in the district of Mayen. The miller's wife had brought a can of water back from Marpingen, poured the contents into a medicine bottle, and stood it in a second-floor window surrounded by candles. Her daughter and many others then claimed they had seen the figure of the Blessed Virgin in the bottle, as well as the figures of angels, the Holy Ghost, and the Marpingen children. In the words of the local priest, this rumour spread 'with unbelievable speed' and as many as 5,000 pilgrims a day flocked from the surrounding area to see the miraculous sight, undeterred by the confiscation of the original bottle by the local mayor or the guard placed on the mill. The miller, his wife, and several accomplices, including an impoverished tailor and a local woman whose religious delusions had earned her the nickname 'the nun of Naunheim', were later prosecuted and gaoled after 450 marks in small change from pilgrims' donations was found in their cellar.[56] Shortly after the episode in Gappenach, a Virgin in a bottle was reported in nearby Mülheim. Large crowds, predominantly female, were observed on the station platforms of Koblenz and Andernach, bound for Mülheim, and there were 'great bands [of pilgrims] on all the high roads'.[57] Between the two incidents a third act of this tragicomic sequence took place in Mayen, where a schoolboy claimed to have seen the Virgin in his ink bottle.[58]

The events that Father Geisbauer had in mind are more likely to have been those which took place closer to home. In the wake of the original apparitions the surrounding areas seemed to be seized with spasms of popular religious frenzy. In January 1877 the 17-year-old daughter of Jakob Bausch in Gronig reportedly saw an apparition; this was followed by similar claims from the Michelsberg, near Wemmetsweiler, and from two villages even closer to Marpingen, Münchwies and Berschweiler.[59] The latter cases involved large groups of children who worked themselves into a state of religious ecstasy. At one point a group of children from Münchwies rushed to Marpingen and burst in on Neu-reuter at 9 o'clock one evening in August 1877, 'bathed in sweat' and asking to take communion.[60] In Münchwies itself, children and adults claimed to have seen

[55] Account of Lewkow events in *FZ*, 7 Aug. 1876.
[56] Details in Berg, *Marpingen*, 29–30; *SMZ*, 27 Mar., 30 Mar., 1 and 5 Apr. 1877; *KZ*, 1 July 1877.
[57] Berg, *Marpingen*, 30; *SMZ*, 7 Apr. 1877.
[58] *SMZ*, 4 Apr. 1877.
[59] *NBZ*, 1 Feb. 1877; *SBZ*, 2 Feb., 15 July, 29 Aug. 1877. See also Mallmann, 'Aus des Tages Last', 166–7.
[60] *Prozeß*, 157.

the devil in miniature form standing next to the Virgin, and dancing round her
in the shape of a dog, a donkey, a cow, and other animals. On one occasion they
had beaten him with such force that—as one woman reported to the parish
priest—he no longer appeared with the Virgin 'because he was in hospital on
account of the many blows'.[61] The Berschweiler incident of the same period had
even darker undertones. A group of children from the village claimed that they
had seen apparitions of the Virgin in Marpingen and been instructed to deliver
souls from purgatory.[62] Back in Berschweiler this group of around a dozen
children, mainly girls, fought violent struggles with the devil in their homes,
watched by large crowds. One scandalized account described how 'eleven girls
rolled on a bed with convulsive twitches and improper movements, while screaming and shouting about the apparitions they were witnessing'.[63] These grim
performances often lasted beyond midnight; afterwards clubs would be banged
on the doors of sceptics and threats shouted out against Protestants in the
denominationally mixed village.[64] Five adults and two children were eventually
convicted on several charges arising out of these events.[65]

   There is no doubt that these manifestations of popular religiosity disturbed
and alarmed the clergy, as well they might. The everyday pattern of religious
observance, already disrupted by the Kulturkampf, was temporarily jolted in a
different way by events in Marpingen.[66] The aftermath of the original apparitions
provided opportunities for distinctly unsaintly characters to take the stage. Those
who orchestrated the frauds in Gappenach and Berschweiler, and the various
young women of dubious morals who claimed visions (one young seer from 'H.'
was 'incapable of turning anyone down, certainly not the young men'), certainly
fell into this category.[67] Perhaps more important, the Marpingen apparitions also
helped to release and give a certain sanction to 'disorderly' popular religious
sentiment, among adults such as the 'nun of Naunheim', but especially among
young people and children. The 'misrule of youth' so evident in the events at
Münchwies, Berschweiler, and Marpingen itself had a frenzied, carnivalesque
element to it, as the normal constraints of authority were cast off.[68]

   [61] LHAK, 442/6442, 78–9: copy of letter from Father Göller to LR Ottweiler, 22 July 1877, forwarded
to RP Wolff Trier.
   [62] LASB, E 107, 127, 160.
   [63] Der Marpinger Prozeß vor dem Richterstuhle der Vernunft von einem Unparteiischen (Vienna, 1881), 29.
   [64] SMZ, 12 Jan. 1878; SPB, 20 Jan. 1878.
   [65] LASB, E 107, 127; VZ, 16 Jan. 1878.
   [66] The disruption of pastoral care during the 1870s may well have had an effect on the conduct of
children. When Bishop Korum later arrived to fill the vacant see of Trier, he lamented the 'many
children who grew up without the discipline and instruction of the church'. See Treitz, Korum, 85.
   [67] On the young woman from 'H.', see the letter to SMZ, 22 Dec. 1876, noting that the poor local
reputation of the woman disillusioned many Catholics about Marpingen itself: for could the apparitions
be taken seriously if they appeared to someone like this? Cf. the young woman Magdalene Müller of
Noswendel, whose character supposedly cast her apparition in an 'unfavourable light': LASB, E 107,
189.
   [68] See N. Z. Davis, 'The Reasons of Misrule: Youth Groups and Charivaris in Sixteenth-Century
France', Past and Present, 50 (1971), 41–75.

Why, asked liberal and Protestant critics, did the Catholic clergy not nip the whole thing in the bud?[69] The answer, of course, is that they tried—certainly when it came to claims about Virgins in bottles, or the obviously unsatisfactory stories of the 'rival children'. Georg Dasbach was one of the first to expose the fraud at the Gappenach mill, in the pages of the Catholic *St-Paulinus-Blatt*. The local clergy also opposed what was happening in Berschweiler and Münchwies.[70] But they were not always successful. It is simply not true that the faithful were, as one Protestant scornfully expressed it, 'used to following their leaders blindly'.[71] Whatever advances clerical discipline had made in previous decades, the heightened atmosphere in the wake of reported apparitions tended to erode popular deference, if only temporarily. Religious enthusiasm, sometimes accompanied by anticlerical malice, made these movements difficult to stop once they were under way. Even after the arrest of the miller of Gappenach, neither denunciations in the Catholic press nor the opposition of the local clergy could stem popular enthusiasm: they were 'no longer masters of the situation'.[72] For her part, the miller's wife wrote to the mayor of Pölch denouncing 'in unprintable terms', not only the civil and judicial authorities, but clergy who had opposed the affair.[73] At Berschweiler the local priest was shown the door by the tailor Thierry when he remonstrated.[74]

The clerical dilemma can be seen in its full complexity if we look at the Münchwies case. The elderly parish priest, Father Göller, opted for a softly-softly approach. He remained silent at first, in the hope that this would see 'the end of the swindle'. Attempting to 'build bridges of understanding', he made only passing reference to the apparitions in his initial Sunday sermons: 'My principle was, on the one hand, through my silence to give them nothing to go on (*keinen Anhaltspunkt zu geben*), but on the other hand to win back those who had strayed, through a policy of leniency.' When this failed, Göller spoke out against the Münchwies children and their supporters, excluding from the sacraments those who would not promise to keep away from the miraculous site. This sowed the seeds of doubt in some of his outlying parishioners; but in Münchwies itself he came up against a wall of 'stubbornness'. The villagers were 'so enamoured of their apparitions' that they pressed the children to continue playing their role as 'children graced by God'. Göller could only extract promises from some of the children that 'although they would continue to go with adults to the spot, they would try to get away if they could, or say nothing about any

[69] See e.g. *DAZ*, 17 Aug. 1876.

[70] Rebbert, *Marpingen und seine Gegner*, 38; *Prozeß*, 142; *Marpinger Prozeß vor dem Richterstuhle der Vernunft*, 29. One of the fiercest clerical critics of Berschweiler was Father Müller of Eppelborn, who had earlier denounced the 'blood-sweater' Elisabeth Flesch, and the curate who supported her, Father Kickerts. See LHAK, 442/6442, 177–8: RP Wolff Trier to MdI Berlin, 12 Jan. 1878.

[71] Berg, *Marpingen*, 13.

[72] *Coblenzer Zeitung und Correspondenzblatt des Deutschen Vereins der Rheinprovinz*, 266 (1877), cit. Berg, *Marpingen*, 29–30.

[73] *KZ*, 1 July 1877.

[74] *SMZ*, 12 Jan. 1878.

apparitions'. When his 'dear, stupid Münchwieser' parishioners reported the blows they had rained on the devil, Göller helplessly expressed the hope that the affair had 'reached its height'. The priest faced additional problems. Disorder grew in the village as the 'night-time mischief' of the apparitions 'was exploited, especially by the grown youth'. Other parishioners paid him back for past rebukes administered to their children, or the reprimanding of their own 'pretensions', by supporting the apparitions 'out of spite'. The situation was exacerbated by the influx of pilgrims, especially from the Bavarian Palatinate, 'whose priests, because they are not yet being burned by it, are not yet willing to extinguish it'. In these circumstances, Göller concluded with some pathos, and a sense of personal hurt, that 'the peace can be maintained most easily, the less mindful I am of my own person, and I must therefore refrain from making any complaint. When they see the error of their ways, they will appreciate such forbearance all the more.'[75]

The apparitions were, as the *Frankfurter Zeitung* sardonically put it, 'infectious'.[76] These episodes were plainly inspired by Marpingen. Many of those involved in them had been there; all derived part of their authority vicariously from their connections with the original apparitions, even if an important part of their appeal also lay precisely in the fact that theirs were *local* miracles, rivalling those in Marpingen. The 'infectiousness' was not restricted, however, to events elsewhere. In Marpingen itself large numbers of children and women claimed visions throughout 1876–7. On 11 and 12 July 1876 there were already three such cases, an 8-year-old boy and two 4-year-olds. There were at least two reported seers the following month, an 11-year-old day labourer's son and a 13-year-old craftsman's son, whose visions occurred on consecutive days.[77] In December the reports showed a variation in the pattern: this time it was six young women who claimed to have seen the Virgin within a short period.[78] Further reports of female and youthful visionaries came in January 1877.[79] A great flood of alleged apparitions then followed, in the months of July and August, between the first anniversary of the original visions and the predicted end of the apparitions. In this period there were around thirty reported visionaries. Some were adults, such as the 28-year-old Franziska Kornbrust of Jochem, near St Wendel.[80] But the great majority were children, mostly in the age range 7–10 and almost all girls. About half these young seers were from outside the village, for Marpingen in these last months took on something of the character of a children's crusade.[81]

[75] LHAK, 442/6442, 76–80: Göller to LR Ottweiler, 22 July 1877, forwarded to RP Wolff Trier.
[76] *FZ*, 7 Aug. 1876.
[77] LASB, E 107, 163, 189, 494; *Prozeß*, 171–2; *MMGE*, 17.
[78] Three came from Morscholz, near Wadern, three from Noswendel, and one from somewhere identified only as 'H.'. See LASB, E 107, 189; *SMZ*, 10 Dec., 22 Dec. 1876; *TLZ*, 13 Dec. 1876.
[79] *MWOL*, 84–5.
[80] *MG*, 32–3.
[81] Cf. the rather ambiguous comment by the author of *MG* (p. 44): 'For now the children too began to make the pilgrimage to Marpingen'.

But the most elaborate apparitions were claimed by children who lived in the village. They reported climbing ladders to heaven and meeting St Peter at the gates, seeing God, the devil with cloven hoofs and a tail, the Holy Ghost and angels, and releasing suffering souls from purgatory.[82]

The popular sentiment sparked off by the apparitions created a movement that raised the question of clerical authority in Marpingen itself. That would have been true even without the further waves of visionaries. As we have seen, pilgrims streamed there without their parish priests, and sometimes in defiance of them. Their behaviour at the site was a far cry from the organized and disciplined devotion the church had sought to foster in previous decades. As one highly critical visitor observed, the clergy had tried to discourage the 'excesses' of the crowds, 'but without success. It favoured the whole business at the beginning, but is now simply not master of a movement over which it has long lost any control.'[83] For all the evident *schadenfreude* with which this view was expressed, it contained a double truth. Automatic deference to clerical authority had broken down; but the clergy itself bore a share of the responsibility for this. Many priests followed their parishioners to Marpingen, rather than leading them, and were eager to accept the authenticity of the original apparitions before any kind of canonical enquiry could be made.

There may have been an element of nervousness here about seeming to be 'lukewarm': it must have demanded considerable self-confidence to resist popular enthusiasm for the miracles. Few priests would have wanted to acquire a reputation as 'governmental' clergy, given that the latter (certainly those who had continued to draw their state salaries during the *Kulturkampf*) sometimes found themselves spat at and attacked.[84] It is therefore possible to argue, as liberals did, that the priests who spoke out against the apparitions were those with the courage to do so—the implication being that those who did not lacked moral fibre.[85] A more plausible argument, as far as the majority of clerical supporters are concerned, is that they were strongly influenced by the circumstances of the *Kulturkampf*. The closing of ranks among Catholics touched clergy as well as laity, and the over-reaction of the state authorities in Marpingen was hardly calculated to enlist clerical support. The brusque contempt shown by state officials to the clergy undermined, rather than reinforced, the clerical impulse to exert its discipline over the faithful. Edmund Radziwill made this point in most telling fashion. The clergy, he suggested, would have been prepared to undertake the most rigorous scrutiny of the apparitions in partnership with the state; 'none would have found it strange or offensive', for example, if clerical interrogations had taken place with 'a hidden policeman or examining magistrate present'.[86]

[82] LASB, E 107, 126–8, 444; *Prozeß*, 193–6; *MG*, 32, 42–3.
[83] 'An der Gnadenstätte', 667.
[84] See *SMZ*, 20 Dec. 1876.
[85] See e.g. the comments of *KZ*, 26 July 1876.
[86] Radziwill, *Besuch*, 23.

But, alas, the state had offered no such partnership. This was the argument mounted by the church for decades, and especially since 1848, namely that the priest made the best policeman. Making all allowances for Radziwill's special pleading, this consideration almost certainly affected clerical reactions to Marpingen.

The *Kulturkampf* also conditioned the response of the clergy in other ways. Just as the heightened mood of the 1870s was likely to prompt spontaneous lay movements that sat awkwardly with clerical control, so the parish clergy had to act in circumstances where the normal hierarchical chain of command did not function with its customary rigour.[87] Moreover, as the zealous curates illustrate, Marpingen drew on the energy of frustrated clergy and was accepted by many with desperate gratitude as a 'sign'. The conduct, the recorded comments, and the letters of the priests who were caught in the investigative net show that the enthusiasts were hardly 'shameless' exploiters of events, but were genuine believers in the 'German Lourdes'.[88] It followed from this belief that other alleged apparitions, however apparently dubious, had to be looked at seriously, if only to discredit imitations that threatened to bring the 'authentic' apparitions into disrepute. Those who claimed to have seen visions of the Virgin in Marpingen could expect to encounter determined clerical interrogation. One of them, the 13-year-old Peter Emmerich of Bardenbach, was hailed by someone inside Neureuter's house as he and his mother returned home in the evening. The man seized him by the arm and led him into the house, where his mother 'half-voluntarily' accompanied him because she could see the parish priest standing in the doorway. Once inside they were led into a room containing various priests and the boy was questioned about his story.[89] Peter Emmerich was then treated gently: he was to ask his father to buy him a picture of the Blessed Virgin to which he could pray.

Would the prospect of benign inquisition, even of clerical wrath, have curbed young (and not-so-young) potential seers? It certainly did little to stem the flow of newly reported apparitions, culminating in the 'rival children' in the summer of 1877. It seems at least as likely that the very gravity with which the clergy weighed these childlike stories reinforced the belief among visionaries acting in good faith that further 'signs' were indeed possible, while persuading those acting in bad faith that they would be accorded respect. Many clergy were plainly reluctant to dismiss even the accounts of the 'rival children', especially as they had claimed their apparitions, not at the site in the Härtelwald but at the Marienbrunnen, the historic site of Marian devotion in the village.[90] Above all, imitative apparitions were likely to be reported for as long as the original visionaries

---

[87] On the improvised hierarchy in Trier during this period, see below, Ch. 11.

[88] For a liberal view that the clergy 'exploited' events in the interests of establishing a German Lourdes, see the long article headed 'Marpingen–Lourdes' in *SMZ*, 22 Aug. 1876. For an even more trenchant argument that the clergy themselves did not believe in the events they were exploiting, see *DAZ*, 17 Aug. 1876.

[89] LASB, E 107, 493–4; *Prozeß*, 171–2.

[90] On the importance of this in the thinking of many priests, see *MG*, 44–5.

claimed that their own apparitions continued, and for as long as those claims continued to be given clerical credence. That, of course, was the point made by liberal critics when they urged the clergy to nip the movement in the bud (or scorned them for failing to do so). These critics took the view, not unreasonably, that the paramount question was how to deal with the claims of Margaretha Kunz, Susanna Leist, and Katharina Hubertus. That was the sticking-point for many clergy. Numerous priests, and almost all of those who actually visited Marpingen, accepted the authenticity of the original visionaries. They defined the problem in a different and twofold sense: how was the sign of grace communicated in the original apparitions to be preserved from diabolical attempts to confuse the children; and how was it possible to prevent the message of the three seers from becoming tainted by association with later imitations ? From this standpoint, clerical misgivings about the course of events in Marpingen by no means led to the conclusion that the original visions were dubious. Quite the contrary: if some priests were worried by the appearance of the devil in the three girls' accounts, others (such as Father Schneider) saw this as proof that the devil was working to undermine the message of hope. And if, by the same token, unworthy and fraudulent apparitions were claimed, this only served to underline the virtue and authenticity of the original visions.

The difficulty of their position anguished many priests. They believed in the possibility of intercession by the Blessed Virgin, of course, just as they believed in the devil as a real force. But they were hardly trained to deal with exceptional events like Marpingen, and the collapse of the decanal and diocesan hierarchy did not help. Most priests seem to have wrestled spiritually with the problem, whether they came down for or against the authenticity of the apparitions. Depending on how they decided, there was a danger of misunderstandings either with their more zealous parishioners, or with the civil authority—and possibly with both. As far as we can judge, the clergy had an ingrained conviction (it is typified by Father Göller in Münchwies) that obedience was the natural condition of their flock, that those who had strayed would, like lost sheep, return to the fold. The enmity of the civil authorities required forbearance of a different but, by the 1870s, not unfamiliar kind. The *Kulturkampf* had accustomed the beleaguered clergy to think in terms of their being tested: the apparitions were perceived as a test over something incomparably more sublime than Prussia's grubby May Laws.

The Parish Priest

Of no one was this more true than the figure at the centre of the whole affair: the parish priest, Jakob Neureuter. As we have seen, Neureuter had long expected his parish to be 'tested' in some way during the *Kulturkampf*.[91] An entry in his

[91] See above, Ch. 2.

notebook makes it clear that when the test came he saw it in personal terms. A series of rough notes reads: 'A test—complete misunderstanding. The matter will melt into nothing; [remain?] completely calm.—They are seeking to triumph over my patience. With respect, gentlemen, you will not succeed.'[92] Neureuter's tendency to view the affair in this way was reinforced by the advice he received from fellow priests. In an effort to console and stiffen the resolve of his friend, Father Eich wrote: 'There is a cross to bear for all good things . . . Endure the test with the patience we see exemplified in Our Lady of Sorrows.' He ended: 'Once more courage and patience . . . It is a test sent by God.'[93]

Neureuter was in his early forties when the apparitions began. He had been in Marpingen, his first parish, for twelve years.[94] After losing a much-loved sister to the smallpox epidemic of 1871, he shared the priest's house with a housekeeper, Johanna Alff, and his dog, Türk. A photograph of Neureuter shows a thoughtful, slightly ascetic face. The son of an artist in Trier, he was a keen painter and musician, and interested himself in improving and cataloguing the mediocre library inherited from his predecessor. Astronomy was another interest, and he owned a telescope.[95] He enjoyed a glass of wine, but his tastes were simple.[96] After the apparitions began Neureuter's character came under intense scrutiny, and the reports agree that he lived frugally and attached very little value to money. The notary Heß from Tholey described a sober and careful man who was 'charitable to a fault' with money. Canon Lorenzi of Trier, whose curate Neureuter had been in Koblenz during the 1860s, painted a similar picture. Neureuter's salary had frequently been given away within a few days; on one occasion he had given a gift of six silver spoons to a man whose furniture was about to be seized for arrears of rent.[97] Perhaps the most impressive testimony came from those who completely disagreed with him over the apparitions. The young legal official Strauß found him very 'sympathetic'.[98] The magistrate Gatzen of Tholey gave him a glowing character reference: Neureuter was generally considered 'the best of all the priests in the whole area', especially because of the unaffected naturalness of his behaviour.[99]

Some took a less generous view of this simple naturalness. For *Landrat* Rumschöttel of St Wendel, Neureuter tended towards 'zealotry and mysticism'.[100]

---

[92] Notebook entry: LASB, E 107, 424. In the undated draft of a letter he made the same point that his patience was being tested, but it would not break.

[93] LASB, E 107, 333: Eich to Neureuter, 15 July 1876.

[94] BAT, 70/3676, 85; Derr, 'Pfarrei Marpingen', 37.

[95] On the books, see above, Ch. 2; on the telescope, *MMGE*, 18.

[96] While the hotel-owner Bonn of Ahrweiler was in Marpingen he had several bottles of Ahr rosé (*Ahrbleichart*) sent from home, and presented them to the priest: LASB, E 107, 236.

[97] Heß to Prince Radziwill, 28 Nov. 1876, letter published in *Germania*, 6 Dec. 1876 (reprinted in *MWOL*, 13–15); *Prozeß*, 199–201.

[98] *Prozeß*, 82.

[99] Ibid. 53.

[100] Ibid. 55.

More friendly observers hinted gently at his ingenuousness and suggestibility.[101] His own notebook entries suggest a man who placed a high value on uncomplicated, childlike faith. On one occasion he wrote: 'If I begin in the morning to reflect on the existence of God, by the evening I am even more stupid than I was in the morning.'[102] Convictions of this sort were obviously important when Neureuter had to react to the apparitions. Equally important was the tightly coiled emotional intensity of the man. We see elements of this in the way Neureuter dramatized the 'test' he faced, and it runs through his reactions to the events of the 1870s. Nearly twenty years later he could still write with a passion laced with self-pity about the lack of generosity of some parishioners during the *Kulturkampf*: 'I put no pressure on the people, but it was striking none the less that during the *Kulturkampf* fifty-four families did not have a single penny to spare for their priest.'[103] His passionate feelings about the experiences he suffered following the apparitions were expressed in the 'bitter words' of an epic poem he composed.[104] A simplicity of faith that tended towards the mystical, and an emotional intensity that tended towards martyred self-pity, were keynotes in the character of the parish priest who faced the events of July 1876 and their aftermath.

Neureuter was absent from Marpingen when the apparitions began. He had left earlier on the day of 3 July to help his friend Father Eich with pastoral duties in Heusweiler. The two priests returned to Marpingen together on the evening of 5 July to find groups of people standing around talking about what had happened, and Neureuter was given an account of events by his housekeeper. The priests discussed the matter and decided it was of little consequence.[105] On the following day, Neureuter took matters in hand, interviewing the village teacher André and a visiting friend of hers called Dubitscher, the parents of the three children, and the visionaries themselves. At this stage he apparently felt no great alarm, cautioning all concerned to exercise restraint and assuming that the matter would soon blow over.[106] His mood was very different a week later. On 13 July he wrote to Eich in Heusweiler: 'The matter which we dismissed initially as a bagatelle appears to rest on truth. The movement it has given rise to has become huge; I am completely at a loss what to do. Please come immediately if possible and help to advise me.'[107] When Eich hurried to Marpingen the same day he found that the nervous parish priest had also sought help in other quarters, for he met Neureuter returning from Alsweiler with two other clergy. Neureuter asked Eich to go immediately to the Härtelwald, even before they had eaten, for

[101] See the comments of Gatzen and Strauß, ibid. 53, 82, 84.
[102] Undated notebook entry: LASB, E 107, 426.
[103] BAT, 70/3676, 158–9: Neureuter to GV Trier, 30 Oct. 1893.
[104] Derr, 'Pfarrei Marpingen', 43. The poem was in private possession, and I have not seen it.
[105] Eich's statement in LASB, E 107, 335; *Prozeß*, 19.
[106] LASB, E 107, 290. See also Neureuter's patchy later account in BAT, B III, 11, 14/4, 1–20.
[107] Eich's statement: LASB, E 107, 335; Eich later gave an almost identical account under oath: *Prozeß*, 12–13.

the crowds had grown and rumours were circulating that the Prussian army
would arrive that evening.[108]

It is hardly surprising that Neureuter should summon assistance—nor, given
the attitude of the civil authorities, that he should later deny summoning it.[109]
The actions of the state represented one of his principal problems. The arrival
of the military on the evening of 13 July set in train a series of events that was to
include the billeting of soldiers in his house, the seizure and interception of
his mail, house searches, arrest, and eventual trial. Neureuter faced repeated
interrogations and the scornful insolence of the gendarmes posted in the village.
He also had to put up with abusive mail. One postcard from Cologne bore the
message: 'I have a billy-goat that milks; can let you have it cheap for your hocus-
pocus.' It was signed 'Margaretha Pimpel, retired priest's cook'. Another from
Wiesbaden, almost incoherent with rage, read: 'Would like to take over the
delivery of hay and thistles to your parish, or are there no longer any donkeys
there? Did you use the ice-pack I sent you correctly, or does it take an entire
Swiss glacier to get your brain working?' This was signed 'Wunderbold, religious
charlatan'.[110] The parish priest also faced constant attack in the liberal press.
Some of this was marked by wit, such as the parody of Goethe's 'Erlkönig' carried
by the Nahe-Blies-Zeitung:[111]

> Wer reutet so spät durch Nacht und Wind?
> Herr Neureuter ist's mit 'nem Marpinger Kind.

Other papers contained personal attacks on the alleged stupidity and cowardice
of the priest.[112] Articles in the Rhein-Curier of Wiesbaden and the Hagener Zeitung
were so defamatory that well-wishers urged Neureuter (in vain) to take legal
action.[113]

The parish priest bore these provocations with a degree of equanimity. He
could console himself that he was being 'tested', and with the belief that these
'misunderstandings' would resolve themselves. In fact, he had as much trouble
coping with his friends as with his enemies. A major problem was the flood of
mail he received, at least before 11 October when the Prussian government began
to intercept it. He was inundated with letters from the clergy, laity, and Catholic
newspapers, containing requests for information, advice, suggestions, and warnings.[114] Others sent him material on Lourdes or the Belgian stigmatist Louise
Lateau, and asked questions about the parallels.[115] The sheer volume of cor-

[108] Prozeß, 12–13, 29.
[109] When first questioned, Neureuter denied he had sent for Eich, claiming that his fellow priest had
arrived in Marpingen by chance: LASB, E 107, 335, 380.
[110] MMGE, 21. The postcards were dated 5 Aug. and 20 Aug. 1876 respectively.
[111] NBZ, 10 Nov. 1876.
[112] On the responses of the liberal press generally, see below, Ch. 9.
[113] LASB, E 107, 399.
[114] Ibid. 170–8; Prozeß, 211–13; Cramer, Die Erscheinungen, 7; MMGE, 19.
[115] e.g. Louis Veuillot sent Neureuter an article about Lourdes from L'Univers: LASB, E 107, 399.

respondence led Neureuter to employ the help of other priests to deal with it. One of them claimed in a newspaper article that the burden of answering them rivalled the situation facing the administrators at Lourdes.[116] The pressure from aristocratic correspondents alone was such that Neureuter felt obliged to invest in a letter-writer's guide for advice on correct forms of address.[117] He was particularly plagued by letters requesting him to send Marpingen water for the sick. In September 1876 he told a priest visiting Marpingen that he was 'snowed under with all kinds of requests, especially concerning the so-called miraculous water, which, partly through lack of time and partly in order not to run into trouble, he was unable to satisfy.'[118] He was eventually forced to announce in the newspaper that he could not send water.[119]

Added to the burden and potential danger posed by his correspondents was the problem raised by the flood of visitors. The pilgrims strained the capacity of the parish church, and Neureuter was kept in the confessional box from early morning until 11 a.m. every day, without being able to satisfy the demand.[120] Visiting priests proved to be a mixed blessing. They offered solidarity, and some helped to relieve the workload. On the other hand they required accommodation and explanations; introductions were needed to the leading actors in the affair; detailed lists had to be drawn up showing the times (starting at 4.30 a.m.) when visiting priests could say mass. Neureuter certainly felt the strain. He later described how a visiting priest 'tortured me with his questions'.[121] Small wonder, then, that he should have welcomed the opportunity to accompany the publicist Dr Thoemes to Trier towards the end of September 1876, for he had 'urgent need of a change from the constant agitation'.[122] In the second week of October he was similarly eager to deliver some materials about Marpingen by hand to Professor Scheeben in Cologne. Together with visits to friends in Koblenz and Bingen, this would provide some 'relief' after 'all the various commotions'.[123]

Burdensome as pressures of this kind were, a still more fundamental problem for Neureuter was the need to reach his own conclusions about the authenticity of the apparitions. This was inevitably complicated by the fact that both friendly and hostile observers were, for different reasons, hanging on his words. His public statements to officials were cautious and reserved. On 14 July 1876, questioned by District Governor Wolff of Trier, he used a formula repeated on other occasions: 'If this is the work of man it will soon disappear; if it is not, it will not

---

[116] Article by Father Schneider in *Germania*, 16 Aug. 1876.
[117] See the bill, and accompanying letter of sympathy for the priest's burdens, from the bookseller Peter Philippi in Trier to Neureuter, 13 Sept. 1876: LASB, E 107, 413. Philippi was a friend of Neureuter's (see ibid. 461).
[118] Conversation with Father Wolf of Neuforweiler: ibid. 396–7.
[119] *Germania*, 21 Dec. 1876.
[120] BAT, B III, 11, 14/4, 8; *MMGE*, 19.
[121] *Prozeß*, 153. The priest in question was the indefatigable Father Wolf.
[122] Thoemes, *Die Erscheinungen*, 81.
[123] Lama, *Die Muttergottes-Erscheinungen*, 47.

be quelled by worldly intervention.'[124] In a statement made to the legal authorities at the end of October Neureuter expressed his uncertainty about aspects of the apparitions, especially the 'rather disturbing' sitting position sometimes adopted by the Virgin and the 'still more questionable' appearances of the Holy Ghost and the devil.[125] A common thread of defensiveness ran through this and other statements, coupled with an apparent determination to highlight secondary features of the apparitions such as the pious singing and praying of the pilgrims.

This is naturally what one might expect from Neureuter in the circumstances. But the evidence suggests that the public posture corresponded closely to the private feelings. The parish priest welcomed the evidence of renewed faith shown by the pilgrims, whatever problems it brought. An entry in his notebook likened the position after the first heavy-handed intervention of the state to the cycle of the Passion: 'Good Friday is already over. The church anticipates the joy of Easter with poetic feeling. It was the same here. It is still Good Friday and the bells are not yet sounding the joy of Easter. I continually think: a time of rapture (*Begeisterung*) must come, free from all Pharisaism—here we have a foretaste.'[126] Neureuter told a Dutch visitor that the apparitions had been sent as a means of 'strengthening the faithful and breaking the shackles of cold materialism'.[127] On another occasion he noted: 'This enthusiasm is doubly miraculous at a time when faith is so often weak and unbelief does its utmost to destroy religion.'[128] A quarter of a century later he would describe the sight and sound of the 20,000 pilgrims gathered in Marpingen on 12 July as 'unforgettable'.[129] But were the children worthy of such inspiring results; was it possible that good had come of something that was, in itself, questionable ? In the early stages, at least, Neureuter's relatively reserved attitude towards the apparitions was not just for public consumption; it reflected his inner uncertainty. He was inclined towards belief by the early cures, particularly that of the 7-year-old Magdalena Kirsch,[130] but as events unfolded he worried about the content of the visions as well as his own vulnerable position. The pressure exerted by parts of the Catholic press, and the expectations of the Catholic public, may indeed have led him to express more confidence in the authenticity of the apparitions than he actually felt. Thus, while subscribers to the *Saar-Zeitung* could read Neureuter's denial of any parallels between events in his own parish and the 'woman in white' visions at Urexweiler, a sympathetic visitor to Marpingen recorded that the priest 'could not restrain a certain anxious feeling when he reflected on the apparitions in Alsace'.[131] Even before the three

---

[124] LASB, E 107, 377–8. Father Anglhuber in Mettenbuch had a similar formulation: the affair would either vindicate itself, or it would 'share the fate of the soap-bubble': SAL, 164/2, 1162, Anglhuber to BA Deggendorf, 8 May 1877.

[125] LASB, E 107, 393–4.

[126] Undated notebook entry: LASB, E 107, 423.

[127] *Germania*, 3 and 4 Feb. 1877.

[128] Notebook entry, 13 July 1876: LASB, E 107, 424.

[129] BAT, B III, 11, 14/4, 7: Neureuter's statement to Bishop Korum, 25 Oct. 1902.

[130] Ibid. 4: Neureuter's statement to Bishop Korum, 25 Oct. 1902.

[131] SZ, 26 July 1876; Cramer, *Die Erscheinungen*, 27–8.

seers reported seeing the devil, Neureuter was troubled by the thought that the apparitions were diabolically inspired.

It is clear that in the early months Neureuter found himself in severe need of spiritual as well as practical help. Any parish priest in his position was bound to face difficulties; they were compounded in Marpingen by the effects of the *Kulturkampf*, which had deprived the parish priest of his bishop. Compare the situation of Father Anglhuber in Mettenbuch. His initial reactions to the apparitions in his parish were as uncertain and nervous as Neureuter's, but he could at least throw himself on the hierarchy for advice. Within days of taking statements from the Mettenbuch seers, Anglhuber made his first visit to Bishop Senestrey in Regensburg.[132] In the months that followed he bombarded bishop and vicar-general with letters, telegrams, queries, and requests for an episcopal visitation. 'What should I do?' was the recurrent theme of the desperate parish priest.[133] In July 1877, uninhibited by soldiers, gendarmes, or the need to secrete his notes, Anglhuber sent a full report to Regensburg and visited the vicar-general to receive further instructions shortly afterwards.[134] The official canonical enquiry and subsequent efforts to suppress the Mettenbuch apparitions did not leave Father Anglhuber with an easy life; but the decisions had been taken out of his hands by the hierarchy.[135] Neureuter had greater *de facto* autonomy, but much more to worry about. The ragged lines of communication with Trier meant that he faced an exceptional problem without the usual sources of support. For practical assistance he could turn to neighbouring and visiting priests; for spiritual guidance he turned elsewhere. His first resort was to his old superior in Koblenz, now Canon de Lorenzi in Trier, to whom he wrote shortly after the apparitions began asking what he should do. De Lorenzi would not go to Marpingen, however, and Neureuter's suggestion that an enquiry be set up, which de Lorenzi put to the cathedral chapter in Trier, was turned down.[136] Some time in early September he sought further theological advice. He requested discussions with a Professor Stolz, and he wrote to the celebrated Mariologist Matthias Scheeben in Cologne, explaining his difficulties and urging Scheeben to visit Marpingen, as he 'didn't know where to turn'. Unlike de Lorenzi, Scheeben agreed to the visit: he went to Marpingen on 11 September and stayed there for the rest of the academic vacation. He formed the opinion that Neureuter was 'struggling with himself'.[137]

[132] BZAR, F 115, Fasc. I: 'Protokolle der Visionäre. Neujahr 1877 mitgeteilt. Metten, d. 24 Dezember 1876'.

[133] See, for example, the following communications in May 1877 alone, all in BZAR, F 115, Fasc. I: Anglhuber to GV Regensburg (telegram), 5 May 1877; Anglhuber to GV Regensburg, 6 May 1877; Anglhuber to Bishop Senestrey, 11 May 1877; Anglhuber to GV Regensburg, 25 May 1877; Anglhuber to GV Regensburg, 26 May 1877.

[134] Ibid.: 'Bericht des Pfarramtes Metten über die behaupteten Erscheinungen der Mutter Gottes . . .', 23 July 1877.

[135] See below, Ch. 11, on the canonical enquiry and its aftermath.   [136] *Prozeß*, 200.

[137] On the contact with Prof. Stolz, see Stolz's letter to Neureuter, 14 Sept. 1876: LASB, E 107, 413; and on Scheeben's visit, *Prozeß*, 174–6. Scheeben was Prof. of Dogmatics at the seminary in Cologne

Scheeben was 'fully convinced' that the apparitions were authentic, and it is possible that his conviction dispelled Neureuter's remaining doubts.[138] For all the qualifications in the parish priest's October statement to the examining magistrate, there is no evidence in notebook entries or the accounts of priests and other visitors suggesting that he had serious doubts beyond September. A priest who talked to him then gained the impression that Neureuter believed in the apparitions.[139] He told a Dutch priest at the end of December: 'I can say only that, before God and my conscience, it is my innermost conviction that the Mother of God has appeared here in Marpingen. And not only that, but that she continues to appear daily in the village.'[140] This was certainly what he longed to believe. The unanimous verdict of all who encountered him is that Neureuter's own faith was of a guileless, unsuspicious kind: a later vicar-general in Trier called him 'credulous'.[141] This view is confirmed by the entries in his notebook. He was moved by the apparently unaffected, childlike simplicity of the story told by the three girls, and impressed by the persistence with which they claimed to be telling the truth.[142] He was, of course, professionally obliged to treat the initial stories with caution, to question the would-be seers and their parents closely. But scepticism went against the grain, and we should not underestimate what it cost Neureuter to suspend belief.

Once convinced, nothing could shake him. In this respect, Marpingen repeated the pattern of Lourdes and other apparition sites. Like Father Peyremale in Lourdes, Neureuter was initially dismissive and sceptical, then went through a period in which belief was marred by doubts, before wholeheartedly embracing the apparitions as a true sign of grace. Thereafter, his emotional commitment to the truth of the apparitions would have made a reversal of opinion painfully, perhaps unbearably, difficult. The harsh treatment meted out to Neureuter and other villagers (including the three girls) after October 1876 only reinforced his faith, for he was inclined to see suffering and martyrdom as proof that a higher cause was at stake. More pragmatically, would the adults and children concerned accept incarceration rather than admit the truth ? When the friendly Catholic legal official Jakob Strauß encountered Neureuter one evening at the house of a priest in Schiffweiler, he recounted the duplicity of Margaretha Kunz at length. Neureuter argued that any changes in the girls' stories were a product of their

and a leading theologian of 19th-cent. Germany: Graef, *Mary*, ii. 118–26; E. Paul, 'Matthias Scheeben', in H. Fries and G. Schwaiger (eds.), *Katholische Theologen Deutschlands im 19. Jahrhundert*, ii (Munich, 1975), 386–408; McCool, *Catholic Theology*, 168, 240.

[138] Scheeben's views are conveyed in a letter from Neureuter to Dicke, 13 Sept. 1876: LASB, E 107, 397.

[139] This was the ubiquitous Father Wolf: LASB, E 107, 397. Unfortunately there is no indication of the period of Sept. to which this applies.

[140] The Dutch priest published an account of his conversations with Neureuter in *Germania*, 3 and 4 Feb. 1877. See also *MWOL*, 83.

[141] This was Karl Kammer. See BAT, B III, 11, 14/6[2]: typed notes drawn up by Kammer, with handwritten heading 'Zu den Akten Marpingen!', dated 26 Nov. 1956.

[142] Notebook entries to this effect in LASB, E 107, 96–7.

homesickness in Saarbrücken, adding that four men (the visionaries of 6 July) had also been imprisoned: 'You do not go to gaol for a lie!' he insisted.[143] Not long afterwards Neureuter published an article in *Germania* in which he expressly declared that there was no truth in stories of a retraction by the girls.[144] On neither occasion did Strauß question Neureuter's good faith, but he felt that the priest had a fixed determination to believe in the apparitions.[145]

Like other clergy, Neureuter took the view that the incidents involving the 'rival children' were a form of perverse compliment paid to the truth of the original, authentic apparitions. He was very sceptical of the claims made by the Münchwies and Berschweiler children,[146] and no less critical of their counterparts in Marpingen. Responding to requests in the Catholic press to give his views on the whole sequence of reported apparitions in the village, Neureuter issued a statement in September 1877. There could be 'nothing but suspicion' concerning the fourteen Marpingen children who had claimed visions since 2 July of that year; but he was 'completely convinced' about the original apparitions.[147] In the following years Neureuter maintained this dual approach. When imitative apparitions continued, he preached against them. In April 1879 he found himself 'obliged for a reason that is exceptionally distressing to return once more to the question of supposed apparitions'. Recent events 'too saddening and shaming' to communicate in church had provided 'incontestable confirmation' that the continuing apparitions were either the devil's work or the product of delusion; the evidence in his possession would lead anyone who heard it to reject the children's accounts with 'disgust'.[148] But when it came to the original visionaries, Neureuter's faith was firm. What one might have expected to be the painful news of Margaretha Kunz's confession appears not to have shaken his conviction;

---

[143] *Prozeß*, 82, 84.

[144] *Germania*, 21 Dec. 1876.

[145] See Strauß's note, LASB, E 107, 81. He took the same view at the later trial. See *Prozeß*, 82–4. It became obvious at the Saarbrücken trial that Neureuter was repeatedly warned about the untrustworthiness of the three girls, esp. Margaretha Kunz, not just by hostile officials but by men sympathetic to the parish priest, such as the Tholey notary and magistrate, Gatzen.

[146] *Prozeß*, 21, 157.

[147] Neureuter's statement of 11 Sept. appeared in both the *SZ* and *Germania*. See LASB, E 107, 443–4; Rebbert, *Marpingen und seine Gegner*, 8.

[148] BAT, B III, 11, 14/4, 52–3: notes of Neureuter sermon preached on the second Sunday after Easter, 27 Apr. 1879. The references to recent events and continuing apparitions in 1879 make it almost certain that 'rival children' were the subject of this sermon: the original visionaries were in convents by that time. The timing of the sermon remains intriguing, however. It occurred in the period between the taking of statements from the 3 girls at a convent in Echternach (Nov. 1878) and the negative judgement on those statements delivered by Bishop Laurent of Chersones (May 1880). It is possible that Neureuter had word of the direction in which Laurent's judgement was tending, and faintly possible therefore that this was the 'exceptionally distressing reason' that prompted his remarks. But this seems unlikely, on balance, for Laurent presented no new evidence on the original case. It would also contradict other evidence that Neureuter never subsequently doubted the truth of the original apparitions. It is more likely that the 'saddening and shaming' occasion was a reference either to the embarrassing testimony recently given by some of the 'rival children' in court at Saarbrücken (Mar. 1879), or to an incident in Marpingen we do not know about.

perhaps it was simply too painful to accept at face value.[149] Neureuter's house-keeper in a later parish, and inhabitants of Marpingen who visited him there, reported that he continued to believe firmly in the apparitions. He told one visitor: 'If it was as certain that we would enter heaven as it is that the Blessed Virgin appeared in the Härtelwald, we should have nothing to fear.'[150] Karl Kammer, a twentieth-century vicar-general in Trier, is surely right to accept that, once convinced, Neureuter was unable to break from his belief in the authenticity of the original apparitions.[151]

Deciding what to believe was one thing; how to act in the summer and autumn of 1876 was another. Neureuter adopted the formal position that it was not for him to pre-empt the church by passing judgement on the truth of the apparitions, or to do the work of the civil authorities by interfering in what was happening in the Härtelwald. His role was to maintain a cautious distance. The Baroness Louisenthal, dining with the parish priest during one of her three visits to Marpingen, found him 'discreetly silent'. When she questioned him, he replied that there were things he could not comment on as he had not been there, and 'as a priest he had to hold himself completely aloof from the matter and wait'.[152] It may be that Neureuter was keen to temper the enthusiasm of the extravagantly pious baroness (he warned her not to believe everything she read in the newspapers), but her account is confirmed by others. To Felix Dicke Neureuter wrote on 13 September that he was still being forced 'to discharge my obligations as a brake on events (*muß ich noch immer meinem Hemmschuhberufe nachkommen*)'. Dicke's later account of the apparitions noted that the restraining expression '*Hemmschuh*' became Neureuter's stock response to demands he did not wish to satisfy.[153] The self-restraint of his own conduct was also emphasized in the report Neureuter later wrote for his bishop.[154]

How far does this square with the facts? It may well be how Neureuter perceived his own role (and, on occasion, how he wanted to perceive it) but his conduct was actually less reticent. Take his treatment of the three girls. It is true that he interviewed them promptly and sternly at the first opportunity, and imposed various injunctions on their behaviour. He forbade the children to talk to non-clerical enquirers, to sign pictures for visitors, or to put questions to the Virgin on behalf of the sick.[155] It is clear, however, that these injunctions followed specific incidents that worried the priest because he felt they opened the door to vanity on the part of the children. They were an attempt to curb 'abuses', not to

---

[149] News of the Kunz confession was first conveyed to Neureuter a few months after Easter 1887. See BAT, B III, 11, 14/3, 63–4: Kunz statement of 26 Jan. 1889.

[150] BAT, B III, 11, 14/6[1]: statement of J. Leist, 9 Jan. 1935. Next to this, in the same folder, is a statement dated 17 Jan. 1935 from Luzie Sartorius, Neureuter's later housekeeper, who also testified to his firm conviction.

[151] BAT, B III, 11, 14/6[2]: Kammer's notes dated 26 Nov. 1956, 'Zu den Akten Marpingen!'

[152] LASB, E 107, 389.

[153] LASB, E 107, 397; *Prozeß*, 26; *MMGE*, 20.

[154] BAT, B III, 11, 14/4, 1–20: Neureuter's report to Bishop Korum, 25 Oct. 1902.

[155] LASB, E 107, 94–5, 161, 296, 319, 325.

deny the validity of the apparitions.[156] Neureuter did not order the children to
stay away from the site in the Härtelwald; he did say a high mass for them in the
parish church, spent time with them almost every day, and gave them booklets
in which to record their visions.[157] There was doubtless an element of attempted
control in this. The regular talks with the girls and the booklets might be seen as
a form of monitoring; the high mass for the visionaries took place on the same
day that Neureuter expressly denied participation in communion to a 'crowd of
children' who were calling for it.[158] It is nevertheless reasonable to ask: who was
controlling whom? Neureuter's position was that of follower rather than leader;
he was caught in the web spun by the visionaries. After the improbable incident
of the funeral procession allegedly sighted over the church graveyard, he could
offer nothing more trenchant than the conventional response: 'that is good, now
go in the church and pray'. A further vision was the result, the first in the
church.[159] In a more poignant moment associated with the same incident, he
joined the girls at prayer by the grave of his dead sister when they claimed to
have seen the Virgin hovering there.[160]

Neureuter similarly lacked the will to impede the cult that developed around
the site. The first words he addressed to his parishioners from the pulpit after
the apparitions urged them to avoid the place 'for the moment' and make their
devotions to the Virgin Mary in the parish church: if God had a purpose in view,
He had ways of making His meaning plain.[161] This was clearly ineffectual, and
we hear no more of attempts to dissuade the village population from visiting the
site. Indeed, Neureuter's request on that first occasion that his parishioners 'avoid
any disorder' amounted to a tacit admission that they were already thronging the
Härtelwald and unlikely to stop doing so. Here was another attempt to prevent
secondary 'abuses', rather than address the primary event critically. Neureuter
settled for an equally lop-sided compromise when it came to visiting pilgrims.
He welcomed the religious enthusiasm that brought them to the village, said
masses for them on request, and heard confessions every morning. Yet he avoided
the confessional box in the afternoons in order 'not to create the suspicion that
he wished to encourage the affair'.[162] Neureuter's behaviour throughout was as
contradictory as that of his fellow priest in Mettenbuch. Father Anglhuber also
emphasized his initial 'fear and mistrust', described how he had spoken sternly
to the visionaries and held himself 'aloof', and made a point of noting how he

---

[156] When he heard that apparitions had been reported in the school, Neureuter similarly forbade the
schoolteacher to put questions to the Virgin through the children. See *MMGE*, 19.

[157] BAT, B III, 11, 14/3, 29; LASB, E 107, 387, 446; *EM*, 54.

[158] This took place on 12 July: *EM*, 54. At the later trial in Saarbrücken, Georg Dasbach argued that
the reading of a high mass (*Hochamt*) rather than a *stille Messe* was normal in Marpingen, as for
example when a young man was conscripted: *Prozeß*, 20. This does not entirely answer the point about
the age of the girls, and the privilege extended to them.

[159] LASB, E 107, 9.

[160] BAT, B III, 11, 14/3, 22–3 .

[161] LASB, E 107, 423: notes of Neureuter's seized by the civil authorities.

[162] BAT, B III, 11, 14/4, 8: Neureuter to Bishop Korum, 25 Oct. 1902; LASB, E 107, 421–2.

had 'forbidden' parishioners to visit the site and done 'everything possible' to dampen down the affair.[163] Yet the priest allowed the visionaries to talk to visitors, gave one of them rosaries for the Virgin to bless, and had in fact (in the words of his bishop) 'completely taken the side of the children'.[164]

It is probable that a combination of reasons led Neureuter, like Anglhuber, to eschew any serious attempt to nip matters in the bud. Not the least important was the growth of his own belief in the apparitions. The formally expressed reluctance to pre-empt a canonical enquiry was undercut by his own evident convictions. Neureuter was powerfully drawn to the Härtelwald. He described how, on the evening of 12 July, he heard singing and praying and turned his telescope on the gap in the bushes made by villagers so that he could see the site. He set off to join them, but 'felt restrained by a hidden force' and turned back. This was subsequently described in many sympathetic accounts as evidence of his restraint.[165] In fact, he later admitted visiting the site on 5 July, the evening on which Nikolaus Recktenwald claimed his cure.[166] Any subsequent efforts to dissuade his flock from visiting the Härtelwald would certainly have lacked moral force.

After army intervention on 13 July the situation changed, of course: Marpingen became an affair of state. Neureuter now had good reason to be seen to distance himself personally from events, but an even better reason to take private pleasure in the clumsily ineffectual efforts of the civil authority. After his own offer to mediate had been brusquely declined there is an unmistakable sense of *schadenfreude* in his reactions to the discomfiting of the mighty state. That the state authorities were prepared to turn Neureuter himself into a martyr would hardly have altered his behaviour; quite the contrary. He bore the personal consequences of declining to call a halt to the popular movement, while suggesting—somewhat disingenuously—that the authorities must live with the consequences of rejecting his good offices. When it was suggested that he intervene to quell popular passions he declared that this was not his role, and made a moral weapon of his own impotence.[167] This impotence was not entirely feigned. It would have been

[163] BZAR, F 115, Fasc. I: 'Bericht des Pfarramtes Metten über die behaupteten Erscheinungen der Mutter Gottes . . .', 23 July 1877. Anglhuber took the same line in his voluminous correspondence with his superiors in Regensburg, contained in the same file. See also SAL, 164/2, 1162, 'Vormerkung' of BA Deggendorf, 3 May 1877.

[164] BZAR, F 115, Fasc. IV, 'Pro memoria über die Mettenbucher Erscheinungen' of Bishop Senestrey, 13 Nov. 1878; Fasc. V, 'Vernehmung des Fr. Xav. Kraus in Regensburg. Nov. 1878. Weitere Vernehmungen in Metten. Dezbr. 1878'.

[165] See e.g. *MMGE*, 18; *EM*, 56–7.

[166] *Prozeß*, 137. This admission in court followed the deciphering by the authorities of an entry in his notebook: LASB, E 107, 271, 386. Father Weichsel at Dittrichswalde also believed personally in the authenticity of the apparitions there; he went a step further by going to the site together with the seers. See 'Bei der Madonna', 30; *Germania*, 24 Oct. 1877; Rebbert, *Marpingen und seine Gegner*, 67–8.

[167] Anglhuber also made a weapon of his own powerlessness, telling the local official in Deggendorf that a direct intervention would be 'ill-advised', things had 'gone too far', his own reputation had already suffered because of his restraint, etc.: SAL, 164/2, 1162, Anglhuber to BA Deggendorf, 5 May 1877.

difficult to stem the movement in Marpingen even if Neureuter had whole-heartedly tried to do so, and even if the state had not inadvertently fanned the flames by its actions. The episodes in Berschweiler and Münchwies were not easily brought to a halt, although the clergy denounced them and co-operated with state officials. As we have seen, the apparitions in Marpingen soon gained general support; Neureuter's own housekeeper went to the Härtelwald.[168] Even such reticence as the parish priest did display earned him suspicious looks.[169] There is some truth in the view of one critic that Neureuter neither wished nor dared to stifle popular piety.[170]

There were, however, two major areas in which Neureuter was compromised by his action as well as his inaction. The first of these concerned publicity for the apparitions. Neureuter was, as we have seen, deluged with requests for infor-mation by Catholic newspaper editors in Germany and beyond. Some visited Marpingen in person. In a letter to Father Dicke during September 1876, Neu-reuter singled out one of these—*Germania* editor Paul Majunke—as a person on whom he had been forced to use the incantation 'Hemmschuh'.[171] But he evidently did not use it on every occasion. From as early as July 1876 he wrote reports of the apparitions and cures for papers that included the *Saar-Zeitung* of Saarlouis, the *Trierische Landeszeitung*, and *Germania* itself.[172] Once Neureuter was himself convinced, these accounts left no doubt about his own views. To later diocesan authorities in Trier, concerned to bury the whole affair, Neureuter's declarations 'could not be called exactly happy'.[173]

The second issue that led Neureuter into a compromised position was the use of the money left by pilgrims. The sums involved were large. The first pilgrims left offerings at the site in the Härtelwald, where coins ranging from small copper and 10-pfennig coins to thaler pieces were deposited. One visiting cabinet-maker described the site as being ringed with flower-pots containing coins; a publican from Tholey saw 'a potato-basket full of money'.[174] Money was later left at the Marienbrunnen and in the parish church.[175] Estimates of the total sums vary. One gendarme estimated that the donations were running at 400–500 marks on special days and 100–150 marks on normal days during the busy summer of 1877.[176] That would give an amount in excess of 1,000 marks a week, an

---

[168] LASB, E 107, 88: testimony of Eva Schwind of Tholey.
[169] LASB, E 107, 380; *EM*, 55. There are, once again, parallels with Mettenbuch, where Father Anglhuber's restraint—half-hearted though it was—earned him a 'reputation as a liberal who believed nothing': SAL, 164/2, 1162, 'Vormerkung' of BA Deggendorf, 3 May 1877.
[170] Berg, *Marpingen*, 13.
[171] LASB, E 107, 397: Neureuter to Dicke, 13 Sept. 1876.
[172] See *MWOL*, 79–80; LASB, E 107, 238.
[173] BAT, B III, 11, 14/6[2]: materials on Neureuter compiled by Karl Kammer, in 'Zu den Akten Marpingen!', 26 Nov. 1956.
[174] LASB, E 107, 213, 215. Ibid. 207 ff. has numerous witness accounts of money being left at the original site.
[175] LASB, E 107, 221–3; *Prozeß*, 159–62.
[176] Detailed estimates and breakdown by gendarmes in LASB, E 107, 224–5.

improbably high figure even given the presence of many free-spending aristocrats. The figures given by parish bookkeeper Jakob Schario were 3,000 marks for 1876 and 4,000 marks for 1877.[177] These were still considerable sums of money. What should be done with it? Left lying around it aroused the suspicion of the authorities and was a source of temptation. There were several cases of theft.[178] It appears to have been gathered up, mainly by women, in receptacles ranging from aprons to a cigar-box, and delivered to the sacristy. The strong implication of several accounts, sympathetic and unsympathetic, is that this was done in such a way that Neureuter himself had no need to handle the money personally.[179] This no doubt provided the parish priest with a form of deniability, and parallels his action in encouraging Konrad Schneider and other priests to go to the Härtelwald on 13 July, while himself remaining at home. It was probably a wise precaution given the presence of gendarmes trying to monitor the movements of the money, and willing to peer into the sacristy when they heard the jingle of coins.[180]

There is no reason to believe that Neureuter found this anything other than an embarrassment; there is certainly no evidence to support the assertion of one detective that he and other clergy cultivated rich pilgrims to secure pecuniary advantages for themselves and the church.[181] He was, however, less than frank. It may be true, as Neureuter claimed, that he waved away pilgrims who tried to leave donations at his house, and did not personally touch money left on the altar in church, but he was undoubtedly aware of the sums being collected from the Marienbrunnen, the church, and elsewhere. He claimed, even more disingenuously, that although he would formerly have welcomed a few groschen to help with church repairs, he became 'completely indifferent' in the new circumstances.[182] Yet Paul Sausseret, a visiting Belgian priest, noted that the parish priest 'was in the happy position of being able partially to renovate the church'. The bookkeeper Schario said that all but a few hundred marks of the money collected went on improving the church. Neureuter himself admitted under questioning that 'much larger than usual' sums of money were left, and were used for the 'restoration of the rather shabby church'.[183]

The most problematic question was the setting up of a fund to construct a chapel in the Härtelwald. This was dear to the hearts of many who wanted to see Marpingen as the 'German Lourdes'. The visionaries reported the Virgin's words

[177] LASB, E 107, 233; Prozeß, 161–2.

[178] BAT, B III, 11, 14/5, 62–8: statement 17 Nov. 1946, of Sister Elisa Haben, niece of Susanna Leist, who described these thefts as the devil's work.

[179] The pattern of collection has been pieced together from accounts in LASB, E 107, 221 ff., and testimony at the Saarbrücken trial in Prozeß, 159–62.

[180] One farcical incident of this kind, on 18 Aug. 1877, is recounted in LASB, E 107, 228–30.

[181] Ibid. 449: report of Meerscheidt-Hüllessem, 28 Oct. 1876. Contrary to the claim of the militant Protestant writer, A. F. vom Berg, there is also no evidence that bottles for sending Marpingen water were found in Neureuter's home. See Berg, Marpingen, 14.

[182] BAT, B III, 11, 14/4, 3: Neureuter to Bishop Korum, 25 Oct. 1902; Prozeß, 161–2.

[183] Sausseret, Erscheinungen, 229; LASB, E 107, 232–3.

that a chapel should be built, and local inhabitants reacted enthusiastically.[184] The cause was taken up in the Catholic press, particularly by a *Germania* correspondent in Paris, Hermann Kühn, who floated the idea in the *Civiltà cattolica* of Rome and also wrote directly to Neureuter.[185] The parish priest received many other letters on the subject, some enclosing money for the purpose. Typical was the letter of a Belgian quarry owner's wife who sent money to assist with the construction of a sanctuarium that Neureuter 'was having built'.[186] As we have seen, the parish priest had offers to build a chapel or sanctuary in the woods.[187] His reactions were, once again, ambiguous. He told two correspondents who wished to send money for a chapel that 'nothing could come of it'.[188] He also claimed that when pilgrims and villagers (including Katharina Hubertus's father) spoke of a chapel, he put them off 'bluntly' with the words 'leave that alone' (*Laßt das noch*).[189] But it appears that what he actually said, to Hubertus at least, was that building a chapel would 'take a lot of money'.[190] Whether this was simply an unfortunate choice of words, or reflected a longer-term design, it is difficult to know. There is equally no firm evidence that a chapel fund was established. What we do know is that Neureuter, together with the Marpingen miller Johann Thomé and probably the bookkeeper Jakob Schario, had commissioned a Bavarian architect to draw up plans for a chapel, and these had been sent to the parish priest.[191] It seems unlikely that the Bavarian architect was working without the prospect of reward, or that no chapel fund had been earmarked in the parish.

In this, as in so much else, Neureuter found himself carried along: by the visionaries, their parents, village enthusiasts, pilgrims, and other supporters of the 'German Lourdes'. There were, of course, those who warned the parish priest that the affair was suspicious, even dangerous. Some were fellow priests; others were officials whom Neureuter liked or respected, such as the magistrate Gatzen and the young Catholic legal official Strauß. But there is no reason to question the fact that, once he had overcome his own doubts, Neureuter believed sincerely in the authenticity of the apparitions. He subsequently bore the burdens this heaped upon him with the stoicism of a martyr being tested, not without a touch of spiritual self-satisfaction. The attachment of the parish priest to the cause of Marpingen, like that of other clergy, was reinforced by the heavy-handed actions of the state. To all of them the degree of coercion used seemed grossly

---

[184] *MWOL*, 24.
[185] *Civiltà cattolica*, 'Correspondenz aus Preußen 19. August [1876]', cited in Berg, *Marpingen*, 15; LASB, E 107, 194: Kühn to Neureuter, 2 Sept. 1876; *Prozeß*, 212.
[186] Letter to Neureuter of 8 Oct. 1876, LASB, E 107, 415.
[187] See above, Ch. 5.
[188] Correspondence with Franz Fisch and W. Richard: *Prozeß*, 206.
[189] *MWOL*, 18, 24; *EM*, 37.
[190] This emerges from Neureuter's testimony at the Saarbrücken trial: *Prozeß*, 19–21.
[191] Testimony of Thomé and Neureuter under oath: *Prozeß*, 167–8. See also LASB, E 107, 195, on the alleged remark made by Thomé and Schario that a 'chapel will be built—no one can stop it'.

disproportionate. From the perspective of those charged with exercising civil authority, things naturally looked different. As they perceived it, the clergy were prime movers in a swindle, possibly a plot, that called for the firmest measures.

The Apparitions and State Repression

One of the most important differences between Marpingen and other German apparition sites of the 1870s was the degree of force employed against it by the state. This cannot be ascribed to some innately repressive character of the Prussian state. After all, Dittrichswalde in the Prussian Ermland, as well as Bavarian Mettenbuch, were spared coercion. What Marpingen revealed was a Prussian state that was indeed latently repressive, but was also cumbersome, inflexible, and unprepared for such incidents, both because it found them profoundly alien, and because bureaucratic parsimony left the normal police presence overwhelmed. The scale of the Marpingen events and the delay before the civil authorities had word of them produced an initial over-reaction by officials on the spot. Once the mailed fist had been shown, the agencies of the state were placed in a quandary. Soldiers, civilian bureaucrats, judicial officials, and policemen found themselves in a situation from which they were unlikely to emerge with either success or credit, and the frustrations of dealing with a refractory population brought instinctive fears and prejudices to the surface. The actions that followed were painstaking and petty, comic and vindictive by turn.

Soldiers, Magistrates, and the 'Irishman'

The lack of early intelligence from Marpingen, and the panic that ensued when word finally arrived, undoubtedly did much to set the repressive tone. Village officials in Marpingen, and particularly the local *Ortsvorsteher*, studiously avoided reporting what was happening. A senior gendarme called Oberleuter, based in St Wendel, was on mounted patrol in the area about a week after the apparitions began, but registered 'nothing out of the ordinary'.[1] The local gendarme, Kinzer, would undoubtedly have raised the alarm, but he was in gaol at the time on an immorality charge.[2] It was Kinzer who, on 11 July, finally alerted the office of the *Landrat* in St Wendel that thousands of pilgrims were streaming to Marpingen. At this point a further problem arose. The *Landrat*, Rumschöttel, was on holiday at the time. The task of responding therefore fell to his deputy, the district

[1] LASB, E 107, 15.
[2] See Neureuter's notebook entry: 'The police would have arrived sooner, but he was in custody because of a sexual offence.' The explanatory note by examining magistrate Kleber ('the reference is to the policeman Kinzer') appears to confirm the substance of this: LASB, E 107, 428.

secretary Hugo Besser, and he leaned heavily on the rural mayor of Alsweiler in deciding how to act.[3] The individual in question was Wilhelm Woytt, a foreman of machines in the St Wendel railway workshops and an ardent liberal. He had already acquired the local nickname the 'Devil of St Wendel' over his part in the Namborn affair, and was engaged in a salary dispute with the Marpingen parish council.[4] Besser and Woytt sent the gendarme Oberleuter to the village on 12 July. He reported that there were thousands of pilgrims gathered in the village whose alarmed reactions to his own arrival reminded him of the battle of Gravelotte.[5] That same evening Besser and Woytt telegraphed the nearest garrison in Saarlouis and requested that troops be placed on alert. Early the next day, Thursday 13 July, there was a further gendarme report that pilgrims had been arriving through the night, and the atmosphere was frenzied. Besser and Woytt, accompanied by Oberleuter and two other gendarmes, then went to Marpingen in person, where Besser in the name of the *Landrat* three times ordered the crowd to disperse under article 116 of the Prussian Criminal Code. Members of the official party later insisted that he did so clearly and distinctly, but it seems likely that many failed to hear because of the loud singing and praying at the site; others reacted with a derision that Woytt believed was directed at him.[6] Unsuccessful, the five men thereupon returned to St Wendel and requested that military assistance be sent.

At 12.30 p.m. the eighty-strong 8th Company of the 4th Rhenish Infantry Regiment, under the command of Captain Fragstein-Riemsdorff, was instructed to proceed to St Wendel where they would be briefed by the *Landrat*'s office.[7] They received instructions from Besser to clear the area, remove non-residents, impose a curfew, and prevent 'excesses' in the public houses. Some time after 6 o'clock in the evening the company set off for Marpingen on a direct cross-country route, using foresters' tracks. At the point where they crossed the old Roman road that ran north–south to the east of Marpingen they spotted a man in clerical garb apparently giving signals to unseen people, but he disappeared into the woods when they hailed him. As the soldiers approached the Härtelwald at around 8 o'clock many people returned to the village, along with the priests Schneider, Schwaab, and Schütz. But a large crowd remained at the apparition site (Woytt estimated their number at 1,500, Captain Fragstein-Riemsdorff at 3,000–4,000) kneeling, singing, and praying. The commanding officer sounded a drum-roll and ordered the crowd to disperse. What happened next was confused, and some of the details were later disputed. The testimony of the soldiers,

  [3] LHAK, 442/6442, 17–18: RP Wolff Trier to Kaiser Wilhelm I, 16 July 1876; *Prozeß*, 149–50. On Besser, see Derr, 'Pfarrei Marpingen', 39; Müller, *St Wendel*, 274.
  [4] On Woytt's occupation, see *Adreß-Kalender . . . Trier* (1876), 190. On his liberal politics—he was a member of the St Wendel council—and the Namborn affair, see above, Ch. 3.
  [5] Testimony in *Prozeß*, 15; also LASB, E 107, 15. Gravelotte was an engagement in the Franco-Prussian war.
  [6] LHAK, 442/6442, 19–20, 133–4; LASB, E 107, 15; *Prozeß*, 14–15; BAT, B III, 11, 14/4, 10.
  [7] *MMGE*, 43, and *MWOL*, 40, both wrongly give it as the 30th Rhenish Infantry Regiment.

like that of Woytt and the gendarmes, emphasized the refractory nature of the crowd: they had sung louder, directed derisory and threatening remarks at the soldiers, and appeared unwilling to believe that force would be used. There were, allegedly, remarks to the effect that 'we have been soldiers too; you can't order us around; you won't do anything to us'. The captain accordingly gave the order to fix bayonets (although not to load rifles) and two platoons went into the crowd in an attempt to disperse it. It is hardly surprising that the sudden arrival of soldiers expecting the worst should have caused concern, and it is certain that their preliminary actions made matters worse. For this was no crisp military manœuvre. In the noise and poor light, there was uncertainty among the soldiers themselves about what was happening: some mistook the drum-roll for an order to load rifles, and had to be ordered to unload. Even witnesses sympathetic to the military noted that there were 'loud screams' from the crowd, and the prevailing mood was understandably one of confusion.[8]

The clearing of the site proceeded with violence. This was not entirely unprovoked. It was untrue, as the miner Peter Kreuz later claimed, that those who were young and fit enough to do so fled, while the old and sick faced the might of the soldiery. That was the stuff of myth: the wounded included the young and fit who stayed to face down the soldiers, and in some cases to issue threats. (Kreuz himself, the son of the notorious day labourer 'Kreuzhannes', had two previous convictions for assault, and was later tried, together with eight other Marpingers, for taking part in an affray in Alsweiler which caused his brother to be charged with unlawful killing.[9]) But it seems fairly well established that the worst the military faced at this stage was taunts and truculence, and that some of the initial accounts they gave were seriously misleading. Lieutenant Lent stated, for example, that one group had tried to unseat him from his horse, leading him to ward them off with his bayonet and the butt-end of his rifle. Other soldiers reported being threatened by clubs. During a later court hearing, however, it became evident that many of these threats and incidents in fact occurred later that evening, and both Lent and his senior officer accepted under oath that there had been no 'resistance'.[10] It was certainly the civilians who came off worst. No soldiers were reported injured during the clearing of the Härtelwald, against more then sixty victims of blows received from rifle-butts or (in a few cases) of cuts from bayonets.[11]

[8] This account of the military intervention has been constructed from 3 major sources: the depositions of military and civilian witnesses in LASB, E 107, 15–19, 31–45; the further testimony given at a later trial in Cologne, reproduced in BAT, B III, 11, 14/4, 27; and the account given by RP Wolff of Trier when briefing the Prussian Minister of the Interior for a later debate in the Prussian parliament, in LHAK, 442/6442, 135–41. There are also descriptions in Cramer, *Die Erscheinungen*, 19–21, Bachem, *Erinnerungen*, 135–7, *MWOL*, 40–1, and *EM*, 58–65.

[9] LASB, E 107, 39, 253 ff.

[10] BAT, B III, 11, 14/4, 27. On the question of resistance, see below, Ch. 8.

[11] LASB, E 107, 17. There were also psychological victims, or so it was claimed. One young villager, Andreas Thomé, who had been mentally ill and emotionally disturbed for 10 years, fell into maniacal raving the day following the military intervention, his family claiming that it had tipped him over the

The violence did not stop at the apparition site. A number of miners and ex-miners, mainly from outside Marpingen, claimed that they were pursued by soldiers and struck.[12] Others who incurred the ire of the soldiers were the carters whose vehicles and horses were an obstacle to the movement of the company. They were dealt with peremptorily when they failed to move.[13] If Fragstein-Riemsdorff wanted some people cleared out of the way, there were others whose attendance he expected—and demanded—in order to service the needs of his men and the company's horses. Above all, he wanted to see the *Ortsvorsteher*, Jakob Geßner, who had followed his earlier silence about the crowds of pilgrims by keeping his head down on 13 July. Geßner was summoned by Woytt, who accused him of 'gross dereliction of duty' and asked why he had not volunteered his services. When Geßner replied that he had to be sent for before he would come, he was told not to use 'insolent language'. The captain then demanded oats for the horses, and the *Ortsvorsteher* claimed there were none to be had in the village. This was not calculated to please the choleric Fragstein-Riemsdorff (Neureuter recorded in his notebook that you could get an idea of what it was like to meet him by throwing water on to a red-hot brick[14]). Woytt admitted of the incident that followed that there were some 'ill-chosen words'; Geßner said that the captain grabbed him by the collar, tightened his grip, and shouted that he would not leave the spot until oats were made available.[15]

The requisitioning of food and drink, including wine, and the billeting of the soldiers on the village proceeded high-handedly through the evening. The soldiers were informed by their senior officer that they should 'eat their fill', and the rounding up of provisions and beds was achieved through the bellowing of orders and much slapping and tupping under the chin, accompanied by leering observations from soldiers that they could do what they liked.[16] Fragstein-Riemsdorff later observed laconically that 'the inhabitants of Marpingen showed themselves to be slack and grudging in the lodging of the men and the procuring of the necessary provisions, etc., so that energetic action and blunt measures were necessary on my part in order to regularize the circumstances of the case (*zur Regelung der desfällsigen Verhältnisse*)'.[17] Billeting was not an entirely novel experience for Marpingen. When mobilized Prussian troops moved into the area almost exactly six years earlier during the Franco-Prussian war, Tholey became

edge. Thomé's case was written up by one liberal paper as an example of the 'religious mania' unleashed by the apparitions themselves. See LASB, E 107, 432–3.

[12] See the cases of Adam Schumacher and Peter Keßler of Wustweilerhof: LASB, E 107, 42; BAT, B III, 11, 14/4, 27. Keßler had a previous conviction from 1869 for causing a public nuisance and resisting arrest.

[13] The case of Paul Bohnenberger of Kleinheiligenwald, an ex-miner, is the one on which we have most detailed evidence, but there were others. See LASB, E 107, 40–1.

[14] Ibid. 427: entry in Neureuter's notebook.

[15] BAT, B III, 11, 14/4, 27.

[16] For some of the notes taken by Neureuter on the mistreatment of villagers and non-residents, see LASB, E 107, 431.

[17] Ibid. 437.

the headquarters of the 1st Army and soldiers were decanted into all the surrounding districts.[18] But in 1876 the circumstances were naturally different. They
recalled a different precedent: the treatment meted out to the population of
Frankfurt by the Prussian army after the Prussian–Austrian war of 1866.[19] Writing
in the *Kölnische Volkszeitung*, Matthias Scheeben suggested that the behaviour of
the army in Marpingen 'was worse than that to be expected of troops in an
occupied country'.[20] One village woman hit on a more melodramatic parallel with
Herod's soldiers and the slaughter of the innocents.[21]

The military occupation of Marpingen was to last two weeks, during which
time the soldiers were billeted on the village at its own expense. The billeting,
requisitioning, and curfew were naturally resented, and some members of the
company behaved provocatively. Sergeant Wolter adopted a habitually mocking
tone, Captain Fragstein-Riemsdorff flew easily into a rage, Lieutenant Hellwig
proved both belligerent and gluttonous. As scandalized stories circulated about
his demands for chicken and coffee from Neureuter's housekeeper, a friendly
sergeant confided to the trainee schoolteacher Metzen that Hellwig was 'the
biggest scoundrel (*Halunke*) in the whole regiment—at home he eats only soaked
potatoes'.[22] Gastronomic excesses apart, however, the soldiers kept to themselves
as far as possible after the rigours of the first evening. The parish priest, on
whom several officers were billeted, seems chiefly to have noticed the unnatural
quiet in his house, especially the retreat into silence of his dog Türk, who spent
most of his time under the sofa bearing a lugubrious expression. For Neureuter,
at least, the passing of the days brought a more relaxed atmosphere. On 17 July
he noted: 'Change of mood. Produced by a cask of beer. A charming picture.'
Irony might be suspected, but for another, less lapidary notebook entry that
described what happened: 'The soldiers are camped out in the meadow and sing
their merry soldiers' songs over a cask of beer.' Neureuter wished that he had
been able to capture the scene in a photograph. At the same time, the captain
became more friendly and the lieutenant more talkative. 'The military *bona fide*',
concluded the priest.[23]

The conduct of the army on the evening of 13 July, like the subsequent costs
of billeting, was to remain a bitterly contested issue for the villagers. Within a
day or two of the military intervention, however, the centre of attention shifted
from soldiers to civilian officials. District Governor Wolff of Trier travelled to St
Wendel on 13 July. On the following day he visited Marpingen to conduct the
preliminary investigation in person, accompanied by Besser, Woytt, and the
district medical officer of health, Dr Brauneck. After some lengthy verbal sparring
with Neureuter, during which he remonstrated with the priest for his failure to

[18] Müller, *St Wendel*, 256–8. The mobilization of 1870 began on 16 July.
[19] For a description, see F. L. Carsten, *Essays in German History* (London, 1985), 187–8.
[20] *KVZ*, 26 Sept. 1876; Bachem, *Erinnerungen*, 136.
[21] Frau Jakob Recktenwald, in a statement given to Father Dicke on 8 Sept. 1876: LASB, E 107, 438.
[22] LASB, E 107, 427: Neureuter's notebook. See also BAT, B III, 11, 14/4, 27.
[23] LASB, E 107, 425: Neureuter's notebook.

quell the movement and asked him rather pointedly whether he held the post of
school inspector (he did), Wolff interrogated the three visionary children, his
questions revolving around the putative part played in events by the parish priest.
He also talked to two of those who claimed to have been cured, Nikolaus
Recktenwald and Magdalena Kirsch.[24] The district governor was evidently satisfied with the results of his visit. On the following day, 15 July, District Secretary
Besser issued a public pronouncement:

On the 13th of this month, a large, unlawful assembly of people, which had gathered in
the woods near the village of Marpingen as a result of alleged apparitions of the Mother
of God, was broken up by the use of military force. Many sick people, some of whom had
come long distances, believed in their simple-mindedness that they would be cured by
placing money at the miraculous spot. The preliminary investigation has already shown,
however, that the instigators (Anstifter) of the miracle were solely bent on defrauding the
credulous population. I herewith warn the inhabitants of the district in the sternest possible
terms against visiting the so-called miraculous place, even after the troops currently ordered
to Marpingen have departed. Any further riotous assembly (Zusammenrottung) at the place
in question will immediately be broken up again with armed force and those involved
subjected to legal penalties.[25]

The pronouncement showed how prematurely Wolff had joined Besser and
Woytt in concluding that deliberate deception lay at the root of the apparitions.[26]
It also signalled clearly the two-track policy that the civil authorities would
henceforth pursue. The first of these was to isolate and prosecute the 'instigators'
supposedly behind the affair; the second was to prevent access to the Härtelwald
in an attempt to rob the popular movement of its momentum. The second policy
might possibly have succeeded, if it had been pursued in conjunction with the
parish priest and the village authorities; but the manner in which the first policy
was pursued made the chances of such co-operation nil. That, in turn, severely
reduced the chances of effectively policing the Härtelwald. As a result, the state
found it difficult to pursue either track of its policy with any great success: stage
by stage it was sucked into actions that exposed it to criticism—or, worse, to
ridicule.

The search for ringleaders began immediately. On the same day as Besser's
public pronouncement, a Saturday, a criminal investigation began under the
direction of the examining magistrate Ernst Remelé and Senior Public Prosecutor
Pattberg of Saarbrücken.[27] They established themselves on the first floor of the
Blaumeier public house and proceeded with a relentless round of interrogations.
The young seers bore the brunt of this. As we have seen, they were questioned
by no fewer than six different officials, not including the medical officer of health,

[24] BAT, B III, 11, 14/4, 11; MWOL, 41–2.
[25] SAStW, C/56, 133: District Secretary Besser's pronouncement of 15 July 1876, in the name of the
Landrat of St Wendel.
[26] This emerges very clearly from RP Wolff's report to Kaiser Wilhelm I on 16 July 1876: LHAK,
442/6442, 17–22, esp. the closing two pages.
[27] BAT, B III, 11, 14/4, 11; MWOL, 42.

Dr Brauneck. Margaretha Kunz believed later that she had been interrogated a total of twenty-eight times.[28] The girls' parents, the parish priest and other clergy, the adult visionaries, and village officials such as schoolteachers and foresters were only the most prominent among the hundreds of witnesses questioned by the indefatigable officials in Marpingen and St Wendel. In their attempts to uncover the mechanics of the 'fraud', the investigators overlooked no detail: who might have acted the part of the Virgin Mary in the woods, who had offered money to the children, who had placed a cross at the site in the Härtelwald, who had suggested that wire be fetched from the Heinitz pit to protect the spot from mass encroachment? Who, indeed, had encouraged the business by publicizing it? When those in charge of the investigation learned that 'a Frau Barbara Backes, the wife of a miner from Marpingen', had supposedly 'taken a keen interest in the apparitions and spoken about them', they decided to question her. Finding three women in the village named Barbara Backes, they interrogated all three.[29] The investigation yielded ten volumes of statements and supplementary material. These were unfortunately lost in Second World War bombing, but the evidence that remains in the form of a 500-page summary drawn up by the examining magistrate Emil Kleber shows that the material ran to considerably more than 3,500 pages.[30]

The taking of statements from suspects and witnesses was the principal means used to identify the alleged instigators of fraud and public disorder. But other methods were also employed. On the very first day of the investigation the houses of the young seers' parents were searched, fruitlessly, for evidence of financial gain from the apparitions.[31] At 8 o'clock one morning a mass identification parade of all the women in the village aged between 25 and 50 was held at the Blaumeier inn. The purpose was to identify the woman who had placed the cross in the Härtelwald reading 'this is the place'. The women were asked individually what they knew of this, and were then instructed to file past three witnesses: a publican, a shoemaker's wife from Tholey, and the 10-year-old daughter of a gendarme. This parading of several hundred women also failed to yield results.[32] Another line of approach involved the disciplining of village figures suspected of having a part in events. On 26 July Neureuter was stripped of his post as a school inspector and replaced by a mine foreman; on 21 August the schoolteacher André was transferred against her will to Tholey.[33]

The measures against Neureuter and André can be read as a sign that no hard

[28] BAT, B III, 11, 14/3, 63–4.
[29] LASB, E 107, 139.
[30] Based on the internal evidence of LASB, E 107, using extreme numbers of the 10 files referred to in the summary. Their contents were as follows: I, 540 pp.; II, 87 pp.; III, 133 pp.; IV, 110 pp.; V, 274 pp.; VI, 327 pp.; VII, 400 pp.; VIII, 528 pp.; IX, 637 pp.; X, 743 pp. This calculation gives a minimum total of 3,779 pages in all.
[31] LASB, E 107, 298–9.
[32] SB, 3 Oct. 1877, 1169; Radziwill, Besuch, 8–9; MWOL, 63; EM, 85.
[33] On Neureuter, see Kammer, Kulturkampfspriester, 159; Derr, 'Pfarrei Marpingen', 38; on André, BAT, B III, 11, 14/4, 11; MWOL, 42–3. André's friend, the schoolteacher Grady of Urexweiler, was

evidence had been uncovered pointing to them (or others) as 'instigators'. By September the investigation of a non-existent plot had stalled. This caused uneasiness in Trier, and unknown to the judicial authorities in Saarbrücken it was decided in Berlin to pursue the matter by other means. The outcome was the arrival in Marpingen of a figure who was to play a key role in the whole affair. This was a detective who worked for the Berlin criminal police in the Templinstraße. His name was Leopold Friedrich Wilhelm Freiherr von Meerscheidt-Hüllessem, but that was not the name he used in Marpingen. The Prussian Minister of the Interior provided him with identity papers that enabled Meerscheidt-Hüllessem to represent himself as an Irish journalist with the *New York Herald*. The alias they hit on for the detective was Marlow.[34]

Meerscheidt-Hüllessem was a specialist in plain-clothes investigations of a political nature. A few years later, during the opening phase of the Anti-Socialist Law enacted in 1878, he headed a group of detectives who maintained a round-the-clock surveillance of Social Democratic leaders such as August Bebel. Some of the actions of his team in these years recalled the 'dirty tricks' practised by the Prussian criminal police in the reactionary era of the 1850s and associated with the names of Karl Hinckeldey and Wilhelm Stieber.[35] They acted as *agents provocateurs* at SPD meetings, in order to have an excuse to break them up. On another occasion Meerscheidt-Hüllessem plied the 16-year-old son of an arrested socialist tailor with beer and cigarettes in an effort to gain information about the friends and political activities of the boy's father.[36] In his guise as an Irish-American journalist, Meerscheidt-Hüllessem deployed a similar repertoire of devices in order to uncover the machinations allegedly afoot in Marpingen.

'James Marlow' arrived in the village on Sunday 1 October. He claimed that he had been on a journey from Hamburg to the Rhine when he decided to see the situation in Marpingen for himself. The visitor was equipped with the visiting cards of Catholic priests and newspaper editors to prove his credentials, and went out of his way to emphasize that he was sympathetic to the position in which Marpingen Catholics found themselves. On his first evening the 'filthy-rich Irishman' bought an estimated 60 litres of beer for miners in Johann Thomé's inn, where he was lodging, while roundly abusing the Prussian police as 'donkeys'

also involuntarily transferred to Alsfaßen in Aug. 1876, 'as a result of the regrettable events in Marpingen': LASB, E 107, 292.

[34] LHAK, 442/6442, 27: MdI Berlin to RP Wolff Trier, 30 Sept. 1876. Wolff was to pass this information on to LR Rumschöttel and OP Pattberg, but he was seemingly unable to do so before the detective's arrival the following day. On 'Marlow's' arrival, see also BAT, B III, 11, 14/4, 12; Rebbert, *Marpingen und seine Gegner*, 23.

[35] On the notorious habits of Stieber and Hinckeldey, see A. Funk, *Polizei und Rechtsstaat: Die Entwicklung des staatsrechtlichen Gewaltmonopols in Preußen 1848–1918* (Frankfurt am Main, 1986), 60–70, and on the modest reforms instituted in 1859–63, 100–3. K. Frohme, *Politische Polizei und Justiz im monarchischen Deutschland* (Hamburg, 1926), shows how much the political police in the 1870s still relied on *agents provocateurs* and spy networks.

[36] D. Fricke, *Bismarcks Prätorianer. Die Berliner Politische Polizei im Kampf gegen die deutsche Arbeiterbewegung (1871–1898)* (Berlin, 1962), 68–71.

and 'scoundrels'.[37] This set the tone of his subsequent actions in Marpingen. He was apprehended by gendarmes on his second day in the village as a result of his incendiary language, and it was only after his arrest that Senior Prosecutor Pattberg learned his true identity and his reason for being in Marpingen.[38] He was no more fastidious in his choice of local confidants. He offered 30 thalers to one village drunkard, Peter Huper, in exchange for information about the person who had decorated the cross in the Härtelwald. Those who witnessed this exchange—they included the teacher Bungert—claimed that Meerscheidt-Hüllessem made the offer with the clear implication that he was not particularly concerned about the accuracy of the information thus obtained.[39] 'Marlow' also cultivated the day labourer Stephan Brill, a man with seven previous convictions for theft who had only recently returned to Marpingen after serving a five-year gaol sentence in Cologne. This was not the only occasion when the detective was undermined by his own deviousness, for Brill apparently persuaded 'Marlow' that he had been among a group of thirty men who had faced the sentries with clubs on the evening of 13 July, in an incident that led to an assault on Sergeant Wolter. In fact, Brill was not released from gaol until 27 July.[40]

It is evident from a later admiring account of his own cleverness published (under a pseudonym) in the *Berliner Tageblatt* that Meerscheidt-Hüllessem took pride in having duped the gullible villagers.[41] In fact the extravagant and inconsistent behaviour of 'the Irishman' aroused suspicion in Marpingen. After observing the way in which 'Marlow' prostrated himself at the Marienbrunnen and drained the cup of water he had drawn from it, Neureuter privately came to the conclusion that this 'oafish', 'idiotic' individual was an improbable Catholic. Others kept their distance.[42] By the time he left Marpingen on Saturday 7 October, the detective seems for the most part to have added only a body of dubious assertions to the prejudices with which he arrived. In his report written on 8 October he argued, for example, that one of the three miners from Theley who had been present in the woods on the evening of 13 July 'must' have been responsible for the attack on Sergeant Wolter; yet Wolter himself later saw all three men and was unable to identify any of them as his assailant.[43] The detective further suggested that the carter and ex-miner Paul Bohnenberger, injured during

[37] Among the printed sources, Thoemes, *Unsere Liebe Frau von Marpingen*, 84 ff. has the most detailed description of 'Marlow's' activities. His account is confirmed in many details by the evidence compiled by the judicial authorities in LASB, E 107, and the documentary record in LHAK, 442/6442. For the incident in Thomé's inn, see Thoemes, 84; Radziwill, *Besuch*, 27.

[38] Meerscheidt-Hüllessem had been asked to 'get in touch' with Rumschöttel and Pattberg: his way of doing this was to get himself arrested and taken to the former, who in turn had him taken to the latter. See LHAK, 442/6442, 27, 29: MdI Berlin to RP Wolff Trier, 30 Sept. 1876; LR Rumschöttel St Wendel to RP Wolff Trier, 2 Oct. 1876. See also *Prozeß*, 43–5.

[39] See Radziwill, *Besuch*, 8.

[40] LASB, E 107, 43; Radziwill, *Besuch*, 27.

[41] Meerscheidt-Hüllessem's account in the *Berliner Tageblatt*, and the replies published by Edmund Prince Radziwill in *Germania*, are reprinted in Radziwill, *Besuch*, 19–27.

[42] Thoemes, *Unsere Liebe Frau von Marpingen*, 91.

[43] LASB, E 107, 18, 43–5.

the clearing of the Härtelwald, had been 'hidden' and looked after by Neureuter until fully recovered. But the parish priest and his housekeeper denied this vigorously—and convincingly, given that army officers were billeted on him at the time.[44] 'Marlow's' report contained many other dubious assertions about Neureuter: that he took money from pilgrims, sold water from the miraculous site, and did not himself believe in the apparitions. It was on the basis of this questionable evidence that Meerscheidt-Hüllessem identified the clergy as the 'instigators' of an attack on the authority of the state.[45]

The local judicial authorities seem not to have been fully convinced of the case made by the detective from Berlin; but the latter's findings undoubtedly initiated a new phase of vigorous state action against the purported ringleaders.[46] The first move came in Berlin on 7 October, when the offices of *Germania* were raided by the criminal police and twenty-seven documents relating to Marpingen seized. The editor, well used to such visits, observed sardonically that 'the officials were as always very polite'.[47] The documents, so *Germania* was informed by police headquarters in Berlin, had been sent to the investigating authorities in Saarbrücken.[48] Four days later, on 11 October, came concerted house-searches of the parish priests in Marpingen, Alsweiler, Heusweiler, and Urexweiler, and of the *Ortsvorsteher* Geßner.[49] Neureuter, who had been away, was seized as he stepped off a train in St Wendel and taken to the *Landrat*'s office for searching and questioning. Only a breviary, a railway timetable, and a purse were found on him, for he had been forewarned on his return journey and passed his notes on the apparitions to a fellow passenger for safe keeping. On returning to Marpingen he found his house in disarray, with cupboards and drawers turned out and his correspondence taken away. The search party consisted of Senior Prosecutor Pattberg, Examining Magistrate Kleber, another examining magistrate from Saarbrücken (probably Ernst Remelé), a locksmith, five gendarmes, and 'Marlow'. The other house-searches involved local magistrates, legal officials

[44] LASB, E 107, 41–2.
[45] Ibid. 198, 449; *Prozeß*, 46. It is a measure of the detective's lack of care with detail that he managed to describe Margaretha Kunz, the youngest of the three visionaries, as the oldest: LHAK, 442/6442, 39–40: Meerscheidt-Hüllessem to RP Wolff Trier, 16 Oct. 1876. LHAK, 442/6442, 31–3: LR Rumschöttel St Wendel to RP Wolff Trier, 9 Oct. 1876, has a fawningly admiring account of the detective's cleverness in 'uncovering' the 'plot'.
[46] LHAK, 442/6442, 31–3: LR Rumschöttel St Wendel to RP Wolff Trier, 9 Oct. 1876, reporting that on the previous day he, OP Pattberg, the examining magistrate, and Meerscheidt-Hüllessem had met in Saarbrücken where they 'discussed and agreed the plan of operation'. On the reservations about the detective's findings, see the marginal query marks made by examining magistrate Emil Kleber against some of Meerscheidt-Hüllessem's claims about Neureuter: LASB, E 107, 449.
[47] *Germania*, 7 Oct. 1876. The documents concerned complaints about the conduct of the army in Marpingen that had been sent to the newspaper: LASB, E 107, 433.
[48] Madai, Police Headquarters Berlin, to the editors of *Germania*, 18 Nov. 1876, in *Germania*, 21 Oct. 1876.
[49] LHAK, 442/6442, 35: LR Rumschöttel St Wendel to RP Wolff Trier, 11 Oct. 1876, noting that the house-searches were taking place as he wrote. Rumschöttel complained that news of the seizures from *Germania* had become known too soon, thus giving the local clergy time to secrete compromising papers.

from Saarbrücken, detectives, and gendarmes. Around thirty gendarmes were employed in all.[50]

The co-ordinated character of the action was underlined when Father Dicke's house in Minden was searched on 21 October. Various notes were seized along with some pressed flowers that bore the suspicious marking *de loco apparitiones*.[51] A second search of Neureuter's house took place on 6 November, in which both Meerscheidt-Hüllessem and Woytt took part, and subsequent searches were made at the offices of the *Saar-Zeitung* and the house of Jakob Schario in Marpingen.[52] From 11 October, mail to the four local parish priests—Neureuter, Schneider, Schwaab, and Eich—was also intercepted.[53] Direct moves against individuals followed. In some cases this took the form of disciplinary administrative action. The Marpingen schoolteacher Bungert, who was also sexton in the parish church and had taught in the village for thirty-six years, was demoted in rank and transferred to Bliesen on 1 November. He was obliged to leave his wife and seven children behind. His replacement took a sterner view of the apparitions.[54] Father Eich of Heusweiler was deprived of his post as school inspector on 15 December 'as a result of his conduct during events at Marpingen, and in the light of the participation with which he is charged in the illegal acts to which those events gave rise'.[55]

Even more ominous action was taken against other alleged prime movers, for on 27 October began a series of arrests. Neureuter was taken into custody at Saarbrücken just after noon that day by a police officer and four gendarmes. According to the priest's housekeeper he was not given time to take a change of clothing.[56] Father Schneider of Alsweiler was arrested in his confessional box on 30 October; the following day seven more people were taken into custody at Saarbrücken. These were the four men who claimed to have seen the Virgin, the village watchman (*Feldhüter*) Jakob Langendörfer, the communal forester Karl Altmeyer, and Angela Kles, the woman suspected of placing flowers by the cross in the Härtelwald, gathering together money left at the site, and reporting to pilgrims on what the Virgin had said. All were questioned individually by Meerscheidt-Hüllessem.[57] The hand of the detective in these events is plain. A telling incident occurred when Nickel Schario travelled to Saarbrücken three days after Neureuter's arrest, seeking permission to visit the priest and ask what he needed.

[50] LASB, E 107, 170; BAT, B III, 11, 14/4, 17, 25; *Prozeß*, 202; Radziwill, *Besuch*, 27; *MWOL*, 56–9.

[51] LASB, E 107, 477.

[52] Radziwill, *Besuch*, 9, 28; *MWOL*, 63; LASB, E 107, 197.

[53] *Prozeß*, 207–8, 213–14. On Neureuter's protracted efforts to claim back his intercepted correspondence, see BAT, B III, 11, 14/4, 21, 41.

[54] LASB, E 107, 141; *MWOL*, 42–3; Rebbert, *Marpingen und seine Gegner*, 14. Radziwill, *Besuch*, 6, wrongly gives the date as 19 Oct.

[55] LASB, E 107, 332. On the Bungert case, see also *SPB*, 7 Jan. 1877, and *MWOL*, 86.

[56] LHAK, 442/6442, 45–6: OP Pattberg Saarbrücken to RP Wolff Trier, 27 Oct. 1876; Radziwill, *Besuch*, 6–7. Neureuter's arrest was regarded as an event of sufficient importance to be recorded in the *Schulthess' Europäischer Geschichtskalender*, 17 (1876), 188.

[57] LASB, E 107, 263, 275–8; Radziwill, *Besuch*, 7–8; *EM*, 84–5; *MWOL*, 62.

The examining magistrate Emil Kleber was willing to grant his approval, but was apparently overruled by Meerscheidt-Hüllessem.[58] Schario's account should not be taken at face value, of course, but it is consistent with other evidence suggesting a degree of tension between the legal official and the detective. In practice Meerscheidt-Hüllessem was dictating the direction, if not the pace, of events: he called four times for the arrest of Neureuter before the examining magistrate finally issued the necessary papers.[59]

The policeman also played a decisive part in the sequence of events that unfolded during the same period and led to the incarceration of the three visionary children. He first talked to them, and especially to Margaretha Kunz, at the beginning of October while playing the role of Marlow. He questioned them for the first time as the detective Meerscheidt-Hüllessem on 11 October. Five further interrogations took place between 24 October and 3 November.[60] The evidence gathered on these occasions underlay the judgement of the Guardianship Court (*Vormundschaftsgericht*) at St Wendel before which the girls appeared on 6 November. The magistrate Comes found the visionaries guilty of disturbing the peace, disorderly conduct, and attempting to profit themselves or a third party by deception. Minors under the age of 12 were not liable under the criminal code, but Comes judged it permissible that they be detained in a reform school.[61] On the evening after the court hearing the children returned with their parents to Marpingen. Three days later, on the morning of 9 November, gendarmes went to the Kunz, Leist, and Hubertus homes, while a fourth stationed himself in the street. Susanna Leist and Katharina Hubertus were taken from their parents, who were told that the girls were to be questioned again by the mayor at the Blaumeier inn and would return in a few hours; they were joined by Margaretha Kunz, who was being looked after by older sisters while her mother visited a married son in Alsweiler. Ten minutes later, the parents of Leist and Hubertus were told by a gendarme that their daughters were to be taken to Saarbrücken, and they should hurry if they wanted to give them anything for the journey. Arriving at the inn, they found a carriage waiting outside, with the children, Mayor Woytt, and a gendarme already inside. They were allowed to throw a change of clothes into the carriage, but refused permission to hand over the food they had quickly packed. The children, they were informed, would be back in three days.

The carriage set off for the station in St Wendel, and the two fathers followed on foot, accompanied by Elisabeth Kunz with a change of clothes for her younger sister. After the one and a half hour walk, they learned that the three girls were in the St Wendel gaol, but were not allowed to speak to them. The little party

[58] Radziwill, *Besuch*, 7.
[59] *Prozeß*, 47.
[60] LASB, E 107, 55–63. These interrogations took place on 24, 27, and 31 Oct., and on 2 and 3 Nov.
[61] Details of the hearing and judgement in BAT, B III, 11, 14/4, 105–6; LASB, E 107, 62; *MWOL*, 69–73.

then followed the children as they were taken to the station, and were joined by Frau Kunz, who had been alerted by another daughter and rushed from Alsweiler to St Wendel in time to see her daughter and the other girls being escorted by gendarmes on to the platform. The parents were, once again, refused access to their children, denied permission to give them food, and told that they could not accompany them to Saarbrücken.[62] The two fathers and Frau Kunz therefore made the fifty-minute journey on the same train, but separately from the official party that escorted their children. Once in Saarbrücken the children and their escort disappeared in another carriage and the parents, deciding to put up in the city for the night, learned unofficially from a clerk of the court where the children had been taken. On the following morning they went to the Prince Wilhelm and Marianne Institute, but feared that presenting themselves might lead to their own arrest. After attempting unsuccessfully to contact a lawyer, they returned to Marpingen later that morning. They were subsequently denied access to the girls, who remained in Saarbrücken for five weeks.[63]

Meerscheidt-Hüllessem played a central part in all this. He may not have achieved everything he wanted (his own recommendation was that Leist and Hubertus be committed to a lunatic asylum on the grounds that they were suffering a 'temporary mental disorder'), but he was the prime mover. Wolff and Pattberg largely reacted to his proposals.[64] Accordingly, it was he who was waiting in St Wendel for the children to arrive, accompanied them on the train to Saarbrücken, and interviewed Margaretha Kunz again on the same day the children were admitted to the institute.[65] The misgivings that the judicial authorities now began to show are understandable.[66] Even allowing for the pathos of the parents' account, this episode constituted perhaps the most frighteningly heavy-handed of all the efforts made to uncover, isolate, and break down the 'instigators' of the apparitions. The original decision in the Guardianship Court caused legal head-shaking; the manner in which that decision was implemented yielded the moral high ground to critics of the state. Along with other arbitrary proceedings, it was to prove a vulnerable point in the legal and political aftermath of the affair.

[62] During their stay at the station, the girls were kept in the first-class waiting room.
[63] BAT, B III, 11, 14/3, 63–4, and ibid. 14/4, 17; Radziwill, *Besuch*, 9–13. Radziwill, 14–16, contains the complaint subsequently drawn up by Radziwill himself on behalf of the parents.
[64] LHAK, 442/6442, 37–49: Meerscheidt-Hüllessem to RP Wolff Trier, 16 Oct. 1876; RP Wolff Trier to OP Pattberg Saarbrücken, 19 Oct. 1876; Pattberg to Wolff, 21 Oct. 1876; Wolff to Pattberg, 23 Oct. 1876; Pattberg to Wolff, 27 Oct. 1876; Wolff to MdI Berlin, 10 Nov. 1876. See also *Prozeß*, 478. I have not been able to find any evidence that (as *MWOL*, 63, claims) Meerscheidt-Hüllessem travelled to Trier on 7 Nov. to encourage Wolff to have the girls consigned to the Saarbrücken institute.
[65] LASB, E 107, 64–5; Radziwill, *Besuch*, 12.
[66] LHAK, 442/6442, 45–9: OP Pattberg Saarbrücken to RP Wolff Trier, 27 Oct. 1876; Wolff to MdI Berlin, 10 Nov. 1876.

Policing the Village

Measures against presumed ringleaders formed one part of a two-pronged policy. The other part consisted of strenuous efforts to prevent the inhabitants of Marpingen, or visitors to the village, from turning the woods into a pilgrimage site. This was to be achieved by heavy policing. On 28 July the army was withdrawn from Marpingen on the orders of the Supreme Army Command of the Rhine Province in Koblenz. The following day the warning went out from the office of the *Landrat* in St Wendel that the further 'influx of superstitious persons into Marpingen' would not be tolerated. Local *Ortsvorsteher* were advised what would happen if processions and pilgrimages took place: the police would make arrests, and if necessary troops would again be sent in at the expense of the districts concerned.[67] Similar warnings went out from other *Landräte* in the area.[68] Extra gendarmes were stationed in Marpingen itself to police the village and the site.[69]

In late August a comprehensive decree was issued, covering a ban on entry to the Härtelwald or Schwanenheck districts without written permission from the mayor of Alsweiler.[70] It prescribed special penalties against those who incited, organized, addressed, encouraged, or attended pilgrimages to the village or open-air meetings in it, against those who failed to disperse after three requests to do so (on the grounds of unlawful assembly), and against visitors who could not satisfy the authorities of their identity and their legitimate reasons for being in Marpingen. A guard-hut was constructed for the gendarmes by the miraculous spring, which they attempted to block up with rubble and mud.[71] The ban on entering the woods was lifted briefly in early November, following a series of arrests, but reimposed after three days.[72] Thereafter, every month brought new decrees, or the reiteration of old ones. A relaxation of the ban on the woods in December was soon followed by a renewed crack-down. At the end of January 1877 the *Landrat* warned that continued 'excesses' against gendarmes would, if necessary, be met by the use of weapons; in February the policing of the woods was strengthened by the arrival of a company of the 8th Rifle Battalion (*Jägerbataillon*); in March restrictions on the Härtelwald and Schwanenheck were once again relaxed, only to be reimposed.[73] Even after the arrival of the Rifle Battalion in Marpingen, the gendarmes remained. From the beginning of September 1876 until the end of the apparitions twelve months later, and beyond,

---

[67] SAStW, C/56, 134, 137–42: proclamation of LR Rumschöttel of St Wendel, 29 July 1876, posted up in the various localities during the following days.

[68] LASB, Best. LRA Saarbrücken, 1, 739: LR Geldern Saarbrücken to local mayors, 13 Aug. 1876.

[69] SAStW, C/56, 144: KR Trier to LR Rumschöttel St Wendel, 2 Aug. 1876, approving the measures of 29 July and the stationing of gendarmes in Marpingen; Müller, *St Wendel*, 274.

[70] LASB, E 107, 156; BAT, B III, 11, 14/4, 11.

[71] LASB, E 107, 350. *MWOL*, 45, wrongly states that this took place in September 1876.

[72] LASB, E 107, 156; *MWOL*, 43.

[73] SAStW, C/56, 165–73; LASB, E 107, 156; *MWOL*, 78–82, 86–91. See also *SMZ*, 13 and 20 Feb. 1877.

there were at least five and usually seven gendarmes posted in Marpingen (at an estimated cost of 90 marks each a month), together with additional gendarmes in Alsweiler, Urexweiler, and Tholey.[74]

The Prussian gendarmerie was organized in military fashion, subject to military discipline, and heavily drawn from the ranks of long-serving NCOs in the army.[75] Gendarmes were mounted, and that was not the only sense in which they looked down on what was happening in Marpingen. Thus gendarme Hentschel: 'In the streets there was an unbroken wave. In quarters and rooms of every kind people of both sexes lodged together. With such a growing influx it is inevitable that swindle, stupidity, and immorality will eventually gain the upper hand.'[76] The gendarmes' behaviour in the village was generally overbearing and sometimes vindictive. One apparently drew himself a drink at Johann Thomé's inn without paying for it; another charged Neureuter with allowing his 'vicious dog to run around off the leash without a muzzle'.[77] The provision of board and lodging to pilgrims was a major source of conflict. Many Marpingers were, undeniably, accommodating visitors in exchange for payment: in the period from 6 August to 2 September 1877 alone, fifty people were charged with the unlawful exercise of a business, and most of these had previous convictions.[78] But it appears equally undeniable that some gendarmes took pleasure in the opportunities that their enquiries provided for petty harassment. The knife-grinder Jakob Salm, for example, stayed in the village every year for a few nights, sleeping for nothing in the barn of a local peasant. He was in Marpingen again during the period of the apparitions. On his last evening in the village he was escorted in a drunken state by two gendarmes to the home of the barn-owner, who was roused and questioned at length about his putative paying guest, and eventually summonsed.[79] Two widowed sisters described their fears about the way in which the regulations on illegal provision of bed and board were enforced. According to their account, gendarmes came to their homes and asked them 'brusquely' (barsch): 'Have you had people staying overnight? Did you give them any food? What did you charge them?' When told by the women that they could no longer remember, one of the gendarmes replied: 'Well, if you don't know, I shall soon find out; I shall have all the people whose names we know come here at your expense and that will be nice and expensive, for they're coming from distant places.'[80]

[74] *MWOL*, 80–2. The estimate of costs was made by Mayor Woytt, quoted in *SMZ*, 29 Sept. 1876. On the costs, see also LHAK, 442/6442, 61–5.

[75] Funk, *Polizei und Rechtsstaat*, 27–31; J. Buder, *Die Reorganisation der preußischen Polizei 1918–1923* (Frankfurt am Main, 1986), 5–6.

[76] LASB, E 107, 167. At least one gendarme stationed in Marpingen already had '*Kulturkampf* experience' in the area. Gendarme Oberleuter was among those keeping watch on a crowd of around 600 Catholics gathered at St Wendel in Aug. 1873 to hear speakers who included Georg Dasbach: SAStW, C/56, 77: report of Mayor Müller of St Wendel, 27 Aug. 1873.

[77] LASB, E 107, 437; BAT, B III, 11, 14/4, 86, 102.

[78] LASB, E 107, 162–4, 167.

[79] BAT, B III, 11, 14/4, 71. The barn-owner was Jakob Saar.

[80] BAT, B III, 11, 14/3, 122: testimony of widows Kunz and Klos, summonsed 3 Jan. 1878.

The restrictions on access to the Härtelwald and Schwanenheck provided more cases of reported arrogance on the part of the gendarmes. Many seem to bear out the words of Father Eich, who wrote in an (intercepted) letter to a fellow priest in October 1876 that the woods were being guarded 'with brutal severity'.[81] Two things stand out in the descriptions we have of incidents that occurred during the policing of the woods. The first is the sheer relish with which villagers were charged for the most minor infractions. One summons for 'an offence against the forest law' during a period when entry to the Härtelwald was allowed under certain conditions charged that the person concerned had placed one foot off the permitted path.[82] There is evidence that some gendarmes preferred the apprehension of offenders to the prevention of offences. On a number of occasions they hid behind bushes in order to catch people drawing water at the spring.[83] There were even suggestions that, like 'Marlows' writ small, they were prepared to provoke offences. In one incident gendarmes allegedly lured a boy into the woods with a 'come here, lad!' On another occasion, two young women setting off at 7 o'clock one morning to draw water were only a few paces into the woods when they saw a gendarme, who seized one of them by the arm and hurried them to the spot where a second gendarme took a statement.[84] Members of the Rifle Battalion also set up what amounted to ambushes.[85]

The second point worth noting is the severity with which inhabitants of Marpingen were, in effect, punished for going about their working lives. It is true that many were drawn to the woods as a result of the apparitions, and particularly to the 'miraculous spring', whether from faith in its curative powers or faith in the ready market for the water among pilgrims, or both. But it is also true that, long before July 1876, the woods provided valuable free resources for the villagers and short cuts to their workplaces for miners and peasants. Both groups, and their wives and daughters, fell foul of the new restrictions. The miner Matthias Barbian was summonsed for taking a short cut through the Härtelwald in August 1876 in order to reach St Wendel station on his way to work; another miner, Michael Kunz, was summonsed the same month for taking a short cut on his return from the pit.[86] This was in fact normal practice among miners working at certain pits—and the army defended its similar approach from St Wendel to Marpingen on 13 July on the grounds that the cross-country route was the most direct. There were also countless summonses against those drawing water and gathering straw or animal feed from the woods, recalling earlier social struggles with the Prussian state over access to the fruits of the forest.

[81] LASB, E 107, 332: Eich to the parish priest of Vallendar, 11 Oct. 1876.
[82] BAT, B III, 11, 14/4, 109 (summons no. 886). See also SB, 3 Oct. 1877, 1170.
[83] BAT, B III, 11, 14/4, 178: the case of the miner Jakob Scheib, with Neureuter's supplementary notes on other, similar occasions.
[84] BAT, B III, 11, 14/4, 110, 114.
[85] BAT, B III, 11, 14/4, 73: testimony of Peter Wald concerning the experience of his 16-year-old son Nikolaus, and 16-year-old Johann Thomé.
[86] BAT, B III, 11, 14/4, 110, 130.

Peasants were also summonsed and fined when they used the woods to reach their own land. The three Meisberger brothers, Peter, Michael, and Wilhelm, had a small plot of just under an acre on which they grew oats, to which normal access was through the Schwanenheck. Michael Meisberger checked the crop on 21 August 1876; the following day all three brothers were apprehended on the path through the wood on their way to harvest it. They received relatively small fines of just over 4 marks apiece.[87] Peter Meisberger's wife was to be involved the following year in a more expensive, and more frightening, experience. She was one of fourteen or fifteen women and girls who went to the Schwanenheck in early May 1877, at a time when Marpingen was suffering a severe shortage of feed and straw. When hailed by gendarmes, all but one of them escaped: Katharina Meisberger, who was seven months pregnant. She was seized by gendarmes and 'strongly pressed (*sehr gedrängt*)' to name her companions. The terrified woman was allegedly 'harassed' (*drangsaliert*) in this way for some time, and told that she would not be charged if she co-operated. She claimed not to know who the others were, however, and eventually received a fine of over 17 marks.[88]

We do not have precise information on the total number of charges brought against persons unlawfully entering the woods. Neureuter preserved scores of summonses served on villagers over the whole period of the apparitions.[89] Apart from the statements and supplementary information he recorded from those involved, this source is useful chiefly in showing the severe financial impact when several members of a family were fined, especially where second offences were involved. Neureuter's collection also suggests a trend towards the more draconian application of the law as time went on. We have, in addition, the evidence of gendarmes' reports from the period 6 August to 2 September 1877, when a total of eighty-six charges were brought on the grounds of unlawful entry into the woods.[90]

By no means all of these charges were brought against natives of Marpingen. The highest weekly total (thirty-six charges in the period 27 August to 2 September 1877) coincided with the high-point in the influx of pilgrims, in the period immediately before the predicted end of the apparitions. Many of these pilgrims must have helped to swell the total. When the village *Ortsvorsteher* Peter Schnur and others requested a lifting of the ban on the woods in August 1877, they were told this could not be done 'until the procession of pilgrims to Marpingen has entirely ceased'.[91] From the outset, the authorities aspired to stem the flow of pilgrims. They could not legally prevent people from visiting Marpingen, but they could, and did, try to obstruct them in petty ways. They could require

---

[87] Ibid. 157, 176.

[88] Ibid. 174–5: details of summons, and the account given by her husband Peter Meisberger to Neureuter.

[89] Ibid. 71–185: summonses relating to this and other offences arising out of the post-apparition policing of Marpingen. Many of the archival file numbers cover more than one summons.

[90] LASB, E 107, 163–4, 167.

[91] Rebbert, *Marpingen und seine Gegner*, 12.

visitors to provide identification, inspect the visitors' books of inns frequently and rigorously, invoke legal statutes dealing with organized processions and the holding of open-air meetings, and make life generally unpleasant.[92]

The Belgian Baroness Drion, who believed her daughter cured by Marpingen water, was sufficiently concerned by the experience of her first visit to the village that, before travelling there a second time, she wrote to Neureuter expressing the hope that the innkeeper with whom she had arranged to lodge would not spread the word around, as she 'was worried about *unpleasantness* with the gendarmes'.[93] In fact, visitors of a more elevated social station were most likely to avoid such unpleasantness—especially if they were in a position to publicize their experiences. Paul Majunke, editor of *Germania* and a member of the Reichstag, was in Marpingen in late August 1876 and was not asked once to present means of identification.[94] Dr Nikolaus Thoemes, an independent Catholic scholar from Baden who wrote an account of the apparitions, arrived in Marpingen on 23 September 1876 and was not asked to provide identification by any of the fourteen gendarmes then in the village until 6 October (although he attributed this to his 'extreme caution'). Even the challenge on 6 October was friendly, and he was told he was welcome to stay if he 'behaved himself quietly'.[95] There were numerous other cases of this sort. In the summer of 1877 there were, as we have seen, dozens of aristocrats in Marpingen. The gendarmes reported waspishly on these 'well-dressed visitors' and 'ladies of high station'; but they generally made no attempt to ask for papers or apprehend them.[96] Exceptions to this tolerant treatment of the well-dressed or high-born were rare. Count Stolberg of Silesia, the brother of a Prussian parliamentary deputy, visited Marpingen in late August 1876 with his wife and mother-in-law. He was taken to the *Landrat*'s office and then to the mayor in St Wendel for questioning before his credentials were eventually accepted.[97] Two aristocratic Belgian women, from Tournai and Charleroi, were arrested in May 1877 for being in Marpingen without adequate means of identification.[98]

Treatment of this kind was familiar to the socially inferior. At almost the same

---

[92] On the statutes that the authorities could use against processions or pilgrimages not of long standing, or that threatened public order, see LHAK, 442/6442, 1–13. The information legally required of those registering at an inn was name, occupation, place of residence, dates of arrival and departure. Mayor Woytt added extra headings (place of birth, place to which travelling, object of journey), although visitors could not be forced to give these details: LHAK, 442/6442, 185–91.

[93] LASB, E 107, 193. A concern not to fall foul of such 'unpleasantness' may be why some actually sought permission to visit Marpingen. See the letters in SAStW, C/56, 158–60.

[94] *Germania*, 18 Dec. 1876.

[95] Thoemes, *Unsere Liebe Frau von Marpingen*, 84, 88–9. In fact, the highly nervous Thoemes took himself off the next day in the direction of the Luxemburg border.

[96] LASB, E 107, 163–8. A sympathetic writer described the experience of one group of obviously well-born visitors at a time of heavy police activity: 'The police were not friendly towards them, but did not prevent them from forming their own views of what had occurred there.' See Cramer, *Die Erscheinungen*, 6.

[97] Report in *TLZ*, 5 Sept. 1876; *MWOL*, 44–5. See also LASB, E 107, 361–2.

[98] LHAK, 442/6442, 71: gendarme report copied by RP Wolff Trier to MdI Berlin, 22 May 1877.

time as Count Stolberg's brush with the law, two servants of Bishop Ketteler of Mainz were arrested in Marpingen because they could not provide means of identification.[99] Two women from the Bernkastel district who arrived in St Wendel during the same period were greeted by a gendarme with: 'I suppose you want to go to Marpingen?' Their claim to have relations in St Wendel (which turned out to be true) was not believed: they were detained and questioned for over an hour, and ordered to leave St Wendel immediately when they proved unable to furnish satisfactory papers.[100] By mid-September 1876 around 400 people had been charged by gendarmes and over 350 convicted in the St Wendel police court on charges of unlawful pilgrimage or unlawful entry into the prohibited woods.[101] The second of these offences at least had the merit of being clearly defined, and it is doubtless true that the Baroness Louisenthal, the Countess Spee, the Princess Thurn und Taxis, and similar high-born visitors were prudent enough—unlike many others—not to court charges by visiting the Härtelwald or Schwanenheck. But when did a pilgrimage become 'unlawful'? The visit of the Princess Thurn und Taxis, with her retinue of seventeen, was plainly not considered to fall under this heading; but the members of a party of thirteen from Furschweiler who also went to Marpingen in the summer of 1877 found themselves sentenced to fines of 15 marks for taking part in an unlawful pilgrimage.[102]

Members of the Catholic clergy also fell foul of the authorities. In some cases reprisals took the form of disciplinary action. Father Winzen of Badenweierbach, like the parish priests of Alsweiler, Heusweiler, Urexweiler, and Marpingen, was relieved of his post as school inspector because he had 'encouraged' events in Marpingen. He was also banned from holding classes on religious instruction.[103] Unlike the other four priests, however, he did not face prosecution. Neureuter, Eich, Schneider, and Schwaab, together with Father Dicke of Minden, were eventually brought to trial in Saarbrücken in 1879 on criminal charges of deception and aiding and abetting deception arising from the Marpingen affair.[104] Other charges were brought against some of these priests. Neureuter, as we have seen, was prosecuted over his dog. Father Eich made the mistake of telling the Sulzbach magistrate who searched his home that seizing a notebook was 'foolish' (einfältig): in January 1877 he was fined 30 marks for defamation.[105] Five months later Edmund Prince Radziwill, a parish priest in Ostrovo, was convicted and

[99] NBZ, 26 and 29 Aug. 1876.
[100] SAStW, C/56, 150–6, which includes a cutting from the Bürger-Blatt für die Kreise Rees, Borken und Cleve [Emmerich], 14 Sept. 1876. The mayor of St Wendel wrote to the local mayor where the women lived; the latter confirmed their identities and could report 'nothing but good' about their characters.
[101] KZ, 15 Sept. 1876.
[102] Details in Kammer, Kulturkampfpriester, 160.
[103] See his correspondence with LR Rumschöttel of St Wendel, cited in MWOL, 86–8; also report in SMZ, 21 Jan. 1877.
[104] LASB, E 107, 332–449, 476–96; Prozeß, 10.
[105] Report in SMZ, 25 Jan. 1877. The case was heard in Saarbrücken on 21 Jan.

fined 20 marks for defamation of Mayor Woytt.[106] Given the ease with which
Catholic priests offended the sensitive and suspicious civil authorities, it was
perhaps as well for his own sake that the hot-tempered Paul Majunke visited
Marpingen in a grey three-piece suit, blue tie, and coral tie-pin, rather than in
the clerical collar to which he was entitled.[107]

In at least one case, a priest was prosecuted for the same offence with which
hundreds of pilgrims and villagers were charged. The visiting Belgian Paul
Sausseret entered the Härtelwald in August 1877 with a group that included a
priest from Bernkastel. An Englishwoman in the group displayed great indignation when the priest was questioned and then charged with holding a public
meeting by a gendarme who emerged, in a manner by then familiar to natives of
the village, from behind a bush.[108] But most of the clergy prosecuted in connection
with Marpingen were charged under *Kulturkampf* legislation concerning illegal
officiation at religious services. In the case of the clergy, the authorities had no
compunction about prosecuting prominent individuals, and the victims include
several well-known figures. In August 1877 the Cologne theologian Matthias
Scheeben was charged with 'performing religious offices in the church'.[109]
Edmund Radziwill was charged with the same offence after saying a mass in the
Marpingen parish church before 200 people.[110] Less prominent priests were also
caught in the net. Scheeben was charged along with a Father Probst from
Waldbreitbach; another priest was fined 20 marks and costs because he baptized
a child when Neureuter was unable to do so.[111] In all, more than twenty priests
were charged with the performance of religious duties in a manner that was illegal
under articles 22 and 23 of the May Laws. They came not only from nearby
areas such as Trier, Hermeskeil, and Simmern, but from Baden, the Palatinate,
the Rhineland, Westphalia, Upper Silesia, and abroad. A number were acquitted
on lack of evidence; those found guilty typically received fines of 20 to 30 marks.
Trials on these charges were still being held in March 1878.[112] Table 7.1 shows
how Marpingen swelled the numbers of priests convicted in the St Wendel area
under these provisions of the May Laws. A comparison with Table 3.3 on p. 109
shows that St Wendel had moved from being the area with the least number of
clerical convictions before July 1876, to one in which the number of convictions
was exceeded only by Trier (town).

[106] *Marpinger Prozeß vor dem Richterstuhle der Vernunft*, 49.

[107] Radziwill, *Besuch*, 42, on Majunke's attire.

[108] Sausseret, *Erscheinungen*, 228.

[109] LASB, E 107, 163. Neureuter was charged at the same time with 'tolerating said offence'.

[110] Details in LHAK, 442/15716. See also Radziwill, *Besuch*, 14.

[111] LASB, E 107, 163; BAT, 70/3676a, 156. This file includes Neureuter's later recollections about
the many fines against priests for illegally celebrating masses.

[112] LHAK, 403/15716: list of legal proceedings against priests charged under articles 22 and 23 of
May 11 law on education and appointment of clergy. See especially 130–1, 134–9, 144–7, 154–5,
158–61.

TABLE 7.1. *Priests convicted after July 1876 of illegally performing clerical duties in the Diocese of Trier*

Trier administrative district		Koblenz administrative district	
Trier (town)	31	Koblenz	12
St Wendel	28 (21*)	Mayen	10
Bitburg	17	Neuwied	7
Saarlouis	17	Cochem	6
Trier (country)	16	Kreuznach	5
Daun	16	St Goar	5
Wittlich	16	Adenau	3
Prüm	15	Ahrweiler	3
Bernkastel	11	Zell	3
Saarbrücken	8		
Ottweiler	7		
Merzig	6		
Saarburg	6		
TOTAL	194		54

*Marpingen-related offences

Source: LHAK, 403/15716: Verzeichnis derjenigen Geistlichen, welche auf Grund # 23 Abs. 2 des Gesetzes vom 11.5.1873 zur gerichtlichen Untersuchung gezogen und verurteilt sind. Diözese Trier.

Mettenbuch: A Bavarian Comparison

Repression of the Marpingen movement affected clergy and laity, villagers and pilgrims. The measures taken—from military intervention to house-searches, from the deceptions of 'Marlow' to the snuffling of the gendarmes—betray a pattern that was coercive, and often vindictive. The contrast with the conduct of Bavarian state officials in Mettenbuch is striking. They faced a very similar set of circumstances: claims of miraculous cures that drew pilgrims from a wide area, the selling of water and the setting up of commercial stalls, a parish priest who was unwilling to say that the apparitions had no foundation. News of what was happening in Mettenbuch also failed to reach Bavarian district officials until several thousand pilgrims were already gathered there.[113] Looked at through bureaucratic eyes, there was as much provocation in the one case as the other.

The local civil authorities in Deggendorf, moreover, like their superiors in the provincial administration at Landshut, were broadly concerned with the same

[113] The first apparitions occurred in Dec. 1876, and the parish priest reported them to his bishop the same month. They were already known to many locally in the early months of 1877, but the influx of pilgrims really began after the alleged cure of Theres Kroiß in Deggendorf in April 1877. The district official in Deggendorf was informed at the beginning of May. See BZAR, F 115, Fasc. I: Father Anglhuber to GV Regensburg, 6 May 1877.

issues as their Prussian counterparts. They wanted, first of all, to investigate the
roots of the affair to determine whether the children's accounts had been 'artificially instigated', and whether clergy and parents had 'encouraged or dis-
couraged the children'. The gendarme Schilterl was accordingly instructed to
look into the question to see whether these suspicions were confirmed. But he
and his men were ordered 'to avoid attracting attention in conducting their
enquiries'.[114] An element of friction was unavoidable here. The district official in
Deggendorf had to make it clear that the vow of silence the priest had requested
of the parishioners concerned could not be maintained against 'legally authorized
organs in the performance of their official duties', and on this issue he won.[115]
Nor did the gendarmes behave unfailingly in accordance with their instructions.
The visionary children were hauled out of bed one evening and asked to show
where they had originally seen the 'lights' of the poor souls; the gendarmes
thereupon fired off several shots to demonstrate that there was nothing there.[116]
On another occasion police read through all the school exercise books of children
who had been asked by a local teacher to write what they knew about 'the new
pilgrimage'. The contents were solemnly taken down as evidence.[117] Father
Anglhuber also complained that he had heard the gendarmes were saying 'the
whole business was instigated by the monastery out of sordid self-interest (*aus
schmutzigem Eigennutz*)'.[118] But this complaint was based on hearsay, and perhaps
the most striking feature of Father Anglhuber's remonstration is the apparently
genuine sense of surprise and hurt that prompted it, and the assumption that the
district official would know better than to accuse him and his fellow Benedictines
of such a thing. Certainly by September 1877, the district official in Deggendorf
was informing the parish priest that the evidence gathered showed that 'no
instruction of the children by other persons had taken place'. He could not
himself believe in the apparitions, said the official, and it seemed clear that the
children were imitating events that had occurred elsewhere, such as Dittrichswalde or La Salette; but after a lengthy discussion with the priest, he concluded
that 'the matter is simply very unclear for the moment'.[119] There is a marked
contrast here with the *Landrat* of St Wendel, to whom the matter at Marpingen
was crystal-clear from the start.

Like the Prussian authorities, those in Bavaria also showed a keen interest in
purported cures. Individual cases were followed up, whether these were local
inhabitants like Theres Kroiß of Deggendorf or visiting pilgrims, and statements

[114] SAL, 164/2, 1162: BA Deggendorf to Anglhuber, 9 May 1877. See also the note dated 4 May,
ibid. and BZAR, F 115, Fasc. I: Anglhuber to GV Regensburg, 11 May 1877, enclosing the letter from
the district official, and Anglhuber's own comments; and Braunmüller, *Kurzer Bericht*, 16.
[115] SAL, 164/2, 1162: BA Deggendorf to Anglhuber, 9 May 1877.
[116] BZAR, F 115, Fasc. I: 'Bericht des Pfarramtes Metten über die behaupteten Erscheinungen der
Mutter Gottes, I: Einleitung bzw. Veranlassung'.
[117] Ibid.: Anglhuber to Bishop Senestrey, 21 Sept. 1877.
[118] SAL, 164/2, 1162: Anglhuber to BA Deggendorf, 8 and 10 May 1877.
[119] BZAR, F 115, Fasc. I: Anglhuber to Bishop Senestrey, 15 Sept. 1877, reporting a discussion of
the previous day.

and medical reports were compiled. But the tone of these enquiries remained very matter-of-fact.[120] The Deggendorf district administration also had the selling of 'miraculous water' investigated. But after gendarmes had carefully measured the meagre flow of water from the Mettenbuch spring (3 litres an hour), and enquiries were made into the possibility that water from other sources was being fraudulently sold, the Deggendorf district official concluded that—even though one of the local water-sellers, the stonemason Gerstl, was 'capable of anything'— there was no clear evidence of deception.[121] This was very much in line with the response of Deggendorf to requests for information from the Lower Bavarian provincial authorities in Landshut. The numbers of pilgrims was 'very moderate', reported Deggendorf; there were, it was true, 'repeated breaches of public order', but they were of 'minor importance', mainly petty theft. A scrupulous distinction was maintained between the incidents directly attributable to the apparitions and those only indirectly connected. One serious assault had occurred on a mentally retarded woman, but the district official quoted his own legal advisers to the effect that prosecutions would be unlikely to succeed against bystanders as accessories, or even (in the absence of a complaint from the victim) against the two main parties involved, at least on the charge of intentional bodily harm.[122] On the larger question of whether grounds existed for police intervention at the site, he was sceptical about whether the laws covering public assembly, or other statutes, were applicable in the circumstances. Without entering into the question of whether police intervention was necessary or well grounded, he expressed doubts about the 'means and possibility of its effective and unchallengeable implementation'.[123] The tone and content of this and other reports strongly suggest that the district official in Deggendorf saw himself as a buffer between local inhabitants and sceptical higher authority. The position taken up towards the bureaucracy in Landshut was that of the cautious man-on-the-spot. On the other side, the parish priest was treated firmly, but always politely, and above all on the explicit basis that church and state were partners and shared the same interest.[124] Once again, it is hard to imagine a greater contrast with the way in which the *Landrat* of St Wendel or the district governor of Trier conceived their roles.

There was a change of personnel in the Deggendorf district office at the end of 1877, in which the issue of Mettenbuch was 'supposedly not without influence'.[125] The new man was certainly tougher. The improvised building of

[120] SAL, Rep 164/2, 1161–3 for evidence on the collection of material relating to cures. 164/15, 814 and 164/18, 697 contain correspondence between the Deggendorf district and the districts of Regen and Viechtach respectively on persons in those districts who had claimed cures. BZAR, F 115, Fasc. I: Anglhuber to GV Regensburg, 25 May 1877 and 21 Sept. 1877, has additional material on the authorities' investigation of cures.

[121] SAL, 164/2, 1163: BA Deggendorf to KR Lower Bavaria, 12 Dec. 1877.

[122] Ibid. On this incident, see above, Ch. 5.

[123] Ibid.

[124] SAL, 164/2, 1162: BA Deggendorf to Anglhuber, 9 May 1877.

[125] BZAR, F 115, Fasc. I: 'Auszug aus einem Briefe des Pfarrers v. Metten an Se. bischöfliche Gnaden vom 31. Dez. 1877'. The regular correspondence between Deggendorf and Landshut is contained in

wooden boards that had been constructed at the site was now torn down as an
unauthorized chapel (*Feldkapelle*). This decision had originally been made in
November 1877, on the advice of forestry officials, but appealed by the owner of
the field on which the chapel stood. The decision was confirmed on 31 January
1878 and carried out in the middle of February.[126] The new incumbent leaned very
heavily on Mayor Heigl of Metten, who had been issuing permits to stallholders in
connection with the apparitions, and complained that the roadside stalls were
unlawful and subject to police action.[127] The language used to describe the
pilgrimage movement also became harsher: 'The Royal District Office is of the
opinion that these [commercial] abuses of the alleged Mettenbuch apparitions
and the other excesses that have occurred as a result of the new pilgrimage should
be eliminated and suppressed with police authority, all the more so as there are
legal grounds for these measures.' The mayor himself, in unison with the parish
priest and parish council, had 'encouraged the endeavours' of the local population
'for obvious reasons'.[128]

For all that, the actions of the state continued to be less than draconian. The
district official recognized that there had been no prior motives of financial gain
on the part of Mettenbuch's inhabitants, and the saga of the stallholders dragged
on into 1879.[129] At the site itself the hut might have been pulled down, but the
land was bought by the Princess Thurn und Taxis, who had a board put up for
the votive offerings of pilgrims and a marble statue of the Immaculate Conception
installed, without any apparent interference.[130] There was no blanket ban on the
woods and no heavy-handed policing of the site. The very complaint about
'excesses' and 'abuses' suggested that the pilgrimage was not in itself regarded

the Deggendorf district files held in the Staatsarchiv Landshut, and the change of personnel is clear
from there, but explicit mention of the decision and the reasoning behind it is absent, and it proved
impossible to locate evidence on this elsewhere. The Landshut archivist was unable to find any files
relating to Mettenbuch, or related matters, from the 'unfortunately in part very unclear indexes to the
files of the Lower Bavarian government' (letter to author, 28 July 1988). The Bayerisches Hauptstaatsarchiv in Munich also appears to contain no material on Mettenbuch (letter to author, 21 July
1988).

[126] SAL, 164/2, 1163: BA Deggendorf to KR Lower Bavaria, 12 Dec. 1877; Braunmüller, *Kurzer
Bericht*, 22–3.
[127] SAL, 164/2, 1161 has the lengthy exchanges between the district official in Deggendorf and the
mayor of Metten, and the situation reports sent by Deggendorf to Landshut, 20 Sept. and 13 Nov.
1878.
[128] SAL, 164/2, 1161: BA Deggendorf to KR Lower Bavaria, 20 Sept. 1878.
[129] SAL, 164/2, 1161: BA Deggendorf to KR Lower Bavaria, 20 Sept. 1878, on the admission that
there had been no prior 'speculative' motives. See the further correspondence in the file on the
continuing problem of commercial stallholders.
[130] Braunmüller, *Kurzer Bericht*, 23–4. The statue was 1.35 m. high and commissioned by the
princess from the Munich artist A. Hess: information kindly provided by the Fürst Thurn und Taxis
Zentralarchiv Regensburg. Nothing could be discovered about the fate of the statue. According to a
note of 5 Dec. 1878, of which the archive also has a copy, Bishop Senestrey talked to the princess and
dissuaded her from becoming further involved in the affair. Her role is discussed in 'Als vor 90 Jahren
viele tausend Wallfahrer kamen. Die Fürstin Thurn und Taxis wollte bei Mettenbuch eine Kirche
bauen', *Deggendorfer Zeitung*, 19 May 1967. A copy of this and other cuttings were kindly made
available by the Stadtarchiv Deggendorf.

as a threat to public order. Gendarmes were still in evidence, but Father Braunmüller, the Metten Benedictine who wrote a popular Catholic pamphlet on the
apparitions, actually praised them for 'furthering' the pilgrimage through the
care with which they protected it from undesirable side-effects.[131] No doubt he
was being diplomatic, but the contrast with Marpingen is nevertheless instructive.
As the pilgrimage movement went on, the district office in Deggendorf continued
to serve as a buffer between local inhabitants and sceptical provincial officials in
Landshut.[132]

Compared with Marpingen, the actions and the tone of Bavarian officialdom
were generally emollient. The chief state prosecutor in the Deggendorf office was
reported as saying, in the presence of other officials, that he did not see why
people had any less right to make the pilgrimage to Mettenbuch than to an
established pilgrimage centre such as Altötting, if they believed in it: 'faith can
neither be decreed nor decreed away'. Nor was the sale of water from the so-
called miraculous spring held to be unlawful, provided it could be shown that
this was indeed the source of the water sold.[133] The decisions of the Deggendorf
official who had to deal with the apparitions in the first crucial months in 1877
drew heavily on the legal advice he received, which tended towards restraint. In
the case of Mettenbuch, legal caution and concern for the rule of law helped to
prevent heavy-handed action; in Marpingen due process was observed only after
the heavy-handedness had already taken place. In Mettenbuch, too, the church
was perceived as a genuine partner by the state. This was true at the top, as well
as locally. The Bavarian Ministry of the Interior, for all its doubts that Regensburg
would interpret the evidence on the apparitions in a way that the state could
welcome, nevertheless believed that material should be provided for the canonical
enquiry in the hope of exerting 'a favourable influence'.[134]

Church–state relations were of course a reciprocal matter. Bavarian government reactions to Mettenbuch were doubtless coloured by evidence that the
church was willing to be co-operative. Clerical supporters of the pilgrimage such
as Fathers Anglhuber and Braunmüller showed awareness of the need to police
the site and prevent 'disorder'.[135] In the Mettenbuch case it was the church, not
the state, that decided to isolate the visionaries and interrogate them under
conditions of confinement; and it was realistic for the Bavarian Ministry of the

[131] Braunmüller, *Kurzer Bericht*, 24–5.
[132] SAL, 164/2, 1164 contains extensive documentation on the case of Theres Köstelbacher, the wife of
an ex-gendarme who had been committed to the district lunatic asylum. Her 2½-year-old daughter claimed
to have seen apparitions in 1881. While the district office expressed frustration with the role of Father
Anglhuber in failing to suppress the matter, it nevertheless presented a strong case for Frau Köstelbacher
as an 'honourable' woman who had no part in instigating the affair. The Lower Bavarian administration
in Landshut was much more sceptical, arguing that motives of financial gain could not be excluded.
[133] BZAR, F 115, Fasc. I: Anglhuber to GV Regensburg, 11 Aug. 1877.
[134] BZAR, F 115, Fasc. I, ad. 21: copy of letter from MdI to Ministry for Church and School Affairs,
Munich 19 Dec. 1877.
[135] Ibid.: 'Bericht des Pfarramtes Metten über die behaupteten Erscheinungen der Mutter Gottes, I:
Einleitung bzw. Veranlassung'.

Interior to try to exert a favourable influence on the canonical enquiry initiated by the Bishop of Regensburg, given the eventual outcome of that enquiry. On the other side, the Bavarian local clergy had less reason to fear and resent the civil power: they did not have to expect repeated interrogation, house-searches, arrest, and prosecution. There was, it is true, a *Kulturkampf* of sorts in Bavaria, extending from the late 1860s into the 1880s. But the fact that it cannot be precisely dated is an indication of its more muted character. The Bavarian *Kulturkampf* was just one episode in a long-running trial of strength between church and state, in which both sides showed a readiness to seek accommodation, and the room for manœuvre of the government was limited in the 1870s by the parliamentary majority of the Catholic Patriotenpartei.[136] The fact that the canonical enquiry in Regensburg could have no direct counterpart in Trier, because the see remained unfilled, was symptomatic of the difference between Bavaria and Prussia. Events like those at Mettenbuch showed up the elements of friction in Bavarian church–state relations, but these could be overcome. Church–state relations in Prussia during the *Kulturkampf* were so bad that violent hostility could easily be sparked off by occurrences such as those at Marpingen.

The Weaknesses of the Prussian State

That does not provide a fully satisfactory explanation of why matters took the course they did in Marpingen. There were, after all, alleged apparitions taking place during the same period in East Prussia, at Dittrichswalde in the Ermland. For many at the head of the Prussian state, not least Bismarck himself, concern about Prussian Poles and security in the east had been an important underlying motive in initiating the *Kulturkampf*.[137] Dittrichswalde might have been this fear made flesh. It was part of a solidly Catholic enclave within a denominationally mixed area; it also fell within a linguistically mixed area that included a high proportion of Polish speakers, as well as Germans and Masurians.[138] The village was little more than thirty miles from the Prussian border with Tsarist Russia, whose Polish subjects had mounted an insurrection in 1863 that Bismarck claimed to see as a movement that aimed ultimately at restoring the Polish borders of 1772, and thus as a threat to the existence of Prussia.[139] The visionaries themselves were Polish-speakers, and some features of the apparitions suggested a quasi-political content. On one occasion the girls saw Polish writing at the feet of the

[136] M. Weber, 'Zum Kulturkampf in Bayern', *Zeitschrift für bayerische Landesgeschichte*, 37 (1974), 93–120; F. Hartmannsgruber, *Die Bayerische Patriotenpartei 1868–1887* (Munich, 1986), 388–93.
[137] On the origins, see Bornkamm, 'Die Staatsidee im Kulturkampf'; E. Schmidt-Volkmar, *Der Kulturkampf in Deutschland 1871–1890* (Göttingen, 1962); and two surveys by Rudolf Morsey, 'Bismarck und der Kulturkampf' and 'Probleme der Kulturkampf-Forschung'.
[138] W. Hubatsch (ed.), *Grundriß zur deutschen Verwaltungsgeschichte 1815–1945. Reihe A: Preußen*, i. *Ost- und Westpreußen* (Marburg, 1975), statistical appendices 1 and 5.
[139] See R. F. Leslie, *Reform and Insurrection in Russian Poland 1856–1865* (London, 1963), and on the threat it posed to Prussia, W. Hagen, *Germans, Poles, and Jews: The Nationality Conflict in the Prussian East, 1772–1914* (Chicago, 1980), 126.

Virgin; on another they claimed that the Virgin spoke of a time of persecution to come.[140] In Dittrichswalde, as in Marpingen, the apparitions were supported by 'well-respected men', and they attracted thousands of pilgrims to a sensitive border region.

Yet the state response to Dittrichswalde was strikingly minimalist. The local *Landrat* of Allenstein visited the village accompanied by just two gendarmes, and closed the immediate area where the apparitions had supposedly taken place.[141] Pilgrims continued to visit Dittrichswalde, but congregated in the village by the church. There were no reports of public disorder, and the official response continued to be low-key. On the Feast of the Assumption in August 1877 an estimated 13,000 pilgrims were in Dittrichswalde, observed by a solitary gendarme.[142]

How can we explain this difference between the actions of the state in one part of Prussia and another? Part of the answer undoubtedly turns on the behaviour of individual officials, and the question of who was responsible for the initial state response.[143] The *Landrat* of Allenstein was at his post when the apparitions began in Dittrichswalde; his counterpart in St Wendel was on holiday when reports first came in from Marpingen. The first move was therefore made by the district secretary, a former NCO of limited imagination and tact. The 1872 *Kreisordnung* laid down that the district secretary should act as short-term deputy for the *Landrat*, but this was in many ways the legacy of a period when the demands on the office were lighter and there were fewer young trainees (*Assessoren*, *Referendare*) to step into the breach. Even in the 1870s, senior officials were often unhappy at the idea of district secretaries exercising authority, and a string of unhappy experiences meant that by the end of the century it became the rule for the more educated trainee officials to deputize.[144] In the case of Marpingen, the hapless Hugo Besser was encouraged in his hard line by an ambitious and bigoted rural mayor with a grudge against the village. Mayor Woytt was later disciplined for physically ill-treating inhabitants of Marpingen: he described them as 'an organized band of thieves' and the Virgin Mary as a 'whore', threatened to empty their coffers, and observed that if he were *Landrat* they would not have a head of cattle left after paying their fines.[145]

[140] *Deggendorfer Donaubote*, 8 Sept. 1877; 'Die Erscheinung der unbefleckt Empfangenen', 60.

[141] *Deggendorfer Donaubote*, 8 Sept. 1877.

[142] 'Die Erscheinung der unbefleckt Empfangenen', 59–60.

[143] In his regional study of officials in East and West Prussia during the *Kulturkampf*, G. Dettmer, *Die Ost- und Westpreußischen Verwaltungsbehörden im Kulturkampf* (Heidelberg, 1958), 116–21, empha-sizes the importance of how individual officials responded.

[144] K. von der Groeben, *Die öffentliche Verwaltung im Spannungsfeld der Politik dargestellt am Beispiel Ostpreußen* (Berlin, 1979), 84–5. For the growing burden on the *Landrat*'s office and the bureaucratic rationalization it brought, see T. Süle, *Preußische Bürokratietradition. Zur Entwicklung von Verwaltung und Beamtenschaft in Deutschland 1871–1918* (Göttingen, 1988).

[145] He allegedly demanded to know from one grieving father whether his 10-year-old child had been carried to the apparition site before his death. Woytt's utterances were testified to by many villagers, and recorded in notes made by Neureuter and Schneider. See LASB, E 107, 354, 425–8, 431, 439;

By the time that *Landrat* Rumschöttel returned, the situation could probably
have been retrieved only with difficulty, given the effects of military intervention.
But Rumschöttel was as little inclined to moderation as his deputy. Installed in
St Wendel as a troubleshooter after 1848, he took an unbending view of his
obligation to maintain order. The Prussian *Landrat* was, of course, expected to
be firm and energetic and to maintain the authority and dignity of the state; but
he was also expected to conduct himself with prudence and moderation, and to
avoid needlessly antagonizing the inhabitants of his district.[146] The right balance
was no doubt difficult to strike; Rumschöttel seems barely to have tried. From
his first appearance in Marpingen he was openly contemptuous and hostile
towards its inhabitants, reinforcing their bitterness. Rather than seeing himself as
a buffer between the local population and higher authority, Rumschöttel painted
the blackest picture of the benighted Marpingers. He was joined in this by District
Governor Wolff in Trier. In Mettenbuch the suspicions of central and provincial
authority were tempered as they passed down the chain of command; in Marpingen the opposite occurred. The senior Prussian legal official Karl Schorn, who
played a small part in the affair, was later highly critical in his memoirs about the
counter-productive behaviour of local administrative officials.[147]

There are, however, more general points to be made about the response of
local officials. For the instinctive attitudes displayed by Mayor Woytt, *Landrat*
Rumschöttel, and his deputy were not confined to St Wendel. We find a similar
nervous belligerence elsewhere in the vicinity—in Merzig, Saarburg, Saarbrücken.[148] One reason was undoubtedly the hostility of Protestant officials to
Catholic 'fanaticism'.[149] Nervousness about the impact of the apparitions on the
miners of the region also played a part. But it is difficult not to link the combination
of anxiety and aggression among local officials to sensitivity about Prussia's (and
Germany's) western border. Of course, one might expect the officials responsible
for Dittrichswalde, on the East Prussian border, to be at least as sensitive,
especially in the 1870s, when the anti-Polish thrust of the *Kulturkampf* went hand
in hand with the Germanization laws of the years 1872–6.[150] Yet, for all the Polish

also Radziwill, *Besuch*, 28. Even RP Wolff in Trier took an extremely defensive line when trying to
justify the mayor's conduct to his superiors in Berlin: LHAK, 442/6442, 141–5.

[146] Groeben, *Die öffentliche Verwaltung*, 47 ff.
[147] Schorn, *Lebenserinnerungen*, ii. 260.
[148] The rural mayors of nearby Eppelborn, and of Canzem-Nittel (Saarburg district) proved as
vindictive in other circumstances as Woytt over Marpingen. See Kammer, *Kulturkampfpriester*, 379,
on the persecution of priests on the run by the mayor of Eppelborn; and LHAK, 442/10419, 175–7:
mayor of Canzem-Nittel to LR Saarburg, 26 Mar. 1875, on priests who 'regularly stir up a rural
population that still lives unfortunately in a state of stupidity', and on the 'fanatical rural population'.
For attitudes on the part of the *Landrat* of Merzig that match those of his opposite number in St
Wendel, see the proclamation of the former, 22 Aug. 1876, in *EM*, 66–7.
[149] Of the officials concerned with Marpingen, Wolff, Rumschöttel, Woytt, and district medical officer
of health Dr Brauneck were all Protestants, and for the most part self-consciously so; Hugo Besser,
however, was a Catholic: LASB, E 107, 440.
[150] Hagen, *Germans, Poles and Jews*, 127–31; Dettmer, *Die Ost- und Westpreußischen Verwaltungsbehörden*, 21–3, 118.

backlash against these policies, Prussia was clearly in the driving-seat; and in the case of the Ermland, acquired during the first Polish partition of 1772, it had been in that position for a century. East Prussia may not, like the gains from the second and third partitions, have served as a laboratory for Prussian administrative reform; but it had been integrated during a long process of state-building. In that sense, there were differences between east and west—differences that were the opposite of what one might expect. The new western territories were of more recent vintage: the Rhine Province had been acquired only in 1815, the area around St Wendel, as we have seen, not until 1834. The Franco-Prussian war was still fresh in the memory, the 'war in sight crisis' had occurred in 1875, and the loyalty of the border population remained a source of anxiety.

Those responsible for the persecution at Marpingen were plainly affected by fears, however unfounded, that French *revanche* lay behind the superstition and religious fanaticism of the apparitions. When the soldiers from Saarlouis first arrived in St Wendel, *en route* to Marpingen, they were apparently told that an insurrection was afoot.[151] The seizure in Saarbrücken during September 1876 of large shipments of devotional materials from France raised the issue of foreign conspiracy in a different guise.[152] When Meerscheidt-Hüllessem compiled a report on Marpingen at the beginning of October, he claimed not only that the villagers were 'cowardly' and 'untruthful', but that their loyalties were French.[153] At the end of the year rumours circulated that a French priest had instigated the whole affair.[154] The response to Marpingen had elements of contingency, but it also reflected the workings of the official mind. Once a hardline policy had been decided on, a tone was then set that inevitably made matters worse by antagonizing local opinion. Thus, by degrees, the state was sucked into further repression, in a manner that resembled a form of occupation, and the authority of the state committed to a position it would hardly have chosen.

The implementation of a hardline policy revealed another important feature of the Prussian state: the shortcomings of its policing. There is a temptation to think of Prussia as uniform and efficient when it came to questions of public order. It was actually neither. The three different kinds of prison jurisdiction to be found within the state were matched by no fewer than six different local police systems.[155] Added to that was the problem that there were too few policemen, a by-product of Hohenzollern parsimony. When the French Rhine-Moselle department became Prussian, the number of gendarmes per head of population fell to

[151] LASB, E 107, 425: Neureuter notebook entry of 18 July 1876.
[152] Ibid. 29, 150–2.
[153] Ibid. 198; *Prozeß*, 46.
[154] LASB, E 107, 155: testimony of trainee schoolteacher Metzen.
[155] Buder, *Die Reorganisation der preußischen Polizei*, 3. On the variations in prison jurisdictions—some controlled by the administrative authorities (as in the Rhine Province), some under the joint control of administration and courts, others run by the office of the public prosecutor—see *FZ*, 25 July 1876.

a third of the previous level.[156] Numbers remained inadequate in later years.[157] The quality of local policing was also suspect. In 1844 the provincial governor of the Rhine Province referred to the 'widespread incapacity' of police officials in the province; in the 1870s the levels of education, experience (and salary) of the Rhenish police remained extremely uneven, but were generally most unsatisfactory in rural areas.[158] Similar problems beset the detective branch: calling in the expert from Berlin was still common during the 1870s, for the standards of education and training of the criminal police in Berlin were far superior to those elsewhere in Prussia, and the decentralization set in train to deal with the wave of crime that followed the Franco-Prussian war had not yet taken effect.[159] The arrival of the self-satisfied Meerscheidt-Hüllessem in Marpingen owed something to a deeper structural problem.

Most important of all, the inadequacy of local policing increased the likelihood of military intervention. This had been a familiar response to civil disturbances during the hungry 1840s, as the Prussian state 'was often forced to resort precipitately and with inappropriate harshness to military action'.[160] The pattern persisted, and for the same reasons, in the troubled 1870s. The Frankfurt am Main beer riots of April 1873 were crushed by a military intervention in which eighteen died. As Lothar Machtan and René Ott observe, reliance on the army in circumstances of this kind 'points to a fundamental dilemma for the exercise of authority in Prussia-Germany, namely the chronic lack of anything other than repressive strategies to cope with explosive social-political conflicts'.[161] Closer to Marpingen in every sense was the precedent set at Trier in March 1874, when the build-up of a large Catholic crowd led the local authorities to call out both infantry and hussars to assist gendarmes in expelling the academic staff of the Trier seminary.[162] Military intervention in Marpingen signified a chronic inflexibility of response. It was, at least in part, a sign of weakness, not strength.

The high-handedness that was so conspicuous in subsequent efforts to winkle evidence from the local inhabitants must also be seen partly as a product of weakness. The sour vindictiveness of administrative officials, examining magistrates, and gendarmes was fed by the sheer frustration of the situation in which they found themselves. They were thwarted, most obviously, by the systematic

[156] R. Koselleck, 'Die Auflösung des Hauses als ständischer Herrschaftseinheit', in N. Bulst, J. Goy, and J. Hoock (eds.), *Familie zwischen Tradition und Moderne* (Göttingen, 1981), 120–1.

[157] On the regular complaints of *Landräte* and District Governors about the shortage of gendarmes, see Funk, *Polizei und Rechtsstaat*, 42.

[158] A. Lüdtke, *'Gemeinwohl', Polizei und 'Festungspraxis'. Staatliche Gewaltsamkeit und innere Verwaltung in Preußen, 1815–1850* (Göttingen, 1982), 157; Buder, *Die Reorganisation der preußischen Polizei*, 7–8.

[159] Buder, *Die Reorganisation der preußischen Polizei*, 14–15.

[160] Koselleck, 'Die Auflösung des Hauses', 120–1. See also R. Tilly, 'Popular Disorders in Nineteenth-Century Germany', *Journal of Social History*, 4 (1971), 14, 21.

[161] L. Machtan and R. Ott, ' "Batzbier!" Überlegungen zur sozialen Protestbewegung in den Jahren nach der Reichsgründung am Beispiel der süddeutschen Bierkrawalle vom Frühjahr 1873' in H. Volkmann and J. Bergmann (eds.), *Sozialer Protest* (Opladen, 1984), 156.

[162] *Bericht über die Gefangennehmung*, 12–16.

lack of co-operation shown by villagers. This is discussed in detail in the following chapter. What made the problem even more frustrating for those attempting to curb and investigate the apparitions was the fact that the recalcitrance of ordinary Catholic citizens was so often supported by sympathetic local officials.

The existence of Catholic officials who were lukewarm, or even openly antagonistic, towards the policies of the *Kulturkampf* was a general and widespread problem for the Prussian state in the 1870s. The difficulty made itself felt to some degree even in the upper and intermediate levels of the administration. District Governor Holzbrinck of Arnsberg in Westphalia was obliged to resign in 1875 because of his lack of enthusiasm for the *Kulturkampf*; ten of the eighteen Catholic *Landräte* in Westphalia were dismissed for the same reason.[163] Similar measures were deemed necessary in the Rhineland, although the numbers involved were smaller. But this was not the level at which the problem was most acute: the proportion of Protestant officials rose in the upper echelons of the administration, and there were also Catholics in the ranks of senior career bureaucrats who were happy to prove themselves 200 per cent loyal.[164] The greatest problem arose at the lowest level of the hierarchy, among local communal and village officials such as rural mayors, village *Ortsvorsteher*, teachers, tax collectors, magistrates, watchmen, foresters, and postmen. Again and again, such men sided with the clergy and popular Catholic sentiment against the senior organs of the state in the struggles of the *Kulturkampf*. The regional and district authorities found, for example, that the banned Mainz Associations continued to be riddled with minor officials, despite all efforts to enforce their resignation. One mayor in the St Wendel district who was loyal to government policy suggested that local schoolteachers should be forced to take an oath on whether they had ever belonged to the organization.[165] In some cases, minor Catholic officials were more actively subversive. One irate letter of denunciation from a brewery owner and part-time magistrate (*Ergänzungsrichter*) in a district near Trier alleged, plausibly enough, that local officials not only did nothing to suppress Catholic organizations, but threw their authority behind efforts to ensure that patriotic celebrations like those for the Kaiser's birthday flopped.[166] Countless local officials also stepped clearly over the line of illegality by aiding priests on the run, protecting them when they returned to read illegal masses and tipping them off if gendarmes were on the way.[167]

[163] Sperber, *Popular Catholicism*, 243. On lukewarm Catholic officials, see also M. L. Anderson and K. Barkin, 'The Myth of the Puttkamer Purge and the Reality of the *Kulturkampf*: Some Reflections on the Historiography of Imperial Germany', *Journal of Modern History*, 54 (1982), 647–86.

[164] On the dominance of Protestant officials in the upper echelons of the bureaucracy, see Bachem, *Erinnerungen*, 38; on '200% loyal' Catholic officials, Sperber, *Popular Catholicism*, 244.

[165] LHAK, 442/7854, 55. Examples of similar cases, and of officials' membership in organizations such as the Saarlouis Catholic Reading Association, in LHAK, 403/6695, 261–2; LHAK, 442/7853, 597, 757–8. Also Kammer, *Kulturkampfpriester*, 110–11, 152.

[166] LHAK, 442/6383, 187–9: Carl Weber of Hermeskeil to RP Trier, 29 Mar. 1875.

[167] Examples abound in local accounts of the *Kulturkampf*, such as Ficker, *Kulturkampf in Münster*, Kammer, *Kulturkampfpriester*, and Schiffers, *Kulturkampf in Stadt und Regierungsbezirk Aachen*.

The problems raised by what happened in Marpingen were of a different order. This was not a question of a forester who belonged to the Mainz Association, a teacher continuing to serve a banned priest as sexton, or even an *Ortsvorsteher* who tipped off an 'illegal' priest about approaching gendarmes. More was at stake on both sides than in other *Kulturkampf* incidents. The state, having defined the apparitions from the outset as a fraud and a serious breach of the peace, had placed its authority on the line and expected co-operation from local officials. The latter faced the very likely prospect of disciplinary action, and even criminal charges if they were seen to behave in an obstructive manner. In the event, in Marpingen as in lesser confrontations elsewhere, the officials concerned were swayed more by religious conviction and local loyalties than by a sense of obligation to the Prussian state.

Resistance from local officials to enforcing measures against Marpingen was widespread. It is true that no Saarland *Landrat* hampered the crack-down. But the authorities faced what was, in some ways, a more awkward problem: a recently retired *Landrat* against whom no disciplinary threats could be made, a rogue elephant. This was Rudolf Baron Lasalle Louisenthal of Dagstuhl, retired from his post as *Landrat* because of a marked absence of enthusiasm for the *Kulturkampf*. On 13 August 1876, *Landrat* Rumschöttel wrote reproachfully to Louisenthal, pointing out that the latter had allegedly promised to help Marpingen financially with the costs of billeting imposed on the village; that he had claimed credit for the withdrawal of troops; and that he had expressed an intention to seek permission from the king to have a chapel built at the apparition site. The letter continued sternly:

It is obvious that such rumours serve to confirm the deluded masses in their mania, and encourage them to commit offences against the legally established order. I have not omitted to inform Your Excellency of this talk, in order to provide you with the opportunity to give the lie to them in a public declaration and thereby contribute to ensuring that this business is not fuelled still more and the poor blinded people are saved from further inevitable and negative repercussions.[168]

A lengthy correspondence ensued, which Louisenthal—clearly enjoying himself at this stage—found 'greatly amusing'. The *Landrat* pressed in vain for an explicit public denial of the rumours on Louisenthal's part; he also adverted to a still more damaging rumour brought to his attention by the authorities in Trier, that 'your wife has even been in Marpingen'.[169] This was undeniably true, and together with related allegations it formed the basis of a further, more threatening letter from an angry regional administration in Trier: 'Your Excellency's household and family', observed Krosigk from the Department of the Interior, 'forms a local centre of ultramontane agitation and for the dissemination

[168] BAT, B III, 11, 14/4, 40, I: LR St Wendel to Louisenthal, 13 Aug. 1876.
[169] BAT, B III, 11, 14/4, 40, II–VI: LR Rumschöttel to Louisenthal, 18 Aug. 1876; Louisenthal to Rumschöttel, 18 Aug. 1876; Rumschöttel to Louisenthal, 19 Aug. 1876; Louisenthal to Rumschöttel, 21 Aug. 1876; Rumschöttel to Louisenthal, 31 Aug. 1876.

of belief in the so-called miraculous apparitions at Marpingen.' The ladies of His Excellency's family had not only visited the apparition site; they had offered their public congratulations to a supposed adult visionary, the 52-year-old Magdalena Müller, and received her at the family seat in Dagstuhl. There was a further sign of gross disloyalty: a comparison of official documents in Louisenthal's hand, and the handwriting of a formal complaint from the Marpingen parish council addressed to Trier and 'containing untruths', led to 'the well-founded suspicion that this submission was inspired, written, and emanated from Your Excellency's family'. The letter closed with an appeal and a threat. It expressed the hope that 'Your Excellency will not close his eyes to the principle that it is the duty of a Royal official, even one on the retired list, to oppose such conduct on the part of his family'. Disciplinary action could hardly be threatened against a retired official, but Trier had found another lever:

Should Your Excellency be unwilling or unable to follow this course, and in future to report to us any similar excesses on the part of your family, we shall find ourselves obliged to file an application for the expulsion of your private family chaplain Emanuel Nicola, who as a foreign priest has been granted special permission to remain in this state in view amongst other things of the position which he occupies in the home of Your Excellency, as a Royal official.[170]

Louisenthal had already been obliged, two years earlier, to mobilize local medical and official support to prevent the expulsion of the aged Nicola (the family priest was 71 years old).[171] Caught between the piety of his family and the pressure coming from St Wendel and Trier, the baron may have been influenced by this neatly managed piece of blackmail. The presssure was certainly applied to a point on which his family—his wife Stefanie, his daughters, and his sister Octavie— would have felt vulnerable. Whatever the reason, the baroness did not return to Marpingen in 1877, after three visits in 1876, and there is some evidence that Louisenthal himself backed away from a public role in protesting about the treatment of the three visionary children.[172]

The Louisenthal case shows how hard the authorities had to work in order to neutralize the opposition even of a retired, albeit prominent, official. At a lower level, threats seem to have had little effect in dissuading minor officials from supporting the Marpingen movement. *Ortsvorsteher* from surrounding villages blithely visited the apparition site.[173] So did numerous male and female school-teachers. Other teachers carried letters on behalf of priests like Schneider and Dicke, after the latter realized that their correspondence was at risk of inter-ception.[174] A measure of the difficulty faced by the authorities was the fact that one visiting teacher, the trainee Fräulein Leidinger from Fürth, was actually

[170] BAT, B III, 11, 14/4, 39: KR Trier to Louisenthal, 19 Dec. 1876.
[171] See LHAK, 442/10419, 47–55, on the earlier dispute over Father Nicola.
[172] See LASB, E 107, 389–90; Radziwill, *Besuch*, 17–18.
[173] LASB, E 107, 102, 134, on the *Ortsvorsteher* Schaefer (Niederhofen) and Brill (Alsweiler).
[174] LASB, E 107, 86–7, 134, 285, 292, 369–99; see also *Prozeß*, 135–6.

investigated on suspicion of having 'played the part of the Virgin Mary' in the woods.[175] Moreover, not all rural mayors conducted themselves like Woytt. Nikolaus Schorn, who claimed to have been cured, was treated with evident pride by Mayor Kordel of Haustadt—mixed, perhaps, with relief that the tailor would no longer be a burden on the parish. The mayor visited Schorn twice at his home and even invited him to take a glass of wine.[176]

It was in Marpingen itself, however, that the tacit support of local officials for the apparitions was most telling, and most frustrating to higher authority. Take the case of Jakob Geßner, village *Ortsvorsteher* when the apparitions began. He was the man responsible for keeping his superiors in the dark about the apparitions during the first ten days, who then proved awkward during the process of requisitioning (his partial deafness was very useful in this). Geßner later participated in a procession to welcome Neureuter home from gaol, and gave permission for guns to be fired in celebration.[177] He also took part in the process of drawing up statements later used as the basis for complaints about the treatment of Marpingen.[178] So did his successor as *Ortsvorsteher*, Peter Schnur, who signed a parish council protest of 4 September, and accompanied the teacher André to Trier in an attempt to have her transfer rescinded.[179] Schnur was heavily implicated in support for the apparitions: one of the first village notables to visit the site (on 5 July), he encouraged Magdalena Kirsch to take her sick child there in search of a cure, and was allegedly involved in the trade with bottled water. Like virtually all the local officials, he also suffered a curious memory-loss when questioned.[180]

The same pattern can be observed in other local officials. The village schoolteachers were compromised in their actions and disingenuous in what they told the investigating authorities. In the course of six interrogations, André made a series of statements that were consistent only in the remarkable lack of light they shed on the role she and others had played in the events.[181] Her male counterpart, Bungert, informed his questioners quite untruthfully that 'on account of his position' he had stayed clear of the apparitions 'from the beginning'.[182] The village watchman Jakob Langendörfer argued that his official duties explained his presence at the Härtelwald, where he prevented pilgrims from trampling nearby

[175] LASB, E 107, 131.
[176] EM, 70.
[177] LASB, E 107, 382; BAT, B III, 11, 14/4, 27: testimony at Cologne trial of Matthias Scheeben; SPB, 25 Feb. 1877. Geßner was fined 30 marks for this last action.
[178] LASB, E 107, 198–200, 436–40.
[179] Ibid. 129, 143.
[180] LASB, E 107, 129, 142–4, 265. Acting *Ortsvorsteher* Backes was also fined and disciplined in June 1877 for allowing unauthorized persons to enter the closed-off area in April: BAT, B III, 11, 14/4, 42: copy of LRA St Wendel to Backes, 2 June 1877.
[181] LASB, E 107, 278–95. The first 3 interrogations took place between July and Nov. 1876, the last 3 between the end of Jan. and the beginning of Mar. 1877. See also *Prozeß*, 143, 183–6.
[182] LASB, E 107, 141.

meadows; but he was also spotted collecting money at the apparition site.[183] The communal forester Karl Altmeyer could recall only that he 'might' have been in the Härtelwald on the day of the military intervention; but he admitted that in August, after the woods were closed, he had shown a monk to the apparition site, after the man had arrived in the village with a note of introduction from Altmeyer's nephew. Why had he not reported this? 'It was not his job to do so, he wasn't the police.'[184]

These officials were, with the exception of the teacher André, locally born people.[185] They were Catholics who took part in the religious life of the village (the teacher Bungert was also sexton in the parish church) and were generally believers in the apparitions. When the state crack-down came from 'outside', their loyalties were predictably enough with the local community. But even had that not been so, it is likely that the administrative, police, and judicial authorities from St Wendel, Trier, and Saarbrücken would have been frustrated in seeking their co-operation. In some of these cases there are grounds for believing that fear of village opinion dictated the actions—and inaction—of local officials. In the case of Jakob Geßner, Wilhelm Woytt considered him lacking in independence: if he had supported the army in its requisitioning efforts, the village 'would have been angry with him'.[186] The source is admittedly tainted; but there is other evidence that Geßner was extremely nervous about his exposed position between the fronts.[187] There is also abundant evidence that André was, at the very least, uncertain about the authenticity of the apparitions, and her reluctance to speak out against them, like her evasiveness and inconsistency under questioning, may well have been linked to her own expressed fear of village sentiment.[188] Similar concerns were evident in other villages during the *Kulturkampf* when, for example, local officials protected 'illegal' priests from arrest. A village mayor in the Saarburg district complained about a case in 1875 when a priest had been tipped off before the gendarme arrived: 'The forester and *Ortsvorsteher*, who live in the parish, out of fear of their own priest and the fanaticized population, do not have the courage to seize the man.'[189] Once again, the anticlerical rancour of the source has to be taken into consideration, but the effects of an oppressive climate of local opinion should not be discounted.

Whether out of conviction or a prudent regard for village opinion, minor officials withheld their co-operation as far as possible. Caught in the cross-fire

[183] Ibid. 257–60.
[184] Ibid. 260–3; *Prozeß*, 13–17.
[185] André was born in Prüm and came to Marpingen, her second teaching job, in 1866.
[186] BAT, B III, 11, 14/4, 27: Woytt's testimony at Scheeben trial.
[187] See, for example, his reactions to the cure of Nikolaus Schorn, whom he tried to hurry out of the village before the gendarmes got wind of it: EM, 69.
[188] On André's lack of belief in the apparitions, see the testimony of supernumerary teacher Lambert Lichtherz (who had known her from her earlier teaching days) and André's successor, Elisa Klein: LASB, E 107, 281; *Prozeß*, 143. On André's stated fears of arousing village antagonism, see above, Ch. 4.
[189] LHAK, 442/10419, 175–7: mayor of Canzem-Nittel to LR Saarburg, 26 Mar. 1875.

between local loyalties and their formal obligations as officials, they were willing to court disciplinary action or criminal charges (and in the case of André, Altmeyer, and Langendörfer, both) rather than act as the agents of a repressive state authority. This set up a vicious circle. The more obstruction the representatives of higher authority found, the more frustrated they became and the more they resorted to repressive methods; yet the more repressive the methods used, the less likely they were to be met with co-operation from officials on the spot. Lack of intelligence from Marpingen, and dark suspicions about the reasons for it, were among the reasons why the initial reaction of authority in St Wendel had been heavy-handed. Subsequent efforts to curb the apparition movement and bring to account those supposedly responsible for 'instigating' it were undertaken in repressive fashion partly for similar reasons. State coercion was the product of an absence of consent and co-operation, even among its own local officials.

8

The Catholic Response

Active and Passive Resistance

Catholic commentators rightly mocked the claims of some local officials that events in Marpingen were a frontal challenge to the authority of the state. The *Trierische Landeszeitung* asked sarcastically whether those who had their homes searched were *pétroleurs*, and insisted that 'no popular rising has taken place'.[1] A pamphlet writer scorned the view that Marpingen represented a 'revolutionary movement'.[2] The conspiracy theory presented a broad target. Yet if Marpingen was no insurrectionary affair, the emphasis laid by Catholic writers on peacefully praying women and children was also misleading. The coercive measures of the Prussian authorities did produce acts and threats of violence in response. Some of the most violent incidents occurred on the evening of 13 July 1876, in the hours after the arrival of the army. While most of the infantry company was engaged in requisitioning and billeting, Lieutenant Lent established a sentry-post at the apparition site. Around 9 o'clock, a group of about thirty men gathered on the edge of the woods, some wearing miners' caps and nearly all carrying sticks or clubs. They mocked and cursed the soldiers, and threats were made ('You scoundrels, you'll pay for this'). Sergeant Wolter was sent out on patrol to disperse them, and they fled; but one turned and hit the sergeant on the hand with a club before continuing his flight. When he refused to obey an order to halt, Wolter fired shots after the man, probably hitting him in the left arm.[3] Six miners or retired miners (three from Marpingen, two from Wustweilerhof, one from Kleinheiligenwald) were later charged with riotous assembly. Three more miners, all from Theley, were suspected of the attack on Wolter and charged with breach of the peace and insurrection, although the identity of the guilty party was never established.[4] There were further incidents in later months. In November the Marpingen

---

[1] Cited in *MWOL*, 57.
[2] *EM*, 38–9.
[3] LASB, E 107, 18.
[4] LASB, E 107, 38–42 on the six, 43–5 on the three from Theley (a carter and a musician were also initially among those suspected of attacking the sergeant). Mallmann, 'Volksfrömmigkeit', 218–19, writes inaccurately of the six miners that 'their list of previous convictions in the records of the

day labourer Stephan Brill was sentenced to four months' imprisonment for
threatening Mayor Woytt and a gendarme with a knife.[5] At the end of January
1877 stones were thrown and shots fired at patrolling gendarmes, two of whom
were injured by stones.[6]

These episodes should not be lightly dismissed, but they hardly add up to
a pattern of sustained violence against the forces of order. The most serious
breaches of the peace took place on the evening of the military intervention,
and some of those questioned by the authorities turned out to be as much the
victims of violence as the perpetrators.[7] Stephan Brill's action seems to have
been an isolated incident and Brill himself had seven previous convictions
(for theft). The sharp response of the *Landrat*'s office in St Wendel (and the
liberal press) to the shots and stone-throwing of January 1877 suggests that
this was also a singular episode; certainly there is no direct evidence that
'patrolling gendarmes were injured again and again by stone-throwing'.[8] It
is worth noting that the investigating authorities gradually came to concentrate
their attention on charges of fraud and deception rather than sedition,
riotous assembly, or breach of the peace, and this was the basis on which
the major trial of those charged in connection with Marpingen eventually
proceeded.

The level of popular violence directed against representatives of the state in
Marpingen was, in fact, comparatively modest. It occurred on a greater scale
in many other parts of the Rhineland and Westphalia during the Kulturkampf.
Protestants who aided the authorities—locksmiths who helped them to force
entry into Catholic churches, for example—risked angry crowds, broken
windows, and physical threats.[9] There were also many cases of violence directed
squarely against officials: a local mayor in Rheine who tried to break up a Pius
Day demonstration in June 1875 was beaten and stabbed by a crowd; the

---

investigation' included 'offences such as physical abuse, resistance to authority, and causing a serious
public nuisance (*grober Unfug*)'. Five of the six had no previous record; the sixth, Peter Keßler of
Wustweilerhof, had a conviction in 1869 for resisting authority and the lesser offence of 'public
nuisance' (*Unfug*). In fact, the lack of previous serious convictions perhaps makes Mallmann's general
point about a 'social movement' better than his own exaggeration.

[5] LASB, E 107, 42; also reported in *KZ*, 24 Nov. 1876 (but without the name being given). Also in
Nov. 1876, the day labourer Johann Dietzler was convicted of violent and threatening behaviour and
resisting arrest in Marpingen, and sentenced to 6 months in gaol, plus 4 weeks for vagrancy. Dietzler,
like Brill, had many previous convictions, and it is not clear what connection, if any, his actions had
with the cause of the apparitions. See *NBZ*, 6 Nov. 1876.

[6] LASB, E 107, 156–7; LHAK, 442/6442, 157–8, RP Wolff Trier to MdI Berlin, 28 Dec. 1877,
reporting later on the same incident; *NBZ*, 1 Feb. 1877; *SZ*, 2 Feb. 1877; *SMZ*, 6 Feb. 1877; *MWOL*,
88–90.

[7] LASB, E 107, 38–45, and above, Ch. 7.

[8] Mallmann, 'Volksfrömmigkeit', 219; also 'Aus des Tages Last', 165. Mallmann's references to
Marpingen in the context of miners, religion, and social protest are nevertheless thoughtful, and build
on his earlier work on the miners' movement, *Anfänge*.

[9] See e.g. Ficker, *Kulturkampf in Münster*, 102–12.

arrest of two men in Emsdetten for firing salutes on the same occasion in 1876 led to a crowd of 200 assembling in front of the local gaol, where they threw stones, demolished the gaol, and released its inmates.[10] In the northern part of the Trier diocese a number of violent confrontations with the Prussian authorities took place, or were only narrowly avoided. An angry crowd gathered in Schweich after the arrest of their priest under the May Laws; villagers in Cues made plans to liberate their imprisoned priest through an attack on the Bernkastel gaol, and were thwarted only because he was swiftly moved to Trier.[11] There were similar violent incidents in the Saarland at Wiesbach, Neunkirchen, Dillingen, and Spiesen, while more locally still the Namborn incident of 1874, when a thousand Catholics stormed the railway station at St Wendel in an effort to free the arrested Father Isbert, demonstrated a level of collective violence that was never remotely approached in Marpingen.[12] Indeed, the use or the threat of physical force against officials in Marpingen, whether by villagers or non-villagers, hardly stands out against the background of a Saarland that was, in the 1870s, a raw and violent community. The gendarmes posted in the village could certainly have found themselves in many more dangerous places. Michael Mallmann is probably right when he argues that in Marpingen 'the aggressions which otherwise broke out in Sunday public house brawls found a new, religiously veiled and sanctioned outlet'.[13] Much the same could be said of Münchwies or Berschweiler. But compared with the intimidation of state officials elsewhere in the diocese during the *Kulturkampf*, or with the levels of everyday violence in the Saarland at that time, the degree of aggression shown towards officials and gendarmes in Marpingen was unremarkable.

Where active resistance did occur, it followed the pattern we find in scores of other towns and villages during the *Kulturkampf*. Threats and physical violence were invariably triggered by a particular incident in which the state caused popular outrage by forceful intervention. Most commonly, as in Cues, Schweich, Wiesbach, Namborn, and many other places, the anger was provoked by the arrest of the parish priest; in Marpingen the actions of the army had a similar effect. The violent phase was usually brief. In those cases where priests were seized provocatively, popular intimidation usually lasted until the outnumbered gendarmes reached the nearest railway station, a symbol of authority as well as the guardian of lines of communication (the storming of St Wendel station during the Namborn incident was highly atypical). Marpingen represented a variation on the theme: violent resistance was brief, concentrated on the evening of 13 July, and it was directed against isolated sentries. The strength of the military and later police presence, and the determination signalled by the authorities, then proved

[10] Sperber, *Popular Catholicism*, 229–30, 232; Scholle, *Preußische Strafjustiz*, has many other examples.
[11] Kammer, *Kulturkampfpriester*, 84, 92–3.
[12] Ibid. 39, 45, 53, 76–7; on Namborn, see above, Ch. 3.
[13] Mallmann, 'Aus des Tages Last', 165.

sufficient to inhibit anything other than sporadic outbreaks of physical resistance.
The Prussian authorities were also assisted, whether they appreciated it or not,
by the firm emphasis of the clergy on legality and non-violence. Marpingen, once
again, falls into a larger pattern. 'Shall we kill them [the gendarmes]?' the crowd
at Spiesen asked their priest; but Father Schieben was able to calm them.[14]
Neureuter also insisted that there be no 'breaches of the law' and 'recommended
to all pilgrims the example of my parishioners, who showed an admirable calm
and patience through all the harassment'.[15] The coercive reserve power of the
state and the calming influence of the clergy worked in the same direction,
reinforcing an everyday disinclination to attack the agents of state authority, at
least in cold blood.[16]

None of this dispelled anger and resentment, or won consent. In Marpingen,
as in other Catholic communities faced with harsh and arbitrary state actions
during the *Kulturkampf* years, the characteristic response was passive resistance.
Here the clergy were very much on the side of their parishioners. In fact, Rome
itself provided moral authority for such a stance. In February 1875 a papal
encyclical declared the May Laws 'null and void' and called upon German
Catholics to practise 'passive resistance'.[17] The clergy, and Catholic intellectuals
such as Peter Reichensperger, interpreted this in the light of resistance and natural
rights theories to mean that while attacks on the authority of the state could not
be justified, passive resistance was 'permissible, indeed necessary' where state
power was itself exercised illegitimately.[18] That became the lodestar of popular
Catholic action in the 1870s. Karl Jentsch, a Catholic priest who defected to the
'Old Catholic' sect over the issue of infallibility, later argued that the Prussian
government had simply been unable to sustain its *Kulturkampf* legislation in the
face of 'many millions practising passive resistance'.[19]

What did this mean on the ground? Across Prussia, a pattern of Catholic
responses can be discerned that was almost crystalline in its regularity. Catholics
refused to co-operate with the authorities, stonewalling when questioned and
finding non-violent ways in which to express their contempt for gendarmes and
other officials: laughter, for example. The attempts of state commissioners to
acquire parish records were hampered, church funds at risk of seizure were

---

[14] See Kammer, *Kulturkampfpriester*, 76. For parallels in Schweich and Münster, see ibid. 92, and
Ficker, *Kulturkampf in Münster*, 101–3.

[15] LASB, E 107, 430–1.

[16] I am not suggesting an automatic 'subject mentality' here. Marpingen earlier in the century and
the revolutionary Mosel communities of Cues and Schweich in 1848 give the lie to that. But it remains
true that in the 1870s deference, partly hardheaded and prudential, generally inhibited attacks on
agents of state authority like soldiers or gendarmes. Once again I find myself in disagreement with
Klaus-Michael Mallmann: the Marpingen movement had elements of violence, but it hardly 'possessed
the characteristics of a latent civil war' (Mallmann, 'Volksfrömmigkeit', 219).

[17] Bachem, *Zentrumspartei*, iii. 299–300.

[18] P. Reichensperger, *Kulturkampf, oder Friede in Staat und Kirche* (Berlin, 1876), 73–83.

[19] Jentsch is cited in Ficker, *Kulturkampf in Münster*, 60.

secreted, church property that was forcibly auctioned found no bidders.[20] Catholics aided refractory priests on the run, accompanied those who were arrested to gaol, and celebrated their release with garlands and gunshot salutes. Those who denounced priests to the authorities were ostracized: a village watchman whose evidence helped to convict a priest in Prüm was taunted as a 'Judas'.[21]

This was the pattern that so frustrated the Prussian authorities in Marpingen. Referring to the early-warning system that always seemed to alert villagers to the approach of officials, one public prosecutor wrote wearily that the entire population 'performed spying duties on every corner and path, in order to bring the activity of the authorities to a standstill'.[22] The most universal form of resistance was sheer dumb insolence. Even sympathetic visitors such as Nikolaus Thoemes, Edmund Radziwill, and other Catholic parliamentarians were struck by the wall of silence they initially encountered from villagers. Radziwill's visit took place after the dissimulations of 'Marlow', and this plainly reinforced the tendency towards 'closed ears and doors'.[23] Men such as Thoemes and Radziwill had the confidence of Neureuter and village notables, however, and after a short time found villagers willing to talk to them. Representatives of the state continued to be frozen out. This was one of the things the gendarme Hentschel found 'endlessly difficult' about service in Marpingen: when the police arrived at the scene of an alleged apparition or miracle, 'finding out the facts from the silent masses [wa]s impossible'. Again, 'if a gendarme is spotted even in the distance everyone shuts up (so verstummt Alles) and not for all the world will they betray anything'.[24] The same treatment was meted out to other officials from whom the investigating authorities hoped to gain information. The rural postman Lohmeyer had spent several hours a day in Marpingen since 1874, but did not have the slightest idea about supporters of the apparitions 'because they keep everything from me as an official and a Protestant'.[25] Villagers were, of course, directly interrogated; but as the examining magistrate Emil Kleber repeatedly had to record, their statements were invariably vague, evasive, and marked by selective amnesia.[26] As we have already seen, the evasiveness may in some cases have been stiffened by moral intimidation. The result, as Meerscheidt-Hüllessem found, was that only

---

[20] The same happened with the property of individual priests. In Schweich, the authorities could not even find takers for Father Thielen's boots and umbrella: Kammer, *Kulturkampfpriester*, 92 On this generally under-researched subject, see Blackbourn, *Populists and Patricians*, 152–5, Sperber, *Popular Catholicism*, 227–33, and Anderson, *Windthorst*, 173–80. Local accounts include, in addition to Kammer, Ficker, *Kulturkampf in Münster*, Jestaedt, *Kulturkampf im Fuldaer Land*, and Schiffers, *Kulturkampf in Stadt und Regierungsbezirk Aachen*.
[21] Kammer, *Kulturkampfpriester*, 36. See also the case of a schoolteacher in Spiesen: ibid. 75.
[22] LHAK, 442/6442, 115–17: SP Petershof's report of 20 Sept. 1877 to MdI Berlin, quotation on 117.
[23] Thoemes, *Unsere Liebe Frau von Marpingen*, 83; Radziwill, *Besuch*, 4.
[24] LASB, E 107, 166–7.
[25] Ibid. 235.
[26] Ibid. 153, 218, 267–71.

the occasional notorious village character with a grudge was prepared to be forthcoming, and this testimony was generally unreliable.

When they were not being cold-shouldered, the hapless officials—the gendarmes especially—were met with sneering looks, derisive laughter, and other demonstrations of contempt against which their rule-books made it impossible to act (although they were plainly enraged). Curtains were pulled in front of their noses; villagers adopted an 'extremely mocking and insolent manner'.[27] The taunting extended to very pointed jokes. One gendarme was told: 'You started off the wrong way round. The *Landrat* and mayor should have announced, "Come, the Blessed Virgin is here"; then nobody would have believed it.'[28] Sympathetic clerical writers picked up this village joke and used it to make a more general (and undeniable) point about the counter-productiveness of state intervention; one even suggested that, in the absence of an early church enquiry, the hostility of officials served a helpful devil's-advocate function.[29] But in glossing the point in this way, clerical writers blunted the meaning it had when addressed by a Marpingen peasant to a gendarme. In its primary context, the joke conveyed mockery and hostility. It was one of the tiny pinpricks with which villagers tormented their tormentors.[30]

In numerous ways, passive resistance in Marpingen sounded variations on a theme found throughout Prussia during the *Kulturkampf*. The house-searches had to be undertaken with locksmiths from outside the village. Villagers worked together with the sexton and members of the church council to secrete money donated by pilgrims, just as their counterparts elsewhere secreted church funds. Father Schneider's housekeeper in Alsweiler hid his notes on Marpingen under a mattress, just as Catholics in other places spirited away parish records. When Father Neureuter was released from gaol on 1 December 1876, he received the festive welcome given to scores of *Kulturkampf* priests of the era, as the young men of Marpingen rode out to meet him on the St Wendel road and provide a guard of honour.[31] The expression and defence of their faith no doubt remained the primary concern for most villagers, but the circumstances turned even that into an implicit act of defiance. The emblems of the apparition movement—the cross that marked the spot and the flowers that adorned it, the lighted candles and pictures, the Marian hymns—became potent symbols of non-compliance with the dictates of the state. Again and again, Catholics in Marpingen were able to seize the moral initiative and place the authorities in a vulnerable, even laughable position. 'Innocent children' became a symbol of moral superiority against the weapons of soldiers and gendarmes. Agents of the state painted themselves into

[27] LASB, E 107, 168–9, 224 ff.
[28] Ibid. 431–2.
[29] EM, 92; MMGE, 60–1.
[30] There is some fragmentary material on village humour directed at gendarmes in BAT, B III, 11, 14/4, 115.
[31] LASB, E 107, 375; *Germania*, 6 Dec. 1876; *MWOL*, 74. The return of Father Schneider of Alsweiler on the same day was marked by the firing of a salute (*Böllerschüße*).

the position of treating the flowers left at 'the place' as evidence of lawbreaking, just as eleven girls in Schweich were imprisoned for being caught in possession of garlands after celebrating the release of their parish priest.[32]

Passive resistance was perhaps most evident of all in the refusal of many Catholics in Marpingen to accept the closing of the Härtelwald and Schwanenheck. The repeated public pronouncements from St Wendel throughout 1876–7 and the numerous summonses for unlawful entry of the forbidden area testify to the frequency with which the ban was broken. If it was the younger and more fleet of foot who most obviously defied this attempted restriction on their movements, there is no doubt that they enjoyed general support in the village. The villagers' sensitivity to their own 'space' and resistance to attempted encroachments on it also had parallels elsewhere. In Münster Catholics resisted a local regulation that opened a narrow road near the bishop's palace to wheeled vehicles and riders, and opposed government proposals to construct a statue at a sensitive site. When the authorities banned the display of flags on the bishop's palace to mark a papal jubilee in 1877, a young woman climbed up to place a wreath of yellow and white flowers on a convenient statue in the Domplatz.[33] In urban Münster, as in rural Marpingen, it is obviously true that in some cases, pragmatic, hard-headed reasons can be given for this stubborn defence of Catholic 'space'. Re-designated road usage in Münster was one aspect of an urban construction boom and a period of economic change that left many Catholics uneasy; the ban on entering the woods was damaging to the economic life of Marpingen. But it is difficult, in either case, to draw a neat distinction between the material and the symbolic. For the woods, like the narrow streets, stood for something more than just a physical space. The refusal of villagers to accept the closing of the woods and their evasion of the patrolling gendarmes recall the earlier, bitter disputes with Prussian officials over access to former communal woodland. In the 1870s, no less than in the 1830s and 1840s, the material and the moral were intertwined. The women and children of Marpingen, as a Catholic newspaper quite accurately pointed out, had not 'built barricades in order to bring down the German Reich'.[34] Yet the Prussian officials whose conspiratorial assumptions the newspaper satirized were not entirely wrong to see a movement of sorts, or at least a vigorous form of communal self-assertion, behind the rejection of their authority in Marpingen.

The Law, the Press, and Politics

This chapter has so far considered everyday forms of Catholic response to the state that had Marpingen itself as their arena. But reaction to the repression of

[32] On the Schweich incident, Kammer, *Kulturkampfpriester*, 94.
[33] Ficker, *Kulturkampf in Münster*, 221–6, 234–5, 241–4. The Governor of Westphalia based in Münster, Kühlwetter, was an exceptionally vigorous supporter of the *Kulturkampf*.
[34] *EM*, 62.

13 July and after also found other means of expression. These alternative ways of fighting back rested on words, not actions. They began with the primary experience of the villagers, but sought to bring the alleged injustices perpetrated on Marpingen to the attention of the world outside. Legal redress, publicity, and political exposure were the three principal, often interconnected channels into which this resistance flowed.

Perhaps the most striking aspect of the moves in this direction is how long it was before they began. Had a similarly heavy-handed intervention occurred in a well-organized Catholic town like Münster, Fulda, or Trier, it is probable that the lawyers and merchants of the Catholic Men's Club or another of the many Catholic associations would have been planning their response within days. While the parish priest and clerical visitors coped with the extra burden of work created by the apparitions, active laymen would have lobbied, petitioned, and taken legal advice. But Marpingen did not have the dense network of Catholic clubs and associations that existed in larger towns. It was, in this sense, 'unorganized' even by comparison with many places of the same size, a fact that may be connected to the complete absence of a native bourgeoisie. As a result, it took some time before decisions were reached in the village on how the resources of the law and public opinion could be used.

The evidence on this process is very fragmentary, but it appears that three individuals or groups were mainly concerned. There was, first and inevitably, Jakob Neureuter, the figure who stood involuntarily at the centre of all the public issues raised by Marpingen. But the parish priest was a sorely beleaguered man in the weeks after 3 July, especially after the military intervention. He was hardly in a position to undertake the organization of a legal or political counter-offensive against the Prussian army, field administration, and Ministry of the Interior. Secondly, an important role was played by village notables and members of the parish council, understandably alarmed at the virtual occupation of Marpingen and its adverse side-effects: the billeting, the charging of its costs to the village, the ban on entering the woods, and the potentially harmful effects on the village economy of the military and later police presence. These, at any rate, were the points the parish council later made in a series of formal complaints.[35] But there is no evidence to indicate whether, in the four or five weeks following the arrival of the army, they were engaged on their own initiative in trying to compile such a litany of grievances; certainly they did not produce one in this period. The catalyst in this situation appears to have been the arrival of outsiders, especially priests. The advent of Fathers Eich, Schneider, and—above all—Dicke removed part of the burden of coping with events from Neureuter's shoulders; it also created some order out of the morass of letters and other paperwork that threatened to drown the parish priest.[36] Their support and advice almost certainly

[35] Details in LASB, E 107, 19–21, 198–9, 434–5. See also LHAK, 442/6442, 152–3, 158–61: RP Wolff Trier to MdI Berlin, 28 Dec. 1877; and Radziwill, *Besuch*, 6.
[36] See above, Ch. 6.

helped to determine the actions that were taken in the first months. An equally important role was played later by Matthias Scheeben, Edmund Prince Radziwill, and Nikolaus Thoemes.

In the second week of August 1876 legal opinion was sought on how Marpingen might challenge the military intervention and the 'excesses' that followed.[37] The trigger here was probably the ban on entering the Härtelwald announced on 8 August. The legal advice was to gather statements from villagers with a view to starting a civil suit, and this was acted on. In the days after 13 August, statements were taken from dozens of witnesses to the behaviour of the army, police, and officials, especially Mayor Woytt. Neureuter took the major role in this, but a good deal of the work was delegated to Felix Dicke. The parish priest was also assisted by the miller Johann Thomé, the church bookkeeper Fuchs, and the recently arrived Dr Nikolaus Thoemes, an independent Catholic scholar from Baden. The net was cast outside the village. Of the six miners charged with riotous assembly on the evening of 13 July, three were non-Marpingers. All were contacted. Two of them, Peter Keßler and Adam Schumacher of Wustweilerhof, sent their account of events that evening via Father Lux of Uchtelfangen. The statement of the third, Paul Bohnenberger of Kleinheiligenwald (the man Neu-reuter was accused of harbouring), was conveyed more circuitously. On the advice of church bookkeeper Fuchs, Bohnenberger gave the statement to his daughter, who had it taken to Marpingen by a feather-dealer. Neureuter even wrote to the convicted confidence trickster Stauder, a shoemaker from the Düs-seldorf area, asking for a detailed description of the events on 13 July and a signed undertaking that he would be prepared to swear to his statement on oath. (This letter found its way back marked 'return to sender', and was later seized by the authorities, along with other correspondence and notes.)[38]

Felix Dicke took the material that had been gathered to a Catholic lawyer called Müller in Koblenz, and reported the lawyer's opinion in a letter to Neureuter on 24 August. Müller was an extremely prudent man (Meerscheidt-Hüllessem later called him 'uncommonly cautious') and his advice was not encouraging. There was, he believed, no realistic possibility of overturning the police regulations imposed on Marpingen by direct legal action. Müller saw little point in his retaining the material that had been gathered; the Marpingen parish council should go through official channels and start by lodging a complaint with the Prussian authorities in Trier.[39] On 4 September, the parish council sent a formal complaint to the administration in Trier, detailing the high-handed actions that had been taken, the intemperate language used by officials, and the automatic assumption that 'fraud' lay behind the apparitions. The document emphasized

[37] LASB, E 107, 24. Neureuter recounts this without giving a name, but the lawyer was probably Herr Müller of Koblenz, who later advised on how to use the statements that had been gathered.
[38] On the mechanics of gathering statements, see LASB, E 107, 216, 436–40. On Stauder, who tried to make money in Marpingen through his supposedly lame daughter, *Prozeß*, 132–5.
[39] LASB, E 107, 25–6, 406–7.

the loyalty of villagers to the Prussian state, and their good behaviour 'despite vexations'. This complaint was formally rejected on 9 September. On 5 September, moreover, the very day that the Marpingen complaint would have arrived in Trier, the district government issued a further proclamation that the 4,000 marks cost of the army billeting in Marpingen was to be met by a tax levy on the village. This prompted further complaints from the parish council, in the drafting of which Neureuter and Thoemes had a major part. One went back to the administration in Trier on 17 September, another to the provincial governor in Koblenz on 28 September, a third to the military General Command of the Rhine Province (also in Koblenz) on 14 October.[40] These documents repeated the earlier grievances, and took up the new provocation of the tax surcharge. The actions of officials in Marpingen were, it was claimed, 'quite unheard of in the whole monarchy'; it was almost as if, having failed to uncover sedition or fraud, they had sought to 'provoke' illegality. There were other, half-muted signs of resentment. Yet the tone was essentially that of loyal, even deferential petitioners, writing more in sorrow than anger. The absence of any political colouring to the apparitions was once again underlined. The response to the surcharge was more 'can't pay' (because of the economic hardships in the village) than 'won't pay'; indeed the document sent to the provincial governor in Koblenz stated that the council would be prepared to pay the surcharge 'without prejudice' out of reserves, although it was felt more appropriate that the costs be borne at provincial or district, not communal, level.[41]

The tone of these documents suggests that Neureuter and members of the parish council still entertained hopes of success through official channels. This was not entirely unrealistic, even if the initial response from Trier had been dusty. But even a successful outcome would necessarily be slow: the lawyer Müller had suggested that the process might have to be pursued right up to the Ministry of the Interior. Meanwhile, in September 1876 the first feverish bout of official visitations and interrogations had ebbed, and the army had been withdrawn; but the ban on the woods remained, and the 4,000-mark surcharge hung over the village. Neureuter had a substantial body of material on the whole course of events since 13 July (he and his helpers began to take down a further series of statements on 8 September); but legal advice suggested that they could not be brought directly before the public in court, for around 11 September Müller reiterated his view that 'a civil action could serve no purpose at all'.[42]

Now, as earlier, Müller advised against publishing the material that had been gathered.[43] That, however, was precisely the use to which it was put. The statements compiled in Marpingen formed the basis, first, for an article on 'The Police in Marpingen' by Matthias Scheeben. This was published on 26 September

[40] Sources as in n. 35.
[41] LASB, E 107, 19–21, 198–9, 434–5; Radziwill, *Besuch*, 6.
[42] LASB, E 107, 26: Dicke to Neureuter, Koblenz 11 Sept. 1876.
[43] LASB, E 107, 25–6, 405.

in the largest-circulation Catholic newspaper in Germany, the *Kölnische Volks-zeitung*.[44] The same material then buttressed a series of articles in *Germania* during October, written by Dr Thoemes. These were not, of course, the first accounts of Marpingen in the Catholic press. But earlier press statements by Neureuter and other priests had been more concerned with the apparitions themselves and the disputed cures; they were essentially reactions to scornful and hostile comment in the liberal press. Scheeben and Thoemes, by contrast, were centrally concerned to publicize the coercive actions of the state.

It is not easy to determine why the case should have been publicized in this way at this time. Müller had warned against such a course; and September was a period of relative quiet in the village, after the first wave of official intervention and before the arrival of 'Marlow'. Frustration over the intransigence of local and district bureaucracies must have played a part, coupled with the depressing prospect of a lengthy series of appeals. Experienced writers like Scheeben and Thoemes were also keen to go public with the Marpingen version of events. But Neureuter was undoubtedly in agreement with the chosen strategy. He played host to Scheeben, received Thoemes warmly, and made material available to both. A letter written by Scheeben to Neureuter on 19 September shows that the parish priest knew of the plan to publicize the role of the army and police, and was aware that this turned the affair more into a question about the abuse of political power than a dispute about the varieties of religious experience.[45] Certainly Scheeben's article marked an important stage in the Catholic counter-attack, for both author and *Kölnische Volkszeitung* editors were summonsed in the wake of it. The result was a trial in April 1877, itself widely publicized, which clearly turned not on the question of the apparitions and cures, or even on allegations of 'deception', but on the appropriateness of the initial state response. Whether intentionally or not, Scheeben had flushed out the state authorities and started to put them on the defensive.[46]

The intervention of Meerscheidt-Hüllessem, and the wave of arrests that followed his visit to Marpingen, provided a further opportunity for Catholic publicists to protest against the misuse of state power. This was especially true of the incarceration of the three visionaries, which led not only to the lodging of legal appeals, but to widespread publicity in the Centre press, especially in *Germania*. A particularly prominent part was played in this campaign by Edmund Prince Radziwill. He arrived at Marpingen in the middle of November 1876, drawn by the belief that police behaviour had become an issue in its own right— 'the second act of the story', as he put it.[47] Radziwill defined his role as 'advocate

---

[44] On the standing of the *Kölnische Volkszeitung*, and the close links it enjoyed with figures like Scheeben in the Cologne seminary and with members of the Cologne cathedral chapter, see Lange, *Die Stellung*, 29, 32.

[45] LASB, E 107, 414: Scheeben to Neureuter, Cologne, 19 Sept. 1877; *Prozeß*, 179.

[46] For Scheeben's trial and its impact, see below, Ch. 10.

[47] Radziwill, *Besuch*, 3.

of the people'.[48] This had a double meaning in practice. As his use of the term *Anwalt* suggests, Radziwill used legal channels in representing the just cause of 'simple villagers' against an intransigent system. In drawing up a complaint about the incarceration of the children and sending it to the Ministry of Justice in Berlin, Radziwill's action resembled that of the 'peasant advocates' who took up legal cases against state officials, moneylenders, and others.[49] At the same time, action on the legal-administrative front was accompanied by publicity in the form of a string of articles in *Germania*.[50] The fact that 'Marlow' chose to publish his own version of events in the *Berliner Tageblatt* was certainly grist to the mill of Catholic publicists such as Radziwill, Thoemes, and others; but injudicious as the policeman's action was, it was probably not decisive. By October 1876, the Catholic press coverage of Marpingen had gained momentum, not least because the issue had moved beyond the apparitions themselves, on which lay and clerical opinion was divided, and became increasingly centred on more explicitly political questions of administration and justice. The apparently unending sequence of arrests, legal judgements, and appeals that began in the autumn of 1876 kept the Catholic press campaign well fuelled. In the end, the combination of due legal process and press scrutiny would make Marpingen at least as great an embarrassment to the Prussian state as it had initially been to clerical and lay Catholics who were sceptical about the 'German Lourdes'.

The legal and press battles sparked off by the actions of the Prussian army, bureaucracy, gendarmerie, and judicial authorities made Marpingen into an eminently political issue. The affair was not only a by-product of the *Kulturkampf*; it became itself part of the political struggle of the 1870s. In his letter to Neureuter on 19 September, Matthias Scheeben referred to the question of 'mak[ing] public the miracle of the police in Marpingen, which is important for the elections'.[51] These were the elections to the Reichstag in January 1877, and one of the editors of the *Kölnische Volkszeitung*, Julius Bachem, later acknowledged that Scheeben's article on Marpingen had indeed been 'heavily used' in the election campaign.[52] The Centre candidate for the constituency that included Marpingen, the lawyer Karl Schmidt of Colmar, told a Boxing Day election rally in St Wendel that he had been to the village and drunk from the spring in the Härtelwald.[53]

---

[48] Radziwill, *Besuch*, 18.

[49] For his approach to the Ministry of Justice, see ibid. 18. From the 1860s and 1870s, the figure of the 'peasant advocate' became institutionalized in peasant associations that took cases to court. One of the most active was the Christian Peasant Association of Trier, led inevitably by Georg Dasbach: BAT, 85/282: materials on Trier Christian Peasant Association; Thoma, *Dasbach*. Between 1884 and 1918 the Trier association fought 13,500 cases against moneylenders and agricultural dealers: Blackbourn, *Populists and Patricians*, 178.

[50] Radziwill, *Besuch*, 17, 25 ff.

[51] LASB, E 107, 414; *Prozeß*, 179.

[52] *Prozeß*, 179.

[53] *Germania*, 2 Jan. 1877. The constituency was Ottweiler-St Wendel-Meisenheim, where Schmidt lost after a bitter campaign to the Free Conservative heavy-industrial magnate Stumm, the same outcome as in the previous election: Bellot, *Hundert Jahre*, 143–7. Voting in the mayoral district that

Marpingen may have helped the Centre Party; but did the Centre Party help Marpingen? To what extent was the legal and press battle in defence of the village taken up at the party-political level? Some of the prominent outsiders who took up the cause were Centre parliamentarians. Both Edmund Radziwill and Paul Majunke sat in the Reichstag as Centre deputies, and the former certainly used his status as a member of parliament in dealings with both gendarmes and the Ministry of Justice. But he was acting as an individual in taking up the Marpingen case. Together with Majunke and the Trier newspaper editor Georg Dasbach, whose papers also publicized the affair, Radziwill belonged to a group of priest-publicists who were Centre parliamentarians, but very much back-benchers.[54] Among senior leadership figures in the Prussian Centre Party, and even in the provincial Rhineland Party, there was no marked enthusiasm to embrace the cause of Marpingen. The lawyer Müller whom Neureuter and Dicke consulted in Koblenz was a local Centre leader, and his advice included the suggestion that the statements collected from villagers be sent to Ludwig Windthorst, the party's national leader.[55] But the sense that comes through from Dicke's visit to Koblenz is that Müller suggested Windthorst's name in order to keep out of the business himself.

The response of the Centre leader to the Marpingen case was always likely to be mixed. Like other prominent figures in the Centre, Windthorst was temperamentally out of sympathy with the kind of faith represented by the *Syllabus of Errors*, the Jesuits, and papal infallibility. ('Even if they cut my head off I won't believe in infallibility,' he once remarked.[56]) He was hardly likely to relish the prospect of taking up the case of the 'German Lourdes' in parliament. It is possible that the Centre leadership, aware of the potential embarrassment, sought to treat Marpingen with benign neglect. The liberal press in the Saarland mocked the party's silence over the affair in 1877, which stood in contrast to its introduction of other, often very minor *Kulturkampf* incidents into budget debates in the Prussian lower house. The silence persisted even when a hostile speaker garnered loud applause in the house for a sardonic reference to the setting up in Marpingen of 'an experimental station on belief in miracles'.[57] On the other hand, by the closing years of the *Kulturkampf* Centre parliamentary leaders were familiar enough with liberal taunts, and hardly likely to be inhibited in the issues they selected to take up. It may be that Windthorst's broken health in the spring of 1877 provides a more prosaic explanation for the delay in placing Marpingen on

included Marpingen was: Schmidt (Centre), 1,551 votes (97.5%); Stumm (Free Conservative), 39 votes (2.5%): *NBZ*, 13 Jan. 1877.

[54] Two clerical Centre Party members of the Bavarian parliament who reportedly visited Marpingen in November 1876 were also modest back-bench figures. See *SMZ*, 18 Nov. 1876.
[55] LASB, E 107, 25–6: Dicke to Neureuter, Koblenz, 24 Aug. 1876, repeated in a letter of 11 Sept. following a further consultation with Müller.
[56] Anderson, *Windthorst*, 126
[57] The speaker was the National Liberal, Ludwig Seyffardt, on 24 Feb. 1877. Speech reprinted in L. F. Seyffardt, *Erinnerungen* (Leipzig, 1900), 188–9. See also report in *SMZ*, 8 Mar. 1877.

the parliamentary agenda in Prussia.[58] By the end of the year the Centre Party
had tabled a motion in the Prussian lower house. For, embarrassing as the
Marpingen events might have been to a Windthorst (or to Julius Bachem, the
Centre politician in whose name the motion was tabled[59]), the reaction to those
events was no less potentially embarrassing to the Prussian government. The
actions of the officials who believed that Marpingen was politically inspired had
helped to bring about what they feared. The full-scale debate that took place in
the Prussian lower house on 15 December 1877 elevated the village briefly to
national renown in parliament as well as press, and it turned on detailed discussion
of how the army and civilian bureaucracy had conducted themselves. This was
to be followed in 1879 by a major trial of defendants from Marpingen during
which the identities of accused and accusers were often unclear.[60]

Occasional acts of violence, passive but sustained non-co-operation, attempts
at legal redress, publicity in the press, a motion in parliament: these represented
different facets of the Catholic response to the state's heavy hand in Marpingen.
They were often complementary: Radziwill publicized the grievances of Marpingen in the press, worked through legal channels, and used his authority as a
member of parliament (*Mitglied des Reichstages*). But there were also dissonances
between the different kinds of response: it is hindsight that makes them appear
neatly dovetailed. It is nevertheless true that real or potential divisions among
Catholics were muted by the tendency to close ranks in the face of a discrimination
and hostility that all had experienced in one form or another. In that sense,
Marpingen reproduced circumstances that occurred again and again during the
Kulturkampf. It made the differences between Catholics weigh less heavily in the
balance by branding all publicly declared Catholics as pariahs. As the Catholic
art historian August Reichensperger put it, 'we ultramontanes are all to some
extent unclear'.[61] In social and cultural terms, men like this had more in common
with their liberal counterparts than with the Mariolatrous Catholic peasant; in
political terms they sided with the peasant. The case of the priest-publicist Paul
Majunke is a particularly telling one. It was not difficult for the *Germania* editor
to sympathize with the beleaguered population of Marpingen, for two years earlier
he had himself been arrested for press offences during a Reichstag session.[62] No
less important, that same incident (a highly controversial one) reduced the
distance that separated the clerical, extravagantly pious, and highly pugnacious
Majunke from lay, religiously austere, and politically more pragmatic Centre
Party leaders like Windthorst and Julius Bachem, for it raised fundamental issues

[58] On the Centre leader's health, see Anderson, *Windthorst*, 200.
[59] The motion in the name of 'Bachem and colleagues' is in *Anlagen zu den Stenographischen Berichten über die Verhandlungen des Hauses der Abgeordneten während der 2. Session der 13. Legislatur-Periode 1877–78*, ii. No. 139, (Berlin, 1878), 1069–73.
[60] See below, Ch. 10, on the parliamentary debate and trial.
[61] L. Pastor, *August Reichensperger*, 2 vols. (Freiburg, 1899), i. 424.
[62] On Majunke's arrest, see M. Stürmer, *Regierung und Reichstag im Bismarckstaat 1871–1880: Cäsarismus oder Parlamentarismus* (Düsseldorf, 1974), 130.

of law and due process. Marpingen had the same effect, the involuntary effect produced by the harsh actions of the state. Whatever the divisions among clerical and lay Catholics over the apparitions, the resulting repression united disparate Catholics around the issues of parental rights, natural justice, and the rule of law.

9

Progress and Piety: Liberal Hostility

To the liberal mind Marpingen was symptomatic of Catholic superstition and credulity. At the same time, resistance to the measures taken by the state confirmed many liberals in their view that Catholics were fractious subjects, led by their clerical masters (and by French example) into disloyalty. In this double set of responses we can see the liberal view of the *Kulturkampf* in microcosm. For the *Kulturkampf*, often depicted as a rather arid squabble between church and state, was actually much more than that. The term itself was coined by Rudolf Virchow, the doctor, pathologist, scientific popularizer, and left-liberal politician. It means literally 'struggle of civilizations', and liberals certainly saw it as a decisive encounter that would shape Germany's future. It was, for them, a conflict between progress and piety, in which material advance, science, and moral improvement were pitted against backwardness, ignorance, and superstition. The terms in which liberals denounced events in Marpingen give a clear picture of their world-view during the 1870s, and their ferocity shows what they felt to be at stake. The enthusiasm with which many, National Liberals in particular, applauded the coercive methods used in the village also gives a measure of the ambivalent relationship between liberal goals and Bismarckian methods.

Superstition versus Civilization

The liberal response to Marpingen was couched in terms that began to emerge around the time of the Trier pilgrimage of 1844, helped to mark the division between Catholics and liberals in 1848, and became more general during the following decades. The Catholic clergy, it was argued, were fanatical and divisive, members of the 'hocus-pocus guild' who kept the people in ignorance—they were, in the common phrase, *Volksverdummer*. Catholicism represented 'stagnation in every respect'; it acted as a 'brake on civilization'.[1] Catholics were a servile mass of the uneducated, with a sprinkling of mystically inclined aristocrats who had nothing better to do than disport themselves from one pilgrimage site to the next. This was the standpoint from which Marpingen was judged, and the

[1] Schieder, 'Kirche und Revolution'; A. Birke, *Bischof Ketteler und der deutsche Liberalismus* (Mainz, 1971), 22–3, 44–5; A. Birke, 'Zur Entwicklung des bürgerlichen Kulturkampfverständnisses in Preußen-Deutschland', in D. Kürze (ed.), *Aus Theorie und Praxis der Geschichtswissenschaft. Festschrift für Hans Herzfeld* (Berlin, 1972), 257–79; Ficker, *Kulturkampf in Münster*, 41.

judgements were harsh. The left liberal Theodor Lucas, a wine dealer in Mülheim, wrote to a political friend in 1877 reporting on the state of things in the Rhine Province: 'The country is flooded with little hate-sheets, which systematically stir up fanaticism, religious mania has made the lowest classes of the people deranged (Marpingen), they try to drag the best characters in the mud in order to rob them of any public effectiveness.'² The National Liberal Ludwig Seyffardt spoke of the 'crass belief in miracles and superstition' and the 'Marpingen swindle'; his fellow liberal Julius Sello argued that stupidity had been exploited by 'clerical secret policemen'.³ It was in the press, however, among what August Reichensperger called the 'liberal newspaper philistines', that these attitudes can be seen most clearly.⁴ Local newspapers were the first into the field against Marpingen. The *Saar- und Mosel-Zeitung* observed on 16 July that 'the crassest stupidity is once again blossoming luxuriantly'.⁵ Subsequent reports anathematized the 'Virgin Mary swindle', 'the most shameful swindle imaginable', and 'this truly abominable case of deception'.⁶ The *Nahe-Blies-Zeitung* in St Wendel took a similarly outraged view of events in the nearby village. The affair was a deception which flourished because of 'habitual stupidity' among the 'stupid masses' and the 'mindless superstition of that area'. The whole business was, in short, 'a colossal swindle basing itself on stupidity'.⁷ The *Saarbrücker Zeitung*, the *St Johanner Zeitung*, and the *Trierische Zeitung* took a similar line.

The major big-city liberal papers—the *Frankfurter Zeitung*, *Kölnische Zeitung*, *Breslauer Zeitung*, *Vossische Zeitung*, *Deutsche Allgemeine Zeitung*, *National-Zeitung*—were, predictably, slower to turn their attention to Marpingen. They were preoccupied in the summer of 1876 with the war in the Balkans, the delicate state of French politics, and the American centennial celebrations. Their domestic gaze in July and August was fixed on the reorientation of German Conservatism, the agrarian question, Reich railway policy, and the first news about candidates for the forthcoming Prussian elections. The *Vossische Zeitung* carried its first news of Marpingen on 18 July; the *Frankfurter Zeitung* followed two days later; other liberal newspapers of record waited until August before they noticed the story, and the lofty *Augsburger Allgemeine Zeitung* ignored it entirely. It also took some time before reports from Marpingen were transferred from the 'miscellaneous' section to the political part of the paper. The left-liberal *Frankfurter Zeitung* was typical. Its first report on events in the village (which it rendered as 'Markingen') appeared on 20 July in the 'miscellaneous' section. Eight days later a further story

² Lucas to Wilhelm Löwe, 4 Nov. 1877: P. Wentzcke, *Im neuen Reich 1871–1890. Politische Briefe aus dem Nachlass liberaler Parteiführer* (Bonn and Leipzig, 1926), 189–90.
³ Seyffardt in Prussian parliamentary speeches of 24 Feb. and 30 Nov. 1877: *Erinnerungen*, 188–9, 195–6; Sello in Prussian parliamentary debate on Marpingen, SB, 16 Jan. 1878, 1165–8.
⁴ The art historian and Centre politician's views can be found in Pastor, *August Reichensperger*, i. 432–7. There are obvious parallels with Nietzsche's bitter epigrams about journalistic philistinism and self-satisfaction—although Nietzsche himself was a vigorous anticlerical.
⁵ SMZ, 16 July 1876.
⁶ SMZ, 22 and 25 July 1876.
⁷ NBZ, 24 Aug., 5, 7, 16, and 19 Sept., 5 and 28 Oct. 1876.

was run in the same section. Not until 31 July was Marpingen granted entry to the political columns.[8]

These papers varied somewhat in tone, between the fierce and the ironic, but the positions they took up resembled those enunciated in the local liberal press. The *Breslauer Zeitung* was probably the most world-wearily sardonic: the news from Marpingen was disagreeable, but hardly the first bitter pill of its kind that had to be swallowed; perhaps the Marpingers should be left to build their German Lourdes ('What would be the harm if some foreign money came into the country?').[9] In its first report, the *Frankfurter Zeitung* noted mildly that 'regrettable excesses have occurred, brought about by "apparitions of the Virgin"'. After reports of apparitions in Posen, it mocked these 'miracles in the east and miracles in the west' and observed that they were evidently contagious.[10] On a later occasion the 'outrageous Madonna-swindle' was branded as 'nonsense', 'mischief', and 'stupidity'.[11] The *Deutsche Allgemeine Zeitung* referred in similar vein to the 'swindle affair', the gatherings of 'the deluded masses' and the 'unhappy victims of fanaticism'.[12] The *Kölnische Zeitung* talked variously of the 'Virgin Mary-swindle', the 'Madonna swindle', and the 'Marpingen Lourdes-swindle', pouring scorn on 'the credulous bigoted masses'.[13] The *National-Zeitung* took exception to the 'unsuccessful Marpingen comedy', and attacked the encouragement of 'stupidity' and 'vulgar superstition'.[14]

Political suspicions obviously fuelled liberal hostility to Marpingen. The *Nahe-Blies-Zeitung*, mixing its metaphors with abandon, argued that 'the heart of the matter in the whole cooking up of the Marpingen swindle is to keep feelings in a state of constant agitation, in order to fish in troubled waters at the forthcoming elections'.[15] Two weeks later the same paper offered a more luridly conspiratorial gloss on the apparitions. Marpingen was designed to increase 'disaffection' with the political status quo among Catholics, fostering 'bitterness' against Prussia and 'hatred' against the German Reich; the appearance of the Virgin was intended to inflame the 'fanatical mob' into 'revolutionary upheaval'.[16] Another local liberal paper reacted to Father Schneider's description of the apparitions with the comment that only 'the premature blabbing of the plotters' had alerted Germany to 'the dangers ahead'.[17] The language of 'ultramontane intrigue' ran through the coverage in the major liberal press, although it was more pronounced in

[8] See *FZ*, 20, 28, and 31 July 1876.

[9] Cited in *Germania*, 13 Jan. 1877. On the generally more moderate line of the paper during the *Kulturkampf* (e.g. it opposed the law expelling the Jesuits) see A. Oehlke, *100 Jahre Breslauer Zeitung: 1820–1920* (Breslau, n.d.[1920]), 198.

[10] *FZ*, 7 Aug. 1876.

[11] *FZ*, 16 and 17 Jan. 1878.

[12] *DAZ*, 17 Aug. 1876. See also issues of 23 Aug., 16, 19, and 28 Nov. 1876.

[13] *KZ*, 13 and 23 Aug., 1 and 6 Sept., and 20 Oct. 1876.

[14] *NZ*, 17 Jan. 1878.

[15] *NBZ*, 24 Aug. 1876.

[16] *NBZ*, 7 Sept. 1876. See also issue of 16 Sept. 1876.

[17] *SMZ*, 24 Aug. 1876.

National-Liberal than in left-liberal newspapers.[18] One of the most serenely confident diagnoses of ultramontane conspiracy came from the *Deutsche Allgemeine Zeitung* of Leipzig. Why, it asked in mid-August 1876, had the movement in Marpingen been allowed to grow to such a dangerous point?[19]

Among all the clerical agitators there is, in our view, not one who is convinced in his heart about the reality of the miraculous events in Marpingen; it was solely the idea of keeping an uncritical population in the necessary state of agitation and hostility against the state and the liberals in order to serve ultramontane ends which, if it did not instigate this swindle in the first place, at least led to its exploitation on the largest possible scale. That is as clear as daylight.

That Marpingen was turned to political use by Catholic editors and parliamentary candidates is undeniable. Even the descriptive accounts of cures and miracles provided by Father Schneider and others had at least an implicitly political message, in so far as they served as a rallying-cry to beleaguered Catholics. It is not surprising that liberals, like state officials, should have reacted allergically. Nor, from the liberal perspective, was the issue purely domestic. An important aspect of the liberal preoccupation with clerical conspiracy within was the link they made with conspiracy without. Given the political situation in the middle of the 1870s, that meant above all France. German liberals were much exercised in these years by the right-wing Catholic revival in France, in which they rightly saw Lourdes being deployed as an important symbol.[20] Many drew directly political conclusions. The *Augsburger Allgemeine Zeitung* drew its readers' attention to the growing strength in France of an 'ultramontane-Jesuit party' that was also a '*revanche*-party'. The 'political dangers of these dark doings' were plain: by awakening the passions of French Catholics, the ultramontane-Jesuit party would ultimately bend the French government to its purposes, which included the restoration of the Papal States, the recovery of Alsace-Lorraine, and revenge against Germany.[21] For the *Saar- und Mosel-Zeitung*, the Virgin of Lourdes was 'the French goddess of revenge'.[22] Others made the same point.[23] In that sense, the universal depiction of Marpingen as a 'Lourdes-swindle' had political connotations linked to the external security of the newly founded German Empire. A sense of uncertainty was, of course, endemic in Germany in the 1870s: the motif of the Catholic enemy within and without had helped to fuel the *Kulturkampf* in the first place. Perhaps more than Bismarck, who liked to play up

---

[18] Cf. *KZ*, 26 Aug. and 3 Nov. 1876, and the long article in *NZ*, 17 Jan. 1878. The treatment of the question in the *Frankfurter Zeitung* and *Vossische Zeitung* was less marked by conspiracy theory.

[19] *DAZ*, 17 Aug. 1876.

[20] See the lengthy articles under the heading 'Die Gründung einer Wallfahrtskirche' in the Sunday supplements of *VZ*, 15 and 22 Oct. 1876.

[21] *Augsburger Allgemeine Zeitung*, 25 Oct. 1876.

[22] *SMZ*, 6 Sept. 1876. See also the political commentary on 19 July 1876, headed 'Frankreich und der Ultramontanismus'.

[23] Cf. *KZ*, 6 June 1877; *NZ*, 17 Jan. 1878.

such fears for domestic political advantage, liberals took the threat seriously.[24] Their nervousness about this putative double enemy was especially acute on the western border. Liberals who opposed extending the Prussian species of self-government to the Rhine Province argued that the region was a 'colony that has to fight for its life, at the moment in the intellectual sense, but as soon as our army is otherwise engaged, in the physical sense too'. If the organs of local administration fell into clerical hands, the Prussian government would be unable to hold the province together and in a few years reliance on the 8th Army Corps would no longer be enough.[25]

The anti-French motif in liberal reactions nevertheless suggests an anxiety that went beyond the party-political, beyond even the security of the German border. It went to the heart of what liberals of both progressive and National-Liberal persuasions saw as the future of the new Imperial Germany, of how it was to develop materially, socially, intellectually. German liberals referred as often as Catholics to Marpingen as a 'German Lourdes', but they drew quite opposite conclusions. At the time of the original Lourdes, liberals had congratulated themselves with the thought that nothing of the kind would be allowed to happen in Germany.[26] In January 1876, less than six months before the Marpingen episode began, one liberal newspaper observed that the efforts of 'zealous priests' had foundered in Germany on the good sense of the German people. It contrasted this happy state of affairs with the situation in France, where 'religious feelings are clearly in a state of much greater agitation, where miraculous apparitions and miraculous deeds occur daily'.[27] That a Marpingen could happen at all was therefore a shock; that it took on such major proportions seemed even more disgraceful in liberal eyes.[28] It was a 'medieval' excrescence in the century of progress, disfiguring a nation liberals liked to regard as the exemplar of modernity. 'Under the sign of exorcisms, stigmatic women, and apparitions of the Virgin', wrote one newspaper, 'the ultramontanes propose to vanquish the spirit of the nineteenth century.'[29] Marpingen confirmed liberals in the original objectives of the Kulturkampf: the struggle of progress against backwardness.

But what did they mean by progress? Liberal values were, in part, a late outcrop of the Enlightenment, in which reason was championed over revelation,

---

[24] Bismarck's playing up of foreign threats for domestic advantage is emphasized in Stürmer, Regierung und Reichstag, and in the works of Hans-Ulrich Wehler, including Bismarck und der Imperialismus (Cologne and Berlin, 1969) and The German Empire 1871–1918 (Leamington Spa, 1985). For a more sceptical view, see O. Pflanze, 'Bismarcks Herrschaftstechnik als Problem der gegenwärtigen Historiographie', Historische Zeitschrift, 223 (1982), 562–99.

[25] Heinrich Sybel to Eduard Lasker, 25 Dec. 1874: Wentzcke, Im neuen Reich, 111–14. Similar dire prognostications about clerical influence on local government were made by the National Liberal Ludwig Seyffardt during a discussion with Bismarck in Jan. 1875: Seyffardt, Erinnerungen, 164–5.

[26] Rebbert, Marpingen und seine Gegner, 9.

[27] NBZ, 22 Jan. 1876.

[28] Even in August, one liberal paper remarked defiantly: 'For the moment we still do not believe that Germany is as ripe for a Lourdes as France, which has been dominated for so long by Jesuits.' See SMZ, 24 Aug. 1876.

[29] NZ, 17 Jan. 1878.

knowledge over ignorance, science over superstition, and the universal over the local or particular. These terms recurred constantly in liberal reactions to Marpingen. The Enlightenment legacy is especially apparent in the way the Manichaean categories of light and dark were employed to describe the struggle between benign liberalism and clerical obscurantism. The alleged instigators of Marpingen were described again and again as the *Finsterlinge*, the 'forces of darkness', bent on shutting out the light of knowledge as they shackled unfortunate Catholics in darkness (*Finsternis*). Here liberal condemnation of Marpingen was of a piece with self-consciously 'enlightened' liberal discourse in the *Kulturkampf* as a whole.[30] The 'stupidity' on display in the Saarland was made to stand for a larger 'superstition'. The 'dead hand' of the church was depicted at work in Marpingen, just as it was held more generally responsible for consigning Catholics to mental sloth and material backwardness. The attack on clerical instigation and exploitation formed part of a broader, more venerable assault on a clergy which kept Catholics 'in leading-strings'.[31] All of this would have seemed familiar to a Diderot or Voltaire. So would the many legends about Marpingen that circulated in liberal circles: the two girls who drowned in a tank of Marpingen water, the supposedly disabled pilgrims *en route* to Marpingen who picked up their crutches and ran to catch the train.[32] These belonged to an Enlightenment form of burlesque that persisted in Imperial Germany in other forms, such as the anticlerical verses of Wilhelm Busch or ribald tales of the nunnery by authors like 'Luzifer Illuminator'.[33] The enlightened strain of liberalism is also plain in the emphasis placed on education (especially by left liberals) as the means to break the clerical stranglehold that made spectacles like Marpingen possible.

Reactions of this kind existed side by side with other, more despairing tones suggesting a belief that 'stupidity' had perhaps reached the point where human nature was no longer capable of improvement, that the darkness might be impenetrable. 'The Marpingers have made themselves immortal with their stupidity,' argued one newspaper, and continued: these 'abysmally stupid people (*bodenlos dumme Leute*) are incorrigible'.[34] Others took Marpingen as the occasion for jeremiads on the growth of stupidity in the world, and registered a sense of 'shame, that our Fatherland, that the century we praise for providing so much

---

[30] See D. Blackbourn, 'Progress and Piety: Liberalism, Catholicism and the State in Imperial Germany', *History Workshop Journal*, 26 (1988), 57–78, for more detailed argument and references.

[31] The phrase 'in leading-strings' is from the *Westfälische Provinzialzeitung*, cited in Ficker, *Kulturkampf in Münster*, 204.

[32] *St-Johanner-Zeitung*, 15 Aug. 1877; Rebbert, *Marpingen und seine Gegner*, 47–50. These stories were, of course, the counterparts to pious legends about sceptics who mocked Marpingen, only to find their horses dead in unnatural circumstances.

[33] The best-known anticlerical works of Wilhelm Busch were *Pater Filucius* and *Die Fromme Helene*, both from 1872. Among the ribald tales were *Pfaffenunwesen, Mönchsskandale und Nonnenspuk. Beitrag zur Naturgeschichte des Katholizismus und der Klöster von Luzifer Illuminator* (Leipzig, 1871), and *Memoiren einer Nonne* (Munich, 1874).

[34] *SMZ*, 19 July 1876.

light, should witness such things'.[35] These passages repay closer attention, for they indicate what liberal attacks on Marpingen owed to the second half of the nineteenth century, rather than to the legacy of the Enlightenment. The bitterness about 'incorrigible' Marpingers suggests the frustration of liberals who had faced three decades of popular Catholic revival symbolized by the 'hocus-pocus' (*Gaukelei*) of Lourdes and Marpingen. It is perhaps understandable if the standard-bearers of rationality found their patience strained by each new example of 'superstition', and came to view the mass of Catholics not only as ill-used, but beyond saving. Pessimism, pathos, and gallows humour run through liberal reactions to Marpingen, their sense of impotent frustration breaking through in intemperate language. For however much liberals peppered their abuse with the epithet 'medieval', the point was that the powers of 'darkness' could no longer be seen as comfortably residual.

Science, 'Mob-Masses', and 'Hysterical Women'

The liberal struggle against the forces of darkness was a post-Enlightenment affair. It was not the eighteenth century they were defending against attempts by clerics to 'vanquish' it, but the nineteenth. The *Kultur* that liberals advocated in the *Kulturkampf* was materialist, technological, and scientific: the culture of the railway, the agricultural field-station, the brave new world of Progress. The vulgar-materialist liberalism of the *Kulturkampf* was a distinguishing feature of the secular crusade against the church in the 1870s. If the state backed down, it would augur ill for the development of the Empire, from the liberal perspective. 'Going to Canossa will bring us no railways,' as one liberal versifier put it with brutal clarity.[36] Hostility to the apparitions was shot through with references to rural backwardness and resistance to material and moral progress.

It was also couched in the language of natural science. The most familiar link between science and liberal politics is the enthusiasm with which Darwinism was taken up by progressive opinion in Germany. One of the earliest examples of this is the speech given by the young Jena zoologist Ernst Haeckel to the Association of German Scientists and Doctors in 1863, where he argued that Darwin stood for 'evolution and progress':[37]

Progress is a natural law that no human power, neither the weapons of tyrants nor the curses of priests, can ever succeed in suppressing. Only through progressive movement are life and development possible. Standing still is in itself regression, and regression carries with it death. The future belongs only to progress!

Similar links between the purported message of Darwin and the course of social

[35] *NZ*, 17 Jan. 1878.
[36] Kissling, *Geschichte*, ii. 295.
[37] A. Kelly, *The Descent of Darwin: The Popularization of Darwinism in Germany, 1860–1914* (Chapel Hill, NC, 1981), 22.

developments were made by other prominent figures. The biologist Friedrich Ratzel, in the preface to a popular work on natural history, observed that his aim was to encourage 'progressive tendencies'. The impact of Darwinism was obvious in the argument for a rational, liberal culture mounted by David Friedrich Strauss in his 1872 work, *Der alte und der neue Glaube*. Popularized versions of the 'progressive' Darwinist creed were expounded by numerous others, and found their way into liberal periodicals like *Die Gartenlaube*.[38] Not all progressive opinion succumbed to the easy embrace of Darwinism. Rudolf Virchow, the progressive man of science *par excellence*, clashed with Haeckel at the 1877 meeting of the Association of German Scientists and Doctors, scolding his former student for prematurely advocating the Darwinian 'hypothesis' on evolution as a fit subject to be taught in the schools.[39] Nevertheless, Virchow began his address with some characteristic remarks about the 'pride' that those assembled were entitled to feel, 'here in the German land of scientific freedom', and made a pointed contrast with France, where progress was threatened by 'ultramontanism'.[40] Virchow also argued forcefully in the Prussian parliament that if evolution were to be proved correct as a theory, the Catholic Church would have to yield to science.[41] By 1875, when the first German edition of Darwin's complete works appeared, the supposed link between Darwinism and the creed of social and political progress had become a commonplace of German liberal thinking, with a sharp anticlerical thrust. The Catholic response, it should be said, was hardly calculated to impress a liberal audience. Virchow's parliamentary efforts were greeted from the Centre Party benches with cries of 'get on to the apes'; *Germania* routinely referred to German Darwinists as 'the ape fanatics'.[42]

Darwinism, used (or abused) in this way, was only one aspect of a larger liberal discourse that combined science and materialism into an anticlerical weapon. Catholic Germany was the embodiment of 'stagnation'. One academic writer in 1872 used an extended irrigation metaphor to prescribe what should be done with the dangerous forces of the Catholic Church: its 'flood-waters' were to be 'carefully canalized and directed into reservoirs (*Bassins*)'; the 'poor residue' could be drained off and left to 'dry out'.[43] Apparition sites were habitually

[38] Kelly, *Descent*, 22–3. See also F. Gregory, *Scientific Materialism in Nineteenth-Century Germany* (Dordrecht, 1977).

[39] R. Virchow, *Die Freiheit der Wissenschaften im modernen Staat. Rede gehalten in der dritten allgemeinen Sitzung der fünfzigsten Versammlung deutscher Naturforscher und Ärzte zu München am 22. September 1877* (Berlin, 1877). See also Virchow, *Glaubensbekenntnis eines modernen Naturforschers* (Berlin, 1873). Virchow was a 'vital materialist', i.e. one owing a debt to the Romantic tradition, rather than a materialist *tout court*: Boyd, 'Rudolf Virchow', 57–60; Kelly, *Descent*, 57–64.

[40] Virchow, *Freiheit der Wissenschaften*, 5–6.

[41] This was in 1879. See Kelly, *Descent*, 64; Bauer, *Rudolf Virchow—Der politische Arzt* (Berlin, 1982), 97.

[42] Boyd, 'Rudolf Virchow', 185. Cf. the attack by J. Rebbert, author of one of the more sober Catholic pamphlets in support of Marpingen, on 'certain progressive "liberals"' who had in common with the Social Democrats that they knew nothing of God and wanted man to be seen 'purely as a developed ape': Rebbert, *Marpingen und seine Gegner*, 16.

[43] Birke, *Ketteler*, 22, 45, 93.

described by liberal commentators as a *Sumpf*, or swamp. The harshness of this
'scientifically' based liberal critique was perhaps most evident in the frequency
with which metaphors of disease were employed. Religious orders were 'out-
growths of diseased aberrations of human social drives'; action should be taken
against them as one would act against 'phylloxera, Colorado beetle, and other
enemies of the Reich'.[44] Virchow, himself a pathologist and popularizer of medicine, could be equally scathing. Visiting Catholic Silesia during a major typhoid
epidemic in 1849, he had observed that the clerically subjugated population was
'lazy, unclean, dog-like in its devotion, and inflexibly averse to any physical or
mental exertion'; the people were 'physically and mentally weak', marked by
'lethargy and bestial submissiveness'.[45] Here, pathology was inextricably tied to
social pathology: disease was a form of social and cultural maladjustment.[46] Most
interesting from the point of view of the enthusiasm unleashed by the Marian
apparitions, Virchow also included 'psychic epidemics' in his account. 'The
artificial epidemics are physical or mental, for mental diseases also occur epi-
demically and tear entire peoples into a mad psychotic movement'.[47]

In the 1870s, Virchow (the 'Pope of medicine') stood at the point where
medical and scientific *gravitas* lent legitimacy to liberal anti-clericalism.[48] His own
interest during that period in the Belgian stigmatist Louise Lateau was part of a
burgeoning contemporary concern with 'mania', 'possession', and 'frenzies'.[49]
Much of this growing body of work was concerned with individual pathological
behaviour. This was true of the case-studies on 'religious mania' and 'religious
hysteria' offered by Krafft-Ebing in his *Lehrbuch der gerichtlichen Psychopathologie*
(1875) and *Lehrbuch der Psychiatrie* (1879–80).[50] Here, as in the contemporary
work of Heinrich Kisch and others, religious ecstasies and visions were reduced to
a form of hysteria resulting from displaced sexuality. Thus, for Kisch, menopausal
women were more predisposed to manifest 'that tendency towards religious
enthusiasm (*Schwärmerei*) which often degenerates into disease'.[51] Others,

[44] A writer in the liberal-nationalist *Im neuen Reich*, cited in Kissling, *Geschichte*, iii. 58.
[45] E. Meyer, *Rudolf Virchow* (Wiesbaden, 1956), 39, 41. See also Boyd, 'Rudolf Virchow', 21–4.
[46] See G. Rosen, *Madness in Society: Chapters in the Historical Sociology of Mental Illness* (Chicago, 1968), 179–80.
[47] Ibid. 180. Virchow believed, like the German specialist on mental disorders Carl Stark, that when the Franco-Prussian war broke out the French might have been gripped by some form of collective insanity: Boyd, 'Rudolf Virchow', 137–8.
[48] See Bauer, *Virchow*, 79, on Virchow as the *Medizinpapst*.
[49] Virchow presented a paper 'Über Wunder' (on miracles) to a Sept. 1873 meeting of the German Association of Natural Scientists in Breslau, in which he denied the validity of Louise Lateau's reported experiences. Text in K. Sudhoff (ed.), *Rudolf Virchow und die deutschen Naturforscherversammlungen* (Leipzig, 1922), 155–64. For German scholarly interest in Louise Lateau, see N.-J. Cornet, *Louise Lateau et la science allemande* (Brussels and Paris, 1875).
[50] Krafft-Ebing, *Lehrbuch der gerichtlichen Psychopathologie*, 200–2 ('Beob. 86. Hysterischer Irresein. (Religiöser Wahnsinn)'); *Lehrbuch der Psychiatrie*, ii. 90–3 ('Die religiöse Verücktheit'); ii. 116–17 ('Transitorische Irreseinzustände'); ibid. iii. 87–90 ('Zur religiösen Verücktheit').
[51] E. H. Kisch, *Das klimakterische Alter der Frauen in physiologischer und pathologischer Beziehung* (1874), cited in P. Gay, *The Bourgeois Experience: Victoria to Freud*, ii. *The Tender Passion* (Oxford, 1986), 287. See Gay generally, 284 ff. on this subject.

Virchow included, were interested in moving beyond the categories of individual 'hysteria' and 'mania', to establish the theme of collective hysteria. Both motifs recurred in liberal treatment of the apparitions at Marpingen and elsewhere. The theme of individual hysteria was the more muted of the two, perhaps because the voice of science in the form of the St Wendel medical officer of health, Dr Brauneck, pronounced judgement that the three visionaries could not be diagnosed in these terms. But repeated efforts were made in the liberal press to brand Marpingen by linking it to the utterances of mental asylum inmates, and it was suggested that supporters of Marpingen, Berschweiler, and Geismühle, were the victims of a collective pathology. The *Rhein- und Ruhr-Zeitung* viewed the Geismühle affair as an 'infectious disease'.[52] Even the *Frankfurter Zeitung*, most sceptical and sardonic of liberal papers when it came to pompous claims about scientific culture, applied the label of 'epidemic popular disease' to Marpingen.[53]

When liberals thought of Catholics in terms of an infestation of Colorado beetle, waters that required draining, or the carriers of an infectious disease, scientific language bore a dehumanizing message. One aspect of the liberal relationship to Catholics that made such a posture easier, and at the same time reinforced it, was class. The angry, bitter contempt displayed towards the Catholic 'masses' was a constant in liberal attacks on the apparitions. Part of this was the old progressive jibe about the idiocy of rural life, what the *Saar- und Mosel-Zeitung* called the 'ignorant rural population'.[54] Automatic surprise was registered that 'even townspeople' should have been drawn to the apparition sites.[55] But the derision extended to the Catholic lower orders more generally. The supporters of Marpingen were, in one account, fanaticized 'mob-masses' (*Pöbel-Massen*).[56] Pilgrims were regularly described as lower-class and ill-educated; one eyewitness even wrote about their 'stupid appearance', before going on to deride the 'screaming of the mob'.[57] The satisfaction with which liberals brandished examples of 'indignation' about the apparitions among propertied or educated middle-class Catholics made the same point in reverse: it underlined the association between Marpingen and the lower orders.[58] One theme in these commentaries was the way in which popular support for the apparitions cut into normal working hours and undermined work-discipline. In one of many examples, the *Saar- und Mosel-Zeitung* described the apparition movement as a 'scandalous' attack on the 'savings, working time, and remaining common sense of our Catholic rural population'.[59]

[52] Cited in *SMZ*, 5 Apr. 1877.
[53] *FZ*, 17 Jan. 1878.
[54] *SMZ*, 15 Aug. 1876.
[55] *KZ*, 6 Sept. 1876, citing the *Rhein- und Ruhr-Zeitung*.
[56] *NBZ*, 19 Sept. 1876.
[57] 'An der Gnadenstätte', 666–9.
[58] *DAZ*, 23 Aug. 1876, on the 'indignation of the educated parts of the ultramontane population'.
[59] *SMZ*, 22 Aug. 1876.

At one level, of course, the liberals presented an accurate broad-brush picture of who the pilgrims were: mainly miners, craftsmen, and peasants, alongside a few prominent aristocrats, with the Catholic bourgeoisie significantly under-represented. But the liberal sociology of apparition crowds also revealed some-thing about liberals themselves. The disdain towards pilgrims reflected a larger unease on the part of liberal notables (*Honoratioren*) when faced with popular sentiment. The propertied and educated middle class were dominant among the parliamentarians, local leadership, and intellectuals of left liberals and National Liberals alike. They viewed property and education as prerequisites for inde-pendence, without which it was difficult to discharge the responsibilities of the mature citizen (*mündiger Bürger*).[60] While left liberals continued to advocate education and the strengthening of property-owning (through cheaper credit, producer co-operatives, and the like) as a means of creating a 'society of citizens' after this liberal image, there are signs of a frustrated liberal disenchantment with what they saw as the shortcomings of an 'ignorant', 'dependent' populace. Nowhere was this more apparent than in liberal anxiety over universal manhood suffrage. Warnings about the dangers it threatened were often couched in terms that recall the harshness of liberal commentary on lower-class pilgrims. The National Liberal historian and politician Heinrich Treitschke rejected a system under which 'the uneducated, immature, and unreliable man would have as much influence as someone who is wise, industrious, and patriotic'. Even a supporter of universal manhood suffrage such as Hermann Schulze-Delitzsch warned about stimulating the 'passions' of the lower orders. He did so in language that, once again, paralleled the liberal response to German apparitions in the way that it dehumanized its subjects. It was, suggested Schulze-Delitzsch, all too easy 'to cross the dark borderline where the animal touches on the human'; and the 'unbound beast', once aroused, would 'tear everything apart with its lion claws'. Another prominent liberal, Max Weber's mentor Hermann Baumgarten, spoke scathingly of 'the dominance of the raw instincts of the masses'.[61]

Popular and political Catholicism, perhaps even more than the independent working-class movement that emerged in the 1860s and 1870s, showed the limits of liberal sympathy for the lower classes. And both demonstrated the limits of liberal optimism. The cult of the Virgin, like the cults of working-class leaders, seemed to liberals to demonstrate the wilful popular rejection of wiser counsel, namely liberal tutelage.[62] These developments drove many liberals into a belea-guered insistence on culture as the property of the educated, and events like those

---

[60] On liberal ideas of citizenship and society, L. Gall, 'Liberalismus und "Bürgerliche Gesellschaft": Zu Charakter und Entwicklung der liberalen Bewegung in Deutschland', *Historische Zeitschrift*, 220 (1975), 324–56.

[61] M. Gugel, *Industrieller Aufstieg und bürgerliche Herrschaft* (Cologne, 1975), 184–8; J. J. Sheehan, *German Liberalism in the Nineteenth Century* (Chicago, 1978), 104–7; W. J. Mommsen, *Max Weber and German Politics* (Chicago, 1985), 6.

[62] On the cult of Ferdinand Lassalle, for example, see Grote, *Sozialdemokratie*. A similar cult grew around the Saarland miners' leader, Nikolaus Warken. See Mallmann, 'Nikolaus Warken'.

at Marpingen reinforced this tendency. In the press and political battles over the meaning of the apparitions, liberals drew a clear line between 'independent, educated, liberal' and 'dependent, ignorant, Catholic'. This was always more likely to induce a backlash among Catholics than to convince them; indeed it provided perfect ammunition for the lay and clerical leaders of Catholic Germany, who were rarely above a spot of demagogy. While the Centre Party leader Ludwig Windthorst observed (with some exaggeration) that the *Kulturkampf* was 'a struggle waged by German professors against the Catholic Church', supporters of the apparitions were happy to assure the faithful that the popular, heartfelt belief in this sign of grace represented a suitable come-uppance for the cold, arrogant liberal prophets of cultural progress.[63] Perceptive liberals could see the same thing. The independently minded left-liberal *Frankfurter Zeitung* saw a direct causal link between 'the ballyhoo about beating the cultural drum' (*der Tamtam der großen Kulturpauke*), or 'stuffing people full of culture' (*Kulturpaukerei*), and 'the Madonnas of the fields, woods, and meadows'.[64]

Liberal disdain for the lower-class character of the apparition movements was joined by distaste for the disproportionate degree of enthusiasm they aroused among women. Once again, the empirical evidence on the over-representation of women among visionaries and supporters of apparitions is undeniable, but the manner in which liberals referred to the role of women at places like Marpingen was also part of a larger liberal tendency to construct their categories of the good and bad citizen in male–female terms. When the statutes of a liberal party branch required that a candidate for membership be 'a man who has reached majority, is of blameless character, and is independent', the gender exclusion was, of course, made necessary by the prevailing laws of association.[65] But in many ways the exclusion of women corresponded to the liberals' own equation of maleness with maturity and civic character. Max Forckenbeck wanted the National Liberals to offer a 'manly defence' of what they had achieved in parliament; Heinrich Kruse of the liberal *Kölnische Zeitung* was praised for the paper's 'firm, manly role' in resisting 'clerical intrigue'; the committee of the anticlerical Deutscher Verein of the Rhine Province congratulated its president, the historian Sybel, on the 'manly demeanour' with which he responded to unjust attacks; Eduard Lasker, in a passionate speech on the rule of law, observed that 'the true man is the independent citizen' (and the reverse was no doubt true).[66] Women were regarded as being too emotional for full participation in public affairs: to involve them in such matters would violate their own nature. They should confine their activities to the private sphere, for they lacked the necessary

[63] Windthorst quoted in Kissling, *Geschichte*, iii. 168.

[64] *FZ*, 16 Jan. 1878.

[65] Statutes of the Progressive Party in Rothenburg, Bavaria: G. Eisfeld, *Die Entstehung der liberalen Parteien in Deutschland 1858–1870* (Hanover, 1969), 132.

[66] O. Pflanze, *Bismarck and the Development of Germany*, 3 vols. (Princeton, NJ, 1990), ii. 354; Wentzcke, *Im neuen Reich*, 126; Seyffardt, *Erinnerungen*, 148–9; Funk, *Polizei und Rechtsstaat*, 115.

independence for true civic engagement.[67] Catholic women aroused particular liberal concern. One object of persistent liberal animus was the nun, the woman who rejected the bourgeois roles of wife and mother and was viewed as the very embodiment of 'medievalism'—of superstition, sloth, and unnatural practices.[68] More important, Catholic laywomen were seen as the cat's-paws of the priest, the weaker vessels through whom the clergy maintained its malign grip.[69] Endless stories were recounted of the priest influencing women inside and outside the confessional box, moulding the character of children through control over the mother and coming between husband and wife in order to influence Catholic men through their womenfolk.[70]

The liberal response to Marpingen contained examples of all these views. The greater susceptibility of girls and women to emotion-laden mysticism was a frequent argument, beginning with the visionaries themselves: 'The maids favoured by the deity (young lads are not quite so suitable for such a high audience) were the heroes of the day.'[71] The local advocates of the apparitions were 'madwomen', those who visited the site 'hysterical women', the stories believed by pilgrims 'old wives' tales'.[72] Liberal accounts sometimes struck a cruel note. One description of pilgrims at Marpingen suggested that 'old women (alte Weiber) would have turned cartwheels with delight if they had been able to do such a thing'.[73] Another described a solitary pilgrim: 'An elderly woman had already adorned her neck with crosses and Marian medals hung on four chains, so that she rattled like a carthorse.'[74] Liberals did not fail to notice that middle-class pilgrims were generally female, and a good deal of ribaldry was directed at pious women from better-off Catholic circles. One writer saw fifty or sixty pilgrims gathered at St Wendel 'dressed in town clothes':

[67] See, once again, Rudolf Virchow, *Über die Erziehung des Weibes für seinen Beruf. Eine Vorlesung gehalten im Hörsaale des grauen Klosters zu Berlin am 20. Februar 1865* (Berlin, 1865). It should be noted, however, that left liberalism was more advanced than any other non-socialist political movement in calling later in the 19th cent. for the public emancipation of women.

[68] A liberal petition in 1869 described closed orders as 'hotbeds of superstition, fornication, and sloth': Anderson, *Windthorst*, 124.

[69] See *SMZ*, 19 July 1876, which observed in the course of an article about 'clerical France' that 'almost all the women allow themselves to be led blindly by the priests'.

[70] Liberal allegations about misuse of the confessional box are cited in B. Duhr, *Jesuiten-Fabeln* (Freiburg, 1891), 479, 746–61. Apocryphal stories were constantly recycled through the liberal press. There are close parallels in French anticlericalism, the classic account being Jules Michelet, *Priests, Women, and Families* (London, 1845). See also T. Zeldin, 'The Conflict of Moralities: Confession, Sin and Pleasure in the Nineteenth Century', in Zeldin (ed.), *Conflicts in French Society* (London, 1970), 13–50. The relationship of women with their priests is something that anti-ultramontane Catholic writers also touched on. See Kraus, *Tagebücher*, 358 (diary entry of 15 May 1875). There is a certain irony here, for Kraus exemplified the issue he was writing about: he enjoyed many very close relations with women, leading in at least one case to great jealousy on the part of the husband. See ibid. 348, 351–2.

[71] *SMZ*, 19 July 1876.

[72] *SMZ*, 18 July 1876; *NBZ*, 21 Oct. 1876; *DAZ*, 17 Aug. 1876.

[73] *SMZ*, 19 July 1876.

[74] 'Bei der Madonna', 30.

They were almost exclusively members of the fair sex, of an age at which one 'is too old to be playful, too young to be without desires'. As they quickly separated themselves off from the 'mob' with turned-up noses and instinctively kept their own company, there emerged a charming collection of chattering old maids (schnatternder alter Jungfern) such as I had never before seen gathered together in one place in such abundance.[75]

An account in the Gartenlaube of Dittrichswalde pilgrims was more concerned with younger Catholic women. As the reporter waited with pilgrims for the train, 'there was a very distinct group that formed around a pious curate, a charming row of young middle-class women aged 17 to 20, with well-developed forms forced into modern dresses and the dove-like expressions so treasured by the Roman clergy'. The train itself was full of 'pilgrims seeking salvation, mainly of the angelic sex'. The reporter shared a compartment with a priest and

eight of the 'delightful children' entrusted to his spiritual supervision [who] found comfortable quarters there. It offered a charming, perhaps rather modern picture of a pilgrimage, as we sat in rows of five, the priest (Geweihete) and I opposite each other while each of us had next to him four young maidens shining with the angelic embellishments of innocence.[76]

One Catholic supporter of the apparitions observed that 'the so-called liberal press courageously assailed and still assails Marpingen in terms that certainly do not suggest calm thought and judgements, but point rather to a vehement passion that finds the Marpingen events very uncomfortable'.[77] It is hard to disagree with this. The language and the analytical categories that liberals brought to their discussion of the apparitions reveal men who were ill at ease and reacted with a verbal barrage that included irony, sarcasm, and bitter denunciation. It is difficult not to see in this the voicing of anxieties within a male, middle-class liberalism about a movement in which women were conspicuous, together with peasants and miners. The class- and gender-specific elements of liberal attacks were joined, as we have seen, by harsh strictures on Catholic backwardness, couched in the language of scientific progress. This also suggests liberals' unease about their own capacity to dispel the powers of 'darkness'. We must try to understand the frustration felt by liberal observers of Marpingen: they saw it as a nonsense, a monstrous provocation, and felt (with some reason) that those Catholics who tried to speak out against the apparitions were drowned by the waves of popular sentiment, or cowed into silence. But frustration breeds its own violence. The liberals' was mainly verbal, but the effect of the language they used was to dehumanize Catholics who were involved in or supported the apparitions. This no doubt made it easier for many liberals to contemplate with equanimity the repression meted out in Marpingen.

[75] 'An der Gnadenstätte', 666. When the 'Virgin in the ink-bottle' incident occurred in March 1877, one liberal newspaper noted sarcastically that the teacher should have let it develop: 'A few ladies of the better class (Honoratiorendamen) would undoubtedly have hurried to the scene, to stare at the miracle and proclaim it to the whole world': Mayener Zeitung, cited in the SMZ, 4 Apr. 1877.
[76] 'Bei der Madonna', 29.
[77] MWOL, 4.

Liberals, Marpingen, and the State

Liberal reactions to the military and police measures were not entirely uniform.
They ranged from the warm support offered by almost all National Liberals to
the doubts expressed by some left-liberal voices. Within the National-Liberal
camp, the response to the official crack-down varied only between the enthusiastic
and the very enthusiastic. The relish with which the National-Liberal mayor
Wilhelm Woytt pursued the adherents of Marpingen was echoed in the party
press. The *Nahe-Blies-Zeitung* devoted a long commentary in early September
1876 to 'the Marpingen Movement', treating the events as an attempt to breed
hatred of the Reich and Prussia among Catholics. It argued that 'peace, security,
and the entire state order' were at stake, and urged those with the power of
authority (*der obrigkeitliche Gewalt*) to 'proceed with maximum energy against
this anti-state and treasonable agitation'. The measures already taken 'could only
be approved. In questions of power, one should not act hesitantly or gently, what
matters is to meet force with force.'[78] A few weeks later, the newspaper took issue
with Catholic complaints:

Like the Poles, our ultramontanes recognize only rights and never obligations towards the
state, and unfortunately it cannot be denied that because of the excessive forbearance and
indulgence of the state government they receive all too much encouragement to persist in
this good-for-nothing viewpoint.

On this occasion, the paper called for the criminal police to be sent in.[79] In
December it advocated the permanent stationing of a squadron of cavalry, or a
battalion of infantry, in St Wendel, suggesting that a new garrison be constructed
there.[80] Other local National-Liberal papers took the same line. After the military
intervention, the editor of the *Saar- und Mosel-Zeitung* observed: 'The rapid
success of the vigorous measures taken proves once again conclusively that in
such situations the only response is to take decisive action without delay, then
these miracle-craving goings-on immediately cease.'[81] That, of course, is exactly
what they did not do, and the following month the paper was still demanding
'energetic counter-measures' against the clerical plot.[82] In October 1876 it invited
the government to conclude from the continuing publicity for Marpingen that
'here the most rigorous determination is indispensable, even if the present occupation of the apparition site has to go on for years'.[83]

[78] *NBZ*, 7 Sept. 1876.
[79] *NBZ*, 5 Oct. 1876.
[80] *NBZ*, 12 Dec. 1876.
[81] *SMZ*, 15 July 1876.
[82] *SMZ*, 24 Aug. 1876.
[83] *SMZ*, 31 Oct. 1876; also issue of 15 Nov. 1876. However, the paper was sympathetic to complaints
about the levy imposed on Marpingen to pay for unwanted extra policing, arguing that the regulations
cited by the local authorities did not apply to such a case. What pilgrims did in Marpingen, argued the
paper, had no more to do directly with villagers than if the Härtelwald had been occupied by gendarmes
because 'a gang of thieves had made it their gathering place': *SMZ*, 29 Sept. 1876.

Major National-Liberal newspapers made similar points. The *Deutsche Allgemeine Zeitung* expressed satisfaction that the Marpingen district had effectively been declared 'in a state of siege (*Belagerungszustand*)', adding, 'one can only hope that these harsh measures will induce calm in the agitated population'.[84] The *Kölnische Zeitung* observed approvingly that the state was not treating Marpingen as a 'harmless game' (*daß man hier keinen Spaß versteht*): all the measures that 'public morality demands of the state' would be taken to resist ultramontane 'hocus-pocus'.[85] Like its local counterparts, the Cologne paper called consistently for 'energetic measures', and praised them when they were taken. When the *Kölnische Zeitung* reported on the searching of priests' homes and the role played by 'Marlow', it rubbed its hands at this 'surprise for our *Finsterlinge*'.[86] The response calls to mind the National-Liberal leader Rudolf Bennigsen, writing cheerfully to his wife in 1875 that a new piece of *Kulturkampf* legislation would 'go off like a bomb under the clericals'.[87] This was the authentic voice of National Liberalism in the 1870s. Vigorous action by the state against the 'clericals' was not only accepted; it was demanded and applauded. National Liberals saw the justification for the suppression of Marpingen, as they saw the justification of the *Kulturkampf* as a whole, in the need to preserve security and order in the new Germany.[88] It was National Liberals, rather than left liberals, who laid particular emphasis on the 'French threat' behind Marpingen (and the 'Polish threat' behind Dittrichswalde): the apparitions were not so much an outrage against universal reason as a blot on national dignity. National Liberals also emphasized the need to maintain law and order—especially order. From this perspective, ultramontanism, like the growing working-class movement (and the 'red curates' who abetted it), presented the alternatives of 'order or chaos'.[89] When it came to confrontations between Catholics and officials or soldiers at Marpingen, National Liberals gave their support to the latter on principle, as the embodiment of order.[90]

Critics of arbitrary state actions in Marpingen, including some within the liberal camp, only reinforced National Liberals' determination: it bolstered their own self-image as men of fixed purpose who, like the Prussian state, were prepared to see things through to the end. Reactions to the apparitions and the

---

[84] *DAZ*, 17 Aug. 1876.

[85] *KZ*, 26 Aug. 1876.

[86] *KZ*, 20 Oct. 1876; also issue of 3 Nov. 1876.

[87] H. Oncken, *Rudolf Bennigsen. Ein deutscher liberaler Politiker*, 2 vols. (Stuttgart and Leipzig, 1910), ii. 280: Bennigsen to his wife, 10 Apr. 1875.

[88] Eduard Lasker, anxious about the implications of the *Kulturkampf* for the rule of law, was the only real dissenting voice among leading National Liberals. He and Bennigsen were the only National Liberals to vote against the expulsion of the Jesuits. See A. Laufs, *Eduard Lasker. Ein Leben für den Rechtsstaat* (Göttingen and Zurich, 1984), 83–8; S. Zucker, *Ludwig Bamberger* (Pittsburgh, 1975), 87–104.

[89] For a linking of the two themes, see the *Badische Landeszeitung* in 1873 (quoted in Machtan and Ott, 'Batzbier!', 158), arguing that such a dangerous war-like situation had arisen domestically 'that all friends of order are required to rally firmly around the flag'; the alternative was 'order or chaos'.

[90] On liberals, the law, and the strong state, see John, *Politics and the Law*, 49–53.

way they were dealt with formed part of a larger National-Liberal siege mentality during the *Kulturkampf*, a mirror-image of the siege mentality among Catholics. Writing on 'the *Kulturkampf* after three years', the *National-Zeitung* observed sternly that there could be no going back, and warned against those with a 'sentimental leaning towards reconciliation'.[91] The party leader Bennigsen also emphasized the arduousness of the task: to settle accounts with the Jesuits and their followers would 'demand a long time, much strength, persistence, and circumspection'.[92] The same theme was sounded in the *Saar- und Mosel-Zeitung*. Pledging its own support to the state, it continued: 'The Prussian state is strong enough, one should be quite clear about that, despite the pygmy army of inflammatory curates (*Hetzkapläne*) and despite all papal curses, to be able to endure the *Kulturkampf*, even if it should last for generations.'[93] Strength, persistence, endurance, lack of sentimentality: this was a catalogue of manly virtues, the self-image with which National Liberals flattered themselves as they 'struggled'—or backed the struggle of the state—against the clerical enemy. The National Liberals were to be rewarded for this unstinting support of the state by Bismarck's decision to end the *Kulturkampf*, for reasons of political opportunism and alarm at the radical implications of the struggle. Marpingen demonstrated the same process in miniature: National Liberals urged no surrender over an affair in which the state eventually backed down with some loss of face.

The left-liberal stance on Marpingen also illustrated a larger problem, although a different one. Left liberals were more alert to the dangers of the repressive state, even when it acted in the name of progress. Against the National-Liberal emphasis on order, they were more inclined to stress the rule of law. Marpingen aroused misgivings on this score. The *Vossische Zeitung* might remark blithely that it took only 'a few soldiers . . . to drive away the apparitions', but it was nevertheless critical of the general handling of events: 'very dubious things have occurred which are difficult to square with the law.'[94] The *Frankfurter Zeitung* was much more critical. While the National-Liberal press ignored the spring 1877 trial of Matthias Scheeben for libelling the Prussian army, the *Frankfurter Zeitung* reported what a miserable figure the prosecution had cut.[95] While liberals habitually used the word *Ausschreitungen*—'outrage', or 'excesses'—to describe the apparitions, the *Frankfurter Zeitung* pinned the label on the conduct of the state.[96] Marpingen, it argued, was a swindle that would have been better dealt with by a 'a manly and honourable word and open discussion' than by gendarmes and 'punitive Prussians' (*Strafpreußen*); the law was the law, however unsympathetic

---

[91] *NZ*, 13 Sept. 1876. While the *Kulturkampf* was a 'possibility' for Bismarck, it was an 'absolute necessity' for the *National-Zeitung*, which consistently argued for the 'strictest prosecution' of the struggle: E. G. Friehe, *Geschichte der 'National-Zeitung' 1848 bis 1878* (Leipzig, 1933), 161.

[92] Oncken, *Bennigsen*, ii. 235–6: Bennigsen to his wife, 21 Nov. 1871.

[93] *SMZ*, 7 Mar. 1877.

[94] *VZ*, 15 Oct. 1876, 17 Jan. 1878.

[95] *FZ*, 30 May 1877.

[96] *FZ*, 17 Jan. 1878.

those who claimed its protection.[97] These reservations about the arbitrary actions taken at Marpingen were of a piece with the concern voiced by some left liberals about the overall character of the *Kulturkampf*. The *Frankfurter Zeitung* once again led the field. It criticized left liberals who supported the *Kulturkampf*, regularly attacked petty measures and imprisonments, and in January 1875 instituted a fortnightly '*Kulturkampf*-calendar' that detailed coercive administrative actions.[98] Among prominent left-liberal politicians, Eugen Richter was especially critical of the authoritarian methods employed in the *Kulturkampf*. These were weapons 'from the armoury of reaction', he argued: liberals who supported their use threatened to undermine their own position.[99] Others saw the dangers, of course, not least Rudolf Virchow, a long-standing opponent of Bismarck and the ethos of 'Borussianism'. Yet Virchow and others swallowed their doubts when it came to the *Kulturkampf*. Why?

The left liberals' response to the apparitions helps to uncover the logic that governed their actions in the *Kulturkampf* as a whole. Left-liberal criticism of the apparitions seldom displayed the positive relish for the wielding of state power that was habitual among National Liberals. The left-liberal emphasis lay more on superstition than conspiracy, more on cultural degradation than the threat to the state. The question was whether their more fastidious concerns could be easily separated from the defence of the powerful state championed by National Liberals. Left liberals were, to some degree, thrown back on the state because of the distance that separated them from popular sentiment. That was the problem with the *Frankfurter Zeitung*'s solution to events like those at Marpingen—the 'manly and honourable word'. The approach itself hinted at the Olympian, patriciaɪ. style of notable politics that characterized left liberals almost as much as their National Liberal counterparts. It was the same approach that led left liberals to dwell distastefully on the stupidity of the lower orders attracted to Marpingen, and permitted politicians like Virchow and Schulze-Delitzsch to speak unabashedly of middle-class 'tutelage' as a key to the social question. The dehumanizing metaphors of 'disease' and 'stagnation' that recurred in left-liberal as well as National-Liberal attacks on apparitions point to the harsher underpinnings of this world-view. German left liberalism lacked the common touch, a problem that was already apparent by the 1870s in the diminishing electoral support for the party. The *Kulturkampf* brought the problem home. The term may have been coined by Virchow, the intention may have been an enlightened crusade against obscurantism; but the reality was a struggle that lacked consent and the methods by which it was conducted were, from the first, coercive and 'Bismarckian'. As a result, left liberals found themselves facing a series of Marpingens.

---

[97] *FZ*, 16 Jan. 1878.

[98] J. Haller, *Geschichte der Frankfurter Zeitung* (Frankfurt am Main, 1911), 246–53.

[99] I. S. Lorenz, *Eugen Richter. Der entschiedene Liberalismus im wilhelminischer Zeit 1871 bis 1906* (Husum, 1980), 116, and 111–25 generally.

The price paid by left liberals for the defence of culture was high. The case of Hermann Schulze-Delitzsch is indicative. A figure known mainly for his effort to organize co-operatives, he welcomed the fact that the Prussian government was prepared to take 'energetic' action against the 'clerical damage to cultural progress'; indeed he called for a 'ruthless struggle' against ultramontanism. This led him to support all the potentially repressive legislation of the *Kulturkampf*, from the original May Laws onwards. Like other left liberals, he was—as his biographer neatly puts it—prepared to take up Bismarck's offer to conduct 'proxy wars' (*Stellvertreterkriege*).[100] The same logic can be seen in the case of Virchow. He was troubled by the content of various *Kulturkampf* laws, but accepted them none the less. As Constantin Frantz observed cruelly, about one such measure: 'Deputy Virchow called [the proposal] dictatorship, and was able to accept the law only with a heavy heart, although he was relieved by the feeling that such a dictatorship was indispensable for the progress of culture.'[101] So it went, too, over Marpingen. Many left liberals were troubled by evidence of coercion and arbitrariness, but few were troubled enough to believe that the costs outweighed the benefits. As a result, the Prussian state, which in the 1850s and 1860s had disciplined and dismissed liberal officials, was now cast by left liberals in the role of progressive cultural steamroller.

[100] R. Aldenhoff, *Schulze-Delitzsch. Ein Beitrag zur Geschichte des Liberalismus zwischen Revolution und Reichsgründung* (Baden-Baden, 1984), 233. A similar point is made in an older work on German liberalism: O. Klein-Hattingen, *Die Geschichte des deutschen Liberalismus*, 2 vols. (Berlin and Schöneberg, 1911–12), ii. 49–55.

[101] C. Frantz, *Die Religion des Nationalliberalismus* (Leipzig, 1872), 105. See also Boyd, 'Rudolf Virchow', 146. The measure in question was the opening shot in the *Kulturkampf*, the abolition of the section of the Prussian Ministry of Public Worship dealing with Catholic affairs.

PART III

The Aftermath

10

The State Climbs Down

Legal Reverses

Was Prussia a state bound by the rule of law? Events in Marpingen caused many to doubt it. After the village schoolteacher André had been summarily transferred to Tholey, Father Schneider wrote to a clerical friend in Trier asking for legal advice on the situation. The reply was that an action of this kind was impermissible without formal disciplinary proceedings—'but in Russia everything is possible'.[1] The equating of Prussia and Russia gives an indication of Catholic bitterness over Marpingen. A friend of Neureuter's from Zwolle wrote in the following terms, in a letter that ironically enough was seized by the authorities, having arrived shortly after the parish priest had been taken into custody:[2] 'Are you ill or in prison; for anything is possible—silence is golden in Germany, even if elsewhere the problem is lead. Moreover, private letters should not be sniffed at by everyone and in Prussia-Germany only the cabinet of the chancellor is private.' The actions of the state in Marpingen worried many beyond the ranks of Catholics, from the *Frankfurter Zeitung* on the left to the *Kreuz-Zeitung* on the right. For the latter, the dubious role played by Meerscheidt-Hüllessem and the treatment of the visionary children were 'weak points that the government might well find it difficult to defend'. Police measures had been an inappropriate choice of weapon, and the government might regret its methods if 'absolutely tangible and convincing evidence' of deliberate deception and criminal actions could not be produced.[3]

That was just what was not forthcoming, with consequences that turned out to be politically embarrassing. The government's case began to unravel within weeks of the wave of arrests in autumn 1876. On 17 November the four adult 'visionaries' were released from remand. They issued a statement on 28 November publicizing their release and claiming that their reputations had been falsely impugned.[4] Just two days later the Superior Court in Saarbrücken considered an appeal against the Guardianship Court decision on which the incarceration of

[1] LASB, E 107, 374–5.
[2] Ibid. 416.
[3] Cited in *MWOL*, 83–4. Compare similar criticisms of Meerscheidt-Hüllessem in the *Kreuz-Zeitung*, cited in Rebbert, *Marpingen und seine Gegner*, 93–4.
[4] LASB, E 107, 250; Radziwill, *Besuch*, 28.

the three visionary children rested. The court overturned the original judgement on the grounds that no evidence had been uncovered showing the children to be guilty of deception or any other offence, and ruled that the decision to send the three girls to the Prince Wilhelm and Marianne Institute had been 'premature'.[5] The government immediately announced its intention to appeal, and the release of the girls was deferred. But they were freed twelve days later, when the Ministry of the Interior in Berlin decided—after receiving a report from Trier—that the government's appeal did not provide sufficient warrant to hold the girls. Prince Radziwill had also requested that a criminal investigation be carried out against the executive of the institute, on the grounds of unlawful deprivation of liberty.[6] Fathers Neureuter and Schneider had, meanwhile, been released on 1 December. They were followed on 20 December by the communal forester Karl Altmeyer, the watchman Jakob Langendörfer and Angela Kles, against whom evidence of placing flowers at the apparition site and gathering money 'had not been corroborated'.[7]

By Christmas 1876, all those who had been remanded were back at home, while evidence of criminal wrongdoing in Marpingen continued to prove elusive. The new year brought a further series of legal reverses. On 30 January, the Court of Appeal (*Obertribunal*) in Berlin upheld the decision of the Superior Court in Saarbrücken against the appeal of the state.[8] The zealous actions of the gendarmes in Marpingen also received a series of tacit rebukes in local courts. At hearings in the Tholey magistrates' court during January and early February, large numbers of pilgrims were acquitted. The same thing occurred at mass appearances before the court in St Wendel of persons apprehended in the Härtelwald (others received token fines of 3 marks). The judgements in St Wendel had a particularly interesting background. The presiding magistrate there, Comes, had had his fingers burned when his Guardianship Court judgement the previous autumn was strongly criticized on appeal and overturned. Whether or not he was affected by this experience, Comes became more circumspect. Noting the huge number of cases coming up that concerned trespass in the Härtelwald, the magistrate visited the site himself on 18 January, together with the senior district forester and the acting *Ortsvorsteher* of Marpingen, to see the circumstances from which the charges arose. The mass acquittals at the next court session in St Wendel followed this visit. Other courts took a similar line. A peasant from Lauschied, tried in Saarbrücken at the beginning of March on a charge of leading an illegal procession to Marpingen, was fined 5 marks rather than the 100 marks demanded by the public prosecutor.[9]

Much more humiliating for the state was the outcome of the legal proceedings

[5] LASB, E 107, 62; Radziwill, *Besuch*, 52–3; *MWOL*, 73.
[6] LHAK, 442/6442, 51 ff.; *MWOL*, 73–4, 77. See also *Germania*, 14 Dec. 1876.
[7] LASB, E 107, 263, 275–8; *MWOL*, 74, 78.
[8] The judgement of the Court of Appeal is given in full in Radziwill, *Besuch*, 53–4.
[9] *MWOL*, 91; *SMZ*, 22 Feb. and 4 Mar. 1877; *Anlagen zu den Stenographischen Berichten* . . . *1877–1878*, ii. 1069–73: No. 139, Bachem und Genossen.

in which the theologian Matthias Scheeben was charged with defaming the Prussian army. He had written an article in the *Kölnische Volkszeitung* suggesting that the troops at Marpingen had conducted themselves worse than if they had been in an occupied country. Scheeben appeared first on 14 April before the Cologne criminal court, where the witnesses called by the state cut such a poor figure that the defendant was acquitted on the grounds that his comments were substantially true. In its judgement, the court noted that Captain Fragstein-Riemsdorff and his officers had placed themselves in a 'seriously compromised' position. The state appealed, and the whole process was repeated at the local court of appeal (*Appellationsgericht*) the following month. Once again, military witnesses talked of the threatening crowds in Marpingen, and the physical attack on Sergeant Wolter. Mayor Woytt testified to the 'obstructive' behaviour of the parish priest and village officials, and described village responses to the soldiers as 'passive resistance in the true sense of the word'. On the other side, a string of villagers appeared before the court with a very different account of events, one that predictably echoed Scheeben's own. They included the carter who had been clubbed, others who had witnessed the military intervention at first hand, and a miller and baker who had been the object of requisitioning sorties.

Senior Prosecutor Crome suggested that 'all the defence witnesses in this matter are unreliable and untrustworthy', a remark that caused a disturbance among the public and led the presiding judge to threaten to clear the court. Why were these witnesses untrustworthy? Because, argued Crome, they had a vested interest in the apparitions and had themselves run foul of the law. The prosecutor went on to paint a picture of 'desperate' circumstances in which the soldiers were being 'mocked by the fanatical populace', the priest stayed at home rubbing his hands over the 'swindle', and local officials proved 'refractory'. 'Gentle methods would have been of little use', he concluded—adding, however, that if rifle butts had to fall, it would have been better if they had fallen not on those who had been 'led astray' but on those who had 'staged the whole affair'. It was left to the defence counsel, Julius Bachem, to point to the initial over-reactions of Woytt and District Secretary Besser, to establish the contradictions in the soldiers' evidence and show that (on their own testimony) any 'resistance' from villagers or other unidentified persons came later in the evening, and did not precede or provoke the charge on the crowd in the Härtelwald.

The defence case was hampered by the fact that the date of the appeal hearing was decided at short notice. Many potential defence witnesses were miners who could not arrange time off from work, while the costs of all who did attend fell on the defence, because the state refused to subpoena them. The presiding judge also seemed more disposed to the prosecution than the defence. When a non-commissioned officer called Burghardt gave a self-exculpatory and very confused account of the charge on the crowd, the presiding judge observed blithely: 'One knows what it is like in such incidents. That happens every day.' Yet the balance of evidence persuaded the court that the original ruling was sound, and in its judgement on 30 May the Court of Appeal expressly noted that Scheeben had accurately described the conduct of the army company. When the state appealed to the court of next instance its case was once again rejected in a judgement of 27 September.[10] On 22 June the facts of the military intervention, and the dubious role of Mayor Woytt, had been aired once again in the course of legal proceedings against Prince Radziwill in the criminal chamber of the Superior Court in Saarbrücken. Just two weeks later, on 7 July, Woytt appeared before the same court. Despite 'extenuating circumstances', he was convicted and fined 50 marks for maltreating a village woman who had come to request a permit to enter the Härtelwald. Woytt's conviction was upheld on appeal three weeks later, and the mayor was ordered to pay the costs of the appeal.[11]

What did this cascade of legal judgements mean? It showed that Prussia was a *Rechtsstaat*, a state in which administrative actions were bound by legal limits. The Prussian concept of the *Rechtsstaat* in this period was not synonymous with the British or French idea of the rule of law (although the practice may not have been all that different). The *Rechtsstaat* was not derived from the notion of law as the product of a sovereign parliament, nor did it imply a theory of the division of powers. It was something conceded by the executive state as a self-limitation on its own actions and those of its administrative agents. The concept of the *Rechtsstaat* was also based on preventing arbitrariness, not on the recognition and enunciation of basic civil rights. Even where 'positive' rights existed, such as the right of assembly, they were subject to executive reservations (*Vorbehalt*): the state reserved the right to define supposed threats to its own position, and within the established legal framework to promulgate exceptional laws (*Ausnahmegesetze*) for that purpose.[12] In short, there were real limits to the rule of law, and Albrecht Funk is right to draw a distinction between the 'liberal *Rechtsstaat*' and the actual '*Rechtsstaat* of the Prussian-German type'.[13] The implications of the *Rechtsstaat* were nevertheless important. Its achievement marked a break in theory and practice with the repressive semi-absolutism that had characterized the era of reaction in Prussia as recently as the 1850s. The effect of the constitutional conflict of the 1860s, and the liberal legal legislation of the 1870s (the law being a sphere to which liberals attached enormous importance) was to create genuine barriers to arbitrary, unpredictable and non-accountable administrative actions. Executive-administrative powers were exercised within a prescribed legal frame-

[10] Details of the Scheeben hearings in LASB, E 107, 17; BAT, B III, 11, 14/4, 27; LHAK, 442/6442, 135–41: RP Wolff Trier to MdI Berlin, 28 Dec. 1877; Bachem, *Erinnerungen*, 136; *FZ*, 30 May 1877.
[11] On the Radziwill and Woytt trials, LHAK, 442/6442, 141–5; *Marpinger Prozeß vor dem Richterstuhle der Vernunft*, 47; *Anlagen zu den Stenographischen Berichten ... 1877–1878*, ii. 1072.
[12] See I. Müller, *Rechtsstaat und Strafverfahren* (Frankfurt am Main, 1980); I. Maus, 'Entwicklung und Funktionswandel der Theorie des bürgerlichen Rechtsstaats', in M. Tohidipur (ed.), *Der bürgerliche Rechtsstaat*, 2 vols. (Frankfurt am Main, 1978), i. 13–81, and other contributions to Part I of i; Funk, *Polizei und Rechtsstaat*, 120–200, esp. 120–6, 195–200. H. Boldt, *Rechtsstaat und Ausnahmezustand. Eine Studie über den Belagerungszustand als Ausnahmezustand des bürgerlichen Rechtstaates im 19. Jahrhundert* (Berlin, 1967), examines the 'state of siege' as one example of exceptional legislation.
[13] Funk, *Polizei und Rechtsstaat*, 126.

work; indeed it is possible to talk of a 'legalization' (*Verrechtlichung*) of police and administration. This was capped by the principle of the legal accountability of the bureaucracy and the institution of the Superior Administrative Court (*Oberverwaltungsgericht*).[14]

This was hardly negligible. We should also remember the considerable degree of autonomy enjoyed by the Prussian legal bureaucracy. Public prosecutors—the *Staatsanwaltschaft*—had fought with some success since their inception in 1849 to subordinate the executive and administrative arms of government to their own authority, especially over the proper observation of the rights of the individual against arbitrary detention (the so-called Habeas Corpus Law of September 1848).[15] This was one of several sources of tension between the Prussian administrative and judicial bureaucracies in the 1870s, as the latter guarded its position and tried to ward off pressure.[16] There were generally more Catholics in the legal bureaucracy than in the field administration, particularly in senior positions, and this may have had some effect on attitudes during the *Kulturkampf*.[17] But the tension was essentially professional, or departmental, as administrative officials pressed for results in cases where state prosecutors and examining magistrates were more sceptical. Clashes arose over standards of proof, for example, an issue that the *Kulturkampf* highlighted.[18] At an important everyday level, harassed legal officials resented the time that had to be devoted to dubious cases. The 1870s marked a period of strain for both administrative and judicial bureaucracies, as a rapidly rising workload was not matched by the creation of new positions, and many of the positions that did exist remained unfilled.[19] The 'overwork and overstrain' on public prosecutors and examining magistrates was especially acute in Prussia, parsimonious as ever, where the lack

[14] D. Merten, *Rechtsstaat und Gewaltmonopol* (Tübingen, 1975), 35–6; H.-J. Strauch, 'Rechtsstaat und Verwaltungsgerichtsbarkeit', in Tohidipur, *Der bürgerliche Rechtsstaat*, ii. 525–47, esp. 530–3.

[15] Funk, *Polizei und Rechtsstaat*, 80.

[16] Funk describes the running battles between *Staatsanwaltschaft* and administrative authorities (*Landräte*, police, ultimately the Ministry of the Interior). By the 1870s a compromise made the police the 'auxiliary organ of public prosecutors', although the actual autonomy of the police, backed by their powerful masters, was considerable. See Funk, *Polizei und Rechtsstaat*, 84–9, 103–5. See also E. Carsten, *Die Geschichte der Staatsanwaltschaft in Deutschland* (Breslau, 1932).

[17] See e.g. the case of Heinrich von Pape, a Westphalian Catholic who was chairman of the Civil Code commission 1874–88: John, *Politics and the Law*, 80–1.

[18] For an example from the 1850s, see LHAK 442/7853, 341–4, 375–6, concerning the statutes of a young men's association set up by Father Dorbach of Bernkastel. The district administration wanted to prosecute over a clause that warned members against 'too familiar relations with members of the opposite sex in the evenings and at night-time and when the person is of a different faith', on the grounds that this constituted an incitement to confessional hatred. The OP at the Superior Court in Trier took a different view and informed the district administration that there was no case to be answered.

[19] For the pressure of new responsibilities on *Landräte*, see Süle, *Preußische Bürokratietradition*, 40–2; on the legal bureaucracy, M. John, 'Between Estate and Profession: Lawyers and the Development of the Legal Profession in Nineteenth-Century Germany', in Blackbourn and Evans (eds.), *The German Bourgeoisie*, 167–8, 178.

of clerical staff, routine copyists, and even standard forms made for 'excessive paperwork'.[20]

Almost all of these tensions were evident in the Marpingen case. There were, in the first place, obvious differences of tone between administrative and judicial officials: *Landrat* Rumschöttel and District Governor Wolff made no secret of their anti-Catholicism; the young trainee legal official Dr Strauß talked to Margaretha Kunz about his own Catholic upbringing. The house-searches and mail interceptions may have gone by the book, the *Landrat* and police working in close co-operation with the legal authorities, but there was still friction. The summary of evidence by the examining magistrate Emil Kleber is larded with sceptical notes, and he was plainly piqued by the high-handed behaviour of the interloper from Berlin, Meerscheidt-Hüllessem.[21] (It was not uncommon for the man from Berlin to be regarded in this way: the Saxon public prosecutor and criminologist Erich Wulffen noted archly that the 'successes of the Berlin criminal police' did not 'find unqualified recognition'.[22]) The judicial authorities were informed belatedly of the criminal commissar's presence in the area; indeed, as the senior prosecutor later noted, the judicial authorities in Saarbrücken knew nothing about events in Marpingen until 14 July, the day after the military intervention.[23] Disgruntlement in Saarbrücken was no doubt exacerbated by shortage of staff, noted in the official Prussian state handbook of 1875.[24] Kleber complained in September 1877 that the Marpingen enquiries were going slowly because since the beginning of the year he had been suffering an 'absolute overloading of business ... just as now I cannot, for the sake of this one matter, neglect or put aside every other case—and in this judicial year I have had to deal with *circa* 600 of these myself, despite the appointment on 1 February of an assistant examining magistrate'.[25]

For all their frustrations, and probably reservations too, examining magistrates like Kleber and Ernst Remelé dutifully gathered evidence against Marpingen suspects, conducting interviews, accompanying the police and administrative officials on house-searches, even granting Meerscheidt-Hüllessem a degree of latitude. And public prosecutors in Saarbrücken, as in Cologne, showed no lack of zeal in presenting their cases. It was in the courts that these cases fell down. The Prussian judiciary was not a rubber stamp of the administration. Liberal judges had, it is true, been purged in the first half of the 1860s under Bismarck's Interior Minister Albrecht zu Eulenburg, but historians are generally agreed that

---

[20] E. Wulffen, *Staatsanwaltschaft und Kriminalpolizei in Deutschland* (Berlin, 1908), 9, 16, 33–4, 57–64.

[21] See above, Ch.7, on the incident witnessed by Nickel Schario in Saarbrücken, where the detective countermanded Kleber's instructions to his own clerk.

[22] Wulffen, *Staatsanwaltschaft und Kriminalpolizei*, 158.

[23] *Prozeß*, 43–5. See LHAK, 442/6442, 27, 29 on the belated arrival of information from Berlin, via Trier, about Meerscheidt-Hüllessem.

[24] *Handbuch über den Königlich Preußischen Hof und Staat für das Jahr 1875* (Berlin, 1874), 883 notes the 'lack of the prescribed number of *Anwalten* and *Advocat-Anwalten*'.

[25] LHAK, 442/6442, 113–14: Kleber's report on the state of the Marpingen enquiry, 17 Sept. 1877.

the judiciary remained substantially independent in the Imperial period.[26] In the 1870s, in an ironic reversal of the position in the previous two decades, it was now liberal enthusiasts for the *Kulturkampf* who complained about 'ultramontane' judgements handed down by some courts. The judiciary largely escaped the purge of pro-Catholic *Landräte* and other administrative officials that took place during the *Kulturkampf*, although there were some politically dictated changes of personnel in the penal sections of superior and appellate courts.[27] These were, however, a measure of their stubborn independence. Prussian courts clearly felt uneasy about some aspects of the *Kulturkampf* and refused to do the bidding of government and administrative bureaucracy.[28] We are fortunate enough to know the views of one senior figure involved in the Marpingen affair, President of the Court Karl Schorn of the Superior Court in Saarbrücken, because he wrote his memoirs. Schorn was critical of the official response to Marpingen: it was 'badly handled' and the problems 'could have been avoided'. Marpingen offered an example of 'how an insignificant matter can be blown up into undeserved importance through clumsiness and lack of understanding'; but for the provocative use of force the apparitions would have been 'soon laughed at and forgotten'. Schorn's criticism extended not only to the treatment of the visionaries and their supporters, but to the prosecutions of visiting priests charged with the unlawful celebration of masses in the village. He pinned particular responsibility on District Governor Wolff in Trier, a 'rigid Protestant', but he also blamed the government for allowing the affair to generate 'such unpleasant scenes and such fruitless agitation'.[29]

Marpingen in Parliament

The chain of events at Marpingen caused similar misgivings within the Prussian government, not excluding the highest levels. Wilhelm I called for a full account at an early stage.[30] In the summer of 1877, Bismarck reportedly observed to a group of visiting Protestant clergymen from Württemberg that gendarmes were not the answer to episodes like those at Lourdes and Marpingen; instead it was necessary to look to the schools. This rapidly made the rounds of the Catholic

[26] Anderson and Barkin, 'The Myth of the Puttkamer Purge', 651, and 656 n. 10.
[27] Ibid. 662.
[28] Sperber, *Popular Catholicism*, 251; R. J. Ross, 'Enforcing the Kulturkampf in the Bismarckian State and the Limits of Coercion in Imperial Germany', *Journal of Modern History*, 56 (1984), 456–82.
[29] Schorn, *Lebenserinnerungen*, ii. 259–61. For Schorn's official position at the time, see *Handbuch über den Königlich Preußischen Hof und Staat für das Jahr 1875*, 833.
[30] LHAK, 442/6442, 15: telegram from Privy Councillor Wilmowski to RP Wolff Trier, 18 July 1876: 'His Majesty expects full report on the Marpingen case'.

press, and was never denied by the chancellor.[31] On the other side, the succession
of legal judgements probably encouraged the Centre Party to move politically. For
what became obvious in the course of 1877 was the discrepancy between the continuing refusal of the administrative authorities, up to the provincial level in
Koblenz, to back down over the various measures imposed against Marpingen,
and the fragile basis of the case against the village that was apparent whenever
the events were subject to legal proceedings. On 15 December, Julius Bachem
and three other members of the Centre Party tabled a motion in the Prussian
lower house, signed by seventy-seven members of the parliamentary group,
calling on the house to demand that the government look into the matter. In its
detailed four-page motion, which drew extensively on the judicial verdicts of the
previous twelve months, the Centre called for the reimbursement of the 4,000
marks surcharge imposed on the village to cover the costs of the military intervention, the rescinding of the ban on entry into the Härtelwald, and disciplinary
proceedings against the officials, especially Woytt, whose actions were irregular
and illegal.[32]

The parliamentary debate on the Centre motion a month later took place
against a tense political background that prompted widespread talk of crisis. One
aspect of this was the heavy legislative load that had been allowed to pile up in
the new Prussia-Germany, threatening to bring government to a halt. Both
national and state parliaments had to consider major commercial, fiscal, social,
and legal legislation, as well as measures affecting relations between church and
state. As the *Vossische Zeitung* argued in January 1878, 'what individual warning
voices have long predicted, namely that the functions of the Reich would falter
and come to a standstill, has now become a commonplace'.[33] This 'inner crisis'
extended to the individual state parliaments, above all the Prussian.[34] By the
beginning of 1878, the backlog of legislation had reached the point that plenary
sessions of parliament were being switched to the evenings to allow parliamentary
committees time to complete their work during the day.[35]

Procedural problems reflected the larger crisis during a watershed period in
the political development of the new Germany. The last years of the 1870s saw a
fundamental change of direction in the Reich. The Great Depression produced
mounting calls for a reversal of liberal commercial policy and the reintroduction
of tariff protection. Trade and taxation issues became increasingly bitter: they
engaged vociferous economic interests and raised fundamental questions about

---

[31] Rebbert, *Marpingen und seine Gegner*, 9–11. Bismarck's reported comments prompted one optimistic Catholic businessman from Paderborn, Robert Goll, to write to the chancellor, pointing out the
virtues of Catholic schools, asking for the Reich Health Office to carry out a full enquiry into the
Marpingen cures, and enclosing a pamphlet on events there. The pamphlet was speedily returned with
a terse acknowledgement of the letter.
[32] *Anlagen zu den Stenographischen Berichten . . . 1877–1878*, ii. 1069–73: No. 139, Bachem und
Genossen. See also LHAK, 442/6442, 121–2.
[33] *VZ*, 20 Jan. 1878.   [34] *NZ*, 16 Jan. 1878.   [35] *NZ*, 15 Jan. 1878.

the way in which government revenue should be raised and divided between the Reich and the individual states.[36] At the same time, Bismarck was trying to free himself from *de facto* dependence on the liberal parliamentary majorities of the 1870s. Liberal support fell in the Prussian elections of 1876, and the Reichstag elections of 1877 removed the liberal majority in the national parliament, although National Liberals and left liberals together still held the largest bloc of seats. Bismarck was also trying to drive a wedge between the two liberal groups. This was the period of the Iron Chancellor's celebrated retreat to his country estates. He divided the period from April 1877 to February 1878 between Friedrichsruh and Varzin, not appearing in Berlin at all. This was partly a result of illness; it was also the result of political brooding and planning. In April 1877 he initiated negotiations with the National-Liberal leader Bennigsen over the entry of National Liberals into the government: these talks were still continuing at the beginning of 1878, causing widespread (and accurate) speculation that the chancellor aimed to shift government policy to the right with National-Liberal help.[37] The *Kulturkampf* was a key element in this political reorientation. By 1877, at the latest, Bismarck was keen to disengage from the struggle against the Catholic Church: it had palpably failed, alarming Protestant Conservatives and reminding Bismarck of his unwelcome dependence on liberal parliamentary strength. The Centre Party was understandably keen for an accommodation on the *Kulturkampf*, and also ready to support a new anti-liberal tariff policy, provided a way could be found to prevent the additional revenues that would accrue to the Reich from upsetting the balance between the federal government and the individual states. This was to be the form taken by the reorientation of German and Prussian politics at the end of the 1870s. The reintroduction of tariffs and the winding up of the *Kulturkampf* took place with support from a new pro-governmental alignment of National Liberals, Conservatives, and Centre Party, the same forces that sealed the 're-founding' of the Empire with their support for the anti-socialist law of 1878.[38]

The debate on Marpingen therefore took place in the middle of a major political crisis, a period of political negotiations, press speculation, and frequent elections, in which the fate of the *Kulturkampf* and the position of the Centre Party were key elements.[39] The deliberations in the Prussian lower house were among the

[36] Rosenberg, *Große Depression*; K. W. Hardach, *Die Bedeutung wirtschaftlicher Faktoren bei der Wiedereinführung der Eisen- und Getreidezölle in Deutschland 1879* (Berlin, 1967), both of whom emphasize the politics of protectionism.
[37] J. F. Flynn, 'At the Threshold of Dissolution: The National Liberals and Bismarck, 1877/78', *Historical Journal*, 31 (1988), 319–40; Pflanze, *Bismarck and the Development of Germany*, ii. 364–82; Stürmer, *Regierung und Reichstag*, 187–215.
[38] Rosenberg, *Große Depression*, 132–54; Sheehan, *German Liberalism*, 181–8; Pflanze, *Bismarck and the Development of Germany*, ii. 445 ff.; G. Schmidt, 'Die Nationalliberalen—eine regierungsfähige Partei? Zur Problematik der inneren Reichsgründung, 1870–1878', in G. A. Ritter (ed.), *Die deutschen Parteien vor 1918* (Cologne, 1973), 208–23; K. D. Barkin, '1878–1879: The Second Founding of the Reich, A Perspective', *German Studies Review*, 10 (1987), 220–35.
[39] Reichstag elections took place in 1877 and 1878, Prussian Landtag elections in 1876 and 1879.

parting shots of the *Kulturkampf*. The Centre Party sought to emphasize the abuses to which the struggle against Catholics had led. The liberals were divided on this, as on almost every other issue on which the politics of the late 1870s turned. The concern of some about the propriety of state actions in Marpingen was offset—among the parliamentarians, more than offset—by a determination to defend those actions, expose 'Catholic superstition', and encourage the Prussian government to continue the struggle with liberal support. The Prussian government was concerned with damage limitation.

The proceedings of the Prussian lower house on Wednesday 16 January opened at 11.15 a.m.[40] Routine business occupied the house for three-quarters of an hour, and it was around noon that the President of the chamber called Julius Bachem to speak to his motion. Bachem had got as far as 'Gentlemen ...' when he was interrupted by noisy demands that he go to the speaker's rostrum. Beginning again, Bachem had time to observe 'I have a sufficiently strong voice ...' before further loud demands that he go to the rostrum led the President to call for order. No more than a minute after beginning his speech for the third time, Bachem had reached the point where he asked the house not to pass judgement on those aspects of the events in Marpingen that 'lay in the realm of the supernatural' when he was interrupted yet again by laughter.[41] These opening exchanges set the tone for the five-hour debate that followed. In an opening speech that was constantly interrupted by shouts and laughter from the liberal benches, Bachem immediately staked out the terrain of the debate. At issue was the conduct of Prussian officials, one of whom, 'namely Mayor Woytt', had acted 'from the basest and most contemptible motives'. This earned a warning from the President to which Bachem responded by citing the evidence of recent court proceedings. Not at issue, continued Bachem, were the apparitions themselves or their theological status: these matters were still subject to an enquiry under canon law, an enquiry delayed by the May Laws that left the diocese of Trier without a bishop. Even if an enquiry were to deem the apparitions authentic, this would by no means entail Catholic belief in their validity. Moreover, argued Bachem, even if those on the other side of the house wanted to believe that the apparitions were based on 'delusion', even if one were in fact to accept for the sake of argument that deliberate deception had been involved, that would not rob the Centre Party motion of its justification.[42]

With this adroit pre-emptive strike, Bachem 'took the wind out of the sails of the *Kulturkämpfer*'.[43] He also moved nimbly on to the offensive by raising two further issues likely to be emphasized by the government and its allies. The minister would undoubtedly refer to the string of other dubious, even fraudulent

[40] The record of the debate is in *SB*, 16 Jan. 1878, 1151–81. Major newspapers carried reports in their 17 Jan. issues.
[41] *SB*, 16 Jan. 1878, 1151.
[42] Ibid. 1151–2.
[43] *FZ*, 17 Jan. 1878.

apparitions in places such as Eppelborn, Berschweiler, and the Gappenach mill; but did not the willingness and ability of the local clergy to nip these matters in the bud show the fruitfulness of state co-operation with the church?[44] Many members of the house, observed Bachem, also regrettably seemed to have brought with them a 'pamphlet bound in green' that defended the role of Mayor Woytt and purported to show that his actions had been found entirely proper. The pamphlet, claimed Bachem, had been financed from Bismarck's notorious 'reptile fund': it had been 'paid for with our money' at a cost of 200 marks, although it was 'not worth a penny'.[45] This was a palpable hit, for the Prussian Ministry of the Interior had indeed financed the pamphlet in question, *Marpingen und das Evangelium* by 'A. F. vom Berg'.[46] Bachem indicated his intention to set the record straight on the mayor's unsavoury behaviour.

What followed was a relentless catalogue of official iniquities. Point by point, Bachem worked his way through the sequence of events. First, the immediate authorities in St Wendel had done nothing; the mayor and the acting *Landrat* had then turned as a first resort to what should have been a last resort, namely the use of the army; and the military intervention had itself been unlawful, because the crowd gathered in the Härtelwald was unthreatening and the order to disperse not properly given.[47] At this point the proceedings once again became unruly:

BACHEM. The actual command given in the Härtelwald on the evening of 13 July and
unanimously attested to by numerous witnesses was 'Attack, forward march, hurrah!'
['Quite right!'—loud unrest—laughter]
I do not envy the gentleman who opined that this was 'quite right'. At that command,
gentlemen, the army forced its way into a defenceless crowd which up to that time had
not been guilty of the slightest unlawfulness, and serious injuries were sustained in this
attack on fellow countrymen with its 'forward march and hurrah'.
['Nonsense!']
Do you not wish to laugh also about the scenes that took place in Marpingen?
[Loud unrest]
Do you not wish to laugh also about the fact that the army seized the bedclothes from
the beds of sick women, that people were mistreated for no reason, that a poor carter
who had committed no crime was crippled by a beating? If you had seen, as I have, the
poor carter, unable even to take the oath with his crippled arm, you would not laugh.
You should be ashamed of such frivolity.
['Bravo!' from the Centre benches. Very loud unrest]
PRESIDENT. Herr Deputy, in the unrest I was not able to hear exactly what you said.
Insofar as I could understand them, you directed at one or more members of the house

[44] *SB*, 16 Jan. 1878, 1153.
[45] Ibid. 1154. On the 'reptile fund' (strictly speaking, the 'Welfenfonds') see Stern, *Gold and Iron*, 266–7; Pflanze, *Bismarck and the Development of Germany*, ii. 101–2.
[46] The booklet, published in Saarbrücken in 1877, began life as a series of articles in the *Evangelisches Wochenblatt* of Neunkirchen, 'Marpingen und seine Wunder'. On the subsidy, LHAK, 442/6442, 81–93, which includes the receipt for 200 marks. Klaus-Michael Mallmann has identified the author as the Protestant Pastor Adam Fauth of Gersweiler: 'Volksfrömmigkeit', 231 n. 171.
[47] *SB*, 16 Jan. 1878, 1154–6.

the words 'You should be ashamed of such frivolity'. I call you to order, Herr Deputy Bachem, for this impermissible expression.

[*Shout of 'Call those who were laughing to order!'—Loud unrest*]

DEPUTY WINDTHORST [Meppen]. Call those who were laughing to order!

PRESIDENT. Herr Deputy Windthorst, it is not your turn to speak. You may not speak without my permission. I request Herr Deputy Bachem to continue.

[*Shout from the Left: 'Call him to order!'*]

DEPUTY WINDTHORST. I wish to speak on a point of order!

PRESIDENT. Points of order are not permitted during a speech. I request Herr Deputy Bachem to continue.

DEPUTY BACHEM. Gentlemen, you will concede that there are so many sensitive points in this matter that move the feelings, that it is forgivable if an expression is used that perhaps breaches the limits of what is permitted, but you will also concede that the expression in question was the result of provocation.

Bachem thereupon resumed his indictment. He carefully avoided making the army the principal object of criticism. It was regrettable that the officers had failed to recognize that the crowd in the Härtelwald was not riotous, and some officers had brought the uniform into disrepute by their conduct: but the army had been placed 'in a completely false position' by Mayor Woytt, as the military authorities had recognized by withdrawing the company after two weeks.[48] This was the central point, as Bachem went on to depict the 'third stage' of the official response, the stationing of gendarmes drawn from all over the Rhine Province in Marpingen, and their high-handed actions. The argument here was two-pronged. On the one hand, Bachem was sharply critical of the powers possessed by the police under the law. Under the relevant legislation of 1850, 'the police in Prussia is so to speak all-powerful'. This was especially true of areas such as the Rhine Province which had no district committee (*Kreisausschuß*) to monitor police actions. In referring to the notorious 'elastic clauses' (*Kautschukparagraphen*) of the 1850 legislation, Bachem was uncomfortably reminding liberals of their own historic opposition to untrammelled police power. If the actions in Marpingen fell within the law, concluded Bachem, then it was high time to rewrite the law. On the other hand, he argued, the measures undertaken in the Saarland were unwarranted even in the elastic terms of the law: it was simply impossible to make a case for the necessity of intervention by the gendarmes on such a scale, given the peaceful behaviour of the populace. In short, a penalty of 4,000 marks had been imposed on the inhabitants of Marpingen to cover the cost of military and police actions they had neither sought nor deserved. It was now the duty of the house and the government to save the village from 'ruin'.[49]

This part of Bachem's speech, concerned with the 4,000 marks in costs and the manner in which they had been incurred, was also the longest part. This was probably inevitable, given the complex sequence of events that had to be outlined, and the constant interruptions that Bachem's account provoked. He spoke much

[48] *SB*, 16 Jan. 1878, 1156.
[49] Ibid. 1157.

more briefly to the other two parts of the Centre Party motion, his arguments now accompanied more frequently by shouts of support from the Centre benches than by the occasional cries of 'Oho!' from the liberals. In calling for the ban on entering the Härtelwald to be lifted, he dwelt particularly on the difficulty of obtaining legitimate access by permission, given the character of Mayor Woytt. Here Bachem redeemed his promise to set the record straight on the conduct of the mayor, by detailing Woytt's conviction in Saarbrücken on the charge of mistreating a woman.[50] The third part of the motion, on the disciplining of officials, followed logically on. Bachem condemned the rush to judgement of the authorities in Trier that deception was afoot, scorned the failure to find evidence of criminality even by the use of dubious methods, and spoke with bitter sarcasm of the roles played by District Governor Wolff, District Secretary Besser and the secret policeman. Once again, however, it was Woytt who received the worst savaging, as Bachem catalogued the vindictive actions and words of the hapless rural mayor. The speech ended with an icily passionate denunciation of the atmosphere of hatred and suspicion bred both by the *Kulturkampf* and by the activities of the Deutscher Verein, the organization established by the historian Heinrich Sybel as a means of keeping government officials up to the mark in the struggle against the clerical enemy:[51]

BACHEM. I further maintain that in the words I have quoted of Mayor Woytt's, a brutal mentality can be demonstrated that is a tragic fruit of the degeneration which, as a result of the *Kulturkampf*

['*Oho!*']

and most particularly as a result of the atmosphere created by the Deutscher Verein

['*Oho!*']

of the ways and means by which the Deutscher Verein seeks to drill and incite the officials in our province, has unfortunately become rooted in parts of officialdom. You have to have seen Mayor Woytt, this nervous, excited man, performing in court, to appreciate the degree of cynical pleasure with which he tormented (*gequält*) the populace.

['*Oho!*']

It was, Bachem concluded, not possible to compensate the inhabitants of Marpingen fully for 'the numerous torments and persecutions' they had been made to suffer; but acceptance of the Centre motion would signify recognition of their just cause.[52] Bachem's speech lasted one and a half hours and was, in the words of one liberal newspaper, 'well-organized and rhetorically flawless'.[53] By the time Bachem sat down, to loud applause from the Centre benches, he had made a

[50] Ibid. 1157–8.
[51] Perhaps the most notorious by-product of the Deutscher Verein's activities was the 'Konitzer affair', when material on officials gathered for the association by a former Krefeld schoolteacher was used for the purpose of blackmail. See *Culturkampf und Spionage oder: Der Proceß Konitzer. Ein Beitrag zur Sittengeschichte der Culturkampfsaera* (Bonn, 1877). The scandal broke in 1877, and greatly embarrassed supporters of the Deutscher Verein: Seyffardt, *Erinnerungen*, 148–9.
[52] *SB*, 16 Jan. 1878, 1158–9.
[53] *VZ*, 17 Jan. 1878.

series of damning charges and pre-empted many of the issues that the government could be expected to raise in its own defence.

The Prussian Minister of the Interior at the time of the Marpingen events, Count Eulenburg, was on extended sick-leave in February 1878 (he retired the following month, to be replaced by his cousin, Count Botho zu Eulenburg). The government put up the liberal-leaning Minister of Agriculture, Dr Rudolf Friedenthal to reply to the Centre motion.[54] Friedenthal tried to establish first that discussion of the matter in parliament was inappropriate.[55] This was partly because of its intrinsic nature: 'it causes me extraordinarily little pleasure to deal in detail with this affair, an affair which is hardly conducive to creating an edifying impression' (shouts of 'quite right!'). In a prurient speech, Friedenthal referred frequently to episodes over which it would be 'inappropriate' to go into detail given the 'impurity' involved. He also argued that it was inappropriate to deliberate in parliament on questions that were still subject to legal action. The investigation was, he announced, 'as good as completed': charges were 'imminent', and they would include not only fraud and related offences, but unlawful assembly, riot, and breach of the peace. This was perhaps the government's strongest card, but the way Friedenthal played it gave an indication of the defensiveness that would characterize his entire speech. Out of respect for the independence of the courts, argued the minister, it would be 'unseemly' to 'interfere with the legal evidence'. This, however, deprived the government of 'a rich mass of material' that would have enabled it to answer the points made by the previous speaker. In raising the expectations of the government's supporters that a major criminal trial was pending, Friedenthal simultaneously lowered expectations about the strength of the case it would present in parliament.

The key to the minister's rejection of the motion was the context of intervention in Marpingen. Unrest had already taken place in Namborn, and local officials were on the alert to take preventive action. In a sentence that slipped easily from hypothesis to proof, Friedenthal observed that in Marpingen 'a riotous movement on a much larger scale might perhaps have developed, which thank God was prevented'. Marpingen, moreover, was only one link in a larger chain of apparitions that had a 'dubious and dangerous character'. Here the minister referred exhaustively to events in Eppelborn, Gronig, Münchwies, Berschweiler, and Gappenach, depicting them as a dangerous epidemic or *Volkskrankheit*, without troubling to explain how episodes that had mostly occurred later could have influenced the decisions to send the army and gendarmes into Marpingen in July 1876. This part of the speech was indeed plump with innuendo. Friedenthal drew attention to the existence of 'social-democratic agitation' in the Saarland, while adding that this had 'no immediate connection' with the case. He alluded to the contemporaneous celebrations at Lourdes, and the popular enthusiasm

---

[54] The minister's speech is in *SB*, 16 Jan. 1878, 1159–65.
[55] Here the minister faithfully followed the briefing he received from RP Wolff in Trier: LHAK, 442/6442, 123–63, RP Wolff Trier to MdI Berlin, 28 Dec. 1877, esp. 145, 161–2.

in Germany for pilgrimage medallions of French manufacture, although he 'attach[ed] no importance to this on its own'. In short, the background to the events in Marpingen, and the length of time in which the local authorities had remained in ignorance, explained the justified concern of the rural mayor and district secretary; and, faced with a 'completely intolerable' situation and a crowd unwilling or unable to listen to them, Woytt and Besser, accompanied only by three gendarmes, had acted with a 'notable degree of prudence and correctness' in calling for military aid, rather than risk taking actions that might have sparked serious disorder. The intervention of the army, in turn, had proceeded regularly: the minister regretted that there had been some more or less serious injuries, but things might have been much worse. The posting of gendarmes in Marpingen was amply justified by the volatility and 'exceptional nature' of the circumstances, as thousands of pilgrims streamed to the village.

The minister's reply to the first part of the Centre motion emphasized the potential dangers of the crowds in Marpingen and the need to preserve order. His response to the second part of the motion, concerning the ban on the Härtelwald, he turned into a conservation issue. The woods represented a 'considerable asset' of the parish, and one that was in danger of being 'devastated', as pilgrims destroyed trees, stripped bark, uprooted plants, and removed soil. At the moment many gave no thought to 'conserving the property of the parish for the future', but there would come a time when pilgrims would no longer bring money into the village and people would be grateful that the government had 'concerned itself with conserving an essential part of parish property for the future'. This was, of course, a classic representation of the Prussian state as the benign embodiment of the general interest. The minister's approach also took him neatly around the many problems associated with the implementation of the ban.

Up to this point, Friedenthal had remained largely on the offensive, while trying to give the impression of fair-mindedness by conceding individual points. He accepted, for example, that the parish priests in Eppelborn, Berschweiler, and elsewhere had conducted themselves 'loyally'; and he conceded that not all the activities of pilgrims in the Härtelwald could be described as 'public nuisance (Unfug)'. As he turned to the third part of the Centre motion, on the role of individual officials, the minister's tone became increasingly defensive and the pro-governmental benches fell very quiet. Friedenthal began with the plea not to take particular episodes in isolation, but to look at 'the situation as a whole'. He then dealt unconvincingly with the charges made by Bachem. The role played by Hugo Besser? The minister apologized that he had not fully understood Bachem's points, and was 'therefore not at the moment in a position to go into details'. And the army? Here the arguments became mired in equivocation. Perhaps individuals had done things better left undone: the minister was 'not in a position to judge'. But those with complaints should have gone the legal route in seeking redress, and done so immediately, 'not one and a half years later, when it is extremely difficult to establish the facts'. Reminded by the noise from the Centre benches about the Scheeben trial, when these very facts had been damningly established, Friedenthal fell back on the argument that the testimony in the Scheeben hearings bore on the guilt or innocence of the accused, not on that of the army officers: ·

I rest my argument on the judgement of all jurists, be their political convictions what they may, that when it is a matter of reaching a positive judgement of such facts on the basis of which certain persons are accused, and when discussion of them comes about in a trial in such a form that the case is concerned with the establishment of the truth respecting the directly accused person, the appearance which matters assume is quite different and is much less to be relied upon, and it is certainly not permissible to place such value on these statements as would be the case in the event of an independent trial having taken place.

Even the minister himself was apparently unconvinced by this serpentine reasoning, for he hurried to note that he did not 'absolutely dispute' the evidence that had been presented in Cologne, and attached 'considerable weight' to the opinion of the judges concerned. Perhaps military improprieties had occurred: it lay in the 'imperfections of human affairs' that even the best measures were not always correctly executed. By the time he came to the case of Wilhelm Woytt, Friedenthal was fully on the defensive. He expressed 'disapproval' of the actions that had led to the mayor's conviction, and acknowledged that Woytt had committed 'improprieties' and made 'regrettable remarks'. All Friedenthal could offer against the demand for disciplinary action was the fact that the mayor had already been punished once in the courts, and had acted in good faith. The minister concluded that the authorities had been obliged to act in Marpingen, and had done so within the law. The second proposition was hardly consistent with much of what he had just conceded in a speech that was generally halting and equivocal. Friedenthal's defence of official actions was repeatedly undermined by vagueness about detail, and suggested an under-prepared minister who had little enthusiasm for his task.[56] Despite the lively applause that greeted the end of the speech, it was an unconvincing performance.

Many deputies had indicated their desire to speak, and the first to be called was Julius Sello, a National Liberal who represented the Saarland seat of Saarbrücken-Ottweiler-St Wendel. He concentrated on defending the actions of Wilhelm Woytt, giving a sympathetic account of the mayor's experiences during the Namborn affair, and doing his best to blacken the character of the woman—Katharina Fuchs—whom Woytt had been convicted of assaulting. Sello's speech was notable for the manner in which he often went beyond the minister in seeking to exculpate official actions. Sello saw no reason to express regret or disapproval

---

[56] The minister apologized for being unable 'to go into detail' about the role played by Besser, was unsure whether it had been the *Landrat* or his deputy who had liaised with the public prosecutor over 'Marlow's' activities ('it is a matter of indifference'), and described the consecration in Lourdes of 'a chapel or a statue'. These were not major issues, but they give the impression of a man who had not mastered his brief. Some of the blame must fall on the patchiness of the information he had received from Trier. See LHAK, 442/6442, 123–63.

THE STATE CLIMBS DOWN

of what Woytt had done to Katharina Fuchs: the mayor had merely 'given her a slap (*ihr einen Klapps gegeben*)'. He outflanked the minister in his insistence that Marpingen was 'not at all a spontaneous gathering of people, but that the business was extremely well planned'; and in contrast to Friedenthal's emollient treatment of the Catholic clergy, he declared that the affair had been exploited by 'clerical secret policemen'.[57] Sello was followed by the Centre deputy Kaufmann. In an obviously prearranged division of labour, he concentrated on the one aspect of the Centre motion that Bachem had passed over briefly: the activities of Meerscheidt-Hüllessem. During a scathing attack on the methods employed by the detective, Kaufmann observed that any recantation on the part of Margaretha Kunz, given the psychological pressure exerted on her, would have no more value than the victim's confession in a witchcraft trial. The Centre deputy concluded that the police measures had only magnified the attention paid to Marpingen: 'It is in the interest of the government that it soon make peace with this poor, harassed parish.'[58]

Both Sello and Kaufmann spoke with a degree of circumspection, and were heard by a well-behaved house. Neither was true of the next speech by the left-wing National Liberal Gustav Lipke. He began by describing Kaufmann's contribution as irrelevant, and ended with the accusation that the Centre Party had done a 'wretched disservice' to its own religion and robbed the house of five hours of its valuable time.[59] Lipke packed the maximum amount of insult into the rest of his short speech, causing constant interruptions as he laid about him. He brushed off the activities of the detective, suggested that Prince Radziwill belonged to a family 'famed more for its Roman and Polish sympathies than its German patriotism', and quoted unnamed Catholic priests in the diocese of Trier who had told him of their 'disgust and outrage' that the 'Marpingen swindle has occurred before the eyes of the civilized world'. Lipke's combative speech ended in tumult. It was at this point that the deputies Hermann Wagener and Count Schack called for closure of the debate. An earlier motion by Wagener had been defeated; this one was accepted.[60] The result was that only three deputies actually contributed to the debate. Those who had asked to be called ran to over a dozen, including heavyweights like Virchow and Rickert from the liberal side, Heeremann and Schorlemer-Alst from the Centre benches. The last word therefore fell to Ludwig Windthorst, the leader of the Centre Party.

Windthorst introduced no new material into the argument. His role, as one of the premier debaters in the house, was to expose the flaws in the case presented by government and liberals.[61] Windthorst's rhetorical gifts were much in evidence: he cited Kant and Rousseau against the anticlericals, drew the attention of the

[57] *SB*, 16 Jan. 1878, 1165–8 for Sello's speech.
[58] Ibid. 1168–71.
[59] Ibid. 1172–3.
[60] Ibid. 1172–3. Wagener was a Conservative, Magnus Count Schack von Wittenau a National Liberal.
[61] Ibid. 1173–80.

government's supporters to Bismarck's misgivings about Marpingen, alluded mischievously to the division between Protestant believers and unbelievers. The camaraderie and theatricality of the parliamentary club were unmistakable in some of the mannered exchanges with prominent liberals like Virchow and Richter, but Windthorst's urbanity, like Bachem's more sober advocacy, did not disguise a cold anger. 'Praying and singing appear to be a danger to the state in this land,' he observed, and there were those in Trier who 'thirsted for the moment when they could turn the cannons on us'. But ideas could not be crushed with bayonets; nor could the 'tyrannical' methods of Mayor Woytt be sanctioned. Windthorst fingered the holes in the minister's statement, but much of his speech emphasized the responsibility of the chamber to protest against government abuses, and was directed at the liberals. Should a parish be 'reduced to beggary' through government measures? Why did members of the house laugh and become impatient when serious allegations were under discussion? Were the noisy demonstrations of opinion whenever Meerscheidt-Hüllessem's name came up to be attributed to a 'love of secret policemen'? Could parliament ignore the 'disgraceful scandal' of 'Marlow'? The house, argued Windthorst, had to support the motion tabled by the Centre deputy Schorlemer-Alst, to set up a parliamentary commission to examine the evidence of official wrongdoing: 'Otherwise you would be saying that the police power could do what it wanted, provided that the objective meets with your approval.' Windthorst's barbs were not lost on his opponents, who interrupted his speech frequently and hissed him at the close. In a debate that was, in Julius Bachem's phrase, 'unusually stormy' the limits of parliamentary etiquette were tested, as they had been in many earlier exchanges on the *Kulturkampf*.[62]

Who were the winners and losers in the parliamentary debate? The Centre Party and the cause it represented were the ostensible losers. No concessions were extracted from the Prussian government: Friedenthal's halting speech conceded that individual acts of impropriety had probably occurred, but the minister was unyielding on the 4,000 marks, the ban on the Härtelwald, and the disciplining of officials. The Centre's speakers met with hostility and ridicule from liberals, and all three parts of its motion were voted down, together with Schorlemer's amendment to establish a parliamentary commission of enquiry into events at Marpingen.[63] But there were undercurrents in the debate that suggest a different conclusion. The very act of bringing events in the village before parliament was an indication that the Centre Party had already begun to appropriate what was once a liberal-progressive speciality, namely the politics of moral outrage based on particular 'scandals'. It was a political style that the Centre was to perfect in the

---

[62] Bachem, *Lose Blätter*, 70, and *Erinnerungen*, 137.
[63] For the divisions, see *SB*, 16 Jan. 1878, 1188. There was no roll-call division, so voting figures are unrecorded.

years to come, with major electoral benefits and considerable political success.[64] In the shorter term, Windthorst's references to Bismarck's concern over Marpingen pointed to the political advantages the party would soon reap as the Prussian government (and especially its dominant figure) tired of a *Kulturkampf* that could not be won. The death of Pius IX just a month after the debate brought the end of the *Kulturkampf* closer. Bismarck's announcement of a new tobacco tax, also in February 1878, was an even more important indicator of the impending sea-change in German politics, which was to bring the Centre Party in from the cold and divide the liberals.[65]

The liberals were the apparent winners in the debate, but appearances were deceptive. Initial reactions, particularly among National Liberals, were scornful and triumphalist. There would be anger, shame, and outrage, argued the *National-Zeitung*, that 'the parliamentary tribune [was] misused for the mocking of common sense and the dragging down of parliamentary institutions'; but Windthorst had rightly been laughed at, and the clericals were conducting a 'rearguard action'.[66] The *Saar- und Mosel-Zeitung* also suggested that the Centre Party had harmed itself with a 'sensationalist motion' that brought 'the monstrous products of crass superstition—even if only indirectly—before the forum of one of the most highly regarded representative institutions in Europe'.[67] Left-liberal newspapers were less sanguine about the debate. They recognized the weaknesses in the government's case, conceded the telling points made by the Centre, and suggested that the noise and laughter from the National-Liberal benches were both 'inappropriate' and a sign of frustration.[68] There were clear signs here of the unease and mutual suspicion that increasingly marked relations within the liberal camp during 1877–8. The willingness of parliamentary National Liberalism, led by its growing right wing, to become the party of Bismarck *sans phrase* was the central issue. By the time of the Marpingen debate this was not only a source of discord between National Liberals and left liberals, but within the National Liberal Party itself. It would shortly lead to a major split.[69]

The great irony, not lost on Windthorst, was that those National Liberals who justified the abuses at Marpingen were tying themselves to a *Kulturkampf* policy that Bismarck was about to jettison. By the beginning of 1878 it was evident to most observers that it was only a question of time before the state sued for peace in its struggle against the church. Meanwhile, embarrassments like Marpingen

[64] I have explored this theme at length in *Class, Religion and Local Politics*, and in *Populists and Patricians*, esp. chs. 7–10.

[65] Windthorst's comparison (*SB*, 16 Jan. 1878, 1177–8) between the treatment of Catholics and alleged government softness towards the Social Democrats also prefigured the change of fronts in 1878, as the struggle against the church was replaced by a struggle against the labour movement that was initially supported by the Centre Party.

[66] *NZ*, 17 Jan. 1878.

[67] *SMZ*, 18 Jan. 1878. See also *KZ*, 17 Jan. 1878.

[68] *VZ*, 17 Jan. 1878; *FZ*, 17 Jan. 1878.

[69] Flynn, 'At the Threshold of Dissolution'; Zucker, *Bamberger*, 87–104; Sheehan, *German Liberalism*, 181–95.

remained. Friedenthal's statement was the real 'rearguard action' in the debate of January 1878. The minister had made no concessions; he had even announced that serious charges were to be brought against the guilty parties in the Marpingen affair. But this only postponed the final reckoning. The government's defeat was ultimately to come, not in the Prussian parliament in Berlin, but in the criminal court in Saarbrücken.

The Trial

Friedenthal had told parliament that an almost completed investigation would lead to serious charges being brought imminently. His statement turned out to be very wide of the mark, and was somewhat disingenuous. Friedenthal must have had a good idea of the slow progress being made. The judicial authorities had already sounded a gloomy note the previous autumn. Shortage of personnel was only one problem; the sheer mass of material and the poor quality of the witnesses also presented 'quite particular difficulties'. The need to investigate new cases of fraud complicated things further, and the examining magistrate Emil Kleber warned that the enquiry would go on for some time.[70] State Prosecutor Petershof also underlined the problems: the investigations repeatedly ran up against a wall of silence, many questions remained 'shrouded in darkness', and until a short time before 'the prospect of a successful criminal prosecution was highly doubtful'. Father Neureuter's papers offered some hope, but in the difficult circumstances it was best not to 'move too quickly'.[71] This bad news was passed to the Ministry of the Interior in Berlin. Shortly before the parliamentary debate the minister heard the same story from District Governor Wolff, who was uncertain whether the instigators of Marpingen could actually be convicted.[72]

The saga continued in the months following the debate. Karl Schorn, who was in a position to know, recalled later that legal proceedings 'gradually ran into the sand'.[73] In February 1878, Neureuter was assured by the examining magistrate Kleber that the enquiry would be concluded 'in the near future'. In July the priest complained to the Minister of Justice about the continuing uncertainty, and the non-return of papers that had been seized.[74] Kleber did not draw up his final report until 9 August, and it was September before the court in Saarbrücken finally announced that charges were to be brought. Problems remained even

---

[70] LHAK, 442/6442, 113–14: Kleber's report of 17 Sept. 1877 on the progress of the enquiry. The 'new cases' may have been Münchwies and Berschweiler, or he may have been referring to the pressure from Trier to bring charges against Dr Thoemes for publicizing Marpingen in his various writings. See ibid. 73–80, 95–103.

[71] LHAK, 442/6442, 115–17: Petershof's comments of 20 Sept. 1877 on the progress of the enquiry.

[72] LHAK, 442/6442, 163: RP Wolff Trier to MdI Berlin, 28 Dec. 1877.

[73] Schorn, *Lebenserinnerungen*, ii. 261.

[74] BAT, B III, 11, 14/4, 22: Neureuter to Minister of Justice, 15 July 1878. The physical evidence was not returned to Neureuter until the beginning of 1880. See ibid. 41: Public Prosecutor's Office Saarbrücken to Neureuter, 26 Jan. 1880.

then. Despite the extraordinary mass of statements, impounded correspondence, and the rest, much of the evidence provided a dubious basis for bringing charges, even on relatively trivial offences like selling Marpingen earth for profit.[75] Some of the original charges had therefore been dropped by the time Kleber drew up his summary of the evidence, and the cases of seven others listed as 'accused' in his report were not pursued by the public prosecutor's office.[76] In the end, twenty individuals were charged and nineteen eventually brought to trial. These were the four surviving parents of the three girls (Johann Leist died before the case came to court); Susanna Leist's sister, Margaretha; the priests Neureuter, Eich, Schneider, Schwaab, and Dicke; the publicist Thoemes; the six adult males who claimed to have seen the apparition; the schoolteacher André, and the forester Altmeyer. The more serious charges were not pursued by the public prosecution. Instead of riot, unlawful assembly, and breach of the peace, all but two of the twenty faced charges of fraud, attempted fraud, or aiding and abetting fraud. District Governor Wolff was doubtful whether even those charges could be proved.[77] The odd two out were charged with the relatively minor offences of inciting disobedience to authority (Father Eich) and refusal to disperse when asked to do so (communal forester Altmeyer).[78] The enquiry had lasted two years; the mountain had laboured to produce a mouse.

The case finally came to trial in March 1879. It was heard in the criminal division of the regional Superior Court in Saarbrücken, established in 1835 to relieve the pressure on the existing superior courts in the Rhine Province, particularly after the transfer to Prussia the previous year of the former Saxe-Coburg territory around St Wendel.[79] The court had already heard other cases arising from Marpingen, including those of Radziwill and Woytt. The trial of the adult principals in the Berschweiler affair on a variety of charges was also held there.[80] But none was followed as closely as this. As the presiding judge noted in his opening remarks, the matter was 'of interest not only in this district, but throughout the whole German Fatherland and beyond the borders of Germany'.[81] On

[75] LASB, E 107, 253–5.

[76] The 7 were Anna Hahn, the brother of Anton Hahn, the only woman among the 6 adult visionaries, and the only one not proceeded against; the wife of another adult visionary, the retired miner Nikolaus Recktenwald; the day labourers Johannes Kreuz ('Kreuzhannes') and Wendel Recktenwald, and the cobbler Michel Puhl; the widow Angela Kles; and the watchman Jakob Langendörfer. Compare the list of accused in LASB, E 107, 31 ff. and 238 ff., with the list of accused at Saarbrücken, in Prozeß, 10–11.

[77] LHAK, 442/6442, 195–8: RP Wolff Trier to MdI Berlin, 25 Feb. 1879.

[78] Prozeß, 9–11.

[79] Hoppstädter and Hermann, Geschichtliche Landeskunde, i. 381–3; E. Landsberg, 'Das rheinische Recht und die rheinische Gerichtsverfassung', in J. Hansen (ed.), Die Rheinprovinz 1815–1915, 2 vols. (Bonn, 1917), i. 167.

[80] See SMZ, 10 and 11 Jan. 1878; SPB, 20 Jan. 1878. The trial took place on 9–10 January, with 14 defendants facing a rich variety of charges: fraud, aiding and abetting fraud, causing a public nuisance through immoral acts, unlawful damaging of trees, embezzlement, slandering officials, and abuse of the sacrament. Seven of the accused were found guilty, seven acquitted.

[81] Prozeß, 11.

Monday 3 March, the opening day of the trial, a large crowd gathered outside
the court building, and by 9 o'clock when proceedings began the courtroom was
packed.[82] The public seats were uncomfortably full throughout the two weeks of
the trial, and stenographers were much in demand by the press.[83] Fearing the
worst, the Prussian administration had also made its plans, lining up sympathetic
newspapers to give a 'true' picture of the trial that would counteract efforts by
the 'ultramontane' press 'to distort, to obfuscate, and to exploit the proceedings
in its own interest'.[84]

This was not a jury trial, and the case was heard by three judges: Presiding Judge
Cormann, recently promoted from the rank of public prosecutor in Koblenz, and
the assistant judges Jerusalem and Reusch.[85] The prosecutor earmarked for the
case was ill with diphtheria. His place was taken by the Senior Public Prosecutor
Pattberg, a man whom his colleague Karl Schorn pointedly described as a 'short-
sighted son of the Protestant Wuppertal'.[86] There were two defence lawyers. One
was advocate Simons from the Saarbrücken court; the other was the ubiquitous
Julius Bachem. Bachem's legal talents were much in demand during the *Kulturkampf*. In the year the Marpingen events began, he had defended the 71-
year-old suffragan bishop of Cologne, Baudri, on May Law charges of illegally
ordaining a priest. The case dragged on through 1876, and Bachem fought it
through the Superior Court and Appeal Court in Cologne, up to the criminal
division of the Appeal Court in Berlin.[87] The following year he appeared for
Matthias Scheeben. The larger ramifications of the Marpingen case, with which
he was already familiar, made Bachem an obvious choice, and he took on the
defence in Saarbrücken at the express wish of his party leader, Windthorst.[88]
The public and those who followed proceedings in the newspapers were treated
to a colourful spectacle, as different worlds were brought together within the
formal confines of the courtroom. Judge Cormann expatiated on the writings
of Pascal; the very last witness testified that Johann Leist had sold him two
draught oxen.[89] An extraordinary array of witnesses appeared. They ranged from

[82] *KZ*, 4 Mar. 1879; *FZ*, 5 Mar. 1879.
[83] *KZ*, 17 Mar. 1879.
[84] LHAK, 442/6442, 195–8: RP Wolff Trier to MdI Berlin, 25 Feb. 1879. The go-between used by
Wolff was *Landrat* Geldern of Saarbrücken, the two newspapers mentioned by name were the *Kölnische
Zeitung* and the *Saarbrücker Zeitung*. The presiding judge had agreed to vet the stenographic transcripts
for accuracy.
[85] *Prozeß*, 9; *Handbuch über den Königlich Preußischen Hof und Staat für das Jahr 1875*, 877, on
Cormann. *Assessor* Jerusalem had also been previously employed in the Lutzerath district of the
Koblenz Superior Court: ibid. 878.
[86] *Prozeß*, 9; Schorn, *Lebenserinnerungen*, ii. 260. The terms *Prokurator* and *Oberprokurator* for public
prosecutor and senior public prosecutor were a residue, like so much else in the Rhenish legal system,
of French influence. The Rhine Province had public prosecutors before the *Staatsanwaltschaft* was
introduced throughout Prussia.
[87] LHAK, 442/10419, 213–34.
[88] Bachem, *Lose Blätter*, 71, and *Erinnerungen*, 138. On Bachem's busy life during the *Kulturkampf*,
when he was in great demand as a political speaker and organizer throughout the Rhineland, see Lange,
Die Stellung, 63, 106, 117, 155, 244.
[89] *Prozeß*, 21, 266–7.

THE STATE CLIMBS DOWN 325

senior government officials, gendarmes, and the infamous Baron Meerscheidt-Hüllessem to Catholic aristocrats and prominent figures in the church; from doctors, lawyers, and merchants to hawkers, peasants, miners, and a chimney-sweep. So many from Marpingen itself were called to give evidence that it was 'as if an entire village community had been assembled'.[90]

The proceedings were, as Bachem described them, 'rich in sensational moments'.[91] On 6 March, Helene Schmidt from the Prince Wilhelm and Marianne Institute in Saarbrücken gave evidence about her conversations there with Margaretha Kunz. At the end of her testimony, Prosecutor Pattberg drew the attention of the court to the possibility that an attempt had been made to interfere with the witness. Schmidt then described an incident at the end of the previous week when a woman had insisted on reading her fortune by turning up cards. The woman had told her she would

take a course she would prefer not to take, but it would bring her good luck, not bad. A man in black had arrived on the train and would come and speak to her, even if she lay on her death-bed. A lady in black was also in the picture; she had something to do with the Catholics. Schmidt would become rich and receive a golden diploma.

Schmidt laughed about the matter, but the presiding judge took the incident seriously, until enquiries revealed that the woman in question was simply a fortune-teller 'of ill repute', not a clerical agent.[92] The following day the trades-woman Amalie Lazarus of Tholey raised the level of tension in the court with allegations that she had been threatened, but her subsequent testimony was anodyne in the extreme.[93] Excitement rose again three days later, when the widow Blies of Marpingen was taken into custody on suspicion of perjury, telling the gendarme who escorted her away that this was her 'road to heaven'.[94]

As the proceedings went on, many of the liveliest moments were furnished by one of the defendants, Dr Nikolaus Thoemes. The incidents in which he was involved were in so many ways indicative of the manner in which the trial was conducted that it is worth considering them in some detail. A teacher's son in his early thirties, Thoemes had been born near Berschweiler, attended school in Trier, and studied jurisprudence in Berlin and Bonn (where he took historical courses from Droysen, Sybel, and Mommsen), before completing his studies in Freiburg and obtaining his doctorate. He was a former editor of the Stuttgart-based *Deutsches Volksblatt*, which he gave up because the newspaper's line on the *Kulturkampf* was too conciliatory.[95] An arresting figure, Thoemes was short, bearded, and wore blue-tinted glasses to disguise the fact that he had only one

[90] *KZ*, 4 Mar. 1879.
[91] Bachem, *Lose Blätter*, 71.
[92] *Prozeß*, 76–7, 84.
[93] Ibid. 95–6.
[94] Ibid. 120, 137.
[95] LASB, E 107, 450; Thoemes, *Unsere Liebe Frau von Marpingen*, 79–82.

eye.[96] He was also a man of exceptionally nervous disposition. Having first visited Marpingen in October 1876 to escape the attentions of a young friend who believed himself possessed, he left in a melodramatic flight that took him over the border to Luxemburg and on to Belgium, believing himself pursued by Prussian police agents.[97] A flying return visit at the end of November suggested another of Thoemes's failings, the tendency to place an unrealistically high value on his own cleverness. He bought a ticket in Mainz for a destination beyond St Wendel, in order to lead potential observers astray, then attracted the attention of the guard at St Wendel by running out of the station in pouring rain.[98]

Nervousness and vanity combined to produce a series of surreal incidents during the Saarbrücken trial. Almost from the beginning, Thoemes sprang into the proceedings at regular intervals as if he were a third defence counsel, arguing with Judge Cormann about miracles, challenging the testimony of the examining magistrate Kleber, and finding it impossible to contain himself on many other occasions when there was testimony that bore on his own conduct, or when he perceived the need to enlighten the court on the 'enigma' of the apparitions.[99] The most serious incident arose out of an angry exchange with the young legal official Dr Strauß, a former schoolmate of Thoemes's in Trier. Asked by the presiding judge to give his opinion of Thoemes, Strauß said that he found the man unsympathetic: in Berlin he had been 'notorious' as an 'utter crank', and his dissertation did not demonstrate sound study. This attack on Thoemes's character, unrebuked by the court, prompted an understandably indignant protest by defence counsel Bachem that the accused should be obliged to 'run the moral gauntlet'. Thoemes decided to pursue the matter himself, and questioned Strauß until he had extracted from the assistant judge the reason for his hostile opinion: he believed Thoemes's dissertation to be plagiarized from St Thomas Aquinas.[100] This episode led to a further exchange the following day. Eva Langendörfer, an aunt of Katharina Hubertus, testifying about the beginning of the apparitions, was rebuked by Judge Cormann for her inability to remember precise dates. Thoemes, alluding to a similar slip by his tormentor of the previous day, requested archly 'that the witness be asked whether she possessed the same level of education as Dr Strauß.' Thoemes was interrupted by the presiding judge, and informed by the prosecution that he now faced a possible slander charge.[101] When the session resumed the following morning, Strauß declined to pursue the slander charge; but Judge Cormann ruled that Thoemes's remarks constituted disorderly

[96] LASB, E 107, 250, 271.

[97] See Thoemes's own highly coloured accounts, in *Unsere Liebe Frau von Marpingen*, 79, 92–104. Examining magistrate Kleber, reporting on Thoemes's paranoia, noted that no order for his arrest was issued at this time; on the other hand, his home in Freiburg was searched: LASB, E 107, 457; Thoemes, *Unsere Liebe Frau von Marpingen*, 98, 106.

[98] Thoemes, *Unsere Liebe Frau von Marpingen*, 109. Kleber noted, not unjustly, that Thoemes 'attributed an exaggerated importance to his own person': LASB, E 107, 455.

[99] *Prozeß*, 28, 40–2, 181–2, 191–2.

[100] Ibid. 83.

[101] Ibid. 98–9.

conduct by disrupting the proceedings of the court. Bachem therefore found himself defending Thoemes in this play-within-the-play. After a lengthy plea the three judges withdrew to deliberate, and Thoemes was fined 25 marks but not given the custodial sentence to which he was liable under the criminal code.[102]

What do these tragicomic episodes tell us about the trial? They indicate, in the first place, the repeated embarrassment caused to defence counsel—and the case they represented—by the testimony and conduct of some defendants' witnesses. As Bachem observed, in his plea on Thoemes's behalf:

you have before you in the accused Dr Thoemes a man who, even in normal circumstances, suffers from great nervous agitation—I might even say, derangment (*Zerrüttung*), so that the accused is often not in a position simply to sit there quietly, but is in continuous motion, as if certain limbs were twitching nervously.

A man who believed he had done nothing more than pursue his interest in theological-mystical questions, plagued by sleeplessness, his state of agitation heightened by the public proceedings, he was

a person whose nervous excitement mounts with every day, so that the accused is no longer in a position fully to recognize his own interests, even to the point of neglecting the need to retain the goodwill of the bench. The defendant has neglected this consideration on many occasions in a manner that the defence finds truly painful. It is my conviction that the condition of the accused is such that he is longer capable of understanding the full meaning of what he is saying, and can therefore hardly be held responsible for his words and the feelings he gives vent to.[103]

Even in a plea for mitigation, these were harsh words that betray more than a hint of exasperation.

Dr Thoemes was an extreme case, but his contribution to the trial was not the only one that undercut Bachem's sober preference for a defence that concentrated on the indignities to which hapless villagers had been subjected by the power of the state. It is notable how Bachem referred to Thoemes's 'theological-mystical questions' in a manner that distanced him from the considerations in question, much as he might have held a gingerbread Virgin distastefully at arm's length. The Centre spokesmen in the Prussian parliamentary debate, led by Bachem himself, had deliberately tried to put such questions on ice. This was impossible in Saarbrücken, given the enlarged and different character of the dramatis personae. The court therefore heard the widow Blies give thanks to the perjury charge for having secured her a way to heaven. It heard the priest-publicist Paul Majunke gratuitously offer his thoughts on Goethe, miracles, and the spiritual world—along with political observations that moved the public prosecutor to further threats of legal action.[104] And the defence counsel were obliged to listen as several of the 'rival children' were called to testify, and variously described seeing a dancing devil and climbing a long white ladder to heaven.[105]

[102] Ibid. 105–9.
[103] Ibid. 107–8.
[104] Ibid. 85–90.
[105] Ibid. 193–6.

If much of this was unwelcome to the defence, it had hardly happened acci-
dentally. Many of the 'sensational' episodes reflected a consistent favouring of
the prosecution by the presiding judge. The exchanges between Strauß and
Thoemes were symptomatic. Not only was Strauß not rebuked for his initial attack
on Thoemes's integrity; the open-ended question to which he was responding was
of a kind that Judge Cormann was reluctant to put to character witnesses for the
defence. The court allowed the dubious testimony of the 'rival children', but did
not—as the defence requested—allow the original three Marpingen visionaries
to be heard.[106] The presiding judge treated the bizarre story of Helene Schmidt
and the fortune-teller with a heavy solemnity that the incident appeared not to
warrant (as the subsequent enquiries showed), and the defence was understandably suspicious when, on the following day, the prosecutor once again
announced that he had received evidence of possible threats against the witness
Amalie Lazarus. After her anticlimactic testimony was over, Bachem became
involved in a sharp exchange with the presiding judge:

BACHEM. Once again we have a dubious story (*dunkle Geschichte*) before us, as we had
    yesterday. In the present case too the defence wishes for the speediest and most complete
    clarification. I must say that it would certainly have been worth while to influence such
    an important witness with threats!
JUDGE CORMANN. It appears from the tone in which defence counsel made his obser-
    vation that he places little value on the testimony.
BACHEM. I certainly wished to indicate immediately the true value of this new dubious
    story.

The senior prosecutor announced that the episode would be investigated, but the
court heard nothing more about it.[107]
    The latitude that the prosecution was allowed in trying to suggest guilt by
association was most evident on the morning of 13 March, two days before the
end of the trial. Johann Ney, a goldsmith from Saarlouis, had been testifying
about an order he received for Marpingen medallions. The order came from 'a
hawker who looked as if he was from the Speicher or the Hunsrück', and had
been placed sometime in the summer of 1876. The precise timing was clearly
important, and the presiding judge devoted much attention to this, without being
able to establish that the order had predated the onset of the apparitions. It was
left to the public prosecutor to turn the place, rather than the time, into a
suspicious circumstance. Disregarding the witness's loose, generic charac-
terization of the hawker (the Speicher was well known for its large population of
itinerants), Pattberg observed that 'all possible steps' had been taken to trace this
man 'from the Speicher'. Why? Because a letter had recently been received by a
Würzburg lawyer addressed to Eduard Kullmann, the apprentice cooper who
had made an attempt on Bismarck's life in May 1878. This anonymous letter

---

[106] *Prozeß*, 32–3; *Marpinger Prozeß vor dem Richterstuhle der Vernunft*, 26–9.
[107] *Prozeß*, 96.

contained a death-threat against the Chancellor, and it had been posted in Illingen, 'near Marpingen'. The public prosecutor continued:

This circumstantial evidence pointed once again to the Speicher. At that time a particular person caught our eye. Herr Hüllessem also went to the Speicher during that period, but the identity of Ney's contact could not be established. This fact assumed an even greater importance because Elisabeth Flesch, the 'blood-sweater' of Eppelborn, also came from the Speicher, and Father Kickerts who was convicted in that case had also been a long-serving priest in the Speicher.

The links in this chain of associations were barely discernible; the innuendo was all too obvious.[108] Judge Cormann merely noted how thorough the investigations had been, before observing coolly that these matters had nothing to do with the present case. Defence counsel Simons thereupon protested about the gratuitous insertion of these 'suspicious facts' into the hearing. The transcript describes Simons as 'extremely agitated'. He and Bachem engaged in some ten minutes of vigorous exchanges with Pattberg and Cormann, arguing that the prosecution had improperly read material into the record suggesting guilt by association. They received little satisfaction, for the presiding judge closed the matter with the observation that he 'concurred entirely' with the explanation given by the public prosecutor for his introduction of the material.[109]

This pattern ran through the trial. The court invariably allowed a greater latitude to the prosecution, holding it to lower standards of relevance than were applied to the defence. The procedural exchanges tell the same story. At no stage did the presiding judge rebuke or restrain the prosecutor, but there were dozens of clashes with the defence lawyers. They took place over the admissibility of evidence, the testimony of particular witnesses, and the rulings of the court. Some of the exchanges were very frosty indeed.[110]

As Bachem noted later, one could not help thinking that the presiding judge had already decided on the guilt of the accused.[111] His sympathies were evident not only in the indulgence he showed towards the prosecution, but in his direct interventions. (Even after the introduction of public prosecutors in Prussia and other states, German judges played a much more active, inquisitorial role in trials than their English counterparts, as was generally the case in Continental judicial proceedings.) At the very beginning of the trial, in emphasizing the importance of the oath, Judge Cormann pointedly used the formulation that the ends did not justify the means. This was a coded but obvious allusion to the Jesuits and their alleged disdain for the truth. He rubbed in the message with a warning that witnesses should not feel that they had to protect church or clergy.[112] In

[108] The association of Marpingen with Elisabeth Flesch was especially disingenuous, given that an investigation had established absolutely no connection between the two cases: LASB, E 107, 131.
[109] *Prozeß*, 188–91.
[110] See e.g. the harsh exchange over the testimony of the gendarme Hentschel: ibid. 163.
[111] Bachem, *Lose Blätter*, 71
[112] *Prozeß*, 12.

questioning members of the clergy, whether defendants or witnesses, Judge Cormann was often peremptory to the point of insolence. He could also be very disingenuous. When the magistrate Gatzen of Tholey (a Catholic) reported Neureuter's expressed conviction that the magistrate would in time come to believe in the apparitions, Cormann seized on this as a suspiciously 'prophetic' utterance.[113] The presiding judge made no effort to hide his distaste for the events that had inspired the trial. After listening to testimony about the popular lore that sprang up around the fallen tree in Urexweiler, he complained 'that the people are not more enlightened'.[114] In this, Judge Cormann's personal feelings probably differed little from those of Julius Bachem. The difference lay in the fact that Cormann seemed predisposed to believe that 'superstition' was intrinsically linked to untruthfulness.

There was a class dimension to all this. Commenting on medical testimony about an alleged cure, the presiding judge lamented the poor air and insanitary conditions to be found in mining villages—a remark that suggested less than complete familiarity with the geography of Marpingen.[115] On another occasion, exasperated with the inability of the witness Eva Langendörfer to recall whether she had been to the Härtelwald on 3 or 4 July, he observed that an apparition was surely a significant event for 'you peasants'.[116] This remark gave rise to an interruption from the public. Its source was an unidentified earlier witness, who apparently shouted out 'Only peasants!'. The incident prompted the presiding judge to remark in the following session that he had 'often had occasion in this court to become acquainted with the violence and brutality of the populace'. On the other hand, the people had great respect for the court; a word sufficed to restore order. It was therefore 'all the more astonishing to hear such a remark from those lips'.[117] Condescension was joined here with chagrin that the rude manners of the populace had penetrated the courtroom.

The hostility of the presiding judge posed problems for the defence, but it can also be read differently—as a sign of unease at the way the case was going. That is the unmistakable impression to be gained from reading through the transcript of the two-week trial. The dramatic episodes punctuated proceedings in which the weight of arguments lay with the defence. The state summonsed no fewer than 170 witnesses, against just twenty-six for the defence; but the prosecution found itself unable to build a convincing case out of the mass of evidence.[118] Many of those summonsed by the state were, in effect, hostile witnesses, but the

---

[113] *Prozeß*, 53.

[114] Ibid. 184–5.

[115] Ibid. 117. The defence lawyer Simons pointed out the inaccurate description of Marpingen as a 'mining village', although his own contention that there were only 'a few miners' there was, if anything, even more wide of the mark.

[116] Ibid. 97.

[117] Ibid. 106–7. The interruption from the public is not directly recorded in the transcript. The phrase used has to be inferred from Cormann's own reference to it the following day.

[118] Ibid. 9, on the numbers of witnesses summonsed.

prosecution had problems even with witnesses whose statements suggested that their testimony would be helpful. One, Emma Walter from the Saarbrücken institute, turned out to be younger than the court records showed, and was unable to testify under oath.[119] Some, including Captain Fragstein-Riemsdorff, failed to attend.[120] Others proved to be poor witnesses. To the evident vexation of the presiding judge and the delight of the defence, the former examining magistrate Emil Kleber admitted to procedural omissions in his questioning of Thoemes that weakened part of the case against the Catholic publicist.[121] Different problems arose with the railway official and former teacher Girard, who testified on the conduct of the visionaries' parents. His evidence was accompanied by energetic gesticulations that provoked laughter in the courtroom public and frequent rebukes from Judge Cormann. He also admitted to drunkenness while in Marpingen.[122]

Many prosecution witnesses did attend, were of age, and gave sober testimony. But what did their evidence add up to? There was abundant and generally convincing testimony, particularly from Herr and Frau Riemer and some of their charges in the Prince Wilhelm and Marianne Institute, that cast Margaretha Kunz in a very poor light.[123] But she and her two companions were not on trial, and the evidence that any of their parents had been engaged in deception was circumstantial at best. It rested on the testimony of witnesses who agreed that the parents had accepted money for boarding guests, but disagreed on the sums involved, and on the ambiguous words shouted up to Margaretha Kunz by her mother from the courtyard of the institute. Frau Kunz swore that she exhorted her daughter to 'tell the truth'; Frau Riemer insisted the words had been 'tell them what you told them before'.[124] The picture of Frau Kunz that emerged from the proceedings may have been unedifying, but it hardly constituted grounds for conviction.

The state found it difficult to prove any pecuniary advantage through fraud. It was able to show that after the apparitions had occurred, many villagers saw Marpingen as another Lourdes and benefited accordingly, but no testimony came close to demonstrating that monetary gain prompted the apparitions in the first place, let alone that orders for pilgrimage medallions and the like had been placed before the event. Again, the state showed that Johann Leist was suspiciously well-off in January 1877; but the defence was able to prove that he had sold two head

[119] Ibid. 72.
[120] Ibid. 15.
[121] Ibid. 41–2. The issue turned on whether Kleber had shown the statements relating to recantations by the three visionaries to Thoemes. To the obvious vexation of the presiding judge, he had not done so; nor could he testify with certainty that he had spoken to Thoemes about the details, although he thought he 'probably' had as Thoemes left the room. By the time of the trial Kleber had become an assistant judge in Cologne.
[122] Ibid. 125–8.
[123] For the evidence of the Riemers, see ibid. 59–68.
[124] Ibid. 66–8.

of cattle that month.[125] To take another example, many witnesses testified to seeing money at the apparition site and elsewhere in the village, but there was a notable dearth of evidence linking this to the accused. In this, as in so many issues concerning the movements and actions of the defendants, accurate identification was crucial. Cases of mistaken identity had plagued the enquiry into Marpingen, understandably enough in a village where one person in ten was called Recktenwald. They continued to dog the trial: the value of Riemer's evidence was partly undercut by his confusion of Frau Leist and Frau Hubertus.[126] To the extent that the charges were capable of being proved in the first place, the prosecution needed witnesses from Marpingen itself who could describe events in detail and identify the persons involved with certainty. It was no surprise, given the nature of the statements taken during the enquiry, that witnesses of this kind were not forthcoming.

The judges faced much the same problem with Marpingers as the examining magistrates had encountered earlier: their reluctance to make incriminating statements.[127] The trial was, of course, taking place nearly three years after the apparitions began, and villagers were not the only ones whose testimony was vague.[128] But it is difficult not to be struck by the procession of witnesses from Marpingen who had apparently modelled themselves on the three wise monkeys. Some had made potentially incriminating statements earlier, which they now withdrew.[129] Others proved remarkably forgetful about dates, places, or individuals.[130] As we have seen, one witness was taken into custody on the grounds of suspected perjury; others were given stern warnings.[131] But there was ultimately little that the judges could do against this collective amnesia.

There was also little to be done about the self-destructive testimony of Meerscheidt-Hüllessem. His proved to be one of the more eventful contributions to the trial, and it did nothing but damage to the prosecution's case. He was sworn in on the morning of Wednesday 5 March, the fifth session of the trial.[132] From the beginning he showed a marked reluctance to be drawn into detail on his activities, a reticence that the presiding judge fully supported. As Judge Cormann handed the detective over for cross-examination, he observed that Meerscheidt-Hüllessem 'could expect to be attacked'. This expectation was certainly fulfilled.

---

[125] *Prozeß*, 266–7.

[126] Ibid. 68.

[127] The presiding judge expressed his exasperation on one occasion that the defence seemed to have found it easy to determine who made the cross placed at the apparition site, whereas a lengthy enquiry had proved fruitless: ibid. 105.

[128] Compare the testimony of Dr Frank from Lebach on statements allegedly made by Father Schwaab, which he could only 'vaguely remember': ibid. 95.

[129] Examples include Peter Schnur, taking back previous testimony about Nikolaus Recktenwald, and Johann Urhahn, recanting earlier statements about the spring in the Härtelwald: ibid. 103–5, 120–1.

[130] e.g. ibid. 168–70, 183.

[131] Ibid. 120–1.

[132] Ibid. 43–50, for Meerscheidt-Hüllessem's testimony and cross-examination.

Defence counsel, led by Bachem, engaged in an explicit and largely successful attempt to discredit the detective. He was questioned about his earliest report on the 'French sympathies' in Marpingen, his dealings with the visionary children and his recommendation that two of them be sent to an insane asylum, his repeated calls for the imprisonment of Neureuter, and his use of Stephan Brill, a man with a long criminal record, as a confidant. Despite the periodic interventions of the presiding judge to protect the witness, Meerscheidt-Hüllessem cut a poor figure. To question after damning question he offered equivocal answers; again and again he 'could not recall' individual details until his own statements were quoted back to him by Bachem or Simons.

The most serious episode turned on the question of the 5 marks the detective offered to Margaretha Kunz. When first asked about this, Meerscheidt-Hüllessem could no longer recall the incident. The relevant passage of his statement was then read out: he 'was in the Kunz house and offered the girl 5 marks in the presence of her mother; the child looked questioningly at her mother, and the mother nodded'. The detective ventured the observation that this did not show he had actually given the money. Even the presiding judge found this difficult to accept. Meerscheidt-Hüllessem then maintained that the 5 marks had been intended 'to win the girl's confidence'. To the crucial question whether Margaretha Kunz had actually accepted the money—or whether she had not, in fact, indignantly rejected it by throwing it on the floor—he responded only: 'I cannot say yes or no.' The point could not be clarified through further cross-examination, for Judge Cormann had already announced that the detective was urgently required back in Berlin by his superiors. To this the defence reluctantly acceded. Later in the trial a witness was called to testify that the money had in fact been given away to the poor. The defence had the two recipients waiting to give evidence, but they were not needed. The court accepted the case made by the defence, and the presiding judge reported on two letters that had been received from Meerscheidt-Hüllessem, 'clarifying'—in fact, correcting—several points in his earlier statements. In the second of these letters he noted coolly that 'the conclusion that the child had taken the money was probably not correct'. Bachem succeeded in having the misleading passage from the original statement read out again in court, pointing out the inference the detective had obviously intended. Judge Cormann could only reply gloomily that he had 'already taxed him with that'.[133] It was a key moment in the trial, signalling the moral as well as evidential collapse of the prosecution case.

The testimony was completed on the afternoon of Thursday 13 March, and the following morning was given over to the reading out of letters to Neureuter and others that had been seized during the enquiry. After a lengthy recess of four and a half hours, Senior Prosecutor Pattberg led off with his closing plea. It was a lengthy speech full of concessions.[134] Pattberg had not expected to prosecute

[133] Ibid. 202–4.
[134] Pattberg's speech occupied all of the afternoon session, from 4.30 to 7.30: ibid. 215–45.

the case, and admitted his lack of familiarity with the mass of written testimony. He also conceded the shortcomings of the case put together by the prosecution. Only two persons had eventually been charged with public order offences, the forester Altmeyer and Father Eich, and Pattberg called for both to be acquitted on grounds of insufficient evidence. He also called for the acquittal of four of those against whom charges of fraud had been brought: Fathers Eich and Schwaab, the schoolteacher André, and Susanna Leist's sister Margaretha. The public prosecutor nevertheless demanded the conviction of the majority of those charged with fraud, or aiding and abetting fraud. The children, he argued, had been demonstrably untruthful, and adults who stood in the dock had encouraged them, even after the visionaries' recantations, for reasons of personal gain or to gain material advantage for the local church. Such infractions 'cannot be strongly enough punished'. Pattberg called for custodial sentences ranging from three years for Magdalena Kunz and Father Neureuter, down to one year for Father Dicke, Dr Thoemes, and four of the five adult visionaries. These were far more severe than the sentences handed down to those found guilty in the Berschweiler case.[135]

The defence had an easier case to make. Simons wasted little breath on the abject failure of the state to prove any of the much-bruited public disorder charges. For the most part he underlined the fact (accepted even by the prosecution) that the accused, along with the rest of Marpingen, had originally believed in the truth of the apparitions. If they had failed to heed the later 'recantations' of the visionaries, then there were powerful reasons for this: suspicion that the recantations might be diabolical in inspiration, the belief that the girls were reacting to chronic homesickness after being taken to Saarbrücken, and distrust of any statements connected with the machinations of the detective from Berlin. On the question of fraud, moreover, the prosecution had not produced a shred of evidence to support the charges.[136] The division of labour between the two defence counsel left Julius Bachem to deal with the more general implications of the case. His closing plea strongly resembled his speech more than a year earlier in the Prussian lower house.[137] Bachem referred to the *Kulturkampf* in underlining the importance of the vacant see in Trier, which impeded a canonical enquiry. He noted the 'monstrous assumption' of guilt that had driven the Marpingen enquiry, and made clerical co-operation with the state impossible. Above all, he spoke at length about the 'recantations' of the three girls, and the psychological background to them. The direction of this argument was obvious, and Bachem came finally to a harsh denunciation of Meerscheidt-Hüllessem:

We are dealing here either with an extremely rash or an extremely unscrupulous man. As one can hardly accept that the Minister of the Interior, in lending support from Berlin to

---

[135] The heaviest sentence in this case was the 10 months' imprisonment imposed on two of the seven who were convicted: *SMZ*, 10 and 11 Jan. 1878; *SPB*, 20 Jan. 1878.

[136] For Simon's plea, *Prozeß*, 245–59.

[137] Bachem's plea, ibid. 260–77.

the authorities here, would send a completely incompetent official, we are left only with the second alternative, and for myself I have no hesitation in saying, in the light of what has happened in these proceedings and of the material on record—which remain vividly in my mind—that I hold this man capable of anything to achieve his ends.

It was a damning judgement, allowed to pass without any intervention from the court.[138] Bachem concluded that juridically and morally the accused had no case to answer; the charges against them were 'unbelievable, even absurd'. He demanded acquittals, in the expectation that 'justice can make good, in so far as it is still possible, the sins of the administrative authorities in this affair'.[139]

The court was adjourned on 15 March. Three weeks later, on 5 April, the judges gave their verdict before another crowded courtroom. It took over two hours to read, and it pronounced all the defendants innocent, with costs awarded against the state.[140] The prosecution immediately announced that it would appeal. The verdict caused 'something of a sensation' among those gathered in the court.[141] There was widespread recognition in liberal circles that the questionable trial had been a failure, while the Catholic press was jubilant. The *St-Paulinus-Blatt* of Trier asked rhetorically: 'Was it really worth starting these grand proceedings in the first place? Should the state not have saved itself the 11,000 marks in witness costs? Was it not obvious from the preliminary enquiry that material evidence was lacking?'[142]

These were all good questions, and they received an implicit answer in the actions that followed from the Prussian authorities. On 9 April, all but two of the fourteen gendarmes stationed in the Härtelwald since 1876 were withdrawn (the last two were withdrawn in November). On 5 May, the acquitted forester Altmeyer, who had been suspended from his post, was reinstated with full arrears of pay. Three days later, Senior Prosecutor Pattberg withdrew the appeal, probably after receiving word from higher up about the costs involved in a process that was likely to yield little reward. One hostile commentator estimated that the enquiry and trial had already cost in excess of 100,000 marks.[143] In 1880, the *Prussian Military Gazette* announced that from 2 March, Colonel Schön, commanding officer of the 30th Infantry Regiment stationed in Saarlouis, Major Walkling, and three captains, including Captain Fragstein-Riemsdorff, had been placed on the retired list. This was the talk of the press, which described the action as 'unheard of' in the Prussian army.[144] Four years later *Landrat* Rumschöttel resigned and retired to Wiesbaden.[145] Police Commissar Meerscheidt-

[138] Ibid. 275; Bachem, *Lose Blätter*, 73–4, and *Erinnerungen*, 140–1.
[139] *Prozeß*, 277.
[140] *Urtheil des Zuchtpolizeigerichts Saarbrücken im Marpinger Prozeße, verkündet am 5. April 1879* (Trier, 1879). See also *Marpinger Prozeß vor dem Richterstuhle der Vernunft*, 48.
[141] *SMZ*, 8 Apr. 1879.
[142] *SPB*, 13 Apr. 1879.
[143] *Marpinger Prozeß vor dem Richterstuhle der Vernunft*, 48–9. The liberal press was already speculating in April that the high costs might jeopardize an appeal: *SMZ*, 12 Apr. 1879.
[144] *Marpinger Prozeß vor dem Richterstuhle der Vernunft*, 49.
[145] Müller, *St Wendel*, 276.

Hüllessem flourished in Berlin through the period of the anti-socialist law when, as we have seen, his methods remained much the same.[146] In the 1890s he was one of those entrusted with maintaining a secret register of suspected homosexuals. This unsavoury activity was to lead to his nemesis after another celebrated trial. In 1900 the banker August Sternberg was tried on charges of immorality. As a result of the gross irregularities by senior police officials that were uncovered during the legal proceedings, Meerscheidt-Hüllessem took his own life.[147]

---

[146] See above, Ch. 7.
[147] Haller, *Geschichte der Frankfurter Zeitung*, 800; Fricke, *Bismarcks Prätorianer*, 71.

11

The Church Stays Silent

The Council of Trent had laid down clearly how the church should proceed when claims of private revelations arose. A rigorous canonical enquiry was to be undertaken. In the case of apparitions, this meant interrogating the visionaries and examining their state of mind, taking statements from other witnesses, and investigating any claims of sudden or miraculous cures. Until the enquiry had been concluded and a formal judgement reached, the clergy was expected to maintain a neutral position; any support for the apparitions by individual priests or members of the laity had a purely private, unofficial status. This procedure was intended to preserve the integrity of the faith and the hierarchy of authority within the church.[1] Matters were rarely so straightforward in practice. It was particularly difficult for the parish priest to remain neutral. Where claims of apparitions did not collapse in the face of his initial remonstrations, the priest in question usually came to the private opinion that there must be something to them. He was all the more likely to adopt a position of benevolent neutrality rather than cool distance, given the popular local support for the apparitions that invariably developed and the consequent danger of cutting himself off entirely from his parishioners. The parish priest, as we have seen, found himself in the middle: clerical caution and the demands of office pulled him in one direction, popular sentiment and often his own instincts pulled him in another. At the same time, any sustained series of apparitions was likely to enlist a variety of individual priests, publicists, and other lay Catholics on both sides of the question. In that respect the German apparitions of the 1870s were no different from La Salette or Lourdes, except that the rapid growth in communications during the third quarter of the nineteenth century made the battle of opinions more fierce and more public. In these circumstances it became even more essential, from the standpoint of the church, that a decisive canonical verdict be pronounced as speedily as possible.

The urgency was perhaps greatest in the case of Marpingen. It achieved the largest resonance, acquired the widest fame and notoriety, became the object of the greatest hopes and fears. Its supporters were hungry for official endorsement of the German Lourdes; the sceptical looked for an end to the nonsense. The

---

[1] See above, Ch. 1.

prospect of a future canonical enquiry was in the minds of everyone who wrote or spoke about the apparitions. Father Neureuter and his fellow priests, the authors of pamphlets, the Catholic press, the Centre Party spokesmen in the Prussian parliament, Julius Bachem at the Saarbrücken trial: all, from their different positions, made a point of emphasizing that only a canonical commission of enquiry could pronounce final judgement. And yet the church never mounted a formal investigation and passed judgement. Why?

A Textbook Enquiry: Mettenbuch

The enquiry conducted by the Regensburg hierarchy into Mettenbuch was a textbook procedure under canon law, and a brief examination of it will suggest some of the reasons for the more muddled response to Marpingen. At the beginning events in the two places followed a similar course. The parish priest, Father Anglhuber, spoke to the Mettenbuch children immediately after their apparitions in December 1876, and to an older male farm servant who believed himself possessed and also claimed to have seen visions. He took detailed statements and 'tried everything to budge them from their claims'.[2] After that the pattern of events was different. Anglhuber had a superior to whom he could report, just as Regensburg could hold the parish priest responsible for his actions. The children stuck to their story and pilgrims arrived in growing numbers, but Regensburg was able to set an enquiry in motion. By early September 1877, a canonical commission of enquiry had been organized and the division of responsibilities between Bishop Senestrey's ecclesiastical counsellors established.[3] The commission met from 21 September to 14 November 1877, with senior clergy from Regensburg joined by medical men. It had the detailed testimony of the parish priest and the statements he had taken down, reports from doctors on alleged cures, and character reports on the visionary children from teachers. There was even a report from the pharmacist Schmid of Regensburg on the 'miraculous' water (it concluded that 'the water in question is *definitely not* to be characterized as good drinking water').[4]

The findings of the commission were negative, but the problem remained of what to do with the visionaries, especially as their apparitions resumed and attracted support from prominent Catholics.[5] There was intense irritation about the pamphlet penned by Father Braunmüller, which had first appeared as a 'short

[2] BZAR, F 115, Fasc. I, Beilage I, 'Protokolle der Visionäre. Neujahr 1877 mitgeteilt. Metten, d. 24 Dezember 1876': statements taken in turn from Theres Liebl, Mathilde Sack, Johann Eikl, Joseph Kraus, Karolina Kraus, Katharina Kraus, and Franz-Xaver Kraus.

[3] BZAR, F 115, Fasc. I: note of Bishop Senestrey's, 5 Sept. 1877.

[4] Ibid. I: 'Akten der bischöfl. Commission, vom 21. Sept. bis 14. Nov. 1877'. Expert testimony (*Gutachten*) can be found in a supplementary volume ('Beilage ad 17'), in Fasc. II, 'Berichte über angebliche Wunder-Heilungen 1878', and in 'Beilage III zu Fasc. I'.

[5] See the heavy correspondence between Father Anglhuber and Regensburg in BZAR, F 115, Fasc. III, 'Briefliche Mittheilungen von Metten und Waldsassen, 1878'.

report' of fifteen pages in spring 1877 and was into a fifth, much enlarged edition by 1878.[6] Regensburg felt that Father Anglhuber was too indulgent towards the visionaries and had been less than discreet: 'as long as this Father Anglhuber remained in communication with the children, any enquiry was illusory'.[7] It was therefore decided to isolate the visionaries. At the beginning of May 1878, Theres Liebl and Karolina Kraus were taken to the Cistercian convent of Waldsassen, to be followed five weeks later by Anna Liebl. They were joined in August by the eldest of the visionaries, Mathilde Sack. Anglhuber had already marked her down as rather too old for visions (her fourteenth birthday fell during the apparitions of December 1876) and took the view that her 'sad family circumstances' had 'impaired the innocence of her heart'. The fact that she was 'talented' meant that she had 'possibly influenced the younger children'. Anglhuber accordingly arranged for Mathilde to be removed from Mettenbuch and placed in the convent of the English Sisters, the Damenstift in Osterhofen, where she was to be subject to 'close observation' by the Mother Superior.[8] But her continued contact with the parish priest and the regime at Osterhofen appeared too indulgent to the bishop, and on 10 August 1878 she joined her fellows in Waldsassen.[9]

The hand of Bishop Senestrey was plainly visible in all of these steps. He was a man who excited strong feelings in the church, a revered and long-serving prelate (he was bishop from 1858 to 1906) who also inspired the most scurrilous gossip.[10] The Catholic priest and academic Franz-Xaver Kraus, always disposed to believe the worst of 'ultramontanes', recorded a story told to him by a Munich law professor that when Senestrey was a parish priest he had been investigated as a suspected accomplice in an abortion, the files on which 'disappeared without trace when he became a bishop'.[11] From a theologian who had attended the First Vatican Council Kraus heard 'how this most brazen spokesman for ultra-montanism in Germany, before he became a bishop and in order to become one, truckled to the government in the basest manner and played the liberal; how Cardinal Reisach was so outraged by the impudent, shameless scoundrel that he

---

[6] Braunmüller, *Kurzer Bericht*. See BZAR, F 115, Fasc. III, Senestrey to Braunmüller, 16 Nov. 1878, and Braunmüller's reply of 19 Nov. 1878. For all Braunmüller's formal disclaimer that he was seeking to pre-empt a canonical judgement, his enthusiasm for the apparitions was unmistakable.

[7] See BZAR, F 115, Fasc. IV, Senestrey's 'Pro memoria über die Mettenbucher Erscheinungen', 13 Nov. 1878. Senestrey's letter to Braunmüller also contained stinging criticism of Anglhuber's conduct, ibid. Fasc. III: Senestrey to Braunmüller, 16 Nov. 1878.

[8] BZAR, F 115, Fasc. I: 'Bericht des Pfarramtes Metten über die behaupteten Erscheinungen ...', V: Verhalten des Pfarrers diesen Erscheinungen gegenüber'.

[9] On the contacts, see for example BZAR, F 115, Fasc. III: Mathilde Sack to Anglhuber, 24 June and 5 July 1878; Anglhuber to Sack, 21 July 1878. Senestrey's thoughts are recorded in Fasc. IV: 'Pro memoria über die Mettenbucher Erscheinungen', 13 Nov. 1878.

[10] See J. Staber, *Kirchengeschichte des Bistums Regensburg* (Regensburg, 1966), 190–7. Senestrey's services are emphasized in P. Mai (ed.), *Ignatius Senestrey: Festschrift zur 150 Wiederkehr seines Geburtstages* (Bärnau, 1968). Mai is also the editor of *Ignatius Senestrey: Eine Selbstbiographie* (Regensburg, 1967).

[11] Kraus, *Tagebücher*, 402–3, entry of 17 Aug. 1879.

wanted to throw him down the steps, etc'.[12] Opinions therefore varied on Senestrey; but nobody doubted that this son of an official and nephew of a vicar-general was a formidable figure. The bishop placed his own imprint on the treatment of the girls. They were confined in Waldsassen because 'I regarded it as absolutely necessary to keep these four girls under my *special* supervision and observation *exclusively* until further notice'. He ordered that they be kept in conditions of isolation and receive no visitors: 'nobody, whatever status and rank he may have, should be allowed to come into contact with the children without special authorization'. They were to be permitted to talk about the apparitions only with their father confessor.[13] The record of the children's stay in Waldsassen shows that they suffered under this regime. They looked frightened, cried, and periodically refused food. Senestrey interrogated the children personally during September and November 1878. The bishop watched his wayward sheep very closely—he even recorded the precise ways in which Karolina Kraus fidgeted during the interrogation of 9 November—and the questioning was rigorous in the extreme.[14]

It was Mathilde Sack whose spirit he was most keen to break. She was kept under especially close observation by Senestrey and a Provincial of the Redemptorist order who was in Waldsassen at the time.[15] They concluded that there was 'no trace' in her of childish innocence; instead of simplicity and piety, they found dissimulation and defiance. In short, she made 'an extremely bad impression' on the two men. It is not difficult to see why. Senestrey had informed himself about Mathilde Sack's chequered life and talked to companions who had known her in earlier years. She knew a song containing so many 'lewd allusions' that 'no innocent girl would allow her mouth to be dirtied by it'—the motif of the sensual, brazen girl runs through Senestrey's judgements. She had been exposed to 'unhealthy' influences at home (her father had read the anticlerical *Gartenlaube*), and had even picked up from somewhere the name Ignaz Döllinger, the most celebrated of the Catholic theologians who broke with the church over infallibility. The Virgin Mary had supposedly said Mathilde should pray for him.[16] An

[12] Kraus, *Tagebücher*, 373–4, conversation of 5 Nov. 1876. Cardinal Reisach was a former Bishop of Eichstätt and Archbishop of Munich who was called to Rome as a cardinal in 1855.

[13] BZAR, F 115, Fasc. IV: 'Protokoll über die vom 20st bis 23st September 1878 zu Waldsassen gepflogenen Untersuchung im Betreff der Mettenbucher Erscheinungen'. When Senestrey talked of 'keeping' the girls in Waldsassen he used the word *behalten*, which also has the sense of 'detain'.

[14] This account of what occurred in Waldsassen is based on BZAR, F 115, Fasc. IV: Senestrey's 'Pro memoria …'; 'Protokoll über die vom 20st bis 23st September 1878 zu Waldsassen gepflogener Untersuchung im Betreff der Mettenbucher Erscheinungen', particularly Senestrey's undated general description of the interrogations; the documentation on the interrogations of Mathilde Sack, Therese Liebl, and Karolina Kraus. There is also relevant material in an unnumbered additional file labelled 'Mettenbuch. Mathilde Sack in Waldsassen'.

[15] Senestrey made very precise arrangements to monitor her: any letters she received were 'without exception' to be brought to his attention; and 'without her knowing it' she was 'constantly kept under close observation'.

[16] Did she require permission to pray for Döllinger, asked Mathilde Sack? 'No', the parish priest had told her; 'Yes', chorused Senestrey and the Redemptorist in Waldsassen.

apostate priest was not expected to provide the subject-matter of a Marian apparition. Nor were 14-year-old girls of Mathilde Sack's background expected to concern themselves with such matters. This comes close to the heart of the confrontation between bishop and servant girl. All accounts agree that Mathilde Sack was spirited and had shown some desire to escape the tribulations of her life by becoming a nun. For Senestrey her spirit was suspicious, and she should be trained in the domestic skills of a 'useful servant'. There was, of course, a further dimension that was crucial from the perspective of the hierarchy. Mathilde Sack threatened to become the object of an unwanted secondary cult. She encountered 'absolute faith and blind trust almost all around her', was regarded by the credulous as 'a being singled out and favoured by God': it was necessary to cut down her status as an 'elevated being'.

Mathilde Sack proved difficult to break down. She was, in Senestrey's words, 'a mistress of lies and misrepresentation', 'cunning enough' to keep her answers short. The bishop pressed her, but 'all exhortations, even the most severe threats, remained unsuccessful'. Then he suggested that if she had seen anything, it was the devil, into whose power she was falling more and more as she persisted in her lies. Still she made no admission. Eventually the pressure told, as Senestrey taxed the girl with 'her wild life and her earlier untruthfulness, depravity, and shamelessness'. Mathilde Sack buckled and confessed to lying; so did the other girls in Waldsassen. Less poised than Mathilde, the younger Theres Liebl and Lina Kraus were pressed to the point that they fell out among themselves and accused each other of lying. The circumstances recall those faced by the three young Marpingen visionaries detained in Saarbrücken, and the results were much the same. By November the church had four confessions. That same month the fifth seer, 11-year-old Franz-Xaver Kraus, was interrogated in Regensburg, then at Metten in December 1878: his answers suggested that Frau Kraus had prompted her two children.[17] In January 1879 a pastoral letter was issued from Regensburg. A canonical enquiry had examined the Mettenbuch apparitions and deemed them to be inauthentic; Catholics in good standing were no longer to lend the apparitions their support.[18]

The enquiry into Mettenbuch proceeded on conventional lines. Despite the equivocal role played by the parish priest, the premature support for the apparitions in Father Braunmüller's pamphlet, and the stubbornness of Mathilde Sack, the hierarchy could regard the outcome with satisfaction. Its success was based on the striking extent to which the church was able to do in the Mettenbuch case what was undertaken by the state in Marpingen. It was Bishop Senestrey or those acting on his authority who took statements from the principals involved, co-operated with members of the medical profession to examine allegedly miraculous

[17] BZAR, F 115, Fasc. V: 'Vernehmung des Fr. Xav. Kraus in Regensburg. Nov. 1878. Weitere Vernehmungen in Metten. Dezbr. 1878'.
[18] Ibid. Fasc. VI: 'Gutachten über die Sache. Entscheidung durch den Hirtenbrief v. 23. Jan. 1879'. A copy of the pastoral letter can be found at the end of the file.

cures, rebuked over-zealous publicists, and detained the visionary children in conditions where they could be observed and interrogated until they confessed. In Mettenbuch, the church launched an enquiry and declared the apparitions inauthentic; in Marpingen the state declared the apparitions inauthentic and launched an enquiry.

Problems in Trier

The contrast brings out the differences between the Bavarian diocese of Regensburg and the Prussian diocese of Trier during the 1870s. It was the Prussian *Kulturkampf* that made the difference, and the *Kulturkampf* that made it impossible to mount an official enquiry into the Marpingen apparitions. There was, in the first place, the damage done to the machinery of church government in Trier. Like every other Prussian diocese, Trier lost its bishop in the course of the struggle between church and state. Bishop Eberhard died in June 1876 and the May Laws made it impossible for the church to elect a successor. When Michael Korum finally came to Trier as the new bishop five years later, he faced 'an expanse of ruins' and a church that had 'atrophied'.[19] Almost a third of all parishes were without a priest, the hierarchical chain of command was under great strain. At the time of the Marpingen apparitions there was no dean in St Wendel, the deanery to which the parish belonged, or in neighbouring Ottweiler.[20] Perhaps more important still, the leadership of the diocese had been driven underground. In the absence of a bishop or a vicar-general, Trier was being run by 'apostolic delegates', the three senior clergy de Lorenzi, Henke, and Reuß, who took the cover-names of the legendary founders of the church in Trier, Eucharius, Valerius, and Maternus. (According to legend they had been sent by St Peter himself.[21]) It was these three men who sought to administer the diocese in the absence of a bishop, coping with the numerous problems posed by the *Kulturkampf* and resisting the efforts made by the Prussian authorities to intercept correspondence and discover their true identities.[22]

These were hardly ideal conditions for setting up a canonical enquiry. That is no doubt why Neureuter seemed so lost in the autumn of 1876, while well-meaning priests offered a variety of suggestions how he might proceed in such irregular circumstances. One referred him to Canon Andreas Laferet in Speyer if he 'needed advice on the canonical handling of the matter'. Another, Dean Heinrichs in Mainz, suggested that Matthias Scheeben might intercede with the

[19] Treitz, *Korum*, 84–6.
[20] *Germania*, 2 Jan. 1877.
[21] A. Heinz, *Glaubenszeugen und Fürsprecher. Die Heiligen des Saarlandes* (Saarbrücken, 1980), 11–16.
[22] Weber, *Kirchliche Politik*, 20–7; Kammer, *Kulturkampfpriester*, 105. They were not the only figures to employ cover-names. In his frequent contacts with Reuß, Windthorst used the name Niewedde; Archbishop Melchers of Cologne went under the name Pomponio.

Archbishop of Cologne (still in post at that time) to mount an enquiry.[23] In fact, the situation in the diocese of Trier was less impossible than it might seem. After all, Eucharius, Valerius, and Maternus did have experience and knowledge of the diocese, and succeeded in holding church government together for five years. Their powers were apparently sufficient to enable them to take action exceeding the requirements of canon law in moving against the few 'state priests' who accepted the May Laws.[24] Any one of the apostolic delegates would have had the authority to head a formal commission of enquiry into Marpingen. *Germania* urged such a step, naming two of them—former Vicar-General de Lorenzi (Eucharius) and Ecclesiastical Counsellor Henke (Valerius)—as ideal for the task, along with two other theologians who held prominent positions in Trier.[25] The newspaper suggested that, with the addition of an unimpeachably 'materialist' senior medical man from Trier, local doctors, and 'other notables', a 'commission of enquiry could easily be brought together, in the face of which any doubt would be stifled'.[26]

It is difficult to believe that *Germania* did not know that this route had in fact already been travelled by Neureuter. He had a quite fortuitous natural connection to the three apostolic delegates unavailable to most parish priests in the diocese, having served as de Lorenzi's curate in Koblenz during the 1860s. As we have seen, Neureuter wrote to his old mentor not long after the apparitions began, urging him to come to Marpingen.[27] De Lorenzi declined (as Senestrey declined to visit Mettenbuch at a similar stage), but he did put Neureuter's request for a canonical enquiry to the cathedral chapter in Trier. The request was turned down.[28] This is not altogether surprising. The Trier cathedral chapter was notoriously divided at the time between 'rationalists' and 'ultramontanes', and there was also the problem that holding a canonical enquiry would be likely to cause further political tensions.[29] In the event of a positive judgement, the position of the apostolic delegates *vis-à-vis* the government might well be worsened—and de Lorenzi was already viewed by the bigoted district governor of Trier as 'the demon of the diocese'.[30] A negative judgement, on the other hand, would play into the hands of the civil authorities and bitterly disappoint the Catholic faithful

[23] LASB, E 107, 190, 204–5: Father Dell of Zell to Neureuter, late Aug. or early Sept. 1876; Dean Heinrichs of Mainz to Cramer, Oct. 1876. Cramer, himself very uncertain what to do, was also in touch with Regent Batsche in Paderborn, who was dubious about the apparitions but appears to have suggested no immediate steps: LASB, E 107, 118–19.

[24] Weber, *Kirchliche Politik*, 23–7.

[25] *Germania*, 2 Jan. 1877. Its further suggestions were Dr Eberhard, regent of the seminary and brother of the dead bishop, and Dr Arnoldi, the brother of Eberhard's predecessor. *Germania* had already made a similar suggestion on 30 Dec. 1876.

[26] *Germania*, 2 Jan. 1877.

[27] See above, Ch. 6.

[28] On these developments, see *Prozeß*, 200.

[29] On the divisons in Trier, see Weber, *Kirchliche Politik*, 2–19, and 23–5, on the particular difficulties that faced the diocese in 1876–7.

[30] Kammer, *Kulturkampfpriester*, 127; Weber, *Kirchliche Politik*, 37, on the government's later opposition to de Lorenzi's episcopal candidacy in 1881.

at a time when Marpingen was still under siege. No wonder, perhaps, that Father
Eich described Valerius (Henke) discussing Marpingen with his 'well-known
half-heartedness'.[31] What was, for Regensburg, a routine enquiry would have
been, in Trier, a politically dangerous luxury from which the church could hardly
emerge without some damage.

The course eventually adopted indicates the practical and political problems
that beset Trier. While Mettenbuch was dealt with within the diocese of Regensburg, the Marpingen case required a more complicated series of steps. At the
beginning of May 1878, exactly at the time that the first two Mettenbuch visionaries were being placed in the convent of Waldsassen, their three counterparts in
Marpingen were sent to the Convent of the Poor Child Jesus in Echternach,
Luxemburg. It is unclear whether this took place with or without the approval of
their parents.[32] Years later, Margaretha Kunz speculated that the move was
intended to 'wrest them' both from the attentions of pilgrims and the continuing
investigation.[33] In fact, the stream of pilgrims had largely dried by May 1878
(although a seasonal boost might have been expected); and the girls had remained
in the world, subject to repeated interrogation, throughout an extraordinarily
lengthy investigation that was now almost complete. The moving of the girls to
Echternach was a first step on the way to a canonical enquiry of sorts.

Why Echternach? With the expulsion of the religious orders, there was no
convent within the diocese of Trier where the girls could be placed. Luxemburg
was in many ways a natural alternative. Trier was hard by the Luxemburg border
and links between the two areas were strong.[34] Historically, the diocese of Trier
had long contained parishes that stretched into Luxemburg.[35] This was ended by
French Revolutionary and Napoleonic armies, and under an agreement between
Rome and Prussia in 1821 the new diocese of Trier stopped short of the border.
But the connection was not broken. In the decades before the *Kulturkampf*,
Luxemburg Redemptorists held missions in the diocese, including Saarland
parishes.[36] Bishop Eberhard of Trier made his *professio fidei* and his episcopal
vows of loyalty to Rome before Bishop Adames of Luxemburg, who—at the
request of the Trier cathedral chapter—also presided at Eberhard's funeral nine
years later.[37] During the *Kulturkampf* the Luxemburg connection proved exceptionally valuable to Trier. De Lorenzi ('Eucharius') referred young couples who

[31] LASB, E 107, 334: Eich to Neureuter, 5 Sept. 1876.

[32] BAT, B III, 11, 14/3, 1; LASB, E 107, 306–7. On the uncertainty over the issue of parental approval,
see the later recollections of Sister Elisa Haben, reporting what she had been told by her mother (who
was Susanna Leist's older sister, Margaretha): BAT, B III, 11, 14/5, 62–8: Sister Elisa Haben to GV
Trier, 17 Nov. 1946.

[33] BAT, B III, 11, 14/3, 59–64.

[34] Many districts within the Trier administrative area contained migrants from Luxemburg. See the
Landrat reports in LHAK, 442/3802.

[35] Marx, *Geschichte der Pfarreien*, i. 176–204.

[36] LHAK, 442/6438, 5–57, 179–83.

[37] Kraft, *Matthias Eberhard*, 105, 242. Suffragan Bishop Kraft was also ordained in 1868 with the
assistance of Bishop Adames: ibid. 132.

wished to be married but lived in a parish with a 'state priest' to sympathetic clergy across the border.[38] Many priests expelled from Trier for contravening the May Laws lived in exile in Luxemburg, where the well-disposed Bishop Adames found them posts.[39] Luxemburg was therefore friendly soil, and Echternach provided a safe house for the visionaries in more than one sense.

There is almost certainly a further reason for the specific choice of Echternach. The Spiritual Director of the Order of the Poor Child Jesus, to which the convent belonged, was also the man who wrote an authoritative judgement on the Marpingen apparitions: Johann Theodor Laurent, titular bishop of Chersones. It is probable that Laurent had already agreed to examine the evidence on the Marpingen case before the three girls were delivered to Echternach. The precise sequence of events remains obscure, but Laurent's career suggests several reasons why he was chosen. Laurent was 72 when the Marpingen apparitions began. He was born in 1804 in what was then French Aix-la-Chapelle (it became Prussian Aachen after 1815), of poor Luxemburg parents who gave him a German upbringing. After studying for the priesthood in Bonn and Liège he was ordained in 1825 and became a priest in Belgium. Laurent identified strongly with the Catholic revival of the 1830s, followed events in Germany closely, and actively supported the Archbishop of Cologne in the 'events' of 1837. The papal nuncio in Brussels brought him to the attention of Rome, where he was Consultor of the Congregation of the Index and a Member of the Academy of the Catholic Religion. Appointed Apostolic Vicar of Luxemburg in 1841, he was denounced by liberals in the Grand Duchy as a fanatical ultramontane and recalled seven years later at the request of the Luxemburg ambassador in Rome after accusations that he had incited revolution against the government. Returning to Aachen, Laurent wrote extensively as a theologian and was one of the founders of the Poor Child order, whose Spiritual Director he became in 1867. Unlike many German bishops, Laurent was a passionate supporter of papal infallibility (he would 'hardly have survived' the failure to pronounce it, according to his friends); but like the German bishops he suffered in the *Kulturkampf*. The Poor Child nuns were expelled from Germany, and the mother-house of the order at Simpelveld in the Netherlands became home to Laurent during the last years of his life.[40]

Many aspects of Laurent's chequered career recommended him as a suitable person to examine the evidence on the Marpingen apparitions. At a time when

---

[38] Kammer, *Kulturkampfpriester*, 105.

[39] Ibid. 39, 49, 117. This well-disposed attitude could not be taken for granted. Exiled Trier priests in Belgium reported again and again the lack of sympathy they encountered from members of the local clergy, who showed no understanding of their German brother-priests and often believed that they were the authors of their own misfortune.

[40] This account of Laurent's life is based on the following sources: K. Möller (ed.), *Leben und Briefe von Johannes Theodor Laurent*, 3 vols (Trier, 1887–9); O. Foesser, 'Johannes Theodor Laurent und seine Verdienste um die Katholische Kirche', *Frankfurter zeitgemäße Broschüren*, NS, 11 (1890), 153–84; J. Goedert, *Jean-Théodore Laurent. Vicaire apostolique de Luxembourg 1804–1884* (Luxembourg, 1957); R. O. M. Claessen, *Johannes Theodor Laurent, Titularbischof Chersones. Sein politisches, sozialfürsorgliches und pastorales Wirken* (dissertation; Bonn, 1983). None mentions Marpingen.

no actual Prussian bishop was available, he was in effect a 'German' bishop without a see, a native-speaker who had been active in German Catholic life since the 1830s and was widely respected. He had spoken at German Catholic assemblies (*Katholikentage*) and had even, in 1862, been proposed as 'papal chancellor' of a putative Catholic University in Germany. His lifetime of work in Luxemburg and the Rhine Province would have made him particularly well known in Trier. He was also a noted Mariologist, and it may have been another prominent Mariologist, Matthias Scheeben, who put Laurent's name forward when his opinion on Marpingen was canvassed. As a titular bishop who had been named to a variety of troubleshooting roles by Rome, and proposed for others, Laurent was an experienced man for a difficult situation.[41]

At Echternach the three Marpingen visionaries were treated more kindly than their counterparts in Waldsassen. For six months, from May until November 1878, their education continued and the nuns were evidently satisfied with their conduct, which was marked by 'childish innocence, trust, and sincerity'.[42] During these months the apparitions were apparently not discussed. In November, a female religious who had lived in Marpingen since August 1877 was sent as Neureuter's intermediary to Echternach, where (with the consent of Dean Clasen) she took a detailed statement from the three girls. The ensuing document ran to forty-nine closely written pages, and largely repeated what the girls had said to numerous members of the clergy on previous occasions. The religious in Echternach believed that they had spoken with 'honesty and open-heartedness'.[43] Some six months later—Margaretha Kunz recalled that it was shortly after the Saarbrücken trial—the three visionaries were visited in Echternach by 'several gentlemen from Trier', who questioned them further and read out the statement they had previously given. The girls agreed that it was accurate.[44]

The girls' account of events had meanwhile been in the hands of Bishop Laurent since November 1878, when it was sent to him at Simpelveld. The evidence suggests that this was all the material he worked with. At this time, many of the notes made by Neureuter were still in the hands of the legal authorities in Saarbrücken; others had been handed temporarily to a Belgian priest to prevent their seizure, and proved difficult to recover.[45] No effort was apparently made to

---

[41] Before his appointment to Luxemburg, Laurent was named by Rome in 1840 as Apostolic Vicar of Hamburg to assist with the 'northern mission' of the church, but his credentials were not accepted by the Hamburg Senate or by other north German governments. He also declined various positions, including the Latin Patriarchy in Constantinople.

[42] BAT, B III, 11, 14/3, 1.

[43] BAT, B III, 11, 14/3, 1–49. The statement is contained in a blue book entitled 'Bericht über die Mutter Gottes Erscheinungen in Marpingen vom 3ten Juli 1876 bis zum 3ten September 1877' ('nebst einer begründeten Beurtheilung derselben durch Bischof Laurent' has been added in a different hand, probably that of the later Trier Vicar-General Karl Kammer). The first page of the book describes the circumstances in which the statement was drawn up.

[44] BAT, B III, 11, 14/3, 63–4.

[45] On the notes that went missing somewhere in Belgium, see BAT, B III, 11, 14/4, 75: Curé Kaes of Liège to Neureuter, 3 Dec. 1877; LASB, E 107, 146–7.

provide Laurent with independent statements or medical evidence about allegedly miraculous cures, or even to collect such material. In short, he was not conducting a canonical enquiry, but delivering an opinion based on the internal evidence of the visionaries' own descriptions. This material alone proved quite sufficient for Laurent. In May 1880, after eighteen months in which he had 'carefully read and deliberated on' the report from Echternach, he wrote out his findings.[46] He saw no reason to doubt the 'honesty and innocence' of the children, and recognized the 'conscientious diligence' of those who had recorded their statements. But the latter had shown themselves 'credulous and lacking in judgement': he felt it necessary to rebuke them for 'presumption' in persistently denoting the apparitions as the Blessed Virgin. Laurent pointedly observed at the close of his preface: 'Only for the purpose of defending the honour of the Blessed Virgin do I feel myself pressed to submit to my judgement her alleged apparitions in Marpingen as they are described in the preceding report from the mouths of the children.' The operative word was 'alleged'.[47]

Laurent took the apparitions at Lourdes as his starting-point: these had been recognized by the church as authentic and 'confirmed by countless incontrovertible miraculous cures'. Lourdes was therefore the 'yardstick' for Marpingen, 'all the more so as the latter unmistakably arose as an imitation of the former'. With this uncompromising statement, the bishop made his position very clear. What remained was a series of carefully marshalled arguments 'against the authenticity of the apparitions in Marpingen'. The apparitions described were, in the first place, 'unworthy' of the Blessed Virgin, from her 'pointless and ghostlike stealing after and following the children', to her appearances in kitchens and barns and her 'frequent changes of dress'.[48] The bishop considered next the language attributed to the apparition, and the numerous exchanges with the children. These also gave cause for serious concern. The words reportedly used by the apparition were 'unseemly and unworthy', a 'mere aping' of Lourdes without dignity; some of the exchanges with the visionaries were 'indecorous and foolish', others 'futile and base'. The 'talkative, even garrulous conversations of the apparition with the children, in which the latter took the initiative' were at odds with all proven apparitions, and the putative Virgin had answered questions that were 'impudent' or 'pert' in a manner likely to encourage vanity.[49] Laurent was equally unhappy with the behaviour of the children during the apparitions, pointing to their initial shrieks of terror and 'later impudence and vulgar familiarity'. The would-be visionaries showed 'an absence of any deep emotion or inspiration' in recounting their experiences, and 'indifference and sullenness'

[46] This is located in BAT, B III, 11, 14/3, 43–52. It is divided by Laurent into 12 sections, I–XII, themselves subdivided into subsections with arabic numerals. These sections and subsections are the ones cited in the following notes.

[47] Ibid. Laurent's signed prefatory comments, headed 'Dignare me laudere Te, Virgo sacrata; | Da mihi virtutem contra hostes tuos!'.

[48] Ibid. I. 1–5.

[49] Ibid. II. 1–4, III. 1–6.

when questioned. Laurent concluded his remarks on the demeanour of the children with an observation that summed up his general attitude: 'Their games with the Christ-child in the meadow, something that occurs only with the greatest contemplative saints, sits ill with their rolling down the hill into the same meadow, an unseemly practice anyway for young girls.'[50]

The bishop was also unimpressed by the reported cures. These had not been properly investigated, and could probably be explained as the product of natural recovery, nervous excitement, imagination, or even diabolical delusion. They certainly did not measure up to the standards required by the church, and some of the means by which the 'cures' were effected (for example, when the children guided the suffering so that they could touch the invisible foot of the Virgin) were dubious. The same applied, in Laurent's judgement, to the 'casual and superficial' appearances of 'poor souls' from purgatory. The description of the Blessed Virgin leading a group of poor souls to the children was 'completely unacceptable'.[51]

After this lengthy catalogue of features that spoke against the authenticity of the apparitions, Laurent's report took on darker tones as he turned to those aspects which positively demonstrated their 'falseness'. He was stung to harsh comments on the 'presumptuous misuse' of language and episodes drawn from the Gospels (on which Laurent had written extensively). The aping of the temptation of the Lord by the devil was a 'sacrilegious mockery'; the appearance of the dove and the voice from above ('This is my dearly beloved son') was a 'hideous sacrilege'. 'Equally sacrilegious' was the aping of the angelic salutation ('Hail, thou that art highly favoured, the Lord is with thee: blessed art thou among women') on the part of 'an apparent angel who, by his boasting that he was the highest angel in heaven, clearly shows himself to be the fallen Lucifer'. The placing of Mary's answer ('Behold the handmaid of the Lord: let it be unto me according to thy word') in the mouth of the apparition was 'even more shocking'. Laurent concluded that 'whoever is not convinced by these sacrilegious games with the most sublime mysteries of religion that the entire apparition and everything pertaining to it is nothing but an infernal delusion (höllische Gaukelei), must have lost all Christian feeling and understanding.'[52]

The references to Lucifer and infernal delusion are important. The episodes where the devil appeared to the children had troubled all the priests who took an interest in Marpingen; for Laurent they were a central point of reference. We need to remember that, for bishops of the period as well as simple priests, the devil was not regarded as a metaphor, a symbolic shorthand for the forces of wickedness. Rather, Satan was a real, physical presence in the struggle between good and evil. Laurent himself had performed an exorcism during his early years in Luxemburg, and we have a grim description of the steps taken to drive the

[50] BAT, B III, 11, 14/3, 43–52: IV. 1–5.
[51] Ibid. V. 1–4, VI. 1–4.
[52] Ibid. VII. 1–4.

devil out of a young woman as she bellowed and writhed while three of Laurent's vicars sought to restrain her. The girl's hands were bound in a stola and she was dragged to the altar of Luxemburg Cathedral. She 'screamed and shrieked for three hours, sometimes like a wolf, sometimes like a bird' while the bishop ordered the devil to obey. Laurent said that the following night had been 'the most terrible of his life': he 'would never forget the sight' when the girl turned on him her 'dreadful devil's face'.[53] True, the Marpingen visionaries were plainly not possessed; but their 'sincerity and truthfulness did not protect them from fantastic and diabolical delusions'. The horror and disgust of Laurent's reaction to the episodes in which they described the appearance of the devil are palpable. Moreover, the consorting together of Mary and the devil, and the request of the Blessed Virgin that the parish priest not come to the site, were indicative. They 'proved' the 'diabolical character and origin' of the apparitions as a whole.[54]

Unseemly, unworthy, sacrilegious, diabolical: these were the characteristics of the Marpingen apparitions that impressed themselves upon Laurent. He accepted that they had probably had a positive effect on prayer and religious devotions; but good often came unwittingly of evil. The enormous popular enthusiasm owed much to the 'ill-advised and unjust, harsh and violent measures of the police'. But the apparitions themselves were inauthentic. Laurent recalled the 'similar events' in Alsace and Mettenbuch, the first rejected by the Bishop of Strasburg, the second 'condemned as fraud and falsehood by the Bishop of Regensburg'. He closed his report by quoting the 'warning of the Saviour' in Mark 13, about false prophets, signs, and miracles.[55]

Secretum

In normal circumstances, this was the point at which the church published and enforced its judgement. To borrow the language of Max Weber, it was where 'the "machinery" of the church' did battle successfully with the 'Catholic form of piety in all of its richness'.[56] What happened in fact was less straightforward. Even where that 'machinery' was in good working order, it was no easy matter to suppress popular piety. In the Mettenbuch case, where a formal canonical enquiry had been undertaken and a pastoral letter issued, Regensburg continued to be plagued by new apparitions, miracle cures, and requests for authentication. The requests flooded in from clergy and laity, in German and Latin, betraying a

[53] Peiper, *Chronik*, 252–3. The young woman, Cathérine Pfefferkorn, was from Lorraine. She believed herself possessed from the age of 16, when she refused money to a group of beggars who replied: 'The devil take you'. See Devlin, *Superstitious Mind*, 249 n. 20.

[54] BAT, B III, 11, 14/3, 43–52: VIII. 1–6, IX.

[55] Ibid. X–XII.

[56] '... the specific Catholic form of piety in all of its richness, is quite a different thing from what I have designated above as the "machinery" of the church—in truth it is antagonistic to this machinery, and has only a meagre chance for the future': Max Weber to Frau Gnauck-Kühne, 15 July 1909 [?], cited in Mommsen, *Max Weber and German Politics*, 123 n. 134.

persistence in 'error' that kept the vicar-general's red pencil busy. The episcopal authorities were not helped by the evident reluctance of Father Anglhuber to comply with the pastoral letter. The parish priest was reminded sharply that the pastoral letter was no mere *circulare* that required a further special decision before being implemented, but a formal judgement that required '*all* priests of the diocese' to enforce it with all necessary measures. He must press for the removal of all devotional objects from the site, and if necessary report those who proved refractory.[57] Five years later, a weary Regensburg still found itself marking letters from the parish priest about further apparitions with impatient marginalia ('Is simply not true!', 'Obvious delusions').[58] The diocesan archive contains a thick folder on the 'carrying out of the judgement, 1879–1881', and no fewer than four further files detailing the problems that Mettenbuch continued to cause the church authorities through the 1880s.[59]

In Trier, the situation presented greater difficulties. The machinery of the church was creaky: there had been no formal canonical commission, and Bishop Laurent's report carried only his personal authority. His judgement was strongly criticized by Matthias Scheeben when he was shown it.[60] The fact that the clash of theological opinion could continue was, of course, a sign of the irregular circumstances that prevailed in Trier. At the time of Laurent's report there was still no bishop to issue a pastoral letter or enforce its contents. Marpingen, moreover, had generated an even greater degree of popular Catholic enthusiasm than Mettenbuch, and it had also produced martyrs. It is true that the hearings in Saarbrücken had produced some embarrassing evidence, especially about Margaretha Kunz. One sympathetic Catholic writer noted in 1881 that 'many who were advocates of Marpingen earlier were influenced by the trial proceedings and even became opponents'.[61] But the final verdict at Saarbrücken had naturally been treated by the village as a triumphant vindication. To condemn the apparitions now, to publish Bishop Laurent's judgement that they were diabolical in origin, sacrilegious, and false would run counter to popular religious sentiment and have the appearance of a betrayal.

The figure who stood reluctantly at the centre of this untidy epilogue to the Marpingen affair was Michael Felix Korum, who was enthroned as Bishop of Trier in September 1881. He was a celebrated and long-serving bishop, the most 'ultramontane' of the four bishops appointed to vacant Prussian sees at the

---

[57] BZAR, F 115, Fasc. VII: BO Regensburg to Anglhuber, 19 Feb. 1879 and 6 May 1879.

[58] BZAR, F 115, 'Mettenbuch 1881–1884' [unnumbered file]: Anglhuber to Regensburg, 14 Mar. 1884; 'Bemerkungen über den Bericht des Pfarrprovisors in Metten, P. J. Ev. Anglhuber', Regensburg 15 Mar. 1884.

[59] BZAR, F 115, Fasc. VII: 'Vollzug der Entscheidung 1879–1881'; 'Mettenbuch 1881–84', 'Mettenbuch 1885', 'Mettenbuch 1887–88', 'Mettenbuch 1886–90' (all unnumbered files).

[60] BAT, B III, 11, 14/4, 44–44a; ibid. 6 [2]: 'Zu den Akten Marpingen!', typed notes by Karl Kammer on Neureuter and Scheeben, 26 Nov. 1956.

[61] *Marpingen vor dem Richterstuhle der Vernunft*, 3.

beginning of the 1880s.[62] Korum's energies went into diocesan reconstruction, in which he showed a marked preference for ceremonial pomp.[63] He was notable for bringing a million visitors to Trier for the enormously successful second displaying of the Holy Coat in 1891.[64] Like his fellow ultramontane, Senestrey, Korum was hardly likely to encourage a secondary Marian cult of proven dubiety. At the same time, restoring the fortunes of the diocese and mending fences with the Prussian regime no doubt made publication of damning evidence about Marpingen equally unattractive.

From the diocesan records in Trier it is possible to reconstruct broadly how the affair was handled, although many details remain unclear. It was evidently decided to sit on the decision reached by Bishop Laurent, while keeping the three visionaries in cloistered seclusion. Susanna Leist fell ill and was brought home to Marpingen, where she died in 1882 at the age of 14—'on the theshold of the convent', as a later supporter of the Marpingen apparitions was to put it.[65] Katharina Hubertus remained with the Order of the Poor Child Jesus, but moved to the mother-house in Simpelveld. There she joined her elder sister Barbara, who had taken the name Sister Irenäa. Katharina took her vows in June 1897, and died as Sister Hugolina on Christmas Eve 1904 in Aachen, probably in the Convent of the Poor Child Jesus there.[66] Her former playmate Margaretha Kunz outlived her by less than a year. She took her vows in 1901, and died in September 1905 as Sister Olympia in the Netherlands at the Steyl convent of the Sisters of Providence.[67] Her death removed the last of the three principals in the Marpingen affair. All had suffered poor health as children, all died young. They were survived by Father Neureuter, who died in retirement at Kesten on the Mosel in 1908, still privately proclaiming his belief in the authenticity of the apparitions.[68] But a quarter of a century after Bishop Laurent's report, Marpingen had still not been laid to rest. Laurent's report itself had not been made public, and villagers received no formal word on the position adopted by the church. Rumours circulated about the three girls. When Susanna Leist died in Marpingen, her last reported words were: 'I *did* see the Blessed Virgin—the others can say what

---

[62] Weber, *Kirchliche Politik*, 72. The other three were Kopp (Fulda), Drobe (Paderborn), and Höting (Osnabrück). On the new bishop, see also Treitz, *Korum*.

[63] On the extraordinary pomp and circumstance of his enthronement, see the description in Weber, *Kirchliche Politik*, 57–8.

[64] Korff, 'Formierung'. Franz-Xaver Kraus was characteristically hostile to the venture and sharply critical of Korum personally, whom he now considered indisputably the 'Chief Pharisee': *Tagebücher*, 580–1, entry of 28 Sept. 1891.

[65] BAT, B III, 11, 14/3, 55: 'Bischof Korum u. Marpingen'; Lama, *Die Muttergottes-Erscheinungen in Marpingen*, 63. On Lama's role as a supporter of Marpingen in the inter-war years, see below, Ch. 12.

[66] Bungert, *Heimatbuch*, 559. Her sister Barbara was born on 19 Nov. 1861, took her final vows on 28 May 1885, and died in Simpelveld the following year, on 11 Nov. 1886.

[67] Ibid.

[68] BAT, B III, 11, 14/6 [1]: statement of Luzie Sartorius, Neureuter's housekeeper in Kesten, 17 Jan. 1935.

they like.'[69] The source for these petulant death-bed words is second-hand and unreliable, but whether Susanna actually used the words or not, the point is that people in Marpingen were prepared to believe that she did.[70] They were equally prepared to believe the rumours that circulated about the continuing claims made by the other two visionaries, and especially by Margaretha Kunz.

Margaretha stayed in Echternach until 1885, when she would have been 17. Four years later she described this as a period of 'spiritual torment' (*geistiges Martirium*): 'I very often accused myself in the confessional of having lied to many people, but even here I could not bring myself to mention the matter.'[71] She left Echternach in October 1885 and entered the household of a Father Kreuzer in Münster as a maid.[72] The town may well have been chosen because (like Katharina Hubertus) Margaretha had an older sister, Maria, who was a novice with the *Klemensschwestern* in Münster.[73] It was in Münster, during her Easter confession of 1887 to a Capuchin Father, that Margaretha first admitted to a priest that she had lied about the apparitions. Several months later she made the same admission in confidence to Father Kreuzer's housekeeper, who conveyed it to the priest. Through this channel word reached Father Neureuter in Marpingen. At the express wish of Neureuter, Margaretha went in February 1888 to the Convent of St Joseph in Thorn, West Prussia. Whether this suggestion was Neureuter's own, or came from Bishop Korum, we do not know. Korum was not present in Thorn, but must have approved the arrangement. At the Convent of St Joseph Margaretha worked, once again, as a maid and took the name Maria Althof.

In January 1889, after almost twelve months in Thorn, she wrote a full confession that began with the words 'I am one of the three children who, nearly thirteen years ago in Marpingen, spread the rumour of having seen the Blessed Virgin and must to my regret make the deeply humiliating admission that everything without exception was one great lie.' The confession is remarkably self-possessed, despite its abject opening. It is written in a clear, mature hand very different from the childish scrawl in which the 8-year-old claimed to have seen the Virgin, and gives every sign of being a freely written personal recollection rather than the stilted product of catechesis. As a confession it is unequivocal, but after the opening paragraph Margaretha shows no evidence of great remorse

---

[69] BAT, B III, 11, 14/5, 62–8: Elisa Haben to GV Trier, 17 Nov. 1946; ibid. 6 [1], 84–90, includes a similar statement dated 17 Nov. 1935.

[70] Elisa Haben was the daughter of Susanna Leist's older sister Margaretha, and these statements are recollections of what she had heard from her mother. Her unreliability is indicated by the fact that she wrongly gives 1887 as the year of Susanna's death.

[71] The following account of Margaretha's life in the 1880s is based, except where otherwise indicated, on her own statement made in Jan. 1889. See BAT, B III, 11, 14/3, 59–65.

[72] This move is ambiguous in Margaretha's own statement. It is confirmed in BAT, B III, 11, 14/6 [2]: GV Trier to Mother Superior Maria Theresa ('or her successor'), the Poor Clares, Münster, 23 Nov. 1956.

[73] BAT, B III, 11, 14/6 [2]: GV Trier to Maria Theresa, 23 Nov. 1956; Bungert, *Heimatbuch*, 559. Maria Kunz was born on 9 Jan. 1864 and took her vows on 18 Aug. 1892. She lived until 1943.

or guilt. It is also striking that at every key juncture in the account it is others who are described as taking the initiative.

Margaretha recalls first how the girls were hurrying home on the evening of 3 July when Susanna Leist called out 'Gretchen, Kätchen, look, over there is a woman in white. Frightened, we looked at the spot she had pointed to and actually saw a white figure, or rather with our imagination already excited and in the half-dark we believed that was what we saw.' As they rushed back into the village their appearance ('we must have looked awful') caused them to be 'bombarded with questions'. According to Margaretha, her own mother was initially sceptical, suggesting that the figure was only 'a cord of wood, and because it was dark you thought you had seen a woman. She was right,' added Margaretha, 'for later I satisfied myself that it was stacked-up wood lying there with the white side pointing outwards.' (She does not, however, say how much later it was that she satisfied herself of this.) At the time she would not be talked out of her story, and all three girls returned to the Härtelwald, primed by Susanna Leist's mother to ask the figure, if they saw her again, whether she was the Immaculate Conception. Margaretha continued:

I saw nothing, but all three of us put the question, then one of them nudged me and said, listen, I am the Immaculately Conceived, although I heard nothing I said, oh yes, we put the second question that had been agreed, what should we do? As if with one voice we both gave the answer, pray devoutly and do not sin.[74] How it was possible I do not know, I know only that I myself neither saw nor heard anything. When we got back to the village Kätchen and I related what had happened.

The adults in the village 'really believed that we had seen the Blessed Virgin': they plied the children with questions to put to her, the cures began, 'and so it went on from day to day'. Visiting priests had questions of their own; they had tried to test the girls, 'but they must have believed too strongly, for no attention was paid to some small discrepancies in our accounts'. In short, the 8-year-olds had stirred up something they only faintly understood, and gone too far to turn back. 'Thousands of people came and went', pilgrims and priests besieged them: 'It was an agitated time, sometimes my imagination was so overstrained by all the questions and answers that I really believed I had seen something.' Margaretha described the arrival of the soldiers, her interrogations, and the five weeks spent in Saarbrücken: she had disavowed her story 'many times', but always claimed that it was true when she was home again. Whether the others had also recanted 'I do not know to this day, for we were always separately interrogated and I always, even in all the later years, anxiously avoided putting any question to the two of them because I believed they might really have seen something, and was afraid of learning the opposite from something they said and thus making my uneasy conscience even worse.' Margaretha closed by bringing the story up to date with an account of her confessions in Münster, and her removal to Thorn.

---

[74] 'Both' refers to Margaretha Kunz and Katharina Hubertus: on this second occasion and for the following 4 weeks Susanna Leist, the original visionary, claimed to have seen nothing.

The written confession, witnessed by a Sister Maria Berthilde, was sent to
Korum in Trier. What happened next is impossible to establish precisely. Bishop
Korum continued to act true to form. He put the confession in a blue envelope
marked *Secretum*, and placed it in his private archive. It was released into the
Marpingen file only by his successor Bishop Bornewasser in 1937. 'In view of
the letter in question [i.e. the confession], the view of Bishop Korum was clear',
as a later senior official in Trier put it: 'the matter was handled discreetly.'[75] For
her part, Margaretha had confessed and was free to exchange the status of
housemaid for that of novice. She returned to Münster, where she entered the
order of the Poor Clares and took the name Sister Maria Stanislaus.[76] It was
probably then, or shortly afterwards, that she and Katharina Hubertus were
summoned to Trier. That, at any rate, is the inference to be drawn from a rather
unsatisfactory later account. In 1905, while in Marpingen for the consecration of a
new parish church, Bishop Korum spoke confidentially to Neureuter's successor,
Father Theodor Schmitt, about the later lives of the two surviving visionaries.
He recalled: 'I had the two Sisters come to me in Trier secretly (*in aller Stille*)
and a proper investigation carried out. The two Sisters admitted to me that they
now believed the apparitions to be delusions, although they had given their
accounts in good faith at the time.' No credence could therefore be given to
earlier statements made by the children.[77]

This statement has a far from perfect provenance. It was written down at an
unspecified date, by two Redemptorist Fathers in Trier, recalling what they had
been told in 1930 by former Marpingen parish priest Theodor Schmitt, who was
himself recalling what he had been told by Korum in 1905 about events that
had occurred in the twenty years before that. This in itself gives cause for
circumspection. There are also several aspects of Korum's statement that require
explanation. Why, for example, did he not make his interview public at the time,
perhaps together with Laurent's damning judgement and Margaretha's written
confession? The explanation for that might well be the same discretion that had
prompted Korum to seal the confession up in the blue envelope: a desire not to
play into the hands of the enemies of the church or to cause pain to the families
concerned. Karl Kammer, the Trier official who handled the twentieth-century

---

[75] BAT, B III, 11, 14/3, 59–65; the blue envelope is preserved as 65. The official in question was Karl
Kammer: see ibid. 5, 92: 'Kurze Übersicht betr. Marpingen', dated 25 Oct. 1947.

[76] Later enquiries by Trier proved unable to establish precisely when Margaretha entered the order.
When, in the 1950s, Trier was able to obtain a copy of a *Sterbebildchen* of the later Sister Olympia, this
recorded that she died in Sept. 1905 after 15 years as a nun. This would give a date sometime in 1890.
But the 15 years may refer to her entry into the Sisters of Providence, and not include her brief period
with the Poor Clares, so that her entry into the latter could have taken place in 1889.

[77] BAT, B III, 11, 14/3, 55: 'Bischof Korum u. Marpingen', a typed copy of a memo drawn up by
Brother Norbert Brühl and signed also by Brother Ballmann of Trier. It is possible that Korum had
the two nuns come to him in Trier somewhat later, *after* reports that Margaretha was talking once more
about the truth of the apparitions, but this is more difficult to square with Korum's reported remarks
of 1905.

repercussions of the Marpingen affair, later offered both reasons for the non-release of the confession.[78] Discretion might explain also the use, even in 1905, of the euphemism 'delusions'. That Trier sought to smother the whole business would hardly be surprising; it was what they had tried to do for a decade.

There remains a mystery, however: why is there no evidence in the diocesan records on Marpingen of any 'proper investigation' of the kind described by Korum? For there is no trace at all of a statement from Katharina Hubertus, from witnesses in Marpingen, from priests who had visited the village, or from those claiming cures; nor are there affidavits from doctors. There is, in fact, no sign of any activity from Trier, or from Father Neureuter acting on instructions from Trier, to support the idea of an enquiry being set afoot at some point in the period 1880–1905. The likeliest answer is the one suggested by later supporters of the apparitions, namely that no such enquiry was carried out.[79] No doubt Bishop Korum did have the two young nuns come to see him in Trier, but it seems unlikely that he did more than that. He had the evidence of Margaretha's confession, but that was unsuitable for public consumption. The story put into circulation with such apparent artlessness in 1905 ('Now I can talk!' Korum supposedly said to the parish priest on that occasion[80]) might be seen as a bland, even sanitized version of events, not entirely true to either the spirit or the letter of what Margaretha had admitted, but designed to save the reputation of the young novice and the church.

This was a strategy with risks attached. It was undermined by the subsequent conduct of Margaretha Kunz. The record of her life as a nun remains incomplete, but as a result of later enquiries about her, first by a maverick twentieth-century supporter of Marpingen and then by Trier, we possess various fragments of information, particularly about the period she spent as a novice with the Poor Clares. She did not stay long with the order, and the weight of evidence suggests that the reason was her reluctance—as in the past—to stand by her admission. It is true that one Mother Superior, Sister Clara, writing in 1913, called her a 'very dear, good little novice', who had left the Poor Clares because she lacked the stamina for such a rigorous order. She had been obliged to keep 'the business of the apparitions' to herself.[81] A much later Mother Superior, Sister Maria Theresa, writing in 1956, also recalled that Sister Maria Stanislaus had been 'much loved'. She had prayed and sung often in the 'Lourdes-grotto' of the convent. According to Sister Maria Theresa, her fellow religious had gained the impression that the parish priest and the secular authorities had been hostile to

[78] BAT, B III, 11, 14/6 [2]: 'Niederschrift über eine Verhandlung mit Pfarrkindern von Marpingen am 19. November 1956 15 Uhr—nach Vereinbarung—bzw. der Marpinger Härtelwaldkapelle und der Erscheinungen 1876/77'.

[79] Lama, Die Muttergottes-Erscheinungen, 64, 68–9. Cf. Lama's justification of his pamphlet in a letter of 8 Mar. 1936 to the Archbishop of Munich and Freising: BAT, B III, 11, 14/6 [1], 84–90.

[80] BAT, B III, 11, 14/3, 55: 'Bischof Korum u. Marpingen'.

[81] BAT, B III, 11, 14/6 [2]: notes taken from a letter of Sister Clara headed 'Dear Baroness', and almost certainly written to the Baroness Drion du Chapois, 5 Oct. 1913.

the apparitions; but no one had heard Margaretha deny the truth of them. It is obvious from this account that Margaretha had talked about Marpingen; indeed we are told that all the nuns believed in the apparitions.[82] A third account goes further. Writing in 1929, the then Mother Superior Sister Maria Antonia reported that no one could remember Margaretha denying the truth of the apparitions. Nuns who had known her considered this out of the question, for on one occasion she had maintained firmly that 'everything happened as I said'. This was what had led to her leaving the Poor Clares, for the senior religious of the order feared that her continued presence might lead to 'unpleasantness' in the form of an enquiry that would jeopardize their strict seclusion and 'pressed for dismissal'.[83]

There is probably an element of euphemism in this last point, and it is reasonable to infer that the main problem was believed to be Margaretha herself and her unwillingness to disavow the apparitions or maintain silence about them. One piece of evidence points in this direction. There are no extant letters or recollections of Margaretha's fellow nuns, but we do have a second-hand account from a 'somewhat older sister who was close to her'. This was probably Maria Kunz, the novice Sister Benedicta of the *Klemensschwestern* in Münster. Her description is consistent with that of Sister Maria Antonia, but less diplomatic. In the words of Sister Benedicta/Maria Kunz, Sister Maria Stanislaus had been dismissed from the Poor Clares because of her stance on apparitions that had not been approved by the church. But she had 'stuck to her views'. When she was dismissed from the order she had been 'utterly unhappy' and—shades of the younger Margaretha Kunz—'almost enraged' (*beinahe wütend*). Maria had been 'sent to calm the young girl' and found her in an 'ailing condition'.[84]

We know, then, that Margaretha Kunz was a young novice who continued to talk about the apparitions (although instructed to remain silent), even to express her continued belief in their validity, and that this led to her departure from the Poor Clares. But this did not prevent her continuing her vocation. Possibly through the intervention of Father Neureuter she was accepted into the Order of the Sisters of Providence, with whom she remained until her death, taking the name Sister Olympia.[85] We have virtually no details of this last period, fifteen

[82] BAT, B III, 11, 14/5, 125: Mother Superior Maria Theresa to GV Trier, 29 Nov. 1956. This is the only source on this subject to be found in the Trier diocesan archives on Marpingen that was generated by a direct enquiry by Trier itself. Sister Maria Theresa notes that many of the convent records (including the investiture book) were destroyed in the war.

[83] BAT, B III, 11, 14/6 [2]: copy of a letter in private hands, from Sister Maria Antonia, Münster, to (?) Baroness Drion du Chapois, 3 July 1929.

[84] Ibid: copy of an undated letter in private hands, written by a Brother Raymund (probably Brother Raymund, born Peter Dörr in Marpingen, 4 Jan. 1882, a monk in Maria Laach) to an unnamed fellow religious. A note on the file suggests that this correspondence also had its origins in the attempt of the Baroness Drion to gather information about Margaretha's life as a nun.

[85] Ibid. GV Trier to Sister Clothilde ('or her successor in office'), Superior of the Sisters of Providence, Münster, 7 Dec. 1956. This letter asks, among other questions: did Father Neureuter arrange for you to accept Sister Olympia?

years out of a life that lasted only thirty-eight years. But there is circumstantial evidence that Sister Olympia did not abandon her insistence that the apparitions 'happened as I said'. Many in Marpingen held to the view that only episcopal pressure had extracted a confession. There were stories similar to those surrounding Susanna Leist that Sister Olympia had affirmed the truth of the apparitions on her death-bed. One writer claimed in the 1930s that copies of a letter to this effect, in which Margaretha withdrew her 'confession', were in broad circulation among villagers.[86]

Regensburg, in much less difficult circumstances, mounted a full-scale enquiry into the Mettenbuch apparitions and publicly denounced them. It then spent a decade trying to enforce the pastoral letter of condemnation. Trier, faced with the problems caused directly and indirectly by the *Kulturkampf*, including the enthusiasm and high expectations aroused by Marpingen, avoided grasping the nettle. The reasons are understandable, and they no doubt included a sense of consideration for the families concerned as well as the embarrassment to the church that must have been caused by releasing material in its possession. But the lack of a clear judgement on the apparitions had unintended consequences. It left the question open in the popular mind, and kept alive suspicion that clerical diplomacy had won a shabby victory and stifled a true relevation. There was lingering resentment both in Marpingen and among its supporters elsewhere that the German Lourdes had been strangled in the cradle. This was to be important in the years ahead.

[86] BAT, B III, 11, 14/5, 122–3; ibid. 6 [2]: GV Trier to Sister Clothilde, 7 Dec. 1936; Lama, *Die Muttergottes-Erscheinungen*, 69.

12

The German Lourdes? Marpingen
in the Twentieth Century

In the 1870s Marpingen was the focus of extraordinary attention as the would-be German Lourdes. Then, for two generations, it became simply a village like many others in the Saarland. The pell-mell growth of the coalfield turned Marpingen into a village of pitmen: by 1910 two-thirds of the population depended on the earnings of 400 miners, a dependence that made them vulnerable during the bitter strikes of 1889–93 and the lay-offs that followed.[1] Mining became not only the principal source of family income, but the axis on which social and recreational life turned; even the physical appearance of the village changed as one-storey miner-peasant houses sprang up along the roads and paths leading out of Marpingen.[2] With the dominance of mining came renewed clerical complaints about excessive drinking, dancing, and late-night unruliness, behaviour that new church-fostered organizations and a popular mission failed to tame.[3] In all of this Marpingen was fairly typical of the experience of Saarland mining villages in the decades before the First World War. The militancy during the strike years was in line with the greater militancy shown by miners from the northern peripheral zone of the coalfield in 1889–93.[4] The tensions between clergy and miners were

[1] Bungert, *Heimatbuch*, 140, 300–7. In 1901 the parish priest noted that 'almost all the inhabitants are miners and are absent the whole week': BAT, 70/3676: Father Schmitt to GV Trier, 3 June 1901. On the rise and fall of the miners' *Rechtsschutzverein* and the strikes of 1889, 1891, and 1892–3, see Mallmann, *Anfänge*, 98 ff., Steffens, *Autorität und Revolte*, 33–107, and Horch, *Wandel*, 320–38.

[2] Bungert, *Heimatbuch*, 306, 319, 326–31, illustrations on p. 331.

[3] Derr, 'Pfarrei Marpingen', 43, 47–8, 51–2; BAT, 70/3676a, 279–83: Father Schmitt's public condemnation of the publican Carl Brill, and complaints about excessive drinking and the moral dangers to the young; ibid. 3676a, 226–7: Margaretha Odermann to Bishop Korum, 7 Sept. 1898, on the 'mischief' of young people. The Recktenwald inn closed down in 1894, because the popular dancing to harmonica music had led to so many brawls among the customers: Bungert, *Heimatbuch*, 336. A mission was held in 1887, and by 1900 Marpingen had a Rosary association, a choral society, a young men's association, and a Childhood of Jesus association, as well as a St Barbara Brotherhood for miners.

[4] In Oct. 1890, 94% of all miners in the St Wendel district belonged to the *Rechtsschutzverein*, compared with only 66% in Saarbrücken, and many leaders of the organization came from the northern zone. The Prussian authorities rightly saw the dormitories of commuting miners as centres of rebellion, and the pits in which the majority of Marpingers worked—Altenwald, Maybach, and Dechen—were among the most militant: Mallmann, *Anfänge*, 104–11, 122, 127, 234–6, 281, 289–90; Steffens, *Autorität und Revolte*, 47, 212–18; Horch, *Wandel*, 383–4.

also typical.[5] They may have been rather worse in Marpingen, where Father Neureuter and his successor Theodor Schmitt found themselves involved in parish disputes over burials, church rebuilding, the conduct of mass, discipline during processions, irregularities in church bookkeeping, where the choral society should keep its flag, even who should do the priest's laundry.[6] The point is that, while Marpingen may have come to resemble Clochemerle, it certainly did not resemble a German Lourdes.[7]

The disputes in the parish turned on money and morals, pastoral affairs and liturgical precedents; they did not revolve around apparitions. Perhaps the most striking aspect of these quarrelsome years is the small part played by the events of 1876–7. Informal pilgrimages to the Härtelwald continued during the 1880s, it is true. A sceptical Westphalian Catholic who went to see for himself reported that the site was 'still much visited', and noted that water from the spring was 'perhaps' still being sold.[8] In 1883 new visionary claims were made by the adolescent Elisa Recktenwald. She reported an apparition of the Immaculate Conception who lamented the suffering and unrepentant world in which sinners turned away from the path of redemption. ('Have I not appeared already to so many children? Yet so few have believed.') The girl described a series of accompanying apparitions: angels, saints, the Christ-child in a communion wafer, a dove fluttering above the head of the parish priest when he preached, visions of the crucifixion and resurrection. She also directed a lamentation to the bishop ('I, poor, forsaken child') that referred to Neureuter excluding her from communion:[9]

I . . . could also have learnt Christian teaching, gone with my fellows to the table of the Lord, but it was denied me. O my Jesus help . . . Now that I must put away childish things, now that the time of danger draws near, that the little ship is to be pushed out into the current. O my God, I have no rudder, no plan for my journey, what is to become of me? I have been turned out from the hearth. If the wolf should come he will tear me apart first before he breaks into the hearth. O Jesus help me.

There is an apocalyptic tone here that exceeds anything to be found in 1876–7, but caution is necessary. The phrasing of the letter suggests (as Trier strongly suspected) that it was written by an adult. Elisa Recktenwald had been one of the

[5] LHAK, 442/6383, 205–32, includes a copy of an 1885 pamphlet by Father Oesterling of Dudweiler deploring the moral degradation of mining communities. See esp. pp. 7–11 of the pamphlet. On the miners' challenge to clerical authority, Mallmann, 'Aus des Tages Last', 176–84.

[6] BAT, 70/3676, 130–3, 160–85, 196–7; ibid. 3676a, 149–59, 226–7, 230–7, 244–67, 279–83; Derr, 'Pfarrei Marpingen', 44–9; Bungert, Heimatbuch, 561–4, 625. The church burial dispute of 1895 caused Neureuter to leave the village. Perusal of the parish records for Eppelborn and Merzig failed to uncover conflicts comparable in scale: BAT, 70/1433–4, 1438 (Eppelborn), and ibid. 3853 (Merzig).

[7] Clochemerle had real prototypes, of course: see the analysis of similar parish disputes in France by R. Magraw, 'The Conflict in the Villages. Popular Anticlericalism in the Isère (1852–1870)', in Zeldin (ed.), Conflicts in French Society (London, 1970), 169–227.

[8] BAT, 70/3676, 11: Heinrich Stratmann of Niederbergheim (Arnsberg district) to Bishop Korum, 25 Sept. 1886.

[9] BAT, 70/3676, 96–8: Elisa Recktenwald to Bishop Korum, 11 Apr. 1883.

'rival children' in 1877, and the apparitions she reported are evidently modelled on those of the earlier years. The most striking point of all is that she found no response: Neureuter moved to discipline Elisa Recktenwald's parents as well as the girl herself, and this apparently remained an isolated incident.[10]

When Father Schmitt came to the village in 1895, he received advice from Trier to 'pay no attention at all to the apparitions', but they seem in fact to have been the least of his worries.[11] Neither the Marpingen parish records, nor the files on the original apparitions, mention further visions in the decades before the First World War, although a 4-year-old girl from Eppelborn did report seeing an apparition of the Virgin Mary in 1901.[12] There were persistent rumours about the alleged recantations of the original visionaries, with documents circulating in the village purporting to deny the truth of any 'confession'. But none of the numerous villagers who clashed with Father Schmitt—not even the tradeswoman Margaretha Odermann, who denounced the priest as an untrustworthy incompetent whose sister was 'not right in the head'—raised the matter of the apparitions in their formal complaints to Trier.[13] Nor did renewed visionary claims add to the problems of the parish priest.

What happened in Marpingen paralleled the general European trend. This was a period when established Marian sites—including approved apparition sites—were developed on a large scale, but there were fewer reports of new apparitions than there had been in the troubled 1860s and 1870s. Unofficial cults that arose seem to have died down quickly. In Marpingen, as elsewhere, it was the First World War and its aftermath that brought about a change.

Renewed Interest

Nineteenth-century Marian apparitions occurred in clusters at times of exceptional political or social stress. The same was true of the period that began in 1914, as war, political upheaval, and economic crisis formed the backdrop to new apparitions across Europe. Those in the hilly Cova da Iria near Fatima became the most celebrated. Fatima was a small Portuguese village in the diocese of Leiria, about eighty miles north of Lisbon. The central visionary, Lucia dos Santos, bore striking similarities to Bernadette Soubirous and other nineteenth-century seers. The 10-year-old shepherdess was the seventh child of a drunken smallholder who had recently lost some of his land; four of the elder sisters who had helped so much in her upbringing had recently left home, two going into domestic service. The context in which the apparitions occurred is also familiar.

---

[10] BAT, 70/3676, 96–8: Neureuter to GV Trier, 30 Apr. 1883. Neureuter noted disapprovingly that Elisa Recktenwald had also written an improper letter to a village boy.

[11] BAT, B III, 11, 14/3, 55.

[12] BAT, 70/1438, 83–8 (Eppelborn parish records).

[13] BAT, 70/3676a, 226–7, 230–1: Margaretha Odermann to Bishop Korum, 7 Sept. and 8 Nov. 1898; Father Schmitt's response, ibid. 232.

While there had been earlier, largely disregarded visions in 1915 and 1916, the apparitions claimed by Lucia and her two shepherd companions began in May 1917, at the same time as bread riots against an unpopular war. The message to the seers warned of war, starvation, and persecution, and they were told to recite the rosary daily 'in order to obtain peace for the world and the end of the war'. Wartime privations and the anticlericalism of the Portuguese government boosted support for the apparitions (70,000 pilgrims were present during the sixth and final apparition in October 1917), and quickly led to the recruitment of Our Lady of Fatima to the clerical cause. The subsequent Catholic-authoritarian regime of Salazar promoted the cult heavily.[14]

European political and economic crises in the early 1930s provided the background to further apparitions. In June 1931, shortly after a left-wing election victory in the newly inaugurated Spanish Second Republic, two children claimed to have seen the Virgin at Ezquioga in the Spanish Pyrenees. The apparitions followed the sacking in May of over a hundred convents and churches, after Cardinal Segura had denounced the republic, and the pilgrimage to Ezquioga gathered strength against a backdrop of anticlerical measures.[15] The following year a series of apparitions began at Beauraing in the Belgian province of Namur, when the 'Virgin with the Heart of Gold' appeared to five working-class children at a time of economic depression and socialist advance. The apparitions gained a large following (150,000 visited the shrine of Beauraing on 5 August 1933), and the cult was taken up by the clerico-fascist Rexists.[16] Then a 12-year-old working-class girl, Mariette Beco, claimed that 'the Virgin of the Poor' had appeared to her eight times between January and March 1933 at Banneux in the Belgian Ardennes. Beauraing and Banneux were followed by a wave of apparitions in Flemish-speaking and Walloon Belgium, at Chaineux, Etikhove, Lokeren, Melen, Onkerzele, Rotselaer, and Tubise. The reported words and prophecies of the Virgin reflected not only the crisis in Belgium, but anxiety about Hitler, appointed German Chancellor in January 1933.[17] The Belgian experience was not unique: 1933 saw Marian apparitions from fifteen different places across Europe.[18] There was an obvious element of imitation in all this—one writer has referred to the Belgian apparitions as an 'epidemic'.[19] Fatima, especially, soon rivalled Lourdes as a form of template: it was to the 1920s and 1930s what

[14] Ernst, Maria redet, 47–53; W. C. McGrath, 'The Lady of the Rosary: Fatima 1917', in Delaney (ed.), A Woman Clothed, 175–211; Perry and Echeverria, Under the Heel, 184–93; Carroll, Cult of the Virgin Mary, 121–3, 173–81.

[15] Holstein, 'Apparitions', 771; Christian, 'Tapping and Defining New Power'; Perry and Echeverria, Under the Heel, 210–11.

[16] Thurston, Beauraing, 1–24; D. Sharkey, 'The Virgin with the Heart of Gold: Beauraing 1932–33', in Delaney (ed.), A Woman Clothed, 215–38; Hellé, Miracles, 201–43; Ernst, Maria redet, 55–8; Perry and Echeverria, Under the Heel, 165, 199–201.

[17] Thurston, Beauraing, 25–44; R. M. Maloy, 'The Virgin of the Poor: Banneux 1933', in Delaney (ed.), A Woman Clothed, 241–67; Ernst, Maria redet, 59–63.

[18] Billet et al. (eds.), Vraies et fausses, table pp. 9–19, here pp. 9–10.

[19] Hellé, Miracles, uses the word in the heading of his chapter on Beauraing.

Lourdes had been to the 1860s and 1870s. At the same time young Catholics, their susceptibilities heightened by crisis, were exposed to the message of Lourdes in a novel way by the first films that began to appear on St Bernadette.[20]

Germany had its own inter-war visionaries and stigmatists. The best known was probably Therese Neumann of Konnersreuth, who was born in Waldsassen where the Mettenbuch visionaries had been taken. Hers proved to be another awkward case for the diocesan authorities in Regensburg.[21] Trier found itself in a similar position. There was, for example, Anna Maria Goebel of Bickendorf, in the diocese of Trier, whose claims of apparitions and stigmata in 1921 were made at the same time as those of Claire Moes just across the border in Luxemburg.[22] Trier was also alarmed in the 1920s by manifestations of mysticism and spiritualism in the Saarland.[23] The crucial year of 1933 issued in a further spate of alleged apparitions. Bernard Billet records six cases between 1933 and 1938, as well as others on the fertile visionary soil of the French Upper Rhine, and his list is probably not exhaustive.[24] The best-publicized began in the Osnabrück parish of Heede in 1937, where the seers were four young girls aged between 12 and 14.[25]

The wave of German apparitions prompted renewed concern with the Marpingen apparitions, but so did those outside Germany. Fatima, Beauraing, Banneux, and the rest seemed to lend the 'German Lourdes' a new significance. Their celebrity contributed indirectly to a renewal of demands that the Marpingen apparitions be properly investigated. The new mood can be traced in the files on Marpingen at the Trier diocesan archive. For decades, bishop and vicar-general were barely troubled by enquiries about the apparitions. Then, in the inter-war years, the sitation was transformed. One of the earliest into the field was a pharmacist from Paderborn, Clemens Schlüter, who began to correspond with Trier in October 1927. He had read a brochure about Marpingen, and felt that the apparitions there were 'in their way much more wonderful than those in La Salette and Lourdes'. It was 'extremely odd' that they had not been authenticated: had the church really done all it could to investigate the events?[26] This lengthy and pious letter elicited a terse five-line note that there was 'no occasion to rake the matter up again'.[27] Schlüter pressed the point and received by return post a reply of studied offensiveness.[28] He now complained that his detailed enquiries had been treated 'in an old-Prussian military manner', and referred darkly to the

[20] A. Ayfre, 'La Vierge Marie et le Cinéma', in Manoir (ed.), *Maria*, v. 807. On the role of cinema in stimulating the imagination of Fernande Voisin at Beauraing, see Hellé, *Miracles*, 162, 216.

[21] Hellé, *Miracles*, 153–87.

[22] Ibid. 181; *Lexikon für Theologie und Kirche*, ed. J. Höfer and K. Rahner, vii (Freiburg, 1962), col. 65. BAT, B III, 11, 14/3, 74–5 on reactions in Trier to the Bickendorf case.

[23] BAT, 70/1438, 58–67 (Eppelborn parish records).

[24] Billet *et al.* (eds.), *Vraies et fausses*, 9–10.

[25] Ernst, *Maria redet*, 64–8.

[26] BAT, B III, 11, 14/3, 66: Schlüter to GV Trier, 16 Oct. 1927.

[27] Ibid. 68: GV Trier to Schlüter, 7 Nov. 1927.

[28] Ibid. 69–70: Schlüter to GV Trier, 9 Nov. 1927, reply of 11 Nov. 1927.

behaviour of senior churchmen. Trier did not deign to reply. Schlüter fired off another (unanswered) salvo four years later, alleging that Trier was infected with the German-Catholic spirit of Ronge, and complaining about the 'utmost meanness' with which it had treated Anna Maria Goebel of Bickendorf.[29] The febrile pharmacist was not alone. Brother Wendelin Quinten (the name suggests he came from the area around Marpingen) wrote from Buenos Aires in passionate support of the apparitions.[30] A postcard arrived from Gelsenkirchen, begging that Marpingen not be forgotten and noting that the Virgin now appeared 'so often in our time'. The writer referred to Fatima, Banneux, Beauraing, and the German apparitions in Heede, ending with a salutation to Mary, 'our great hope'.[31]

Trier could afford to disregard these individual expressions of the inter-war spirit. Much more awkward was the case of a publicist, Friedrich Ritter von Lama. He came from the Austrian branch of a Catholic aristocratic family with connections throughout Europe, and was born in Salzburg in September 1876.[32] (In an age when General Ludendorff was not alone in the mystical importance he attached to dates and numbers, the fact that Lama was born in the same year as the Marpingen apparitions impressed many as a significant coincidence.) Lama spent much of the 1920s preparing a scholarly study of Pope Benedict XV's peace initiative of 1917.[33] His interests also tended strongly towards the mystical and apocalyptic, and he wrote on the seventeenth-century prophet and mystic, Batholomäus Holzhauser of Bingen, and on Therese of Konnersreuth.[34] Lama was a great supporter of Marian apparitions. Critical of cautiously rational church hierarchies in what he saw as a time of moral crisis, he viewed such revelations as an antidote to the 'great apostasy' of the post-war period. He developed a passionate interest in Marpingen, and published a booklet in 1934 arguing that it should become the German Lourdes.[35]

The diocesan authorities in Trier learned of the booklet a week before Christmas 1934, and wrote a letter of remonstration to the author, outlining the conclusions Bishop Korum had drawn and presenting the affair as a piece of

[29] Ibid. 71, 74–5: Schlüter to GV Trier, 13 Nov. 1927, Schlüter to Bishop of Trier, 3 Dec. 1931. BAT, B III, 11, 14/4, 20, contains a note by Neureuter on the cure in 1877 of the 10-year-old son of the cobbler Franz Schlüter of Paderborn, who is presumably either Clemens Schlüter himself or a close relation.

[30] BAT, B III, 11, 14/3, 134.   [31] Ibid. 147. Emphasis in original.

[32] See the materials on Lama's life gathered by the Marpinger Michael Marx, in BAT, B III, 11, 14/6 [1], 91–3.

[33] F. von Lama, Deutschlands Unglück 1917—und jetzt? Die Friedensvermittlung Papst Benedikt XV. und ihre Vereitlung durch den deutschen Reichskanzler Michaelis (August–September 1917) (Munich, 1932), based on 'twelve years' study' (preface).

[34] See Bartholomäus Holzhauser's 'Deutschland wach auf!' Die berühmte prophetische Busspredigt an Deutschland des heiligmässigen Binger Dekans (1613–58), edited and introduced by F. von Lama. (I was able to consult the 1953 reissue of this volume in the British Library, published in the Credo-Reihe of Wiesbaden); F. von Lama, Der Weg der Therese Neumann von Konnersreuth 1898–1935 (Colmar, 1935).

[35] Lama, Die Muttergottes-Erscheinungen; BAT, B III, 11, 14/3, 94a: Father Biegel to GV Trier, 19 Dec. 1934 reports the appearance of the booklet, and there is a copy of it, ibid. 111. I have a later (undated) edition published in Altötting.

superstition.[36] Lama replied that he had 'of course' received the imprimatur of
the appropriate clerical authorities (he was living at the time in Gauting, outside
Munich), and observing insolently that he had believed the Korum story to be 'the
unfounded gossip of irresponsible people' and, more insolently still, that if Korum
had indeed formed such a conclusion, Divine Providence was to be thanked that
'such an erroneous judgement' had never been published.[37] This was highly disingenuous, for Lama had already been briefed on the situation by a senior retired
theologian in Trier, as the vicariate-general pointed out.[38] Trier now worked successfully to have the imprimatur removed from Lama's booklet.[39] It may also have
had a hand in two Saarland newspapers running very hostile reviews early in 1935.
These outlined the position of the church, praised its 'rationality', and warned
of the 'great dangers' in the recent trend towards excessive belief in mysticism,
prophecies, and apparitions.[40] In subsequent correspondence with the church
authorities in Trier and Munich, the Austrian publicist laboured his good faith.[41]
In a letter to the editor of the hostile *Saar-Zeitung* of Saarlouis, however, he
violently defended his position, criticized the inadequacy of the earlier enquiry,
and expressed his determination to appeal to Rome over attempts to block his
'right' to disseminate the booklet. He added, with magnificent aplomb, that the
canon in Munich responsible for this had immediately suffered a stroke, and the
suffragan bishop of Trier had been called to meet his maker. He repeated these
blasphemous observations in a letter to the parish priest of Marpingen.[42]

Removal of the imprimatur did not take Lama's booklet out of circulation, or
prevent it from reawakening interest in Marpingen. The author also found
another way of publicizing the German Lourdes. A devoted follower of the
stigmatist Therese Neumann, he belonged to the so-called 'Konnersreuth circle'
which published a variety of bulletins, pamphlets, and books.[43] In February 1936,
Die Stimme Mariens. Sendbote der Muttergottes-Erscheinungen, a supplement to the
weekly paper put out by the circle, began a series on Marpingen.[44] Trier again
intervened with the relevant clerical authorities, this time in Regensburg, requesting that the editors be asked to stop publication immediately:[45]

We take the liberty of adding that in recent times the *Sendbote der Muttergottes-Erscheinungen*
has often spread alarm in the church and that it fosters an unhealthy piety in the Christian
people. At the present time there is every reason to hold fast to the revealed truths of the

[36] BAT, B III, 11, 14/3, 97a: GV Trier to Lama, 24 Dec. 1934.
[37] Ibid. 98a: Lama to GV Trier, 4 Jan. 1935.
[38] Ibid. 99c: GV Trier to Lama, 16 Jan. 1935; and ibid. 99: Professor Emeritus Jakob Marx to GV
Trier, 8 Jan. 1935, confirming that he had informed Lama of the background.
[39] Ibid. 99d, 101: GV Trier to GV Munich, 16 Jan. 1935, reply of 21 Jan. 1935.
[40] The two newspapers were the *Saar-Zeitung* and the *Saarbrücker Landeszeitung*. See ibid. 103, 112.
[41] Ibid. 99c: Lama to GV Trier, n.d.
[42] Ibid. 103: Lama to editor of *Saar-Zeitung*, 23 Feb. 1935; ibid. 119, Lama to Father Biegel, 27 Feb.
1935.
[43] Hellé, *Miracles*, 185; Lama, *Der Weg der Therese Neumann von Konnersreuth*.
[44] Copy in BAT, B III, 11, 14/3, 126.
[45] Ibid. 127: GV Trier to BO Regensburg, 17 Feb. 1936.

faith and oppose with all our force the excessive mania for spreading the message of new apparitions among the faithful.

Regensburg was sympathetic, unsurprisingly in view of its own difficulties with Mettenbuch and Therese of Konnersreuth, but there was little it could do. After previous warnings the imprimatur had already been withdrawn, and the publication appeared without it.[46]

Trier complained about the effect of these outside initiatives, but such interventions depended on local consent. Brother Wendelin in South America had his contacts in Marpingen, and when Friedrich von Lama investigated he found plenty of village witnesses to the original apparitions who were ready to express their indignation that no proper enquiry had been held. A travel agent who decided a few years later to organize trips to Marpingen must also have been confident that pilgrims would find the welcome (and the apparition narrative from locals) that they expected.[47] The evidence makes it clear that the villagers' interest in the apparitions was reawakened in the inter-war years. This was not just a response to the growing enthusiasm from outsiders; it was also fuelled by the uncertainties and anxieties of the post-war period in Marpingen itself.

The war cost the village seventy-two young men, leaving more than 350 bereaved family members.[48] It had an impact on every aspect of village life, causing dislocation of the local economy, disrupting schools, and wreaking demographic mayhem (the birth-rate halved in 1914–17, then doubled in 1919–23).[49] Even the ethnic homogeneity of the village was affected with the arrival of Slav immigrants.[50] War was followed by revolution. In Marpingen revolutionaries gathered in rooms at the Dewese inn, and the local gendarme was disarmed by members of the Workers and Soldiers Council wearing red armbands.[51] There is a slightly theatrical air to this episode, and the revolution in the Saarland generally possessed neither the political radicalism nor the violent class conflict of its counterparts in Berlin, central Germany, or the Ruhr. The strikes of 1918–19 nevertheless signalled a return to the desperate militancy of the 1890s, given new shape by the revolution. Membership of the left-wing miners' union, the Alter Verband, expanded rapidly, and the newly founded Communist Party (KPD) was buoyant: by 1932 it was winning a regular 25 per cent of votes cast in the Saarland.[52] The KPD was most successful in coalfield towns like Dudweiler, but there were also 'red enclaves' in the Catholic hinterland to the north, such as the

[46] Ibid. 128: BO Regensburg to GV Trier, 19 Feb. 1936.
[47] Ibid. 130–3, 135–9. See also below.
[48] Bungert, *Heimatbuch*, 244, 264–5.
[49] Keuth, 'Die wirtschaftliche Entwicklung', 121; Bungert, *Heimatbuch*, 244; Derr, 'Pfarrei Marpingen', appended tables.
[50] The Russian-born Johann Chrustalew, who settled in Marpingen and married a local girl in 1921, began a process that would gather pace in later decades: BAT, 70/3679, 53–6.
[51] Bungert, *Heimatbuch*, 245.
[52] From 1,250 members in 1913, the Alter Verband grew to 40,000 by 1920: Horch, *Wandel*, 483. The membership fell away again after that date, but the propensity to strike did not. On the KPD, H. Weber, *Die Wandlung des deutschen Kommunismus* (Frankfurt am Main, 1969), 391; and the statistical

strongly Communist village of Lockweiler.[53] Marpingen was no Lockweiler, but the left did acquire new strength after the war. In 1923 we find the new parish priest, Father Ferdinand Gerhard, leaning heavily on miners who had joined the Alter Verband by denying them absolution: if he followed the practice elsewhere and gave in, argued Gerhard, he would 'thereby strengthen the Free Trade Union and play into the hands of communism'. He gave the number of Alter Verband members as over 100, of whom forty-six were 'openly proclaimed communists'. They were, he complained, 'incorrigible'.[54]

War also brought French military occupation and a fifteen-year period (1920–35) in which, under the terms of the Treaty of Versailles, the Saarland was severed from Germany and administered by League of Nations commissioners under strong French influence.[55] The artificially created 'Saargebiet' of this period has been described by one writer as a 'political homunculus'.[56] The Prussian state mines passed into French hands as 'compensation' for German military depredations, and the area was integrated into the French economic, currency, and customs system. Nationalist resentment, the work-tempo demanded by new masters in the mines, and other disadvantages that followed from the French connection, especially the inferior French social security provision, all generated conflict.[57] Miners, ex-miners, and their families faced particular problems. A long strike in 1923 which led to harsh emergency legislation was the result of unmet wage demands, the situation complicated by the problems of a dual-currency area at a time of German hyperinflation. (When Father Gerhard wrote to Trier in 1923 he included 500 marks for return postage.) The chronic devaluation of the mark also threatened the livelihoods of those drawing social benefits from the period before the French take-over of the pits. This was part of a larger problem, for the new French regime refused to assume responsibility for accident benefits, miners' pensions, and payments to injured ex-servicemen or war widows, and the Reich disputed its share of responsibility. This caused anxiety that affected every community in the Saarland, where the 16,000 disabled ex-servicemen, war widows, and dependent children were joined by nearly as many pit-pensioners, widows, and orphans.[58] This was bound to affect Marpingen.

tables on *Landesrat*, district, and communal elections in L. Bies, *Klassenkampf an der Saar 1919–1935. Die KPD im Saargebiet* (Frankfurt am Main, 1978), 207–10.

[53] Horch, *Wandel*, 661 n. 213. There were similar red enclaves south-east of Saarbrücken in the Warndt, such as the village of Ludweiler: Bies, *Klassenkampf*, 39–40.

[54] BAT, 70/3679, 14–15: Gerhard to Bishop Bornewasser, 20 July 1923. As in the Saarland (and indeed Germany as a whole), the KPD appealed especially to the young in Marpingen. See Bies, *Klassenkampf*, 37, 47–8, 64.

[55] K. Schwabe, 'Die Saarlandfrage in Versailles', *Saarheimat*, 29 (1985), 17–20.

[56] Bies, *Klassenkampf*, 19.

[57] Herrmann and Klein, 'Zur sozialen Entwicklung', 140–2; and Bungert, *Heimatbuch*, 245–7 for a Marpingen perspective.

[58] There were 14,400 dependent on mining pensions and payments: T. Balk, *The Saar at First Hand* (London, 1934), 112. Balk, 112–18, describes the anxieties of these 30,000 out of a total population of only 800,000.

Although employment diversified in the inter-war years, as quarrying and construction firms established themselves in the village and others found employment in the steelworks, mining grew in importance as agriculture declined. The number of miners touched 600: with dependants they accounted for 70 per cent of the population in 1927.[59]

Insecurity and material distress became widespread at the end of the 1920s. Employment in mining fell steeply after 1926. In that year the pits provided a livelihood for over 77,000 men; during the next six years the figure fell steadily to under 50,000. Other sectors like iron and steel, quarrying, and construction expanded in the mid-1920s, but all were hit by the depression.[60] By December 1932 a quarter of the labour-force was unemployed.[61]

The arrival of communism in the village, rule by League of Nations commissioners and French mine officials, anxieties over pensions, mass unemployment: these were the troubled circumstances of inter-war Marpingen. The immediate event that prompted renewed disputes over the apparitions was another by-product of the war. One of the combatants from the village, Heinrich Recktenwald, swore an oath at the front that if he survived he would have a chapel built to the glory of the Virgin Mary. The place where he chose to build it was the apparition site in the Härtelwald.[62] Recktenwald was a prominent figure in post-war Marpingen, a building contractor (albeit with debts) and commander of the village fire brigade.[63] The *Gemeindevorsteher*, Peter Brill, also backed the scheme; so did members of the parish council. Recktenwald and his supporters initially tried to obtain church approval. Jakob Biegel, who succeeded Gerhard as parish priest in 1927, heard about the idea as soon as he arrived in the village, and tried to head Recktenwald off, suggesting that he switch his attention instead to the Marienbrunnen. The former parish priest Theodor Schmitt then attempted unsuccessfully to use his influence.[64] Recktenwald and a companion presented the proposal to Canon Karl Kammer in Trier, who also tried to persuade him to fulfil the oath in a less contentious manner—by adding to the Marian altar in the parish church, or building a simple Marian chapel. 'Displeased' when Kammer proved unyielding, the men then tried to work on Vicar-General Tilmann, again without success. 'They hoped for a great pilgrimage to Marpingen, in which they saw an opportunity for their village,' was Kammer's lapidary comment.[65] On

[59] Bungert, *Heimatbuch*, 248–9, 302, 307. Mining employment in the village peaked in 1927.
[60] Of all the unemployed in the Saarland in the late summer of 1932 40% were construction workers. One measure of the collapse in building activity is provided by cement production, which by 1932 was at barely half the level of three years earlier: Bies, *Klassenkampf*, 55.
[61] Herrmann and Klein, 'Zur sozialen Entwicklung', 140–2.
[62] BAT, B III, 11, 14/6 [2], contains a letter from his widow to Vicar-General Karl Kammer of Trier, 7 Mar. 1956, enclosing copies from Recktenwald's wartime diary and detailing his 'miraculous survival'.
[63] Bungert, *Heimatbuch*, 495. On Recktenwald's indebtedness, BAT, B III, 11, 14/3, 77: report of Father Jakob Biegel to GV Trier on the proposal to build a chapel, undated (but early Feb. 1933).
[64] BAT, B III, 11, 14/3, 77: Biegel to GV Trier, early Feb. 1933.
[65] Ibid. 14/5, 92: 'Kurze Übersicht betr. Marpingen', Trier, 25 Oct. 1947.

instructions from Trier, Biegel tried to dampen his parishioners' zeal by announcing from the pulpit that an enquiry into the apparitions had proved negative.[66]

The movement was strengthened with the dramatic news reported by two women who had visited Konnersreuth in October 1931, that the stigmatist Therese Neumann had answered 'yes' three times when asked whether the Marpingen apparitions were genuine. One of the women was Elisa Brill, a 74-year-old miner's wife in Marpingen who had been present as an adolescent at some of the apparitions in 1876–7.[67] Her companion was almost certainly a slightly younger widow, Gertrauda Kastel of St Ingbert, who had visited Marpingen 'in the first days' ('often barefoot') and become friendly with Frau Brill at the beginning of the 1930s.[68] The sceptical parish priest asked both women not to discuss the matter until further enquiries could be made in Bavaria: 'They kept their word so well that eventually not only the whole village but the entire district was full of the story.'[69] Father Biegel managed to suppress a newspaper article about Konnersreuth and Marpingen. But the chapel plan had now regained momentum, and the process of seeking civil permissions for construction went ahead despite clerical disapproval. In June 1932 the parish council agreed to make land available. At a time of high unemployment among construction workers in the village, the project was seen as a useful work-creation scheme, and local business people saw material advantages in a pilgrimage chapel. 'On the one hand this revolts me, on the other hand it forces me to be careful,' reported a worried parish priest.[70] The council even expressed itself willing to assume the costs, but this was vetoed by the Saarland authorities, fearful that the council would be financially overburdened. A Chapel Association was therefore formed, with Brill as treasurer, and the chapel was built with voluntary donations and gifts of materials.[71] Trier learned that construction had gone ahead without clerical permission when it was asked at the end of January 1933 to consecrate the nearly completed chapel.[72]

'A True Apparition Mania': The 1930s

The chapel proved to be the focus of a renewed apparition movement. This began with a sustained campaign to have the chapel consecrated, which included approaches to Trier from Recktenwald himself, Peter Brill, and the Marpingen

[66] BAT, B III, 11, 14/3, 77: Biegel to GV Trier, early Feb. 1933.

[67] Ibid. 113: deposition of Elisabeth Brill, 6 May 1935. Elisa Brill was unrelated to the *Gemeindevorsteher* Peter Brill.

[68] Ibid. 115: deposition of Gertrauda Kastel, 6 May 1935.

[69] Ibid. 14/3, 77: Biegel to GV Trier, early Feb. 1933.

[70] Ibid.

[71] Ibid. 14/6 [2], has the most detailed evidence on the origins of the chapel, including bills showing the costs of materials, etc., passed on by former parish priest Nicklas (by then in Steinberg/Saar) in a letter to GV Trier of 27 Aug. 1964. Also Bungert, *Heimatbuch*, 237–9, which includes a picture of the chapel.

[72] BAT, B III, 11, 14/3, 76: *Gemeindevorsteher* Brill to GV Trier, 27 Jan. 1933; also BAT, B III, 11, 14/5, 92.

ex-servicemen's association.[73] When Trier remained adamant that it would not 'foster superstition', a petition was sent, emphasizing the 'movement among the people' in support of the Virgin of Marpingen.[74] Elisa Brill then requested a personal interview with the bishop, on the grounds that her visit to Konnersreuth had furnished 'favourable evidence that, despite distortion and misrepresentation, cannot be argued away'. This also met with a predictably dusty response.[75] It was Frau Brill who injected new life into this stalemate. In October 1934, Father Biegel reported to his superiors that she had 'caused excitement in our village and the whole district' with claims that she had seen the Virgin Mary, accompanied by the three visionaries of 1876, in the parish church. Admonished that she must keep quiet about these 'delusions', she thereupon claimed a further vision of the Virgin in the new chapel, with the result that growing numbers of pilgrims were descending on the village. Fearing that the matter would 'continue to cause a stir', a harassed Biegel requested instructions.[76] This was the beginning of what Trier would later describe as 'a true apparition mania'.[77]

What followed was in many ways a re-run of 1876–7, with significant variations. Unlike 1876, there was a bishop and a functioning vicariate-general in Trier, which tried to stamp out the movement. They were unsuccessful, however, and the situation on the ground was similar in a number of ways to the earlier period. Biegel, like Neureuter, was caught in the crossfire between official restraint and popular enthusiasm. In May 1933 he complained to his superiors that he had been placed under pressure to support the consecration of the chapel: 'a refusal would now create great pastoral difficulties for me'. But there was to be no concession from Trier on this.[78] Biegel then tried to 'divert attention' from the chapel and apparition cult by making the Marienbrunnen next to the parish church an alternative focus of devotional activity. In 1933 he had already instituted candle-lit processions there; three years later the housing of the Marienbrunnen was reconstructed as a miniature chapel.[79] This did not work, and Elisa Brill's claims struck a chord in the village, especially when further visionaries announced themselves. The first was Frau Brill's friend Gertrauda Kastel.[80] She was followed in 1937 by a Frau Maldemer from Bildstock, who had become known for claiming visions and stigmata—according to a local priest she was a woman with 'an unusually powerful craving for recognition'. Beginning at Whitsuntide 1937, she supposedly saw apparitions of the Virgin Mary in the Härtelwald, and despite

[73] Ibid. 78–9, 82–3: GV Trier to Brill, 15 Feb. 1933; Heinrich Recktenwald to GV Trier, 6 May 1933; Biegel to GV Trier, 11 May 1933, reporting on the background to Brill's visit to Trier; Committee of *Kriegerverein* Marpingen to GV Trier, 13 Aug. 1933; reply of 17 Aug. 1933.

[74] Ibid. 84–5

[75] Ibid. 87–8: Elisa Brill to GV Trier, 10 Jan. 1934; reply of 12 Jan. 1934.

[76] Ibid. 90: Biegel to GV Trier, 19 Oct. 1934.

[77] Ibid. 14/6 [2]: GV Trier to Father Nicklas of Marpingen, 6 Dec. 1954.

[78] Ibid. 14/3, 80–1: Biegel to GV Trier, 11 May 1933; reply of 15 May 1933.

[79] Ibid. 129a: Biegel to GV Trier, 5 July 1935, 5 June 1936. Bungert, *Heimatbuch*, 554, mentions these changes, without referring to the problems that prompted them.

[80] BAT, B III, 11, 14/3, 115: deposition of Gertrauda Kastel, 6 May 1935.

her dubious character (she had misappropriated money from a rosary association) it was 'beyond doubt' that Frau Maldemer had found 'many who believe her'.[81]

In gender terms, we therefore have a familiar pattern. It was (in the phrase used later by Trier) 'hysterical women' who claimed to have seen apparitions.[82] Village women were also, once again, the most prominent supporters of these new claims. Almost all of the forty-eight signatories who 'witnessed' a vision vouchsafed to Frau Brill and Frau Kastel were women.[83] The men who sought consecration of the chapel were apparently concerned (in the view of the parish priest) that 'they lacked sufficient authority to prevent erratic and exaggerated behaviour, particularly on the part of the women'.[84] One of the episodes that may have fuelled this concern followed the arrival in the village of a Frau Captain Müller, who adopted the name 'story-teller' (*Märchentante*) and claimed to be an artist. She offered to paint the chapel without payment, a proposition likely to go down well in Marpingen, but in the event her efforts failed to please and the cost of her materials, plus free board and lodging, turned out to be higher than expected. More than that, 'everyone in Marpingen believed that they should have their say over the chapel, and went there and placed statues and flowers just as they wanted, producing a regular motley'.[85] The picture that emerges from the detailed accounts of the parish priest therefore bears some similarities to 1876–7. The core of the devout who welcomed the apparitions was female, but the seal of approval was given by local male notables, including the men at the head of the movement to have the chapel consecrated, who had more worldly reasons to welcome the renewed interest in the village. (The chapel brought in 1,500 marks in 1935.[86]) There was some tension between the two. What is strikingly different from the 1870s is the absence, at least in the accounts we have, of any real part played by children in the whole affair. In 1876–7, the movement began with young seers, and was continued by other youthful visionaries—the 'rival children'. In the 1930s the movement began with one elderly widow and was continued by others. It is tempting to speculate that widowed women had something akin to the same painful position in the post-war period that 'orphaned' children had sixty years earlier.

The flow of pilgrims to Marpingen also grew as it had done in the 1870s. In 1934, the parish priest was still referring mainly to the excitement caused in the immediate vicinity. Then the radius widened and the numbers rose. Friedrich von Lama claimed in 1935 that 10,000–15,000 a year were visiting the village.[87] He

[81] BAT, B III, 11, 14/3, 143: Biegel to GV Trier, 24 May 1937. On Frau Maldemer's character, see ibid. 144–5: Dean Klee of Bildstock to GV Trier, 26 May 1937.

[82] BAT, B III, 11, 14/6 [2], GV Trier to Father Eduard Huber of Kippenhausen, Lake Constance, 30 Aug. 1962; ibid. 14/3, 144–5: Dean Klee of Bildstock to GV Trier, 26 May 1937.

[83] Ibid. 114.

[84] Ibid. 129d: Biegel to GV Trier, 25 June 1936.

[85] Ibid. 129a: Biegel to GV Trier, 5 June 1936.

[86] Ibid. 129d: Biegel to GV Trier, 25 June 1936.

[87] Ibid. 103: Lama to editor of *Saar-Zeitung*, 23 Feb. 1935.

was, of course, likely to give a generous estimate, but his figure is not implausible. By July 1935 Father Biegel was reporting the arrival of 'more and more pilgrims'.[88] A year later he noted that Marpingen had been 'much visited in the last years. Hardly a day goes by when there are no pilgrims here, and they do not come just from the immediate vicinity. This year there have already been whole groups (20–40) from Pirmasens, Mayen, Cologne, Mönchen-Gladbach and Saarbrücken.' In Biegel's view, 'the stream of pilgrims can no longer be stemmed, but it must be directed into the right channels'. As he noted, the publicity given to Marpingen by Lama had encouraged pious visitors.[89] So had the enthusiastic support of maverick clergymen like Valentin Vogt, the incumbent of a Westerwald parish until forced to step down in November 1935. He had 'through his peculiarity, which obviously derives from pathological tendencies, for a long time created difficulties and worries for us', as his superiors in Cologne wearily reported to Trier; but it would be 'hopeless to try and disabuse him of his ideas'.[90]

Valentin Vogt recalls some of the clerical enthusiasts of the 1870s. Another development in Cologne recalls the commercial exploitation of the original apparitions. Trier learned from Biegel in autumn 1936 that a travel bureau in Cologne was advertising group visits to Marpingen. The parish priest's copy of the advertisement had come from Limburg an der Lahn, suggesting wide dissemination.[91] The publicity sheet spoke of the many thousands who had visited Belgian apparition sites in recent years, and announced that 'the longing in hopeful souls' in Germany had been fulfilled. '*Mary has also appeared in Germany!*' it screamed. Why had nothing further been heard about this? 'The answer to this question is certainly a very sorry one. *We could in fact have a second Lourdes in Germany today,* if our leading personalities and Catholics of that period had been alert and had understood the call of the Blessed Virgin.' The publicity gave an uncritical account of the apparitions, comparing them with Lourdes, Beauraing, and Banneux, and added that it was more necessary than ever to recognize Mary's role as intercesssor 'today when our people is striving for recognition and to rise again, today when our church has been subject like our people to a purification and the young church is to shine with a new brilliance'. After giving details of the excursion, the advertisement added a final note: as the Gestapo had banned all trips to the Belgian apparition sites until further notice, there was an even stronger reason to visit Marpingen.[92] The clerical authorities in Cologne placed warnings in the archdiocesan newspaper about the travel bureau (Herr Brand, its proprietor, was well known to them), but the damage had been done.[93] The warnings clearly did not prevent pilgrims from making the trip.[94]

[88] Ibid. 122: Biegel to GV Trier, 5 July 1935.
[89] Ibid. 129d: Biegel to GV Trier, 25 June 1936.
[90] Ibid. 136–7: GV Trier to GV Cologne, 30 Nov. 1936; reply of 8 Jan. 1937.
[91] Ibid. 130: Biegel to GV Trier, 27 Oct. 1936.
[92] Ibid. 131–3: copy of advertisement from the *Pilgerbüro Köln*, Palmstraße 47.
[93] Ibid. 137: GV Cologne to GV Trier, 8 Jan. 1937.
[94] Ibid. 143: Biegel to GV Trier, 24 May 1937.

Herr Brand's motives were no doubt commercial, but the terms in which he couched his advertisements remind us of the stark political background against which support for the new Marpingen apparitions grew. Here there are further parallels with the events of the 1870s although, once again, they are not exact. The saga of the Härtelwald chapel and the new wave of apparitions took place at a time when German Catholics faced problems of a kind they had not faced since the *Kulturkampf*, from a regime that owed virtually none of its popular support to Catholics. For, at the very moment that the chapel was completed, Hitler became German chancellor, and the campaign to have the chapel consecrated coincided with the Nazi campaign against the church and Catholic organizations. This took a variety of forms, from the ideological assault of Alfred Rosenberg's 'paganism' to the heavy pressure on Catholic occupational and youth organizations to disband themselves. The offensive was largely concerned until 1935 with the 'outworks' of Catholic Germany, but it entered a new, more threatening phase in 1936–7 with the dismantling of denominational schools and a Nazi campaign to drive Catholics from the church.[95] In the Rhineland, from which many Marpingen pilgrims came, the prominent trials of regular and secular clergy on foreign currency and immorality charges were particularly brazen and threatening.[96]

Where should the renewed apparition movement be placed within a larger picture of the Catholic response to such intimidation? Only a tiny proportion of practising Catholics deserted the church under pressure. Even at the high-point of the Nazi campaign in 1937, the 100,000 who left represented less than half of 1 per cent of all Catholics.[97] Most of the faithful found themselves torn between fear and resignation, and the desire to make some demonstration of allegiance to the church. Under certain circumstances this demonstration could take the form of open resistance to the Nazi regime. One such case was the forceful and public protest in Oldenburg against the removal of crucifixes from schools in 1936.[98] Similar crucifix struggles took place in the Ermland, and in the Saar-Palatinate.[99]

---

[95] For an introduction to this large subject, see G. Lewy, *The Catholic Church and Nazi Germany* (London, 1964), and J. S. Conway, *The Nazi Persecution of the Churches, 1933–1945* (London, 1968). See also D. Albrecht (ed.), *Katholische Kirche im Dritten Reich. Eine Aufsatzsammlung zum Verhältnis von Papsttum, Episkopat und deutschen Katholiken zum Nationalsozialismus 1933–1945* (Mainz, 1976); K. Gotto and K. Repgen (eds.), *Kirche, Katholiken und Nationalsozialismus* (Mainz, 1980). A useful early collection of materials is J. Neuhäusler, *Kreuz und Hakenkreuz. Der Kampf des Nationalsozialismus gegen die Katholische Kirche und der kirchliche Widerstand* (Munich, 1946).

[96] H. G. Hockerts, *Die Sittlichkeitsprozesse gegen katholische Ordensangehörige und Priester 1936/37* (Mainz, 1971).

[97] U. von Hehl, 'Das Kirchenvolk im Dritten Reich', in Gotto and Repgen (eds.), *Kirche, Katholiken und Nationalsozialismus*, 73.

[98] J. Noakes, 'The Oldenburg Crucifix Struggle of November 1936: A Case Study of Opposition in the Third Reich', in P. D. Stachura (ed.), *The Shaping of the Nazi State* (London, 1978), 201–33.

[99] On the Ermland, see G. Reifferscheid, *Das Bistum Ermland und das Dritte Reich* (Cologne and Vienna, 1975), 173 ff.; on the crucifix struggle at Frauenholz in the Saar-Palatinate (diocese Trier), which included a 'school strike' by parents, see Neuhäusler, *Kreuz und Hakenkreuz*, 118–19, and B. Vollmer, *Volksopposition im Polizeistaat. Gestapo- und Regierungsberichte 1934–1936* (Stuttgart, 1957), 88.

There were many other individual instances of open opposition to aspects of the Third Reich on the part of clergy and laity, attracting penalties that ranged from warnings and fines to incarceration or execution. This can be seen as part of the resistance—the *Widerstand*—within Nazi Germany. More common, however, was a more muted phenomenon that historians have come to call *Resistenz*.[100] This was widespread in Catholic regions. It might take the form of grumbling, the ubiquitous *Nörgelei*, but it also expressed itself in large-scale support for processions and celebrations that had a tacit message for the regime. In the years 1934–7, unusually large crowds gathered for Corpus Christi Day processions and for scheduled pilgrimages like the Procession of Relics in Aachen.[101] The security forces were right to see an element of defiance in this.[102]

The broad spectrum of 'resistance' to the Third Reich suggests obvious parallels with the period of the *Kulturkampf*. This holds true even down to the way in which, say, funerals became the site of small political struggles, as priests refused to accept wreaths embellished with swastikas.[103] Indeed, the precedent of the *Kulturkampf* exercised numerous minds after the Nazi seizure of power. In the first months of the regime, Hermann Goering (thinking tactically) and the Catholic Vice-Chancellor Franz von Papen (thinking wishfully) agreed that 'a *Kulturkampf* would be a disaster for the young state'.[104] Three years later, as the pressures on Catholics mounted, Cardinal State Secretary Pacelli (the later Pope Pius XII) believed that a *Kulturkampf* was under way.[105] The same perception existed at less elevated levels. As early as March 1934, Catholic newspapers in the Rhineland and Bavaria ran very pointed stories about the imprisonment during the *Kulturkampf* of Bishop Eberhard of Trier, the contemporary import of which was not lost on the Gestapo.[106]

The apparitions of the 1930s, like those of the earlier period, clearly found a response in part because of the threatening political circumstances. In one case,

---

[100] The concept of *Resistenz*, with its suggestion of 'immunity' rather than outright resistance (*Widerstand*), and its concern with the sphere of 'everyday life', was developed by Martin Broszat. See his 'Resistenz und Widerstand', in Broszat *et al.* (eds.), *Bayern in der NS-Zeit*, 6 vols., iv (Munich, 1981), 691–709. See also I. Kershaw, *The Nazi Dictatorship* (London, 1989), 151, 156–7; and for examples of the approach in action, in addition to the 6-vol. Bavarian project cited above, see I. Kershaw, *Popular Opinion and Political Dissent in the Third Reich: Bavaria 1933–1945* (Oxford, 1983); and D. Peukert, *Inside Nazi Germany: Conformity, Opposition and Racism in Everyday Life* (Harmondsworth, Middx., 1989).

[101] See Hehl, 'Das Kirchenvolk', 70–1, 74–5, and the many Rhineland examples in Vollmer, *Volksopposition*, 129, 184–5.

[102] Cf. Gestapo use of the word *Widerstand* in a report from Aachen on 5 Apr. 1935: Vollmer, *Volksopposition*, 181.

[103] See e.g. ibid. 184.

[104] B. Stasiewski (ed.), *Akten deutscher Bischöfe über die Lage der Kirche 1933–1945*, i. *1933–1945* (Mainz, 1968), 96–7: report of the visit of Bishops Berning and Kaller to Vice-Chancellor von Papen, 25 Apr. 1933.

[105] Pacelli, in an exchange of notes with the German ambassador to the Vatican von Bergen, 29 Jan. 1936, cited in Reifferscheid, *Das Bistum Ermland*, 263 n. 7.

[106] On Rhineland newspapers, and Gestapo reactions, see Vollmer, *Volksopposition*, 31; on a similar story in the *Bayerische Kurier*, see Zipfel, *Kirchenkampf in Deutschland 1933–1945* (Berlin, 1965), 309.

apparitions from the 1870s actually became a focus for official church defiance. In October 1934, Bishop Kaller of the Ermland led a procession of 50,000 to the apparition site in Dittrichswalde, where he preached in such warm terms to the 'dear Polish people' (on whom pastoral restrictions had just been imposed) that he caused 'displeasure and indignation in Nazi circles'.[107] The exercise was repeated two years later.[108] Support for the new apparitions in the 1930s was a more spontaneous affirmation of Catholic identity. Going to Heede or Marpingen—and, until the Gestapo closed the border, Banneux or Beauraing—was less organized than participation in an official pilgrimage or procession, and less obviously political than the crucifix struggles. But it was also less private than mere grumbling, and at least quasi-political, if only because the authorities in the 1930s (as in the 1870s) were disposed to view such collective movements of the faithful with suspicion. That is why they closed the Belgian border to pilgrims, and intervened at Heede.[109]

For locals and non-locals, Marpingen occupied a singular position because, thanks to the Treaty of Versailles, it was both German and non-German. Under the terms of the treaty the Saarland remained under League of Nations auspices until the population was invited to vote on its future in 1935. From Hitler's assumption of power in January 1933 until the plebiscite of January 1935, a region that could be crossed in half an hour by express train became a centre of European attention and a cockpit of political struggle. On the one hand, the Saarland was spared the open violence and repression of Nazi Germany: a multi-party system continued and the media of communications remained formally untrammelled. The church and Catholic organizations were free from Nazi pressure, while the Saarland became a haven for Communist militants on the run and a centre from which anti-Nazi literature could be smuggled into the Third Reich. In that sense it was no different from neighbouring Belgium, Luxemburg, or France.[110] On the other hand, the Saar clearly was different. The Nazis had no scruples about kidnapping opposition militants across the German border, and for two years the Saarland was subjected to propaganda from the Third Reich. Above all, the indigenous population felt itself to be German, and therefore faced an invidious choice. As Germans they chafed at their treatment by League commissioners and the French, and looked forward to rejoining the Fatherland; but by 1935 a 'yes' vote in the plebiscite also entailed the dubious embrace of the Third Reich. The Communists on the Saar were obvious opponents of this, and as the plebiscite approached they were joined in their campaign for the 'status

---

[107] Reifferscheid, *Das Bistum Ermland*, 105. Dittrichswalde was one of four large-scale pilgrimages mounted in the diocese in 1934: ibid. 117–20. See also Lama, *Muttergottes-Erscheinungen*, 72.
[108] Reifferscheid, *Das Bistum Ermland*, 158; see also table 7, a photograph of the 1936 gathering.
[109] On state intervention at Heede, Ernst, *Maria redet*, 64–8.
[110] Vollmer, *Volksopposition*, 29, 53, cites two Saxon communists eventually arrested at Aachen in Feb. 1934 after sojourns in Czechoslovakia, Austria, Switzerland, Luxemburg, France, The Netherlands, Belgium—and the Saarland. See also the contemporary account by Balk, *The Saar at First Hand*, and Bies, *Klassenkampf*, 104–6, on the region as a centre of Communist organization after Jan. 1933.

quo' by both Social Democrats and dissident Catholics led by Johannes Hoffmann, editor of the *Neue Saar-Post*. It was a dirty campaign, in which the opponents of reunion were always at a disadvantage. They were subjected to widespread intimidation by supporters of a 'German Front' movement that enjoyed much greater financial muscle and support from the Reich. Supporters of the 'status quo' also faced the strong desire among Saarlanders to be part of the Reich 'despite Hitler', something that may have been eased by the Nazis' temporary soft-pedalling of the campaign against the church in Germany and was certainly encouraged by the church hierarchy in the Saarland, which threw itself strongly behind the 'yes' campaign. In the event, a full 90 per cent voted 'yes' to reunion.[111]

This provided the backdrop to the 'apparition mania' of the 1930s. The plebiscite campaign left a bitter after-taste. In Marpingen, as elsewhere in the region, some of the more determined opponents of reunion emigrated.[112] For the vast majority (in the Marpingen area it was 96 per cent) who had voted 'yes' with varying degrees of enthusiasm, the outcome of the plebiscite left them in the same position as other Germans. Indeed, the satisfactory settlement of the Saar question removed a major tactical reason for Nazi reticence towards the church, as Catholics in other parts of Germany had feared.[113] There were some concessions to local Catholic sensibilities (in not pressing the 'New Heathenism' movement, for example), but religious organizations came under pressure and 1936-7 saw systematic attacks on the denominational school.[114] The experience of Marpingen seems to have been mixed. The Franciscan nuns who had established themselves in the village in 1901 and moved into more spacious accommodation on the Kirchberg in 1930, continued to perform their charitable works without interference.[115] In other spheres there were immediate changes. On the same day that the Nazi local government regulations of 1935 took effect in the Saarland, the Marpingen *Gemeindevorsteher* Peter Brill—that keen supporter of the Härtelwald chapel—was replaced by a Nazi nominee. Local council meetings operated subsequently under the *Führer*-principle. The two rival village choirs (a legacy

---

[111] On the plebiscite of 13 Jan. 1935, and the political conflicts that preceded it: E. Kunkel, *Für Deutschland—gegen Hitler* (Saarbrücken, 1968); P. von der Mühlen, *'Schlägt Hitler an der Saar!' Abstimmungskampf, Emigration und Widerstand im Saargebiet 1933–1935* (Bonn, 1979); P. Siegmann, 'Vor vierzig Jahren. Der Kampf um den 13. Januar 1935. Tagebuch-Auszüge', *Zeitschrift für die Geschichte der Saargegend*, 22 (1974), 224–325. These concentrate on the left opposition, but also have material on the Catholic opponents of rejoining Germany. On the latter, see also Lewy, *Catholic Church and Nazi Germany*, 182–201; H.-W. Herrmann, 'Die Volksabstimmung vom 13. Januar 1935', *Saarheimat*, 29 (1985), 21–4.

[112] Bungert, *Heimatbuch*, 257–8.

[113] There were rumours in the Rhineland in Nov. 1934 that a 'Kulturkampf' would follow settlement of the Saar question: Vollmer, *Volksopposition*, 111, 130.

[114] Neuhäusler, *Kreuz und Hakenkreuz*, 109; Vollmer, *Volksopposition*, 85–92, 185–6.

[115] Bungert, *Heimatbuch*, 564–5. During the war the convent housed refugees, and later served as a field hospital. Before the Franciscans came, two previous attempts by nuns to settle in the village had proved fruitless, one of the many sources of friction between Father Schmitt and his parishioners, who accused him of failing to welcome the nuns: BAT, 70/3676a, 233–7, 244–67, 279–83.

of Father Schmitt's troubled incumbency) were merged by dictat in 1935.[116] Previous associational activity, much of it under clerical auspices, was restricted, while organizations like the Hitler Youth and League of German Girls were encouraged. The miners' provident association escaped dissolution only by affiliating itself to a life assurance company.[117]

The support among German Catholics in the 1930s for new apparition sites in Heede and in Belgium can hardly be understood without some reference to the threatening political climate. The same applies to the renewed popularity of Dittrichswalde and Marpingen, by-products of an earlier *Kulturkampf*. The renewed outcrop of apparitions in Marpingen can certainly be attributed to the stimulus of the chapel, to particular groups in the village, and to the indirect influence of figures such as Friedrich von Lama; but it is difficult not to see the growing numbers of pilgrims to Marpingen in 1935–6 partly as a response to the increasing pressures under which Catholics lived. For pilgrims from beyond the Saarland, travel to Marpingen was—as the travel agent, Herr Brand, pointed out—easier now that the region was part of the Reich. For Catholics in the Saarland, the fact that it was now part of the Reich may have been a further reason to make the pilgrimage.

For the hierarchy, the political circumstances made the apparitions an extra embarrassment. The position in the 1930s was not the same as it had been in the 1870s. At the height of the Bismarckian *Kulturkampf* there was no bishop in Trier or any other Prussian diocese. Faced with Hitler, however, the Fulda Bishops' Conference made conciliatory noises and a Concordat with the new regime was signed in July 1933. Only three bishops were to be chased off their thrones during the Third Reich, and Dr Bornewasser of Trier was not among them. Compared with the 1870s, the lines of command in the diocese remained intact: not until the war placed new strains on diocesan organization did any signs of breakdown appear. Unlike his hapless predecessor sixty years earlier, Father Biegel received regular advice from his superiors on what to do about the apparitions. That advice was not new, of course, and there is no reason to doubt that Trier was genuinely sick of Marpingen. At the same time, the renewal of the apparition movement at a politically charged moment must have caused additional uneasiness.

Bishop Bornewasser belonged neither to the more critical members of the German hierarchy (Galen of Münster, Faulhaber of Munich), nor to those who at different times showed themselves most tame (Berning of Osnabrück, Gröber of Freiburg).[118] Addressing Catholic youth in Trier Cathedral, Bishop Bornewasser announced that 'with raised heads and firm step we have entered the new Reich and we are prepared to serve it with all the might of our body and

---

[116] Bungert, *Heimatbuch*, 462–3, 625.

[117] Ibid. 258, 617.

[118] Lewy, *Catholic Church and Nazi Germany*, on the positions taken by different members of the hierarchy.

soul'.[119] When the Holy Coat was exhibited once again in Trier, the bishop and Vice-Chancellor Papen sent a joint telegram assuring Hitler of their 'steadfast participation in the work of resurrecting the German Reich'.[120] There was nothing exceptional about these expressions of sentiment; they did no more than elaborate the line laid down by the Fulda Bishops' Conference, and reflected political prudence as well as the convergence of episcopal and Nazi views on certain points (anti-communism, the emphasis on authority and the family). But Bornewasser's position was, in one respect, exceptionally vulnerable: together with Bishop Sebastian of Speyer, he was faced with the choice of supporting the 'yes' campaign in the Saar plebiscite, or exposing Catholics to the charge that they were 'unpatriotic'. Both chose the former course, and tried to claim the result as a victory for Catholic loyalty.[121]

The heavy pressure exerted on Trier during the campaign was a foretaste of things to come. The price to be paid for antagonizing the Nazi authorities was well known. Many priests from the diocese of Trier (including a number from the Saarland) were among those who were imprisoned in Koblenz, Trier, St Wendel, and elsewhere before being transported to Dachau.[122] Bishop Bornewasser continued his policy of discretion during the peacetime years, before joining other members of the episcopate in effusive support for the war effort.[123] It is hardly surprising that Trier preferred not to stir up trouble over Marpingen, which it firmly believed anyway to be a product of superstition. The contrast with the conduct of Bishop Kaller in the Ermland is none the less striking. Dittrichswalde had the same status as Marpingen, having remained unrecognized by successive bishops.[124] Bishop Kaller chose to make Dittrichswalde a symbol by leading a pilgrimage to the apparition site, and this was of a piece with his general policy towards the Nazi regime. As early as February 1933 he went beyond the coded statement issued by the Fulda Bishops' Conference by urging Catholics to vote for the Centre Party in the March elections.[125] In the way he addressed Polish members of his flock, in his encouragement of mass pilgrimages, and his bold pioneering of a 'peripatetic church' (*wandernde Kirche*) in the Ermland, he was responding not only to the local problems of the Catholic diaspora, but to the National Socialist challenge. Bishop Kaller's willingness to court disapproval ended with his arrest by the Gestapo.[126]

[119] Ibid. 100.
[120] Ibid. 104; but note (p. 110), Bornewasser's scepticism about Papen and the organization of Nazi-leaning Catholics (the AKD) he had encouraged.
[121] Ibid. 182–200; Vollmer, *Volksopposition*, 151–3, 165–6; and the works cited above in n. 111.
[122] Neuhäusler, *Kreuz und Hakenkreuz*, 346–7.
[123] Lewy, *Catholic Church and Nazi Germany*, 228; G. Zahn, *German Catholics and Hitler's War* (London and New York, 1963).
[124] Reifferscheid, *Das Bistum Ermland*, 117. Diocesan pilgrimages were organized during the First World War to older cult centres like Heiligelinde, Crossen, and Glottau—but not to Dittrichswalde.
[125] Lewy, *Catholic Church and Nazi Germany*, 28–9.
[126] Reifferscheid, *Das Bistum Ermland*, 85–96, 105–8, 260–1. The other two bishops to be expelled from their dioceses were Legge of Meissen and Sproll of Rottenburg.

Their attitudes to Marpingen and Dittrichswalde are a touchstone of the different ways in which Trier and the Ermland responded to Nazi intimidation. This is implied in the pointed mention Lama makes in his booklet on Marpingen of Bishop Kaller's Dittrichswalde pilgrimage. There is an obvious defence of the prudent course. Defiance exacts a price, often paid by others, and the more barbaric the regime, the more dreadful the price is likely to be. From an institutional point of view, accommodation had allowed the church to outlast earlier threats (although the contrast between the conduct of the hierarchy in the 1870s and the 1930s remains striking). What is particularly interesting for our purposes is the convergence—at the very least—between criticism of the 'over-diplomatic' position of the hierarchy on Marpingen, and the more general criticism levelled by many individual Catholics in the 1930s against their spiritual leaders, under the watchword 'shepherds awake!'[127] The sorrowful complaints that rained into Trier, urging a less 'diplomatic' posture over the apparitions, take on a different colouring when we view them against the political background of the Third Reich. That is especially true of the indefatigable Friedrich Ritter von Lama, an awkward customer certainly, a pest no doubt to a harassed vicar-general, but a man who also lost his life at the Stadelheim concentration camp in 1944. He supposedly suffered a heart attack, but a doctor who saw the body believed the signs were consistent with strangling. Lama's son was murdered by Nazis the following year.[128]

Wax and Wane: The Post-War Years

The Lamas belonged to the fifty million victims of Hitler's war. The dead were joined by the millions more who suffered bereavement or separation from their families, lost their homes, or became 'displaced persons'. Wartime suffering, post-war privations, and political turbulence contributed to the largest of all the modern waves of Marian apparitions. Sixty-five separate cases were recorded during the years 1947–50.[129] They were global in their incidence (the visions of a young Carmelite postulant at Lipa in the Philippines attracted particular attention), but the apparitions occurred above all in wretched Europe.[130] They were reported in east and west, from Italy, Spain, France, Ireland, and Britain, from Poland, Romania, and Hungary, and from the in-between land of Austria.[131]

---

[127] Hehl, 'Das Kirchenvolk', 71.
[128] BAT, B III, 11, 14/6 [1], 91–3: material on Lama gathered by Michael Marx.
[129] Billet et al. (eds.), Vraies et fausses, 9–19, table.
[130] On Lipa, see Ernst, Maria redet, 93–7.
[131] The Italian apparitions (one was a moving statue) occurred in Ghiaie di Bonate, Tre Fontane, Perugia, Gimigniano, and Marta; the French cases were in the Île Bouchard, Bouxières, and Espis; the Spanish apparitions took place in Codosera, in the Badajoz province of Estramadura. There were two Irish apparition sites, in Galway and Co. Mayo. The sole British case in this period was in Stockport, Lancashire. Marian apparitions in Eastern Europe were reported from Cluj (Romania), and Hasznos (Hungary), while weeping statues were claimed in Lublin and elsewhere in Poland. See Ernst, Maria

Historians have rightly detected a strongly anti-communist colouring to this new visionary wave, and this was true not only of eastern Europe.[132] Many saw communism as a punishment for faithlessness, and stories abounded of former 'reds' converted by the loving presence of the Virgin.[133] Rome was not above encouraging these sentiments, pressing the Fatima message about the conversion of Russia on the post-war faithful. The French Jesuit Henri Holstein has emphasized the link between the spate of apparitions and 'the troubled post-war years'. But the meaning of the post-war apparitions should not be narrowed to the anticommunist message. War (or rather, peace) was prominent in the messages delivered by the Virgin, and the apparitions of the period had a notably apocalyptic tone. Holstein was struck by the prevalence of morbid fantasies, prophecies, and revelations: the 'current of Marian messianism' was reminiscent of those who had once beseeched Jesus 'to restore the Kingdom of Israel'.[134] The Benedictine Damascus Zähringer noted a similar tone in German apparitions of the time. These included Pfaffenhofen (1945–6), Forstweiler (1947), Munich (1947–55), Fehrbach (1948), Düren (1949–50), Würzburg (1949), Heroldsbach (1949–52) and Remagen (1950).[135] Bärbel Ruess in Pfaffenhofen recounted the Virgin's words that warned of the devil's work but held out the hope of peace on earth when Christ would rule all the peoples of the world as the King of Peace.[136] In the desperate, emotionally charged atmosphere of post-war Germany, it is not surprising that Our Lady of Marpingen was looked to once again for consolation.

The war had brought bereavement to Marpingen on a dreadful scale: 212 men were killed or reported missing in action out of a total male population (including children) of some 1,650.[137] The village faced mounting air-raids from autumn 1944, the celebrated West Wall (built partly with Marpingen hardstone) proving useless against American air superiority. Pits and schools closed as miners and children worked on defences against the US 3rd Army, but although the offensive was temporarily halted in the Ardennes, by February 1945 the front had moved close to Marpingen. By then, as villagers watched the retreating German soldiers and the daily stream of refugees dragging handcarts over the clogged and bomb-damaged roads, they had come to share the defeatism and elemental desire for peace that was widespread in the Saarland.[138] On the night of 18 March 1945 a

redet, 69–75, 85–92; Holstein, 'Apparitions', 771–2; Billet et al. (eds.), Vraies et fausses, 9–19; Perry and Echeverría, Under the Heel, 232.

[132] Christian, 'Religious Apparitions and the Cold War in Southern Europe'; Perry and Echeverría, Under the Heel, 231–57.
[133] Ernst, Maria redet, 73–5, 85–92.
[134] Holstein, 'Apparitions', 773, 776. On the spate of celestial omens and prophecies in France at the end of the Second World War, and their apocalyptic tenor, see also Devlin, Superstitious Mind, 145–50.
[135] D. Zähringer, 'Muttergotteserscheinungen', Benediktinische Monatschrift zur Pflege religiösen und geistigen Lebens, 26 (1950), 29–40. See also Holstein, 'Apparitions', 772; Höfer and Rahner (eds.), Lexikon für Theologie und Kirche, vii, col. 65; Billet et al. (eds.), Vraies et fausses, 11–14.
[136] Ernst, Maria redet, 76–84.
[137] Bungert, Heimatbuch, 264–5.
[138] M. Steinert, Hitler's War and the Germans (Athens, Ohio, 1977), 296, 304.

child was killed in Marpingen during the rush to claim food supplies left behind by the retreating German army; early the following morning American troops entered the village.[139] In July a second round of French military occupation began, just fifteen years after the first had ended. The vulnerable borderland became once again a political football, and the civilian population paid the price of war in homelessness, food shortages, rationing, requisitions, and dismantled industrial plant. The population of the Saar coalfield faced a particularly bitter experience. During the chaotic wartime evacuation they had often been taunted by their German hosts as 'Saar French', 'Frenchies', or 'Gypsies', and up to three-quarters returned home. Now they were treated as Germans by the French.[140]

In this potent atmosphere, a new surge of interest in Marpingen began. Villagers petitioned Trier yet again for the consecration of the chapel.[141] Despite serious transport difficulties, the apparition site also attracted pious visitors. In September 1946, the widow of the chapel-builder Heinrich Recktenwald wrote to Trier, claiming that 'every day many pilgrims come from near and far'.[142] As it happens, we possess two visitors' books signed by pilgrims to the Härtelwald chapel during the period 12 August–18 October 1947.[143] They contain over 1,500 names, an average of twenty-two a day, although 450 of these came on 15 August, the Feast of the Assumption. The numbers involved—the equivalent of 8,000 a year—are smaller than those drawn to some of the new post-war apparition sites, or to Marpingen itself in its heyday, but they suggest substantial regional interest. This is confirmed by the visitors' books, which show that pilgrims came particularly from the industrial towns and villages to the south. The great majority of signatories were women, who described themselves variously as wife, housewife, widow, and war widow. Among the men there was the occasional electrician, peasant, or 'apprentice', with railwaymen present in larger numbers, but the great majority were active or retired miners.

The pattern of the 1870s and 1930s also repeated itself in the pressure brought to bear on the ecclesiastical authorities by outside enthusiasts. Even during the war Trier had to respond to an article in the Roman periodical *Pastor bonus* with a reminder that the apparitions had not been authenticated.[144] After 1945, some of the old cast of pre-war characters returned to action. Pharmacist Schlüter of Paderborn was one. He tried 'repeatedly' to organize pilgrimages to Marpingen and wrote letters to Trier in which piety was laced with sarcasm about ecclesiastical diplomats. He added a poignant post-war footnote: '4 children, 2 sons and

[139] Bungert, *Heimatbuch*, 259–65.
[140] On the evacuation, Steinert, *Hitler's War and the Germans*, 62–3, which argues that the Saarlanders sought consolation in the church; on the status of the post-war Saarland, R. H. Schmidt, *Saarpolitik 1945–1957*, 3 vols. (Saarbrücken, 1959–62), i and ii; on Marpingen in this period, Bungert, *Heimatbuch*, 292–4.
[141] BAT, B III, 11, 14/5, 79–91.
[142] Ibid. 61: Maria Recktenwald to suffragan bishop of Trier, 24 Sept. 1946.
[143] Ibid. 14/7–8: 'Pilgerliste'.
[144] Ibid. 14/5, 3: GV Trier to *Pastor bonus*, 25 Jan. 1943. The Nov. 1942 issue of the periodical that had contained the offensive reference to Marpingen is filed ibid. 4–60.

2 daughters, who died as victims of the most terrible of all wars, were also great venerators of the Immaculate Conception'.[145] The would-be visionary Frau Maldemer of Bildstock was now dead, but another widow from Bildstock took up the baton and wrote asking for the Härtelwald chapel to be consecrated.[146] Friedrich von Lama was also dead, but a new publicist emerged to try the patience of the vicariate-general. Richard Wenz, a writer in Cologne who had apparently been inspired by seeing the film The Story of Bernadette, announced in November 1948 that he intended to write a novella about Marpingen, dealing with the question from a psychological angle. A predictably tart response from Trier inspired him to some frenzied observations about 'sophistical materialists'.[147]

These lay initiatives were accompanied once again by the efforts of the clerical awkward squad. Susanna Leist's niece, born in 1895 and a nun since 1922, wrote expressing her belief in the authenticity of the original apparitions and requesting consecration of the chapel.[148] The immediate post-war years also brought the first signs of trouble from another member of the Leist family who had followed a religious vocation: Father Eduard Leist, ordained in 1928 at the age of 26 and a parish priest in the Palatinate. In the spring of 1948, Trier learned that Leist was creating 'unrest' in a parish near Marpingen (St Laurentius in Hirzweiler) by preaching sermons that urged pilgrims to visit the Härtelwald. The new parish priest in Marpingen since 1946, Anton Nicklas, joined his complaints to those of the priest in St Laurentius. Nicklas had 'succeeded in stemming the pilgrimage to the Härtelwald, but because of these sermons more and more people want to go there. Is it not now finally time to announce the truth about Marpingen?' Trier tried to curb Father Leist's activities with an approach to his superiors in Speyer.[149] But it was clearly not yet prepared to make the details of the Marpingen case public.

In the short term, the policy of stonewalling worked. From 1948 until 1954 the activity around Marpingen appeared to subside. Trier, it is true, had to field a variety of enquiries about the apparitions. The most lurid came from a Rome-based Redemptorist, who favoured the diocesan authorities with an account of the persistent failure by the hierarchy in German-speaking Europe to recognize true revelations and miracles. His list included Anna Katharina Emmerich, Therese Neumann, and Barbara Weigand, 'the seer of Schippach', as well as Philippsdorf, Marpingen, Dittrichswalde, Heede, and the post-war apparitions

[145] Ibid. 77, 100: Schlüter to GV Trier, 31 Oct. and 14 Dec. 1947 (quotation from the first letter). On Schlüter's repeated efforts to organize pilgrimages, see ibid. 14/6[2]: GV Trier to BO Limburg, 25 Sept. 1951.
[146] Ibid. 14/5, 71–2: Katharina 'Hassdenteufel' to GV Trier, undated but received 30 Aug. 1947. On the death of Frau Maldemer, ibid. 76: Dean Klee of Bildstock to GV Trier, 21 Oct. 1947.
[147] Ibid. 113–20: Wenz to GV Trier, 10 Nov. 1948; GV Trier to Wenz, 15 Nov. 1948; Wenz to GV Trier, 19 Nov. 1948; GV Trier to Wenz, 23 Nov. 1948.
[148] Ibid. 62–8: Sister Elisa (born Berta Haben) to GV Trier, 17 Nov. 1947. Brief details on Sister Elisa and photograph in Bungert, Heimatbuch, 560.
[149] Ibid. 101: Nicklas to GV Trier, 20 Apr. 1948. Ibid. 102–12 has further complaints to Trier, plus correspondence of Trier with Father Leist's superiors in Speyer.

at 'Paffenhofen' (*sic*). The moral he drew owed nothing to understatement: the senior clergy and their allies who suppressed the message and harassed the messengers had ended badly, in suicide and madness, with horribly distended bodies, or driven from a burning bishop's palace in their underclothes.[150] There is no record of a response to this. Trier did reply to several other correspondents who requested a meeting with the bishop on the subject of the Härtelwald chapel, or urged that the 'enquiry' into the apparitions be reopened.[151] Perhaps the most optimistic was a disabled pensioner from Stuttgart, who tried to sell the vicariate-general a Marpingen commemorative medal.[152] Approaches of this kind met with stern injunctions about obedience to church authority. Slightly more complicated was the case of Herr Höcht of Limburg, who publicized Marpingen through statements in a 1951 issue of his journal, *Der grosse Ruf*, and tried to organize a pilgrimage the same year. Höcht was related to the suffragan bishop of Regensburg, and had support in the Curia for a booklet he had written on *Fatima and Pius XII*, but an approach to the Limburg diocesan authorities succeeded in stopping his Marpingen activities.[153]

These remained isolated cases, and they matched the sporadic activity in Marpingen itself. On the seventy-fifth anniversary of the original apparitions, in July 1951, 'a few infatuated agitators (lay people) . . . organized a candle-lit procession without permission'.[154] Three months later Maria Recktenwald, the chapel-builder's widow, asked to see the official documents on Marpingen, but was refused.[155] Otherwise, until 1954, the village gave the impression of pastoral tranquillity. Then the issue flared up again to such a degree that Trier was forced, after nearly eighty years, to reconsider its policy of sitting on the evidence. Why?

A reconstruction of the tangled record suggests several new elements that interacted with each other. First, new interest was aroused by the efforts of outsiders with village connections to reopen the case. One of them was Michael Marx, an ex-miner from Guidesweiler, whose aunt Anna Brill had lived near the Härtelwald. Returning to Marpingen in 1955, Marx encountered an old friend Nickel Leist. He and Marx had been born one day apart in 1885, and first went down the Altenwald pit together on the same day in 1901 as 16-year-olds. Leist showed his friend a large bundle of manuscripts and correspondence that had been gathered by Friedrich von Lama, and Marx conceived the idea of reissuing the Austrian's booklet. Nothing apparently came of this; but the project certainly

---

[150] BAT, B III, 11, 14/6 [2]: Brother Clemens Henze to GV Trier, 15 Nov. 1950. These dreadful fates had supposedly befallen those who dealt with Barbara Weigand.

[151] Ibid: correspondence with Nikolaus Urhahn of Quierschied (Jan.–Feb. 1953) and the pensioner Jacob Paul of Lebach (Feb.–May 1954).

[152] Ibid: W. Rütgers to GV Trier, undated.

[153] Ibid: BO Limburg to GV Trier, 19 Sept. 1951; GV Trier to BO Limburg, 29 Sept. 1951, copied to BO Speyer, Mainz, and Cologne; BO Limburg to GV Trier, 5 Oct. 1951; GV Trier to BO Limburg, 8 Oct. 1951.

[154] On the procession, ibid: BO Limburg to GV Trier, 19 Sept. 1951 (with enclosed newspaper clipping); and reply of 25 Sept. 1951.

[155] Ibid: Maria Recktenwald to GV Trier, 16 Oct. 1951; and reply via Father Nicklas of 19 Oct. 1951.

stirred up older village memories, and—in conjunction with the materials gathered by Marx on other apparitions, including La Salette and Pellevoisin—probably helped to revive the feeling that the original apparitions had never been properly investigated. Thus the idea of the 'German Lourdes' was carried back into the village.[156]

The role of Father Eduard Leist was more direct. As we have seen, Trier had been obliged to inform the diocesan authorities in Speyer about his activities in 1948. In 1954 he was reported to be visiting the Härtelwald again, and accused of fostering the apparition cult.[157] The following year, the harassed parish priest in Marpingen reported once more that Leist had been in the Härtelwald, praying with a group of women: 'the episcopal authorities in Trier and Speyer seem, for him, not to exist'.[158] He was also seen in the chapel during the same period. On 5 November 1955, Trier notified its opposite number in Speyer that Father Leist had now been forbidden to perform his clerical offices anywhere in the diocese ('his disobedience causes great vexation and sabotages our efforts to suppress the cult in the Härtelwald'), and Speyer threatened him with canonical punishment if he used the chapel.[159] The unrepentant Leist spread the story of his disciplining, which he apparently wore as a badge of honour.[160]

It is unclear to what extent Leist brought new pilgrims to Marpingen. He certainly encouraged processions to the Härtelwald and lent legitimacy to the cult, but we have very little information about pilgrims in this period. We know that three or four buses brought pilgrims (mainly from Quierschied) on 3 July 1955, and the following year a senior cleric in Trier referred tantalizingly to the fact that new female 'seers' had helped to reopen the question of the apparitions.[161] Indirect evidence is provided by the non-Marpingen signatories of a 1954 petition calling for the consecration of the chapel. They were, according to the covering note, 'almost exclusively members of the working class', and the signatories came mainly from Quierschied, Neunkirchen, and Wellesweiler, with a smaller number from Urexweiler, Berschweiler, Illingen, and Contwig. Only a handful were from Alsweiler, Tholey, or St Wendel.[162] In other words, the pattern is consistent with earlier periods, when support for the apparitions came principally from the industrial towns and villages to the south. On the other hand, the 399 non-Marpingen signatories constituted only 20 per cent of the total. This confirms

---

[156] Ibid. 14/6 [1] consists of the various materials gathered by Marx, as well as some notes on his activities.

[157] Ibid. 14/6 [2]: Nicklas to GV Trier, 19 July 1954; GV Trier to BO Speyer, 22 July 1954. The evidence from Speyer casts some doubt on whether Leist had been the author of an appeal for public support; ibid: BO Speyer to GV Trier, 4 Aug. 1954.

[158] Ibid: Nicklas to GV Trier, 19 Oct. 1955.

[159] Ibid: GV Trier to BO Speyer, 5 Nov. 1955.

[160] Ibid: BO Speyer to parish of Marpingen, 22 Dec. 1955.

[161] On the 1955 pilgrims, ibid: Nicklas to GV Trier, 18 Aug. 1955; on the 'female seers', ibid. 14/5, 122–3: report by Karl Kammer on a meeting in Marpingen organized by the Bishop of Trier in Nov. 1956.

[162] Copy of petition, dated 28 Sept. 1954, ibid. 14/6 [2].

the impression that the real focus of activity in the mid-1950s was the village itself. Significantly, perhaps, a pilgrimage organized by the apparition supporters in 1956 was not to Marpingen, but from the village to the Dutch convent where Margaretha Kunz had died.[163]

The evidence certainly suggests that the main role played by Leist, like Michael Marx, was within the village. Both had Marpingen connections, but Leist's were especially strong. His brother-in-law Johann Klein was a publican in the village, and the parish priest saw Leist and his relations as a key link in the burgeoning 'Härtelwald movement': 'the eighty communists of the parish have not caused me as many unhappy hours as he and his family'.[164] The core of the movement included Frau Maria Recktenwald, the former *Gemeindevorsteher* Peter Brill, who had put his weight behind the chapel in the 1930s, and the current mayor Neis.[165] This movement pressed repeatedly for consecration of the chapel, and organized candle-lit processions to the Härtelwald in 1955 and 1956. Father Nicklas tried, like his predecessors, to deflect these activities on to the 'official' site of the Marienbrunnen. On the Feast of the Assumption in 1955 he organized a candle-lit procession there; but after it was over the supporters of the apparitions took their lights and music on to the Härtelwald, where they had arranged for the area around the chapel to be 'bathed in Bengal lights'.[166] By this time the parish priest was gloomily convinced that 'the activity of the Härtelwald movement is not dying down, on the contrary it is increasing. I have the impression that they are absolutely determined to go on (*daß sie den Zug ins Verbissene nimmt*).'[167]

Did Father Nicklas identify the prime movers correctly? At first sight, the 1954 petition appears to support the charge of a strong Leist–Recktenwald axis to the movement. Trier, no doubt taking its lead from the parish priest, clearly thought so. Someone went through the petition, carefully underlining every 'Leist' and 'Recktenwald' signature: they found 243 out of 1,569 Marpingen signatures, a total of 15.5 per cent. But this was hardly any more than one would expect on a random basis, given that these were the two most common village names.[168] Much more striking is the overall number of Marpingen signatories: 1,569 out of a total population of around 3,800.[169] Few children appear to have signed, and even allowing for some duplicate signatures, the conclusion must be that a substantial majority of village adults put their names to the petition. This does not contradict the parish priest's claims about the core of the movement, which

[163] BAT, B III, 11, 14/6 [2]: Nicklas to GV Trier, 24 Aug. 1956. During this period, Father Leist had a Dutch priest staying with him, ostensibly learning German.
[164] Ibid: Nicklas to GV Trier, 28 Feb. 1956 (the second of the two letters bearing that date).
[165] Ibid: Nicklas to GV Trier, 28 Feb. 1956 (the first letter of that date).
[166] Ibid: Nicklas to GV Trier, 18 Aug. 1955.
[167] Ibid.
[168] In 1932, Leists and Recktenwalds made up 15.8% of the village population; in 1978 the two names still accounted for 11.3% of the total: calculated from the tables in Bungert, *Heimatbuch*, 183–92.
[169] The Marpingen population was 3,610 in 1951, 4,208 in 1961.

recalled the leading role played by village notables in the 1870s and 1930s, but it does suggest that the movement enjoyed formidable support.

One reason for this was no doubt an old one. As the former *Gemeindevorsteher* Peter Brill observed to the parish priest: 'Surely nobody can deny that the Härtelwald brings money into the village.'[170] The material dreams of a German Lourdes had not been abandoned. But support for the apparition movement was also given new life in the mid-1950s when it became interlocked with politics. In one way or another, a political note had been sounded by many post-war supporters of Marpingen. Trier's Redemptorist correspondent in Rome believed there was a connection between the loss of German territory in Bohemia and the Ermland, and the failure to authenticate the Philippsdorf and Dittrichswalde apparitions: he expressed the fear that the Bishop of Trier would lose his 'beautiful Saarland'.[171] Richard Wenz, the writer who wanted to devote a novella to Marpingen, lectured during the same period on the 'Thirty Years War of the SPD (from 1918 until 1948)'.[172] In the late 1940s, village supporters of the apparitions also emphasized the political context, and these arguments became more emphatic in the mid-1950s. The 1954 petition claimed that the failure to consecrate the chapel had 'created bitterness everywhere, and in the last resort only provides grist for the Communist mill'. It continued:

We live at a time in which the devastating flood-tides of anti-religious communism threaten to break through all barriers. Yet every Catholic House of God and every Marian chapel is a thorn in the side of communism. And now this enemy of the church no. 1 is to have the further pleasure of witnessing how our lovely Marian chapel is still to be denied consecration by the church despite all requests.

The petition concluded with a plea in the name of 'countless devotees of the Virgin from near and far' that the bishop 'no longer extend a welcome to such anti-Marian machinations'.[173] A few months later a group of Marpingen men wrote to Trier asking once again for the chapel to be consecrated and suggesting that 'Protestants and Communists' took malicious pleasure in the failure to do so.[174]

The cold war formed only one part of the political background to the renewed movement to have the chapel consecrated. There was also the question of the Saarland's own uncertain status. From the summer of 1945 France treated the area differently from the rest of its zone of occupation, introducing French currency and establishing customs posts on the border with Germany. After elections in 1947 that were dominated by French-approved parties, a new constitution established the Saarland as a region independent of Germany, integrated into the French economic system, its defence and diplomatic representation assumed by France. Maria Recktenwald, petitioning for the consecration of the

---

[170] BAT, B III, 11, 14/6 [2]: Nicklas to GV Trier, 28 Feb. 1956 (second letter).
[171] Ibid: Brother Clemens Henze to GV Trier, 15 Nov. 1955.
[172] Ibid. 14/5, 116: Wenz to GV Trier, 19 Nov. 1948.
[173] Ibid. 14/6 [2]: unsigned covering note to petition of 28 Sept. 1954.
[174] Ibid: letter of Marpingen residents to Bishop Wehr, 1 Feb. 1955.

chapel in 1947, observed that 'we are living now through a time of the greatest imaginable need and despair', and argued that the French and their political allies on the Saar (the Mouvement pour le Rattachement de la Sarre à la France: MRS) were abusing the veneration of Mary by encouraging pilgrimages to Lourdes for their own political purposes. How much better, she suggested artfully, if pilgrims made their devotions to the Blessed Virgin nearer home.[175] The status of the Saarland remained provisional and contested. From 1952, however, efforts were made to resolve the future of the region through a policy of 'Europeanization', and in 1954 French Prime Minister Mendès-France and Federal Chancellor Adenauer agreed that a plebiscite should be held in October the following year, when Saarlanders would be able to vote 'Yes' or 'No' to a proposal for autonomy within the emerging western European community of states. In the event, 68 per cent of the votes were cast against the proposal, and the Saarland joined the Federal Republic two years later.[176]

The foremost figure in the group campaigning for consecration of the chapel was Nikolaus Kopp, leader of the local Christian Democratic Party.[177] In the highly charged 1955 plebiscite campaign the party in the Saarland called for the 'No' vote that would mean a return to Germany, and in this period the cause of the Christian Democrats and the cause of the chapel became closely identified.[178] Kopp gave the address at a procession to the chapel at the end of May 1955.[179] Father Leist was seen in the chapel with a female entourage, praying and explaining how voters should cast their ballots in the plebiscite. These developments caused resentment among the 'Yes' voters (there were more than 700 in the village) some of whom began to refer to the 'CDU chapel'. Only a sudden family death prevented a festive celebration of the 'No' result in the chapel.[180]

It is understandable that the Marian cause should have become so politicized in Marpingen during these years, for in this it only followed the lead given by Rome. Pope Pius XII, who declared the dogma of the Assumption in 1950, was fiercely devoted to Mary and fervently anti-communist. The two causes often

---

[175] BAT, B III, 11, 14/5, 80–2: Maria Recktenwald to Bishop Bornewasser of Trier, 24 Oct. 1947 (as covering note to hand-delivered petition). On the Saarland politics of this period, see Schmidt, Saarpolitik, ii.

[176] Schmidt, Saarpolitik, iii. The agreement to hold the plebiscite owed much to the improvement of Franco-German relations as a result of Adenauer's own policy and the fact that Germany's division dampened French fears. The two-thirds 'No' vote had several causes, among them the desire to be part of the 'economic miracle' in the Federal Republic, scepticism over autonomous status at a time when European integration had suffered several short-term set-backs, and German-national sentiment fostered by the plebiscite campaign.

[177] BAT, B III, 11, 14/6 [2]: Kopp's letter to Bishop Wehr of Trier, 2 Mar. 1955, following up the collective letter and the earlier petition, identifies him as the leading figure. Trier's reply of 9 Mar. 1955 to Father Nicklas enclosed a letter (not in the file) that the priest was instructed to read out to Kopp. On Kopp as the CDU leader, see Nicklas to GV Trier, 19 Oct. 1955.

[178] Konrad Adenauer, the Christian Democratic chancellor of the Federal Republic, formally supported a 'Yes' vote.

[179] BAT, B III, 11, 14/6 [2]: Nicklas to GV Trier, 18 Aug. 1955.

[180] Ibid: Nicklas to GV Trier, 7 Nov. 1955.

became fused. The dogmatization of the Assumption is difficult to separate from its cold war background, while in his own supplications the Pope called on the Virgin to 'annihilate the dark plans and the wicked work of the enemies of a united and Christian humanity'. Pius XII praised the 'Wonderful Madonna of Fatima' and offered the faithful a Mary with a militantly anti-communist face. All of this came to a head in 1954, the 'Marian Year' and the centenary of the Immaculate Conception being promulgated.[181] The significance of this was unlikely to escape supporters of the Marpingen apparitions—one request for consecration of the chapel made by Nikolaus Kopp and others pointedly remarked on the 'Marian Year'.[182] In 1954, the Saarland even issued three postage stamps depicting the Virgin Mary.[183] More pertinently, perhaps, the Pope's enthusiasm for Fatima was answered by a new wave of revelations and miracles. In 1953 there had been a weeping Madonna at Syracuse in Sicily, which was recognized by the local bishop in little over three months.[184] In 1954 there was a renewed rash of apparitions, eighteen in all, ranging climatically from Newcastle upon Tyne to St Tropez.[185]

Fatima, however, was one thing, St Tropez—or Marpingen—quite another. The new apparitions of 1954 remained unrecognized, and the attempt in Marpingen to use the new mood to further old business met with a dusty response. The undertaking was all too obviously self-serving. Trier was hardly likely to look on it more favourably when it learned that the cause had been adopted by the village left as well as the right. For the May 1956 elections the local Social Democrats prepared a pamphlet in which, sandwiched between demands about local bus-stops and the final 'Watchword: German Reunification', there were some observations about religion from the SPD candidate, watchmaker Bernhard Leist. He rebuked the 'so-called Christian parties' for challenging the religious credentials of the Social Democrats: the future would show that candidates on the SPD list had 'a more ready ear for a genuinely Christian concern of our community (Härtelwald) than the gentlemen from the most-Christian CVP had in the past'.[186] Local SPD backing for the Härtelwald movement was reinforced by articles in the socialist *Allgemeine Zeitung* of Saarbrücken, probably written by Robert Bonner, whose mother was a supporter of Marpingen. The articles criticized the unwillingness of the church authorities to recognize the apparitions or allow Father Leist to visit the site; and for the 3 July 1956, the paper advertised a festive eightieth anniversary procession to the Härtelwald.[187]

---

[181] Perry and Echeverria, *Under the Heel*, 242–6.

[182] BAT, B III, 11, 14/6 [2]: letter of Marpingen men, including Kopp, to Bishop Wehr, 1 Feb. 1955.

[183] L. Ropars, 'Notre Dame et la philatélie', in Manoir (ed.), *Maria*, v. 814.

[184] Höfer and Rahner (eds.), *Lexikon für Theologie und Kirche*, vii, cols. 64–5.

[185] Billet *et al.* (eds.), *Vraies et fausses*, 15–16.

[186] BAT, B III, 11, 14/6 [2]: Nicklas to GV Trier, 24 Aug. 1956, enclosing copy of pamphlet. The CVP (Christliche Volkspartei) were the local Christian Democrats.

[187] Ibid: Nicklas to GV Trier, 7 Aug. 1956, on the articles; Nicklas to GV Trier, 24 Aug. 1956, notes the advertisements for the 3 July anniversary. On the likely authorship by Robert Bonner, see BAT, B III, 11, 14/5, 128: Nicklas to GV Trier, 10 Feb. 1957, enclosing a further clipping from the paper and explaining the circumstances.

For a long time Trier turned a completely stony face to this renewed agitation. As Father Nicklas was sternly informed: 'The events in Marpingen are reminiscent of Heroldsbach and cannot be tolerated. It is impossible to use force against such mischief, but it should not be approved or furthered in any way.'[188] Great efforts were made to prevent the activity of Father Leist, and the parish priest was repeatedly told that he must drill obedience into his parishioners. If necessary he should threaten them with removal of the sacraments.[189] Father Nicklas was eager to follow instructions, particularly when it came to the nefarious activities of Father Leist, for the two priests plainly enjoyed very poor relations. But when it came to his parishioners, the local priest was awkwardly cast as the man in the middle. In trying to implement official church policy, he succeeded only in causing bad blood in the village. Like previous incumbents, he found that exhortations could weaken his own authority. He confided helplessly in August 1955: 'My words carry no weight. It has reached the point that I am described as a troublemaker if I read out an announcement from the episcopal authorities.'[190] After a stiffening note from Trier, he confided to his superiors in October 1955 that he had still not brought himself—after nearly two months—to threaten the Christian Democrat Kopp with removal of the sacraments, and faced the prospect with trepidation. He noted also that people 'drew back' when he sought information about the will-o'-the-wisp Leist.[191]

It may have been this damage to clerical authority, or simply a recognition that the problem of Marpingen would not go away, that caused a change of tactics in Trier. Whatever the reason, 1956 saw a series of new developments. When Maria Recktenwald wrote yet again to Trier in January, she was invited to discuss the question of the chapel with a senior official, Karl Kammer.[192] This was a clear break with earlier policy. The meeting took place on 4 February. Margaretha Kunz's confession was read to Frau Recktenwald, and she agreed to stop her agitation on behalf of a 'Härtelwald pilgrimage'. Kammer put it to her that consecration of the chapel could not be considered until pictures of the 'so-called Madonna of Marpingen' had been removed and the building turned into a genuine war memorial dedicated, perhaps, to Our Lady of Sorrows. Reporting to the parish priest, Trier made it clear that full consecration would follow only after a lengthy probationary period. But the episcopal authorities were clearly looking for an acceptable compromise solution: 'the vexation of the Härtelwald chapel must be settled'. The position of the chapel was to be regularized by transferring responsibility from the local council which formally owned it and the self-appointed chapel committee which actually maintained it to the parochial

---

[188] BAT, B III, 11, 14/6 [2]: GV Trier to Nicklas, 6 Dec. 1954.
[189] Ibid: GV Trier to Nicklas, 6 Aug. 1954, 6 Dec. 1954, and 23 Aug. 1955.
[190] Ibid: Nicklas to GV Trier, 18 Aug. 1955.
[191] Ibid: Nicklas to GV Trier, 19 Oct. 1955.
[192] Ibid: Maria Recktenwald to GV Trier, 24 Jan. 1956; reply of 31 Jan. 1956.

church council. Meanwhile, Trier was prepared to consider withdrawing the ban on Father Leist celebrating mass in Marpingen.[193]

The auspices for this solution were not particularly good. Father Nicklas noted the practical difficulties involved in removing all traces of the 1876 apparitions from the chapel. More worrying, from his perspective, were the personalities involved. Frau Recktenwald was 'a woman who promises kingdoms that are not in her power'; Father Leist was a man who did not keep his word; all the supporters of the apparitions were unreliable ('I have been acquainted for years with the underhand methods of the Härtelwald movement'). Nicklas noted that even as the proposal was being launched to rid the chapel of its link with the apparitions, a stall had opened up next to it selling candles and postcards.[194] On the question of Father Leist and his right to celebrate mass, Trier left things to the judgement of the parish priest; on the main point—reaching a settlement over the chapel—it pressed on, asking for details about the ownership and inventory.[195] It did so despite evident scepticism about the truthfulness of chapel supporters, and the conflicting signals coming from those supporters. While Frau Recktenwald wrote in a spirit of accommodation, Johann Klein wrote to remind the bishop that a prominent, recently deceased cleric had been a believer in the Blessed Virgin of Marpingen.[196] Trier persisted also despite regular reports from the parish priest recounting the further activities of the Härtelwald movement.[197] There can have been no doubt in Trier about the degree of recalcitrance in Marpingen, for Father Nicklas's letters were matched by correspondence from the other side accusing the parish priest of unreasonableness and egoism.[198] Replying to one of Johann Klein's many complaining letters, the vicariate-general wrote in exasperation: 'People in Marpingen appear simply neither to know nor recognize the duty of obedience to the established church authorities.'[199] Pastoral relations in the village were obviously in a poor state; but as they worsened, this may have reinforced the view in Trier that it must try to settle the matter if this could be done without a climb-down.

The Marpingen council met on 7 November 1956. Its deliberations lasted five hours, and the issue of the chapel—the tenth item on the agenda—absorbed so much time that eight other items were not discussed at all. In the event a final

[193] Ibid: GV Trier to Nicklas, 21 Feb. 1956, which gives a full account of the meeting between Kammer and Frau Recktenwald. The consideration of a concession to Leist may have been in response to a letter from the priest, passed on by Speyer, in which he requested the lifting of the ban because of the ill health of his sister and brother-in-law; ibid: Leist to GV Trier, 9 Feb. 1956.
[194] Ibid: Nicklas to GV Trier, 28 Feb. 1956 (first letter).
[195] Ibid: GV Trier to Nicklas, 5 Mar. 1956.
[196] Ibid: Maria Recktenwald to GV Trier, 2 Mar. 1956; Johann Klein to Bishop Wehr of Trier, 16 Aug. 1956. The scepticism in Trier can be gauged from the marginalia (presumably Kammer's) on the undated memorandum of 1956 submitted by Mayor Neis of Marpingen to Trier; ibid: 'Zur Klarstellung über den Kapellenbau in Marpingen'.
[197] Ibid: Nicklas to GV Trier, 12 Mar., 13 July, 7 and 24 Aug. 1956.
[198] Ibid: Johann Klein to GV Trier, 23 Oct. 1956; Mayor Kunz to GV Trier, 10 Nov. 1956.
[199] Ibid: GV Trier to Johann Klein, 31 Oct. 1956, copied to Father Nicklas.

decision was postponed. Instead a resolution was passed agreeing to what the parish priest had hoped would be a last resort: a meeting with Ecclesiastical Counsellor Kammer and Bishop Wehr.[200] Accordingly, on 19 November, an all-party delegation from the council numbering sixteen men, accompanied by the parish priest, presented itself in Trier.

This meeting took place eighty years after the original apparitions, and was novel in two respects. Trier had never before entertained a formal delegation from the village, and it had never before laid out in detail the grounds for rejecting the authenticity of the apparitions. For although the meeting had been arranged to resolve the issue of the chapel, it was centrally concerned with the question of what had happened in 1876. Karl Kammer, who was in charge of proceedings, took the meeting through the various documents in the possession of the church authorities, including Bishop Laurent's judgement and Margaretha Kunz's confession. That, said Kammer, was the reason why the chapel could not be consecrated on the present basis, however much villagers might cling to their belief in the apparitions. After some critical observations about Friedrich von Lama's booklet, the ecclesiastical counsellor asked for questions. There were many of these from the assembled village politicians: why had there been no full enquiry, what of the miraculous cures, had Margaretha Kunz not retracted her 'confession', why had it not been made public at the time, and could an appeal be made to the Holy Office in Rome? Kammer fielded the questions patiently, while conceding nothing and omitting some of the more awkward points (such as the evidence of Neureuter's continuing belief in the apparitions). It is not clear whether he succeeded in convincing his audience. Mayor Kunz apparently represented the general feeling: he remained of the view that the apparitions had been genuine, but supported the proposal that the parochial church council assume responsibility for the chapel. This was agreed, and the four and a quarter-hour meeting ended on a conciliatory note, Father Nicklas having pressed for agreement and expressed his wish to reach an understanding with Father Leist.[201]

The meeting left many loose ends. Some of them concerned the documentation of the apparitions. Much of what we know about the later lives of the visionaries is a result of the efforts made by Trier immediately after the November 1956 meeting to track down missing information. They scored several successes with the religious orders to which the girls had belonged. The lacunae in the archive suggest that it was much more difficult to round up the letters, photographs, and recollections in private hands.[202] Defeat in this modest undertaking reflected the failure of the 1956 meeting to resolve the larger issue. Peace did not break out between Father Nicklas and Father Leist. When the two priests met, shortly after

[200] BAT, B III, 11, 14/6 [2]: Nicklas to GV Trier, 13 Nov. 1956.
[201] Ibid. for an account of the meeting drafted by Karl Kammer: 'Niederschrift über die Verhandlung mit Pfarrkindern von Marpingen am 19. November 1956 15 Uhr—nach Vereinbarung—bez. der Marpinger Härtelwaldkapelle und der Erscheinungen von 1876/77'.
[202] A list of the materials sought by Trier can be found ibid: GV Trier to Nicklas, 24 Nov. 1956.

Christmas 1956, the parish priest agreed to a *rapprochement*. When Trier was informed by Mayor Kunz that this had not occurred, it wrote crossly to ask Nicklas why: 'You are causing the greatest embarrassment to your superior authority.'[203] The hapless parish priest reported that the meeting in Trier had changed nothing. The 'Leist–Klein party' remained incorrigible; the council would not pass control of the chapel to the parochial church council; and the mayor had used the occasion of the Saar returning to Germany (to 'the Reich', as Nicklas put it) to praise Father Leist as a 'national martyr'. The 'Christian political camp' was split, and the mayor was openly boasting that he had successfully carried an ecclesiastical-disciplinary case against the parish priest.[204] Father Nicklas, troubled by rheumatism, village hostility, and the fear that he was to be made the sacrificial victim of the agreement, was obviously sensitive; but he had much to be sensitive about. Both the Christian-Democratic group based on the Leist inn, and elements in the SPD, continued their propaganda on behalf of the Marpingen apparitions, asking why they had not been acknowledged as a German Lourdes or Fatima.[205]

Trier was also concerned that its attempt at compromise had failed. Recalling the popular support for the Heroldsbach apparitions, it reminded the parish priest—unnecessarily—that 'you must be extraordinarily careful'.[206] The following year, Father Nicklas left Marpingen after twelve torrid years. The centenary of Bernadette Soubirous's apparitions was in 1958, and Trier had hoped that after agreement was reached on the Härtelwald chapel, the site might be safely domesticated in that year as a Lourdes-grotto.[207] But the agreement broke down, the chapel was never consecrated, and supporters of the apparitions wanted more than a bland Lourdes-grotto in the Härtelwald. For them, Marpingen was still the German Lourdes. Trier received songs and poetry from a seer who believed that Marpingen would become the most important centre of Marian pilgrimage in the world, greater even than Lourdes or Fatima.[208] A priest from Homburg informed Trier about pilgrimages to Marpingen organized by female parishioners: 'One has the impression that Marpingen appears to them as a would-be Lourdes (*ein verhindertes Lourdes*), which—if the church does nothing for it—they as lay people must help to achieve renown and recognition as a place of pilgrimage.' The women were collecting money to finance a major church on the site, which they visited ('without priests!') to sing and pray.[209] Pilgrims

---

[203] Ibid: GV Trier to Nicklas, 1 Feb. 1957. This followed a letter from Kunz to GV Trier, for the attention of Kammer, on 28 Jan. 1957.

[204] Ibid: Nicklas to GV Trier, 7 Feb. 1957.

[205] On the continuing support for the apparitions from the *Allgemeine Zeitung* in Saarbrücken, and SPD supporters in Marpingen, see BAT, B III, 11, 14/5, 128–9: Nicklas to GV Trier, 10 Feb. 1957 (enclosing newspaper cutting), and ibid. 14/6 [2]: GV Trier to Nicklas, 12 Feb. 1957, commenting laconically that 'there has been no improvement in the (red) population of Marpingen'.

[206] Ibid. 14/6 [2]: GV Trier to Nicklas, 12 Feb. 1957.

[207] Ibid: GV Trier to Nicklas, 5 Mar. 1956.

[208] Ibid. 14/5, 130.

[209] Ibid. 14/6 [2]: Dean Rembor of Homburg/Saar to GV Trier, 27 Sept. 1962.

continued to disturb the church authorities in Trier until the early 1960s. A Frau
Hetterich in Jägersburg 'made propaganda for Marpingen' and organized a bus
trip.[210] The Palatinate, stamping ground of Eduard Leist, continued to harbour
enthusiasts, and Saarbrücken also sent pilgrims to the village.

Then, in the early 1960s, the ecclesiastical archive simply falls silent: there is
no further evidence of Marpingen causing anxiety. The cult did not entirely
disappear. We learn from the historian of the village that the centenary of the
apparitions in July 1976 was marked by lighted processions, singing, and prayers
in and around the chapel, with many pilgrims present. Services were even
conducted by outside priests, at least in the early stage of celebrations—a sign,
perhaps, that Trier had given up its long struggle to suppress such things, and
was now content to treat the declining cult with benign neglect.[211] The decline is
no great surprise. Over the period of a century, interest in Marpingen rose and
fell in rhythm with apparitions elsewhere in Europe. The Härtelwald achieved its
greatest fame in the 1870s, the peak decade of nineteenth-century apparitions.
The sagging interest of the later nineteenth and early twentieth century followed
a European pattern; so did the revivals of the 1930s and the post-war period.
The 1960s and 1970s were mean years for Marian apparitions. In the period
1947–54 an average of twelve new ones was reported annually; in 1955–75 the
figure was three.[212] There was, it is true, a small flurry of apparitions in the 1960s.
At San Damiano in Italy, the peasant woman 'Mamma Rosa' claimed no fewer
than 3,000 apparitions, beginning in October 1964, the content of which had a
clearly conservative thrust directed against the liberal reforms of Vatican II.[213] In
the same period four young girls at Garabandal in north-west Spain claimed to
have seen Our Lady of Mount Carmel 2,000 times (they were the first visionaries
to be televised).[214] But these were the exceptions that proved the rule. For the
most part, the pattern of the 1960s and 1970s saw the development of long-
standing, recognized apparition (and other pilgrimage) sites at the expense of
obscure, would-be Lourdes. Knock had some 700,000 visitors a year, Lourdes
itself around three and a quarter million, 228,000 of them German.[215]

The 1980s brought another wave of new Marian apparitions. The majority of
these were reported outside Europe, in Africa (Egypt, Uganda, Kenya) and
Central and Latin America (Nicaragua, Venezuela, Chile).[216] The combination

[210] BAT, B III, 11, 14/5, 141.

[211] Bungert, Heimatbuch, 239.

[212] Billet et al. (eds.), Vraies et fausses, 20.

[213] Baumer, Wallfahrt, 19–21.

[214] Nolan and Nolan, Christian Pilgrimage, 1, 102, 201, 286–7, 326; Perry and Echeverria, Under the
Heel, 264–5. An enquiry launched by the Bishop of Santander came out against the apparitions, but
the cult was not suppressed.

[215] Turner, Image and Pilgrimage, 138; Marnham, Lourdes, 183, appendix 1, from which I have
calculated the number of German visitors. By the 1970s, there were about a thousand Christian sites
that received at least 100,000 pilgrims a year.

[216] Perry and Echeverria, Under the Heel, 302–4, 307–9; Nolan and Nolan, Christian Pilgrimage, 377
n. 81.

of economic distress, political turbulence, and 'great fears' that spawned them (the Virgin in Uganda referred to Aids as a divine scourge) is reminiscent of earlier European apparitions. Within Europe itself, the visions claimed by a group of children in Medjugorje have the hallmarks of a Croatian Lourdes or Fatima: humble seers in an obscure village, a background of political crisis, a church divided in its response, and the development of a vastly popular (and heavily commercialized) new devotional site.[217] There is good reason to think that current uncertainties and presentiments of the end of the millennium may provide fertile soil for further visionary claims in Europe, west as well as east. The widespread newspaper reports and television programmes on events like those in Medjugorje are also likely to spawn imitative claims of apparitions, like those that followed Lourdes, Fatima, and Banneux. Or a maverick priest may help a new cult to emerge. That was the case with the dubious Virgin of Surbiton in 1986, and it was the writings of a retired priest that drew as many as 300,000 pilgrims to the tiny Palatine village of Ranschbach between 16 February and 11 April 1983, to see the Blessed Virgin of Kaltenbrunn and take the 'miraculous' waters.[218] The affair led to a tenfold increase in the price of local land, the temporary closure of the spring, and police intervention. It seems unlikely, though, to lead to the construction of a basilica or tourist hotels.

Lourdes and Fatima continue to flourish, warmed by the approval of Pope John Paul II. They have been joined in the 1980s by a considerable number of new would-be Lourdes, from Medjugorje to Ranschbach. Marpingen is neither official nor novel, and there is little doubt that the fire has gone out of the apparition cult in the village. Since 1976 it has shown none of the vigour in its second century that was so often evident in its first hundred years. This is partly a matter of key individuals. Many of those who revived the cult in the 1930s and fostered it through the 1940s and 1950s were the same people. Most of them were born in the nineteenth century; often they could boast direct links to the visionary families of the 1870s. The twentieth-century cult became sclerotic as its greatest supporters aged. The very fact that, by the 1950s, a 'Härtelwald movement' was identifiable suggests the weakening hold of the cult on the spontaneous village imagination. The political crises of twentieth-century Germany, and the special problems of the Saarland, gave the Madonna of Marpingen an extra lease of life; but the cult could not survive the stability and well-fed complacency of the Federal Republic. Marpingen changed greatly from the 1950s. The Leists and Recktenwalds made up a steadily falling proportion of an increasingly mixed and mobile population. The miners whose families had always provided such powerful support for the apparitions diminished in numbers

[217] R. Laurentin, *Is the Virgin Mary Appearing at Medjugorje?* (Washington, DC, 1984); S. Kraljevic, *The Apparitions of Our Lady at Medjugorje, 1981–1983: An Historical Account with Interviews* (Chicago, 1984); Perry and Echeverrzia, *Under the Heel*, 304–7.
[218] On Surbiton, see *Surrey Comet*, 14 Mar. 1986 ('Visions to Make Town into Another Lourdes'); on Ranschbach, see Kleemann, 'Marpingen und die Marienerscheinungen', 57; Nolan and Nolan, *Christian Pilgrimage*, 225.

as the pits closed. By 1972 there were fewer than 200 miners in the village and the numbers were declining sharply. Marpingen had become a commuter town. By the 1970s, a growing proportion of those in employment worked outside the village: in 1970 it was 73 per cent, up from 52 per cent in 1951, and far above the Saarland average. They no longer worked in the coalfield, but as officials and white-collar workers in St Wendel and Saarbrücken.[219] Marpingen has achieved prosperity, but through the economic miracle rather than the miracles witnessed in the Härtelwald. The village has no tourist hotels, promenades, or bottled-water plants; but its inhabitants boast a high level of car ownership and a strikingly modern housing stock. Marpingen has creature comforts, discothèques, and a gliderdrome. The apparitions do not animate villagers as they did earlier generations.

The chapel still stands in the Härtelwald, although the houses now come up closer to the wood. The building has been maintained, and the path from the chapel to the spring has been marked by Stations of the Cross. The area around the spring itself is equipped with seating that also shows signs of care. Outside the chapel are little wooden boards, in a standard design, announcing 'Maria hat geholfen'—Mary helped. It is the kind of thing that can be seen at countless Marian shrines. Inside, it is possible to buy memorabilia of the apparitions— Lama's booklet, for example, or a candle with the words 'I am the Immaculately Conceived' running around a picture of the Virgin and Child and the inscription underneath: 'The Blessed Virgin of Marpingen, 3 July 1876'. But there seems no reason why these should disturb a bishop or a vicar-general. They are gentle reminders only of the time when Marpingen promised, or threatened, to become the German Lourdes.

[219] Bungert, *Heimatbuch*, 307–17.

Conclusion

The events examined in this book had a simple beginning. Three young girls in an obscure Saarland village claimed to have seen an apparition of the Virgin Mary, and neither threats nor promises could budge them from their claims. What happened after that turned Marpingen into a place of celebrity and notoriety. It was bruited as the German Lourdes, drawing pilgrims from throughout the new Empire and beyond; priests descended on the village with their notebooks and hundreds of miraculous cures were made public. The apparitions also engaged the attention of Prussian officials, soldiers, examining magistrates, and gendarmes; even Bismarck and Wilhelm I took notice. The events became the subject of legal deliberation and parliamentary debate. Marpingen came to serve as an anticlerical shorthand for Catholic infamy, the butt of acerbic newspaper comment and popular jokes. The immediate reverberations of this remarkable episode made themselves felt for several years. Even decades later, after Marpingen had apparently returned to obscurity, the upheavals of the twentieth century breathed new life into the apparition movement. The force of that movement was not spent until the 1960s. Only then did the career of the German Lourdes become a matter of history.

The present book has looked at these events in detail, but also tried to draw out their larger significance. Why, in the first place, did they occur as they did, where they did, and when they did? Private revelations were a part of Christian culture from the beginning, but until the late Middle Ages they had generally been experienced by saints and clergy, or at least by adult lay people, usually men. The visionary peasant girl was a more familiar figure in the early modern period, but it was not until the nineteenth century that apparitions became associated predominantly with young children and women from humble backgrounds. This fact can be linked to a number of changes. One was the earlier age at which children were brought into the life of the church in the nineteenth century, together with the accompanying 'feminization' of religion. Another was the tendency for the church to move, in some respects, closer to popular sentiment. In the austere atmosphere of the Catholic enlightenment, and into the early nineteenth century, the church tried to extirpate popular 'superstition'; in the decades of religious revival that followed it was more willing to go with the grain of popular belief. It tried to channel or domesticate such beliefs, most obviously by encouraging devotion to the Virgin Mary. Festivities associated with spring fertility became celebrations of Mary's month of May. Pilgrimages to local saints credited with dubious powers were transformed into Marian pilgrimages.

Sodalities or brotherhoods that had become too worldly were refounded and
dedicated to the Blessed Virgin.

The Catholic revival in nineteenth-century Europe, only now receiving the
attention it deserves from historians, was centred on the figure of the Virgin Mary.
Her growing presence could be seen not only in new doctrine (the Immaculate
Conception) and the naming of new congregations, but in liturgical changes,
Marian hymns and new popular devotions. Catholic children growing up during
the papacy of Pius IX lived in a world permeated by images of the Virgin Mary,
and apparitions were one aspect of this. Visions of Mary became increasingly the
most common visions of the nineteenth century: that was another distinguishing
feature of the period after the French Revolution compared with earlier centuries.
This can be ascribed partly to the general Marianization of the church in these
years, but even more to the fact that the church chose to authenticate and
celebrate a number of apparitions as exemplary. Most notable among them were,
of course, the visions of Bernadette Soubirous in 1858, taken by Rome as a
vindication of the doctrine of the Immaculate Conception promulgated just four
years earlier. The outcome was that Lourdes became a kind of template, a
stimulus to future visionaries, however much the church might condemn the
frequently unsatisfactory results.

Marpingen provides an excellent illustration of what all this meant in practice.
A village in which, up to the 1840s, religious duties were performed without
enthusiasm and successive parish priests encountered surly hostility, it became
an exemplar of the Catholic revival in the third quarter of the nineteenth century.
Throughout the diocese of Trier this religious renewal was strongly associated
with the Virgin Mary. In Marpingen a Marian well was restored and a discredited
village practice (the oath of 1699) replaced by a brotherhood dedicated to the
Sacred and Immaculate Heart of Mary. A new parish priest arrived, who placed
his own painting of the Virgin and Child in the church and sermonized enthusiastically to his flock about Lourdes. His message was echoed by a village schoolteacher. None of this drove out popular belief in the mysterious power of certain
rocks and trees, or vanquished the idea that poor souls from purgatory walked
abroad as ghosts—witness the many 'women in white' in the area during the
1870s. The stories told by priest and teacher about a Virgin Mary who appeared
to simple peasant children was more likely to overlay popular belief than to
replace it. In this sense, the ground was well prepared by July 1876, when the
Marpingen visionaries made their first claims on a day that saw 100,000 Catholics
gathered for inaugural celebrations in Lourdes.

Marpingen had in common with other apparition sites not only its new-found
and heavily Marianized piety, but its former 'bad reputation'—a point that
devotees of La Salette and Lourdes also liked to emphasize. The resemblances
did not stop there. Many places that greeted apparitions enthusiastically felt
themselves to be in some way overshadowed by their neighbours. Many were
located close to powerful religious foundations or long-established pilgrimage

centres; others were dominated by the commercial weight or political muscle of a neighbouring town. All of this was true of Lourdes, and it was also true of Marpingen. The village had lived for centuries in the shadow of Tholey abbey, its tithe-lord until French Revolutionary armies arrived. (The abbey of Metten stood in the same relationship to Mettenbuch, the Bavarian apparition site of the 1870s.) The merchants and moneylenders of Tholey continued to play an important but resented part in the economic life of the village. Slightly further away, St Wendel was a regional market centre on whose craftsmen the village was dependent for any substantial project, such as church rebuilding; it was an important pilgrimage centre and the seat of local political power; and unlike Marpingen, it had the railway. Even neighbouring Alsweiler, although smaller in population, gave its name to a local mayoralty. Marpingen was one of the largest villages in the area, but it might be described as 'inert', a place associated with nothing in particular except perhaps a reputation for truculence. It was not the only apparition site that took special pleasure in its new celebrity.

This raises important questions about the geography of apparitions. They are, of course, associated with inaccessible and barren spots. In Latin America the Virgin has favoured landscapes of mesquite, in Europe rocky uplands—areas of sheep and goats, low-yield arable, and quarrying, not the fertile European plains. This apparently clear-cut picture confirmed supporters of the apparitions in their belief that Our Lady sought out the obscure for a sign of special grace; it suggested to opponents that everything could be attributed to the idiocy of rural life. The reality is a little more complicated. Apparition sites were indeed generally poor, but they were hardly cut off from the world. How could they be in an era of state-building, furious diocesan organization, and the encroaching market? By the third quarter of the nineteenth century the railway and the telegraph had arrived close to communities like this, even if they had not yet reached them. The movement of itinerant workers and the trade in wool, animal skins, or quarry stone brought contact with a larger world, even if that contact was not always happy. If we interrogate the cliché of the remote apparition site, we find that they were not always so remote after all, but had been at least partially penetrated by the forces of change. Their problem was not that they were isolated, but that they were marginal. That is what fuelled the sense of being overshadowed by neighbours who were richer or more powerful.

This analysis certainly fits the case of Marpingen. The village was commonly described as remote or inaccessible ('not marked on normal maps'). Situated in the raw Saar–Nahe hill country, most of its population struggled to make a living from agriculture, weaving, and stone-cutting, even if poverty was less stark than in La Salette or Knock. Indebtedness, emigration, and conflict with the state over the use of communal woodland—these marked out the difficulties villagers faced. The problems were real enough, but they were not the problems of an isolated, unchanging world. In the century before the apparitions Marpingen was doubly transformed. First, its agriculture was commercialized by the loss of communal land, the consolidation of holdings, and the developing market in real property. As the nineteenth century went on, the old crises of dearth were replaced by new crises associated with periodic price-depression and dependence on the moneylender or 'usurer'. Marpingen was part of a European trend, one that caused widespread rural resentment against distant exploiters or their local proxies (Jewish moneylenders being an obvious target, as they were in Saarland villages, including Marpingen). Sometimes, especially from the 1870s, these resentments were organized through peasant associations, credit or co-operative organizations, or systematic efforts to challenge usury in the courts. Such efforts invariably required 'outside' leaders, whether a maverick lawyer, a priest, or a local politician with links to larger networks of power. Apparitions generally occurred in places that were not organized in this way, although Knock may be the exception that proves the rule. Organizations of this or any other kind were certainly conspicuous by their absence in Marpingen and surrounding areas, by contrast with the northern region of the Trier administrative district or the southern Saarland.

Marpingen was also subject to change of a second, more striking kind in the generation before the apparitions. Like so much of rural Europe its population faced pressure from a sharply rising population. One response to this was the once-for-all option of permanent migration to the town, or emigration. The rapid urbanization of the nineteenth century, and the masses of emigrants crowded into the 'steerage' on their way to the New World, have received plenty of attention. Less familiar, but equally important in disturbing old patterns of life, peasants engaged in auxiliary occupations, laboured to build railways or canals, turned themselves into worker-peasants or became seasonal migrant workers. For Marpingen the proximity of the Saarland coalfield proved decisive. As 'black California' grew in the decades after the middle of the nineteenth century, poor wages and housing shortages made it difficult to recruit a sufficiently large resident labour-force for the Prussian state mines. What developed, instead, was the characteristic 'peasant-miner' of the Saarland, as peasants from the peripheral zone of the coalfield commuted on a weekly basis to the pits. By the 1870s Marpingen was dependent on the income brought in by peasant-miners of this kind. But the transformation exacted a price. The men spent six days a week away from home, crowded in insanitary accommodation, policed by an authoritarian mines administration, disliked by many miners already settled in the coalfield as bumpkins who threatened wage-rates. Every week the peasant-miners also left behind them women and children who faced extra burdens. Marpingen was not entirely a village without men (*Weiberdorf*), but the relations between men and women, adults and children, everything from the organization of farm labour to family marriage strategies—all were necessarily affected by a change of such magnitude. I have tried to suggest how this upheaval might have prepared some of the ground for the apparitions of 1876.

To the importance of place we must add the importance of time. Modern

European apparitions have occurred in clusters, usually at periods of particular stress. The triggers have most commonly been economic crisis, epidemic, war, and political persecution. The 1860s and 1870s were particularly rich in apparitions, rivalled only perhaps by the late 1940s and early 1950s. It was a period when the map of Europe was reshaped by war, church–state conflicts flared, and economies faltered. In Marpingen these crises came together to feed a mood of desperation. The village was situated in a region that had changed hands many times from the late eighteenth century, and in 1870 it experienced a further bout of mobilization and post-war epidemics. The examples of Philippsdorf and Alsace-Lorraine suggest that borderlands were especially prone to apparitions. Then, in the 1870s, the village suffered the double impact of economic crisis and political persecution. Historians continue to disagree about whether there was a 'Great Depression' in Germany in the years 1873–96, but nobody doubts that the 1870s saw a severe economic downturn. It was especially serious for agriculture and heavy industry, the two principal sources of income in Marpingen. The *Kulturkampf* reached its height in the same years. There was no bishop in Trier by 1876: the diocese had been, in the emotive contemporary phrase, 'orphaned', together with numerous parishes. The attempt in Namborn, close to Marpingen, to seize a priest on the run had led to one of the most serious civil disturbances by Catholics anywhere in Prussia during the *Kulturkampf*. Communal tension in the denominationally mixed Saarland had been growing for some time: during the 1870s it added a further ingredient to a potent cocktail of Catholic fears. In the area around Marpingen, lacking the clubs and organizations that schooled the Catholic response to persecution elsewhere, the mood was one of desperation and longing for some kind of deliverance.

Many elements therefore went into making Marpingen possible. There was, of course, nothing inevitable about the way the apparitions then developed into a major contemporary cause. Many other cases of the kind simply petered out, collapsing through indifference or nipped in the bud by figures of authority, whether familial, clerical, or official. That this did not occur in Marpingen is itself significant. Why these particular apparitions acquired the momentum they did requires explanation at different levels, and raises questions that go to the heart of Prussian rule in the Bismarckian period. But the starting-point must be the visionaries themselves, their families, and fellow villagers.

The classic modern visionary was a young girl of humble background and poor health whose emotional and material security had been threatened. Bernadette Soubirous at Lourdes was the sickly daughter of a bankrupted miller arrested for theft; she had been neglected by her mother and ill-treated by a foster-mother. Margaretha Kunz, by common consent the leading figure among the three Marpingen seers, had lost her father in a mill accident before her birth; she had seen her mother fail in litigation over rights to the mill, her sisters go into domestic service, her brothers go down the pit. It was not so much endemic poverty (neither family had belonged to the poor), but the shock of becoming declassed and the threat to family respectability that stands out in the lives of these and other visionaries. Mathilde Sack, the dominant figure in the Mettenbuch apparitions, shared a strikingly similar background. We can see in detail in the case of Margaretha Kunz how her dramatic pronouncements altered the way in which she was perceived. The status of visionary brought consolations in the form of attention, gratitude, and wonderment (although not, perhaps, any marked increase in affection). What this new position also brought was a temporary suspension, even an inversion, of the everyday rules that normally bound a girl like Margaretha Kunz. It conferred authority and compelled adult respect. This sudden reversal of fortune resembled what we find in Cinderella and other folktales, with the Mother of God in the role of Fairy Godmother.

All of this can be illustrated in considerable detail in the Marpingen case. But it is not the whole story. The evidence suggests that the Marpingen visionaries were not the sole authors of their story, and would have been unable to sustain their position without the active encouragement of others. That meant, in the first instance, families and close relations. Reading the many sympathetic published accounts of Marpingen would lead one to believe that the seers' parents showed exemplary scepticism and restraint when the apparition was first reported to them. In fact, they and a small group of relations and neighbours did much to shape the girls' story by making suggestions of their own and by 'improving' the raw narrative. The account of a woman in white was topped and tailed so that it resembled a Blessed Virgin modelled after Lourdes that others would recognize. This version of the apparitions first gained acceptance in the part of Marpingen nearest to the Härtelwald, spreading into the rest of the village through kinship and friendship networks, especially among women. The local success of the apparitions was sealed, however, when the cause was taken up by men. The two fathers and a number of neighbours were the first in the field; they were soon followed by village notables and officials, men of 'good reputation' and figures of authority. This is important. There is always the temptation to see a movement of this kind as the property of an underclass, just as there is an understandable inclination to stress the way that an event such as an apparition propelled children and women into the limelight. Neither of these propositions is entirely false, but neither stands up on its own. The many 'rival children' who claimed apparitions in 1877 suggest elements of a broader revolt against parental authority—but none of these children gained anything like the credence given to the original visionaries. Women also had a central role in the movement that developed after July 1876—but all contemporary accounts of Marpingen chose to emphasize the gravity of events by pointing out that men had also 'seen' and been cured. Similar considerations apply to the social distribution of support for the Marpingen apparitions. The movement that developed certainly attracted labourers, poor peasants, and miners—but it also won the active support of those who counted for most in the village.

The very few sceptics in Marpingen took the view that what swayed village men in general, and village notables in particular, was the prospect of material gain. For the apparitions attracted pilgrims, and pilgrims spent money. This argument should not be overstated. Anyone who has read the evidence would probably conclude that most villagers, male and female, sincerely believed in the authenticity of the apparitions, accepting that Marpingen had been singled out for a sign of grace. Where there was an admixture of more worldly considerations, these were just as likely to take the form of pride in 'village originality' and satisfaction that Marpingen had finally made a name for itself. Scoring points over neighbours like Tholey and Urexweiler was its own reward. As for the money to be made from pilgrims, the more Marpingen became commercialized, the larger the sums that flowed into the pockets of outsiders such as the wholesalers of devotional kitsch and the stallholders or hawkers who sold it. Nevertheless, the material rewards to Marpingen were not negligible and the prospect of becoming the German Lourdes held out hope of greater bounty in the future. The hotels and promenades never materialized. But while the pilgrims still came, villagers of all classes reaped short-term rewards by providing them with food, drink, and accommodation as well as containers to carry home 'miraculous' Marpingen water.

Historians have recently started to pay some attention to modern pilgrims, understandably so when pilgrimages could set hundreds of thousands of people in motion. This became even more apparent in an age of mass communications. As Marpingen and other German apparition sites of the 1870s showed, the railway—that archetypal symbol of 'modernity'—could carry pilgrims to their goal as easily as it carried anticlerical scientists to their conferences. The broad profile of those who went to Marpingen is clear. The lower social classes predominated: miners, peasants, craftsmen, servants, and a significant minority of tradespeople and others from the lower middle class (this group seems to have been even better represented at Mettenbuch). Aristocrats came in large numbers, but the business and professional middle classes hardly at all. There was also a gender gap, women notably outnumbering men in all classes—another sign of the 'feminization' of nineteenth-century Catholicism. Pilgrims went for a variety of reasons: as an act of penance, to give thanks to the Virgin Mary or request her intercession, or simply to bear witness. Many sought cures for themselves or a loved one, reminding us of the shortcomings of contemporary medicine and the widespread distrust towards doctors, especially in rural and mining communities. The pilgrimage also had a festive, ludic quality: it was a break from everyday constraints that offered sociability and a sense of community with new companions. Those who went to Marpingen generally did so without their priests, and the pilgrimage had a more unbuttoned, less disciplined aspect than we associate with the new model pilgrimages to official sites in this period.

Priests went to Marpingen as individuals, of course, and in large numbers. Their presence is invariably noted in contemporary accounts; it also shows up in other kinds of evidence, from the record of arrests for illegal celebration of mass to the reports that many priests published in the press. Marpingen highlights the importance of the 'priest-publicist'. Historians have written about the more celebrated figures, such as Georg Dasbach and Paul Majunke (both of whom played a role in Marpingen); unsung village clergy like Fathers Eich, Dicke, and Neureuter underline just how crucial the priest-publicist had become in this period. The other group of priests whose contribution stands out are curates, an often frustrated group whose prospects were blighted by the *Kulturkampf*. Again, we are already familiar with one particular subgroup of these, the 'red curates' who argued the cause of workers; Marpingen provided another cause to engage frustrated energies. What stands out most obviously, however, is the divided reaction of the clergy to the apparitions. All were formally required to suspend judgement pending a canonical enquiry: in practice true believers were offset by anxious sceptics and others who wrestled painfully with the 'unsatisfactory' aspects of the Marpingen story. The most difficult position was certainly occupied by the parish priest, Jakob Neureuter. He was in many ways typical of the intensely Mariolatrous clergy that emerged from the more independent and ultramontane seminaries in the third quarter of the nineteenth century, although his scholarly leanings lifted him a little above the run of rural priests. (Few of his fellows had been the curate to a future vicar-general; few possessed a telescope.) When it came to the events of July 1876, Neureuter was plainly oppressed by his responsibilities and painfully undecided about the apparitions. Once he had decided they were authentic, however, he believed with a characteristic passion. Neureuter was never an 'instigator' as some government officials alleged, but in numerous ways he lent legitimacy to the apparitions.

As Margaretha Kunz noted in her later confession, pilgrims and priests as well as villagers helped to shape the visionaries' account—and made it more difficult for them to retract their story altogether. Beyond a certain point, what they said took on a life of its own. But it was the reactions of the Prussian state that perhaps did most to keep up the momentum of the apparitions. The greater the onslaught against the village, the harder it was for the three girls to back down; and the more martyrs the apparition movement claimed, the harder it was for supporters to accept that the story had no foundation. The Prussian state unwittingly inflated the importance of Marpingen, turning it into a major cause. Events surrounding the apparitions unfolded, like so much of the *Kulturkampf*, according to the law of unintended consequences.

To ask why the Prussian state responded as it did in Marpingen, and with what eventual results, is to pose fundamental questions about bureaucracy, army, law, and politics in the Bismarckian era. Consider, first, the heavy-handed intervention. There were naturally specific local reasons for the way things developed, as there must be in any event of this kind. The course of events would have been different if the initial tone had not been set by the bigoted Woytt and the hapless Besser, if *Landrat* Rumschöttel and District Governor Wolff had shown more restraint, if the secret policeman 'Marlow' had never been sent. But, as the

Russian proverb has it, 'if my grandmother had a beard, my grandmother would be my grandfather'. Marpingen shows the importance of the contingent, but it was no chapter of accidents. Most of the elements that allowed Marpingen to blow up into a major incident revealed deep-seated attitudes among Prussian officials: the tendency to treat Catholics as untrustworthy subjects, suspicion of the clergy, an allergic response to anything that seemed to threaten public order. The location of Marpingen in the Saarland, near the French border, only made things worse. The resort to military intervention was also nothing exceptional: it occurred with regularity during the *Kulturkampf*, but not only then.

The vigour of the response to Marpingen throws light on several features of the Prussian state in these years. One is the violence with which the *Kulturkampf* was prosecuted. This 'struggle of civilizations' still appears in many general accounts of the period as a rather arid dispute between church and state that turned on the education and appointment of clergy. It was actually a more fundamental conflict over the future shaping of German society; and, as recent historians have started to show, it was also more violent than such anodyne accounts might suggest. The breaking down of church doors to arrest illegal clergy, the hunting down of priests who went on the run, the issuing of wanted notices for bishops, the seizure of church property and papers, the habitual use of gendarmes and soldiers against Catholic crowds: all were a routine part of the *Kulturkampf*. Marpingen was just one episode that attracted particular public attention. Yet the repression there also highlighted weaknesses in the Prussian state. They included the growing demands on the *Landrat*'s office that placed it under severe pressure, the lack of policing that compelled resort to the army, the patchy provision and poorly developed quality of criminal investigation that led the Ministry of the Interior to send in the man from Berlin. The apparitions triggered an instinct to repress, but the heavy-handed response was not necessarily a sign of strength.

Marpingen was not the only episode in the *Kulturkampf* where Prussian state officials painted themselves into a corner. Stung into a show of force, they found that Catholics sullenly refused to capitulate. Contemporaries of different political persuasions referred to this as passive resistance. At first sight the term may seem overblown. What did Catholic responses to *Kulturkampf* persecution have in common with 'resistance' in its more familiar guise, during the Third Reich? In fact the two had a good deal in common. Historians of the 1930s have increasingly talked in recent years of *Resistenz*, to denote something less than heroic resistance, more an alienation from established authority that expressed itself in small acts of everyday defiance. That is what we find during the *Kulturkampf*, exemplified in Marpingen. A community closed ranks, refused to accept the imposition of no-go areas, refused to co-operate with the legal investigation, refused to accept the moral authority of gendarmes. Dumb insolence and scornful laughter marked the pinpricks of everyday resistance to authority. As occurred so often in the *Kulturkampf*, the position of the Prussian state was made much worse because it could not count on the allegiance of its own officials at the most humble level—village *Ortsvorsteher*, schoolteachers, forester, watchman.

There were of course many differences between the 1870s and the 1930s. An obvious one was the existence of a functioning press, public opinion, and parliaments in Imperial Germany. The opportunities they provided were used by the defenders of Marpingen, culminating in a debate on the floor of the Prussian lower house in which the government was forced to justify its actions. In Imperial Germany, scandalous behaviour by state officials could and did become scandals. Such actions were also subject ultimately to the rule of law, to the constraints of the *Rechtsstaat*. The official case against Marpingen started to unravel in the Prussian courts. A key figure like Mayor Woytt was convicted, numerous Catholic defendants were acquitted. After a protracted investigation (much resented by some of the legal officials involved) and a good deal of bluster about serious charges, a trial eventually took place at Saarbrücken in 1879. Few of the serious charges survived the investigation, and not one of the defendants was convicted. The authorities decided not to waste money on a fruitless appeal. Many loose ends remained, it is true. Responsible officials and soldiers either remained in post, or were dealt with discreetly; the most provocative actor in the whole affair, the Baron Meerscheidt-Hüllessem alias Marlow, was discredited in open court but remained free to conduct his nefarious business. Yet, on balance, the Marpingen case ended in failure and embarrassment for the Prussian government and administrative authorities.

Marpingen also revealed some of the weaknesses of liberalism in Bismarckian Germany. The apparitions represented, in liberal eyes, everything they opposed: backwardness, superstition, disorder, the power of the priest, and the rule of the ignorant mob. However much we may try to sympathize with the position liberals believed themselves to occupy—many clearly saw themselves as beacons of enlightenment in a world succumbing to the worst mass instincts—their reactions to Marpingen were harsh and revealing. The bitter diatribes of press and politicians against 'credulous' villagers, 'stupid' pilgrims, and 'hysterical' women tell us much about liberalism itself. Reactions of this kind suggest a creed powered by scientific (or pseudo-scientific) certainty and committed to 'progress', that great shibboleth of the age, yet uncertain of its own capacity to shape the world accordingly. Just as the actions of the Prussian state denoted weakness as much as strength, so the violent bombast of liberal rhetoric denoted impotence (which is perhaps why liberals repeatedly emphasized their own 'manliness'). The dehumanizing of their clerical enemy eased the way for liberal support of repressive state measures against them. In this sense, Marpingen was a perfect example of the liberal dilemma in the *Kulturkampf*. If, in some respects, Bismarck found himself the unwitting champion of a liberal crusade, the liberals for their part found themselves defending actions that were hard to square with their own values. A few isolated voices said as much; most went along with the logic of the situation. By the time of the Prussian parliamentary debate on Marpingen, it was becoming plain that liberals had obtained the worst of all possible worlds. National Liberals especially, the dominant political grouping of the 1870s, were left defending positions on Marpingen that even the Ministry of the Interior was quietly vacating. Compromised and divided, they were soon to be ditched by Bismarck as an ambiguous liberal era came to an end.

In the short term, what happened at Marpingen was the sort of incident that made the *Kulturkampf* an embarrassment to Prussian state and liberalism alike. Conversely, the Catholic Church emerged from the conflict unbowed, even with enhanced moral authority. In the longer term, however, Marpingen was to prove at least as great an embarrassment to the church. Most apparition movements fell into one of two categories. The great majority subsided, or were suppressed by clerical authority; a small number of cases were held up by the church as exemplary and developed with all the resources of a formidable organization. The apparitions at Mettenbuch in Bavaria showed the former process at work. An untrammelled diocesan hierarchy undertook the enquiry that in Marpingen was undertaken by the state, isolating and interrogating the would-be visionaries, gathering medical evidence, subjecting the findings to detailed scrutiny. The outcome was a pastoral letter that proclaimed the apparitions inauthentic. Even this textbook judgement took a full decade to enforce, much to the frustration of Regensburg, and it may be that we are inclined to exaggerate the iron discipline of the church. Anticlericals, Old Catholics, and renegade Jesuits talked and wrote so often about the fearsome machinery of the church that it is tempting to take them at their word. Things did not necessarily look so simple to a harassed vicar-general. What is certain is that Marpingen was never subject to a full canonical enquiry; and that left the way open for its supporters to continue claiming it as the 'German Lourdes'. The reasons for this hybrid status are plain. The diocese of Trier was hard hit by the *Kulturkampf*—without a bishop, administered by papal legates using code-names. Perhaps even more important, any decision on Marpingen would have created problems for the church in these highly sensitive years. The negative conclusions reached by Bishop Laurent in 1880 were therefore not made public, and Michael Korum continued this course of action—or inaction—as the new Bishop of Trier. It was a potentially hazardous strategy, and it backfired. The grumbles and rumours of the decades before the First World War posed no great threat; but the circumstances of the 1930s, 1940s, and 1950s revived the apparition movement on a scale that caused great embarrassment to Trier and to successive parish priests in Marpingen. We are familiar with the efforts made by the church to develop approved apparition sites like Lourdes and Fatima. In Marpingen the church spent its energy trying to prevent the development of an unofficial site by villagers, maverick priests, publicists, and tour operators. It was not notably successful. Demographic and social change in the village probably did more than the exercise of clerical authority to end the movement.

This book had its starting-point in a series of striking events during the uneasy first decade of the new Germany. Those events remain at the core of the book. To explore their implications has involved ranging much wider: from the late eighteenth century to the 1960s, from the economic history of the Saarland to the social history of medicine, from the devotional revolution in the Catholic Church to the overburdened field administration in Bismarckian Prussia. In an obvious sense, the nature of the events themselves led me to try and bring together these and other sub-themes in the book—the different histories that would normally be considered apart from each other. But the attempt to join these different realms of experience, to connect the disparate, also expresses my own convictions about history. I have tried to show the interlacing of the economic, the social, the political, the cultural. By the same token, and from the same conviction, I have tried to use a range of conceptual tools in writing about the apparitions. Power, class, status, gender—all have something to contribute to our understanding of Marpingen and its reverberations.

Richard Wenz, an obscure contemporary of Heinrich Böll in post-war Cologne, wanted to make a work of fiction out of Marpingen, rather as Émile Zola and Franz Werfel turned Lourdes into novels. The Saarland apparitions certainly had their share of drama, whether tragedy or farce—and, as I have tried to show, supporters and opponents alike soon made Marpingen into the story they wanted it to be. Take Margaretha Kunz, the improbable figure at the centre of this book, if not quite its heroine. Depending on whom we listen to, she was an innocent peasant child, a recipient of a special sign of grace, a symbol of ignorance, a cat's-paw of her mother, an incorrigible liar, and a suitable case for treatment. In this particular instance the evidence allows us to come to some fairly firm conclusions, even if the various constructs retain their importance. It is less obvious what larger conclusions we should draw from the Marpingen apparitions. I want to suggest three.

What happened reminds us, first, of the power of religion in nineteenth-century Europe, something that still receives too little attention in general textbooks on the period. In the case of Catholicism, a more centralized and disciplined institutional church was certainly one aspect of this. So too, however, was the sort of popular religion that surfaced at Marpingen, where orthodox faith mingled with animistic and quasi-magical folk beliefs. This book has sought to demonstrate the existence of these two strands, the importance of the interplay between them, and the problems as well as the opportunities that this created for the church. I have tried, secondly, to throw new light on the Prussian state in the Bismarckian period from an unfamiliar angle. We have, on the one hand, seen in damning detail the unlovely Prussia of brusque officials, high-handed soldiers, and disreputable secret policemen. Yet the apparitions show other, perhaps less familiar aspects of the Prussian state—the problems that arose from penny-pinching policing, the anxieties felt by officials with a mounting burden of administration and paperwork, the notable absence of that much-vaunted Prussian efficiency. In the end, moreover, press, public opinion, parliament and—

above all—the law functioned in such a way that the cause of the villagers was ventilated and, to a considerable degree, vindicated. The findings of this book suggest, in line with other evidence, that neither 'Prussia-Germany' nor Prussia itself should be viewed as simply authoritarian. The reality is richer and more interesting.

If there is a red thread running through this book, it is the theme of modernity—or 'modernity', perhaps, for few terms have earned such a right to be placed in inverted commas. That provides a third, more tentative conclusion to this study. At one level, Marpingen can be seen as a form of revolt against modernity, against modern economic life and the modern state, by communities whose church had recently hurled its anathemas against 'modern civilization'. Contemporary officials and liberals were outraged that such things could happen in the century of progress. As a battle of faith against reason, superstition against science, Marpingen seems to fit into a familiar pattern, and some will see uncomfortable parallels with our own time. Others, looking at the actions taken against villagers, or at the dehumanizing, pseudo-scientific language that was used to justify those actions, will find uncomfortable parallels of a different kind. Either conclusion can plausibly be drawn from the evidence in this book; neither is fully satisfactory. It is unhelpful and condescending to regard the visionaries and their supporters as ignorant, irrational peasants, and to laud their opponents as the sorely tried upholders of reason. But it is no less condescending or problematic simply to invert these moral judgements. Marpingen did not represent a clash between tradition and modernity, but fed off many conflicts of an uneven, uneasy modern world. Any larger conclusions we wish to draw from these events must surely be ambiguous, like modernity itself.

BIBLIOGRAPHY

A. ARCHIVAL SOURCES

Bistumsarchiv Trier (BAT)
Abt. B. III *11, 14*
3: Bericht über die Mutter Gottes Erscheinungen in Marpingen vom 3ten Juli 1876 bis zum 3ten Sept. 1877 nebst einer begründeten Beurtheilung derselben durch Bischof Laurent.
4: [Untitled file on apparitions.]
5: Marpingen 1935–62, 1971.
6 [1]: [Untitled file on apparitions.]
6 [2]: Marpingen 1950–64.
7: Pilgerliste 1944–7.
8: Pilgerliste 1944–7.

Abt. 70: Pfarrakten
1433: Pfarrei Eppelborn, Seelsorge 1827–76.
1434: Pfarrei Eppelborn, Seelsorge 1882–1929.
1438: Pfarrei Eppelborn, 1916–48 [1916–54].
3676: Pfarrei Marpingen, Seelsorge 1838–90.
3676a: Pfarrei Marpingen, [Seelsorge] 1893–1914.
3677: Pfarrei Marpingen, Vermögensverwaltung 1910–47 [1910–59].
3678: Pfarrei Marpingen, Bauakten u. Kunst 1876–1953.
3679: Pfarrei Marpingen, Seelsorge 1915–54.
3680: Stiftungen der Pfarrei Marpingen 1829–1948.
3853: Pfarrei Merzig, Geistliche und weltliche Verwaltung 1869–95.

Abt. 85: Personal-Akten Dasbach, Friedrich Georg
281–2b: [Untitled files with miscellaneous material on Dasbach's journalistic, organizational and political activities.]

Landeshauptarchiv Koblenz (LHAK)
Bestand 403: Oberpräsident der Rheinprovinz
6683–7: Die Festtage u. deren Feier.
6695: Die Teilnahme der Lehrer u. Beamten an Vereinen deren Tendenzen als staatsgefährlich erkannt werden (Verein deutscher Katholiken, Verein zum geheiligten Herzen Jesu). 1872–6.
7558: Die Ausführung des Reichsgesetzes vom 4. Mai 1874; Unbefugte Ausübung von Kirchenämtern; Orts-Ausweisungen von Geistlichen usw. 1874–5.
8806: Verhalten der von Geistlichen, Lehrer usw. bei den Wahlen. 1852–1911.
9658–9: Sonn- u. Feiertagsmärkte und deren Verlegung, 1853–80.
10447: Katholische Bruderschaften und Vereine, 1826–95.
10611–12: Die Kirchlichen und Pfarrverhältnisse in den Kreisen: St Wendel, 1838–73, 1874–91.
10860: Die Kreisschulinspektoren im Regierungsbezirk Trier, 1874–93.

13676: Beschwerden über kath. Geistliche in gemischten Ehe-Angelegenheiten, 1849–1910.

15716: Verzeichnis derjeniger Geistlichen, welche auf Grund Art. 23, Abs. 2 des Gesetzes vom 11.5.1873 zur gerichtlichen Untersuchung gezogen und verurteilt sind. Diözese Trier.

15722: Die Ausführung des Reichsgesetzes vom 4. Mai 1874; Unbefugte Ausübung von Kirchenämtern; Orts-Ausweisungen Geistlichen usw. 1874–83.

15846: Der Gebrauch der Kirchenglocken 1875–89.

16730: Angelegenheiten von Geistlichen, insbes. Gesuche bei Stellensetzungen, politische Spannung mit der kath. Geistlichkeit im Bistum Trier 1848–50.

Bestand 442: Bezirksregierung Trier

1505: Die Verzeichnisse der Ein- u. Ausgewanderten 1871–76.

3802: Statistische Notizen über stattgefundene Einwanderungen 1845–60.

3963: Wirken u. Verhalten der kath. Missionen u. der Jesuiten 1850–1900.

6383: Die im Regierungsbezirk Trier bestehenden (katholischen) Vereine sowie das Vereinswesen im Allgemeinen, 1849–95.

6438: Sammlungen zur Unterstützung des Papstes; Adressen an denselben; Sammlungen für die Karlisten in Spanien; kath. Vereine. 1861–89.

6442: Das Abhalten von öffentlichen Prozessionen und Wallfahrten resp. Bittgängen. Mutter-Gottes-Erscheinungen in Marpingen, Münchwies, Berschweiler.

6660: Das Verhalten der Beamten und der Geistlichkeit bei den Wahlen zum Abgeordnetenhaus und überhaupt in politischer Hinsicht, 1866–88.

7853–4: Die politischen, kirchlichen u. religiösen Vereine, 1845–74, 1874–87.

10419: Ausweisungen kath. Geistlicher, 1874–84.

10420: Verzeichnisse der in Strafanstalten inhaftierten kath. Geistlichen, 1874–78.

Landesarchiv Saarbrücken (LASB)

Bestand: Landratsamt Saarbrücken

1: Polizeinachrichten aus dem Kreise darin u.a. Berichte über politische Versammlungen 1819–84.

Bestand: Dep. Landkreis St Wendel

265: Haupt-Akten betr. Gemeindefinanzen, Bd. I: Aug. 1864–Juni 1928.

476: Haupt-Akten betr. Forstwesen, Bd. I: Mai 1835–Sept. 1894.

Bestand: Einzelstücke Nr. 107

Zusammenstellung des wesentlichen Inhalts der Untersuchungs-Acten betreffend die Mutter-Gottes-Erscheinungen in Marpingen. Saarbrücken den 9. Aug. 1878. Kleber, Untersuchungsrichter.

Stadtarchiv St Wendel (SAStW)

Abt. C: Fürstentum Lichtenberg und preußische Zeit

2/56: Revolutionäre Bewegungen und politische Umtriebe, Mainzer Verein, Bergmännischer Rechtsschutzverein, verbotene Wallfahrten und Prozessionen, öffentliche Versammlungen, 1848–1908.

Bischöfliches Zentralarchiv Regensburg (BZAR)

Generalia F 115

Fasc. I (mit Beilage I): Erste Mittheilung mit Protokollen über Vernehmung der Kinder; Bericht des Pfarramtes Metten über Erscheinungen und angebliche Wunderheilungen, etc.

Fasc. II: Berichte über angebliche Wunder-Heilungen 1877.

Fasc. III: Briefliche Mittheilungen von Metten und Waldsassen, 1878.
Fasc. IV: Untersuchung der Angaben der Mettenbucher Mädchen in Waldsassen—1878 u. 1879.
Fasc. V: Vernehmung des Fr. Xav. Kraus in Regensburg. Nov. 1878. Weitere Vernehmungen in Metten. Dezbr. 1878.
Fasc. VI: Gutacten über die Sache. Entscheidung durch den Hirtenbrief v. 23 Jan. 1879.
Fasc. VII: Vollzug der Entscheidung, 1879–81.

This collection also includes the following unnumbered files:

Angebl. Erscheinungen in Mettenbuch 1878.
Metten—Untersuchungen der Muttergotteserscheinungen in Mettenbuch.
Mettenbuch, 1881–4.
Mettenbuch, 1885.
Mettenbuch, 1887–8.
Mettenbuch, 1886–90.
Mettenbuch. Mathilde Sack in Waldsassen.

Staatsarchiv Landshut (SAL)
Rep. 164/2: Bezirk Deggendorf
1161: Wunderheilungen u. Wundererscheinungen in Mettenbuch, 1878.
1162: Ditto, 1877 [1877–9], I. Teil.
1163: Ditto, 1877 [1877–8], II. Teil.
1164: Angebliche Muttergotteserscheinungen in der Mettenbucher Waldschlucht, 1881 [1881–4].

Rep. 164/15: Bezirk Regen
814: Angebliche Wunderheilungen in Mettenbuch, 1877 [1877–8].

Rep. 164/18: Bezirk Viechtach
697: Wundererscheinungen und Wunderheilungen bei Mettenbuch, 1877 [1877–8].

Fürst Thurn und Taxis Zentralarchiv Regensburg (TTZ)
Akten des Fürstlichen Hofmarschallamtes (HMA)
2699: Hofmarschallamts-Rechnung. Belege 1877/8.
2700: Hofmarschallamts-Rechnung. Belege 1878/9.

Bundesarchiv Koblenz (BAK)
Nachlaß Hertling
7: Briefe an die Schwester Gisberta Bd. 1, 1862–98.
10: Briefe an die Gattin Anna geb. von Biegeleben Bd. 2, 1876–8.
28: Schriften u. Reden Hertlings.
45: Schriftwechsel mit Franz Brentano, 1869–1912.

Stadtarchiv Deggendorf (SAD)
B 21: Chronik der Stadt Deggendorf 1868–1911 [printed material].

B. NEWSPAPERS

Augsburger Allgemeine Zeitung
Deggendorfer Donaubote
Deggendorfer Zeitung
Deutsche Allgemeine Zeitung

Frankfurter Zeitung und Handelsblatt
Germania
Kölnische Volkszeitung
Kölnische Zeitung
Nahe-Blies-Zeitung
National-Zeitung
Saar- und Mosel-Zeitung
Saar-Zeitung
Saarbrücker Zeitung
St Johanner Zeitung
St-Paulinus-Blatt
Trierische Landeszeitung
Trierische Zeitung
Vossische Zeitung

C. OFFICIAL PUBLICATIONS, REFERENCE WORKS

Adreß-Kalender für die Bewohner des Regierungs-Bezirks Trier (Trier, 1871, 1876).
Anlagen zu den Stenographischen Berichten über die Verhandlungen des Hauses der Abgeordneten während der 2. Session der Legislatur-Periode 1877–78, ii (Berlin, 1878).
Bärsch, Georg, *Beschreibung des Regierungs-Bezirks Trier*, 2 vols. (Trier, 1849).
Beck, Otto, *Beschreibung des Regierungsbezirks Trier*, 3 vols. (Trier, 1868–71).
The Catholic Encyclopedia, ed. Charles G. Herbermann *et al.*, 15 vols. (New York, 1907–12).
Fremantle, Ann, *The Papal Encyclicals in their Historical Context* (New York, 1956).
Handbuch des Bistums Trier (Trier, 1952).
Handbuch der historischen Stätten Deutschlands, vii. *Bayern*, ed. Karl Bosl (Stuttgart, 1961).
Handbuch der Kirchengeschichte, ed. Hubert Jedin, vi. 1. *Die Kirche zwischen Revolution und Restauration* (Freiburg, 1971); vi. 2. *Die Kirche zwischen Anpassung und Widerstand (1876 bis 1914)* (Freiburg, 1973).
Handbuch über den Königlich Preußischen Hof und Staat für das Jahr 1875 (Berlin, 1874).
Das Katholische Deutschland: Biographisch-bibliographisches Lexikon, ed. Wilhelm Kosch, 3 vols. (Augsburg, 1930–8).
Das Königreich Württemberg. Eine Beschreibung von Land, Volk und Staat (Stuttgart, 1863).
Lexikon der Marienkunde, ed. K. Algermissen, L. Böer, C. Feckes, and J. Tyciak, ii (Regensburg, 1957).
Lexikon für Theologie und Kirche, ed. J. Höfer and K. Rahner, 10 vols. (Freiburg, 1957–67).
Lorenzi, Philipp de, *Beiträge zur Geschichte sämtlicher Pfarreien der Diöcese Trier*, i. *Regierungsbezirk Trier* (Trier, 1887).
Overbeck, Hermann, and Sante, Georg Wilhelm (eds.), *Saar-Atlas* (Saarbrücken, 1934).
Saarländische Bibliographie (Saarbrücken, 1964).
Schulthess' Europäischer Geschichtskalender, 17–18 (1876–7).
Stenographische Berichte über die Verhandlungen der durch die Allerhöchste Verordnung vom 3. Oktober 1877 einberufenen beiden Häuser des Landtages. Haus der Abgeordneten (Berlin, 1878), ii, 46th Sitting, 16 January 1878.

D. PRINTED SOURCES ON MARPINGEN AND OTHER APPARITIONS

'An der Gnadenstätte von Marpingen', *Die Gartenlaube* (1877), 666–9.
Bachem, Julius, *Lose Blätter aus meinem Leben* (Freiburg, 1910).
—— *Erinnerungen eines alten Publizisten und Politikers* (Cologne, 1913).

'Bei der Madonna von Dietrichswalde', *Die Gartenlaube* (1878), 29–30.

Berg, A. F. vom [Adam Fauth], *Marpingen und das Evangelium* (Saarbrücken, 1877).

Braunmüller, Benedikt, *Kurzer Bericht über die Erscheinungen U. L. Frau bei Mettenbuch* (Deggendorf, 1878).

Cramer, W., *Die Erscheinungen und Heilungen in Marpingen, Gläubigen und Ungläubigen erzählt* (Würzburg, 1876).

'Die Erscheinungen der unbefleckt Empfangenen in Dittrichswalde', *Der Sendbote des göttlichen Herzens Jesu*, 14 (1878), 56–62.

Die Erscheinungen in Marpingen im Jahre 1876. In geordneter Reihenfolge nebst den damit zusammenhängenden Ereignissen zusammengestellt (Saarlouis, 1877).

'Die Erscheinungen zu Dittrichswalde', *St-Bonifatius-Kalender für das Jahr 1879*, 147–59.

Frohschammer, J., 'Die Glaubwürdigkeit der Wunderheilungen in Lourdes und Marpingen', *Die Gartenlaube* (1878), 164–7.

Huysmans, Joris Karl, *The Crowds of Lourdes* (London, 1925).

'L. v. H. Ein Niederländer in Marpingen', *Germania*, 26, 27 Dec. 1877.

Lama, Friedrich von, *Die Muttergottes-Erscheinungen in Marpingen (Saar)* (Karlsruhe, 1934; Altötting, n.d.).

Laurentin, René (with Billet, Bernard, and Galland, Paul), *Lourdes. Dossier des documents authentiques*, 7 vols. (Paris, 1958–66).

Majunke, Paul, *Die Wunder von Lourdes* (Berlin, 1873).

'Marpingen als Reliquie', *St-Bonifatius-Kalender für das Jahr 1881*, 141–55.

Marpingen und seine Gnadenmonate. Mutter-Gottes-Erscheinungen früherer Zeiten kurz erzählt, ausführlich aber die von Marpingen dargestellt in den Ereignissen vom 3. Juli 1876 bis 3. Sept. 1877 von einem Priester der Diöcese Münster, der wiederholt Marpingen besucht hat (Münster, 1877).

Die Marpinger Mutter-Gottes-Erscheinungen und wunderbaren Heilungen. Dem katholischen Volke dargestellt von einem geistl. Priester aus der Diöcese Paderborn (Paderborn, 1877).

Der Marpinger Prozeß vor dem Richterstuhle der Vernunft von einem Unparteiischen (Vienna, 1881).

Der Marpinger Prozeß vor dem Zuchtpolizeigericht in Saarbrücken. Nach stenographischer Aufnahme, ed. Georg Dasbach (Trier, 1879).

Marpingen—Wahrheit oder Lüge?—Dem christl. Volke vorgel. v. einem Unbetheiligten (Münster, 1877).

Mettenbucher Wallfahrts-Büchlein. Eine Sammlung von Marien-Gebeten nebst einer kurzen neuesten Geschichte der Wallfahrt Mettenbuch von einem Weltgeistlichen (Deggendorf, n.d.).

Radziwill, Edmund, *Ein Besuch in Marpingen. Nebst einem Anhang, enth. alle Correspondenzen u. Actenstücke, welche über die Marpinger Angelegenheit in letzter Zeit in der 'Germania' erschienen sind* (Berlin, 1877).

Rebbert, Joseph, *Marpingen und seine Gegner. Apologet. Zugabe zu d. Schriften u. Berichten über Marpingen, Mettenbuch u. Dittrichswalde* (Paderborn, 1877).

Sabbatier, J., *Affaire de La Salette* (Paris, 1857).

Sausseret, Paul, *Erscheinungen und Offenbarungen der allerseligsten Jungfrau Maria*, 2 vols. (Regensburg, 1878).

Schorn, Karl, *Lebenserinnerungen. Ein Beitrag zur Geschichte des Rheinlands im neunzehnten Jahrhundert*, 2 vols. (Bonn, 1898).

Thoemes, Nikolaus, *Die Erscheinungen in Marpingen. Historische Darstellung nach an Ort und Stelle gesammelten schriftlichen und mündlichen Mittheilungen und nach eigenen Erfahrungen* (Stuttgart, 1877).

Thoemes, Nikolaus, *Unsere Liebe Frau von Marpingen. Geschichtliche Darstellung nach persönlichen Forschungen und Erlebnissen* (Trier, 1878).

Urtheil des Zuchtpolizeigerichts von Saarbrücken im Marpinger Prozeße, verkündet am 5. April 1879 (Trier, 1879).

'Wunder in Elsaß', *St-Bonifatius-Kalender für das Jahr 1893*, 89–104.

Zähringer, Damascus, 'Muttergotteserscheinungen', *Benediktinische Monatschrift zur Pflege religiösen und geistigen Lebens*, 26 (1950), 29–40.

Zola, Émile, *Lourdes*, transl. E. Vizetelly (London, 1894).

'Zwei Tage in Lourdes', *Die Gartenlaube* (1876), 602–6.

E. OTHER PRINTED SOURCES

Bachem, Julius, 'Wir müssen aus dem Turm heraus', *Historisch-Politische Blätter*, 137 (1906), 376–86.

Balk, Theodor, *The Saar at First Hand* (London, 1934).

Beaumont, Barbara (ed.), *The Road from Decadence: From Brothel to Cloister. Selected Letters of J. K. Huysmans* (London, 1989).

Beck, Otto, *Die Waldschutzfrage in Preußen* (Berlin, 1860).

—— *Land- und volkswirthschaftliche Tagesfragen für den Regierungsbezirk Trier* (Trier, 1866).

—— *Die ländliche Kreditnoth und die Darlehenskassen im Regierungsbezirk Trier* (Trier, 1875).

Bericht über die Gefangennehmung des Herrn Bischofs Dr. Matthias Eberhard sowie über die Austreibung der Professoren aus dem bischöflichen Priesterseminar zu Trier (Trier, 1874).

Bernhardt, August, *Geschichte des Waldeigentums, der Waldwirtschaft und Forstwirtschaft in Deutschland*, 3 vols. (Berlin, 1872–5).

Busch, Wilhelm, *Die Fromme Helene* [1872], *Gesamtwerke in Sechs Bänden* (Hamburg, 1982), iii. 7–118.

—— *Pater Filucius* [1872], *Gesamtwerke in Sechs Bänden*, iii. 183–220.

Cornet, N.-J., *Louise Lateau et la science allemande* (Brussels and Paris, 1875).

Culturkampf und Spionage oder: Der Prozeß Konitzer. Ein Beitrag zur Sittengeschichte der Culturkampfsaera (Bonn, 1877).

Dasbach, Georg Friedrich, 'Der Wucher in den Dörfern des trierischen Landes', *Schriften des Vereins für Sozialpolitik*, 35 (1887), 151 ff.

Frantz, Constantin, *Die Religion des Nationalliberalismus* (Leipzig, 1872).

Hüsgen, Eduard, *Ludwig Windthorst* (Cologne, 1911).

Jaskowski, Friedrich, *Verlauf und Fiasko des Trierer Schauspiels im Jahre 1891* (Saarbrücken, 1891).

Kartels, J. J., 'Die wirthschaftliche Lage des Bauernstandes in den Gebirgsdistricten des Kreises Merzig', *Schriften des Vereins für Sozialpolitik*, 22 (1883), 187–239.

Knebel, E. R., 'Der Wucher im preußischen Saargebiete', *Schriften des Vereins für Sozialpolitik*, 35 (1887), 121–50.

Krafft-Ebing, Richard von, *Lehrbuch der gerichtlichen Psychopathologie* (Stuttgart, 1875).

—— *Lehrbuch der Psychiatrie auf klinischer Grundlage für practische Ärzte und Studirende*, 3 vols. (Stuttgart, 1879–80).

Kraft, Johann Jakob, *Matthias Eberhard. Bischof von Trier. Ein Lebensbild* (Trier, 1878).

Kraus, Franz-Xaver, *Tagebücher*, ed. Hubert Schiel (Cologne, 1957).

Lama, Friedrich von, *Deutschlands Unglück 1917—und jetzt? Die Friedensvermittlung Papst Benedikt XV. und ihre Vereitlung durch den deutschen Reichskanzler Michaelis (Aug.–Sept. 1917)* (Munich, 1932).

—— *Der Weg der Therese Neumann von Konnersreuth 1898–1935* (Colmar, 1935).

—— (ed.), *'Deutschland wach auf!' Die berühmte prophetische Busspredigt an Deutschland des heiligmäßigen Binger Dekans [Bartholomäus Holzhauser] (1635–58)* (Wiesbaden, 1953 edn.).

Lefebvre, Ferdinand F. M., *Louise Lateau of Bois d'Haine: Her Life, her Ecstasies, and her Stigmata. A Medical Study* (London, 1873).

Martin, Thérèse, *Autobiography of a Saint*, transl. Ronald Knox (London, 1960).

Memoiren einer Nonne (Munich, 1874).

Michelet, Jules, *Priests, Women, and Families* (London, 1845).

Nießen, Heinrich, *Geschichte des Kreises Merzig* (Merzig, 1898).

Northcote, J. Spencer, *Celebrated Sanctuaries of the Madonna* (London, 1868).

Petit, L, 'Une epidémie d'hystéro-démonopathie, en 1878, à Verzegnis, province de Frioul, Italie', *Revue Scientifique*, 41 (10 Apr. 1880), 974A–975A.

Pfaffenunwesen, Mönchsskandale und Nonnenspuk. Beitrag zur Naturgeschichte des Katholizismus und der Klöster von Luzifer Illuminator (Leipzig, 1871).

Reichensperger, Peter, *Kulturkampf, oder Friede in Staat und Kirche* (Berlin, 1876).

Rost, Hans [Johannes], *Die wirtschaftliche und kulturelle Lage der deutschen Katholiken* (Cologne, 1911).

Seyffardt, Ludwig Friedrich, *Erinnerungen* (Leipzig, 1900).

Siegmann, Paul, 'Vor vierzig Jahren. Der Kampf um den 13. Januar. Tagebuch-Auszüge', *Zeitschrift für die Geschichte der Saargegend*, 22 (1974), 224–325.

Spiele für Knappenvereine (Paderborn, 1874).

Stasiewski, Bernhard (ed.), *Akten deutscher Bischöfe über die Lage der Kirche 1933–1945*, i. *1933–34* (Mainz, 1968).

Stürzbecher, Manfred (ed.), *Deutsche Ärztebriefe des 19. Jahrhunderts* (Göttingen, 1975).

Viebig, Clara, *Das Weiberdorf. Roman aus der Eifel* (Berlin, 7th edn., 1901).

Virchow, Rudolf, *Über die Erziehung des Weibes für seinen Beruf. Eine Vorlesung gehalten im Hörsaale des grauen Klosters zu Berlin am 20. Februar 1865* (Berlin, 1865).

—— *Glaubensbekenntnis eines modernen Naturforschers* (Berlin, 1873).

—— *Die Freiheit der Wissenschaften im modernen Staat. Rede gehalten in der dritten allgemeinen Sitzung der fünfzigsten Versammlung deutscher Naturforscher und Ärzte zu München am 22. Sept. 1877* (Berlin, 1877).

—— 'Über Wunder' [1873], in Karl Sudhoff (ed.), *Rudolf Virchow und die deutschen Naturforscherversammlungen* (Leipzig, 1922), 155–64.

Wentzcke, P., *Im neuen Reich 1871–1890. Politische Briefe aus dem Nachlaß liberaler Parteiführer* (Bonn and Leipzig, 1926).

F. SECONDARY WORKS: BOOKS AND ARTICLES

Abel, Wilhelm, *Massenarmut und Hungerkrisen im vorindustriellen Europa* (Hamburg, 1974).

Agulhon, Maurice, *Marianne into Battle: Republican Imagery and Symbolism in France 1789–1880* (Cambridge, 1981).

Alber, Wolfgang, and Dornheim, Jutta, '"Die Fackel der Natur vorgetragen mit Hintansetzung alles Aberglaubens." Zum Entstehungsprozeß neuzeitlicher Normsysteme im Bereich medikaler Kultur', in Jutta Held (ed.), *Kultur zwischen Bürgertum und Volk* (Berlin, 1983), 163–81.

Albrecht, Dieter (ed.), *Katholische Kirche im Dritten Reich. Eine Aufsatzsammlung zum Verhältnis von Papsttum, Episkopat und deutschen Katholiken zum Nationalsozialismus 1933–1945* (Mainz, 1976).

Aldenhoff, Rita, *Schulze-Delitzsch. Ein Beitrag zur Geschichte des Liberalismus zwischen Revolution und Reichsgründung* (Baden-Baden, 1984).

Amery, Carl, *Die Kapitulation oder deutscher Katholizismus heute* (Reinbek, 1963).

Anderson, Margaret Lavinia, *Windthorst: A Political Biography* (Oxford, 1981).

——and Barkin, Kenneth D., 'The Myth of the Puttkamer Purge and the Reality of the

Kulturkampf: Some Reflections on the Historiography of Imperial Germany', *Journal of Modern History,* 54 (1982), 647–86.

Aretin, Karl Otmar von, *The Papacy in the Modern World* (London, 1970).

Aubert, Roger, *Le Pontificat de Pie IX (1846–1878)* (Paris, 1950).

Ayfre, A., 'La Vierge Marie et le Cinéma', in H. Manoir (ed.), *Maria, Études sur la Sainte Vierge,* v (Paris, 1958), 793–810.

Bachem, Karl, *Vorgeschichte, Geschichte und Politik der deutschen Zentrumspartei,* 9 vols. (Cologne, 1927–32).

Bade, Klaus J., *Vom Auswanderungsland zum Einwanderungsland* (Berlin, 1983).

——— (ed.), *Labour and Migration in 19th- and 20th-Century Germany* (Leamington Spa, 1987).

Bär, M., *Die Behördenverfassung der Rheinprovinz seit 1815* (Bonn, 1919).

Bark, T., *Vertragsfreiheit und Staat im Kapitalismus* (Berlin, 1978).

Barkin, Kenneth D., '1878–1879: The Second Founding of the Reich, A Perspective', *German Studies Review,* 10 (1987), 220–35.

Bauer, Arnold, *Rudolf Virchow—Der politische Arzt* (Berlin, 1982).

Baumer, Iso, *Wallfahrt als Handlungsspiel. Ein Beitrag zum Verständnis religiösen Handelns* (Frankfurt am Main and Berne, 1977).

——— 'Kulturkampf und Katholizismus im Berner Jura, aufgezeigt am Beispiel des Wallfahrtswesens', in G. Wiegelmann (ed.), *Kultureller Wandel im 19. Jahrhundert* (Göttingen, 1978), 88–101.

Becker, Josef, *Liberaler Staat und Kirche in der Ära von Reichsgründung und Kulturkampf* (Mainz, 1973).

Becker, Winfried, 'Der Kulturkampf als europäisches und als deutsches Phänomen', *Historisches Jahrbuch,* 101 (1981), 422–46.

Bellot, Josef, *Hundert Jahre politisches Leben an der Saar unter preußischer Herrschaft (1815–1918)* (Bonn, 1954).

Bensusan, S. L., *Some German Spas: A Holiday Record* (London, 1925).

Berenson, Edward, *Popular Religion and Left-Wing Politics in France, 1830–1852* (Princeton, NJ, 1984).

Bies, Luitwin, *Klassenkampf an der Saar 1919–1935. Die KPD im Saargebiet* (Frankfurt am Main, 1978).

Billet, Bernard et al. (eds.), *Vraies et fausses apparitions dans l'Église* (Paris, 1973).

Birke, Adolf, *Bischof Ketteler und der deutsche Liberalismus* (Mainz, 1971).

——— 'Zur Entwicklung und politischen Funktion des bürgerlichen Kulturkampfverständnisses in Preußen–Deutschland', in D. Kürze (ed.), *Aus Theorie und Praxis der Geschichtswissenschaft. Festschrift für Hans Herzfeld* (Berlin, 1972), 257–79.

Birtsch, Günter, 'Soziale Unruhen, ständische Gesellschaft und politische Repräsentation. Trier in der Zeit der Französischen Revolution', in Ernst Hinrichs et al. (eds.), *Mentalitäten und Lebensverhältnisse: Beispiele aus der Sozialgeschichte der Neuzeit: Rudolf Vierhaus zum 60. Geburtstag* (Göttingen, 1982), 143–59.

Blackbourn, David, *Class, Religion and Local Politics in Wilhelmine Germany: The Centre Party in Württemberg before 1914* (London and New Haven, Conn., 1980).

——— *Populists and Patricians: Essays in Modern German History* (London, 1987).

——— 'Progress and Piety: Liberalism, Catholicism and the State in Imperial Germany', *History Workshop Journal,* 26 (1988), 57–78.

——— 'The Catholic Church in Europe since the French Revolution', *Comparative Studies in Society and History,* 33 (1991), 778–90.

——— and Eley, Geoff, *The Peculiarities of German History: Bourgeois Society and Politics in Nineteenth-Century Germany* (Oxford, 1984).

——— and Evans, Richard J. (eds.), *The German Bourgeoisie: Essays on the Social History of the German Middle Class from the Late Eighteenth to the Early Twentieth Century* (London, 1991).

Blanning, Timothy C. W., *The French Revolution in Germany: Occupation and Resistance in the Rhineland 1792–1802* (Oxford, 1983).

Blasius, Dirk, *Bürgerliche Gesellschaft und Kriminalität. Zur Sozialgeschichte Preußens im Vormärz* (Göttingen, 1976).

—— *Kriminalität und Alltag. Zur Konfliktgeschichte des Alltagslebens im 19. Jahrhundert* (Göttingen, 1978).

Blessing, Werner K., *Staat und Kirche in der Gesellschaft. Institutionelle Autorität und mentaler Wandel in Bayern während des 19. Jahrhunderts* (Göttingen, 1982).

Boldt, Hans, *Rechtsstaat und Ausnahmezustand. Eine Studie über den Belagerungszustand als Ausnahmezustand des bürgerlichen Rechtsstaates im 19. Jahrhundert* (Berlin, 1967).

Bornkamm, Heinrich, 'Die Staatsidee im Kulturkampf', *Historische Zeitschrift*, 179 (1950), 41–72, 273–306.

Bourdieu, Pierre, 'Marriage Strategies as Strategies of Social Reproduction', in R. Forster and O. Ranum (eds.), *Family and Society: Selections from the Annales: Économies, Sociétés, Civilisations* (Baltimore, 1976), 117–44.

Boyd, Byron Albert, 'Rudolf Virchow: The Scientist as Citizen', dissertation, University of North Carolina, Chapel Hill, 1981.

Broszat, Martin, 'Resistenz und Widerstand', in Broszat *et al.* (eds.), *Bayern in der NS-Zeit*, 6 vols. (Munich, 1977–83), iv (1981), 691–709.

Budde, Heiner, *Die 'roten Kapläne'. Priester an der Seite der Arbeiter* (Cologne, 1978).

Buder, Johannes, *Die Reorganisation der preußischen Polizei 1918–1923* (Frankfurt am, Main, 1986).

Bungert, Wilhelm, *Heimatbuch Marpingen* (Marpingen, 1980).

Bury, J. B., *History of the Papacy in the Nineteenth Century* (London, 1964).

Bynum, Caroline W., *Holy Feast and Holy Fast: The Religious Significance of Food to Medieval Women* (Berkeley, Calif., 1987).

Bynum, William F., and Porter, Roy (eds.), *Medical Fringe and Medical Orthodoxy 1750–1850* (London, 1987).

Callahan, William J., and Higgs, David (eds.), *Church and Society in Catholic Europe of the Eighteenth Century* (Cambridge, 1979).

Camporesi, Piero, *Bread of Dreams: Food and Fantasy in Early Modern Europe* (Oxford, 1989).

Carroll, Michael P., *The Cult of the Virgin Mary: Psychological Origins* (Princeton, NJ, 1986).

—— *Catholic Cults and Devotions: A Psychological Inquiry* (Kingston, Ont., Montreal, and London, 1989).

Carsten, Ernst, *Die Geschichte der Staatsanwaltschaft in Deutschland* (Breslau, 1932).

Carsten, Francis L., *Essays in German History* (London, 1985).

Cauzons, Thomas de, *La Magie et la sorcellerie en France*, iv (Paris, 1911).

Chadwick, Owen, *The Secularization of the European Mind in the Nineteenth Century* (Cambridge, 1975).

Chickering, Roger, *We Men Who Feel Most German: A Cultural Study of the Pan-German League, 1886–1914* (London, 1984).

Christian, William A., *Apparitions in Late Medieval and Renaissance Spain* (Princeton, NJ, 1981).

—— 'Religious Apparitions and the Cold War in Southern Europe', in Eric Wolf (ed.), *Religion, Power and Protest in Local Communities: The Northern Shore of the Mediterranean* (Berlin, 1984), 239–66.

—— 'Tapping and Defining New Power: The First Months of Visions at Ezquioga, July 1931', *American Ethnologist*, 14 (1987), 140–66.

—— *Person and God in a Spanish Valley* (2nd edn.; Princeton, NJ, 1989).

Claessen, Robert O. M., *Johann Theodor Laurent, Titularbischof von Chersones. Sein politisches, sozialfürsorgliches und pastorales Wirken* (dissertation; Bonn, 1983).

Clark, Samuel, *Social Origins of the Irish Land War* (Princeton, NJ, 1979).

Clear, Catriona, *Nuns in Nineteenth-Century Ireland* (Washington, DC, 1988).

Cobb, Richard, *The People's Armies* (New Haven, Conn., and London, 1987).

Cohn, Norman, *The Pursuit of the Millennium* (London, 1957).

Connelly, Owen, *Napoleon's Satellite Kingdoms* (New York, 1969).

Conway, John, *The Nazi Persecution of the Churches, 1933–1945* (London, 1968).

Conze, Werner, and Kocka, Jürgen (eds.), *Bildungsbürgertum im 19. Jahrhundert*, Part 1: *Bildungsbürgertum und Professionalisierung in internationalen Vergleichen* (Stuttgart, 1985).

Cooter, Roger (ed.), *Studies in the History of Alternative Medicine* (London, 1988).

Cragg, Gerald R., *The Church and the Age of Reason 1648–1789* (London, 1960).

Craig, Gordon A., *Germany 1866–1945* (Oxford, 1978).

Cranston, Ruth, *The Miracle of Lourdes* (New York, 1955).

Crawford, E. Margaret, 'Indian Meal and Pellagra in Nineteenth-Century Ireland', in J. M. Goldstrom and L. A. Clarkson (eds.), *Irish Population, Economy, and Society: Essays in Honour of the late K. H. Connell* (Oxford, 1981), 113–33.

Daly, Mary, *The Church and the Second Sex* (New York, 1968).

Danckert, Werner, *Unehrliche Leute. Die verfemten Berufe* (Berne, 1963).

Darnton, Robert, *The Great Cat Massacre and Other Episodes in French Cultural History* (New York, 1984).

Davis, Natalie Zemon, 'The Reasons of Misrule: Youth Groups and Charivaris in Sixteenth-Century France', *Past and Present*, 50 (1971), 41–75.

—— *The Return of Martin Guerre* (Cambridge, Mass., 1983).

Delaney, John D., *A Woman Clothed with the Sun: Eight Great Apparitions of Our Lady in Modern Times* (New York, 1960).

Delius, Walter, *Geschichte der Marienverehrung* (Munich, 1963).

Derr, Hermann, 'Geschichte der Pfarrei Marpingen', dissertation (Trier, 1935).

Dettmer, Günter, *Die Ost- und Westpreußischen Verwaltungsbehörden im Kulturkampf* (Heidelberg, 1958).

Devlin, Judith, *The Superstitious Mind: French Peasants and the Supernatural in the Nineteenth Century* (London and New Haven, Conn., 1987).

Dipper, Christof, 'Volksreligiosität und Obrigkeit im 18. Jahrhundert', in W. Schieder (ed.), *Volksreligiosität in der modernen Sozialgeschichte* (Göttingen, 1986), 73–96.

Dirvin, Joseph I., 'The Lady of the Miraculous Medal: Paris 1830', in J. D. Delaney (ed.), *A Woman Clothed with the Sun* (New York, 1960), 63–86.

Ditscheid, Aegidius, *Matthias Eberhard, Bischof von Trier, im Kulturkampf* (Trier, 1900).

Douglas, Ann, *The Feminization of American Culture* (New York, 1978).

Duhr, Bernhard, *Jesuiten-Fabeln* (Freiburg, 1891).

Dülmen, Richard van, 'Religionsgeschichte in der historischen Sozialforschung', *Geschichte und Gesellschaft*, 6 (1980), 36–59.

Ecker, Franz, and Ecker, Alfred, *Der Widerstand der Saarländer gegen die Fremdherrschaft der Franzosen 1792–1815* (Saarbrücken, 1934).

'Ehrung für Karl August Schleiden', *Saarheimat*, 24 (1980), 129–30.

Eisfeld, Gerhard, *Die Entstehung der liberalen Parteien in Deutschland 1858–1870* (Hanover, 1969).

Eley, Geoff, 'Hans Rosenberg and the Great Depression of 1873–96', in Eley, *From Unification to Nazism* (London, 1986), 23–41.

Engelhardt, Ulrich, 'Zur Entwicklung der Streikbewegungen in der ersten Industrialisierungsphase und zur Funktion von Streiks bei der Konstituierung der Gewerkschaftsbewegung in Deutschland', *Internationale Wissenschaftliche Korrespondenz zur Geschichte der deutschen Arbeiterbewegung*, 15 (1979), 547–69.

Ernst, R., *Maria redet zu uns. Marienerscheinungen seit 1830* (Eupen, 1949).

Evans, Richard J., *Death in Hamburg: Society and Politics in the Cholera Years 1830–1910* (Oxford, 1987).

—— 'Epidemics and Revolutions: Cholera in Nineteenth-Century Europe', *Past and Present*, 120 (1988), 123–46.

Farr, Ian, 'Populism in the Countryside: The Peasant Leagues in Bavaria in the 1890s', in Richard J. Evans (ed.), *Society and Politics in Wilhelmine Germany* (London, 1978), 136–59.

Fehn, Klaus, 'Das saarländische Arbeiterbauerntum im 19. und 20. Jahrhundert', in Hermann Kellenbenz (ed.), *Agrarisches Nebengwerbe und Formen der Reagrarisierung* (Stuttgart, 1975), 195–214.

—— *Preußische Siedlungspolitik im saarländischen Bergbaurevier (1816–1919)* (Saarbrücken, 1981).

Ficker, Ludwig, *Der Kulturkampf in Münster*, ed. Otto Hellinghaus (Münster, 1928).

Finucane, Ronald C., *Miracles and Pilgrims: Popular Beliefs in Medieval England* (London, 1977).

Flynn, J. F., 'At the Threshold of Dissolution: The National Liberals and Bismarck, 1877/78', *Historical Journal*, 31 (1988), 319–40.

Foesser, O., 'Johann Theodor Laurent und seine Verdienste um die Katholische Kirche', *Frankfurter zeitgemäße Broschüren*, NS 11 (1890), 153–84.

Fohrmann, Ulrich, *Trierer Kulturkampfpublizistik im Bismarckreich* (Trier, 1977).

—— 'Georg Friedrich Dasbach—Gedanken über einen Ultramontanen', in *Soziale Frage und Kirche im Saarrevier* (Saarbrücken, 1984), 79–108.

Fox, Nikolaus, *Saarländische Volkskunde* (Bonn, 1927).

Frevert, Ute, *Krankheit als politisches Problem 1770–1880* (Göttingen, 1984).

—— 'The Civilizing Tendency of Hygiene: Working-Class Women under Medical Control in Imperial Germany', in John C. Fout (ed.), *German Women in the Nineteenth Century* (New York, 1984), 320–44.

Fricke, Dieter, *Bismarcks Prätorianer. Die Berliner Politische Polizei im Kampf gegen die deutsche Arbeiterbewegung (1871–1898)* (Berlin, 1962).

Friehe, Ernst Gerhard, *Geschichte der 'National-Zeitung' 1848 bis 1878* (Leipzig, 1933).

Frohme, Karl, *Politische Polizei und Justiz im monarchischen Deutschland* (Hamburg, 1926).

Funk, Albrecht, *Polizei und Rechtsstaat: Die Entwicklung des staatsrechtlichen Gewaltmonopols in Preußen 1848–1918* (Frankfurt am Main, 1986).

Furlong, Monica, *Thérèse of Lisieux* (London, 1987).

Gabel, K. A., *Kämpfe und Werden der Hüttenarbeiter-Organisationen an der Saar* (Saarbrücken, 1921).

Gall, Lothar, 'Die partei- und sozialgeschichtliche Problematik des badischen Kulturkampfes', *Zeitschrift für die Geschichte des Oberrheins*, 74 (1965), 151–96.

—— 'Liberalismus und "Bürgerliche Gesellschaft": Zu Charakter und Entwicklung der liberalen Bewegung in Deutschland', *Historische Zeitschrift*, 220 (1975), 324–56.

—— *Bismarck, the White Revolutionary*, 2 vols. (London, 1986).

Galot, Jean, *L'Église et la femme* (Paris, 1965).

Gatz, Erwin, *Rheinische Volksmission im 19. Jahrhundert* (Düsseldorf, 1963).

Gay, Peter, *The Bourgeois Experience: Victoria to Freud*, ii. *The Tender Passion* (Oxford, 1986).

Geertz, Clifford, *The Interpretation of Cultures: Selected Essays* (London, 1975).

Gibson, Ralph, *A Social History of French Catholicism 1789–1914* (London, 1989).

Gillett, Henry Martin, *Famous Shrines of Our Lady*, 2 vols. (London, 1949–53).

Ginzburg, Carlo, *The Cheese and the Worms: The Cosmos of a Sixteenth-Century Miller* (London, 1980).

Göckenjan, Gerd, *Kurieren und Staat machen. Gesundheit und Medizin in der bürgerlichen Welt* (Frankfurt am Main, 1985).

Goedert, Joseph, *Jean-Théodore Laurent. Vicaire apostolique de Luxembourg 1804–1884* (Luxemburg, 1957).

Götten, Josef, *Christoph Moufang: Theologe und Politiker 1817–1890* (Mainz, 1969).

Gotto, Klaus, and Repgen, Konrad (eds.), *Kirche, Katholiken und Nationalsozialismus* (Mainz, 1980).

Goubert, Josef, and Cristiani, L., *Messages et apparitions de la Sainte Vierge de 1830 à nos jours* (Paris, 1952) [transl. as *Marienerscheinungen. Erscheinungen und Botschaften der Mutter Gottes von 1830 bis auf unsere Tage* (Recklinghausen, 1955)].

Graef, Hilda, *Mary: A History of Doctrine and Devotion*, 2 vols. (London, 1963–5).

Gregory, Frederick, *Scientific Materialism in Nineteenth-Century Germany* (Dordrecht, 1977).

Grenze als Schicksal—150 Jahre Landkreis Saarbrücken (Saarbrücken, 1966).

Groeben, Klaus von der, *Die öffentliche Verwaltung im Spannungsfeld der Politik dargestellt am Beispiel Ostpreußen* (Berlin, 1979).

Grote, Heiner, *Sozialdemokratie und Religion* (Tübingen, 1968).

Grotjahn, Alfred, *Soziale Pathologie* (Berlin, 1915).

Gugel, Michael, *Industrieller Aufstieg und bürgerliche Herrschaft* (Cologne, 1975).

Hagen, William, *Germans, Poles, and Jews: The Nationality Conflict in the Prussian East, 1772–1914* (Chicago, 1980).

Hales, E. E. Y., *Revolution and Papacy, 1769–1846* (London, 1960).

Haller, Johannes, *Geschichte der Frankfurter Zeitung* (Frankfurt am Main, 1911).

Hansen, Joseph (ed.), *Die Rheinprovinz 1815–1915*, 2 vols. (Bonn, 1917).

Hardach, Karl W., *Die Bedeutung wirtschaftlicher Faktoren bei der Wiedereinführung der Eisen- und Getreidezölle in Deutschland 1879* (Berlin, 1967).

Hardach-Pinke, Irene, and Hardach, Gerd (eds.), *Deutsche Kindheiten 1700–1900* (Kronberg, 1978).

Harrison, J. F. C., *The Second Coming* (London, 1979).

Hartmannsgruber, Friedrich, *Die Bayerische Patriotenpartei 1868–1887* (Munich, 1986).

Hegel, Eduard, *Die Katholische Kirche Deutschlands unter dem Einfluß der Aufklärung des 18. Jahrhunderts* (Opladen, 1975).

Hehl, Ulrich von, 'Das Kirchenvolk im Dritten Reich', in Gotto and Repgen (eds.), *Kirche, Katholiken und Nationalsozialismus*, 63–82.

Heimatblätter für den Stadt- und Landkreis Deggendorf, 10 (1963).

Heinen, Ernst, 'Antisemitische Strömungen im politischen Katholizismus während des Kulturkampfs', in Ernst Heinen and Hans-Julius Schoeps (eds.), *Geschichte in der Gegenwart. Festschrift für Kurt Kluxen zu seinem 60. Geburtstag* (Paderborn, 1972), 259–99.

Heinz, Andreas, *Glaubenszeugen und Fürsprecher. Die Heiligen des Saarlandes* (Saarbrücken, 1980).

—— 'Im Banne der römischen Einheitsliturgie. Die Romanisierung der Trierer Bistumsliturgie in der zweiten Hälfte des 19. Jahrhunderts', *Römische Quartalschrift für Christliche Altertumskunde und Kirchengeschichte*, 79 (1984), 37–92.

—— 'Marienlieder des 19. Jahrhunderts und ihre Liturgiefähigkeit', *Trierer Theologische Zeitschrift*, 97 (1988), 106–34.

Heitjan, Franz Emil, *Die Saar-Zeitung und die Entwicklung des politischen Katholizismus an der Saar von 1872–1888* (Saarlouis, 1931).

Hellé, Jean, *Miracles* (London, 1953).

Heller, Geneviève, 'Körperliche Überbelastung von Frauen im 19. Jahrhundert', in Arthur

E. Imhof (ed.), *Der Mensch und sein Körper von der Antike bis heute* (Munich, 1983), 137–56.

Hentschel, Volker, *Wirtschaft und Wirtschaftspolitik im wilhelminischen Deutschland* (Stuttgart, 1980).

Heriot, Angus J., *The French in Italy, 1796–1799* (London, 1957).

Herrmann, Hans-Walter, 'Die Volksabstimmung vom 13. Januar 1935', *Saarheimat*, 29 (1985), 21–4.

——and Klein, Hanns, 'Zur sozialen Entwicklung im Landkreis Saarbrücken', in *Grenze als Schicksal—150 Jahre Landkreis Saarbrücken* (Saarbrücken, 1966), 132–44.

Herzlich, Claudine, *Health and Illness: A Social Psychological Analysis* (New York and London, 1973).

——and Pierret, Janine, *Illness and Self in Society* (Baltimore and London, 1987).

Hickey, Stephen H. F., *Workers in Imperial Germany: The Miners of the Ruhr* (Oxford, 1985).

Hobsbawm, Eric, *Primitive Rebels: Studies in Archaic Forms of Social Movement in the 19th and 20th centuries* (Manchester, 1959).

——*The Age of Revolution 1789–1848* (London, 1962).

——'Mass-Producing Traditions', in E. J. Hobsbawn and T. Ranger (eds.), *The Invention of Tradition* (Cambridge, 1983).

——*The Age of Empire 1875–1914* (London, 1987).

Hockerts, Hans Günter, *Die Sittlichkeitsprozeße gegen katholische Ordensangehörige und Priester 1936/37* (Mainz, 1971).

Hoffmann, Alfons, 'Aberglaube und religiöse Schwärmerei in der Pfalz im 19. Jahrhundert', *Archiv für mittelrheinische Kirchengeschichte*, 27 (1975), 203–13.

Hoffmann, H., *Landwirtschaft und Industrie in Württemberg* (Berlin, 1935).

Hohorst, Gerd, Kocka, Jürgen, and Ritter, Gerhard A. (eds.), *Sozialgeschichtliches Arbeitsbuch II: Materialien zur Statistik des Kaiserreichs. 1870–1914* (Munich, 1978).

Holmes, Douglas R., *Cultural Disenchantments: Worker Peasantries in Northern Italy* (Princeton, NJ, 1989).

Holstein, Henri, 'Les Apparitions Mariales', in Manoir (ed.), *Maria. Études sur la Sainte Vierge*, v (Paris, 1958), 757–78.

Hoppstädter, Kurt, *Die Entwicklung der Saarländischen Eisenbahnen* (Saarbrücken, 1961).

——'"Eine halbe Stunde nach der Schicht muß jeder gewaschen sein". Die alten Schlafhäuser und die Ranzenmänner', *Saarbrücker Bergmannskalender* (1963), 77–9.

——and Herrmann, Hans-Walter, *Geschichtliche Landeskunde des Saarlandes*, i. *Vom Faustkeil zum Förderturm* (Saarbrücken, 1960); ii. *Von der fränkischen Landnahme bis zum Ausbruch der französischen Revolution* (Saarbrücken, 1977).

Hopkins, James K., *A Woman to Deliver her People: Joanna Southcott and English Millenarianism in an Era of Revolution* (Austin, Tex., 1982).

Horch, Hans, *Der Wandel der Gesellschafts- und Herrschaftsstrukturen in der Saarregion während der Industrialisierung (1740–1914)* (St Ingbert, 1985).

Hubatsch, Walter (ed.), *Grundriß zur deutschen Verwaltungsgeschichte 1815–1945. Reihe A: Preußen*, i. *Ost- und Westpreußen* (Marburg, 1975).

Huerkamp, Claudia, *Der Aufstieg der Ärzte im 19. Jahrhundert* (Göttingen, 1985).

——'The History of Smallpox Vaccination in Germany: A First Step in the Medicalization of the General Public', *Journal of Contemporary History*, 20 (1985), 617–35.

Hufton, Olwen, 'Women in Revolution, 1789–96', *Past and Present*, 53 (1971), 90–108.

Iggers, Georg (ed.), *The Social History of Politics: Critical Perspectives in West German Historical Writing since 1945* (Leamington Spa, 1985).

Ilgen, Theodor, 'Organisation der staatlichen Verwaltung und der Selbstverwaltung', in J. Hansen (ed.), *Die Rheinprovinz 1815–1915* (Bonn, 1917), i. 87–148.

Jeggle, Utz, *Kiebingen: Eine Heimatgeschichte* (Tübingen, 1977).

Jestaedt, Winfried, *Der Kulturkampf im Fuldaer Land* (Fulda, 1960).

John, Michael, *Politics and the Law in Late Nineteenth-Century Germany* (Oxford, 1989).

—— 'Between Estate and Profession: Lawyers and the Development of the Legal Profession in Nineteenth-Century Germany', in D. Blackbourn and R. J. Evans (eds.), *The German Bourgeoisie* (London, 1991), 162–97.

Kammer, Karl, *Trierer Kulturkampfpriester* (Trier, 1926).

Keinemann, Friedrich, *Das Kölner Ereignis: Sein Widerhall in der Rheinprovinz und Westfalen*, 2 vols. (Münster, 1974).

Kelly, Alfred, *The Descent of Darwin: The Popularization of Darwinism in Germany, 1860–1914* (Chapel Hill, NC, 1981).

Kennedy, John S., 'The Lady in Tears: La Salette 1846', in J. D. Delaney (ed.), *A Woman Clothed with the Sun* (New York, 1960), 89–112.

Kent, John, 'A Renovation of Images: Nineteenth-Century Protestant "Lives of Jesus" and Roman Catholic Alleged Apparitions of the Blessed Virgin Mary', in D. Jasper and T. R. Wright (eds.), *The Critical Spirit and the Will to Believe* (Basingstoke, 1989), 137–52.

Kershaw, Ian, *Popular Opposition and Political Dissent in the Third Reich: Bavaria 1933–1945* (Oxford, 1985).

—— *The Nazi Dictatorship* (London, 1989).

Keuth, Paul, 'Die wirtschaftliche Entwicklung im Landkreis Saarbrücken', in *Grenze als Schicksal—150 Jahre Landkreis Saarbrücken* (Saarbrücken, 1966), 109–31.

Kindleberger, Charles, *Manias, Panics and Crashes: A History of Financial Crises* (London, 1978).

Kissling, Johannes Baptist, *Geschichte des Kulturkampfes im Deutschen Reiche*, 3 vols. (Freiburg, 1911–16).

Kitchen, Martin, *The Political Economy of Germany 1815–1914* (London, 1978).

Kleeman, Siegfried, 'Marpingen und die Marienerscheinungen', *Gemeinde Marpingen, Heimatkundliche Lesestoffe*, 23 (1984), 57–65.

Klein, Ernst, 'Bergfiskus und Kirche an der Saar im 19. Jahrhundert', *Zeitschrift für die Geschichte der Saargegend*, 23/24 (1975–6), 157–93.

Klein, Hanns, 'Geschichte des Landkreises Saarbrücken', in *Grenze als Schicksal—150 Jahre Landkreis Saarbrücken* (Saarbrücken, 1966), 37–108.

—— 'Die Saarlande im Zeitalter der Industrialisierung', *Zeitschrift für die Geschichte der Saargegend*, 29 (1981), 93–121.

Klein-Hattingen, Oskar, *Die Geschichte des deutschen Liberalismus*, 2 vols. (Berlin and Schöneberg, 1911–12).

Kocka, Jürgen, 'Theorien in der Geschichtswissenschaft', in P. Leidinger (ed.), *Theoriedebatte und Geschichtsunterricht* (Paderborn, 1982), 7–27.

Korff, Gottfried, 'Politischer "Heiligenkult" im 19. und 20. Jahrhundert', *Zeitschrift für Volkskunde*, 71 (1975), 202–20.

—— 'Formierung der Frömmigkeit. Zur sozialpolitischen Intention der Trierer Rockwallfahrten 1891', *Geschichte und Gesellschaft*, 3 (1977), 352–83.

—— 'Heiligenverehrung und soziale Frage. Zur Ideologisierung der populären Frömmigkeit im späten 19. Jahrhundert', in Günter Wiegelmann (ed.), *Kultureller Wandel im 19. Jahrhundert* (Göttingen, 1978), 102–11.

—— 'Zwischen Sinnlichkeit und Kindlichkeit. Notizen zum Wandel populärer Frömmigkeit im 18. und 19. Jahrhundert', in J. Held (ed.), *Kultur zwischen Bürgertum und Volk* (Berlin, 1983), 136–48.

—— 'Kulturkampf und Volksfrömmigkeit', in W. Schieder (ed.), *Volksreligiosität in der modernen Sozialgeschichte* (Göttingen, 1986), 137–51.

Koselleck, Reinhart, 'Die Auflösung des Hauses als ständischer Herrschaftseinheit', in N.

Bulst, J. Goy, and J. Hoock (eds.), *Familie zwischen Tradition und Moderne* (Göttingen, 1981), 109–24.

Kraljevic, S., *The Apparitions of Our Lady at Medjugorje, 1981–1983* (Chicago, 1984).

Kramer, Karl Sigismund, 'Ehrliche/unehrliche Gewerbe', *Handwörterbuch zur deutschen Rechtsgeschichte*, i. (Berlin, 1971), 855–8.

Krämer, Wolfgang, *Geschichte der Stadt St Ingbert*, 2 vols. (St Ingbert, 1955).

Kselman, Thomas, *Miracles and Prophecies in Nineteenth-Century France* (New Brunswick, NJ, 1983).

Kuczynski, Jürgen, *Geschichte des Alltags des deutschen Volkes 1600–1945*, iv. *1871–1918* (Berlin, 1982).

Kunkel, Ernst, *Für Deutschland—gegen Hitler* (Saarbrücken, 1968).

Küppers, Kurt, 'Die Maiandacht als Beispiel volksnaher Frömmigkeit', *Römische Quartalschrift für Christliche Altertumskunde und Kirchengeschichte*, 81 (1986), 102–12.

Labisch, Alfons, ' "Hygiene ist Moral—Moral ist Hygiene"—Soziale Disziplinierung durch Ärzte und Medizin', in C. Sachße and Florian Tennstedt (eds.), *Soziale Sicherheit und soziale Disziplinierung* (Frankfurt am Main, 1986), 265–85.

Lacher, Hugo, 'Das Jahr 1866', *Neue Politische Literatur*, 14 (1969), 83–99, 214–31.

Lademacher, Horst, 'Wirtschaft, Arbeiterschaft und Arbeiterorganisationen in der Rheinprovinz am Vorabend des Sozialistengesetzes', *Archiv für Sozialgeschichte*, 15 (1975), 111–43.

Ladurie, Emmanuel Le Roy, *Montaillou: Cathars and Catholics in a French Village 1294–1324* (London, 1978).

—— *Carnival: A People's Uprising at Romans 1579–1580* (London, 1980).

Landsberg, Ernst, 'Das rheinische Recht und die rheinische Gerichtsverfassung', in J. Hansen (ed.), *Die Rheinprovinz 1815–1915*, 2 vols. (Bonn, 1917), i. 149–95.

Lange, Josef, *Die Stellung der überregionalen katholischen deutschen Tagespresse zum Kulturkampf in Preußen (1871–1878)* (Frankfurt am Main and Berne, 1974).

Langner, Albrecht (ed.), *Säkularisation und Säkularisierung im 19. Jahrhundert* (Munich, Paderborn, and Vienna, 1978).

Lannon, Frances, *Privilege, Persecution, and Prophecy: The Catholic Church in Spain 1875–1975* (Oxford, 1987).

Lanternari, Vittorio, *The Religions of the Oppressed: A Study of Modern Messianic Cults* (London, 1963).

Larkin, Emmet, 'The Devotional Revolution in Ireland, 1850–75', *American Historical Review*, 77 (1972), 625–52.

Latourette, Kenneth S., *Christianity in a Revolutionary Age*, i. (New York, 1958).

Laufer, Wolfgang, 'Bevölkerungs- und siedlungsgeschichtliche Aspekte der Industrialisierung an der Saar', *Zeitschrift für die Geschichte der Saargegend*, 29 (1981), 122–64.

Laufs, Adolf, *Eduard Lasker. Ein Leben für den Rechtsstaat* (Göttingen and Zurich, 1984).

Laurentin, Réne, *The Life of Cathérine Labouré 1806–1876* (London, 1983).

—— *Is the Virgin Mary Appearing at Medjugorje?* (Washington, DC, 1984).

—— 'Apparitions of Our Lady in Africa', *Soul Magazine*, Mar.–Apr. 1986.

—— and Durand, Albert, *Pontmain. Histoire authentique*, 3 vols. (Paris, 1970), i. *Un signe dans le ciel*.

Lee, Joseph, *The Modernisation of Irish Society 1848–1918* (Dublin, 1973).

Lenhart, Ludwig, 'Die Bonifatius-Renaissance des 19. Jahrhunderts', in *Sankt-Bonifatius. Gedenkgabe zum zwölfhundertsten Todestag* (Fulda, 1954), 533–85.

Leslie, Robert F. D., *Reform and Insurrection in Russian Poland 1856–1865* (London, 1963).

Lewy, Guenter, *The Catholic Church and Nazi Germany* (London, 1964).

Lillig, Karl, 'Die Wallfahrtskapelle vom "Heiligen Kreuz und den Sieben Schmerzen Mariä" bei Medelsheim', *Saarheimat*, 23 (1979), 273–6.

Lochet, Louis, *Muttergottes-Erscheinungen* (Freiburg, 1958).

Lorenz, Ina Susanne, *Eugen Richter. Der entschiedene Liberalismus im wilhelminischer Zeit 1871 bis 1906* (Husum, 1980).

Lüdtke, Alf, 'The Role of State Violence in the Transition to Industrial Capitalism: The Example of Prussia from 1815 to 1848', *Social History*, 4 (1979), 175–221.

—— '*Gemeinwohl*', *Polizei und 'Festungspraxis'. Staatliche Gewaltsamkeit und innere Verwaltung in Preußen, 1815–1850* (Göttingen, 1982).

Lyons, F. S. L., *Ireland since the Famine* (London, 1973).

McCool, Gerald A., *Catholic Theology in the Nineteenth Century* (New York, 1977).

McGrath, William G., 'The Lady of the Rosary: Fatima 1917', in J. D. Delaney (ed.), *A Woman Clothed with the Sun* (New York, 1960), 175–212.

Machtan, Lothar, 'Zur Streikbewegung der deutschen Arbeiter in den Gründerjahren (1871–1873)', *Internationale wissenschaftliche Korrespondenz zur Geschichte der deutschen Arbeiterbewegung*, 14 (1978), 419–42.

—— *Streiks im frühen deutschen Kaiserreich* (Frankfurt am Main, 1983).

—— and Ott, René, ' "Batzbier!" Überlegungen zur sozialen Protestbewegung in den Jahren nach der Reichsgründung am Beispiel der süddeutschen Bierkrawalle vom Frühjahr 1873', in H. Volkmann and J. Bergmann (eds.), *Sozialer Protest* (Opladen, 1984), 128–66.

McLeod, Hugh, *Religion and the People of Western Europe 1789–1970* (Oxford, 1981).

McManners, John, *The French Revolution and the Church* (London, 1969).

Magraw, Roger, 'The Conflict in the Villages: Popular Anticlericalism in the Isère (1852–1870)', in T. Zeldin (ed.), *Conflicts in French Society* (London, 1970), 169–227.

Mai, Paul, (ed.), *Ignatius von Senestrey: Eine Selbstbiographie* (Regensburg, 1967).

—— (ed.), *Ignatius von Senestrey: Festschrift zur 150 Wiederkehr seines Geburtstages* (Barnau, 1968).

Mallmann, Klaus-Michael, ' "Haltet fest wie der Baum die Äst". Zur Rolle der Frauen in der Bergarbeiterbewegung 1892/93', *Saarheimat*, 24 (1980), 89–92.

—— *Die Anfänge der Bergarbeiterbewegung an der Saar (1848–1904)* (Saarbrücken, 1981).

—— 'Nikolaus Warken', in Peter Neumann (ed.), *Saarländische Lebensbilder*, i. (Saarbrücken, 1982), 127–52.

—— 'Volksfrömmigkeit, Proletarisierung und preußischer Obrigkeitsstaat. Sozialgeschichtliche Aspekte des Kulturkampfes an der Saar', in *Sozialfrage und Kirche im Saar-Revier* (Saarbrücken, 1984), 213–21.

—— ' "Aus des Tages Last machen sie ein Kreuz des Herrn"? Bergarbeiter, Religion und sozialer Protest im Saarrevier des 19. Jahrhunderts', in W. Schieder (ed.), *Volksreligiosität in der modernen Sozialgeschichte* (Göttingen, 1986), 152–84.

Maloy, Robert M., 'The Virgin of the Poor: Banneux 1933', in J. D. Delaney (ed.), *A Woman Clothed with the Sun* (New York, 1960), 241–67.

Manoir, D'Hubert du (ed.), *Maria. Études sur la Sainte Vierge*, iv–v (Paris, 1956–8).

Marnham, Patrick, *Lourdes: A Modern Pilgrimage* (London, 1980).

Marrus, Michael, 'Pilger auf dem Weg. Wallfahrten im Frankreich des 19. Jahrhunderts', *Geschichte und Gesellschaft*, 3 (1977), 329–51.

Marx, Jakob, *Geschichte der Pfarreien der Diözese Trier* (Trier, 1923).

Masani, Rustom Pestonji, *Folklore of Wells, Being a Study of Water-Worship in East and West* (Bombay, 1918, reprinted 1974).

Maus, Ingeborg, 'Entwicklung und Funktionswandel der Theorie des bürgerlichen Rechtsstaats', in Mehdi Tohidipur (ed.), *Der bürgerliche Rechtsstaat*, 2 vols. (Frankfurt am Main, 1978), i. 13–81.

Medick, Hans, and Sabean, David Warren (eds.), *Interest and Emotion: Essays on the Study of Family and Kinship* (Cambridge, 1984).

Mergen, Josef, *Die Auswanderungen aus den ehemals preußischen Teilen des Saarlandes im 19. Jahrhundert*, i. *Voraussetzungen und Grundmerkmale* (Saarbrücken, 1973).

Mernissi, Fatima, 'Women, Saints and Sanctuaries', *Signs*, 3 (1977), 101–12.

Merten, Detlev, *Rechtsstaat und Gewaltmonopol* (Tübingen, 1975).

Meyer, Ernst, *Rudolf Virchow* (Wiesbaden, 1956).

Miegge, Giovanni, *The Virgin Mary: The Roman Catholic Marian Doctrine* (London, 1955).

Mitchell, Allan, 'Bürgerlicher Liberalismus und Volksgesundheit im deutsch–französischen Vergleich 1870–1914', in Jürgen Kocka (ed.), *Bürgertum im 19. Jahrhundert*, 3 vols. (Munich, 1988), iii, 395–417.

Molitor, Hansgeorg, *Vom Untertan zum Administré. Studien zur französischen Herrschaft und zum Verhalten der Bevölkerung im Rhein-Mosel Raum von den Revolutionskriegen bis zum Ende der napoleonischen Zeit* (Wiesbaden, 1980).

Möller, Karl, *Leben und Briefe von Johannes Theodor Laurent*, 3 vols. (Trier, 1887–9).

Mommsen, Wolfgang J., *Max Weber and German Politics* (Chicago, 1985).

Mooser, Josef, 'Soziale Mobilität und familiale Plazierung bei Bauern und Unterschichten', in N. Bulst, J. Goy, and J. Hoock (eds.), *Familie zwischen Tradition und Moderne* (Göttingen, 1981), 182–201.

—— 'Religion und Sozialer Protest. Erweckungsbewegung und ländliche Unterschichten im Vormärz am Beispiel von Minden-Ravensburg', in H. Volkmann and J. Bergmann (eds.), *Sozialer Protest* (Opladen, 1984), 304–24.

Morsey, Rudolf, 'Bismarck und der Kulturkampf. Ein Forschungs- und Literaturbericht 1945–1957', *Archiv für Kulturgeschichte*, 39 (1957), 232–70.

—— 'Probleme der Kulturkampf-Forschung', *Historisches Jahrbuch*, 83 (1964), 217–45.

Mosse, Max, and Tugendreich, Gustav, *Krankheit und soziale Lage* (Munich, 1913, reprinted Göttingen, 1977).

Mühlen, Patrick von der, *'Schlägt Hitler an der Saar!' Abstimmungskampf, Emigration und Widerstand im Saargebiet 1933–1935* (Bonn, 1979).

Müller, Ingo, *Rechtsstaat und Strafverfahren* (Frankfurt am Main, 1980).

Müller, Jutta, *Die Landwirtschaft im Saarland. Entwicklungstendenzen der Landwirtschaft eines Industrielandes* (Saarbrücken, 1976).

Müller, Max, *Die Geschichte der Stadt St Wendel* (St Wendel, 1927).

Müller, Michael, *Säkularisation und Grundbesitz. Zur Sozialgeschichte des Saar-Mosel-Raumes* (Boppard, 1980).

Müller-Lyer, Franz, *Soziologie der Leiden* (Munich, 1914).

Nair, Gwyneth, *Highley: The Development of a Community 1550–1880* (Oxford, 1988).

Neame, Alan, *The Happening at Lourdes, or the Sociology of the Grotto* (London, 1968).

Neary, Thomas, *The Light of the Day* (Knock, Co. Mayo, 1974).

—— *I Comforted Them in Sorrow: Knock 1879–1979* (Knock, Co. Mayo, 1979).

Neher, A., *Die wirtschaftliche und soziale Lage der Katholiken im westlichen Deutschland* (Rottweil, 1927).

Neuhäusler, Johann, *Kreuz und Hakenkreuz. Der Kampf des Nationalsozialismus gegen die Katholische Kirche und der kirchliche Widerstand* (Munich, 1946).

Niethammer, Lutz, 'Anmerkungen zur Alltagsgeschichte', *Geschichtsdidaktik*, 5 (1980), 231–42.

—— and Brüggemeier, Franz, 'Wie wohnten Arbeiter im Kaiserreich?', *Archiv für Sozialgeschichte*, 16 (1976), 61–134.

Noakes, Jeremy, 'The Oldenburg Crucifix Struggle of November 1936: A Case Study of Opposition in the Third Reich', in Peter D. Stachura (ed.), *The Shaping of the Nazi State* (London, 1978), 210–33.

Nolan, Barbara, *The Gothic Visionary Perspective* (Princeton, NJ, 1976).

Nolan, Mary Lee, and Nolan, Sidney, *Christian Pilgrimage in Modern Western Europe* (Chapel Hill, NC, 1989).

O'Brien, Susan, '*Terra Incognita*: The Nun in Nineteenth-Century England', *Past and Present*, 121 (1988), 110–40.

Oehlke, Alfred, *100 Jahre Breslauer Zeitung: 1820–1920* (Breslau, n.d. [1920]).

Ohlert, Konrad, 'Das Volksschulwesen', in J. Hansen (ed.), *Die Rheinprovinz 1815–1915* (Bonn, 1917), ii. 1–25.

Oncken, Hermann, *Rudolf von Bennigsen. Ein deutscher liberaler Politiker*, 2 vols. (Stuttgart and Leipzig, 1910).

Oraison, Marc, 'Le Point de vue du médecin psychiatre clinicien sur les apparitions', in B. Billet (ed.), *Vraies et fausses apparitions dans l'Église* (Paris, 1973), 123–47.

Pastor, Ludwig, *August Reichensperger*, 2 vols. (Freiburg, 1899).

Paul, Eugen, 'Matthias Scheeben', in Heinrich Fries and Georg Schwaiger (eds.), *Katholische Theologen Deutschlands im 19. Jahrhundert*, ii (Munich, 1975), 386–408.

Pauli, Kurt, 'Der Arbeiterbauer im Saarland', dissertation (Heidelberg, 1939).

Peiper, Albrecht, *Chronik der Kinderheilkunde* (Leipzig, 1951).

Pelger, Hans, 'Zur sozialdemokratischen Bewegung in der Rheinprovinz vor dem Sozialistengesetz', *Archiv für Sozialgeschichte*, 5 (1965), 377–406.

Perry, Nicholas, and Echeverría, Loreto, *Under the Heel of Mary* (London, 1988).

Peukert, Detlev, *Inside Nazi Germany: Conformity, Opposition and Racism in Everyday Life* (Harmondsworth, Middx., 1989).

Pflanze, Otto, 'Bismarcks Herrschaftstechnik als Problem der gegenwärtigen Historiographie', *Historische Zeitschrift*, 223 (1982), 562–99.

—— *Bismarck and the Development of Germany*, 3 vols. (Princeton, NJ, 1990).

Pope, Barbara, 'Immaculate and Powerful: The Marian Revival in the Nineteenth Century', in Clarissa Atkinson, Constance Buchanan, and Margaret Miles (eds.), *Immaculate and Powerful: The Female in Sacred Image and Social Reality* (Cambridge, Mass., 1985), 173–200.

Purcell, Mary, 'Our Lady of Silence: Knock 1879', in J. D. Delaney (ed.), *A Woman Clothed with the Sun* (New York, 1960), 147–71.

Rahner, Karl, *Visions and Prophecies* (London, 1963).

Ramsey, Matthew, 'The Politics of Professional Monopoly in Nineteenth-Century Medicine', in Gerald L. Geison (ed.), *Professions and the French State 1700–1900* (Philadelphia, 1984), 225–305.

Reichert, Franz Rudolf, 'Das Trierer Priesterseminar im Kulturkampf (1873–1886)', *Archiv für mittelrheinische Kirchengeschichte*, 25 (1973), 65–105.

Reif, Heinz, *Westfälischer Adel 1770–1860* (Göttingen, 1979).

Reifferscheid, Gerhard, *Das Bistum Ermland und das Dritte Reich* (Cologne and Vienna, 1975).

Reinalter, Helmut, *Aufklärung—Absolutismus—Reaktion. Die Geschichte Tirols in der zweiten Hälfte des 18. Jahrhunderts* (Vienna, 1974).

Retter, Hein, *Spielzeug. Handbuch zur Geschichte und Pädagogik der Spielmittel* (Weinheim and Basle, 1979).

Rivinius, Karl Josef, 'Die sozialpolitische und volkswirtschaftliche Tätigkeit von Georg Friedrich Dasbach', in *Soziale Frage und Kirche im Saarrevier* (Saarbrücken, 1984), 109–82.

Ropars, Louis, 'Notre Dame et la Philatélie', in H. Manoir (ed.), *Maria. Études sur la Sainte Vierge*, v (Paris, 1958), 813–14.

Rosen, George, *Madness in Society: Chapters in the Historical Sociology of Mental Illness* (Chicago, 1968).

Rosenbaum, Heidi, *Formen der Familie. Untersuchungen zum Zusammenhang von Familienverhältnissen, Sozialstruktur und sozialem Wandel in der deutschen Gesellschaft des 19. Jahrhunderts* (Frankfurt am Main, 1982).

Rosenberg, Hans, *Große Depression und Bismarckzeit. Wirtschaftsablauf, Gesellschaft und Politik in Mitteleuropa* (Berlin, 1967).

Ross, Ronald J., 'Enforcing the Kulturkampf in the Bismarckian State and the Limits of Coercion in Imperial Germany', *Journal of Modern History*, 56 (1984), 456–82.

Rubner, Heinrich, 'Waldgewerbe und Agrarlandschaft im Spätmittelalter und im 19. und 20. Jahrhundert', in Hermann Kellenbenz (ed.), *Agrarisches Nebengewerbe und Formen der Reagrarisierung* (Stuttgart, 1975), 97–108.

Rudé, George, *The Crowd in the French Revolution* (Oxford, 1967).

—— *The Crowd in History* (London, 1981).

Saam, Rudolf, 'Die industrielle und siedlungsgeographische Entwicklung Dudweilers im 18. und 19. Jahrhundert', *Zeitschrift für die Geschichte der Saargegend*, 22 (1974), 95–125.

Sabean, David Warren, *Power in the Blood: Popular Culture and Village Discourse in Early Modern Germany* (Cambridge, 1984).

St John, Bernard, *The Blessed Virgin in the Nineteenth Century: Apparitions, Revelations, Graces* (London, 1903).

Schauff, Johannes, *Die deutschen Katholiken und die Zentrumspartei* (Cologne, 1928).

Schieder, Wolfgang, 'Kirche und Revolution. Sozialgeschichtliche Aspekte der Trierer Wallfahrt von 1844', *Archiv für Sozialgeschichte*, 14 (1974), 419–54.

—— (ed.), *Volksreligiosität in der modernen Sozialgeschichte* (Göttingen, 1986).

Schiffers, Heinrich, *Der Kulturkampf in Stadt und Regierungsbezirk Aachen* (Aachen, 1929).

—— *Kulturgeschichte der Aachener Heiligtumsfahrt* (Cologne, 1930).

Schmidt, Gustav, 'Die Nationalliberalen—eine regierungsfähige Partei? Zur Problematik der inneren Reichsgründung, 1870–1878', in Gerhard A. Ritter (ed.), *Die deutschen Parteien vor 1918* (Cologne, 1973), 208–23.

Schmidt, Robert H., *Saarpolitik 1945–1957*, 3 vols. (Saarbrücken, 1959–62).

Schmidt-Volkmar, Erich, *Der Kulturkampf in Deutschland 1871–1890* (Göttingen, 1962).

Schmolke, Michael, *Adolf Kolping als Publizist. Ein Beitrag zur Publizistik und zur Verbandsgeschichte des deutschen Katholizismus im 19. Jahrhundert* (Münster, 1966).

Schneider, Bernhard, 'Die Trauben- und Johannesweinsegnung in der Trierer Bistumsliturgie vom Spätmittelalter bis zum ausgehenden 19. Jahrhundert', *Archiv für mittelrheinische Kirchengeschichte*, 37 (1985), 57–74.

Schock, Ralph, 'Johann Anton Joseph Hansen', in Peter Neumann (ed.), *Saarländische Lebensbilder*, ii (Saarbrücken, 1984), 161–84.

Scholle, Manfred, *Die Preußische Strafjustiz im Kulturkampf 1873–1880* (Marburg, 1974).

Schulte, Regina, 'Dienstmädchen im herrschaftlichen Haushalt. Zur Genese ihrer Sozialpsychologie', *Zeitschrift für bayerische Landesgeschichte*, 41 (1978), 879–920.

Schwabe, K., 'Die Saarlandfrage in Versailles', *Saarheimat*, 29 (1985), 17–20.

Segalen, Martine, *Love and Power in the Peasant Family* (Oxford, 1983).

Sharkey, Don, 'The Virgin with the Golden Heart: Beauraing 1932–33', in J. D. Delaney (ed.), *A Woman Clothed with the Sun* (New York, 1960), 215–38.

Sheehan, James J., *German Liberalism in the Nineteenth Century* (Chicago, 1978).

Showalter, Elaine, *The Female Malady: Women, Madness and the English Culture 1830–1980* (London, 1987).

Siegrist, Hannes (ed.), *Bürgerliche Berufe. Zur Sozialgeschichte der freien und akademischen Berufe im internationalen Vergleich* (Göttingen, 1988).

Simpson, Eileen, *Orphans* (New York, 1987).

Soziale Frage und Kirche im Saarrevier (Saarbrücken, 1984).

Sperber, Jonathan, *Popular Catholicism in Nineteenth-Century Germany* (Princeton, NJ, 1984).

Spree, Reinhard, *Health and Social Class in Imperial Germany: A Social History of Mortality, Morbidity and Inequality* (Oxford and New York, 1988).

Staber, Joseph, *Kirchengeschichte des Bistums Regensburg* (Regensburg, 1966).

Steffens, Horst, 'Arbeitstag, Arbeitszumutungen und Widerstand. Bergmännische Arbeitserfahrungen an der Saar in der zweiten Hälfte des 19. Jahrhunderts', *Archiv für Sozialgeschichte*, 21 (1981), 1–54.

—— *Autorität und Revolte. Alltagsleben und Streikverhalten der Bergarbeiter an der Saar im 19. Jahrhundert* (Weingarten, 1987).

—— 'Einer für alle, alle für einen? Bergarbeiterfamilien in der 2. Hälfte des 19. Jahrhunderts', in Toni Pierenkemper (ed.), *Haushalt und Verbrauch in historischer Perspektive* (St Katharinen, 1987), 187–226.

Steinert, Marlis, *Hitler's War and the Germans* (Athens, Ohio, 1977).

Stern, Fritz, *Gold and Iron: Bismarck, Bleichröder and the Building of the German Empire* (London, 1977).

Strauch, Hans-Joachim, 'Rechtsstaat und Verwaltungsgerichtsbarkeit', in M. Tohidipur (ed.), *Der bürgerliche Rechtsstaat* (Frankfurt am Main, 1978), ii. 525–47.

Stürmer, Michael, *Regierung und Reichstag im Bismarckstaat 1871–1880: Cäsarismus oder Parlamentarismus* (Düsseldorf, 1974).

Süle, Tibor, *Preußische Bürokratietradition. Zur Entwicklung von Verwaltung und Beamtenschaft in Deutschland 1871–1918* (Göttingen, 1988).

Tackett, Timothy, 'The West in France in 1789: The Religious Factor in the Origins of Counterrevolution', *Journal of Modern History*, 54 (1982), 715–45.

Tenfelde, Klaus, 'Ländliches Gesinde in Preußen. Gesinderecht und Gesindestatistik 1810 bis 1861', *Archiv für Sozialgeschichte*, 19 (1979), 189–229.

Thoma, Hubert, *Georg Friedrich Dasbach. Priester, Publizist, Politiker* (Trier, 1975).

—— 'Wie es zur Gründung des "Paulinus" kam', *Paulinus* [Trier], 20 Apr. 1975.

Thurston, Herbert, *Beauraing and Other Apparitions: An Account of some Borderline Cases in the Psychology of Mysticism* (London, 1934).

Tilly, Charles, *The Vendée* (London, 1964).

Tilly, Richard, 'Popular Disorders in Nineteenth-Century Germany', *Journal of Social History*, 4 (1971), 1–40.

Tohidipur, Mehdi (ed.), *Der bürgerliche Rechtsstaat*, 2 vols. (Frankfurt am Main, 1978).

Treiber, Hubert, ' "Wie man wird, was man ist." Lebensweg und Lebenswerk des badischen Landpfarrers Ambros Oschwald (1801–1873) im Erwartungshorizont chiliastischer Prophezeiungen', *Zeitschrift für die Geschichte des Oberrheins*, 136 (1988), 293–348.

Treitz, Jakob, *Michael Felix Korum, Bischof von Trier 1840–1921* (Munich, 1925).

Turi, Gabriele, *'Viva Maria!' La reazione alle riforme leopoldine (1790–1799)* (Florence, 1969).

Turner, Victor, 'Pilgrimages as Social Processes', in Turner, *Dramas, Fields, and Metaphors: Symbolic Action in Human Society* (Ithaca, NY, 1974), 166–230.

—— *Process, Performance and Pilgrimage: A Study in Comparative Symbology* (New Delhi, 1979).

—— and Turner, Edith, *Image and Pilgrimage in Christian Culture: Anthropological Perspectives* (Oxford, 1978).

—— —— 'Postindustrial Marian Pilgrimage', in James Preston (ed.), *Mother Worship* (Chapel Hill, NC, 1982), 145–73.

Veith, Ilza, *Hysteria: The History of a Disease* (Chicago, 1965).

Viethen, Eva, 'Tradition und Realitätseignung—Bergarbeiterfrauen im industriellen

Wandel', in Helmut Fielhauer and Olaf Bockhorn (eds.), *Die andere Kultur. Volkskunde, Sozialwissenschaften und Arbeiterkultur* (Vienna, Munich, and Zurich, 1982), 241–59.

Vierhaus, Rudolf, 'Preußen und die Rheinlande 1815–1915', *Rheinische Vierteljahrsblätter*, 30 (1965), 152–75.

'Visions to make Town into Another Lourdes', *Surrey Comet*, 14 Mar. 1986.

Volkmann, Heinrich, and Bergmann, Jürgen (eds.), *Sozialer Protest: Studien zur traditioneller Resistenz und kollektiver Gewalt in Deutschland vom Vormärz bis zur Reichsgründung* (Opladen, 1984).

Vollmer, Bernhard, *Volksopposition im Polizeistaat. Gestapo- und Regierungsberichte 1934–1936* (Stuttgart, 1957).

Walsh, William J., *The Apparitions and Shrines of Heaven's Bright Queen*, 4 vols. (New York, 1904).

Warner, Marina, *Alone of All her Sex: The Myth and Cult of the Virgin Mary* (London, 1976).

Weber, Christoph, *Kirchliche Politik zwischen Rom, Berlin und Trier 1876–1888* (Mainz, 1970).

—— *Aufklärung und Orthodoxie am Mittelrhein 1820–1850* (Munich, Paderborn, and Vienna, 1973).

Weber, Eugen, 'Religion and Superstition in Nineteenth-Century France', *Historical Journal*, 31 (1988), 399–423.

Weber, Hermann, *Die Wandlung des deutschen Kommunismus* (Frankfurt am Main, 1969).

Weber, Margot, 'Zum Kulturkampf in Bayern', *Zeitschrift für bayerische Landesgeschichte*, 37 (1974), 93–120.

Weber-Kellermann, Ingeborg, *Die Kindheit. Kleidung und Wohnen, Arbeit und Spiel* (Frankfurt am Main, 1979).

Wehler, Hans-Ulrich, *Bismarck und der Imperialismus* (Cologne and Berlin, 1969).

—— 'Neoromantik und Pseudorealismus in der neuen "Alltagsgeschichte"', in Wehler, *Preußen ist wieder chic* (Frankfurt am Main and Berlin, 1983), 99–106.

—— *The German Empire 1871–1918* (Leamington Spa, 1985).

Weindling, Paul, 'Hygienepolitik als sozialintegrative Strategie im späten Deutschen Kaiserreich', in Alfons Labisch and Reinhard Spree (eds.), *Medizinische Deutungsmacht im Sozialen Wandel des 19. und frühen 20. Jahrhunderts* (Bonn, 1989), 37–55.

Weyand, Helmut, 'Stückelteilung und Bannrenovation im Oberamt Schaumburg. Ein Beitrag zur Untersuchung Grundherrlicher Bauerndörfer des 17./18. Jahrhundert', *Zeitschrift für Agrargeschichte und Agrarsoziologie*, 20 (1972), 161–85.

Windell, George C., *The Catholics and German Unity, 1866–71* (Minneapolis, 1954).

Wirtz, Rainer, 'Die Begriffsverwirrung der Bauern im Odenwald 1848. Odenwälder "Excesse" und die Sinsheimer "republikanische Schilderhebung"', in Detlev Puls (ed.), *Wahrnehmungsformen und Protestverhalten. Studien zur Lage der Unterschichten im 18. und 19. Jahrhundert* (Frankfurt am Main, 1979), 81–104.

Wulffen, Erich, *Staatsanwaltschaft und Kriminalpolizei in Deutschland* (Berlin, 1908).

Wunder, Heide, *Die bäuerliche Gemeinde in Deutschland* (Göttingen, 1986).

Zahn, Gordon, *German Catholics and Hitler's War* (London and New York, 1963).

Zang, Gert (ed.), *Provinzialisierung einer Region. Zur Entstehung der bürgerlichen Gesellschaft in der Provinz* (Frankfurt am Main, 1978).

Zeldin, Theodore, 'The Conflict of Moralities: Confession, Sin and Pleasure in the Nineteenth Century', in Zeldin (ed.), *Conflicts in French Society* (London, 1970), 13–50.

Zenner, Maria, 'Probleme des Übergangs von der Agrar- zur Industrie- und Arbeiterkultur im Saarland', in *Soziale Frage und Kirche im Saarrevier* (Saarbrücken, 1984), 65–78.

Zipfel, Friedrich, *Kirchenkampf in Deutschland 1933–1945. Religionsverfolgung und Selbstbehauptung der Kirchen in der nationalsozialistischen Zeit* (Berlin, 1965).

Zucker, Stanley, *Ludwig Bamberger* (Pittsburgh, 1975).

INDEX